PENGUIN REFERENCE

MEDICINE, PATIENTS AND THE LAW

Margaret Brazier has been a Professor of Law at the University of Manchester since 1990. She has written widely on medical law and ethics. She chaired a review of laws relating to surrogacy from 1996 to 1998 and chaired the Retained Organs Commission from 2001 to 2004. She is the Editor of the *Medical Law Review*.

Emma Cave graduated in law in 1995 (MJur 1997; PhD 2002) and is a lecturer in tort and medical law at the University of Leeds. Her research interests include research ethics, and legal and ethical issues in reproductive medicine, and she is author of *The Mother of All Crimes*, published in 2004. She was the co-author of Chapter 16 of the third edition of *Medicine, Patients and the Law*.

Medicine, Patients and the Law

Fourth Edition

Margaret Brazier and Emma Cave

PENGUIN BOOKS

In memory of
L. T. Jacobs 1914–85
and
Harry Street 1919–84

PENGUIN BOOKS

Published by the Penguin Group
Penguin Books Ltd, 80 Strand, London WC2R ORL, England
Penguin Group (USA) Inc., 375 Hudson Street, New York, New York 10014, USA
Penguin Group (Canada), 90 Eglinton Avenue East, Suite 700, Toronto, Ontario, Canada M4P 2Y3
(a division of Pearson Penguin Canada Inc.)
Penguin Ireland, 25 St Stephen's Green, Dublin 2, Ireland (a division of Penguin Books Ltd)
Penguin Group (Australia), 250 Camberwell Road, Camberwell, Victoria 3124, Australia
(a division of Pearson Australia Group Pty Ltd)
Penguin Books India Pvt Ltd, 11 Community Centre, Panchsheel Park, New Delhi – 110 017, India
Penguin Group (NZ), 67 Apollo Drive, Rosedale, North Shore 0632, New Zealand
(a division of Pearson New Zealand Ltd)
Penguin Books (South Africa) (Pty) Ltd, 24 Sturdee Avenue, Rosebank, Johannesburg 2196, South Africa

Penguin Books Ltd, Registered Offices: 80 Strand, London WC2R ORL, England

www.penguin.com

First edition published 1987
Second edition published 1992
Third edition published 2003
Fourth edition first published in hardback by Lexis Nexis Butterworths 2007
Published in paperback 2007
1

Copyright © Margaret Brazier, 1987, 1992, 2003
Copyright © Margaret Brazier and Emma Cave, 2007
All rights reserved

The moral right of the authors has been asserted

Printed in England by Clays Ltd, St Ives plc

ISBN: 978-0-141-03020-3

Preface

Keeping up to date with the pace of developments in medicine, law and ethics gets no easier. Just as was the case with the last edition in 2003, no sooner is a chapter completed then some novel development throws the authors into disarray. Sharing the job between two of us has been an immense bonus. Emma Cave (who wrote Chapter 16 in the last edition) was, thankfully, happy to take on half the load. Drafts of each chapter have flown to and fro across the Pennines.

Each chapter of this book could easily grow into a book in its own right. Inevitably, this edition is longer than the last. We hope that it remains readable to a broad audience. Every one of us, whether as a patient or as a health professional, has a stake in how law regulates medicine. As before, we do not attempt to cover mental health law as such. To do so would double the length of the book. We do, in Chapter 6, address crucial questions about mental capacity and consent to treatment. As medical care involves women and men, as both doctors and patients, we use the pronouns she and he interchangeably. We could not be comfortable with the 'old' legal tradition of using only the male pronoun, and he/she (or s/he) seems intolerably clumsy.

We remain in debt to Professors Harry Street and Gerald Dworkin who were initially to have co-written this work with Margaret Brazier. Harry Street's untimely death, and Gerald Dworkin's many other commitments, prevented those original plans coming to fruition. We want to thank all our colleagues at Manchester, Leeds and elsewhere for their unstinting help and advice. Colleagues from the disciplines of law, bioethics and medicine have listened patiently as we tried out ideas on them, and advised us as the work progressed. We owe a particular debt over many years to Maureen Mulholland, Marie Fox, Jean McHale, Suzanne Ost, John Harris and Charles Erin. We thank Sara Fovargue, Anne-Maree Farrell, Sarah Devaney, Sheelagh McGuinness and Kirsty Keywood, who have helped us with materials and patiently read draft chapters for us, and Elizabeth Maliakal, and David and Helen Pickworth for their invaluable advice on the practical implications of recent reforms. We also thank our students who often challenge our views and force us to think again on many issues. We are especially grateful to Catherine Thurlow who prepared much of the typescript and polished all the final drafts of the chapters. This edition could not have been written without the support and encouragement of our families, Rodney and Victoria Brazier, and Simon, Hannah and Tom Cave.

Any criticism of medical practice in this book is the result of academic endeavour and not personal experience. We are grateful for the care our families have received from general practice and NHS hospitals. We care passionately about the NHS. Were all care of the standard that we have received, this book would be shorter.

No book on this subject is ever wholly up to date. This book is (we trust) up to date to 28 February 2007.

Introduction

The law's relationship with medicine has become a highly publicised affair. Rarely a day passes without media coverage of some new controversy surrounding medical practice or medical ethics. Cases relating to the rights and responsibilities of doctors and patients feature regularly in the Law Reports. The medical profession finds itself in the limelight. One day the doctor is hailed as a saviour, the next she is condemned as authoritarian or uncaring. Advances in medical science, extending life at one end and bringing new hope to the childless at the other, have given rise to intricate problems of law and ethics. At every level of medical practice, law plays a role. Doctors cannot escape the reach of the law. For many medical practitioners, the rise in the number of malpractice claims is their main concern. Although, as we shall see, the rapid increase in clinical negligence claims now seems to be levelling out, doctors still fear an epidemic of US proportions. Patients still find the pursuit of any grievance frustrating. Despite significant reforms of the civil justice system, litigation is expensive. In 2007, people also seek a greater say in their own treatment. Patients are no longer prepared to be patient. The extent to which patients have a right to determine their own treatment is a question for the law. How far patients who claim rights are also subject to responsibilities is increasingly debated.

It is not only the narrow question of our own health needs that concerns people today. Many recent scientific developments are themselves controversial. Research on embryos, 'saviour siblings', human cloning, organ retention – all excite controversy. Older controversies – about abortion and euthanasia – get no less difficult with time. The purpose of this book, then, is to examine how medical practice is regulated, to analyse the rights and responsibilities of doctors and patients, to look at the provision of compensation for medical wrongdoing or error, and to explore the framework of legal rules governing those delicate questions of life and death when medicine, morals and the law overlap. It is easy to perceive law's relationship with medicine as one of conflict, mirroring conflict between doctors and their patients. We suggest that this is a 'false' conflict. What the medical profession, patients and the public have a need for are that:

(1) the medical profession be properly regulated;

(2) where possible, the rights and obligations of patients, doctors and other health professionals are clearly defined;

(3) there is an adequate, fair and rational system of compensation for patients suffering injury;

(4) there are effective means of investigating medical accidents and errors; and

(5) the law (together with professional guidelines) offers comprehensive guidance on those areas of medical practice of moral and ethical sensitivity.

Sources of law

In contrast to most European countries, the law of England is not to be found neatly encapsulated in any code. The task of the non-lawyer seeking to establish her rights or ascertain his duties is far from easy. The law relating to medical practice is to be discovered in a variety of sources. Parliament has enacted a number of statutes governing medical practice. The regulation of medical practice and the disciplining of the defaulting doctor have traditionally been entrusted by Act of Parliament to the General Medical Council (GMC), by virtue of the Medical Act 1983. That Act has already been substantially amended, and further reforms radically altering the powers of the GMC are imminent. The organisation of the health service has been governed by a series of statutes, now consolidated in the National Health Service Act 2006. The Medicines Act 1968 is concerned with the safety of drugs. A number of other Acts of Parliament, such as the Abortion Act 1967 and the Human Fertilisation and Embryology Act 1990, the Human Tissue Act 2004 and the Mental Capacity Act 2005, are crucially relevant to questions about medicine, patients and the law. An Act of Parliament can create only a general framework of legal rules. Acts of Parliament, therefore, commonly empower government ministers to make subsidiary regulations known as Statutory Instruments. These regulations may determine crucial questions. For example, most of the duties of general practitioners within the NHS are dealt with by regulations and not by Act of Parliament.

It is impossible today to understand the legal rules governing the practice of medicine without reference to European law. In matters within the jurisdiction of the Treaty of Rome and subsequent treaties, notably the Treaty of Amsterdam, the European Union is empowered to make laws affecting all Member States. This may be by way of regulations, which immediately and directly become law in the UK, or by way of directives which oblige the UK Government to introduce an appropriate Act of Parliament to give effect to the directive. In 1985, a Community directive on liability for unsafe products resulted in the Consumer Protection Act 1987 which, as we shall see in **Chapter 10**, introduced strict liability for defective drugs. The Clinical Trials Directive, promulgated in April 2001, obliged the UK to introduce reforms of the law governing medical research. This was done by way of a new set of regulations – the Medicines for Human Use (Clinical Trials) Regulations 2004. Provisions of the European Union treaties themselves may be invoked to make a case for greater rights for patients. This is how Diane Blood won her case to be allowed to be inseminated with her dead husband's sperm abroad.

The European Union must not be confused with the European Convention on Human Rights. That Convention is a separate treaty to which the UK is a party. The Convention seeks to establish the rights of the individual and directly addresses questions such as rights to life, to privacy, and to found a family. The Human Rights Act 1998 renders rights granted by the Convention enforceable against public authorities in the UK. As we shall see, the 1998 Act has the potential to transform medical law and offer a clearer articulation of patients' rights.

Conventions, statutes and statutory regulations alone, be they British or European legislation, by no means paint the whole picture of English medical law. Much of English law remains judge-made, the common law of England. Decisions, judgments handed down by the courts, form precedents for determining later disputes and define the rights and duties of doctors and patients in areas untouched by statute. The common law largely governs questions of compensation for medical accidents, the patient's right to determine her own treatment, parents' rights to control medical treatment of their children and, as we shall see, several other vital matters.

We deal with English law. The common law is not confined to England. Decisions of courts in the USA, Canada and elsewhere are mentioned from time to time. Such judgments do not bind an English court. They can be useful as examples, or warnings, showing us how the same basic principles of law have developed elsewhere. Finally it must be remembered that, for the lawyer, Scotland counts as a foreign country. Scotland maintains its own independent legal system and, post-devolution, enjoys the power to legislate independently on most issues relating to medical care. Scotland has, for example, enacted its own Human Tissue (Scotland) Act 2006. On many of the questions dealt with in this book, English and Scottish law coincide. Occasionally, the law in England and Scotland diverges. We confine ourselves to stating the law as it applies in England and Wales, though the problems of law and medicine embodied in the book are common to the UK as a whole.

Part I

Part I of this book begins by seeking to examine the overall framework of medicine today. How does the law seek to ensure that patients are treated by competent, qualified doctors practising ethical medicine? Does the General Medical Council, which for over a century and a half has regulated the medical profession, meet patients' needs? What rights do we enjoy in the context of health care and how has the Human Rights Act 1998 affected medical law? Law can, at best, only set basic standards of behaviour. So we explore some of the ethical principles and dilemmas in modern medicine. Then, in the final chapter of this first part, we examine that critical component of any doctor-patient relationship – the necessity for trust and confidence. Can we be assured that our doctors will respect our privacy so that we can feel confident enough to be wholly frank with them? In what exceptional circumstances should that duty of confidence be breached to fulfil some more pressing responsibility to others?

Part II

In this part, we examine what remedies the law affords a patient dissatisfied with the medical care which he or she has received. A patient may feel that he has not been fully consulted or properly counselled about the nature and risks of treatment. He may have agreed to treatment and ended up worse, not better. Consequently, the patient may seek compensation from the courts. Or he may simply want an investigation of what went wrong, and to ensure that his experience is not suffered by others. It is the rise in litigation that has caused so much anxiety among doctors.

The law relating to medical errors, often described as medical malpractice, operates on two basic principles: (1) the patient must agree to treatment; and (2) treatment must be carried out with proper skill and care on the part of all the members of the medical profession involved. Any doctor who operated on or injected, or even touched, an adult patient against her will might commit a battery, a trespass against the patient's person. A doctor who was shown to have exercised inadequate care of his patient, to have fallen below the required standard of competence, would be liable to compensate the patient for any harm he caused her in the tort of negligence. In short, to obtain compensation, the patient must show that the doctor was at fault. And if she sues for negligence, she must show that the doctor's 'fault' caused her injury. Three overwhelming problems are inherent in these two simple statements.

First, how do courts staffed by lawyer-judges determine when a doctor is at fault? We shall see that judges in England used to defer largely to the views of doctors. Recent case law, however, suggests that judges are now more ready to scrutinise medical practice. Establishing what constitutes good practice will still cause the court some difficulty. The courts remain dependent on expert evidence and a clash of eminent medical opinions is not unusual.

Second, as liability, and the patient's right to compensation, is dependent on a finding of fault, doctors naturally feel that a judgment against them is a body blow to their career and their reputation. Yet a moment's reflection will remind the reader of all the mistakes she has made in her own job. A solicitor overlooking a vital piece of advice from a conference with a client can telephone the client and put things right when he has a chance to check what he has done. A carpenter can have a second go at fixing a door or a cupboard. An overtired, overstrained doctor may commit a momentary error which is irreversible. He is still a good doctor despite one mistake.

Third, the doctor's fault must be shown to have caused the patient harm. In general, whether a patient is treated within the NHS or privately, the doctor only undertakes to do his best. He does not guarantee a cure. The patient will have a legal remedy only if he can show that the doctor's carelessness or lack of skill caused him injury that he would not otherwise have suffered. So, if you contract an infection and are prescribed antibiotics which a competent doctor should have appreciated were inappropriate for you or your condition, you can sue the doctor only if you can show either (1) that the antibiotic prescribed caused you harm unrelated to your original sickness (for example, caused a violent allergic reaction), or (2) that the absence of appropriate treatment significantly delayed your recovery. In both cases you must prove that, had the doctor acted properly, the harm would have been avoided.

We shall see, therefore, that the law is a remedy only for more specific and serious grievances against a doctor. It is in any case an expensive and unwieldy weapon. Many patients have complaints, particularly about hospitals, which do not amount to actionable negligence. They complain about being kept waiting, inadequate visiting hours, or rudeness on the part of NHS staff. We shall look in this part at extra-legal methods of pursuing complaints against a hospital or a doctor, and we consider if the whole system for compensating medical errors should be replaced by a no-fault compensation scheme. Nor do we limit our examination to faults alleged against medical practitioners. Many medical mishaps arise from the dangers inherent in certain drugs. We consider the liability of the drug companies and attempts by government to ensure that available medicines are safe.

Finally, we should say a word about legal 'language' today. The person who initiates a legal action, for example a patient suing a doctor for battery or negligence, used to be referred to as the plaintiff. When Lord Woolf recommended radical reforms of the civil justice system, some of which are discussed in **Chapter 8**, he also proposed that old-fashioned language should be changed into plain English. So today, the patient bringing a claim against a doctor is simply called the claimant. Where we discuss cases decided before 1999, we use the old term plaintiff. In discussion of contemporary cases and problems, we use the new approved style of claimant. Defendants, thankfully, remain just that – defendants.

Part III

The first two parts of this book focus on the relationship of doctors and patients, both the framework of that relationship and how the law deals with conflict when a patient is dissatisfied with the care that he has received. Part III looks at the dramatic questions in medical law where what is at stake is not only what an individual patient may be entitled to, but also what society should allow. The range of questions addressed is broad. Some questions are omitted simply on grounds of space. We consider if parents who find themselves with an unplanned child after receipt of negligent medical advice or treatment should receive compensation to meet the cost of raising that child. What duties are owed to an unborn child, and should pregnant women continue to enjoy legal immunity from liability to their future children? We venture into the troubled waters of the reproductive technologies, seeking to explain and analyse the law governing such matters as the creation of 'saviour siblings', human cloning, hybrid embryos. But we also attempt to address practical questions – how to define parental status, and access to information about gamete donors. Medical research, transplantation and the especial problems around the medical care of children are addressed. We end (appropriately) by examining laws relating to the end of life, and debates about euthanasia.

Law matters

Medical law has altered beyond recognition in the 20 years since the first edition of this book. No-one who reads a newspaper or watches television can be unaware of the sorts of questions which we address. On an almost weekly basis, new initiatives or new laws are proposed. Sometimes it seems as though the dizzying pace of reform reflects little thought about the whole picture. More attention is paid to policy and ethical debate than law. There is insufficient rigorous analysis of what the limits of the law's remit should be.

One set of lawyers, doctors and patients groups address the adequacy (or inadequacy) of malpractice litigation. Ethicists, journalists, and legal theorists join doctors and theologians in debating the grand moral dilemmas of medicine. Lay people tend not to get much of a chance to have their say until some controversy breaks, such as the scandals around organ retention. For all these reasons, this book seeks to concentrate more on law than ethics, and to attempt to locate our discussions of the law in a practical context. We hope that we can dispel the myth that law is 'boring'. We hope that our discussion may cast some light on what the role of the law should be in the context of modern medicine.

Contents

Part I
MEDICINE, LAW AND SOCIETY

Contents

Part II
MEDICAL MALPRACTICE

Contents

Chapter 7
CLINICAL NEGLIGENCE 155

Chapter 8
MALPRACTICE LITIGATION 185

Contents

Part III
MATTERS OF LIFE AND DEATH

Chapter 14
ABORTION AND EMBRYO RESEARCH 351

Chapter 15
DOCTORS AND CHILDREN 375

Contents

Chapter 19
THE HUMAN BODY AND ITS PARTS 469

Chapter 20
THE END OF LIFE 485

INDEX 517

Table of Cases

A

Table of Cases

B

C

Decisions of the European Court of Justice are listed below numerically. These decisions are also included in the preceding alphabetical list.

Table of Statutes

Table of Statutory Instruments

Table of European and International Material

Part I

MEDICINE, LAW AND SOCIETY

Chapter 1

THE PRACTICE OF MEDICINE TODAY

1.1 Few professions still stand so high in public esteem as medicine.[1] None the less the final years of the twentieth century, and first years of the twenty-first, dealt a blow to the reputation of the medical profession in the UK. Scandal after scandal beset doctors. Surgeons carrying out cardiac operations on infants in Bristol were found to have continued to operate despite incurring higher death rates for such surgery than their peers. The Bristol Inquiry[2] uncovered a 'club culture'. Vulnerable children were not the hospital's priority. Care was badly organised; the standard of care was poor and openness non-existent. In Bristol,[3] and in Liverpool,[4] evidence emerged of hospitals retaining children's organs without their parents being told that only parts of their children's bodies were returned to them for burial. Subsequently, it became apparent that organ retention in relation to children and adults was a widespread practice. A gynaecologist was struck off the medical register after years of gross malpractice involving bungled operations, removing women's ovaries without their consent, and a record of appalling rudeness to patients.[5] Harold Shipman was convicted of 15 counts of murder and later found to have killed at least 215 of his patients.[6] A general practitioner, Clifford Ayling, was convicted of indecent assault on twelve female patients.[7] Between 2002 and 2005, staff cuts and poor communication led to the deaths of new mothers in London maternity units.[8] Nor were the doctors alone in

---

[1] See R Tallis, *Hippocratic Oaths: Medicine and Its Discontents* (2004) Atlantic Books, p 102.

[2] *Learning from Bristol: The Report of the Public Inquiry into Children's Heart Surgery at the Bristol Royal Infirmary 1984–1995* (2001) CM 5207(1) (hereafter the Bristol Inquiry).

[3] The Inquiry into the Management of Care of Children Receiving Complex Heart Surgery at the Bristol Royal Infirmary Interim Report, *Removal and Retention of Human Material* (available at www.bristol-inquiry.org.uk).

[4] *The Royal Liverpool Children's Inquiry Report* (2001) HC 12–11 (hereafter the Redfern Report).

[5] Department of Health, *Report of the Committee of Inquiry into How the NHS Handled Allegations About the Conduct of Richard Neale* (2004) Cm 6315. See Chapter 9 at 9.2.

[6] See http://www.the-shipman-inquiry.org.uk/. See further below.

[7] Department of Health, *Committee of Inquiry – Independent Investigation into how the NHS Handled Allegations about the Conduct of Clifford Ayling* (2004) Cm 6298.

[8] Healthcare Commission, *Investigation Into 10 Maternal Deaths at, or Following Delivery at Northwick Park Hospital, North West London Hospitals NHS Trust, Between April 2002 and April 2005* (August 2006).

their misery. The conviction of Beverly Allitt of the murder of four of her child patients dented the reputation of nurses too.[9] Disturbing reports of degrading treatment of learning-disabled people in NHS establishments surfaced in 2006.[10] All these so-called 'scandals' have a common factor. They involved not just the wrongdoing of one person, but a failure within the NHS to ensure a safe service of the quality that patients and their families are entitled to expect.

What are the implications for medical regulation? Four distinct tiers of regulation have been identified.[11] First, personal regulation involves a doctor's individual commitment to a code of ethics, found in part in documents such as the Hippocratic Oath and the General Medical Council's *Good Medical Practice* guidance.[12] We consider the ethical responsibilities of doctors in Chapter 3. Second, team-based regulation requires all health care professionals to take responsibility for their team's performance and conduct. Third, professional regulation, which we consider in the next section, is undertaken by statutory regulators such as the General Medical Council (GMC).[13] Finally, work-based regulation involves a system of clinical governance and performance management which we consider in the latter half of this chapter. The various tiers of regulation do not always work in harmony. As we shall see, work-based regulation is designed not only to enhance patient safety, but also to ensure the economic accountability of NHS organisations. Job freezes and staff cuts have an impact on the level of care a hospital can provide. Economy may compromise safety and reduce the ability of the individual doctor to offer the kind of care that she might wish to.

Angels or demons?

1.2 Praised to the skies for their triumphs, few individuals attract greater public odium than the doctor or nurse who falls from her pedestal. The revulsion occasioned by Nazi atrocities in the concentration camps was nowhere as marked as in the case of Dr Mengele. The thought that he used his skills as a doctor, taught to him that he might heal and comfort the sick, to advance torture and barbarism still causes horror today, more than half a

---

9   Department of Health, *The Allitt Inquiry: Independent Inquiry Relating to Deaths and Injuries on the Children's Ward at Grantham and Kesteven General Hospital During the Period February to April 1991* (1994).

10 Healthcare Commission and the Commission for Social Care Inspection, *Joint Investigation into the Provision of Services for People with Learning Disabilities at Cornwall Partnership NHS Trust* (2006).

11 According to the GMC, *Proposals on Healthcare Professional Regulation* (2006), para 8.

12 In essence, the doctor must seek to be a good person, a tradition dating back to the work of the nineteenth century physician, Thomas Percival: see below at 3.2.

13 We concentrate on the role of the GMC. Other professional regulators include the General Chiropractic, Dental, Optical and Osteopathic Councils, the Nursing and Midwifery Council, the Health Professions Council, the Royal Pharmaceutical Society of Great Britain and the Pharmaceutical Society of Northern Ireland. The Council for Healthcare Regulatory Excellence oversees them all: see below at 1.12. Note that there are proposals to extend the remit of the General Medical Council to cover the regulation of other heath professionals. See GMC, *Proposals on Healthcare Professional Regulation* (2006), para 104.

century after the end of the Nazi era. The transformation of a supposed angel of mercy into the angel of death makes the blood run cold.

Public passion is rightly aroused by the likes of Mengele and Shipman. Passion is never far away from everyday relationships between doctor and patient. Clients usually remain unemotional about their solicitor. If he does a good job they may appreciate him. If he is incompetent they sack him. He will rarely be loved or hated. The family doctor arouses more intense feelings. When doctors meet their patient's expectations, they are rewarded by admiration and affection. Woe betide them if they do not. One error, one moment of exasperation or insensitivity, may transform a beloved doctor into a hate figure. The hospital consultant enjoys or endures a similarly ambivalent role. Consultants were once accorded godlike status. They inspired awe visiting the ward attended by a retinue of junior doctors and nurses. Their exalted status insulated them from personal contact with patients and protected them from the sort of complaints voiced freely to nursing staff. They paid a price. Gods are expected to work miracles. They are not expected to be subject to human error. When a consultant proved to be human, when medicine could not cure, the patient found it hard to comprehend failure and rightly or wrongly – often wrongly – regarded the doctor as personally incompetent.

Medical attitudes are changing, if slowly. Family doctors are becoming a different breed. Many try hard to persuade patients to see their doctor as a partner in promoting good health. Doctors are urged to prescribe less freely and to talk more to their patients. The good GP is as interested in the prevention of ill health as its cure. A new generation of consultants is taking over in the hospitals. They are (in most cases) less grand and more prepared to listen to patients and nursing staff.

One, or even several, 'bad apples' should not destroy the reputations of thousands of other medical practitioners who do their job diligently and compassionately. The medical profession should not be punished for Shipman's bizarre and apparently motiveless murders. Nor should the reputation of surgery be tarnished just because two of their number in Bristol were culpably incompetent. The heart of the problem and the damage to the 'image' of medicine is that too little was done by other doctors to identify and remedy such failings. It seems amazing that no colleague noted or acted on evidence of the number of apparently healthy patients on Shipman's list who died suddenly, in certain cases even in his surgery. An anaesthetist who worked with the Bristol surgeons tried several times to raise his concerns about their competence with his superiors. His complaints were cavalierly dismissed. The Public Interest Disclosure Act 1998, which protects employees who disclose information in the public interest from victimisation, did not prevent his career in Britain stalling and he emigrated to Australia. None the less, as the Bristol Inquiry Report[14] put it, events even at Bristol did not disclose,

> ... an account of bad people. Nor is it an account of people who did not care, nor of people who wilfully harmed patients. It is an account of people who cared greatly about human suffering, and were dedicated and well-motivated.

14 The Bristol Inquiry, p 1.

Sadly some lacked insight and their behaviour was flawed. Many failed to communicate with each other, and to work together effectively for the interests of their patients. There was a lack of leadership, and of teamwork.

There are certain features of the profession of medicine which will render doctors more vulnerable to attack than other professionals. The doctor deals with the individual's most precious commodity, life and health. On a mundane level she may determine whether Patient X is to be sanctioned to enjoy seven days off work for nervous exhaustion brought about by overwork, or classified as another malingerer.[15] At the other end of the scale, the doctor may hold in his hands the power of life and death. He is the man with the skill and experience. In his hands, as the patient sees it, rests the power to cure. As Ian Kennedy has said, the patient appears before the doctor '... naked both physically and emotionally'. It is hard to overstate the power vested in doctors.[16] The price of power is that those who exercise it must expect constant scrutiny from those subject to it and from the public at large. The age of deference is past. Doctors cannot be surprised when failure, incompetence or controversy attract equal notoriety. Unfortunately, representatives of the profession sometimes react in an over-defensive manner, exacerbating the original criticism or complaint.

Entitlement to practise

1.3 One of the crucial functions of regulation is to ensure the competence of professionals offering services to the public. So who is entitled to practise medicine? The GMC maintains a register of medical practitioners. However, no law expressly prohibits any unregistered or unqualified person from practising most types of medicine or even surgery. A criminal offence is committed only when such a person deliberately and falsely represents himself as being a registered practitioner or as having a medical qualification.[17] The rationale of the criminal law is that people should be free to opt for any form of advice or treatment, however bizarre, but must be protected from rogues claiming a bogus status and from commercial exploitation of untested 'alternative' medicine.

Few might quarrel with the liberality of the law where the unqualified 'practitioner' limits himself to advice. What if an unqualified person practises surgery? Any physical contact with a patient permitted under the impression that he is dealing with a 'real doctor' will be a criminal assault. A biology teacher who set himself up in private practice in Lancashire was imprisoned for assault causing grievous bodily harm for carrying out gynaecological operations on unsuspecting women.[18] A more difficult question is raised

---

[15] I Kennedy, *The Unmasking of Medicine* (1981) Allen & Unwin, Chapter 1, pp 9ff.

[16] Kennedy, *The Unmasking of Medicine*, p 8.

[17] Medical Act 1983, s 49; and see *Younghusband v Luftig* [1949] 2 KB 354; *Wilson v Inyang* [1951] 2 KB 799. Unregistered practitioners are expressly prohibited from certain fields of practice, eg venereal disease (see the Venereal Disease Act 1917). They are also barred from holding certain positions (see the Medical Act 1983, s 47).

[18] He was initially sentenced to six years' imprisonment. His sentence was reduced on appeal to 18 months. See also *R v Tabassum* [2000] Lloyd's Rep Med 404, CA.

where the patient agrees to surgery by an unregistered and unlicensed practitioner knowing full well that he is not dealing with a registered and licensed medical practitioner. We would tentatively suggest that a prosecution for assault would still succeed even if nothing went wrong with the 'operation'. The consent of the 'victim' of an assault is not always a defence when bodily harm is done.[19] The public interest in preventing unqualified persons from engaging in surgery may be sufficient to render the 'doctor's' conduct punishable as a crime.

A tradition of self-regulation: to be consigned to history?

1.4 By virtue of the Medical Act 1983, the regulation of the medical profession is currently entrusted to the profession itself, acting through the GMC. This continues a tradition of self-regulation, endorsed by Parliament, dating back to 1858. Prior to 1858, there were in effect three separate medical professions – the physicians, the surgeons and the apothecaries. The Royal Colleges of Physicians and Surgeons wielded great power. Those colleges, joined later by others (for example, the Royal College of Obstetricians and Gynaecologists), continued to control specialist education and specialist practice. Self-regulation has long been the hallmark of the learned professions. The Bar Council used to enjoy extensive powers to regulate barristers, and the Law Society enjoyed a similar jurisdiction over solicitors. Doctors' patients and lawyers' clients were increasingly unconvinced that the professional regulators protected public interests. The GMC came under especially vigorous attack. Its composition was seen as too biased in favour of the doctors, and its capacity to ensure that patients were treated by competent doctors truly fit to practise was doubted. Thus, although the Medical Act 1983 remains on the statute book, Statutory Instruments in 2002[20] and 2006[21] have radically amended that Act. A White Paper published in February 2007 signals further reform.

The Medical Act 1983 (Amendment) Order 2002 sets out the central tenet of all attempts to reform the GMC. It amends the 1983 Act, so that section 1A says simply:

> The main objective of the General Council in exercising their functions is to protect, promote and maintain the safety of the public.

Historically, while the GMC has policed admission to the medical register, little was done to ensure a doctor continued to be competent, and up to date, in her practice. She remained 'licensed' to practise, unless disciplinary proceedings, or health or performance procedures, were invoked against her. Initial registration established that a doctor in her twenties starting out in practice satisfied set criteria for competence. Twenty years after she left medical school, was she still competent? Amendments to Part III of the 1983 Act introduce a

---

19 *R v Brown* [1996] AC 543, HL; and see *Consent in the Criminal Law* (Law Commission Consultation Papers No 139 Part XIII, 1995).

20 The Medical Act 1983 (Amendment) Order 2002, SI 2002/3135.

21 The Medical Act 1983 (Amendment) and Miscellaneous Amendments Order 2006, SI 2006/1914.

scheme for revalidation of medical competence. The GMC will issue doctors a licence to practise on first registration. Then, as we shall see, doctors will be required to renew that licence every five years, proving their continued competence. Revalidation is highly controversial and these new provisions have yet to come into force.

If the absence of processes to monitor doctors' competence caused public concern, what were seen as feeble and apparently prejudiced disciplinary proceedings to deal with complaints against doctors aroused anger.[22] The antique concept of 'infamous conduct in a professional respect' was replaced by the notion of 'serious professional misconduct' in the Medical Act 1969. Critics still argued that the threshold of what constituted such misconduct was set too high, and when such a finding was made, penalties were too lenient. Thus in 2002, the whole of the existing system for disciplining defaulting doctors, dealing with sick doctors and addressing underperforming doctors was revised. The process of reform proceeds at dizzying speed. Critics are still unsatisfied.

Dame Janet Smith's inquiry[23] into the Shipman debacle led to a review of medical regulation by the Chief Medical Officer (CMO), Sir Liam Donaldson. The CMO published a consultation document, *Good Doctors, Safer Patients*, in July 2006, concluding that the GMC is 'too secretive, too tolerant of sub-standard practice and too dominated by the professional interest, rather than that of the patient'.[24] Sir Liam recommended a further shake up of the GMC. In February 2007 the Government responded with a White Paper entitled *Trust, Assurance and Safety – The Regulation of Health Profession-als*.[25] It signals an end to self-regulation of the disciplinary process. In future, an independent body is likely to carry out the adjudication of fitness to practise cases.[26]

Composition of the General Medical Council

1.5 Who regulators are influences how confident the public will be in the process and objectivity of the regulatory framework. In 1983, the GMC comprised 104 members. The lay element was less than 25 per cent. Doctors chosen by their peers dominated the Council. Such a large Council is on any analysis an unwieldy organisation to govern any profession, and in 2002 a

---

[22]   See D Irvine, *A Doctors' Tale* (2003) Radcliffe Medical Press, in particular sections 3 and 4. Sir Donald Irvine was the President of the GMC from 1995–2002.

[23]   Fifth Report of the Shipman Inquiry, *Safeguarding Patients: Lessons From the Past— Proposals for the Future* (2004) Cm 6394 (hereafter the Shipman Inquiry).

[24]   Department of Health, *CMO's Report, Good Doctors, Safer Patients: Proposals to Strengthen the System to Assure and Improve the Performance of Doctors and to Protect the Safety of Patients* (2006), para 60 (hereafter *Good Doctors, Safer Patients*). Published simultaneously was the Department of Health, The Regulation of Non-Medical Health Care Professionals (2006). Though the two reach similar conclusions, there are divergences. A consultation period ran from July–November 2006.

[25]   Secretary of State for Health, *Trust, Assurance and Safety – The Regulation of Health Professionals*, White Paper (2006) Cm 7013 (hereafter Trust, Assurance and Safety).

[26]   *Trust, Assurance and Safety*, para 4.36.

new Council of no more than 35 members was established.[27] Nineteen members are elected by the profession, two doctors are appointed by the Academy of Medical Sciences and the universities, and 14 lay people are appointed by the Appointments Commission.[28] Lay representation on the Council rose to 40 per cent to reflect the GMC's commitment to professionally-led regulation in partnership with the public. In his 2006 review, the CMO has recommended that *all* members should be independently appointed by the Appointments Commission and a President elected from its members.[29] In response, the GMC agreed that the constitution of the Council should change again.[30] It proposed equal proportions of medical and lay members with no in-built majority (medical or otherwise) in order to create a 'balanced composition'. The February 2007 White Paper supports this proposition. There should no longer be a professional majority. In future there will be a minimum of parity of membership between professional and lay council members. All members will be appointed by the Appointments Commission.[31]

So what does the GMC do? At the time of writing, the GMC has four principal functions:

(1)   To provide advice for doctors on ethics and standards of professional conduct.
(2)   To oversee medical education.
(3)   To maintain a register of qualified doctors.
(4)   To discipline doctors.

A fifth role, revalidation, is already provided for in amendments to the Medical Act 1983 not yet brought into force. Let us examine role each in turn.

Advisory function

1.6 First, the Council is charged with providing advice for doctors on ethics and standards of professional conduct, standards of professional performance and medical ethics.[32] Reference to this advice is made throughout this book. The core guidance is contained in *Good Medical Practice*, which was first produced in 1995 and was comprehensively revised in 2006. The 2006 version emphasises the importance of partnership between doctors and patients, and places new weight on equality and diversity. Most importantly, it clarifies the standard of professional conduct which underpins the GMC's fitness to practise procedures. The aim is to achieve greater certainty and consistency in both patient expectations and doctors' professional standards.

---

[27] Medical Act 1983, Sch 1, Pt 1, para 1(3) as amended by SI 2002/3135, Art 4.
[28] The NHS Appointments Commission (a special health authority) was abolished by s 57 of the Health Act 2006 and replaced by the Appointments Commission (a non-departmental public body).
[29] *Good Doctors, Safer Patients*, recommendation 43.
[30] GMC, *Proposals on Healthcare Professional Regulation*.
[31] *Trust, Assurance and Safety*, para 1.12.
[32] See s 35 of the Medical Act 1983 as amended by SI 2002/3135.

Medical education

1.7 Second, the Council sets standards and outcomes for undergraduate medical education and the first year of training after graduation.[33] On completion of the medical degree, a new section 10A[34] of the Medical Act 1983 will ensure that provisionally registered, newly-qualified doctors receive more consistent and rigorous training. A two-year Foundation Programme is being rolled out to bridge the gap between medical school and specialist or GP training. The GMC currently regulates the first year of the Foundation Programme (F1). Historically, regulation focused purely on a doctor's experience. This is set to change.[35] In order to achieve full registration at the end of their 'F1' year, doctors will need to demonstrate that they have reached *outcomes* set by the GMC's Education Committee.[36] It is expected that this part of the 2006 Order will come into effect in August 2007.

Doctors who have successfully completed the F1 year, undergo their second Foundation Programme year (F2). Historically, control of postgraduate medical education rested with the Royal Colleges of Medicine. Much of the Colleges' power passed to the Postgraduate Medical Education and Training Board (PMETB),[37] which promotes postgraduate medical education for all medical specialties.[38] The PMETB regulates F2s and further postgraduate training. At the end of the F2 year, doctors will compete for training in their chosen speciality or GP training which in turn will lead, subject to assessment, to a Certificate of Completion of Training (CCT) or a Statement of Eligibility for Registration in General Practice.[39]

The CMO proposed that in the interests of consistency and better co-ordination of medical training, the GMC should hand over responsibility for the undergraduate curriculum and the first year of the Foundation Programme to the PMETB. The GMC argues that this would 'damage regulatory coherence, fragment responsibilities and work against patient interests'.[40] The Council accepts that better co-ordination is required, but argues that the combined undergraduate, postgraduate and continuing education of doctors would be better placed with the GMC than the PMETB. The February 2007 White Paper partially accepts the GMC's recommendations:

---

[33] GMC, *Tomorrow's Doctors: Recommendations on Undergraduate Medical Education* (2003); GMC and PMETB, *Principles of Good Medical Education and Training* (2005); GMC, *The New Doctor – Transitional Edition* (2005). See also the GMC's proposals to introduce changes to the undergraduate curriculum and make assessment more robust: GMC Education Committee, Final Report, *Strategic Options for Undergraduate Medical Education* (2006).

[34] SI 2006/1914, Pt III, Art 24.

[35] See GMC, *The New Doctor – Transitional Edition*, which sets down the new outcome-based framework.

[36] SI 2006/1914, Art 21 will amend s 5 of the Medical Act 1983 accordingly.

[37] Established under the General and Specialist Medical Practice (Education, Training and Qualifications) Order 2003, SI 2003/1250.

[38] The revised postgraduate curriculum was written by the Academy of Medical Royal Colleges Foundation Committee and Modernising Medical Careers: see http://www.mmc.nhs.uk/.

[39] SI 2003/1250, Pt III.

[40] GMC, *Proposals on Healthcare Professional Regulation*, para 36.

the GMC will develop a new undergraduate board and continue its professional development board, while the PMETB will continue to fulfil its role as postgraduate board. In future, better co-operation will be required of the two organisations.[41]

Maintaining a register

1.8 Third, the GMC is charged with the maintenance of the 'list of registered medical practitioners'. Doctors listed on the medical register have full, provisional or limited registration. 'Provisional' registration is for new medical graduates. Doctors with 'full' registration are eligible for unsupervised medical practice. Equivalent qualifications from other Member States of the European Union must be recognised by the Joint Committee on Higher Medical Training, soon to change its name to the Joint Royal Colleges of Physicians Training Board.[42] 'Limited' registration is given to certain international medical graduates (IMGs), but will gradually be replaced with full registration when the 2006 Order[43] comes into force.[44]

Registration alone used to be sufficient to permit a doctor to practise medicine and hold herself out as a medical practitioner. Amendments to the Medical Act 1983[45] (yet to come fully into force) will additionally require that doctors hold a licence to practise from the GMC. Such a licence will be granted at registration. Revalidation will require regular renewal of the licence.

Until recently, the GMC exercised no control over specialist qualifications. A doctor was registered as a medical practitioner, and then, in theory at least, could practise in whatever specialty he chose. NHS hospitals might be unlikely to employ an obstetrician who had not gained membership of the Royal College of Obstetricians and Gynaecologists. The private patient had to check for herself whether her obstetrician had expertise in obstetrics. Now, in addition to the 'general' medical register, there is a specialist and a GP register.[46] All are accessible online. The GP register is a list of GPs eligible to work in the UK. It does not include GP registrars (trainee GPs). It provides information for patients and aids pre-employment checks.[47] The specialist register identifies medical practitioners by their specialties, accreditation and qualifications. The Joint Committee on Higher Medical Teaching, which will become the Joint Royal College of Physicians Training Board in March 2007, undertakes the actual accreditation of specialists. Practising in a specialty

[41] *Trust, Assurance and Safety*, para 5.9.
[42] In March 2007.
[43] SI 2006/1914, Pt II abolishes limited registration. Part IV sets down new arrangements for the registration of persons qualifying outside the EU.
[44] Note, however, that the Department of Health changed the immigration rules for postgraduate doctors in 2006. Doctors that were considered 'in training' for immigration purposes are now viewed as 'in employment' and require the necessary work permits.
[45] SI 2002/3135, Pt V inserts a new Part IIIA, 'Licence to Practise and Revalidation' into the Medical Act 1983. This provision has not yet been brought into effect.
[46] Both set up under SI 2003/1250, Pt IV.
[47] See recommendations in *Trust, Assurance and Safety*, para 6.10, that the register might be further developed to provide a 'single authoritative source of information on doctors, including disciplinary action by employers and alert notices'.

outside the specialism on the register is still not prohibited. The specialist register acts as a source of information rather than a 'guarantee' of the specialist's competence.

Revalidation

1.9 Registration is evidence that the doctor on entry to the register satisfied criteria for medical competence. The GMC itself recognised that it was not enough to maintain standards by acting after complaints are made about a doctor's practice. So, the GMC adopted proposals to ensure monitoring of medical practice. The revalidation process, under which doctors are to be revalidated every five years to ensure their general fitness to practise and compliance with *Good Medical Practice* guidance, was due to be implemented in April 2005,[48] but the Fifth Report of the Shipman Inquiry[49] highlighted a number of serious concerns. In particular, section 29A of the Medical Act 1983, as amended, which imposes a duty on the GMC to set up a revalidation scheme, defines revalidation as an 'evaluation' of a doctor's fitness to practise. Dame Janet was concerned that the process set to begin in April 2005 was formative rather than evaluative.[50] The concept of revalidation had been watered down:

> By 2004, revalidation (on a five-yearly basis) would involve a statement from a doctor's employer, confirming the lack of any significant concerns and documentary evidence of participation in an annual process of peer-appraisal. ... Furthermore, the consequences of failing to revalidate were not made explicit: would a practitioner have to cease to practise, or would they 'limp on' in substandard practice, through to the next revalidation cycle?[51]

Consequently, in December 2004, Lord Warner announced that the scheme would be postponed pending the outcome of the CMO's consultation on medical regulation.[52]

The CMO now recommends a revised and more rigorous scheme of revalidation. His recommendations are generally endorsed in the February 2007 White Paper.[53] Revalidation should be broken down into two distinct procedures: re-licensing and re-certification. Doctors on the medical register would be called upon to prove their competence in order to be 're-licensed'. The GMC would retain responsibility for re-licensing, for a doctor's basic competence. New 'GMC Affiliates' would apply amended NHS appraisal procedures at a

---

48   SI 2002/3135, Pt V.
49   Chapter 26.
50   Shipman Inquiry, paras 27.261–27.262.
51   *Good Doctors, Safer Patients*, para 50.
52   See Department of Health, *CMO's Review of Medical Revalidation, A Call for Ideas* (3 March 2005), accessible online at www.dh.gov.uk.
53   *Trust, Assurance and Safety*, para 2.7. Though, contrary to the CMO's report, the White Paper proposes (at p 7) three streams of revalidation depending on whether the professional is an employee of an approved body (such as a nurse or paramedic), someone performing services commissioned by primary care organisations or a health care provider, such as an osteopath, who falls outside the other two categories.

local level. Supervised practice, or a break from practice, might be imposed on doctors found wanting, followed by re-assessment at a later date.

As we have seen, from August 2007, UK specialist training programmes will lead to the conferral of a Certificate of Completion of Training. New specialists will require this certificate in order to be placed on the specialist register. Similarly, those entered on the GP register will require a Statement of Eligibility for Registration in General Practice. Existing specialists and GPs who have not undergone the new training must apply to the PMETB for entry to the GP/specialist registers, demonstrating by virtue of their previous experience and training that they reach the required standard.[54] 'Recertification', as proposed by the CMO, will require renewal of specialist certificates every five years. The powers of the Royal Colleges would be increased under the proposals. They would be responsible both for specialist qualifications and for re-certification.

The GMC supports the CMO's twin track revalidation system 'in principle',[55] mindful of the costs and difficulties inherent in rolling out the scheme. It is unclear whether revalidation will take the form of a single national scheme or will be tailored to the requirements of the specific medical specialities. A consultation will be will undertaken to determine how best to proceed.[56]

Disciplining doctors: fitness to practise

1.10 Ethical standards, education and competence are crucial components of effective regulation. How the regulator deals with complaints that a professional is not fit to practise is the most important issue for its 'clients'. Dissatisfaction with the GMC's handling of accusations of professional misconduct resulted in a radical overhaul of all the GMC's procedures for dealing with misconduct, sick doctors and underperforming practitioners. On 1 November 2004,[57] new fitness to practise criteria were introduced. The separate streams of health, performance and conduct were abandoned. Now complaints about doctors involve an analysis of their fitness to practise in the round. The aim is to create a general overview of the doctor's fitness to practise.

Under section 35C(2) of the Medical Act 1983, as amended, impairment can result from all or any of the following:

(a) misconduct;
(b) deficient professional performance;
(c) a conviction or caution in the British Islands for a criminal offence, or a conviction elsewhere for an offence which, if committed in England and Wales, would constitute a criminal offence;
(d) adverse physical or mental health; or

---

[54] SI 2003/1250, Arts 11–14.
[55] GMC, *Proposals on Healthcare Professional Regulation*, paras 73–81.
[56] *Trust, Assurance and Safety*, para 2.12.
[57] The General Medical Council (Fitness to Practise) Rules Order of Council 2004, SI 2004/2608.

(e)   a determination by a body in the United Kingdom responsible under any enactment for the regulation of a health or social care profession to the effect that his fitness to practise as a member of that profession is impaired, or a determination by a regulatory body elsewhere to the same effect.

Better communication between the GMC and the doctor's employers is encouraged by disclosing complaints to employers at an earlier stage in the process.[58] A simplified two-stage procedure, investigation and adjudication, has been introduced. At the investigation stage, the case examiners (one medical and one lay) can refer the doctor to an interim orders panel where there is a clear need to protect patients or the public interest.[59] The panel has the power to impose an interim order restricting or suspending the doctor's right to practise pending the full investigation.[60] Where the public interest is not threatened, the GMC has since advised that a single test which emphasises the GMC's duty to the public is applied to determine whether a doctor should be referred to a fitness to practise panel for a full hearing:

> The Investigation Committee or case examiner must have in mind the GMC's duty to act in the public interest which includes the protection of patients and maintaining public confidence in the profession, in considering whether there is a realistic prospect of establishing that a doctor's fitness to practise is impaired to a degree justifying action on registration.[61]

At this stage the GMC may issue a warning: a measure introduced for cases which call for an official response, but which are not serious enough to justify restrictions on the doctor's registration, when either 'there has been a significant departure from *Good Medical Practice*' or 'a performance assessment has indicated a significant cause for concern'. The warning may be used at either the investigation or adjudication stage.

The reformed procedure attempts to address the criticism that the GMC acts as both prosecutor and judge. Yet whilst the new fitness to practise panellists are 'independent' they are selected and trained by the GMC, so arguably the separation of powers problem has been only partially resolved.[62] The panellists apply the following, much simplified single test:

> Do the findings we have made show that the doctor's fitness to practise is impaired to a degree justifying action on registration?[63]

If the answer is 'no', then a warning can be issued[64] or no further action taken. If the answer is 'yes', then the panel have four options:

(1)   erasure from the medical register (except in health cases),
(2)   suspension from the register for a maximum of twelve months,

---

[58]   Medical Act 1983, s 35B.
[59]   Medical Act 1983, s 35C(8).
[60]   Medical Act 1983, s 41A.
[61]   GMC, *Making Decision on Cases at the End of the Investigation Stage: Guidance for Case Examiners and the Investigation Committee* (2006), para 14.
[62]   Shipman Inquiry, paras 27.204–27.210.
[63]   GMC, *Media Briefing Paper: The GMC Reforms: Making Fitness to Practise Fit for Practice* (6 December 2004).
[64]   Medical Act 1983, s 35D(3).

(3)   conditional registration and
(4)   undertakings, for example, to take medical treatment for a condition impairing fitness to practise.[65] The panel must provide reasons for their decision.[66]

As we have seen, the Medical Act 1983 was further amended in 2006.[67] At the time of writing, a timetable for implementation is still being discussed. The 2006 Order requires that all doctors will need to show that their fitness to practise is not impaired at the point of registration. Failure to declare relevant factors could lead to the doctor being struck from the register. Doctors will be required to carry professional indemnity or insurance cover from the point of registration and failure to do so could amount to impaired fitness to practise.

Too little, too late?

1.11 Do the reforms of the GMC go far enough? The Fifth Report of the Shipman Inquiry suggested not.[68] Whilst Dame Janet Smith stopped short of suggesting that the GMC should be deprived of its fitness to practise function, she contended that many of the defects present in the old system survive the reforms. Whilst the new concept of 'impairment of fitness to practise' is 'all-embracing', it lacks clarity of meaning. No standard had been set for impairment of fitness to practise, making it difficult to define and recognise.[69] The solution, according to Dame Janet, lies in the development of agreed standards, criteria and thresholds. Without these, doctors will not know what conduct is likely to result in action on their registration, users will find it difficult to determine the appropriate body to which their complaint should be directed, employers will make mistakes in referral of cases to the GMC, and GMC rulings will remain inconsistent.[70]

In the CMO's report of 2006, Sir Liam Donaldson judged that whilst the all-encompassing 'impaired fitness to practise' goes a long way toward streamlining the labyrinthine process of dealing with performance complaints, it swaps one circular definition for another. Without better guidance as to what constitutes impairment, the shortcomings of the old system remain. Doctors and patients alike need to know what it is to be a 'good doctor'. Clear standards need to be incorporated into doctors' contracts. In response to the CMO's report, the GMC issued comprehensive new guidance, *Good Medical Practice* in 2006,[71] with links to external guidance and examples of fitness to practise cases. For example, when deciding what course of treatment is in the best interests of a child, a doctor might, in certain circumstances, act contrary to the law by restricting his analysis to the child's *medical* best interests. Wider, welfare interests should be factored into the decision. Practical guidance is being developed by the GMC, informing doctors of the relevant factors

[65]   Medical Act 1983, s 35D(3).
[66]   *Threlfall v General Optical Council* [2004] EWHC 2683 (Admin).
[67]   SI 2006/1914.
[68]   Shipman Inquiry, Chapters 25 and 27.
[69]   Shipman Inquiry, para 25.42.
[70]   Shipman Inquiry, paras 27.221–27.222.
[71]   See http://www.gmc-uk.org/guidance/good_medical_practice/index.asp.

to consider when making this assessment.[72] More is yet to be done. The February 2007 White Paper indicates that the standards should 'be adapted to address the skills and competencies required for career grade doctors who specialise in specific fields of practice.'[73] Doctors need to know specifically what is required of them.

Medical students are not exempt from the process of change. Since the GMC published *Tomorrow's Doctors* in 1993, medical schools have been required to have in place fitness to practise procedures. Between 2000 and 2004, there were 92 cases leading to 23 students being forced to abandon their studies,[74] but the procedures are vague and inconsistent. The CMO recommends that students are awarded 'student registration' with the GMC and that each medical school have a 'GMC affiliate' to operate procedures in line with those in place for registered doctors.[75] Consultation has begun on draft guidance for medical schools and students, issued by the GMC in January 2007.[76]

The GMC is still reeling from the 2004 reforms,[77] but the critics are far from satisfied. Substantial changes to fitness to practise procedures are recommended by the CMO. Recommendations 2–10 relate to the creation of new 'GMC Affiliates' who will react to complaints and concerns at a local level. Their creation will add a monitoring function to the GMC. Only the more serious cases will be referred to the central GMC. Affiliates will have a power to agree a 'recorded concern' which does not affect registration. Recorded concerns will be reviewed by a national committee which will have the power to refer a doctor for further assessment or investigation. The February 2007 White Paper supports these recommendations in principle and the Secretary of State will seek approval to establish a network of GMC Affiliates through primary legislation.[78] The Affiliates will not be attached to individual institutions. Rather, they will exist at a regional level in England and a national level in Scotland, Wales and Northern Ireland.[79] This goes some way to allaying fears that the GMC Affiliates as proposed by the CMO would be 'copper's narks',[80] policing individual trusts and hospitals. The Affiliates will lead regional medical regulation support teams. Various approaches will be piloted prior to full roll-out. In smaller organisations, such as primary care organisations, medical directors and others in similar roles are likely to take on some of the roles originally envisaged by the CMO for the GMC Affiliates.[81] All doctors on the medical register will be assigned a relevant Affiliate or other

---

[72]   GMC, *Children and Young People: Doctors' Roles and Responsibilities* (Draft for Consultation) (2006).

[73]   *Trust, Assurance and Safety*, para 2.9.

[74]   GMC, 'Student Fitness to Practise' *GMC Today* (Feb/Mar 2006).

[75]   *Good Doctors, Safer Patients*, recommendation 23.

[76]   GMC and Council on Heads of Medical Schools, *Guidance on Student Fitness to Practise* (*Draft*) (2007). See also *Trust, Assurance and Safety*, paras 6.6–6.7, which recognises that each regulator should employ measures according to the risks inherent in the particular profession and requires regulators to issue a progress report in January 2008.

[77]   SI 2004/2608.

[78]   *Trust, Assurance and Safety*, para 3.31.

[79]   *Trust, Assurance and Safety*, para 3.31.

[80]   S Boseley, 'Doctors to Face Independent Review in Cases of Misconduct' (2006) Guardian, 15 July.

[81]   *Trust, Assurance and Safety*, paras 3.32, 3.35.

'responsible officer', who will have the power to require doctors to attend meetings to resolve patient complaints.[82]

The White Paper endorses the recommendation of both the CMO and the Shipman Inquiry, that the standard of proof applied by tribunals should no longer be the criminal 'beyond reasonable doubt' standard. Instead, the civil 'balance of probabilities' standard will apply, as it does in cases governed by the majority of health regulators. However, the civil standard proposed in the White Paper is a sliding standard which can be flexibly applied: the more serious the matter, the greater the degree of probability required.[83]

Most controversially, the CMO recommended that in serious fitness to practise cases, which cannot be dealt with locally, investigatory powers will be retained by the GMC but the formal adjudication will be undertaken by an independent tribunal. The White Paper endorses this view.[84] The GMC will no longer be prosecutor, judge and jury. Instead, it will take on a role akin to the Crown Prosecution Service. More doctors are likely to come before the tribunal and, given the new standard of proof, more are likely to be found lacking.

Whilst the GMC accepts that the channels of communication between national and local systems need improvement, it expressed doubts as to whether Affiliates are the answer.[85] Neither will the reader be surprised to learn that the GMC does not see the need for a separate and independent tribunal for serious cases.[86] The GMC argues that the 2004 reforms, which created a distinction between investigation and adjudication, have resulted in substantial improvement. In 2005, the GMC heard 273 fitness to practise cases, out of which only twelve doctors appealed. Of those, only six were successful.[87] The Government is clearly not convinced. Change is required to ensure public and professional confidence. The GMC's days of self-regulation are numbered.

Appeals to the High Court and the Council for Healthcare Regulatory Excellence

1.12 A doctor whose fitness to practise is found to be impaired has a right of appeal to the High Court.[88] If the White Paper is endorsed and the GMC hands over its powers of adjudication to a tribunal, then it too will have a right of appeal to the High Court.[89] Acting on proposals in both the NHS Plan and the Bristol Inquiry Report,[90] sections 25–29 of the National Health Service Reform and Health Care Professions Act 2002 established a Council

---

82 *Trust, Assurance and Safety*, para 3.37.
83 *Trust, Assurance and Safety*, para 4.6.
84 *Trust, Assurance and Safety*, para 4.36.
85 GMC, *Proposals on Healthcare Professional Regulation*, paras 82–89.
86 GMC, *Proposals on Healthcare Professional Regulation*, paras 65–82.
87 GMC, *Proposals on Healthcare Professional Regulation*, para 66.
88 See s 28 of the National Health Service Reform and Health Care Professions Act 2002.
89 *Trust, Assurance and Safety*, para 4.36.
90 See the Bristol Inquiry, pp 349–350.

for the Regulation of Health Care Professionals, now renamed the Council for Regulatory Health Excellence. This Council has overarching powers to control the 13 regulatory bodies of all the health care professions, from the GMC to the Nursing and Midwifery Council to the General Optical Council.[91] In addition to promoting best practice, it reports to Parliament on the performance of the regulatory bodies and may appeal decisions that appear unduly lenient to the High Court.[92] Around 1.3 per cent of cases received by the CRHE are referred to the High Court under section 29 of the 2002 Act.[93] This function has caused some disquiet on the basis that the criteria for determining undue leniency include the 'maintenance of public confidence in regulation', which might potentially go beyond the merits of the case.[94] In 2004, the Court of Appeal clarified the CHRE's powers.[95] Not only may it refer cases to the High Court when it is of the view that regulators have acted too leniently in applying 'penalties', it may also do so when the regulator acquits a health care professional. Thus, even if a doctor is acquitted by the GMC, the CHRE may refer him to the High Court which may impose a sanction. Mason and Laurie point out that the element of double jeopardy such doctors are subjected to has potential to offend their rights under Article 6 of the European Convention of Human Rights.[96]

Regulating the NHS

1.13 The first part of this chapter examined the regulation of individual doctors. We now turn to methods by which NHS organisations are regulated.

Supervising, managing and protecting employees

1.14 Individual doctors face sanctions when they fall short of good medical practice. But what of the employing organisation? Poor treatment often has several causes. Poor doctors are created by poor systems. In 2000, a 31-year-old father was admitted to hospital for minor knee surgery. The operation was a success, but he went on to develop an infection which resulted in toxic shock syndrome from which, tragically, he died. Doctors Misra and Srivastava had failed to diagnose the infection and were convicted of gross negligence manslaughter in 2003,[97] and suspended from the medical register by the GMC in 2005. In 2006, Southampton University Hospital NHS Trust became the first NHS trust to be prosecuted under the Health and Safety

---

[91]   See, for example, *Council for the Regulation of Healthcare Professionals v General Medical Council* [2005] EWHC 579 (Admin).

[92]   In *Trust, Assurance and Safety*, para 4.17, it is proposed that CHRE develop common protocols for investigation across the regulators.

[93]   Council for Healthcare Regulatory Excellence, *Annual Report 2005–6*, para 2.4.

[94]   See, for example, Editorial, 'Concerns Raised About CHRE's Powers and Its Use of Spin Doctors' (2004) 273 *The Pharmaceutical Journal* 578.

[95]   *Ruscillo v Council for the Regulation of Health Care Professionals; the GMC, CHRP v NMC and Truscott* [2004] EWCA Civ 1356.

[96]   JK Mason and GT Laurie, *Mason and McCall Smith's Law and Medical Ethics* (7th edn, 2006) OUP, p 19. See also A Samanta and J Samanta, 'Referring GMC Decisions to the High Court' (2005) 330 *British Medical Journal* 103.

[97]   See below at 7.21.

at Work Act 1974 for failing to manage the two junior doctors adequately. The Trust pleaded guilty to a charge of improper supervision and was fined £100,000 and ordered to pay £10,000 costs.[98]

Organisations must take measures to protect their employees adequately. Work-related stress amongst NHS staff is widespread.[99] Long working hours exacerbate the problem. Stressed doctors put patients at risk. The European Working Time Directive,[100] implemented in 1998,[101] laid down minimum requirements in relation to working hours for everyone, but for doctors the rules could be – and were – circumvented in a number of ways. There have been two recent changes to the law in this respect. First, the 2003 European Court of Justice ruling in *Jaeger*[102] affected the way on-call staff's working hours were calculated. Now, on-call staff resident at work out of hours are considered to be 'working' whilst on duty, whether or not they are called to the bedside. Second, trainee doctors were initially excluded from the regulations, putting them at particular risk of psychological distress.[103] However, since 2004[104] trainees' working weeks must not exceed 58 hours, and they have entitlements to daily and weekly rest breaks. Troublingly, in an organisation of finite resources, is it possible that the psychological burden is being shifted rather than reduced? Junior doctors are better protected, but is this at the expense of senior doctors?

Governance

1.15 NHS organisations are responsible for a rigorous system of clinical governance. Clinical audit and quality improvement are given high priority. A formal requirement for clinical audit in the NHS was introduced in 1989.[105] But the system was found lacking by the Bristol Inquiry, which recommended that clinical audit should be at the core of a system of local monitoring of performance.

At a national level, too, audit and monitoring are entrenched in the modern NHS. The Department of Health assesses and reports on the performance of health care organisations on an annual basis. The Commission for Health Improvement (CHI) issued the first 'star ratings' in 2003. In 2004, the CHI became the Commission for Healthcare Audit and Inspection, known as the

---

[98] See 'Trust Guilty Over Death Doctors' (2006) BBC News, 11 January (available at http://news.bbc.co.uk).
[99] See 'Work Stress Finding in NHS Survey' (2006) BBC News, 6 March (available at http://news.bbc.co.uk).
[100] (EC) 93/104.
[101] SI 1998/1833.
[102] Case C-151/02 *Landeshauptstadt Kiel v Norbert Jaeger* [2003] ECR I-8389.
[103] J Firth-Cozens, 'Emotional Distress in Junior House Officers' (1987) 295 *British Medical Journal* 539.
[104] Working Time (Amendment) Regulations 2003, SI 2003/1684.
[105] Secretaries of State for Social Services, Wales, Northern Ireland and Scotland, *Working for Patients* (1989) Cm 555.

Healthcare Commission,[106] chaired by Professor Sir Ian Kennedy. The Commission investigates serious service failings either at the instigation of patients, NHS staff and the media, or resulting from its screening processes. It has a monitoring function and can visit unannounced at NHS and independent health care organisations in order, for example, to check their compliance with hospital acquired infection measures.[107]

In 2005 the 'star ratings' were replaced with a broader 'annual health check', in which the Commission details the safety, effectiveness and efficiency of health care services. In its 2006 report, improvements in capacity are noted along with concerns regarding patient safety and the quality of services for the most vulnerable patients (such as older people and mental health patients).[108] Whilst increased investment has led to some improvement, recent reforms of the NHS have resulted in spiralling costs.

Reforming the NHS

1.16 Many books have been written about the NHS.[109] Here we give a brief introduction to recent initiatives. Since 1974, the NHS has been subject to a constant stream of political reform. Recently, the numerous NHS Acts have been consolidated into the National Health Service Act 2006.[110] It comes into force in March 2007, but effects little change.

What matters is how publicly-funded NHS care is delivered and its implications for patients, and for their legal rights. In 1991, NHS hospital trusts were first created and the NHS was divided into 'purchasers' and 'providers'. In 1995, the Conservative Government introduced the internal 'market' and GP fund-holding. The Government's philosophy was that local health authorities or GP fund-holders would seek out the best quality and best value hospital treatment and other secondary care for all their patients. Hospital trusts would compete to attract patients. GP fund holding was abolished by the incoming Labour Government in 1997. Twenty-eight strategic health authorities (SHAs) were created in 2001 to manage the performance of the NHS locally. Three hundred and three primary care trusts (PCTs) were created to provide health services. Less emphasis was placed on financial management and many NHS organisations incurred deficits. New emphasis was placed on decentralisation: a patient-led NHS. Focus on patient choice led to the reinstatement of competition between trusts in 2004, and in 2006 mergers

---

[106] Set up under s 41 of the Health and Social Care (Community Health and Standards) Act 2003. The Healthcare Commission incorporates CHI, the Mental Health Act Commission and the National Care Standards Commission (which oversaw the independent health care sector).

[107] See Commission for Healthcare Audit and Inspection, *A Snapshot of Hospital Cleanliness in England* (2005).

[108] Commission for Healthcare Audit and Inspection, *State of Healthcare 2006* (2006).

[109] Recent examples include M Tempest, *The Future of the NHS* (2006) XPL Publishing and the controversial A Pollock, *NHS Plc: The Privatisation of our Healthcare* (2005) Verso Books.

[110] As well as the National Health Service (Wales) Act 2006 and the National Health Service (Consequential Provisions) Act 2006.

resulted in the number of SHAs being reduced to ten and PCTs to approximately 100, creating units of a size reminiscent of the regional offices and health authorities abolished in 2001. The NHS, it seems, has come full circle.

The reformulation of PCTs and SHAs and the introduction of foundation trusts, payment by results, practise-based commissioning and independent sector treatment centres placed intense financial pressures on NHS organisations. Despite substantial investment,[111] the 2005/06 unaudited English NHS accounts revealed a net deficit of £536m.[112] The Audit Commission blames the impact of national policies and decisions, in addition to local management problems and local health economy problems.[113] NHS trusts with a deficit are responsible for recovering their financial position, usually within four years.[114] In some cases, external accountants are imposed on NHS trusts to find savings. Trusts working to make up for last year's deficits must make cuts for this year's patients. Staff cuts, closed wards,[115] and delayed and cancelled work have NHS workers running scared. Financial accountability necessarily limits the impact of clinical accountability, which seeks to limit inconsistencies and improve patient care.

Primary care

1.17 Primary care is the 'front line' of the NHS. The local surgery is often the patient's first point of contact. There she can see a range of health care professionals, such as nurses, GPs or midwives and access a range of services. PCTs were first established in 2000. They plan and commission services for the locality, from GPs and hospitals, to pharmacies and NHS Direct. From April 2003, 75 per cent of the NHS budget devolved to PCTs.[116] PCTs must work within a strict budget (which may be increased if targets are met) which they receive directly from the Department of Health. Commissioning is central to the reformed NHS. PCTs can commission NHS trusts, NHS foundation trusts, NHS or independent sector treatment centres and other independent sector providers. By 2008, PCTs will be able to commission any health care provider meeting NHS standards and budget. PCTs can devolve some of their responsibilities. They can give GP practices (or groups of GP practices)[117] indicative budgets and allow them to become more directly involved in the

---

[111] Department of Health, *Delivering the NHS Plan: Next Steps on Investment, Next Steps on Reform* (2002).

[112] Audit Commission, *Audit Commission Review of the NHS Financial Management and Accounting Regime* (July 2006); and see King's Fund, *King's Fund Response to Health Select Committee Inquiry on NHS Deficits* (June 2006), p 1.

[113] *King's Fund Response to Health Select Committee Inquiry on NHS Deficits*, p 3.

[114] Under s 10 of the NHS and Community Care Act 1990, 'Every NHS Trust shall ensure that its revenues is not less than sufficient, taking one year with another, to meet outgoings properly chargeable to revenue account'. Consolidated in the National Health Service Act 2006, Sch 5, para 2(1).

[115] Though see *R (on the application of Morris) v Trafford Healthcare NHS Trust* [2006] EWHC 2334 (Admin) on the duty to engage in public consultation prior to ward closure.

[116] Department of Health, *Sustaining Innovation Through New PMS Arrangements* (2004), p 7.

[117] GP practices frequently group together to make commissioning decisions.

commissioning of services that best suit their particular patients. At the end of 2006, 'Practice Based Commissioning', as it is called, had near universal coverage. The intention is to increase the variety of services and providers, so enhancing convenience for patients.[118]

Freedom comes at a price. Not only is it accompanied by responsibility to provide services that represent value for money, but it inevitably leads to differences in the way PCTs and individual GP practices allocate resources – resulting in the proliferation of the controversial 'postcode lottery'.[119] Some PCTs may be prepared to fund drugs which others consider too costly. In 2006, the CMO[120] concluded that the 'inappropriate variations in clinical practice' could not be explained by differing health needs of patients or their economic status. He called for the better sharing of knowledge by the National Institute for Health and Clinical Excellence and tighter controls to benchmark provision.

Secondary care

1.18 Secondary care has also been subject to reform in the effort to drive down waiting lists and improve patient choice. Three initiatives have emerged. The first concerns the creation of a wider range of providers. Patients referred by their GPs for hospital diagnostic or treatment procedures have previously been presented with little choice or flexibility. Elective procedures were frequently delayed or cancelled due to the unpredictability of priority emergency surgery. From 2006, the aim is for NHS patients to be able to choose from a menu of four or five different providers when their GP refers them for hospital treatment or diagnosis. Among these may be a treatment centre. The Treatment Centre Programme established both NHS and independent sector treatment centres (ISTCs), which aim to make elective treatment efficient and convenient.[121] Positive results of quality monitoring are emerging,[122] but in 2006 the Health Select Committee[123] revealed a number of concerns, including inadequate communication and follow-up, poor resources when operations go wrong and differing standards.

The second initiative gives more freedom to hospitals. Foundation trusts were established by the Health and Social Care (Community Health and Standards) Act 2003.[124] Whilst subject to NHS inspection and standards, they are independent not-for-profit public benefit corporations with unique governance arrangements. Under these terms, investment from both the public and private sectors is encouraged. They are authorised by 'Monitor', an independent

---

[118] Department of Health, *Commissioning a Patient-Led NHS* (2005).
[119] See King's Fund, *Local Variations in NHS Spending Priorities* (August 2006).
[120] *On the State of the Public Health: Annual Report of the Chief Medical Officer 2005* (July 2006), Chapter 2.
[121] Department of Health, *Growing Capacity: Independent Sector Diagnosis and Treatment Centres* (2002).
[122] National Centre for Health Outcomes Development, *Preliminary Overview Report for Schemes GSUP1, OC123, LP4 and LP5: ISTC Performance and Analysis Service* (2005).
[123] HC 934-II.
[124] Consolidated in the National Health Service Act 2006, Part 2, Chapter 5 (ss 30–65).

regulator, and governed by people elected from and by the membership base (which includes patients, the public and staff). The Government is committed to giving all NHS trusts the opportunity to apply for foundation trust status by 2008.

The third initiative is a new rule-based, transparent NHS tariff. Every procedure carries a fixed price and hospitals are paid for what they do: 'payment by results' (PbR), or more accurately payment by activity. PbR replaces block contracts and locally agreed prices in the NHS, aiming to reward efficiency and encourage patient choice and diversity. However, specialist hospitals have voiced concern that the rather simple tariff does not take into account the greater complexity of specialist procedures, which may result in the most difficult procedures being lost at a regional, and perhaps even at a national, level. Services that patients need may cease to be available.

Specialist regulators

1.19 As we have seen, work-based regulation involves a system of clinical governance and performance management. Much of this sort of 'regulation' has been decentralised. To ensure common standards across the country, special 'regulators' may be created to monitor local activity. Most are independent of government, at least in theory. Four examples have already been given: we have seen that 'Monitor' regulates foundation trusts; that the Council for Healthcare Regulatory Excellence regulates professional bodies such as the GMC; that the Postgraduate Medical Education and Training Board supervises postgraduate medical education; and the Healthcare Commission promotes improvement of quality.

Medicines and devices are licensed and regulated by the Medicines and Healthcare Products Regulatory Agency, set up in 2003. We examine the role of the MHRA in licensing products in Chapter 10 and in monitoring and regulation of clinical research in Chapter 16. In the latter case, regulation by the MHRA is complemented by internal NHS research and development governance arrangements, and by independent research ethics committee scrutiny (sometimes by specialist committees such as the Gene Therapy Advisory Committee). In addition, the MHRA is advised by specialist boards. Since 2005, these comprise the Commission on Human Medicines, the Committee on the Safety of Devices, the British Pharmacopoeia Commission and two committees dealing with complementary and alternative medicines: the Herbal Medicines Advisory Committee and the Advisory Board on the Registration of Homeopathic Products. The MHRA also has a range of expert advisory groups.

The Mental Health Act Commission is a specialist health authority which was set up under section 121 of the Mental Health Act 1983 to keep the Act under review. In 2008, it will merge with the Healthcare Commission and the Commission for Social Care Inspection in order to create a streamlined body with regulatory functions covering both health and social care. The National Institute for Health and Clinical Excellence (see Chapter 2) produces guidance for the NHS on public health, health technologies and clinical practice and the National Patient Safety Agency (see Chapter 16) oversees the Central Office for Research Ethics Committees, and monitors the safety of care through reporting and analysing 'near misses' involving NHS patients.

Finally, certain kinds of medicine may be deemed to pose particular risks or arouse exceptional ethical controversy. In these cases a specialist regulator is created, often combining both functions of regulating the individual practitioner and the quality of the overall service. The numbers of such specialist authorities proliferated after the establishment of the Human Fertilisation and Embryology Authority (HFEA) in 1990. Creating a quango seemed to be the answer to any controversy arising from medical advances. Such regulatory authorities sought to combine medical and scientific expertise with experience from other relevant walks of life and allow a strong lay voice in regulation. So the Human Tissue Act 2004, which came into force in 2006 (see Chapters 18 and 19), creates a Human Tissue Authority (HTA)[125] to regulate all matters concerning the removal, storage, use and disposal of human tissue (except for gametes and embryos, which are already regulated by the Human Fertilisation and Embryology Authority, created by section 5 of the Human Fertilisation and Embryology Act 1990 – see Chapter 13). A Government White Paper proposes that the Human Tissue Authority and the Human Fertilisation and Embryology Authority should be merged to form a new Regulatory Authority for Tissue and Embryology (RATE).[126] RATE, which is expected to be operational by 2009, will be smaller than the combined HFEA and HTA, but will be assisted by the technical advice from expert advisory panels.

In 1997, the United Kingdom Xenotransplantation Interim Regulation Authority (UKXIRA) was created following the publication of *Animal Tissue into Humans*.[127] However, in 2003 a review was conducted by the Secretary of State for Health with the aim of reducing the number of 'arm's length bodies' by 50 per cent.[128] UKXIRA[129] was one of the casualties and was abolished in December 2006. The MHRA and research ethics committees will regulate xenotransplantation from now on. The abolition of UKXIRA and the forced marriage of the HFEA and the HTA may well dilute both the necessary specialist advice in relation to controversial areas of medicine and suppress the lay voice.

---

[125] See the Human Tissue Act 2004, ss 13–15 and Sch 2. Note that although different legislation (the Human Tissue (Scotland) Act 2006) applies in Scotland, the HTA will perform various roles in Scotland.

[126] *Review of the Human Fertilisation and Embryology Act: Proposals for Revised Legislation* (*Including the Establishment of the Regulatory Authority for Tissue and Embryos*) (2006) Cm 6989.

[127] Report of the Advisory Group on the Ethics of Xenotransplantation, *Animal Tissue into Humans* (1996); Department of Health, *The Government Response to 'Animal Tissue into Humans'* (1997).

[128] Department of Health, *Reconfiguring the Department of Health's Arm's Length Bodies* (2004).

[129] See HSC 1998/126.

Whither the NHS?

1.20 The NHS does not stand still. Nor should it. It is an organisation for the people and must evolve to take account of changing needs. We have briefly examined systems of regulation at local, organisational, and national levels. Regulation serves a variety of purposes which do not always coincide. Economic accountability may result in a health service that represents value for money; resource allocation decisions and their local variations will inevitably result in injustice to some. Aggrieved patients may look to the law for redress, both if they are denied treatment or if they are harmed by substandard treatment. Increased regulation is supposed to benefit patients. The public is increasingly critical of 'facile political sloganeering'.[130] There remains much to do to ensure confidence in both the 'new' systems for regulating medical professions and the NHS itself.

---

[130] See I Heath, 'In Defence of National Sickness Service' (2007) 334 *British Medical Journal* 19.

Chapter 2

DOCTORS' RESPONSIBILITIES: PATIENTS' RIGHTS

2.1 When we are ill we want to be treated by competent doctors – that is why debates about regulation of the medical profession are so crucial. However, we may also wish to assert our own rights, especially in the context of decision-making. Patients are no longer content to be passive recipients even of 'good' care. They want a say in what 'good' care comprises. The pace of medical developments is such that, particularly in the context of reproductive medicine and genetics, new questions surface daily around the implications of certain kinds of treatment. These may concern entitlement to treatment, or how far choices about treatment belong to individual patients alone. Or they may focus on the role of the state. Or the interests of commerce may be involved. How does the law begin to address patient rights in 2007? What relevance does Human Rights Act 1998 have to medicine?

Medical law, Ian Kennedy and Andrew Grubb declared,[1] is essentially '... a sub-set of human rights law'. The fundamental nature of the relationship between doctors and patients amply proves their point. At stake within the realm of medical law is our right to make our own decisions about how we live our lives and how we die. Our interests in privacy and in family life, in having or not having children, are central to our dealings with health professionals. So the Human Rights Act 1998 might be expected to transform health care law radically. The importance of the Act should not be underestimated. Lord Irvine, the Lord Chancellor, reflected thus:

> Which Convention Rights may be relevant in the medical field? The answer, here, and I suspect elsewhere is 'more than you might guess'.[2]

However, the European Convention on Human Rights (the Convention to which the 1998 Act gives domestic effect) addresses only a limited range of rights. There is no *positive* right to health care; there is no equivalent to Article 25 of the Universal Declaration of Human Rights. For the most part what the Convention confers are *negative* rights – ie prohibitions against

---

[1] I Kennedy and A Grubb, *Medical Law: Text and Materials* (3rd edn, 2000) Butterworths, p 3.

[2] Lord Irvine of Lairg, 'The Patient, the Doctor, their Lawyers and the Judge: Rights and Duties' (1999) 7 *Medical Law Review* 255 at 261.

certain kinds of infringement of basic freedoms. Moreover, the Human Rights Act 1998 does not (whatever the media says) incorporate the Convention into English law. It renders the Convention enforceable against *public authorities*. The 1998 Act is relevant to disputes about enforced treatment or arguments that the Government is violating patients' privacy. Where what is at stake is a failure by the NHS to provide certain sorts of care, or concerns about allowing, for example, insurers to demand medical details about you, the utility of the Act will need to be tested. We shall see that the European Court of Human Rights has interpreted the Convention as imposing positive obligations in some cases. The extent of such positive obligations remains unclear.

Even when a patient can bring her claim squarely within the ambit of a Convention right, she may find that the violation of her right is found to be justified. Many Convention rights are qualified. A good example is Article 8(1) – the right to respect for private and family life. In certain circumstances, Article 8(2) provides that infringement of the right may be justifiable; a violation of a patient's privacy could be held justified on grounds of public health, or for the protection of health or morals, as long as that infringement is proportionate. That means that interference with the individual's right must be shown to be 'necessary in a democratic society'. Moreover, Articles of the Convention may 'contradict' each other in certain circumstances, for example Article 2 (life) and Article 8 (privacy). Finally, the jurisprudence of the European Court of Human Rights expressly endorses a doctrine oddly entitled the 'margin of appreciation'. That is, national jurisdictions will be allowed a degree of freedom in defining their own criteria of public policy (morality). English courts will still enjoy some degree of discretion to determine English views of ethical dilemmas in medicine.

Nor should you expect the European Court of Human Rights itself to be startlingly radical in relation to health care. Many European countries adopt a conservative approach to health care rights. For example, in relation to fertility treatment and embryology, France restricts access to heterosexual couples where the woman is of normal childbearing age, Italy has recently enacted legislation radically curtailing options for fertility treatment and effectively giving the force of law to Roman Catholic doctrine.[3] Be wary of arguments that English law violates the Convention where a consequence would be that other European countries are also in breach. Remember that, as the supreme arbiter of the Convention, the European Court of Human Rights is an international court with judges representing several jurisdictions.

It should be also noted that, in practice, English courts referred to, and deferred to, the European Convention on Human Rights for several years prior to 1998 in developing the common law. The Human Rights Act 1998 does not replace or eliminate existing common law principles. Although the common law relating to health care has developed piecemeal, with an apparent emphasis on wrongs rather than rights, in many instances the existing law may suffice to vindicate rights endorsed in the Convention.

---

[3] See R Fenton, 'Catholic Doctrine Versus Women's Rights: The New Italian Law on Assisted Reproduction' (2006) 14 *Medical Law Review* 73.

Decisions of the English courts so far that address the Human Rights Act tend not to declare new rights, but review whether the existing common law 'rights' are sufficient in the light of the Convention.

How the Human Rights Act 1998 works[4]

2.2 Understanding how the Human Rights Act 1998 works is crucially important to assessing how the Act may affect health care law. As we have noted, the Act does not directly incorporate the European Convention on Human Rights. In a claim against a private litigant, the claimant cannot sue for violation of Convention rights. The Act, first, requires that primary and subordinate legislation be interpreted where possible in a way which is compatible with Convention rights[5] and renders it 'unlawful for a public authority to act in a way which is incompatible with a Convention right'.[6]

'Convention rights' are the fundamental rights and freedoms[7] set out in Articles 2 to 12 and 14 of the Convention, Articles 1 to 3 of the First Protocol (concerning rights to property, education and free elections) and Articles 1 and 2 of the Sixth Protocol (abolishing the death penalty). Section 11 of the Act makes it crystal clear that Convention rights are in addition to, not in substitution for, rights and freedoms already endorsed at common law. It may seem odd that no express provision of the Act requires that judges develop the common law in a manner consistent with Convention rights. However, as noted above, English judges already, wherever possible, seek to ensure that the common law is consistent with such rights. More importantly, section 6 of the Act, which makes it unlawful for any public authority to act in a way incompatible with Convention rights, provides that courts are classified as public authorities. A judge hearing a patient's claim must, by virtue of section 6, consider compatibility with Convention rights and ensure consistency between common law and Convention rights.

However, the domestic rules on precedent are unaffected. If a decision of the Court of Appeal contradicts a decision of the European Court of Human Rights, the Court of Appeal in subsequent cases is bound by its previous decision. Only a higher court (the House of Lords in this example) could hold that the Court of Appeal case was wrongly decided on the basis that it conflicts with a decision in the European Court of Human Rights.[8]

Where a claim alleging violation of a Convention right involves legislation, section 3 of the Act requires any court or tribunal to seek to interpret that rule in a way which is compatible with the relevant Convention right. However, if such an interpretation is not possible, the courts are not granted powers to

---

[4]   An excellent introductory text to the Act is: J Wadham, H Mountfield, A Edmundson, C Gallagher, *Blackstone's Guide to the Human Rights Act 1998* (4th edn, 2007) OUP.

[5]   Human Rights Act 1998, s 3.

[6]   Human Rights Act 1998, ss 6–8.

[7]   Human Rights Act 1998, s 7.

[8]   *Kay v Lambeth London Borough Council, Price v Leeds City Council* [2006] UKHL 10. Applied in *R (on the application of Johnson) v Havering London Borough Council* [2007] EWCA Civ 26 (see below at 2.3).

strike down legislation. The judicial role remains limited by doctrines of Parliamentary sovereignty.[9] Section 4(2) provides that:

> If the court is satisfied that the provision is incompatible with a Convention right, it may make a declaration of that incompatibility.

The Government should then act to amend legislation to 'cure' the relevant incompatibility. Section 10 enables them to do so by secondary legislation making a 'remedial order'. Failure to act to remove the stated incompatibility would give rise to a claim against the UK before the European Court of Human Rights at Strasbourg. The dissatisfied patient could bring another claim suing the Government itself.

This can be illustrated by considering a controversial provision of the Human Fertilisation and Embryology Act 1990, which has been the subject of a declaration of incompatibility. Section 28(6)(b) of the 1990 Act provides that if the sperm of any man is used after his death, he is not to be treated as the father of the child. Diane Blood[10] fought a long battle to be able to undergo insemination with her deceased husband's sperm. She ultimately gave birth to two sons after fertility treatment abroad. Section 28(6)(b) meant that the boys' birth certificates recorded the father as 'unknown'. Mrs Blood and her sons succeeded in their contention that the 1990 Act violated their rights to respect for private and family life endorsed by Article 8 and, in response, Parliament enacted the Human Fertilisation and Embryology (Deceased Fathers) Act 2003.

For the health care professional, the most crucial element of the Human Rights Act 1998 is the provision that 'Convention rights' are directly enforceable against public authorities, and that an individual who considers that her rights have been violated by a public authority can sue for damages. Where an individual considers that a public authority has acted in breach of Convention rights, a number of rather different outcomes must be considered. First, in many cases, the self-same rights conferred by the Convention are already recognised by the law of torts. For example, Article 5 provides for a right to liberty and security and protects the citizen against arbitrary detention. The ancient tort of false imprisonment protects that same fundamental interest. A patient alleging unlawful detention in hospital may not need to resort to claiming a breach of Article 5. He can sue in false imprisonment. In determining whether his detention was lawful, the court will be mindful of the provisions of Article 5 and the jurisprudence of the European Court of Human Rights.[11]

---

[9] For an introductory account of how the Act works, see L Betten, *The Human Rights Act 1998 – What it Means* (1999) Brill; C Gearty, *Principles of Human Rights Adjudication* (2004) OUP.

[10] Mrs Blood brought an application for judicial review of s 28(6)(b) and the incompatibility of that provision with Convention rights was conceded: see JK Mason and GT Laurie, *Mason and McCall Smith's Law and Medical Ethics* (7th edn, 2006) OUP, p 825; and see below at 13.7.

[11] But a lacuna in the law allowing the detention of adults lacking capacity under the common law doctrine of necessity was held to breach Article 5 in *HL v United Kingdom* (2005) 40 EHRR 32; see below at 2.8.

The position is more complex when a Convention right is not so well established in domestic law. Privacy was not, though the common law is developing rapidly. The claimant might then choose to bring his claim directly under the Human Rights Act 1998, alleging breach of Article 8 (which requires respect for private and family life). If he elects for a Convention remedy alone, he can sue under the Act only if the defendant is a public authority. Were we to discover that the Department of Health was bugging our offices, suing a Government department would be straightforward. What if a tabloid newspaper splashed our medical history all over its front page? There is an argument that the newspaper, too, might be classified as a public authority, for section 6(3)(b) classifies as a public authority 'any person certain of whose functions are functions of a public nature'.[12]

Suppose, however, a private individual (a colleague, for example), invades our privacy by steaming open private correspondence and finding letters from our doctors revealing an embarrassing medical complaint. What then? In practical terms, often some common law remedy may be found within which to frame a cause of action. The 'snooper' who peers through windows or opens our mail could be liable for harassment or trespass to goods. If no common law remedy can be identified so that the defendant appears to be immune from liability, Article 6 of the Convention comes into play. Article 6 grants a right that, in determination of his civil rights and obligations, everyone is entitled to a fair trial. It grants a right of access to justice. If no remedy for violation of Article 8 (right to privacy) appears to exist, the court must in effect develop a remedy (as in relation to privacy the Court of Appeal seems to have sought to do),[13] or the court acts unlawfully in failing to implement Article 8. Further, the Government is in breach of the Convention in failing to provide a legal remedy, violating the citizen's right to access to justice.

Article 6 will affect the development of the English law in two ways. Relatively rarely, Article 6 will come into play because the common law offers *no* remedy for violation of a Convention right. More commonly, the Article will be invoked in order to overcome some restriction on the claimant's common law right. For example, in one recent case the High Court ruled that there was a breach of Article 6(1) when a 14-year-old witness was called upon at short notice and without legal representation to consent to the disclosure of her medical records as evidence in a sexual abuse case.[14] The High Court held that the child's right to privacy under Article 8(1) had been breached.

Who can be sued?

2.3 As we have seen, the Human Rights Act 1998 does not define public authority. Section 6(3) provides that public authority includes: (a) a court or

---

[12] See below at 2.3.
[13] *Douglas v Hello Magazine* [2001] 2 All ER 289, CA; *A v B (A Company)* [2002] 2 All ER 545, CA; *Campbell v Mirror Group Newspapers Ltd* [2003] 1 All ER 224, CA. But see also *Wainwright v Home Office* [2003] UKHL 53, where the court deferred any responsibility for the creation of a tort of privacy to Parliament.
[14] *R (on the application of B) v Stafford Combined Court* [2006] EWHC 1645 (Admin). See Chapter 4 at 4.12.

tribunal, and (b) any person certain of whose functions are of a public nature. What does this mean for the NHS? National Health Service trusts, including primary care trusts (PCTs), are public authorities. So are bodies such as NHS research ethics committees. 'Quangos' such as the Human Fertilisation and Embryology Authority (HFEA) are equally clearly public authorities, as are regulatory bodies such as the General Medical Council. Individual health professionals, doctors and nurses working within the NHS, are performing functions of a public nature and face potential claims under the 1998 Act (although normally such claims would be brought against their employer). GPs and other non-employed NHS personnel might be more directly in the firing line.

Professionals in private practice and private hospitals raise tricky questions. Whilst a doctor is a public authority in relation to their NHS functions, the same does not apply to doctors in private practice. So if Patient A contracts with Dr B to carry out surgery at Clinic C, paying out of his own pocket or via private health insurers, the relationship is entirely private. However, if Patient A later sues Dr B or Clinic C, in determining the nature of his redress, the court must seek to develop the common law consistently with the Convention on Human Rights. If this is not possible, Patient A may have redress against the Government under Article 6 for violating his right to a fair trial to determine his civil rights and obligations.

What about independent treatment centres? Do private clinics treating NHS patients perform functions of a public nature? They will not be regarded as 'core' public authorities under section 6 of the 1998 Act, but might they be viewed as 'hybrid bodies' under section 6(3)(b)? As we have seen, under section 6(3)(b) a public authority includes 'any person certain of whose functions are of a public nature'. However, section 6(5) provides that: 'In relation to a particular act, a person is not a public authority ... if the nature of the act is private.' The test, therefore, relates to the particular act of which complaint is made. The European Court of Human Rights has held, for example, that by delegating responsibilities to private schools the UK government cannot escape liability under the Convention.[15] The question is whether the act is a private act, or the discharge of a public function?[16]

It was held in *R (on the application of Heather) v Leonard Cheshire Foundation (Cheshire)*[17] that a charity responsible for providing a home and care for a number of disabled people paid for by the local authority was neither a 'core' nor a 'hybrid' public authority for the purposes of the Human Rights Act 1998. It was created by private individuals. It was not obliged to accept publicly-funded residents, nor was it closely regulated by the state. In *Aston Cantlow PCC v Wallbank*[18] the House of Lords held that a parish church council was not a public authority, but Lord Nicholls urged a

---

[15] See *Costello-Roberts v United Kingdom* (1993) 19 EHRR 112 at para 27.
[16] See *Aston Cantlow and Wilmcote with Billesley Parochial Church Council v Wallbank* [2003] UKHL 37, per Lord Nicholls at para 16.
[17] [2001] EWHC Admin 429. Might the very detailed regulation of licensed private fertility clinics bring such clinics within the scope of the 1998 Act?
[18] See n 16 above: [2003] UKHL 37.

'generously wide scope to the expression "public function" in section 6(3)(b)'.[19] Does this throw doubt on the Court of Appeal decision in *Cheshire*? In 2007,[20] a case on similar facts to *Cheshire* was heard in the Court of Appeal. The Secretary of State intervened to submit that *Cheshire* was incorrectly decided. However, the Court of Appeal were bound by their earlier decision[21] and confirmed that a private care home used by a local authority was not a public authority under section 6(3)(b). This limited definition of public functions is, we submit, unlikely to survive in the House of Lords.[22] NHS patients treated in private institutions await further clarification.

Who can sue?

2.4 Only a person who is a 'victim' of the alleged violation of the European Convention on Human Rights can bring a claim under the Human Rights Act 1998. The concept of victim derives from the Convention and jurisprudence of the European Court of Human Rights. A victim must be actually and directly affected by the act or omission which is the subject of the complaint. There is no direct provision for interest groups to sue to vindicate Convention rights.

What does this mean in practice? Obviously a claimant who is detained in hospital against her will can ground a claim on Article 5 (although a claim in false imprisonment will usually suffice).[23] A person who alleges that he has been experimented on without consent may have a claim under Article 3 (prohibiting inhuman or degrading treatment) or Article 8.[24] However, it may be difficult for individuals to fund claims about important principles. Interest groups will want to use the Convention to challenge and change existing law (eg the ban on voluntary euthanasia). Will they be able to do so, given interest groups cannot sue as groups? It is not necessary to show that a claimant has actually already suffered from the consequences of an alleged violation. 'Victims' need only show a real risk of being directly affected by a breach. Gay men in Northern Ireland were allowed to challenge laws criminalising all homosexual conduct.[25] Abortion centre counsellors acting with women wishing to receive advice successfully challenged Irish laws prohibiting dissemination of any information about abortion.[26] Representative interest groups involving groups of victims are able to gain standing under the 1998 Act.

---

[19] [2003] UKHL 37 at para 11.
[20] *R (on the application of Johnson) v Havering London Borough Council* [2007] EWCA Civ 26.
[21] See *Kay v Lambeth London Borough Council, Price v Leeds City Council* [2006] UKHL 10 (and see above at 2.2).
[22] Note Buxton LJ's (obiter) reservations about the Court of Appeal judgment in *Cheshire* at paras 67–80.
[23] But see *HL v United Kingdom* (2005) 40 EHRR 32, discussed below at 2.8.
[24] For a discussion of the application of Articles 3 and 8 in this context see *R (on the application of B) v S* [2005] EWHC 1936 (Admin), where a patient contested a decision by doctors that he lacked capacity to decide and could therefore be forced to undergo treatment in his best interests.
[25] *Dudgeon v United Kingdom* (1982) 4 EHRR 149.
[26] *Open Door and Dublin Well Women v Ireland* (1992) 15 EHRR 244.

Convention rights

2.5 Reference will be made to relevant Convention rights throughout the chapters which follow. All that we do now is give a brief overview of those Convention rights which are likely to have the most significant impact on the rights and obligations of doctors and patients in England.[27]

Article 2

2.6 Article 2 provides that 'Everyone's right to life shall be protected by law.' This might be invoked to challenge a number of entrenched principles of English law. Consider the following questions. Could a patient whose life (health) is endangered by refusal of treatment (eg denied expensive chemotherapy) use Article 2 to obtain a court order demanding that he be given priority in treatment?[28] Article 2 does impose on the state a positive obligation to intervene to protect people whose lives are at real and immediate risk.[29] But what limits may or must be placed on such a right? When does such a right crystallise? Is it an absolute right entitling the patient to any possible treatment? How are competing rights of other patients to be addressed? Remember that such a right would necessarily impose an obligation to provide publicly-funded care. The European Court of Human Rights has made it clear that where protection from disease requires use of state resources, individual countries are left considerable freedom to assess their own aims and priorities.[30]

Article 2 will also affect legal issues surrounding allowing patients to die. It was suggested that Article 2 might render decisions that it is lawful to withhold/withdraw treatment in certain circumstances unlawful, in particular that it might alter the law on withdrawing artificial nutrition and hydration from patients in a persistent vegetative state.[31] However, in *NHS Trust A v M, NHS Trust B v H*,[32] the then President of the Family Division (Elizabeth Butler-Sloss P) ruled that Article 2 does not impose an obligation to prolong life in such cases.

Finally, could Article 2 affect laws permitting abortion or case law denying foetuses any legal personality? Could the judgment in *St George's Healthcare NHS Trust v S*[33] be subjected to a foetal life challenge? Refusing to strike

---

[27] See R Lilley, C Newdick, P Lambden, *Understanding the Human Rights Act: A Tool Kit for the Health Service* (2001) Radcliffe Press; A Garwood-Gowers, J Tingle (eds), *Health Care Law: The Impact of the HRA 1998* (2001) Cavendish.

[28] This argument was raised in *R (on the application of Rogers) v Swindon NHS PC Trust* [2006] EWCA Civ 392 (see below at 2.18) but the court found that the policy of the primary care trust to refuse to fund the appellant with the breast cancer drug Herceptin was irrational and therefore unlawful. Therefore it did not need to go on to consider whether the PCT breached Article 2 or Article 14 of the European Convention on Human Rights: at para 83, per Sir Anthony Clarke MR.

[29] See *Osman v United Kingdom* (1998) 29 EHRR 245.

[30] *Osman v United Kingdom* (1998) 29 EHRR 245.

[31] *Airedale NHS Trust v Bland* [1993] 1 All ER 821, HL.

[32] [2001] 1 All ER 801. See also *NHS v D* [2000] 2 FCR 577.

[33] [1998] 3 All ER 673; see below at 12.18.

down national abortion laws, the European Commission has not applied Article 2 to foetuses in the first trimester of pregnancy.[34] And in *Vo v France*[35] the European Court of Human Rights confirmed that the question of when a right of life accrued fell within the margin of appreciation allowed to contracting states.

Article 3

2.7 Article 3 provides that 'No one shall be subjected to torture or inhuman or degrading treatment or punishment'. It has been suggested that this could be used to challenge failure to provide treatment or poor quality treatment. Does being left on a trolley constitute degrading treatment? It seems unlikely.[36] We should never forget the original evils that the Convention was framed to prevent.

Are laws prohibiting voluntary euthanasia contrary to Article 3? An argument might run linking Articles 3 and 8. The case could be put, for example, that a patient dying of some terrible degenerative disease or suffering acute pain from terminal cancer was, by being denied the option of active euthanasia, subjected to inhuman and degrading treatment, contrary to Article 3. Moreover, if her doctor, or some other third party, was willing to help her die, preventing them from doing so might violate her privacy contrary to Article 8. We shall see that when Dianne Pretty,[37] a woman dying of motor neurone disease, sought to invoke Articles 3 and 8 to support her claim that her husband should be granted immunity from prosecution if he helped her to commit suicide, her claim failed. The House of Lords refused to interpret Article 3 to affirm a right to die with dignity. Her further appeal to the Strasbourg Court also failed.[38] Nor can Article 3 be relied upon to compel doctors to continue futile or inappropriate treatment. Leslie Burke, who suffers from a degenerative neurological condition, cerebellar ataxia, fought for the right to artificial nutrition and hydration in the event that he is unable to voice his wishes. He unsuccessfully sought to invoke Articles, 2, 3, 8 and 14 to challenge guidance from the General Medical Council which stated that where a patient's disease is severe and the prognosis poor, artificial nutrition and hydration will not always be appropriate, even if death is not imminent.[39]

---

[34] See *Bruggeman and Scheuten v Federal Republic of Germany* (1981) 3 EHRR 244; *Paton v British Pregnancy Advisory Service* [1981] 2 EHRR 408. See Chapter 14 at 14.14.

[35] [2004] ECHR 326. See Chapter 14 at 14.15.

[36] See *R v North West Lancashire Health Authority, ex p A, D & G* [2000] 1 WLR 977, CA.

[37] See *R (on the application of Pretty) v DPP* [2001] UKHL 61 (discussed below at 20.6); and see *Rodriguez v British Columbia A-G* (1993) 82 BCLP (2d) 273.

[38] *Pretty v United Kingdom* [2002] 2 FLR 45. At the time of writing, Kelly Taylor, who suffers from Eisenmenger's syndrome and is in constant pain, is launching a case in the High Court arguing that a refusal to allow doctors to increase her morphine dose to induce unconsciousness breaches Article 3. Taylor has prepared an advance statement refusing artificial hydration and nutrition in the event that she loses capacity. See C Dyer, 'Allow me to Die, Terminally Ill Woman Urges Court' (2007) Guardian, 13 February and Chapter 20 at 20.3.

[39] General Medical Council, *Withholding and Withdrawing Life-Prolonging Treatments: Good Practice in Decision-Making* (2002). Paragraph 16 provides: '... Doctors must take account of patients' preferences when providing treatment. However, where a patient

2.7 Doctors' responsibilities: patients' rights

The Court of Appeal and the European Court of Human Rights turned his claim down.[40] Doctors cannot be forced to administer treatment which they believe to be clinically unnecessary, futile or inappropriate.

Article 3 will raise other questions about our existing common law. Might certain forms of non-consensual treatment fall foul of Article 3?[41] Consider cases relating to feeding anorexic patients. What effect might Article 3 have on principles relating to consent to clinical research and research involving patients incapable of giving consent?

Article 5

2.8 The relevant parts of Article 5(1) provide:

> Everyone has the right to liberty and security of person. No-one shall be deprived of his liberty save in the following cases and in accordance with a procedure prescribed by law:
>
> ...
>
> (e) the lawful detention of persons for the prevention of the spreading of infectious diseases, or persons of unsound mind, alcoholics or drug addicts or vagrants.

We have seen that the common law tort of false imprisonment already gives protection to the liberty and security of persons. However, a lacuna in mental health law came to light in *R v Bournewood Community and Mental Health Trust, ex p L*.[42] L was a 49-year-old man who had autism and lacked capacity. He was an in-patient at Bournewood Hospital but was not detained under the provisions of the Mental Health Act 1983. Instead, he was detained in his best interests, under the common law doctrine of necessity.[43] The High Court held that L's detention was lawful and proper. But the case was successfully challenged in the European Court of Human Rights in *HL v United Kingdom*:[44] detention under the common law was arbitrary and lacked sufficient safeguards. It was therefore incompatible with Article 5.[45] A change to the Mental Capacity Act 2005 is envisaged so as to close the 'Bournewood gap'.

Article 6

2.9 Article 6 provides that:

wishes to have a treatment that – in the doctor's considered view – is not clinically indicated, there is no ethical or legal obligation on the doctor to provide it ...'.

[40] *R (on the application of Burke) v General Medical Council* [2005] EWCA Civ 1003; *Burke v United Kingdom* (2006) App No 19807/06.

[41] See *Herczegfalvy v Austria* (1992) 18 BMLR 48; *R (N) v M* [2003] 1 WLR 562, CA.

[42] [1998] 3 All ER 289, HL.

[43] *F v West Berkshire Health Authority* [1989] 2 All ER 545.

[44] (2004) App No 45508/99.

[45] See K Keywood, 'Detaining Mentally Disordered Patients Lacking Capacity: The Arbitrariness of Informal Detention and the Common Law Doctrine of Necessity' (2005) 13 *Medical Law Review* 108 at 108–115. New proposals to close the 'Bournewood gap' were unveiled in June 2006: see Chapter 6 at 6.8.

In the determination of his civil rights or obligations or of any criminal charge against him, everyone is entitled to a fair and public hearing within a reasonable time by an independent and impartial tribunal established by law.

Could Article 6 impede attempts to reduce litigation, for example by excluding any right to sue within a no-fault scheme?[46] In 2004, Article 6 was successfully invoked by an ophthalmic optician when the General Optical Council found her guilty of serious professional misconduct.[47] The Committee had a duty under Article 6 to give reasons for its decision within a reasonable time.

Article 8

2.10 Article 8 will have far-reaching effects. Article 8(1) provides: 'Everyone has the right to respect for his private and family life, his home and his correspondence.' Note the wording, the right is a right to *respect*. Does that connote an absolute claim to privacy? As with Article 2, the question arises of what kind of obligations Article 8 creates. Does it impose positive obligations on the state to act to promote a right to privacy or simply a duty not to interfere with privacy?[48] It is clear that some sort of positive obligation is imposed by Article 8. Then we have to consider how to define parameters of private and family life. Prohibition of contraception, for example, obviously constitutes an interference with that right – interfering with intimate relationships. However, does regulation of third parties involved in assisted conception fall into the same category? In some cases, one person's right to private life may conflict with another's right to family life. Imagine A tests positively for an inherited form of bowel cancer. A's children have a one in four chance of inheriting the condition also, but A refuses to inform her estranged daughter of this possibility. Does respecting A's privacy violate her daughter's right to family life or her right to life under Article 2?

What is clear is that Article 8 is strongly influencing the development of medical law. As was recognised by Coleridge J in 2003,

> The advent of the Human Rights Act 1998 has enhanced the responsibility of the court to positively protect the welfare of these patients and, in particular, to protect the patient's right to respect for her private and family life under Art 8(1) of the European Convention ...[49]

Thus in *Glass v United Kingdom*,[50] the Strasbourg Court held that a child's right to privacy was breached when he was given diamorphine against the wishes of his mother. Doctors believed the twelve-year-old boy was dying and sought to administer the drug as a palliative measure. His mother disagreed

---

[46] See *Osman v United Kingdom* (1998) 29 EHRR 245.

[47] *Threlfall v General Optical Council* [2004] EWHC 2683 (Admin). However, in *Abu-Romia v General Medical Council* [2003] EWHC 2515 (Admin), the High Court found that the GMC had sufficient evidence to reach its conclusion: see paras 55, 57, per Wall J.

[48] See *R v North West Lancashire Health Authority, ex p A, D & G* [2000] 1 WLR 977, CA.

[49] *D v NHS Trust (Medical Treatment: Consent: Termination)* [2003] EWHC 2793 (Fam) at para 31.

[50] [2004] 1 FLR 1019.

and argued that diamorphine would diminish his chances of recovery. Doctors administered it none the less. They did not seek a court order, though they had ample time to do so. In these circumstances, their failure to secure a declaration from the court that such treatment was lawful contravened Article 8(1). Consequently, where there is dispute as to the best interests of a patient, there should be a court order unless urgent treatment is necessary.[51]

We will see in Chapter 4 that the common law duty of confidentiality is changing in terminology, if not in substance, to the extent that, in 2004, Lord Nicholls recommended that the tort should be renamed, the 'misuse of private information'.[52] Could Article 8 be used to prevent certain information ever being sought from individuals? The Government conceded that insurers could require applicants for insurance to give results of certain genetic tests including tests for Huntington's Chorea. Does such a policy violate Article 8? Could it be justified under Article 8(2)? Article 8(2) graphically illustrates the qualified nature of certain Convention rights. It provides:

> There shall be no interference by a public authority with the exercise of this right except such as is in accordance with the law and is necessary in a democratic society in the interests of national security, public safety or the economic well-being of the country, for the prevention of disorder or crime, for the protection of health or morals, or for the protection of the rights and freedoms of others.

Note the width of potential exceptions to Article 8(1).[53] The jurisprudence of the European court illustrates both the complexity of Article 8 and judicial conservatism on its part of the European Court of Human Rights.[54]

Article 9

2.11 Article 9 protects religious freedom, providing:

> Everyone has the right to freedom of thought, conscience and religion; this right includes freedom to change his religion or belief and freedom, either alone or in community with others and in public or private, to manifest his religion or belief, in worship, teaching, practice and observance.

> Freedom to manifest one's religion or beliefs shall be subject only to such limitation as are prescribed by law and are necessary in a democratic society in the interests of public safety, for the protection of public order, health or morals, *or for the protection of the rights and freedoms of others.*

In *Re J*,[55] for example, the rights and freedoms of a non-practising Christian mother and the welfare of the child were balanced against a Muslim father's

---

[51] See *R (on the application of Burke) v General Medical Council* [2005] EWCA Civ 1003, per Lord Phillips MR at para 77.
[52] *Campbell v Mirror Group Newspapers Ltd* [2004] UKHL 22 at para 14.
[53] *Z v Finland* (1997) 25 EHRR 371; *MS v Sweden* (1997) 45 BMLR 133; *Brown v United Kingdom* [1997] 24 EHRR 39.
[54] *Rees v United Kingdom* [1986] 9 EHRR 56; *Cossey v United Kingdom* [1990] 13 EHRR 622; *B v France* (1992) 16 EHRR 1.
[55] *Re J (Child's Religious Upbringing and Circumcision)* [2000] 1 FLR 571, per Thorpe LJ at para 12. See also *Re S (Specific Issue Order: Religion: Circumcision)* [2004] EWHC 1282 (Fam). Female circumcision was prohibited in the UK under the Prohibition of Female

wish to manifest his religion by having his son circumcised. The Court of Appeal held that a failure to sanction the operation did not offend the father's rights under Article 9.

As we shall see, English courts have on a number of occasions overruled parental objections to treatment of their children contrary to their faith.[56] The classic example is where a court orders that a blood transfusion is given to a child of Jehovah's Witness parents. The parents might argue that requiring that their child undergo a transfusion violates the family's religious freedom and their right to respect for their family life (Article 8). Do the rights of the child, especially her right to life under Article 2, trump the parents' claims?

Article 10

2.12 Nor must Article 10 be overlooked. Article 10 guarantees freedom of expression, a right embracing freedom of the press. All too often Articles 8 and 10 conflict and the courts must embark on a delicate balancing exercise.[57]

Article 12

2.13 Finally, Article 12 might be thought to guarantee a right to reproduce as it states that:

Men and women of marriageable age have the right to marry and found a family according to the national laws governing the exercise of that right.

Could Article 12 be used to challenge limitations on access to fertility treatment? It has been held by the Court of Appeal and the Strasbourg Court that Articles 8 and 12 were not infringed when a prisoner was refused the right to services which would enable the artificial insemination of his wife.[58]

Convention on Human Rights and Biomedicine

2.14 It will be apparent that patients' rights are not centre-stage in the European Convention on Human Rights. To raise a question about patients' rights, the relevant dispute must somehow be fitted into the pigeonhole of general rights. A further European convention, the European Convention on

Circumcision Act 1985 (replaced by the Female Genital Mutilation Act 2003). See generally, AR Gatrad, A Sheikh, H Jacks, 'Religious Circumcision and the Human Rights Act' (2002) 86 *Archives of Childhood Diseases* 76.

[56] See *Re S (A Minor) (Medical Treatment)* [1993] 1 FLR 376; discussed below at 15.9.

[57] Graphically illustrated in *H (A Healthcare Worker) v Associated Newspapers Ltd and H (A Healthcare Worker), N (A Health Authority)* [2002] Lloyd's Rep Med 210, CA, and see *Campbell v Mirror Group Newspapers Ltd* [2004] UKHL 22.

[58] *R (on the application of Mellor) v Secretary of State for the Home Department* [2001] EWCA Civ 472; *Dickson v Premier Prison Service Ltd* [2004] EWCA Civ 1477; and *Dickson v United Kingdom* (2006) App No 00044362/04, [2006] 2 FCR 1. And see H Codd, 'Regulating Reproduction: Prisoners' Families, Artificial Insemination and Human Rights' (2006) 1 *European Human Rights Law Review* 39.

Human Rights and Biomedicine (the Bioethics Convention)[59] directly addresses doctor-patient relationships. This Convention (agreed in 1997) by states party to the (main) Human Rights Convention has not been signed or ratified by the UK. We are not yet a party to that treaty. Even if and when the UK does ratify this Convention, it will not have direct force. A patient will not be able to sue for violation of a right granted by the Convention. Nor is there any right of individual petition to the European Court of Human Rights at Strasbourg. None the less, articles of the European Convention on Human Rights may be interpreted with reference to the much fuller explanations and definitions of human rights offered in the Bioethics Convention.

Access to health care[60]

2.15 Provided a decision is made fairly and rationally, the European Court of Human Rights is reluctant to interfere with the rationing decisions of Member States.[61] In *Scialacqua v Italy*,[62] the European Commission held that there was no breach of Article 2 when the Italian health service refused to pay for drugs that allegedly improved the patient's condition, though the Commission did recognise that the state might be under an obligation to meet the costs of medical treatment essential to save life. Article 3 might be invoked if the refusal of treatment constitutes 'inhuman or degrading treatment'[63] and Article 14 if the decision discriminates on the ground of disability or age. It has been held that Article 8 does not impose a positive obligation to provide treatment.[64] If the European Convention on Human Rights fails to endorse a direct unequivocal right to health care, can we construct such a right from other sources? First let us briefly consider how rationing decisions are made in the NHS.

NICE[65]

2.16 The National Institute for Health and Clinical Excellence (NICE) is established as a special health authority,[66] and its principal function is to advise primary care trusts about whether to fund new medicines or other treatments, having regard to 'the promotion of clinical excellence and the

---

[59] See HDC Roscam-Abbing, EH Hondius, JH Hubben (eds), *Health Law, Human Rights and the Biomedicine Convention* (2005) Martinus Nijhoff Publishers.
[60] See C Newdick, *Who Should We Treat? Rights, Rationing and Resources in the NHS* (2nd edn, 2005) OUP.
[61] See E Jackson, *Medical Law: Texts and Materials* (2006) OUP, pp 92–94.
[62] (1998) 26 EHRR CD 164. See also D O'Sullivan, 'The Allocation of Scarce Resources and the Right to Life under the European Convention on Human Rights' (1998) *Public Law* 389 at 394–395.
[63] Note that in *Price v United Kingdom* (2002) 34 EHRR 53 the prison authorities breached Article 3 in their deficient care of a prisoner who was a thalidomide victim.
[64] *R v North West Lancashire Health Authority, ex p A, D and G* [2000] 1 WLR 977, CA.
[65] See Newdick, *Who Should We Treat? Rights, Rationing and Resources in the NHS*, pp 203–211.
[66] See the National Institute for Clinical Excellence (Establishment and Constitution Order) 1999, SI 1999/220 as amended by SI 1999/2219.

effective use of available resources in the health service'.[67] NICE does two jobs, seeking to ensure that NHS patients receive effective treatments, but also attempting to ensure that the NHS gets value for money. We are principally concerned here with that second, difficult and controversial job. A drug that offers a young father suffering from cancer two or three extra years of life to be with his children will be perceived as of incalculable value by his family. But can the NHS afford it? It has been suggested that NICE bases its guidelines for England and Wales on the appropriate treatment of patients with specific diseases and conditions on the basis of the cost per quality adjusted life year (QALY),[68] and adopts a cost per QALY of about £30,000.[69] Since 2002, NHS organisations are required, normally within three months, to fund treatments recommended by NICE in its technology guidance. Its clinical guidance is not mandatory, though it does provide a benchmark for the management of clinical conditions by local health care organisations. Are clinicians free to ignore the advice? Will the guidelines define the standard of care in negligence cases?[70] At the very least, a clinician defending a negligence claim is likely to be called upon to justify divergence with the guidance.[71] And what if the guidance NICE produces is flawed? NICE's decisions are subject to judicial review.[72] Its decision will always arouse anger from those refused a treatment because it is said not to be cost-effective.[73]

A right to health care?

2.17 Before looking at the case law, let us reflect for a moment on what a right to health care might involve. Article 25 of the Universal Declaration of Human Rights provides:

> Everyone has the right to a standard of living adequate for the health and well being of himself and his family including food, clothing and medical care.

Other rights within Article 25 can be easily defined and quantified. Basic needs for food and clothing alter little from one person to another. Desires may vary widely, but no-one would argue that they have a fundamental human right to caviar and champagne every day. Basic needs for medical care vary widely. A baby born prematurely at 24 weeks may consume as much health care resource in his first week of life as others do in a lifetime. What constitutes 'need' is hotly debated. Treatment for pneumonia falls comfortably into a definition of need, but where would you place surgery to eliminate

---

[67] See Newdick, *Who Should We Treat? Rights, Rationing and Resources in the NHS*, p 205.

[68] See Chapter 3 at 3.6.

[69] See J Raffery, 'NICE: Faster Access to Modern Treatments? Analysis of Guidance on Health Technologies' 323 *British Medical Journal* 1300.

[70] See A Samanta, J Samanta, M Gunn, 'Legal Considerations of Clinical Guidelines: Will NICE Make a Difference?' (2003) 96 *Journal of the Royal Society of Medicine* 133.

[71] See Mason and McCall Smith's Law and Medical Ethics, p 424.

[72] K Syrett, 'Nice Work? Rationing Review and the Legitimacy Process' (2002) 10 *Medical Law Review* 1 at 18. On a recent challenge by Pfizer and Eisai Ltd to NICE's guidance on Alzheimer's drugs such as donepezil, see 'Drug Watchdog Faces Legal Review' (2006) BBC News, 17 November (available at http://news.bbc.co.uk).

[73] See MD Rawling and AJ Culver, 'National Institute for Clinical Excellence and Its Value Judgments' (2004) 329 *British Medical Journal* 224. (The authors are, respectively, the Chair of NICE and the Vice Chair between 1999 and 2003).

varicose veins? Note the World Health Organisation definition of health as '... a state of complete physical mental and social well-being and not just the absence of disease or infirmity'. What would a right to health so defined involve and whose duty is it to ensure that we enjoy such health?

Ultimate responsibility for the health of the NHS lies with the Secretary of State for Health. The National Health Service Act 2006 now provides in section 1:

> The Secretary of State must continue the promotion in England of a compre-
> hensive health service designed to secure improvement—
> (a)   in the physical and mental health of the people of England, and
> (b)   in the prevention, diagnosis and treatment of illness.[74]

Section 3 of the 2006 Act imposes on the Secretary of State a further duty to provide, to such extent as he considers necessary to meet all reasonable requirements, services including hospital accommodation, medical, dental, nursing and ambulance services and such other services as are required for the diagnosis and treatment of illness. High-sounding sentiments and expressions of political will these may be, but is there any legal significance in this 'duty' imposed on the Health Minister? Do patients have a right to health care? Judges were once wary of involving the courts in disputes about allocation of resources or priorities for treatment. Three developments signal change. First, there are signs of greater judicial activity in relation to access to health care. Second, the European Court of Justice has established a limited right to access to other national health systems if your own cannot provide the care you need without undue delay. Finally, once again, Government ministers are offering 'guarantees' of speedier, fairer treatment.

Challenging NHS resource decisions

2.18 In the domestic courts, early attempts to challenge decisions about access to health care met little success. In 1979, four patients who had spent long periods awaiting hip-replacement surgery went to court, alleging that the Health Minister had failed in his duty (then imposed by the National Health Service Act 1977) to promote a comprehensive health service and to provide hospital accommodation and facilities for orthopaedic surgery. The patients alleged (1) that their period on the waiting list was longer than was medically advisable, and (2) that their wait resulted from a shortage of facilities, caused in part by a decision not to build a new hospital block on the grounds of cost. The patients asked for an order compelling the Minister to act, and for compensation for their pain and suffering. The Court of Appeal[75] held that (a) the financial constraints to which the Minister was subject had to be considered in assessing what amounts to reasonable requirements for hospital and medical services and (b) the decision as to what was required was for the Minister, and the court could intervene only where a Minister acted utterly unreasonably so as to frustrate the policy of the Act. An individual patient

---

[74]   Previously the National Health Service Act 1977, s 1.
[75]   *R v Secretary of State for Social Services, ex p Hincks* (1980) 1 BMLR 93, CA. See also *R v N and E Devon Health Authority, ex p Coughlan* [1999] Lloyd's Rep Med 306, CA.

could not claim damages from the Minister for pain and suffering. The patients lost the immediate legal battle. They gained valuable publicity. And the courts did not entirely abdicate control over the Minister: a public-spirited patient resigned to getting no damages himself could (by way of an application for judicial review) still challenge a Minister whom he could allege had totally subverted the health service (for example a Minister using his position and powers exclusively to benefit private medicine at the expense of the NHS).[76]

The Court of Appeal rejected any legally enforceable right to health care actionable by a patient for his own benefit. Did any such right exist against local health providers? In 1987, the parents of two sick babies who needed cardiac surgery sought to enforce such a right on their sons' behalf. They applied to the divisional court for a court order that their sons be operated on. The health authority explained that lack of resources and lack of trained nurses meant that each baby kept missing out on his operation to other more urgent cases. The court refused to make an order that the operation be carried out immediately.[77] The parents had no right to demand immediate treatment for their sons. The health authority could do only what was reasonable within their limited resources, human and financial. It is difficult to see what else the court could have done in these cases. The court could not provide the resources needed to operate on all sick babies. In effect, the judges were being asked to decide that Baby X needed surgery more urgently than Baby Y, and judges are not qualified to make clinical judgments.

In *R v Cambridge District Health Authority, ex p B*,[78] the Court of Appeal again demonstrated reluctance to become involved in questions of allocation of resources. B was a ten-year-old girl suffering from non-Hodgkin's lymphoma. In 1994, she received a bone marrow transplant from her sister. In 1995, she became ill again. The doctors treating her considered no further treatment should be given to prolong B's life. B's father obtained advice that there was a possible course of treatment. With further intensive chemotherapy, B stood a 10–20 per cent chance of remission sufficient to allow a second bone marrow transplant to succeed. The transplant itself stood a 10–20 per cent chance of success, offering B at best a 4 per cent chance of 'recovery'. The treatment package would cost about £75,000. The health authority refused to fund B's treatment. They argued (1) that such 'experimental' treatment was not in B's best interests and (2) that given the minimal prospects of successful treatment the cost could not be justified. Other demands on the limited budget took priority.

The trial judge, Laws J, was not convinced by the authority's case. He issued an order requiring the authority to reconsider the evidence in support of their

---

[76] Chances of success are not high, and the Government of the day could always change the law; however, they can be made to do it openly and not be permitted to pay lip service to a duty to a public health service which may have been abandoned.

[77] *R v Central Birmingham Health Authority, ex p Walker* (1988) Times, 26 November; *R v Central Birmingham Health Authority, ex p Collier* (1988) Times, 6 January, CA. See the highly critical analysis of Collier in Newdick, *Who Should We Treat? Rights, Rationing and Resources in the NHS*, pp 98–100.

[78] [1995] 2 All ER 129, CA.

decision not to treat B They must do more than 'merely toll the bell of tight resources'.[79] The authority appealed. The Court of Appeal backed them unequivocally, rejecting Laws J's attempt to require greater transparency in decisions about allocating resources. The Appeal Court rested their decision largely on clinical grounds, on evidence from doctors that the aggressive treatment proposed was not in B's interests, despite the contrary view of B's father and the child herself. Sir Thomas Bingham MR summed up judicial attitudes to problems in allocation of health care resources when he commented:

> Difficult and agonising judgments have to be made as to how a limited budget is best allocated to the maximum advantage of the maximum of patients. That is not a judgment which the court can make. In my judgment, it is not something that a health authority can be fairly criticised for not advancing before the court.[80]

So when will the courts intervene to question decisions about whom to treat, or what treatment patients may be entitled to? Judges do assert the power to assess the reasonableness of decision-making by NHS authorities, just as they will hold other public bodies to account for the reasonableness of their decision-making processes. In *R v St Mary's Hospital Ethical Committee, ex p Harriott*,[81] Mrs Harriott had been refused treatment by the IVF (test-tube baby) unit. The unit's informal ethical advisory committee had supported the doctors' decision not to treat Mrs Harriott because she had been rejected by the local social services department as a potential adoptive or foster mother and because she had convictions for prostitution offences. She challenged their decision. The judge held that the grounds for refusing her treatment were lawful. But he said refusal of treatment on *non-medical* grounds could be reviewed by a court. It would be unlawful to reject a patient because of her race or religion or other irrelevant grounds. A patient denied renal dialysis or surgery because the consultant in charge refuses to treat divorced people, or new Labour Party members, might well have a remedy. However, judges, it must be remembered, tend to be conservative. In *R v Sheffield Health Authority, ex p Seale*,[82] the judge refused to interfere with a health authority's decision to refuse fertility treatment to older women (defined as any woman over 35).

Successful challenges to decisions about provision of health care often depend on the patient identifying some obvious flaw in the decision-making process.[83] In *R v North Derbyshire Health Authority, ex p Fisher*,[84] the health authority refused to fund the costly drug beta-interferon for any patient with multiple sclerosis. They operated a blanket ban on provision of the drug, failed to make any assessment of individual patients' needs and ignored a circular from the Department of Health advising that serious consideration be given to providing beta-interferon to certain categories of patients with multiple

---

[79]   (1995) 25 BMLR 16 at 17.
[80]   [1995] 2 All ER 129 at 137, CA.
[81]   *R v Ethical Committee of St Mary's Hospital, ex p Harriott* [1988] 1 FLR 512.
[82]   (1994) 25 BMLR 1.
[83]   See Newdick, *Who Should We Treat? Rights, Rationing and Resources in the NHS*, Chapter 5.
[84]   [1997] 8 Med LR 327.

sclerosis. The judge held that the authority failed to take a reasoned decision after consideration of all the relevant factors.

A notable 'victory' for patients denied access to treatment is found in *R v North West Lancashire Health Authority, ex p A, D & G*.[85] The defendant health authority refused to pay for gender-reassignment surgery for the applicants. Such surgery was classified by the authority as a low priority along with cosmetic procedures such as face-lifts or hair transplants. Transsexuals should be provided with psychiatric and psychological services, but the authority would not 'commission drug treatment or surgery that is intended to give patients the physical characteristics of the opposite gender'. Statements in the policy document about exceptional cases based on overwhelming clinical need made it abundantly clear that in reality such a case would never be conceded. No-one would be a sufficiently *exceptional* case to qualify. The Court of Appeal quashed the decision to refuse treatment to the applicant as 'irrational'. The authority had failed to evaluate the medical evidence relating to transsexuality. They paid lip service to the notion that the applicant's condition constituted illness, but dismissed forms of effective treatment without proper consideration. The authority did not:

> ... in truth treat transsexualism as an illness, but as an attitude or state of mind which does not warrant medical treatment. ... [T]he ostensible provision that it makes for exceptions in individual cases and its manner of considering them amount effectively to the operation of a 'blanket policy' against funding treatment because it does not believe in such treatment.[86]

Another patient victory, this time in relation to unlicensed drugs, occurred in *R v Swindon NHS Primary Care Trust*.[87] The Court of Appeal, overturning the High Court decision, held that Swindon Primary Care Trust's funding policy for the (as yet) unlicensed drug Herceptin was irrational and unlawful. Herceptin was licensed for late-stage HE-II, an aggressive form of breast cancer. Ann Marie Rogers (the applicant) was in the early stage of the disease. Some trusts provided Herceptin in such cases, despite the fact that it was neither licensed nor approved by NICE. The Health Secretary, Patricia Hewitt, had previously announced that Herceptin, which costs £26,000 a course, should not be refused purely on grounds of cost. Trusts will still be able to refuse treatment where cost is a factor but, in this case, Swindon PCT had declared that cost was irrelevant to its decision. The court held that there was therefore no rational basis for refusing to treat Mrs Rogers. What, then, would provide a rational basis for refusal of unlicensed treatment? Resource availability, combined with clinical need and individual circumstances.

The courts are beginning to show themselves prepared to scrutinise the process by which health care providers make decisions about what kinds of treatment they will provide and who will have access to such treatment. However, if the health care provider can demonstrate that it has fully considered the case made to it and addressed all the relevant considerations, but ultimately determined that other treatments and other claims must be

---

[85] [2000] 1 WLR 977, CA.
[86] [2000] 1 WLR 977, CA, per Auld LJ.
[87] [2006] EWCA Civ 392.

given priority, courts remain unlikely to intervene. Nor is going to court likely to advance your treatment to the head of the waiting list.

Strict limits are placed on waiting times. The Government has set a target that by 2008 there will be a maximum wait of 18 weeks between GP referral and treatment in hospital. Some doctors are dubious about strategies based on waiting lists. Hospitals anxious to avoid sanctions will find themselves treating less urgent cases first just because that patient has been waiting longer. 'Guarantees' of timely treatment or surgery raise other questions too. Unless entrenched in statute, will this still fall short of a legal right to health care? Against whom might any right be enforceable?

Treatment abroad

2.19 In 2002, the NHS began to fund treatment in Europe. A patient requiring a knee-replacement might be sent to Belgium or Germany rather than be kept waiting in pain for months in the UK. But first he has to receive authorisation from the PCT.

Much publicity was given to the decision of the European Court of Justice[88] that if a patient living in one Member State of the European Union faced *undue delay* in receiving treatment in his home country, his state insurance system must be prepared to pay for him to have treatment in another Member State where treatment is available more speedily. A patient forced to wait years for a hip-replacement in England might demand to be sent to Germany where such surgery can be performed within weeks. Do we now enjoy a 'European' right to health care?[89]

In *R (on the application of Watts) v Bedford Primary Care Trust*,[90] a 74-year-old woman was informed by Bedford PCT that she would have to wait a year for a bi-lateral hip-replacement. She applied to have the operation in France under the Community law E112 scheme, but the PCT refused and reduced her wait to four months. Mrs. Watts, who was wheelchair-bound and in constant pain, went ahead with the operation in France, without the PCT's authorisation. The PCT refused to reimburse her because four months was the 'normal' waiting time for a hip-replacement. In the High Court, Munby J held that 'undue delay' might be evident even if a patient is treated within NHS waiting time targets. Unfortunately for Mrs Watts, he held that there was no evidence of undue delay in her case. Munby J treated with scepticism the view that, on the basis of his decision, thousands of NHS patients would flock abroad for treatment.

---

[88] Case C-157/99 *BSM Geraets-Smits v Stichting Ziekenfonds VGZ and Peerbooms v Stichting CZ Groep Zorgverzekeringen*. See European Community Regulation (EC) 1408/71 establishing the E112 form, which enables pre-authorised cross-border care.

[89] See T Hervey and J McHale, *Health Law and the European Union* (2004) CUP; and see *Mason and McCall Smith's Law and Medical Ethics*, Chapter 3 (by M Aziz).

[90] [2004] EWCA Civ 166.

Both Mrs Watts and the Department of Health appealed to the Court of Appeal, which referred the matter to the European Court of Justice.[91] The ECJ held that when determining whether a proposed waiting time is acceptable, Member States must apply 'an objective medical assessment of the clinical needs of the person concerned in the light of all of the factors characterising his medical condition'.[92] While the NHS is given powers of authorisation, it must be impartial and objective[93] – it cannot use NHS waiting times to determine the definition of 'undue delay'. If patients wait longer than doctors advise, regardless of targets, the NHS must refund the costs where patients pay for treatment elsewhere in Europe.[94] Yet 'undue delay' is still undefined. Medical assessments are inherently subjective. A doctor's opinion may differ from those of his colleagues on such issues as medical condition, history and prognosis. In the case of Yvonne Watts, the NHS failed to set out the criteria for the grant of refusal of prior authorisation. It is difficult to see how the NHS can rectify this situation so as to prevent further legal action.

The cost to the NHS of sending patients abroad will drain resources here, exacerbating existing difficulties. Unsurprisingly, the Government is exploring other strategies, including initiatives with the independent sector. The ECJ ruling in *Watts* concerned freedom to provide services under Article 49 of the EC Treaty. The NHS is not obliged to authorise or pay for hospital treatment provided by private hospitals on this basis.

The Health Act 1999 moved responsibility for arranging NHS care to primary care trusts.[95] Section 18 of the 1999 Act imposes a duty of quality:

> It is the duty of each Health Authority, Primary Care Trust and NHS Trust to put and keep in place arrangements for the purpose of monitoring and improving the quality of health care which it provides to individuals.[96]

Failure to address provision of timely treatment on the part of a PCT is an obvious breach of section 18. Good care is timely care. Will the courts offer a remedy to patients aggrieved by the failure of their PCT to provide timely treatment, or to provide the treatment of their choice? The remedy many patients may seek is compensation. Imagine that a patient is told that she will have to wait another twelve months for her hip-replacement, in contravention of Department of Health guidelines. She borrows money from the bank and pays £8,000 to have her operation privately. If she is to recover that sum from her PCT, the courts will have to overrule *ex p Hincks*[97] and allow a claim for

[91] Case C-372/04 *R (on the application of Watts) v Bedford Primary Care Trust* [2006]. See JV McHale, 'Rights to Medical Treatment in EU Law' (2007) 15 *Medical Law Review* 99.
[92] At para 79.
[93] At para 115.
[94] At paras 113–114.
[95] The Health Act 1999 amended the NHS Act 1977, ss 16A and 16B (now consolidated in the National Health Service Act 2006, ss 18, 19 and Sch 3). See also s 228 of the National Health Service Act 2006 (replacing s 8 of the National Health Service Reform and Health Care Professions Act 2002).
[96] Words in s 18 (1) inserted by the National Health Service Reform and Health Care Professions Act 2002, s 37(1).
[97] *R v Secretary of State for Social Services, ex p Hincks* (1980) 1 BMLR 93, CA.

breach of statutory duty against the NHS.[98] Once again, money to compensate patients will deplete funds to treat patients. If the patient cannot raise the costs of private treatment herself, will the court grant on order requiring the PCT to arrange her operation immediately, if need be in the private sector, but paid for by the NHS? Perhaps they may. A court will at least require from a PCT a cogent explanation for delay. This scenario does not involve a judge saying, treat this patient and not some other patient in greater need. It entails a court requiring the PCT, a public body, to establish that in *not* using the powers they have to arrange this patient's care, they acted *reasonably*. Budgets remain relevant factors. A right to treatment 'on demand' is unlikely to emerge. What we may see develop in the next few years is a legal right to an equitable process of decision-making about NHS treatment. In other contexts, one positive impact of the Human Rights Act has been to encourage judges to scrutinise public authorities' decisions more vigorously, particularly where life may be at stake.[99]

---

[98]   But consider the possibility of damages for breach of the Human Rights Act 1998: see Newdick, *Who Should We Treat? Rights, Rationing and Resources in the* NHS, pp 125–126.
[99]   *R v Lord Saville of Newdigate, ex p A* [1999] 4 All ER 860, HL. And see Newdick, *Who Should We Treat? Rights, Rationing and Resources in the NHS*, pp 121–125.

Chapter 3

MEDICINE, MORAL DILEMMAS AND THE LAW

3.1 Medical ethics make news, but are far from new. From the formulation of the Hippocratic Oath in Ancient Greece to the present day, doctors have debated among themselves the codes of conduct which should govern the art of healing. These days philosophers, theologians, lawyers and journalists insist on joining the debate. Outside interest, or interference as doctors sometimes see it, is not new either. Hippocrates was a philosopher. The Christian churches through the centuries have asserted the right to pronounce on medical matters of spiritual import, such as abortion and euthanasia, and to uphold the sanctity of life. All other major religions across the world similarly pronounce on matters of medical ethics.[1] In the UK today, in considering the impact of faith on medical ethics and practice greater attention needs to be paid to traditions other than the Christian faith.

The Hippocratic Oath makes interesting reading. Its first premise is that the doctor owes loyalty to his teachers and his brethren. Obligations to exercise skill for the benefit of patients' health come second. Abortion, direct euthanasia and abetting suicide are prohibited. Improper sexual relations with patients are banned. Confidentiality in all dealings with patients is imposed. In 2,500 years these basic precepts of medical practice changed little. Dramatic changes in the kinds of moral and ethical problems confronting the doctor have appeared only in the last 50 years or so.

The art of the Greek philosopher-physician has become a science for many practitioners. Science has given the doctor tools to work marvels undreamed of by earlier generations. *In vitro* fertilisation (IVF) and gamete donation to assist infertile couples to have children are no longer seen as extraordinary. The technology to create artificial gametes is on the horizon, so a man who produces no natural sperm might be able to father a child via sperm 'constructed' from other cells in his body. A family with a child dying of certain genetic diseases can be helped to create a 'saviour sibling'. Tests will

---

[1] See, for example, DB Sinclair, *Jewish Biomedical Law: Legal and Extra-Legal Dimensions* (2003) OUP; *The Islamic Code of Medical Ethics* (1981) International Organisation of Islamic Medicine; A Sheikh and AR Gartrad, *Caring for Muslim Patients* (2000) Radcliffe Medical Press; SC Cromwell, *Hindu Bioethics in the Twenty-First Century* (2003) State University of New York Press.

ensure that the new baby does not suffer from her sibling's disease, and is an exact tissue match for her. Then stem cells taken from the newborn infant's umbilical cord may constitute a 'cure' for the elder child.

Creating a human clone looks technically feasible now that mammalian cloning has proven possible. Reproductive cloning attracts much media attention and disapproval, but it is the potential for therapeutic cloning, better described as stem cell therapy, which excites doctors and scientists. The possible uses of embryonic stem cells hold out the hope of being able to replace damaged cells in patients with diseases such as Parkinson's disease. Further in the future, some suggest that stem cells can be used to grow new organs to replace diseased kidneys or livers.[2]

Babies born at ever earlier stages in gestation, or born with severe abnormalities, can be offered a chance of survival by amazing developments in neonatal intensive care. Some forms of foetal handicap are correctable by surgery carried out while the baby is still in the womb. Ventilators keep alive accident victims whose heart and lungs have given up. Dialysis and transplant surgery save kidney, liver and heart patients from certain death. The list of technological 'miracles' is endless. They have placed in the hands of doctors powers which humanity once ascribed to God alone.

Technological progress has been matched by social change. People are less willing to accept without question the decisions of those who exercise power, be they judges, politicians or doctors. Paternalism is out of fashion. Feminists ask why doctors should determine which infertile women receive treatment. Lawyers and philosophers, not to mention parents, wonder why the doctor is best qualified to judge whether a baby's quality of life is such as to make life-saving surgery desirable. The power of the doctor to end life, whether by switching off a ventilator or by deciding not to give a patient a place in a dialysis unit, disturbs us all. These moral dilemmas are just as acutely felt by doctors. Their difficulties are accentuated by the fact that new technology cannot be made available to all those in need: there is just not enough money or resource in the National Health Service. Above all, the medical profession in 2007 faces a society deeply divided on virtually every moral question. The public demands a say in medical decision-making on sensitive ethical issues. Yet, from the 'hot potato' of whether doctors should help couples to have a 'saviour sibling' to help their dying child, through the debates on abortion to euthanasia, the doctor who seeks guidance from public opinion will discover division, bitterness and confusion.

Questions of medical ethics arise throughout the field of medical practice. Most medical students receive education in ethics as an integral part of their studies and several texts address medical ethics in detail.[3] Increasingly, those

---

2   See I Kuehnle, MA Goodall, 'The Therapeutic Potential of Stem Cells From Adults' (2002) 325 *British Medical Journal* 372.

3   Excellent texts on medical ethics include: TL Beauchamp and JF Childress, *Principles of Biomedical Ethics* (5th edn, 2001) OUP; R Gillon, *Philosophical Medical Ethics* (1996) John Wiley; JM Harris, *The Value of Life* (1985) Routledge; J Jackson, *Ethics in Medicine* (2005) Polity Press; and see generally, H Kuhse and P Singer (eds), *A Companion to*

scholars who address the ethics of medicine speak of *bioethics* rather than *medical* ethics. The change of terminology is not merely semantic. The most difficult dilemmas begin in the laboratory, not at the bedside. Consider xenotransplantation, whereby animals might be genetically-engineered to produce organs compatible for transplant into humans with organ failure. The essential question is whether science should continue to pursue the research that may transform such possibilities into reality. Scientists need education in ethics as much as doctors. Equally importantly, the term bioethics is seen as less doctor-centred than medical ethics. All health professionals confront ethical dilemmas.

This book focuses on doctors. Much of what we say is relevant to other health professionals too, but each health profession faces its own particular variant of ethical debate.[4] While the ethics of the doctor-patient relationship are touched on throughout this book, it is not and does not purport to be a book about medical ethics, or bioethics. Never the less, two fundamental issues of ethics do need to be introduced at this juncture. Are ethics more than etiquette? How does society today understand and implement concepts of the sanctity of human life?

Ethics not etiquette

3.2 Were you to peruse the ethical guidance provided for doctors in the nineteenth and early twentieth century, what you might find would have scant relationship to what most of us today think of as medical ethics. The physician was envisaged as an English gentleman,[5] and as long as he behaved in a gentlemanly and benevolent fashion, his own conscience and integrity would guide him towards ethical solutions in dilemmas surrounding how to treat a patient.[6] Professional bodies, notably the General Medical Council (GMC), did offer somewhat more concrete advice (doctors were prohibited from sexual relationships with their patients or their patients' wives, they should not take advantage of their privileged access to patients' homes, they must avoid misuse of alcohol or drugs, they were not to tout for custom, nor disparage other doctors, they must refrain from any sort of collaboration with unqualified practitioners[7]) but, in essence, this advice centred on gentlemanly behaviour. Although there can be no doubt that some of the injunctions issued in earlier days had beneficial effects on patient care, what was styled ethics

Bioethics (1998) Blackwell. For a succinct introduction to bioethics in the context of medical law, see E Jackson, *Medical Law: Text, Cases and Materials* (2006) OUP, Chapter 1.

4 See IE Thompson, KM Melia, KM Boyd, *Nursing Ethics* (5th edn, 2006) Churchill Livingstone; MA Santaro, TM Gorrie (eds), *Ethics and the Pharmaceutical Industry* (2005) Cambridge University Press; P Lamden (ed), *Dental Law and Ethics* (2002) Radcliffe Medical Press; British Register of Complementary Practitioners, *Code of Ethics and Practice for Members* (December 2001).

5 This model of 'ethics' was initiated by the Manchester physician Thomas Percival, in his book *Medical Ethics*, first published in 1808; see CD Leake (ed), *Percival's Medical Ethics* (1927) Williams & Wilkins.

6 See Gillon, *Philosophical Medical Ethics*, Chapter 5.

7 See, for example, GMC 'Bluebook', *Professional Conduct: Fitness to Practise* (April 1985).

had at its core a code of etiquette. Doctors should conduct themselves in a particular way, they should show professional solidarity, and practise benevolent paternalism.

The scale of grossly unethical abuse of medicine revealed in the wake of the Second World War destroyed any complacent culture of paternalist medicine. A series of codes of medical ethics were promulgated internationally. Moral philosophers began to subject medicine to a much more rigorous critical analysis. 'Critical' medical ethics emerged, offering a framework within which ethical dilemmas could be the subject of debate and reflection. Beauchamp and Childress's seminal book *Principles of Biomedical Ethics* proved especially influential.[8]

Beauchamp and Childress formulated four basic principles – autonomy, beneficence, non-maleficence and justice – as a framework for ethical conduct. Today, the four principles are a fashionable subject for attack[9] but they do not, and never sought to, provide easy answers to particular questions or to offer a comprehensive ethical analysis. They do, as Gillon says, '… help us bring more order, consistency and understanding to our medico-moral judgments'.[10] The influence of the four principles, and their delicate relationship with legal principles, is such that any study of the law relating to health care should give a brief account of them.

Respect for autonomy: self-determination

3.3 Autonomy literally means self-rule (as opposed to heteronomy – rule by others). We should respect autonomous choices made by other people. Crude paternalism is the antithesis of respect for autonomy. Non-consensual treatment of a patient, even for her own good, violates her autonomy. Gradually, as we shall see in Chapters 5 and 6, English law, via principles governing consent to treatment, clothed the moral principle of autonomy in legal reality.

Respect for autonomy does not demand unthinking deference to any choice made by another human being. To demand respect, a choice must be maximally autonomous – an informed and free decision made by someone with the capacity to make such a choice. A very young child will 'choose' not to go to the dentist and 'choose' not to be injected with antibiotics. His choice will be dictated by the nastiness of the procedure involved. He is not able to weigh the benefits of good dental care, or antibiotics to cure his streptococcal infection, against the immediate unpleasantness. An older person with severe mental disabilities may be similarly disabled from making any real choice. A

---

[8]   (1st edn, 1979) The Free Press, (5th edn, 2001) OUP. See also RM Veatch, *A Theory of Medical Ethics* (1981) Basic Books Inc; HT Engelhard, *The Foundation of Bioethics* (2nd edn, 1996) OUP.

[9]   For example, K Clouser and B Gert, 'A Critique of Principalism' (1996) 15 *Journal of Medicine and Philosophy* 219. And see J Savelescu *et al*, 'Festschrift Edition of the Journal of Medical Ethics in Honour of Raanan Gillon' (2003) 29 *Journal of Medical Ethics* 265–312.

[10]   See Gillon, *Philosophical Medical Ethics*, p viii.

paranoid schizophrenic may be led by his 'voices' to refuse treatment because he knows that the doctor is 'Satan'. The preferences expressed in such cases are not autonomous choices.

In setting boundaries of mental capacity, the law struggles with the concept of what constitutes an autonomous choice. The temptation to regard a choice you disagree with as non-autonomous is strong. The outcome of the choice should be irrelevant. A woman who rejects surgery for breast cancer where the prospects of complete recovery are good because she cannot tolerate any mutilation of her breast makes a decision that we may see as bizarre. The Jehovah's Witness rejecting a blood transfusion does so on the basis of an interpretation of the Bible which not all of us share. Their choices remain autonomous choices, made by people able to reason and on the basis of adequate information.

Beneficence: do good

3.4 An injunction to act beneficently requires doctors to frame their actions to benefit their patients. The needs of the patient should be the professional's pre-eminent concern. A patient should never be a means to an end. What does such a pious hope mean in practice? The ethics of clinical research have attracted much philosophical attention. The failure of doctors to act beneficently and the treatment of human subjects as little more than research tools explains that emphasis on research ethics. Ethical professionals should put the individual's welfare first, even if to do so conflicts with their own interests (for example, their research objectives).

Another problem with beneficence might be that it could be seen as just another name for paternalism. The beneficent doctor does what he thinks is best for the patient. If natural childbirth is dangerous for the patient and the child she carries, must the beneficent doctor perform a Caesarean section whether she likes it or not? The answer is no, because beneficence demands respect for autonomy. The professional should offer his judgement on what is good for the patient, but doing good for her requires that ultimately he accepts *her* decision on what is good for her.

Translating the ethical imperative of beneficence into legal principle is tricky. The law imposes a duty of care owed by doctor to patients. That duty, however, generally involves not doing harm. English law does not impose any duty to be a Good Samaritan. Once a patient is admitted to hospital, staff must provide him with adequate and competent care. A doctor or nurse who witnesses a road accident but passes by on the other side commits no legal wrong. Yet if she fails to help when she could easily do so, she fails to act beneficently.[11]

---

[11] Though she may face disciplinary proceedings as GMC guidance requires that in an emergency a doctor must provide to anyone at risk the assistance she could reasonably be asked to provide. General Medical Council, *Good Medical Practice* (2006) GMC, paragraph 11.

Beneficence illustrates an important point about law and ethics. Ethics demand a higher standard of behaviour than the law requires. A competent surgeon who removes a patient's gallstones without mishap fulfils her legal duty of care. If she dismisses the patient's complaints of pain with scorn, makes him feel like a child and treats him as just another patient number, is she acting ethically?

Non-maleficence: do no harm

3.5 Raanan Gillon[12] says of non-maleficence: 'Among the shibboleths of traditional medical ethics is the injunction *Primum non nocere* – first (or above all) do no harm'. Gillon does not challenge the principle of non-maleficence as such. Its importance is self-evident; what he rightly points out is that principle cannot be absolute. Medicine often involves doing harm. Removing an inflamed appendix inevitably involves a degree of harm, risk, pain and scarring. The benefits obviously outweigh the harm in that case. Practices which avoid all risk have ultimately done more harm than good. Sometimes agonising dilemmas arise, as was the case in relation to the conjoined twins, Jodie and Mary, separated by surgeons in Manchester in 2000.[13] Without surgery both girls would die. Separating Mary from her sister would and did result in her death. 'Do no harm' to Mary meant not doing good for Jodie.

Justice[14]

3.6 '[T]he idea that justice is a moral issue that doctors can properly ignore is clearly mistaken.'[15] Few would disagree with a proposition that doctors should treat patients justly. 'Justice' in this context might be interpreted as meaning that patients are entitled to be treated fairly and equally by their doctors. The Queen should be treated no differently from a homeless person brought into Casualty after he is found unconscious in a doorway. Health professionals should not show preference for patients who enjoy a particular status, or provide sub-standard care for patients of whom they disapprove.

Alas justice is much more complex. Within the NHS resources are limited. Not every treatment can be offered to every patient who may derive clinical benefit from such treatment. Imagine that the Queen and the homeless person both needed a liver transplant. The demand for donor livers far exceeds supply. How should a just decision be made about whether either of them should receive a transplant? The Queen is 81, but in good health. The homeless person is 35, but is an alcoholic and his general health is poor. Other contenders compete for livers, a number of them younger than the Queen and in better health than the homeless person.

12 See Gillon, *Philosophical Medical Ethics*, p 80.
13 See *Re A (Minors) (Conjoined Twins: Separation)* [2000] Lloyd's Rep Med 425, CA.
14 See generally, C Newdick, *Who Should We Treat? Law Patients and Resources in the NHS* (2nd edn, 2005) OUP.
15 See Gillon, *Philosophical Medical Ethics*, p 87.

We might agree that the Queen should not get a transplant just because she is the Queen.[16] We might agree that the homeless person should not be refused a transplant just because he is homeless. Is it relevant that if he continues to drink after surgery, the transplant is likely to fail? Even if he overcame his addiction his lifestyle may militate against success. Poor diet and no settled home will make it difficult for him to comply with the post-operative regime necessary to avoid rejection of the donor liver. There is a lively debate about how far lifestyle and/or 'fault' should affect access to NHS resources.[17]

The complexity of notions of distributive justice in health care, coupled with scarcity of resources, has resulted in health economists entering the debate. They have advanced the merits of an exercise based on 'quality adjusted life years' (QALYs), which measure health as years of life after treatment weighted by the patient's quality of life. QALYs embody an attempt to provide an objective framework to assess how society should determine priorities for treatment.

Both the Queen and the homeless person may do badly on a QALY test. Life post-transplant is unlikely to generate for anyone years of full health. Let us award the Queen ten years[18] of 0.75 health and the homeless person 20 years at 0.25 health, the cost being the same for both 'patients'. The Queen scores 7.5, the homeless person scores 5; both will almost certainly lose out to younger, fitter patients. QALYs trigger another question. Should anyone get a liver transplant? Compare liver transplants with hip-replacements. A woman of 50 having a hip-replacement for arthritis may generate 15–20 QALYs at lower cost. Yet arthritis is not life-threatening. It is perhaps not surprising then, as we shall see, that the English courts have been reluctant to engage in questions of health resources.

NICE[19] has no such option. The National Institute for Clinical Excellence was set up as a special health authority in 1999 to produce clinical practice guidance and promote transparency of research allocation decisions. It became the National Institute for Health and Clinical Excellence in 2005. It is often difficult to ascertain the method used by NICE to determine whether or not a particular treatment is cost-effective, but the QALY has undoubtedly been influential.[20] John Harris criticised NICE's interpretation of the QALY when allocating resources to Alzheimer's patients. He accused NICE of evaluating patients rather than treatment.[21]

---

[16] She can of course simply opt for private care. Is it unjust that those who can pay can obtain whatever treatment they desire?

[17] See, for example, MJ Underwood and JS Bailey, 'Should Smokers be Offered Coronary Bypass Surgery?' (1993) 306 *British Medical Journal* 1047; S Hall, 'Smokers and Alcoholics Should Pay for Operations' (2006) *Guardian*, 29 June.

[18] Given her mother's longevity this does not seem an unreasonable assumption.

[19] See E Jackson, *Medical Law* (2006) OUP, pp 76–82.

[20] See S Hill, S Garattini, J Van Loenhout, B O'Brien, K De Joncheere, *Technology Appraisal Programme of the NICE: A Review by WHO* (2003) WHO, p 31.

[21] J Harris, 'It's Not NICE to Discriminate' (2005) 31 *Journal of Medical Ethics* 373. Alzheimer's patients, he claimed, were judged by NICE as 'not cost effective to society'. See reply in K Claxton and AJ Culyer, 'Wickedness of Folly? The Ethics of NICE's Decisions' (2006) 32 *Journal of Medical Ethics* 373. More recently, NICE faces judicial review after

Autonomy and patients' responsibilities

3.7   Of Beauchamp and Childress's four principles, autonomy became *de facto* the dominant principle – especially in legal debate. So dominant did that one principle become that Daniel Callaghan declared:

> Nothing has exasperated me so much as the deference given in bioethics to the principle of autonomy.[22]

The emphasis on autonomy has meant, as Draper and Sorrell explain:

> Medical Ethics is one-sided. It dwells on the ethical obligations of doctors to the exclusion of those of patients.[23]

And in *R v Collins and Ashworth Health Authority, ex p Brady*, Kay J commented:

> ... it would seem to me a matter of deep regret if the law has developed to a point in this area where the rights of the patient count for everything and other ethical values and institutional integrity count for nothing.[24]

The problem is that the notion of autonomy has become distorted. Autonomy is wrongly understood as simply a right to what 'I want'. The doctor becomes little more than a technician delivering what the consumer-patient demands.[25] As Onora O'Neill[26] has eloquently pointed out, such an interpretation of autonomy is mistaken. Autonomy involves

> ... privacy, voluntariness, self-mastery, choosing freely, choosing one's moral position and accepting responsibility for one's choices.[27]

O'Neill adds to that list 'self-control' and 'self-determination'.[28] Expressing a non-reflective preference is not a manifestation of autonomy. Responsibility requires reflection on how our choices affect others. Making a case that patients owe ethical duties to others, including their doctors, is relatively easy. Clothing such ethical responsibilities with legal force is a harder task.[29] Reflecting, however, on patients' responsibilities forces us to consider the

---

restricting the drugs available on the NHS to treat mild to severe Alzheimer's. See M Barriaux and S Boseley, 'Third Company Joins Lawsuit Against NICE' (2006) Guardian, 18 November.

[22]   D Callaghan, 'Can the Moral Commons Survive Autonomy?' (1996) *Hastings Center Report* 41.

[23]   H Draper and T Sorrell, 'Patients' Responsibilities in Medical Ethics' (2002) 16 *Bioethics* 335.

[24]   [2000] Lloyd's Rep Med 355 at 367.

[25]   See M Brazier and N Glover, 'Does Medical Law Have a Future?' in D Hayton (ed), *Law's Future(s)* (2000) Hart Publishing, p 371.

[26]   See O O'Neill, *Autonomy and Trust in Bioethics* (2002) CUP; O O'Neill, *A Question of Trust* (2002) Reith Lectures.

[27]   See R Faden and T Beauchamp (in collaboration with NMP King), *A History and Theory of Informed Consent* (1986) CUP, p 7.

[28]   See O O'Neill, *Autonomy and Trust in Bioethics*, p 22.

[29]   See M Brazier, 'Do No Harm – Do Patients Have Responsibilities Too' (2006) 65 *Cambridge Law Journal* 397.

growing support for a view of communitarian ethics.[30] In judging the ethics of a particular course of action, the impact on the community, not just the individual, must be evaluated.

Virtue ethics and the ethics of care

3.8 Virtue ethicists counter the dominance of autonomy in medical ethics by stressing the benefit of doing the right or virtuous thing in a given situation.[31] If your friend asks you for money with which he might travel to Switzerland to engage the services of the assisted-suicide clinic because he is suffering intolerably from a terminal condition, you may agree to help him because you respect his right to make his own choices, or alternatively, from a virtue ethics standpoint, you might help simply because benevolence, kindness and generosity requires it. Principalists revere autonomy, but it has less relevance to a virtue ethicist who might argue that decisions about death or abortion should be based on compassion.[32]

Feminists, too, find conventional theory lacking on the basis that it fails to take account of gender-specific disparities. Attention is directed to areas where women's interests have traditionally been neglected, such as birth control and pregnancy. But the resulting theories have significance far beyond reproductive issues. Harvard psychologist Carol Gilligan's 'Ethic of Care'[33] emphasises the importance to women of relationships. Instead of basing ethical theory on abstract principles, such as autonomy, the ethic of care addresses issues at a personal level. Health must be contextualised, physical and emotional needs must be taken into account.

To whom (or what) do we owe ethical obligations?[34]

3.9 Principles of medical ethics often conflict. If an obstetrician performs a Caesarean section without a woman's consent, he violates her autonomy. If he does not intervene and the child dies or is born severely disabled, he has done harm to the child. Withdrawing treatment from a patient in a permanent vegetative state may be seen to harm him. Yet continuing to keep him alive can equally be classified as harming him. Money spent on sustaining such a patient over several years deprives others of treatment in a cash-strapped NHS. Keeping X alive may be an injustice to Y. The 'trump card' invoked to demand that the foetus and the patient in persistent vegetative state (PVS) be

---

30   Note that JK Mason and GT Laurie declare their 'partial adherence to community ethics'. See JK Mason and GT Laurie, *Mason and McCall Smith's Law and Medical Ethics* (7th edn, 2006) OUP, p 6. And see D Callaghan, 'Principalism and Communitarianism' (2003) 29 *Journal of Medical Ethics* 287.

31   See generally, R Hursthouse, *On Virtue Ethics* (1999) OUP.

32   See, for example, L Van Zyl, *Death and Compassion: A Virtue-based Approach to Euthanasia* (2000) Ashgate; R Hursthouse, 'Virtue Ethics and Abortion' (1991) 20 *Philosophy and Public Affairs* 223–246.

33   C Gilligan, *In a Different Voice* (1982) Harvard University Press.

34   See Gillon, *Philosophical Medical Ethics*, Chapters 7 and 8.

accorded priority centres around beliefs in sanctity of life. What we mean by sanctity of life, and whether it is a trump card, is hotly debated.

The sanctity of life: Judaeo-Christian tradition[35]

3.10 For the devout Roman Catholic sanctity of life is straightforward. Human life is a gift from God and is literally sacred. Any act which deliberately ends a life is wrong. Life begins at conception. Therefore, abortion, and research on, or disposal of, an artificially-created embryo, a test-tube embryo, is never permissible. Life ends when God ends it. No degree of suffering or disability justifies a premature release effected by us.

Yet even so there remain grey areas in the application of belief that life is sacred. Abortion is banned because the only intent of that operation is to kill the child. The Roman Catholic Church forbids abortion even when pregnancy threatens the woman's life. However, a pregnant woman with cancer of the womb may be allowed a hysterectomy, albeit the child will then die. This is called the 'doctrine of double effect': the operation for cancer incidentally destroys the child but that was not its primary purpose.

At the other end of life, the Church, while condemning euthanasia, does not demand that extraordinary means be taken to prolong life. Where is the line drawn? Should a severely disabled baby be subjected to painful surgery with a low success rate? Must antibiotics be administered to the terminal cancer patient stricken with pneumonia? The doctrine of double effect, and the application of a distinction between ordinary and extraordinary means to preserve life have generated substantial literature and debate.[36] Even accepting that areas of doubt exist, the orthodox Roman Catholic remains fortunate in the security of her beliefs on the sanctity of life, beliefs shared by many fundamentalist Christians of the Protestant tradition.

Other practising Christians, who subscribe in essence to the doctrine of the sanctity of life, see further problems once they seek to apply their faith. Contraception is morally acceptable to the majority, and to many Roman Catholics now (although still officially prohibited by the Church). The exact point when life begins and becomes sacred becomes of the utmost importance to determine the morality of certain contraceptive methods. Abortion to save a mother's life is accepted by many Christians, as it always has been in the Jewish and Muslim faiths. A child's life deserves protection but not at the expense of his mother's. This step taken, the extent to which the child's life may be sacrificed to his mother's has to be ascertained. Is a threat to the mother's mental stability sufficient? What about the women who suffer rape? What is the status of the early embryo created in the test-tube? These and many other issues have caused dissent within the Church of England and other

---

[35]   See J Finnis, *Natural Law and Natural Rights* (1980) OUP; O O'Donovan, *Begotten or Made* (1984) OUP.

[36]   See, for example, the debate between J Finnis and J Harris in J Keown (ed), *Euthanasia Examined: Ethical, Clinical and Legal Perspectives* (1995) CUP.

Christian traditions. For example, a number of eminent Anglican theologians[37] argue that research on the early embryo is acceptable and raises no conflict within Christian doctrine. Other Anglicans remain adamantly opposed to any form of destructive research on embryos. None the less, the adherent of any religious faith enjoys a framework of belief. The sanctity of life has meaning for them because that life was given by God.

The sanctity of life in a secular society

3.11 Many people still subscribe to some form of belief in a divinity or higher power. Churches are popular for weddings and funerals, and thriving communities of Jews and Muslims remain committed to their traditions. Britain today is an overwhelmingly secular society where the majority of the population is uncommitted to any religious creed and those people practising any religious faith are a minority.[38] How many people retain a general belief in God as the Creator is open to question. For those who do not, what meaning has the sanctity of life? If life is not bestowed by God, on what grounds is it sacred?

There can be no doubt that belief in the sanctity of life does survive the absence of religious belief. Taking life is as reprehensible to many agnostics and atheists as it is to believers. Many non-believers have been more consistent in fighting for the sanctity of life than have certain warmongering Christian priests, or those Christians who in the USA gather round the jails to celebrate the death penalty's return. What in a secular society is the basis of the sanctity of human life? To most people who are not philosophers the answer is simple: there is a deep and embedded instinct that taking human life is wrong. Life is a most precious possession.[39] All other possessions, all potential joys, depend upon its continued existence. An attack on one individual's right to life which goes unchecked threatens us all. Our autonomy is undermined. Our security becomes precarious. The move away from a concept of life as God-given, however, has certain consequences. If, at the basis of belief in the sanctity of life, there is a perception of the freedom of the individual, of the joy that life can bring, then the quality of life comes into account. The right of the foetus to come into possession of his own life, his own freedom, must be balanced against his mother's rights over her own life and body. When pain and disability cause an individual to cease to wish to live, then he may be free to end that life. It is his to do with as he wishes. Individual choice becomes central to applying the concept of the sanctity of life. No one must interfere with an adult's choices on continued life.[40] Whether any other adult can be compelled to assist a fellow to end his life raises more difficult questions. The concept of freedom of choice offers little guidance where an individual is incapable of choice. Never the less this

---

[37] See, for example, K Ward, 'An Irresolvable Debate' in A Dyson and J Harris (eds), *Experiments on Embryos* (1989) Routledge, Chapter 7.

[38] On the secularisation of bioethics, see E Jackson *Medical Law: Text, Cases and Materials*, pp 9–23.

[39] See R Dworkin, *Life's Dominion: An Argument About Abortion and Euthanasia* (1993) Harper and Collins.

[40] See G Dworkin, RG Frey and S Boy, *Euthanasia and Physician Assisted Suicide For and Against* (1998) CUP.

uncertain position commands a fair degree of generous support. People have an intrinsic right to life. Life is sacred, but not 'inviolable'.

Sanctity of life: a different perspective[41]

3.12 A number of philosophers attack the very notion that 'taking human life is intrinsically wrong'. Life is seen as having no inherent value. Life has value only if it is worth living. Taking life is wrong because 'it is wrong to destroy a life which is worth living'.[42] Side by side with a move to concentrate attention on the quality of life alone comes a redefinition of human life deserving of protection. It is *persons*,[43] not all human animals, whose lives have value. With such a perspective, unless there is capacity for self-awareness, for the individual to recognise himself as a functioning human person able to relate to other persons, he has no life of the quality and kind which must be preserved. Certain consequences follow. A person who can reason must be allowed to judge for himself whether continued life is worth it. A human who cannot reason for himself, who is not a person, may have that judgment made for him by others. Providing painless release for a person who considers his life not worth living, or an individual whose capacity for self-awareness has gone, so that he has ceased to be a 'person', becomes a moral action. The unborn are not 'persons'. They have no rights against their mothers who *are* persons. Abortion is moral and it may even be considered immoral not to abort a seriously damaged foetus. Research on embryos to benefit existing persons, whether by improving treatment for infertility or seeking a cure for congenital disease, is not only morally permissible, but almost a moral imperative. Euthanasia of the hopelessly brain-damaged with no hope of recovery is entirely acceptable and may, in strictly controlled circumstances, be non-voluntary.

Sanctity of life and the medical profession

3.13 No doubt the disparity of views among the general population is reflected in the personal views of many doctors. Doctors, however, have to take decisions on matters others merely debate. How far and in what fashion is the sanctity of life a central medical ethic? The Declaration of Geneva[44] included the following undertaking:

> I will maintain the utmost respect for human life from time of conception; even under threat, I will not use my medical knowledge contrary to the laws of humanity.

---

[41] See in particular, two persuasive and lively works: J Glover, *Causing Death and Saving Lives* (1977) Penguin; JM Harris, *The Value of Life* (1985) Routledge & Kegan Paul. And see H Kuhse (ed), *Unsanctifying Human Life: Essays on Ethics* (2001) Blackwells.

[42] Glover, *Causing Death and Saving Lives*, Chapter 3.

[43] Harris, *The Value of Life*, Chapter 1.

[44] For the Hippocratic Oath, Declaration of Geneva and other codes of medical ethics, see *Mason and McCall Smith's Law and Medical Ethics*, Appendices A–D, pp 741–749.

When the Declaration was first formulated in 1947, 'the utmost respect for human life' no doubt imported to most doctors a prohibition on abortion, at any rate where the mother's life was not in danger, and a complete ban on any form of euthanasia. The Declaration was amended and updated in Sydney in 1968. By 1968, abortion on grounds other than immediate danger to the mother had been legalised in Britain and parts of the USA. Within a decade debate was to flourish within respected medical circles as to whether keeping alive all disabled babies was right, and whether prolonging the life of the sick and elderly had not been taken to extremes by modern medicine. The Declaration was amended again in 1984, 1994, 2005 and 2006. The most recent version contains an undertaking which simply reads:

A physician shall always bear in mind the obligation to respect human life.

What, then, does the obligation to respect human life entail? What it does not entail, and what has never existed in any code of medical ethics, is an injunction to preserve life at any price. The prevention of suffering is as much the doctor's task as the prolonging of life. Alas, the two cannot always be complementary. The doctor struggling to interpret and apply his obligation to respect life faces a number of quandaries.

The beginning and end of life

3.14 An admonition to respect human life would be easier to adhere to if there was agreement as to when life begins and ends. Few biologists see the fertilisation of the woman's egg as the beginning of a new life. They argue that egg and sperm are living organisms and point out that many fertilised eggs fail to implant. The fertilised egg may split into two and, in rare cases, grow not into a baby but a hydatiform mole. Fertilisation is just one step in a continuing process. At what stage then does life begin and attract respect? We have noted the argument that the foetus has no status because it is not a person. A growing view appears to be that the foetus as potential life attracts increased status as it grows to full human likeness.[45] This gradualist perception of the embryo resulted in the support for embryo research from most doctors' organisations in 1990, helping to ensure that Members of Parliament eventually voted to permit research for a period of up to 14 days in the Human Fertilisation and Embryology Act 1990.

The influence of the medical profession is discernible too in more recent debates on human cloning. Nuclear substitution is a technique in which a nucleus with its complete complement of DNA is removed from a cell taken from the organism to be cloned. The nucleus is inserted in an egg cell that has had its own nucleus removed. The egg cell, now carrying the DNA from the first organism, is encouraged to divide and develop into an embryo that is genetically identical to the donor of the DNA. Experiments on mammals, such as those which produced Dolly, the most famous sheep in the world, suggest that it will be possible to produce human clones using this process. However,

[45] See, for example, M Reichlin, 'The Argument from Potential: A Reappraisal' (1997) 11 *Bioethics* 1–23.

it need not be taken as far as reproductive cloning producing a new person: it is also possible to collect stem cells, undifferentiated cells with the potential to divide indefinitely and give rise to more specialised tissue cells, from a cloned embryo. As we have noted, such therapeutic cloning – 'stem cell therapy' – could be used to provide tissue grafts, or ultimately transplant organs, to treat the donor of the DNA. Doctors and scientists mostly oppose reproductive cloning, but back therapeutic cloning. Their views carried the day with the British Government.[46]

The end of life, too, no longer has a definite marker. It can no longer be equated with the cessation of breathing and heartbeat as the development of life-support machines to replace heart and lung functions during surgery or after traumatic injury demonstrate that life can go on although the heart has stopped. When, then, does death occur? A definition of death as the irreversible cessation of all activity in the brain stem[47] is generally accepted within the medical profession, although some doctors still occasionally express public doubts. For the lay public the decision to agree to switch off the life-support machine of a relative causes individual anguish, and anxiety occasionally surfaces that a desire for organs for transplantation might prompt too swift a pronouncement of death.[48] The moral dilemma relating to dying arises a stage before brain stem death. A person may suffer irreversible brain damage, be comatose and yet still show signs of some activity in the brain stem. He is not dead according to the current definition of death. Some argue that this definition should be extended to include the irreversibly comatose. For those who regard human life as of value only where the individual can recognise himself as a person, loss of consciousness is equated with physical death.[49] If a patient is in PVS having lost all cortical function should we regard him as dead? Was Tony Bland alive in any real sense?[50] Is such a move really euthanasia by the back door? The question of continuing to keep alive the unkindly named 'human vegetable' will not go away. It must be faced, not by a surreptitious moving back of the moment of death but by addressing ourselves to the question of whether the doctor may ever kill.[51]

Killing and letting die

3.15   Caring for a patient as he dies in peace and dignity may be the last service a doctor can perform. Doctors and nurses tending the terminally ill in hospices are accorded the highest respect. The doctor's obligation to relieve suffering may on occasion cause him to refrain from prolonging life. Asked

---

[46]   The Human Reproductive Cloning Act 2001 prohibits the placing in a woman of an embryo created otherwise than by fertilisation. Additional safeguards are proposed in the Secretary of State's *Review of the Human Fertilisation and Embryology Act* (2006) Cm 6989. The Human Fertilisation and Embryology Act 1990 as amended by the Human Fertilisation and Embryology (Research Purposes) Regulations 2001, SI 2001/188 sanctions the use of embryos for research purposes, subject to licensing.

[47]   *Re A* [1992] 3 Med LR 303.

[48]   See Chapter 17 and also I Kennedy, *The Unmasking of Medicine* (1981) Allen & Unwin, Chapter 7.

[49]   Glover, *Causing Death and Saving Lives*, pp 43–45.

[50]   See *Airedale NHS Trust v Bland* [1993] AC 789, HL; discussed below at 20.9.

[51]   See Chapter 20.

whether a doctor should invariably invoke every weapon of medical progress to prevent death, people of every shade of opinion would answer, no. For the Roman Catholic, the test would be whether 'extraordinary means' must be resorted to in order to prolong that life. Extensive surgery on a dying cancer patient offering only weeks more life would be ruled out. Antibiotics to cure a sudden, unrelated infection pose a more difficult moral dilemma. Never the less for most of us, religious or irreligious, this satirical rhyme sums up our attitude;

Thou shalt not kill; but needst not strive

Officiously to keep alive.

Scratch the surface of this popular attitude and problems emerge. What amounts to 'officiously' keeping alive? Is the doctor alone to judge when a life is worth living? Lawyers and philosophers often enjoy the argument such issues generate, doctors on the whole do not. They have to provide answers. Where a patient is sane, conscious and an adult, the dilemma has today a relatively easy answer – albeit no less painful. The patient decides whether treatment continues. The doctor, if he has been frank with the patient, has little choice but to leave it to the patient. He cannot lawfully give treatment without the patient's consent.[52] Once a patient has decided to reject further treatment the doctor must normally desist. Suicide, if refusing treatment can be so classified, is no longer a crime. The freedom of the individual to make his own moral choices, where he is able to, is largely unquestioned. A more acute dilemma arises where the patient cannot make his own decision. Here the distinction between killing and letting die takes a central role. Asked if a doctor, or anyone else, should be allowed to smother a brain-damaged patient, the average person may recoil in horror. When a parent at the end of his tether does the same to his dying and profoundly disabled child he may attract public sympathy and understanding, though public attitudes to 'mercy killing' are not consistent.[53]

Not surprisingly, then, the distinction between killing and letting die has not been allowed to go unchallenged. It is subject to a three-pronged attack:

(1)   Technology makes the distinction between letting die and killing difficult if not impossible to put into practice.

(2)   It is argued that there is no valid moral distinction between killing and letting die.

(3)   Some writers have maintained that directly and painlessly killing a patient is a morally superior decision to leaving him to a slow undignified death.[54]

The problems posed for the doctor by the technology at his disposal cannot be side-stepped. An accident victim rushed into hospital is put on a life-support machine. All that can be done is done for him. He proves to be irreversibly

---

[52]   See *B v NHS Hospital Trust* [2002] 2 All ER 449.

[53]   See the case of Wendolyn Markrow, who received a suspended prison sentence after killing her disabled son: A Asthana, 'Hell of the Carers Driven to Breaking Point' (2005) *Observer*, 6 November.

[54]   And see Lord Browne-Wilkinson in *Airedale NHS Trust v Bland* [1993] AC 789 at 885.

brain-damaged but not brain-dead. Failing to put him on a machine would have meant allowing him to die. Is disconnecting the machine killing him[55] (though comatose patients disconnected from life-support machines have lived on for several years in some cases)?[56] Into which category, killing or letting die, does not feeding the patient fall? A newborn baby with severe disabilities may never demand food, may be unable to feed naturally from breast or bottle. Is omitting to tube-feed that baby killing or letting die? What about failing to operate to remove a stomach obstruction? Into which category does failure to perform delicate and painful surgery to relieve hydrocephalus (water on the brain) fall? The difficulties of applying the distinction in practice can be enumerated endlessly.

So, why not abandon the distinction altogether? Several apparently persuasive arguments can be made in favour of such a change of direction.[57] The concept of the value of human life as dependent on self-awareness and the quality of life renders it moral to end a life once self-awareness has gone, or, as in the case of a newborn baby, where it has never developed. A patient still able to reason but living in pain, distress and disability retains the right to make his own judgement on his quality of life. If he is unable to reason the decision may be taken from him. Once quality of life, not life itself, is the determining factor, it follows that directly killing the patient may be a moral imperative: if the patient's quality of life is such that life has no instrumental value, is it not kinder to end that life painlessly rather than let it drag on for more days, weeks or months in undignified 'sub-human' misery? If one accepts the basic premise that the value of human life is solely dependent on life being objectively 'worth living' then, logically, progress to acceptance that a doctor may sometimes kill his patient must follow.

Pure logic does not, however, govern most human reactions. *Involuntary*[58] euthanasia, ending a patient's life without any direction from him or a proxy acting on his behalf and without reference to his interests, is universally excoriated. *Non-voluntary* euthanasia, ending a life on the invitation of a proxy speaking for the patient and on the basis of a considered judgment of the patient's best interests receives some support,[59] often invoking the justification of beneficence. *Voluntary* euthanasia, assisting a competent patient who desires to die, has a growing number of committed advocates. None the less, any form of active euthanasia causes some disquiet and fears of a 'slippery slope' that modest legalisation of voluntary euthanasia in limited circumstances may rapidly metamorphose into a ready acceptance of less than

---

[55]   *B v NHS Hospital Trust* [2002] 2 All ER 449; and see I Kennedy, 'Switching Off Life Support Machines: The Legal Implications' [1977] *Criminal Law Review* 443.

[56]   See I Kennedy, 'The Karen Quinlan Case: Problems and Proposals' (1976) 2 *Journal of Medical Ethics* 3.

[57]   J Rachels, 'Active and Passive Euthanasia' (1975) 292 *New England Journal of Medicine* 78. See also Glover, *Causing Death and Saving Lives*, Chapters 7 and 15; Harris, *The Value of Life*, Chapter 4.

[58]   On the problems of terminology, see below at 20.1; and see *Mason and McCall Smith's Law and Medical Ethics*, Chapter 17.

[59]   See L Doyal, 'Dignity in Dying Should Include the Legalisation of Non-Voluntary Euthanasia' (2006) 2 *Clinical Ethics* 65.

voluntary euthanasia.[60] The arguments against are dismissed with some scorn by the philosophers proposing a change of attitude. Suggestions that doctors are 'playing God' ought to cut little ice unless you believe in God. Fear that powers to kill may be misused could be alleviated by proper controls. Instinctive revulsion is seen as an uninformed response.

The distinction between killing and letting die is unlikely to go away. First, the conception of life as in some sense 'sacred' in itself has a greater hold on the population as a whole than its detractors appreciate. Even if many do not subscribe to belief in the God of the Bible, the Talmud and the Koran, belief in a Creator of sorts is more widespread. Belief that humanity must set limits on what humanity may do is deeply ingrained. Killing those who cannot speak for themselves remains taboo. Second, the vision of the slippery slope to euthanasia (real or illusory)[61] for the unfortunate and the dissenter operates to deter acceptance of non-voluntary euthanasia. Today the hopelessly brain-damaged, tomorrow the mentally-disabled, the day after opponents of the government, is the fear of many. Finally, and practically most importantly, even if the exercise of judging objectively quality of life is carried out in all good faith, how can it be achieved? Who will sit in judgment?

Sanctity of life and the law[62]

3.16 Legislating on moral and ethical issues created fewer problems for the Victorian parliamentarian. Applying the common law posed no dilemma for the judge. He knew what was right and what was wrong. The Victorian was unperturbed by doubt, unconcerned by any feeling that his decision should mirror the moral attitudes of society as a whole. Divisions in moral attitudes, although they did exist, were not as deep as those pertaining today. Nor were the problems of medicine as complex. Death remained then an independent agent largely beyond the doctor's skill to combat.

Yet, despite the plethora of ethical problems created daily by modern medicine and the changed moral climate, the law changes slowly. No statute expressly addresses the fate of the newborn infant with multiple disabilities who in an earlier age would have died whatever had been done for her.[63] Every attempt to legislate on euthanasia has stalled in its progress through Parliament. The first test-tube baby, Louise Brown, was born in July 1978. It was not until twelve years later that Parliament enacted the Human Fertilisation and Embryology Act 1990, finally regulating IVF. Before that Act, the Abortion Act 1967 stood alone as a legislative attempt specifically designed to tackle developments in medicine and altered moral outlooks. And the Abortion Act

---

60   See J Keown, *Euthanasia, Ethics and Public Policy: An Argument Against Legalisation* (2002) CUP, Chapter 1.

61   See S Smith, 'Evidence for the Practical Slippery Slope in the Debate on Physician-Assisted Suicide and Euthanasia' (2005) 13 *Medical Law Review* 17.

62   See G Williams, *The Sanctity of Life and the Criminal Law* (1958) Faber & Faber; PDG Skegg, *Law, Ethics and Medicine* (1984) Clarendon Press; *Mason and McCall Smith's Law and Medical Ethics*.

63   See Nuffield Council on Bioethics, *Critical Care Decisions in Fetal and Neonatal Medicine* (2006).

was piloted through Parliament not by the government of the day, but by David Steel MP by means of a Private Member's Bill. The troubled history of that Act, a compromise which pleases few, perhaps explains why governments of all political colours shy away from entering the battlefields on sanctity of human life. Attempts to amend the Human Fertilisation and Embryology Act 1990, which originally sought to reduce the time-limit for abortion,[64] unleashed a bitterness and outburst of vitriolic abuse unknown in even the most hard-fought party-political battle. In 2005, foetal politics surfaced briefly once again. On the basis of new evidence of foetal development and advances in the care of premature babies there were renewed calls for a reduction in the time-limit. The Prime Minister side-stepped the issue, proclaiming that abortion is not a political issue, but a matter for individual conscience.[65]

Political disinclination to engage in debate on the sanctity of life means that, to a large extent, the regulation of the medical profession on issues of life and death has been left to the common law. In drawing up and applying codes of practice on the treatment of the critically ill newborn, the brain-damaged and the dying, the medical profession acts within the constraints of the criminal law of murder and manslaughter. The law stays its hand from laying down medical codes of practice and so the doctor's exposure to the law can be brutal. Struggling to decide on whether treatment should continue, a doctor acts within the guidelines agreed within his own profession, but these lack any statutory force. Ninety-nine times out of a hundred he can comfort himself with the thought that no one will question his decision in the grey areas between living and dying. On the hundredth occasion he may face the spectre of prosecution for murder or attempted murder. The distinction between killing and letting die does not operate in the criminal law to debar a charge of murder. Allowing a patient to die, when it was the doctor's duty to treat him, and when the doctor knew that and intended that death would ensue, is as much murder as stabbing the patient to death.

The crucial issue once more is what is the content of the doctor's duty? When is it his obligation to prolong life? Left to decide that issue according to conscience and professional opinion most of the time, doctors not unnaturally are resentful that intervention – when it comes – may take the form of criminal prosecution for murder. Doctors do not see themselves as murderers. Even the most vehement and passionate member of *Life* (the UK's leading pro-life charity), believing as he will that medical decisions as to the care of the newborn are frequently wrong, and err too often on the side of withholding treatment, would not place the doctor on the same moral plane as the man murdering in the course of robbery.

The reaction of the medical profession has often been that the law should keep out of medical ethics. Proposals to replace the existing and hazy common law

---

[64]   But ultimately resulted in a 'liberalisation' of the law on late abortions: see section 37 of the 1990 Act (and see below at 14.10).
[65]   'Abortion Not a Poll Issue' (2005) BBC News, 15 March, accesssible at www.news.bbc-.co.uk.

with detailed legislative rules attract little enthusiasm.[66] Procedural rules about consultation, reference to codes of practice and the keeping of records of decision-making appear more acceptable. What doctors might welcome is legislation which additionally promises immunity from prosecution to the doctor following the correct process. Such legislation would check the maverick. It would ensure that no one doctor whose standards deviate markedly from his fellows could pursue a course of treatment or non-treatment of patients unacceptable to the majority. However, it would enshrine in the law a principle that such decisions are for doctors alone. The rest of us would be excluded from any right to a say on these matters of life and death.

The ultimate decisions about life and death are not simply medical decisions.[67]

This was the view expressed in an editorial in the *British Medical Journal* over 25 years ago. We concur wholeheartedly. The meaning and application of the sanctity of life is not a matter to be left for doctors to decide and philosophers to argue over. The law's involvement to ensure that society's expectations are met is inevitable. The law is far from perfect in its operation. Reform in a society divided in its moral judgements is hard to formulate. Detailed legislation is probably undesirable, even if such legislation were to be agreed on. The variation in the circumstances confronting the doctor is too great. Rules cannot be invented that would meet every possible dilemma the doctor may face. The doctor's judgment cannot and should not be excluded. What can be done, if there is a will to do so, is to stimulate greater debate on the codes of practice under which the doctor works. Greater legal and lay involvement in their development should be encouraged. The gap between lawyer and doctor needs to be bridged. Doctors complain that lay people do not understand the full implications of the problems presented by the disabled and the dying and do not appreciate the complexity of modern medical technology; only greater openness and a greater willingness to involve those outside the medical profession in decision-making will bring about better understanding. Only better understanding of the problems of medicine will bring about better law-making.

However much any government might prefer to remain aloof from debates on medicine and morals, developments in the uses of human tissue, genetics, embryology and assisted conception have forced the British, and other European and Commonwealth governments, to legislate.

(1)   Legislation may be designed to protect patients from possible abuses, to prevent what is perceived as an undesirable practice creating risks of exploitation.

(2)   Legislation may be needed because gaps in the existing law place people in a legal limbo. For example, if A donates an egg which is fertilised and implanted in B who carries and gives birth to the child, who in the law is the child's mother? Such questions of family law and status may be

---

[66]   J Havard, 'Legislation Is Likely to Create More Difficulty than it Resolves' (1983) 9 *Journal of Medical Ethics* 18. And see below at 15.3.
[67]   [1981] *British Medical Journal* 569.

complex and sometimes controversial. Clear statutory answers are essential to safeguard the interests of the child.

(3) Developments in genetics and biotechnology may create, or exacerbate, several legal problems. Who owns genetic information, and how should access to that information be controlled? What property rights accrue from body products? If cells from a patient's body are used to develop a remedy to some disease, can she claim the ensuing profit made by a drug company? If a healthy gene taken from a patient's embryo is used and inserted to replace a defective gene from his sister's embryo, to whom does the gene belong? Can human genes be patented? All these questions require a legal answer and, if legislation does not provide the answer, expensive litigation proliferates.

(4) Inadequate, unclear laws generate distrust and anger. The fuzzy, toothless provisions of the Human Tissue Act 1961[68] contributed immensely to the outrage and agony occasioned by revelations of organ retention practices.[69]

(5) Finally, the most difficult of all aspects of legislation in this area is to decide what kinds of procedures are acceptable in our society. Are there medical possibilities whose implications are such that, though possible, they should be prohibited by law? The United Kingdom sanctions strictly controlled stem cell therapies, ie therapeutic cloning. Most of Europe outlaws cloning altogether.

Legislating on what is permissible is fraught with difficulty. Emotions run high. In 1990 anti-abortion campaigners flooded Parliament with model foetuses. Pro-embryo research lobbies played to the cameras with touching and well-timed stories of the joy brought to previously infertile women by their 'test-tube' babies. Scientific possibilities are hard to grasp and science fiction scenarios abound. Test-tube baby technology creates fears of Aldous Huxley's *Brave New World*. But above all, each side in the moral debate is convinced that they are right and the other is irretrievably wrong. What tends to be overlooked is that, in many ethical debates today, there is no answer that will be accepted as unchallengeably right. The question for legislators is not to find a right answer, to achieve a moral consensus, but to determine how in a liberal, democratic society legislation can be formulated in the absence of such consensus. To evade that task is to give the scientists free rein to do as they see fit. To criticise them with hindsight is unfair and unproductive. Theologians, ethicists, lawyers and (indeed) all citizens must be prepared to grapple with these awkward moral dilemmas and, probably, be ready to compromise.

---

[68] Now repealed, see below at 19.2.
[69] *The Royal Liverpool Children's Inquiry Report* (2001) HC 12–11; see Chapter 19 at 19.2.

Chapter 4

A RELATIONSHIP OF TRUST AND CONFIDENCE

Whatever, in connection with my professional practice, or not in connection with it, I see or hear in the life of men, which ought not to be spoken of abroad, I will not divulge, as reckoning that all such should be kept secret.

The Hippocratic Oath

I will respect the secrets which are confided in me, even after the patient has died.

Declaration of Geneva (as amended 1968, 1983, 2006)

4.1 Doctors, like priests and lawyers, must be able to keep secrets. For medical care to be effective, for patients to trust their doctor, they must have confidence that they can talk frankly to her. An obligation of confidence to patients lies at the heart of all codes of ethics. Comparison of the quotations above shows that the obligation is not always absolute. The Ancient Greek physician undertook not to divulge that which ought not to be spoken of abroad. He presumably judged what fell into that category. The Declaration of Geneva is more stringent. *Any* information given by a patient in confidence must be kept secret for ever. A moment's reflection reveals the problems inherent in both absolute and relative obligations of confidence. An absolute obligation leaves the doctor powerless to do anything but try to persuade his patient to allow him to take action when a patient tells him he is HIV positive but is still sleeping with his wife, or when a mother confesses her violent impulses towards her baby, or when examination reveals that the patient may be a rapist sought by the police. On the other hand, a relative obligation, which leaves the doctor free to breach confidence when he judges that some higher duty to another person or to society applies, may deter patients from seeking necessary treatment. This may damage not only the patient but also those very people vulnerable when the doctor treats and does not 'tell'. The wife whose husband receives no advice about 'safe sex' and HIV, and the baby whose mother seeks no counsel may be more vulnerable if fears of breach of confidence prevent the husband and the mother getting any help at all.

In this chapter we look at the law on confidentiality as it affects doctors and adult patients, and examine the role of the medical profession in enforcing the ethical obligation of confidence. The special problems affecting confidentiality and parents and children are considered in Chapter 15. The vagueness and complexity of the law may surprise some. The number of occasions when the law compels the doctor to breach confidence may shock many. The chapter also explores what the patient is entitled to be told. From the patient's viewpoint the doctor's obligation of confidence exists to prevent the doctor from passing on information about the patient to third parties. A relationship of trust requires that this should not happen. It also requires that the doctor be frank with the patient. Information about the patient should generally not be withheld from him. How far is the patient entitled to frankness from his doctor?[1]

Breach of confidence

4.2 The law on breach of confidence[2] has developed in a haphazard fashion.[3] The core obligation requiring doctors to respect patient confidences derives from the common law. Judges have shown themselves willing to act to prevent the disclosure of confidential information in a wide variety of circumstances. A duty to preserve confidences has been imposed in settings as diverse as trade or research secrets confided to employees,[4] marital intimacies,[5] intimate disclosures to close friends[6] and Cabinet discussion.[7] Often the obligation of confidence arises as an implied term of a contract, as is the case with the employee bound by his contract of employment to keep his employer's business to himself. But the obligation of confidence can equally arise where no contract exists, or has ever existed, between the parties.

There is a public interest in keeping certain types of information private, and this is particularly true of medical information. In a very early case, action was taken to prevent publication of a diary kept by a physician to King George III.[8] Much later, in 1974, a judge put the doctor's duty thus:

> … in common with other professional men, for instance a priest and there are of course others, the doctor is under a duty not to disclose, [voluntarily] without the consent of his patient, information which he, the doctor, has gained in his professional capacity, save … in very exceptional circumstances.[9]

Today any attempt to understand the law governing medical confidentiality must take account of the Data Protection Act 1998 and Article 8 of the European Convention on Human Rights, which states that: 'Everyone has the right to respect for his private and family life, his home and his correspondence'. The European Court of Human Rights has consistently upheld the right to privacy in relation to medical records. But it is not an unqualified right. The court has upheld seizure of medical records in criminal proceedings[10] and use of records in connection with social security benefits.[11] In *Z v Finland*[12] the court said:

---

[1]   See JE Thompson, 'The Nature of Confidentiality' (1979) 5 *Journal of Medical Ethics* 57.
[2]   See generally, R Pattenden, *The Law of Professional-Client Confidentiality: Regulating the Disclosure of Confidential Personal Information* (2003) OUP.
[3]   See Law Commission Report No 110, *Breach of Confidence* Cmnd 8388, para. 3.1; and see G Jones, 'Restitution of Benefits Obtained in Breach of Another's Confidence' (1970) 86 *Law Quarterly Review* 463.
[4]   F Gurry, *Breach of Confidence* (1984) Clarendon Press, Chapters 8 and 9.
[5]   *Argyll v Argyll* [1967] Ch 302.
[6]   *Stephens v Avery* [1988] 2 All ER 477.
[7]   *Attorney-General v Jonathan Cape Ltd* [1976] QB 752.
[8]   *Wyatt v Wilson* (1820) unreported, but referred to in *Prince Albert v Strange* (1849) 41 ER 1171 at 1179.
[9]   *Hunter v Mann* [1974] QB 767 at 772.
[10]   *Z v Finland* [1997] 25 EHRR 371.
[11]   *MS v Sweden* [1997] 45 BMLR 133.
[12]   [1997] 25 EHRR 371 at para 95.

Respecting the confidentiality of health data is a vital principle in the legal systems of all the Contracting Parties to the Convention. It is crucial not only to respect the sense of privacy of a patient but also to preserve his or her confidence in the medical profession and in the health services in general.

In England, the Human Rights Act 1998 came into force in 2000, rendering the Convention Articles enforceable against public authorities. In the USA, an all-inclusive cause of action for invasion of privacy is recognised. The House of Lords rejected this approach in *Wainwright v Home Office*,[13] but the various aspects of English law which protect privacy, including the common law action for breach of confidence, have developed to take account of Article 8. The terminology has changed dramatically, leading Lord Nicholls to call for the renaming of the tort:

> The continuing use of the phrase 'duty of confidence' and the description of the information as 'confidential' is not altogether comfortable. Information about an individual's private life would not, in ordinary usage, be called 'confidential'. The more natural description today is that such information is private. The essence of the tort is better encapsulated now as misuse of private information.[14]

Yet behind the talk of Convention rights lie the common law principles developed incrementally by the judiciary. In the leading case on breach of confidence, *Campbell v Mirror Group Newspapers Ltd*,[15] to which we shall return, the House of Lords balanced human rights, rather than the traditional concepts of private and public interests, but Lord Hope commented that: 'It seems to me that the balancing exercise to which that guidance is directed is essentially the same exercise, although it is plainly now more carefully focussed and more penetrating.'[16] In essence, Article 8 of the European Convention on Human Rights strengthens the principles long contained in the common law action for breach of confidence.

The basic general principles are these:

(1)   The courts will intervene to restrain disclosure of information where the information is confidential in nature and not a matter of public knowledge, or trivial in nature.

(2)   Where information is found to be private and confidential, disclosure requires justification in the public interest.[17]

(3)   Once an obligation of confidence is created it binds not only the original recipient of the information but also any other person to whom disclosure is made by the recipient when that other person knows of the confidential status of the information. As well as acting in advance to prevent the disclosure of confidential information, the courts may where appropriate award compensation after information has been improperly disclosed.

---

[13]   [2003] 3 WLR 1137.
[14]   *Campbell v Mirror Group Newspapers Ltd* [2004] UKHL 22 at para 14.
[15]   [2004] UKHL 22 at para 157.
[16]   [2004] UKHL 22 at para 86.
[17]   *W v Egdell* [1990] 1 All ER 835 at 846, CA; *Campbell v Mirror Group Newspapers Ltd* [2004] UKHL 22.

4.2 A Relationship of Trust and Confidence

In *AG v Guardian Newspapers (No 2)*,[18] Lord Goff stipulated a further requirement of the common law duty of confidence: that the information is entrusted to another person in *circumstances* imposing an obligation not to use or disclose that information without the consent of the giver of the information. An initial confidential relationship is not required.[19] The test did not pose a problem in the context of the doctor-patient relationship. The relationship of any doctor with any patient, NHS or private, imports an obligation of confidence. More recently there has been a change of emphasis. In *Campbell v Mirror Group Newspapers Ltd*[20] (which did not involve a doctor-patient relationship), the *circumstances* in which the information was obtained were irrelevant. The *nature* of the information was of paramount importance. Applying the new terminology, it remains the case that a 'reasonable expectation of privacy'[21] can be established when a patient divulges information about her health to her doctor.

The difficult area of medical confidentiality does not lie in establishing a *general* duty of confidence, but in determining what amounts to 'very exceptional circumstances' justifying breach of that duty. First, disclosure will always be justified legally when the doctor is compelled by law to give confidential information to a third party. This may be by way of an order of the court to disclose records in the course of some civil proceedings, or may be under some statutory provision, such as those Acts of Parliament requiring that specified diseases be notified to the health authorities. Doctors, unlike lawyers, enjoy no professional privilege entitling them to refuse to give evidence in court. We shall return to this later. Second, it is clear that the doctor may voluntarily elect to disclose information in certain circumstances. Where there is a public interest in disclosure of confidential and private information, the court will consider whether harm (to either physical or moral integrity) may be caused to someone as a result.[22] The public interest in disclosure must be balanced with the public and private interests in maintaining confidentiality. Thus, disclosure of private information requires justification.

In early judgments, the public interest 'defence' tended to concern disclosure of crime: 'there is no confidence in the disclosure of iniquity'.[23] Gradually it has been accepted that that defence is not limited to crime, or even misconduct. In *Lion Laboratories Ltd v Evans* (which considered the disclosure of confidential information suggesting that a breathalyser device, the Intoximeter, was unreliable), Griffiths LJ said:

> I can see no sensible reason why this defence should be limited to cases where there has been wrongdoing on the part of the plaintiffs ... it is not difficult to

---

[18] [1990] 1 AC 109.
[19] [1990] 1 AC 109 at 281. See also *Douglas v Hello Ltd* [2001] 2 All ER 289.
[20] *Campbell v Mirror Group Newspapers Ltd* [2004] UKHL 22.
[21] *Campbell v Mirror Group Newspapers Ltd* [2004] UKHL 22, per Lord Nicholls at para 21.
[22] *R v Department of Health, ex p Source Informatics Ltd* [2000] 1 All ER 786; *Campbell v Mirror Group Newspapers Ltd* [2004] UKHL 22.
[23] *Gartside v Outram* (1856) 26 LJ Ch 113 at 114.

think of instances where, although there has been no wrongdoing on the part of the plaintiff, it may be vital in the public interest to publish a part of his confidential information.[24]

In *X v Y*[25] a tabloid newspaper acquired, in breach of confidence from a health authority employee, information identifying two general practitioners who were continuing to practise after having been diagnosed as HIV positive. The authority sought an injunction prohibiting publication of their patients' (the doctors') names. The newspaper argued that the public at large, and the doctors' patients in particular, had an interest in knowing that doctors were HIV positive. Rose J reviewed the evidence about transmission of HIV from doctor to patient where the doctor had received proper counselling about safe practice. He found that the risk to patients was negligible. Far greater risks arose from the possibility that if they could not rely on confidential treatment, people with AIDS, or who feared they might have AIDS, would not seek medical help. The judge, granting the injunction, said:

> In the long run, preservation of confidentiality is the only way of securing public health; otherwise doctors will be discredited as a source of education, for future individual patients will not come forward if doctors are going to squeal on them. Consequently, confidentiality is vital to secure public as well as private health, for unless those infected come forward they cannot be counselled and self-treatment does not provide the best care ...[26]

By contrast, in *W v Egdell*[27] the Court of Appeal sanctioned a breach of confidence by a psychiatrist. W had been convicted of the manslaughter of five people and of wounding two others. He was ordered to be detained indefinitely in a secure hospital. He could be released only by order of the Home Secretary if he were found to be no longer a danger to public safety. As a step towards eventual release he sought to transfer to a regional secure unit. The transfer was not approved by the Home Secretary and W then applied to a mental health review tribunal for a conditional discharge. In support of his application his solicitors arranged for an independent psychiatric report from Dr Egdell. Dr Egdell's report was not favourable. He judged that W was still a dangerous man with a psychopathic personality, no real insight into his condition and a morbid interest in explosives. Unsurprisingly W's solicitors withdrew their application for his discharge but they did not pass on the report to the tribunal or the hospital where W was detained. Dr Egdell was concerned by the fact that his report was not passed on. He ultimately sent his report to the medical director of W's hospital and agreed that a copy of that report should be forwarded to the Home Secretary. W sued Dr Egdell for breach of confidence.

The Court of Appeal made it crystal clear that Dr Egdell did owe W a duty of confidence. Had he sold his story to the press or discussed the case in his memoirs, Dr Egdell would have been in breach of confidence. But the duty of confidentiality is not absolute. The public interest in medical confidentiality

[24] *Lion Laboratories Ltd v Evans* [1984] 2 All ER 417 at 433.
[25] [1988] 2 All ER 648.
[26] [1988] 2 All ER 648 at 653.
[27] [1990] 1 All ER 835; applied in *R v Crozier* [1991] *Crim LR* 138, CA.

must be balanced against the public interest in public safety. If Dr Egdell's diagnosis was right, W remained a source of danger to others and he was entitled to communicate his findings to the director of the hospital now detaining W and to the Home Secretary, who would have the final say on if and when W should be released into the community.

X v Y and *W v Egdell* do not mean that a doctor may *never* disclose that a patient is HIV positive, or that he may *always* disclose his concerns about a patient's mental health. In each case the powerful interest in maintaining confidentiality must be balanced against the danger ensuing if confidentiality is not breached. Only where there is a clear and significant risk of the patient causing harm to others which cannot be abated by any other means may confidence be breached.

As we have noted, more recently judicial assessment of public and private interests has involved the careful balancing of Convention rights. *Campbell v Mirror Group Newspapers Ltd*[28] involved the disclosure of information concerning the health of a famous fashion model. Although the information was disclosed by the *Mirror* newspaper, rather than a medical practitioner, there are clear implications for medical privacy. At first instance, Naomi Campbell was awarded £3,500 in damages, but the Court of Appeal reversed the decision holding that disclosure was in the public interest. The House of Lords balanced Campbell's right to privacy under Article 8 of the European Convention on Human Rights, protected by the common law duty of confidentiality, with the freedom of the press, protected under Article 10 of the Convention. Both are qualified rights and neither has pre-eminence over the other. Campbell had previously falsely stated that she was not a drug addict. She was powerless to object, therefore, when the *Mirror* newspaper published information to the contrary. However, she did object to the publication of furtively-taken photographs and articles proving that she was attending Narcotics Anonymous. This, she maintained, was a breach of confidence for which she was entitled to compensation under the Data Protection Act 1998. By a 3:2 majority, the House of Lords found in her favour, overturning the decision of the Court of Appeal. The special nature of medical information was recognised by Baroness Hale, who stated:

> It has always been accepted that information about a person's health and treatment for ill health is both private and confidential. This stems not only from the confidentiality of the doctor-patient relationship but from the nature of the information itself.[29]

Baroness Hale, made the following points:

(1)   The information about Campbell's attendance at Narcotics Anonymous was private and confidential 'because it related to an important aspect of Miss Campbell's physical and mental health and the treatment she was receiving for it. It had also been received from an insider in breach of confidence … .'

(2)   Because it was private, its publication required specific justification.

---

[28]   [2004] UKHL 22.
[29]   [2004] UKHL 22 at para 145.

(3)   'Some [types of speech] are more deserving of protection in a demo-
        cratic society than others.' Where disclosure carries little risk of harm to
        a person's physical or moral integrity, where for example 'a public
        figure has a cold or a broken leg', it might be justifiable. Note however,
        that Baroness Hale was balancing Article 8 and Article 10 rights. Her
        words do not necessarily imply that less protection will be given to a
        breach of confidence relating to 'trivial' health matters where there is
        no competing public interest in their disclosure.

(4)   The breach of confidence had potential to cause Miss Campbell harm.
        Her Article 8 privacy rights took priority over the public interest in
        freedom of the press under Article 10.

Article 8, like the common law, imposes only a relative obligation of
confidence.[30] Consider the scope of Article 8(2):

> There shall be no interference by a public authority with the exercise of this
> right except such as is in accordance with the law and necessary in a democratic
> society in the interests of national security, public safety or the economic
> well-being of the country, for the prevention of disorder or crime, for the
> protection of health or morals, or for the protection of the rights and freedoms
> of others.

There has been little case law governing the relevance of Article 8(2) in
medical confidentiality, but imagine the following scenario. X undergoes
genetic tests to establish whether she has a gene rendering her susceptible to
breast cancer. The test proves positive. A potential employer or insurer seeks
to ascertain if she has undergone such a test and to find out the results.
Doctors breach confidence if they release test results without the patient's
consent. So the employer or insurer will simply demand that information from
the patient herself. She is free to refuse to divulge her test results. The
consequence may be that she is turned down for the job, or refused insurance.
Her 'right' to privacy means little.

Could Article 8 establish a right to keep personal information secret? Alas, an
employee or insurer may seek to invoke one of the justifications for violating
privacy set out in Article 8(2). In X's case, where what is established by tests is
a susceptibility to breast cancer, a 'defence' based on the protection of the
health or freedom of others invoked by an employer is unlikely to succeed.
Were she a potential airline pilot with a genetic susceptibility to heart failure,
the balance of argument might be different. Another argument that might be
advanced in X's particular case is one based on protection of 'economic
well-being'. Can employers or insurers be forced to take on poor risks? Note,
though, that Article 8(2) speaks of the economic well-being of the country, not
of individual businesses. A further twist to the tale is this. Does X's daughter
have any right to information about X? Could she argue that her right to life
(Article 2) and 'family life' (Article 8(1)) impose an obligation on X to disclose
information to her, to inform her decisions about whether to seek genetic

---

[30] See also *R (on the Application of B) v Stafford Combined Court* [2006] EWHC 1645
      (Admin), discussed below at 4.12.

testing?[31] Defining the scope of a right to medical privacy will prove more difficult than establishing that such a right exists.

In the context of genetic privacy, the Human Genetics Commission (HGC)[32] was established to develop policy and advise the government on the regulation of genetics. The HGC is reviewing whether individuals applying for insurance policies[33] have a right to genetic privacy and what such a right entails. In May 2001, the HGC advised that there should be a three-year moratorium, except in relation to tests for Huntington's Chorea, preventing insurers from seeking access to genetic test results in relation to policies worth less than £500,000. Subsequently, in October 2001, the insurers themselves, via the Association of British Insurers, agreed a voluntary five-year moratorium in relation to life insurance policies worth less than £500,000, and other insurance policies worth less that £300,000.[34] The voluntary moratorium on predictive genetic testing was extended until 2011 in 2005.[35] It seems likely that ultimately the HGC will press for laws to protect genetic privacy. Would it make sense to legislate more generally to safeguard medical privacy?

Breach of confidence: the General Medical Council

4.3 The exact ambit of the public interest defence as it affects doctors is difficult to ascertain, despite key judgments of the High Court[36] and the Court of Appeal.[37] Should, or rather may, the doctor inform on any patient whom he suspects of a crime, however trivial? What other circumstances justify the invocation of the public interest to override the patient's interest in confidentiality? Guidance available to doctors comes primarily from the General Medical Council (GMC) and we shall consider that guidance a little later, for despite the underlying authority of the law of confidence, the enforcement of medical confidentiality often rests in practice with the GMC.

The civil action for breach of confidence is an excellent weapon for restraining threatened breaches of confidence. It is less effective in compensating the victim of a breach of confidence, except in a commercial setting. If a trade secret is revealed by an employee and the employer loses profits, his loss can be measured by the courts and appropriate compensation ordered. A breach of medical confidence rarely results in monetary loss, but will give rise to

---

[31] See R Gilbar, *The Status of the Family in Law and Bioethics: The Genetic Context* (2005) Ashgate; R Gilbar, 'Medical Confidentiality Within the Family: The Doctor's Duty Reconsidered' (2004) 18 *International Journal of Law and Policy and the Family* 195.

[32] See http://www.hgc.gov.uk.

[33] See T Sorell, 'The Insurance Market and Discriminatory Practices' in J Burley and J Harris (eds), *Companion to Genethics* (2002) Blackwell, Chapter 29.

[34] S Mayor, 'UK Insurers Agree Five Year Ban on Using Genetic Tests' (2001) 323 *British Medical Journal* 1021.

[35] HM Government and Association of British Insurers, *Concordat and Moratorium on Genetics and Insurance* (2005).

[36] *X v Y* [1988] 2 All ER 648.

[37] *W v Egdell* [1990] 1 All ER 835, CA; *H (A Healthcare Worker) v Associated Newspapers Ltd and N (A Health Authority)* [2002] Lloyd's Rep Med 210, CA.

indignity and distress for the patient. In *Cornelius v De Taranto*[38] the judge at first instance awarded the claimant £3,000 in damages for mental distress caused by 'unauthorised disclosure of the confidential information'. The Court of Appeal did not upset the award of damages. However, even if damages are now available for distress, such damages may be costly to obtain, and complaining to the GMC is likely to remain the preferred remedy in many cases of breach of confidence. None the less the courts, not the GMC, are the ultimate arbiters of the scope of the doctor's duty of confidentiality, even though judges have tended to look to the GMC's guidelines on confidentiality in formulating the legal rules.[39]

Any improper disclosure of information obtained in confidence from, or about, a patient can constitute impairment of fitness to practise on the part of the doctor. Again the crucial issue is: when is a disclosure improper? The GMC gives both general[40] and detailed[41] guidance. We consider first information where the identity of the patient is disclosed, what the GMC describes as 'personal information'. The doctor's duty is to maintain strict confidentiality. The GMC recognises that patients have a 'right' to confidentiality. The death of the patient does not absolve the doctor from this duty.[42] In this respect the doctor's ethical obligation is stricter than his legal duty. The law of confidence probably does not protect the patient's secrets after death. Any doctor deciding to disclose information 'must be prepared to explain and justify [his] decision'.

The 2004 guidance warns doctors to be vigilant in protecting confidential information. It rightly notes that many improper disclosures of information are accidental. Notes should not be left lying around. Consultations with patients should not take place where they can be overheard by other patients or by staff not involved in the care of the patient.

Where a considered decision is made to disclose voluntarily information about a patient,[43] disclosure would be justifiable in the following categories of cases:

(1)   When the patient expressly consents to disclosure. The doctor must ensure that the patient understands what is to be disclosed, the reasons for disclosure and the consequences thereof. The patient must be told to whom information will be given and how much information will be disclosed.

(2)   When information is shared within a health care team caring for the patient. The GMC makes it clear that every effort must be made to ensure that the patient is aware that information about him may be

---

[38]   (2001) 68 BMLR 62. In 1981, the Law Commission had recommended the award of damages for distress. And see the Scottish decisions *AB v CD* (1851) 14 D 177; *AB v CD* (1904) 7 F 72. See also JK Mason and GT Laurie, *Mason and McCall Smith's Law and Medical Ethics* (7th edn, 2006) OUP, p 289.

[39]   See *X v Y* [1988] 2 All ER 648; *W v Egdell* [1990] 1 All ER 835 at 843 and 850, CA.

[40]   GMC, *Good Medical Practice* (2006), para 37.

[41]   GMC, *Confidentiality: Protecting and Providing Information* (2004).

[42]   GMC, *Confidentiality: Protecting and Providing Information*, para 30.

[43]   Doctors do not act unlawfully if they disclose information when required to do so by statute or under court order. The law cannot condemn a doctor for conduct compelled by the law. See GMC, *Confidentiality: Protecting and Providing Information*, paras 18–21.

disclosed to other health professionals working with his doctor and that, if a patient does not want certain information about him revealed to others, his wishes must be respected. Doctors must make sure that everyone within the team to whom information is disclosed understands that they are bound by a legal obligation of confidence.

(3) All doctors in clinical practice should participate in clinical audit. Provided it is undertaken by the team providing the care, or their support staff, personal information may be disclosed if the patient has been informed and has not objected. If the patient objects, it is necessary to make an assessment as to whether safe care can be provided without it. Where audit is undertaken by an external organisation, express consent should be obtained unless the data can be anonymised.

(4) In circumstances of emergency, and when the patient cannot be consulted herself, information may, and should, promptly be passed on to those involved in her care. If a patient is brought unconscious into Casualty, staff may properly share all relevant information about her so, for example, her GP could properly disclose her relevant medical history to hospital staff.

(5) Difficult questions arise when doctors believe that a patient lacks the capacity to give consent to disclose information. The GMC advises doctors to try to persuade the patient to allow appropriate persons, including family members, to be involved in the consultation. If the patient refuses but the doctor is 'convinced that it is essential, *in their medical interests*, [the doctor] may disclose relevant information to an appropriate person or authority ...'.

(6) 'Personal information may be disclosed in the public interest, without the patient's consent, and in exceptional cases where patients have withheld consent, where the benefits to an individual or to society of the disclosure outweigh the public and the patient's interest in keeping the information confidential. In all cases where you consider disclosing information without consent from the patient, you must weigh the possible harm (both to the patient, and the overall trust between doctors and patients) against the benefits which are likely to arise from the release of information'.

The GMC's 2004 guidance narrows and structures the discretion granted to doctors to disclose information about their patients. Confidentiality is given the emphasis it deserves and, as we shall see, much more specific guidance about potentially difficult dilemmas for doctors is spelled out in some detail. However, awkward questions still bedevil the extent to which doctors may lawfully[44] disclose information without consent in, first, the patient's own interests and, second, the public interest.

---

[44] The courts have stressed that care must be taken to limit information to those who 'need to know' and to ensure that the recipient of that information understand the requirements of confidentiality; see *W v Egdell* [1990] 1 All ER 835 at 850, CA.

Disclosure where the patient lacks capacity

4.4 Let us consider cases (4) and (5) above. In both cases, the doctor judges that the patient lacks the capacity to consent to disclosure. Under the Mental Capacity Act 2005 there is a presumption of capacity. A person will only be shown to lack capacity in relation to a specific decision where she is unable to make a decision for herself[45] by virtue of the fact that she cannot understand, retain, weigh or use the information relevant to the decision.[46] Under section 5 of the Act, those providing care for someone who lacks capacity will not incur legal liability provided they have properly assessed her capacity and act in her best interests. The Act provides a checklist for determining best interests.[47] The individual who lacks capacity may have previously made a written statement, or appointed a Lasting Power of Attorney, which must be taken into account – as must the views of carers and family.

Where the patient clearly lacks capacity, the GMC recognises the value of disclosing information to her family. Under section 4(7) of the Mental Capacity Act 2005 the doctor has a duty, where practicable, to consult appropriate persons about the patient's treatment. Discussing the condition of an unconscious patient in Casualty and seeking advice on her treatment with colleagues and family members is proper and lawful.[48] However, where a patient is conscious and withholds consent to disclosure, doctors should be wary of releasing information to the family in her 'medical interests'. Under section 4, best interests include, but are not limited to, medical interests. The patient's beliefs, values, and past and present wishes must also be taken into account.

Disclosure to protect the patient

4.5 What if a patient is very ill, but retains capacity? A doctor may believe that it is kinder to ignore a patient's plea to keep knowledge of her illness from her family, or even to spare the patient pain by not telling her how close she is to death. Earlier GMC guidance expressly allowed doctors, albeit 'rarely', to bypass the patient and entrust information which might be damaging to her to her family. Information could even be withheld from the patient. That now appears to be outlawed by the GMC: if the patient retains the capacity to make her own decisions, i e she remains mentally competent, the legal basis for compassionate paternalism is shaky.[49] But what if death or serious injury may result to the patient? Can disclosure to protect the patient be made in such circumstances? Article 8 imposes only a relative obligation and that may be limited under Article 8(2) 'for the protection of health or morals'. The latest

---

[45]   Mental Capacity Act 2005, s 2(1). On the 2005 Act generally, see below Chapter 6.
[46]   Mental Capacity Act 2005, s 3.
[47]   Mental Capacity Act 2005, s 4.
[48]   See *R (on the application of S) v Plymouth City Council* [2002] EWCA Civ 388.
[49]   GMC, Confidentiality: Protecting and Providing Information.

formulation of the GMC guidance suggests that it is in the public interest to override a competent patient's privacy for the protection of his *own* health or morals.[50] Paragraph 24 states:

> In cases where there is a serious risk to *the patient* or others, disclosures may be justified even where patients have been asked to agree to a disclosure, but have withheld consent (for further advice see paragraph 27).[51] (*Emphasis added.*)

Respectfully, we submit that whilst it is acceptable in limited circumstances to disclose information in order to protect third parties, doing so to protect the competent patient is of dubious legality. English law upholds the competent patient's right to withhold consent to treatment even if death should result. It does so out of respect for the patient's privacy. Similarly, the patient may risk injury or death by withholding consent to the disclosure of information to a third party. That is his right. Consider the patient who refuses to consent to a further round of potentially life-saving chemotherapy. The patient is entitled to confidentiality and entitled to require that it be maintained even when it is contrary to his medical interests. If the patient places a ban on communication with any third party then the doctor must respect that ban. A desire to protect the patient is properly beneficent. May doctors not protect patients from themselves? The law affords doctors no such privilege.

Disclosure in the public interest

4.6 Case (6) above invokes the general 'public interest' defence available in any action for breach of confidence. These issues generate the most sensitive questions surrounding medical confidentiality, seeking to justify breaching patient's confidences to protect the public interest and safeguard other people.

Serious crime

4.7 Let us look first at the most obvious public interest given to justify breach of confidence, the prevention or detection of a serious crime. When may, or

---

[50] Note that the NHS *Code of Practice* makes no reference to disclosure to protect the patient in the public interest; see *Confidentiality: NHS Code of Practice* (2003) Department of Health.

[51] Paragraph 27 of the Guidance states: 'Disclosure of personal information without consent may be justified in the public interest where failure to do so may expose the patient or others to risk of death or serious harm. Where the patient or others are exposed to a risk so serious that it outweighs the patient's privacy interest, you should seek consent to disclosure where practicable. If it is not practicable to seek consent, you should disclose information promptly to an appropriate person or authority. You should generally inform the patient before disclosing the information. If you seek consent and the patient withholds it you should consider the reasons for this, if any are provided by the patient. If you remain of the view that disclosure is necessary to protect a third party from death or serious harm, you should disclose information promptly to an appropriate person or authority. Such situations arise, for example, where a disclosure may assist in the prevention, detection or prosecution of a serious crime, especially crimes against the person, such as abuse of children.' It is possible that the GMC's paternalism is grounded in a parallel provision in s 7 of the Data Protection Act 1998 (as modified by SI 2000/413, Art 5(1)), which restricts patient access to personal data where it is likely to cause them serious harm. We explore this provision at 4.16.

even should, a doctor inform the police about criminal conduct on the part of a patient? Contrary to popular myth, a doctor is under no general obligation enforced by the criminal law to contact the police. Unless a statute specifically so provides, a doctor does not commit any offence by failing to tell the police of any evidence he may have come across professionally which suggests that a patient may have committed, or is contemplating, some crime.[52] A criminal offence is committed only when a doctor or anyone else accepts money to conceal evidence of crime.[53] Section 19 of the Terrorism Act 2000 imposes a duty on everyone, including doctors, to inform the police if they believe or suspect certain offences concerning funding terrorist activity have been committed. Although many statutes require doctors to disclose information if asked to do so by police,[54] doctors are not compelled to volunteer that information. In many cases, a doctor will none the less judge that he should do so where others are at risk.

So, in the case of most crimes, the choice is the doctor's. Criminal law will not penalise him for not informing the police. Will he be in breach of confidence if he elects to do so? Judges early last century were divided on the issue of whether a doctor was justified in going to the police after attending a woman who had undergone a criminal abortion. Hawkins J condemned such a course as a 'monstrous cruelty' and doubted whether such a breach of confidence could ever be justified,[55] where Avory J saw the doctor's duty to assist in the investigation of serious crime as always outweighing his duty to his patient.[56] More recent judgments appear to support Avory J's view, although they deal with confidential relationships outside the medical field, suggesting that the public interest justifies disclosure of *any* crime or misdeed committed or contemplated.[57]

Within the doctor-patient relationship freedom to disclose in the public interest should be more limited in scope. Unless commission of any crime disentitles the criminal from normal standards of medical care, disclosure should be strictly limited. Doctors who suspect that another person is at risk of physical injury at their patient's hands must be free to act to protect that person. Preventing harm to others outweighs the private and public interests in confidentiality. Volunteering evidence of less serious crimes committed by patients to the police may be seen as less straightforward. The GMC advises that disclosure is more readily defensible in relation to serious crime,[58] 'especially crimes against the person, such as abuse of children'.[59] What the doctor should not do is hand over to the police information on each and every patient who transgresses the law. Parliament has legislated in numerous cases to compel breach of medical confidence. The courts should not be zealous to

---

[52] Criminal Law Act 1967, s 5(5).
[53] Criminal Law Act 1967, s 5(1).
[54] For example, section 172 of the Road Traffic Act 1988 (information identifying the driver of a car involved in a road accident).
[55] *Kitson v Playfair* (1896) Times, 28 March.
[56] Birmingham Assizes (1914) 78 JP 604.
[57] *Initial Services Ltd v Putterill* [1968] 1 QB 396 at 405.
[58] GMC, *Confidentiality: Protecting and Providing Information*, para 27.
[59] See also Royal College of Paediatrics and Child Health, *Responsibilities of Doctors in Child Protection Cases with Regard to Confidentiality* (2004).

add to that list. The law should limit justifiable breach of confidence to *serious* crime and interpret the term *serious* strictly.

The flaw in this argument may be that a doctor found to be in breach of confidence for disclosing a crime could be condemned by a court or the GMC for taking steps to combat crime, performing a moral duty cast on every citizen. The doctor is distinguished from other citizens by the presence of a positive legal duty to his patient. Enforcing his duty to his patient benefits the public as well as the patient. The Court of Appeal has expressly recognised a public interest in the maintenance of medical confidentiality.[60] Medical confidentiality is at the root of good health care. Should the courts, however, find that as upholders of the law they cannot condemn those who help bring lawbreakers to justice, the alternative solution is to fall back on the ethical standard set by the GMC, and hold that breach of confidence is justified only in case of grave or serious crime. The doctor may not break the law if he discloses details of petty crimes, but he may be punished for professional misconduct. The legal and ethical standards do not need to be exactly the same.

Next arises the question of disclosure where crime is not an issue. The law no longer limits the concept of public interest disclosure to crime alone, nor does the GMC in its ethical guidance to doctors. Defining exactly when the doctor may disclose on this more general basis is exceptionally difficult. May he tell a wife that her husband is HIV positive? What if a doctor is treating a fellow health professional who is HIV positive but continues to carry out risky surgery? Or what if a general practitioner knows that a patient continues to drive when her eyesight or epilepsy renders her a danger on the roads? In all cases, the doctor must first do his utmost to obtain the patient's consent to disclosure. If persuasion fails, what may the doctor do? He must balance his duty to the patient against the risk threatening other individuals. It is clear that he may, in an appropriate case, inform an appropriate public body.[61] The GMC expressly addresses the case of patients unfit to drive who refuse to accept medical advice. A doctor may lawfully contact the DVLC (Driver and Vehicle Licensing Centre) if a patient unfit to drive absolutely rejects advice to surrender his licence. Similarly where colleagues are medically unfit to practise, the GMC puts the safety of patients first.

Communicable diseases

4.8 *X v Y*[62] concerned the proposed disclosure of information identifying two GPs who had been diagnosed as HIV positive. As we have seen, the judge granted an injunction on the basis that the risk to patients was negligible. But consider the following example. A surgeon is HIV positive. It is not uncommon for surgeons to cut themselves in the course of surgery so that there is

---

60   *W v Egdell* [1990] 1 All ER 835, CA.
61   See *Hubbard v Vosper* [1972] 2 QB 84; *Church of Scientology v Kaufman* [1973] RPC 635 (disclosure of matter threatening the health of members of the public). See also see Gurry, *Breach of Confidence*, pp 334–338.
62   [1988] 2 All ER 648; see above at 4.2.

blood-to-blood contact between surgeon and patient, and a number of doctors have contracted HIV from patients. Certain forms of surgery, now styled 'exposure-prone procedures', carry a real risk of cross-infection between surgeon and patient. Public concern about health workers transmitting HIV to patients prompted the GMC to give further and specific guidance on the ethical issues surrounding not just HIV and AIDS, but serious communicable diseases[63] (hepatitis B,[64] for instance, is much more infectious than HIV but transmitted in the same manner). A doctor reporting a colleague who refuses to avoid endangering patients when he risks transmitting such a disease acts lawfully. The GMC expressly advises that:

> ... when a doctor knows, or has good reason to believe that, a fellow health worker is infected with a serious communicable disease and that that person has not sought or followed advice to modify his practice to protect his patients the doctor must inform the appropriate regulatory authority and an appropriate person in that health worker's employing authority.

A surgeon or, for example, a midwife, carrying out procedures where there is an unavoidable risk of transmitting a blood-borne disease poses such a risk of harm to her patient that the public interest in confidentiality is outweighed by the need to safeguard the patient.[65]

Can this *public* interest in disclosure justify disclosure, not only to a public body or official but also to an individual at risk? If an HIV positive surgeon refuses to refrain from unprotected intercourse or to tell his wife of his condition, can she be warned of the danger she faces? The GMC advises that doctors *may* disclose such information to known sexual contacts. Doctors are urged to do all they can to persuade the infected person himself to inform sexual partners. If persuasion fails then the doctor should consider whether he should inform any sexual partner at risk of infection. Would the law support a doctor who did so? In defamation a defence of qualified privilege protects any communication which the maker has a duty to impart and the recipient a legitimate interest in receiving. No defence of qualified privilege as such exists in breach of confidence.[66] The defence is that the public interest demands disclosure. Private interests alone are not usually enough. However, where a genuine risk of physical danger, of injury or disease is posed to any third party, the public interest in individual security is sufficient to justify disclosure to that person so that she can protect herself appropriately. When the doctor reasonably foresees that non-disclosure poses a real risk of physical harm to a third party he ought to be free to warn that person, especially if that person too is his patient. The courts should not be over-zealous to prove him wrong. Similarly, in such cases, if the doctor thinks it more appropriate to contact the third party's GP, he should not be condemned. None the less, risk of harm

---

63 GMC, *Serious Communicable Diseases* (1997).
64 M Brazier and J Harris, 'Public Health and Private Lives' (1996) 4 *Medical Law Review* 171.
65 Similar arguments prevail where other forms of disease may impair the doctor's judgement. For example, if a doctor has reason to believe that a patient, who is also a health worker, is so mentally disturbed that he poses a threat to his own patients, once again the appropriate authority should be alerted to the risk: see *Woolgar v Chief Constable of Sussex Police* [1999] 3 All ER 604, CA.
66 Law Commission Report No 110, *Breach of Confidence* Cmnd 8388, paras 6.94–6.96.

must be established. A simple belief that someone else, spouse or relative, is entitled to information is insufficient, even if they have an interest – a legitimate and not merely prurient interest – in the matters at stake.[67] That is not enough. The balance of public interest in favour of preserving confidentiality should be displaced only by a significant danger of physical harm.

Openly identifying a health care worker who is HIV positive will thus rarely be lawful. A more difficult question arose in *H (A Healthcare Worker) v Associated Newspapers Ltd and N (A Health Authority)*.[68] H tested positive for HIV while working as a health care professional for a health authority, identified in court proceedings only as N. The health authority proposed to carry out a 'look back' exercise to notify patients treated by H and invite them to undergo HIV testing if they so chose. H first sought an injunction to prevent N from notifying his patients and carrying out the 'look back' study. He provided details of at least some of his NHS patients with the utmost reluctance and refused to supply any information about his private patients. H argued that, in his particular case, the risk to patients of HIV was so low that it did not justify breach of his, or his patients', clinical confidentiality.

Before H's case against the health authority could be heard, the *Mail on Sunday* heard about the case. The newspaper planned to publish a story about H's condition and his dispute with the health authority. He sought a second injunction to prevent publication of any details identifying him personally, or identifying either the health authority that employed him or his medical specialty. A temporary injunction was granted to him in the term he sought. The newspaper retaliated with the headline 'Judge's gag over AIDS threat to patients'.

Gross J upheld the ban on publishing details of H's identity, but would have allowed publication of the health authority's identity and H's specialty. H appealed. He argued that if the nature of his specialty and the name of his employing authority were in the public domain, he himself would be readily identifiable by a significant number of people, including some of his patients. The Court of Appeal acknowledged that H's case involved a difficult balancing exercise. They concluded that a ban on identifying the health authority should be imposed. Disclosing N (the health authority)'s identity would be likely to '… set in train a course of events' that could result in disclosure of H's identity and compromise his first action against the health authority to prevent the health authority conducting the 'look back' study. Patients might also be harmed by discovering the risk to themselves without immediate access to proper advice and counselling. The Appeal Court, however, was not convinced that a ban on identifying H's specialty was necessary. Such a restraint would inhibit legitimate debate on a matter of public interest. The Court of Appeal in *H (A Healthcare Worker) v Associated Newspapers Ltd and N (A Health Authority)*[69] granted more legitimacy to the interest in freedom of expression and public debate about the risks of HIV transmission

---

[67] For example, that a parent might legitimately want to know if an adult daughter was HIV positive.
[68] [2002] Lloyd's Rep Med 210, CA.
[69] [2002] Lloyd's Rep Med 210, CA.

and infected health workers than Rose J did in *X v Y*.[70] The influence of Article 10 of the European Convention on Human Rights (guaranteeing freedom of expression) is plainly seen.

Genetics[71]

4.9 Especially difficult questions touching on confidentiality arise in relation to genetic screening and genetic counselling. This is a complex subject which we can give only cursory attention here. Tests which reveal that the individual patient suffers from, or is a carrier of, a genetic disease often indicate that other family members are at risk of the same disease.[72] Consider a simple example. Jenny, a medical student, having completed her initial course in genetics, becomes concerned about her family history. There appears to be a pattern of paternal relatives succumbing to dementia and premature death. After counselling she consents to a test for Huntington's Chorea. The test proves positive. Huntington's is an autosomal dominant genetic disease which means that if a parent has the affected gene, any child has a 50 per cent chance of inheriting Huntington's. The disease does not manifest itself until early middle age when the affected person succumbs over several years to progressive dementia and early death. Jenny's diagnosis necessary means that one of her parents must also have the affected gene, and that each of her siblings is at 50/50 risk, as will be any child whom Jenny may bear. If Jenny refuses to consent to genetic counsellors contacting her family, would the interests of those family members justify a breach of confidence? If Jenny's elder brother had just married and he and his wife were hoping to start a family, would the potential harm to the child justify disclosure?[73]

Defamation

4.10 Whatever the problem before him, a doctor must not forget that the law ultimately determines when overriding interests justify a breach of confidence. The role of the law of defamation must not be overlooked. Disclosure of any confidential information, even when every word is true, may be the subject of an action for breach of confidence. If the doctor is mistaken and information disclosed by him proves to be untrue, he may face a further action for defamation. Any statement causing responsible citizens to think less of a person or to avoid his company may be defamatory. Diagnoses of alcoholism, venereal disease and HIV are all examples of possible defamatory remarks.

[70] [1988] 2 All ER 648.
[71] See, generally, GT Laurie, *Genetic Privacy: A Challenge to Medico-Legal Norms* (2002) CUP.
[72] Fully and eloquently discussed in *Mason and McCall Smith's Law and Medical Ethics*, pp 219–228. And see Nuffield Council on Bioethics, *Genetic Screening: The Ethical Issues* (1993) and *Genetic Screening: Ethical Issues*, 2006 Supplement (www.nuffieldbioethics.org). See also Gilbar, *The Status of the Family in Law and Bioethics: The Genetic Context.*
[73] See D Bell and B Bennett, 'Genetic Secrets and the Family' (2001) 9 *Medical Law Review* 130; L Skene, 'Genetic Secrets and the Family: A Response to Bell and Bennett' (2001) 9 *Medical Law Review* 162.

Suspicion of child abuse is another. In defamation the doctor has a complete defence if what he has stated is true. Additionally, he has a defence of qualified privilege if, first, he reasonably believed his statements to be true, and second, he communicated with a person with a legitimate interest in the relevant information. Informing the police of suspected violence to a child is privileged even if the doctor's suspicions prove to be unfounded. Informing an employer that an employee is an alcoholic is generally not. The issue of whether the communication was justified is one and the same in the law of confidence and defamation.

A duty to disclose?

4.11 There are clearly circumstances when the doctor's duty of confidence to his patient may be overridden by his duty to safeguard a third party from physical harm. If he mistakenly decides in the patient's favour and the risk of harm to someone else materialises, is the doctor at risk of a lawsuit by the injured party? Normally where a risk of injury is readily foreseeable and a person has the ability to eliminate that risk, or at any rate to minimise it, a duty to take the necessary action will arise. For example, an education authority which failed to ensure that small children could not get out of their nursery school and on to a busy road were found liable, not just to any child on the road, but to a lorry driver injured in an incident caused by a straying child.[74]

The student medical centre at the University of California was held liable for failing to warn a young woman of the risk posed to her by one of their patients.[75] The girl's rejected lover sought psychiatric help at the centre. He told staff there of his violent intentions towards the girl and that he had a gun. The staff warned the police, who decided to take no action. The medical centre said nothing to the girl. She was murdered by their patient soon afterwards. Her family sued the University for negligence. The medical centre was found liable for failing to breach their patient's confidence and warn the girl of the threat to her life.

On similar facts, an English court would be less likely to find a doctor negligent. First the court would have to determine whether, in the special circumstances of medical confidentiality, a duty to breach confidence could be countenanced. In the case of the education authority held liable for the escape of the infant, their duty to child and to lorry driver was one and the same. The doctor is faced with a stark conflict of duty.[76] If the doctor *may* lawfully breach his patient's confidence, does he have a duty to do so to safeguard the individual at risk? The courts in England are reluctant to make A liable for a wrong committed by B.[77] So the injured individual would have to satisfy the

---

74 *Carmarthenshire County Council v Lewis* [1955] AC 549.
75 *Tarasoff v Regents of University of California* (1976) 551 P 2d 334; see *Mason and McCall Smith's Law and Medical Ethics*, pp 269–271, 719–721.
76 See *Palmer v Tees Health Authority* [1999] Lloyd's Rep Med 351, CA.
77 See *Smith v Littlewoods Organisation Ltd* [1987] 1 All ER 710, HL. Nor is there in English law, unlike Continental civil law, a 'duty to rescue': see A McCall Smith, 'The Duty to Rescue and the Common Law' in M Menlowe and A McCall Smith (eds), *The Duty to*

court that the doctor's knowledge of the risk to him was sufficient to make it 'just and reasonable'[78] for the doctor to be required to act to protect him. At its highest, the doctor's duty may be set as an obligation to consider and assess the risk to the third party. The Californian medical staff did their best. They informed the police. The extent of the doctor's duty to third parties in England would appear to be as follows. He must not ignore any risk to other people created by his patient. He must weigh his duty to his patient against his duty to society and other individuals. If he acts reasonably on the evidence before him in the most awesome of dilemmas, the court will not penalise him if he proves to be wrong.

Compulsory disclosure

4.12 The circumstances in which doctors may choose to disclose information about their patients may worry patients and create problems for doctors. The doctor's legal dilemma is solved when the law compels him to disclose information.

First, a doctor must give any information required by a court of law. Privilege, in the sense of being free to refuse to give evidence relating to professional dealings with clients, is something usually enjoyed by lawyers alone and not shared by any other professional colleagues.[79] A doctor can be subpoenaed to give evidence just like anyone else. Nor can he withhold anything from the court. He does not have to volunteer his views or expertise but whatever questions he is asked he must answer. Just as he can be called to the witness box, so his records can be called up before the courts. The only protection for medical confidentiality lies in the judge's discretion. Judges will try to ensure that confidence is breached only to the extent necessary for the conduct of the trial. The doctor may be unhappy at having to break trust with his patient but he can at least be reassured that he is at no legal risk. Any breach of confidence made as a witness in court is absolutely privileged.

In exercising their powers to order disclosure of evidence or documents, courts strive to balance justice and confidentiality. In *D v NSPCC*[80] the plaintiff sought to compel the NSPCC to disclose who had mistakenly accused her of child abuse. The court refused to make the order. The public interest in people feeling free to approach appropriate authorities to protect young children outweighed the plaintiff's private interest in unearthing her accuser. Thus there will be some cases where the courts may refuse to help a party seeking to discover who gave damaging information about him to the police or some other body. The courts may find that the public interest outweighs the private

---

Rescue (1993) Dartmouth. And note the restrictive approach of many American courts to *Tarasoff v Regents of University of California*: see N de Haan, 'My Patient's Keeper' (1986) 2 *Professional Negligence* 86.

[78] *Peabody Donation Fund (Governors) v Parkinson* [1984] 3 All ER 529, HL.
[79] See JV McHale, *Medical Confidentiality and Legal Privilege* (1993) Routledge.
[80] [1977] 1 All ER 589.

rights of the affected party. A similar balance of public versus private interest may also apply where the doctor is not a potential defendant but merely a witness.

Particularly sensitive information may be allowed to be withheld from the court in the public interest. So in *AB v Glasgow and West of Scotland Blood Transfusion Service*[81] a Scottish court refused to order disclosure of the identity of a blood donor who had allegedly supplied infected blood. The doctor's protection depends on the judge's discretion. In *R (on the application of B) v Stafford Combined Court*,[82] the High Court held that the Crown Court breached TB's right to privacy contrary to Article 6(1). TB was a 14-year-old witness in a criminal case against a man alleged to have sexually abused her. The Crown Court ordered disclosure of her medical records relating to psychiatric counselling she had received. In accordance with the Criminal Procedure Rules 2005 (which were at the time under review,[83] leading May LJ to confine his decision to the facts), the application was served on the NHS Trust but not on TB. The Trust was concerned that releasing the records without giving TB a chance to make oral representations would breach their duty of confidence. In response the Crown Court judge called TB at short notice whereupon, unrepresented, she reluctantly agreed to the disclosure. TB sought judicial review of the Crown Court decision to order disclosure. The High Court held that TB's right to privacy under Article 8(1) had been breached. Neither was the interference justified within the terms of Article 8(2).

Next, the doctor may be compelled to hand over information to the police or other authorities before any trial commences. Several statutes demand that the doctor answer questions if the police come and ask him. If a statute imposes a duty on 'any person' to answer police questions, 'any person' includes a doctor.[84] His profession confers no exemption or privilege upon him. Where no specific statutory power aids the police in their investigation of a crime the question becomes whether, if they believe a doctor holds records or other material constituting evidence of a crime on the part of a patient, they can search the doctor's premises and seize the relevant material. The Police and Criminal Evidence Act 1984 grants police access to medical records, but imposes certain safeguards. A search warrant to enter and search a surgery, hospital or clinic for medical records or human tissue or fluids taken for the purposes of medical treatment may be granted only by a circuit judge[85] and not, as is usually the case, by lay magistrates. The judge is directed to weigh the public interest in disclosure of the material against the general public interest in maintaining confidentiality.

Beyond the scope of the criminal law, several further examples of compulsory disclosure must be noted. Provision is made for compulsory notification of

---

[81]   1993 SLT 36.
[82]   [2006] EWHC 1645 (Admin).
[83]   Now amended by SI 2006/2636.
[84]   *Hunter v Mann* [1974] 1 QB 767.
[85]   Police and Criminal Evidence Act 1984, ss 8–14 and Sch 1.

certain highly infectious diseases and of venereal disease.[86] AIDS is not a notifiable disease in the UK. The Public Health (Control of Disease) Act 1984 expressly states that cholera, plague, relapsing fever, smallpox and typhus shall be notifiable diseases and makes provision for other diseases to be so categorised at times of epidemic. Successive governments have resisted pressure to make HIV/AIDS a notifiable disease.[87] Again the question is one of balancing the competing public interests, the interest in patients seeking advice and treatment for disease, and the interest in protecting the health of those at risk from infection. HIV is not in the same league as diseases such as cholera. The cholera carrier immediately places his casual contacts at risk; if he is untreated, he can do little to minimise that risk. Cholera spreads like wildfire. HIV is much less infectious and, by acting responsibly, the patient can reduce the risk to others. To act responsibly he needs professional help and should not be deterred from seeking help by fear that his doctor will be forced to 'squeal' to the authorities.

Accidents at work and instances of food poisoning are notifiable. Abortions must be reported. Details of drug addicts are required under the Misuse of Drugs Act 1971. Births and deaths have to be notified by doctors as well as registered by families.

Finally, a number of organisations concerned with health administration may require information in the course of performing their functions. These include the NHS Ombudsman, the Department of Health and other NHS authorities.[88] Many of the items on the long list of circumstances when a doctor can be forced to hand over information concerning his patients can be justified on grounds of public interest. The trouble is that the list grows haphazardly. Only in the case of HIV has the question of competing public interests and private rights been expressly addressed. What is needed is a review of medical confidentiality to examine all instances of compulsory disclosure and clarify when the public interest overrides the general benefit of preserving confidentiality. Legislation compelling disclosure should be express rather than simply including the doctor in a general requirement that any person gives information. Parliament should address the problem directly and not leave it to the judiciary to interpret ambiguous statutory provisions. An opportunity for such a review might have been offered by the highly controversial section 60 of the Health and Social Care Act 2001 (see now sections 251–252 of the National Health Service Act 2006).[89] Section 60(1) provided that:

> The Secretary of State may by regulation make such provision for and in connection with requiring or regulating the processing of prescribed patient information for medical purposes as he considers necessary or expedient—

---

[86] The National Health Service (Venereal Diseases) Regulations 1974, SI 1974/29, make provision for the tracing of sexual contacts, but also seek to ensure that the identities of patients and contacts remain confidential.

[87] Though provisions for detention in the Public Health (Control of Disease) Act 1984 do extend to people with AIDS: see below at 6.19.

[88] But powers must be used with proper regard for the patient's right to privacy under Article 8 of the European Convention on Human Rights: see *A Health Authority v X* [2001] EWCA Civ 2014.

[89] See P Case, 'Confidence Matters: The Rise and Fall of Informational Autonomy in Medical Law' (2003) 11 *Medical Law Review* 208.

(a)   in the interest of improving patient care, or
(b)   in the public interest

As the Health and Social Care Bill progressed through Parliament, fears were voiced that Ministers would use this power to drive a coach and horses through the common law protection of medical privacy. In a concession to opponents of the move, a Patient Information Advisory Group was established with whom the Secretary of State must consult on any regulations to be made under section 60. Since December 2001, the Patient Information Advisory Group has approved 125 applications under section 60. Now six years old, this 'transitional' measure is still much utilised, particularly by researchers.

The Data Protection Act 1998

4.13 The Data Protection Act 1998 offers statutory protection to control the use and processing of all forms of 'personal data'.[90] This includes all medical and health records, whether the records are manual or computerised. The individual about whom information is held is designated the 'data subject' and the person or organisation responsible for holding that information is styled the 'data controller'. The 1998 Act applies to all kinds of information held about us, not just health records. We are, however, concerned here only with its application to health records. 'Health records' are defined as:

any record which:
(a)   consists of information relating to the physical or mental health or condition of an individual, and
(b)   has been made by or on behalf of a health professional in connection with the care of an individual.[91]

'Health professional'[92] is broadly defined to include doctors, dentists, nurses and most kinds of other 'conventional' health professionals (but not most complementary medicine practitioners).[93] The Act is lengthy, complex and not compelling reading. The fundamental points to emphasise are these. Any processing of data, including alteration of health records, retrieval of or use of records, and *disclosure* or erasure of records must be done in conformity with the Act. Any 'personal data' from a health record that is information relating to a living and identifiable patient is subject to stringent controls. Whenever such data is processed one at least of the conditions of Schedule 2 to the 1998 Act must be met. These include that the patient gave consent to processing, that processing is necessary to protect the 'vital interests' of the patient, or necessary in the administration of justice or for the purpose of the legitimate interests of the data controller. Consent need not be explicit. Notices in GP

---

[90] Defined in *Durant v Financial Services Authority* [2003] EWCA Civ 1746 (which did not concern health records) as information focusing on the individual rather than a third party, incident or event in which the individual participated.
[91] Data Protection Act 1998, s 68(2).
[92] Data Protection Act 1998, s 69.
[93] The Data Protection Act 1998 does include osteopaths and chiropractors. The definition would appear to cover all health professionals subject to statutory regulation.

surgeries and clinics about possible uses of information may suffice. A broader range of justifications for disclosure than the common law allows is sanctioned by Schedule 2.

Health records fall within the category of 'sensitive personal data' and are granted additional protection by the 1998 Act. 'Sensitive personal data' is defined to include any information about a person's physical or mental health or condition. 'Sensitive personal data' may only be processed, and therefore only disclosed, either with the *explicit* consent of the patient or in the following circumstances:

(1)   to protect the vital interests of a patient who cannot consent on his own behalf or where the data controller cannot reasonably be expected to obtain consent, or to protect the vital interests of another person where the patient has unreasonably withheld consent to disclosure;

(2)   in connection with the administration of justice, or disclosure is required by law; and

(3)   for medical purposes by a health professional, which involves only disclosure to another person bound by a similar duty of confidentiality.

This is not an exhaustive list. (For instance, specific provision is made in relation to research and we address this later, in Chapter 16.)

The Secretary of State is empowered to add further conditions allowing the lawful processing of 'sensitive personal data'. He has done so *inter alia* to allow the disclosure of health records in professional disciplinary proceedings involving health professionals, and to allow various NHS authorities to investigate mismanagement or malpractice.[94] A wide, all-embracing provision allows processing without consent where it is in the substantial public interest and necessary for the discharge of any function designed to protect the public against dishonesty, malpractice or service failure. It must necessarily be carried out without the explicit consent of the patient 'so as not to prejudice the discharge of that function'.

The range of exceptions to the duty of non-disclosure under the Data Protection Act 1998 mean that its scope is little greater than the obligation of confidentiality imposed by common law. The force of the 1998 Act lies in its remedies. A patient suspecting misuse of his health records can apply to the data controller to cease processing records when what is being done causes, or is likely to cause, him substantial and unwarranted damage or distress.[95] A person who has suffered damage or distress as a consequence of violation of the 1998 Act has a right to compensation. He does not need to prove financial loss. However, the data controller may in defence of such a claim establish that he had taken all reasonable care to comply with the Act.[96] Most crucially, section 14 of the Act allows a patient to apply to the court to correct inaccurate health records. He can act to ensure that misinformation about his health is not perpetuated for all time.

---

[94]   SI 2000/417.
[95]   Data Protection Act 1998, s 10.
[96]   Data Protection Act 1998, s 13.

eHealth

4.14 Health records are currently both electronic and written. The use of written records and incompatibility between electronic systems can cause delays and errors in research, audit and patient care. The solution, according to the Government, is a controversial £12 billion national computer system – the 'National Programme for Information Technology in the NHS', which was launched in 2002. At its core will be the NHS Care Records Service, which 'NHS Connecting for Health' (an agency of the Department of Health) is responsible for delivering. Patients' demographic details, together with relevant parts of their NHS patient clinical records will be uploaded onto a national database to be accessed by any approved medical staff. Smartcards are being issued to relevant NHS staff to ensure that access is secure. Patient data will be mobile, reducing errors and enhancing consistency and coordination. The implications for patient privacy are worrying. There is some way to go before the support of doctors and patients is secured.[97] Patients consent will be implied rather than express and the opportunity to opt out of the scheme is limited.[98]

As we move away from a personalised health service and witness the introduction of new data systems, the British Medical Association[99] question whether the traditional confidentiality model is sustainable. They raise the possibility of a wholesale change in outlook whereby a data protection/health governance model is put in place to oversee information-sharing across the NHS.

Anonymised data

4.15 Most of what has been said so far relates to information from which the identity of the patient can be ascertained. For many purposes, however, anonymised data about patients and their diseases is needed or wanted by diverse bodies. Anonymised information may be necessary to carry out clinical audits, to compile statistics about health needs or for epidemiological purposes. Many of us might applaud such purposes. Commercial organisations such as drug companies may also seek access to such information to help them with marketing or product development. The GMC gives extensive advice on anonymising data and its disclosure.[100] It urges doctors to explain to their patients how such data is used and what benefits flow from exchange of information. Does confidentiality apply to anonymised information?

In *R v Department of Health, ex p Source Informatics Ltd*[101] the applicants were a data collection company. They persuaded GPs and pharmacists to supply them with anonymised information about prescribing habits. They

---

[97]   National Audit Office, *The National Programme for IT in the NHS*, HC 1173 (2006) The Stationary Office, para 8.
[98]   See The BigOptOut.org, accessible at http://www.nhsconfidentiality.org.
[99]   BMA, *Confidentiality as Part of the Bigger Picture* (2005).
[100] See GMC, *Confidentiality: Protecting and Providing Information*.
[101] [2000] 1 All ER 786, CA.

then sold this information to drug companies. The Department of Health issued a document ruling that to disclose such information without patient consent constituted a breach of confidence. The company challenged the ruling. The trial judge found that anonymisation did not remove the obligation of confidence. Transfer of anonymised data might in certain cases be justifiable – for example to ensure clinical audit – but information about patients was in all cases confidential, whether the patient was identifiable or not. The Court of Appeal disagreed. Disclosure of anonymised information, it ruled, did not violate the interests which obligations of confidentiality protect. The patient's privacy is not violated. He is not vulnerable to any harm. Patients have no property in information about them. Ethical safeguards now surround anonymised data.[102] The law restricts itself to controlling information about us only where we can be identified. GPs, pharmacists and drug companies may still profit from information derived from us.

Patients' access to records[103]

4.16 We turn now to the opposite side of the coin. Patients expect their doctors to keep their secrets. Can the doctors have secrets from their patients? The law of confidence prevents doctors from improperly disclosing information from or about their patients. What if the patient seeks information about herself? When can a patient demand to see his records?

Until November 1991, the answer to this simple question was confusing. A patient who started legal proceedings was able to obtain a court order giving her and her advisers access to her health records. The difficulties in getting access to health records by any other means prompted patients who only wanted to know what had gone wrong with their treatment to bring legal action, even though they did not particularly want or need monetary compensation. From 1987, the Data Protection Act 1984 gave patients limited access to computerised health records. Then the Access to Health Records Act 1990 offered access to manual records,[104] but only records compiled after November 1991. An attempt to assert a common law right of access to all records, including records compiled before 1991, failed.[105] The Data Protection Act 1998 repeals and replaces most of these prior rules.[106] Section 7 of the 1998 Act establishes a right for data subjects to have access to all personal data relating to them held by the data controller. For our purposes this means that patients have a *prima facie* right to access of all their health records,

---

[102] See, for example, BMA, *Confidentiality and Disclosure of Health Information* (1999), *Confidentiality as Part of the Bigger Picture* (2005).

[103] See generally on the implications of record-keeping for medical confidentiality, *Report on the Review of Patient-Identifiable Information* (1997) HMSO (The Caldicott Report).

[104] See also the Access to Medical Reports Act 1988 granting access to reports supplied to employers and insurers.

[105] *R v Mid-Glamorgan Family Health Services, ex p Martin* [1995] 1 WLR 110.

[106] Note that the Data Protection Act 1998, rather than the Freedom of Information Act 2000, governs access to personal data.

whether manual or computerised. However, the 1998 Act, like its predecessors, allows the Secretary of State to exempt or modify rights of patient access to health records.[107]

Access is not unlimited. Certain sorts of information held for research, historical or statistical purposes are exempted from access. Special rules are laid down where information about a patient also discloses information about some third party. A host of other exemptions and limitations apply. Most crucially, access to health records may be refused where release of information would be likely to cause serious harm to the physical or mental health or condition of the patient or any other person.[108] In deciding whether to refuse access, NHS authorities are required to consult the health professionals currently responsible for the patient's care.[109]

On the face of it, such exclusions from rights of access seem reasonable. A patient whose mental health is fragile and who may be devastated by a full account of his diagnosis and prognosis may be thought to be 'better off' not knowing the true state of affairs. Of course, when he is refused access he may imagine an even worse scenario. The crux of the problem, though, is the way in which relevant NHS authorities, and doctors in particular, will use the exclusions. Suppose a patient is diagnosed as having terminal cancer. His doctor decides not to tell him, and advises the health authority to refuse access to records because *he* judges that the patient could not cope with the truth. What can the patient do? Section 7 of the Data Protection Act 1998 allows him to apply to the court, so a judge can decide if access has been improperly refused.

Medical and legal attitudes to patients' 'right to know' have altered. The GMC expressly acknowledges the importance of sharing information with patients. Doctors are admonished that patients[110] '... have a right to information about any condition or disease from which they are suffering'. The Court of Appeal has moved away from its previously entrenched position, that doctors decide what patients have a right to know. Lord Woolf[111] has asserted that patients should be told about any '... significant risk which would affect the judgment of a reasonable patient'. With luck, the Data Protection Act 1998 will provide a legal framework within which a culture of openness will flourish. Fears that such a culture will result in patients being faced with unwanted information are misplaced. No-one is obliged to seek access to his records.

Finally, the access provisions of the Data Protection Act 1998 apply only to living patients. Consequently, a small part of the Access to Health Records Act 1990[112] is preserved to enable executors of a deceased person's estate or members of his family to gain access to his records in an appropriate case.

---

[107] See section 30(1) of the Data Protection Act 1998.
[108] Data Protection (Subject Access Modification) (Health) Order 2000, SI 2000/413, Art 5(1).
[109] Data Protection Act 1998, s 7.
[110] GMC, *Confidentiality: Protecting and Providing Information* (2004), paras 6–8.
[111] *Pearce v United Bristol Healthcare NHS Trust* [1991] PIQRP 53, discussed below at 5.7.
[112] Data Protection Act 1998, s 3(1)(f).

NHS practice

4.17 It is important to note that within the NHS crucial decisions on patient confidentiality and access to records may be made not by health professionals but by health service administrators. A manager, not a doctor or nurse, may decide, for example, to allow police access to patient records.[113] We have already examined the role of the GMC in enforcing the ethics of confidentiality. Their jurisdiction is limited to medical practitioners. The Nursing and Midwifery Council (NMC) enforces similar stringent ethical rules for nurses. Doctors as well as patients have expressed concern that a patient's notes are seen by an unnecessary number of persons. They complain that decisions as to when to disclose records are taken too often by administrators, and that administrators are not subject to the control of the GMC or the NMC. Doctors fear they may be less concerned about confidentiality.

Such fears should be misguided. All NHS staff are subject to the law on confidence. Information confided by the patient to her doctor remains legally confidential when passed by the doctor to NHS clerks for filing and preserving in NHS files. The NHS Code of Practice 2003[114] makes it clear that confidentiality binds everyone working within the NHS. Disclosure within the service is justified only if required in the context of the patient's health care. Disclosure to third parties outside the service is permissible only with the patient's consent, save in exceptional cases. The exceptions, for example, where disclosure is required by law or in cases of serious crime, correspond closely to the exceptions sanctioned by the GMC. Generally decisions on disclosure should always be taken by a medically-qualified person and where possible it should be the doctor caring for the patient. Guidelines are enforced by the sanction of disciplinary action, or even dismissal, against staff members who break them.

---

[113] See Pheby, 'Changing Practice on Confidentiality: A Cause for Concern' (1982) 8 *Journal of Medical Ethics* 12.
[114] *Confidentiality: NHS Code of Practice* (2003) Department of Health

Part II
MEDICAL MALPRACTICE

Chapter 5

AGREEING TO TREATMENT

5.1 There would be little support today, even from the most paternalistic doctor, for the proposition that every sick adult should be compelled to accept whatever treatment his doctor thought best. No one suggests that adults who stay away from dentists out of fear and to the detriment of their dental and general health should be rounded up and marched to the nearest dental surgery for forcible treatment. Few would deny the right of the adult Jehovah's Witness to refuse a blood transfusion, even if in doing so she forfeits her life. Medical treatment normally requires the agreement of the patient. The right of the patient, who is sufficiently rational and mature to understand what is entailed in treatment, to decide for herself whether to agree to that treatment is a basic human right. The right to autonomy, to self-rule rather than rule by others, is endorsed by ethicists as a right to patient autonomy. Two of their Lordships in *Chester v Afshar*[1] signalled that a patient's right to autonomy and dignity should today be accorded the highest priority by English law. Lord Steyn declared that in '... modern law, paternalism no longer rules'.[2] We shall, however, have to consider just how far such theory translates into practice.

This chapter considers only the relatively easy case of mentally-competent adults. Such an adult has an inviolable right to determine what is done to his or her body. Later, in Chapters 6 and 15, we look at the law in relation to patients lacking capacity and to children, and also address circumstances where legislation may endorse compulsory medical treatment. A person who intentionally touches another against that other's will commits a trespass to that person just as much as coming uninvited on to the person's land is a trespass to his land. The tort of battery is committed. Where a person consents to contact no battery is committed. So a boxer entering the ring cannot complain of battery when he is hit on the chin by his opponent. Battery is any non-consensual contact. Conduct which constitutes the crime of battery will generally also amount to the crime of assault. We should also note that contacts resulting in serious bodily harm may still constitute a *criminal* assault, even when such contacts are wholly consensual. English law does not

---

[1]   [2004] UKHL 41 at paras 17 and 24.
[2]   [2004] UKHL 41 at para 16.

allow you to consent to, for example, sado-masochistic practices that cause actual injury to you.[3] Any such 'injury' must be justified by some good purpose. Medical treatment and surgery are acknowledged to be such purposes.[4] So, more controversially, are contact sports, thus justifying the boxers' mutual exchange of blows.[5] There remains a question of whether any kind of maverick or extreme 'surgery' might be beyond the privilege usually accorded to medicine and surgery.[6]

How do the rules relate to doctors? Any doctor examining a patient, or injecting or operating on a patient, makes contact with that patient's body. Normally he commits no wrong because he does so with the patient's agreement. Should a doctor fail to obtain a patient's agreement, should he force himself on a patient, he commits the tort of battery, and the crime of assault. Not only does he infringe on his patient's autonomy, he also violates her bodily integrity.[7] That crude scenario is unlikely, but what of the surgeon who correctly decides to treat cancer of the bone in the right leg by amputating that leg, but by error amputates the wrong leg, the left leg? Once the error is discovered the poor patient has to endure a further operation to remove the right leg. Or what if a patient's notes are mixed up and a woman who was scheduled for and consented to an appendectomy is given a hysterectomy? Both unfortunate victims can sue the surgeon in battery. They did not consent to the operation performed. In a Canadian case, a woman who expressed her wish to be injected in her right arm was injected by the doctor in her left. She sued in battery and succeeded.[8]

In all the above examples, the surgeon or some other member of the hospital staff has been careless. So the patient could normally sue in negligence too. However, there are differences between the two torts. In battery, a patient need not establish any tangible injury. The actionable injury is the uninvited invasion of his body. This is important. A doctor may, on medically unchallengeable grounds, decide that an operation is in the patient's best interests. He goes ahead. The patient's health improves. Yet if the operation was done without consent, a battery has still been committed. A doctor who discovered that his patient's womb was ruptured while performing minor gynaecological surgery was held liable to her for going ahead and sterilising her there and then. She had not agreed to sterilisation.[9] A woman whose ovaries were removed without her express consent similarly recovered for battery.[10] The

---

3   *R v Brown* [1993] 2 All ER 75, HL.
4   See *Attorney General's Reference (No 6 of 1980)* [1981] 2 All ER 1057; Law Commission Consultation Paper No 139, *Consent in the Criminal Law* (1995) HMSO.
5   See *R v Coney* (1882) 8 QBD 534.
6   For example, extreme 'cosmetic' surgery involving amputation or gross facial disfigurement.
7   And so breaches Article 8 of the European Convention on Human Rights: see *Glass v United Kingdom* [2004] 1 FLR 1019, ECtHR.
8   *Allan v New Mount Sinai Hospital* (1980) 109 DLR (3d) 634.
9   *Devi v West Midlands AHA* [1980] 7 CL 44. And see *Williamson v East London and City Health Authority* [1998] Lloyd's Rep Med 6 (woman consented to removal of breast implants but not to a mastectomy).
10 *Bartley v Studd* (1995) in 2 *Medical Law Monitor*, 15 July 1997 (the surgeon was disciplined by the GMC).

essence of the wrong of battery is unpermitted contact. There is no requirement that the patient prove that if he had been asked to consent to the relevant treatment he would have refused.

Two further points should be noted. Battery may be alleged by a patient who *says* he did not consent. First, on whom does the onus of proof lie? It has been held in England that the onus of proof lies on the patient. He must establish that he did not agree.[11] Second, for what will the patient be compensated? In negligence, we shall see that a defendant is only liable for the kind of damage which he reasonably ought to foresee. In battery, the test may be more stringent. The defendant may be liable for all the damage which can factually be shown to flow from his wrongdoing. A doctor who injected a patient in the 'wrong' arm would be liable in battery *and* negligence for any unwanted stiffness in that arm, and for any adverse reaction which he ought to have contemplated in view of the patient's history. He would not be liable in negligence for a 'freak' reaction. In battery he might be so liable. Nonetheless, judges in England have sought to limit the scope of battery when it overlaps with negligence. They strive to avoid subjecting a surgeon to liability in battery.

A significant disadvantage with the tort of battery as a means of vindicating patients' rights is that for a claim to lie in battery traditionally there had to be direct *physical* contact between doctor and patient. A patient who agreed to take a drug orally, having been totally misled as to the nature of the drug, could not sue in battery. Had the doctor injected him with that self-same drug, a claim in battery would lie. Recently the courts have developed the criminal law to allow prosecution for causing grievous bodily harm where no direct physical contact took place.[12] So it is possible that if a doctor deceived a patient into taking a dangerous drug that made her seriously ill, the doctor could face criminal charges.

A right to say no?

5.2 Will the law ever set limits to a competent person's right to refuse treatment? Are we free to reject life-saving treatment which others might consider it 'wicked folly'[13] to refuse? The theory is clear. In *Re T (Adult: Refusal of Medical Treatment)*,[14] Lord Donaldson declared that an adult patient '... has an absolute right to choose whether to consent to medical treatment, to refuse it or to choose one rather than another of the treatments being offered'.[15] Such an absolute right to autonomy '... exists notwithstanding that the reasons for making the choice are rational, or irrational, unknown or even non-existent'. In *Re T*, a young woman of 20 had suffered serious injuries in a road accident. She was 34 weeks pregnant and consented to a

11 *Freeman v Home Office* [1984] 2 WLR 130.
12 *R v Ireland and R v Burstow* [1998] AC 147, HL; *R. v Dica* [2004] 3 All ER 593, CA.
13 See, for example, the judgment of Lord Alverstone in *Leigh v Gladstone* (1909) 26 TLR 139, authorising forcible feeding of a suffragette prisoner.
14 [1992] 4 All ER 649, CA.
15 [1992] 4 All ER 649 at 652–653, CA.

Caesarean section on the following day. Later that evening she was visited by her mother, a devout Jehovah's Witness. T was not herself a baptised Witness. After her mother's visit, T told doctors that she would not agree to any blood transfusion before or during surgery. She first enquired whether alternatives to whole blood were available, and was assured that such alternatives existed. She was given a form to sign evidencing her refusal of transfusion and absolving the hospital from liability for failing to administer blood should she haemorrhage. After delivery of a stillborn child, T lapsed into a coma and suffered life-threatening internal bleeding. The hospital argued that they could not lawfully give her a blood transfusion. Her boyfriend and father sought a court order authorising a life-saving transfusion. Notwithstanding his ringing endorsement of patient autonomy, Lord Donaldson and his brethren in the Court of Appeal granted that order.

The Court of Appeal held that, on the facts of the case, T's refusal of treatment was not an autonomous judgement. Her decision was 'flawed':

(1)   The combination of the effect of her injuries and the medication she was taking impaired her mental capacity to decide whether or not to agree to blood transfusions.

(2)   T lacked sufficient information to make a decision to refuse transfusion. While she was told there were alternatives to whole blood, she was not advised about their limited utility or warned that there were circumstances where, without transfusion, her life would be at risk. Lord Donaldson[16] criticised doctors, whom he suggested were more anxious to disclaim any possible legal liability than to ensure that T was given comprehensible and comprehensive information.

(3)   Pressure from T's mother may have constituted undue influence, rendering her purported refusal of blood transfusion less than independent and voluntary.

These factors were felt to cloud the nature of T's decision and caused the Court of Appeal to conclude that T's rejection of blood could be disregarded. The right of the individual to decide whether to accept medical treatment is paramount but in '... cases of doubt, that doubt falls to be resolved in favour of preservation of life, for if the individual is to override the public interest, he must do so in clear terms'.

It may be tempting to regard *Re T* as judges saying one thing (upholding the rhetoric of autonomy) and doing another (rejecting a belief which caused a young woman to risk sacrificing her life). *Re T* requires careful scrutiny. Do the facts in *Re T* support judicial doubts whether T ever made a truly voluntary and sufficiently informed choice to reject life-saving treatment?[17]

---

[16]   [1992] 4 All ER 649 at 663, CA.
[17]   It may always be especially difficult to judge competence retrospectively: see *NHS Trust v T* [2005] 1 All ER 387.

Subsequent judgments have upheld the principle of autonomy articulated in *Re T*[18] In *Airedale NHS Trust v Bland*,[19] Lord Goff reiterated that the:

> ... principle of self-determination requires that respect must be given to the wishes of the patient, so that if an adult of sound mind refuses, however unreasonably, to consent to treatment or care by which his life would or might be prolonged, the doctors responsible for his care must give effect to his wishes, even though they do not consider it to be in his best interests to do so.

In *B v An NHS Trust*,[20] Butler-Sloss P ruled that it was unlawful for doctors to refuse to switch off a ventilator keeping Ms B alive. Ms B had suffered a haemorrhage in her spinal cord which left her paralysed from the neck down and wholly dependent on a ventilator to breathe. She asked her doctors to switch the ventilator off. She considered that death was preferable to survival in such a state. Her doctors disagreed. They thought that she could enjoy a reasonable quality of life living in a spinal rehabilitation unit. They expressed strong conscientious objections to 'killing' Ms B. When she first indicated her wish to have the ventilator switched off, psychiatrists questioned Ms B's mental capacity. However, she was ultimately adjudged competent to make her own decisions. The judge ruled that continuing to ventilate Ms B against her will constituted an assault on her and awarded her nominal damages of £100. She ordered that arrangements be made to transfer Ms B to a unit where doctors would be prepared to comply with her request. Butler-Sloss P unequivocally endorsed the value of patient autonomy. The crux of the matter will always turn on the capacity of the individual to make a valid choice – a subject explored further in the next chapter.

In *Re T*, Lord Donaldson's recognition of an unqualified right to refuse treatment as long as the adult patient was competent to make that decision was subject to a controversial *caveat*. He contended that an exception to that right might exist in '... a case in which the choice may lead to the death of a viable foetus.'[21] Pregnant women, and women in labour, might be excluded from the normal right to self-determination. A series of controversial cases followed *Re T* in which judges ordered women to submit to Caesarean sections. In *Re S*,[22] Sir Stephen Brown P invoked Lord Donaldson's *dictum* to authorise Caesarean surgery to save the life of the woman's unborn child. Other judgments[23] tended to rely more heavily on the judge's ruling that at the time she refused 'necessary' surgery, the woman's capacity to make decisions was impaired. Ultimately the Court of Appeal clarified the law. A pregnant woman 'of sound mind' retains exactly the same right to accept or refuse treatment as any other adult. The unborn child enjoys no legal personality entitling the court to force its mother to submit to any form of intervention

---

[18] See *Secretary of State for the Home Department v Robb* [1995] 1 All ER 677 (forcible feeding of mentally-competent prisoners is unlawful), *Re C (Adult. Refusal of Medical Treatment)* [1994] 1 All ER 819 (patient entitled to order prohibiting amputation of leg even if the leg became gangrenous).

[19] [1993] 1 All ER 821 at 866; and see Lord Mustill at 889.

[20] [2002] EWHC 429 (Fam); discussed further at 6.3.

[21] [1992] 4 All ER 645 at 653, CA.

[22] [1992] 4 All ER 671.

[23] For example, *Rochdale Healthcare (NHS) Trust v C* [1997] 1 FCR 274.

she elects to decline.[24] The mother's right to autonomy is not diminished or reduced merely because her decision may '... appear morally repugnant'.[25] Adults can say no to treatment as long as their mental capacity is unimpaired. Identifying when a person lacks capacity may be tricky, however, and judges may be naturally reluctant to stand by and watch a pregnant woman and her child both die.[26]

What is meant by consent?

5.3   Consent is mandatory but what actually constitutes 'consent'? It need not usually be written.[27] Consent may be implied from the circumstances. If a patient visits his general practitioner complaining of a sore throat and opens his mouth so that the doctor can examine his throat, he cannot complain that he never expressly said to the doctor, 'You may put a spatula on my tongue and look down my throat.' A patient visiting Casualty with a bleeding wound implicitly agrees to doctors or nurses cleaning and bandaging the wound. In an American case an immigrant to the USA complained that he had not consented to vaccination. It was found that he had bared his arm and held it out to the doctor. His action precluded the need for any verbal consent.[28]

A patient for whom surgery or any form of invasive investigation is proposed will normally be asked to sign a consent form. The Department of Health issues guidance on consent to treatment and produces model forms for use within the NHS. The Department's aim is to ensure that health care professionals appreciate the need to give patients the information to which they are entitled. The model form for routine surgery, investigation or treatment is shown below.[29]

Patient identifier/label

Name of proposed procedure or course of treatment (include brief explanation if medical term not clear) ....

....

Statement of health professional (to be filled in by health professional with appropriate knowledge of proposed procedure, as specified in consent policy)

I have explained the procedure to the patient. In particular, I have explained:

---

[24]   *Re MB (Caesarean Section)* [1997] 8 Med LR 217, CA; *St George's Healthcare NHS Trust v S* [1998] 3 All ER 673.

[25]   *St.George's Healthcare NHS Trust v S* [1998] 3 All ER 673 at 692.

[26]   See, for example, *Bolton Hospitals NHS Trust v O* [2003] 1 FLR 824. The rights of pregnant women are dealt with more fully at 12.16–12.18.

[27]   Sometimes legislation such as the Human Fertilisation and Embryology Act 1990 requires written consent: see *R v Human Fertilisation and Embryology Authority, ex p Blood* [1997] 2 All ER 687, CA, discussed below at 13.7. See also ss 2(5) and 3(5) of the Human Tissue Act 2004.

[28]   *O'Brien v Cunard SS Co* 28 NC266 (Mass. 1891).

[29]   Special forms are provided, for example, to cover surgery where there are doubts about the patient's mental capacity, or in relation to sensitive procedures such as sterilisation. See also the Department of Health's *Reference guide to consent for examination or treatment* (www.doh.gov.uk/consent).

The intended benefits ....

....

....

Serious or frequently occurring risks ....

....

Any extra procedures which may become necessary during the procedure

☐   blood transfusion ....
☐   other procedure (please specify) ....

I have also discussed what the procedure is likely to involve, the benefits and risks of any available alternative treatments (including no treatment) and any particular concerns of this patient.

☐ The following leaflet/tape has been provided ....

This procedure will involve:

☐ general and/or regional   ☐ local   ☐ sedation
    anaesthesia   anaesthesia

Signed   Date ....
Name (PRINT) .... Job title ....

Contact details (if patient wishes to discuss options later) ....

Statement of interpreter (where appropriate)

I have interpreted the information above to the patient to the best of my ability and in a way in which I believe s/he can understand.

Signed .... Date ....

Name (PRINT) ....

Top copy accepted by patient: yes/no (please ring)

Statement of patient   **Patient identifier/label**

Please read this form carefully. If your treatment has been planned in advance, you should already have your own copy of page 2 which describes the benefits and risks of the proposed treatment. If not, you will be offered a copy now. If you have any further questions, do ask – we are here to help you. You have the right to change your mind at any time, including after you have signed this form.

I agree to the procedure or course of treatment described on this form.

I understand that you cannot give me a guarantee that a particular person will perform the procedure. The person will, however, have appropriate experience.

I understand that I will have the opportunity to discuss the details of anaesthesia with an anaesthetist before the procedure, unless the urgency of my situation prevents this. (This only applies to patients having general or regional anaesthesia.)

I understand that any procedure in addition to those described on this form will only be carried out if it is necessary to save my life or to prevent serious harm to my health.

I have been told about additional procedures which may become necessary during my treatment. I have listed below any procedures **which I do not wish to be carried out** without further discussion. ....

....

....

Patient's signature .... Date ....

Name (PRINT) ....

A witness should sign below if the patient is unable to sign but has indicated his or her consent. Young people/children may also like a parent to sign here (see notes).

Signature .... Date ....

Name (PRINT) ....

Confirmation of consent (to be completed by a health professional when the patient is admitted for the procedure, if the patient has signed the form in advance)

On behalf of the team treating the patient, I have confirmed with the patient that s/he has no further questions and wishes the procedure to go ahead.

Signed .... Date ....
Name (PRINT) .... Job title ....

Important notes: (tick if applicable)

☐   See also advance directive/living will (eg Jehovah's Witness form)
☐   Patient has withdrawn consent (ask patient to sign /date here) ....

The form is detailed. It attempts to ensure that patients appreciate that they are entitled to ask questions and to demand explanations about what is to be done to them, and covers anaesthetic procedures as well as surgery. Patients are not passive recipients of what doctor thinks best. However, a form is no more than some evidence of what the patient has agreed to. What is important is the substance of what the patient is entitled to be told and has been told, and what is then done to him. Clearly any action expressly prohibited by the patient, that is additional procedures which on the form he states '*I do not wish to be carried out without further discussion*' would constitute a battery if imposed on the patient.

What sort of authority does the provision in the form about additional procedures necessary to save life or serious injury to health confer on the doctor? This would not affect liability in the cases discussed earlier, of the doctor who sterilised a patient in the course of minor gynaecological surgery or the surgeon who removed a woman's ovaries without her consent (see 5.1). Neither measure was immediately necessary to preserve the woman's health. The doctor is only authorised to carry out further surgery without which the patient's life or health is immediately at risk. A surgeon discovering advanced cancer of the womb while performing a curettage may be justified in performing an immediate hysterectomy. Delay might threaten the woman's life. A doctor discovering some malformation, or other non-life-threatening condition, must delay further surgery until his patient has the opportunity to offer her opinion.

The use of the model form is not compulsory within the NHS and practice varies widely. In private hospitals and clinics a quite different form may be used. What would be the effect of a form within which a patient consented to any procedure that the surgeon saw fit to embark on? In the absence of the clearest evidence that the patient fully understood the 'blank cheque' which he handed to his doctor, such a form will be virtually irrelevant. Any consent form is no more than one piece of evidence that the patient did, in fact, consent to what was done to him.[30] If the patient can show that despite the form he did not give any real consent to the procedure carried out, the surgeon will be liable in battery.

How much must the doctor tell the patient: real consent?

5.4 We have seen that for consent to be real the patient must be told what operation is to be performed and why it is to be done. The doctor certifies on the consent form that he has explained the proposed operation, investigation or treatment to the patient. What exactly must the doctor explain? All surgery under general anaesthetic entails some risk. Many forms of surgery and medical treatment carry further risk of harm, even if they are carried out with the greatest skill and competence. Patients have argued that if an operation entails an inherent risk then they cannot be said to have given a real consent to that operation if they were not told of the risk. They had inadequate information on which to make a proper decision. They could not give an 'informed consent' and therefore a claim in battery should lie. Alternatively, they argue that if a claim in battery does not lie, they ought to be able to sue for negligence. The doctor's duty of care encompasses giving adequate information and advice. If he has given the patient inadequate information

30   See *Chatterton v Gerson* [1981] 1 All ER 257.

and the patient agreed to a risky procedure from which injury did ensue, the doctor, it is argued, is responsible for that damage.

Let us look first at the argument that if risks or side-effects inherent in an operation are not disclosed, then the patient has not really consented at all and the surgeon is liable for battery. In *Chatterton v Gerson*,[31] Miss Chatterton pursued such a claim. She suffered excruciating pain in a post-operative scar. Dr Gerson proposed an operation, but the operation failed to relieve her symptoms. A second operation was carried out. Miss Chatterton was no better and subsequently lost all sensation in her right leg and foot with a consequent loss of mobility. She claimed that while Dr Gerson was in no way negligent in his conduct of the surgery, he failed to tell her enough for her to give her 'informed consent'. Her claim in battery failed. The judge said that a consent to surgery was valid providing that the patient was 'informed in broad terms of the nature of the procedure which is intended'. Any claim in relation to inadequacy of information about the risks or side-effects of treatment, or availability of alternative treatment, should be brought in negligence.

By contrast, a patient who agreed to an injection which she understood to be a routine post-natal vaccination, but which was in fact the controversial long-acting contraceptive Depo-Provera, succeeded in battery. Her doctor failed the test set in *Chatterton v Gerson*. He obtained her agreement to the injection leaving her totally unaware and indeed misleading her, albeit in good faith, as to the nature of what was being done to her.[32] A dentist who deliberately misled patients to persuade them to agree to unnecessary dental treatment was also held liable in battery. His fraud vitiated the apparent consent given him by his unfortunate patients.[33] A bogus doctor, who persuaded several women to allow him to examine their breasts, claiming that he was conducting research into breast cancer, was convicted of indecent assault.[34] The women's 'consent' depended on their belief that he had medical qualifications and that the contact to which they agreed had a proper medical purpose.

Other attempts to claim in battery, where the nature of what was to be done was honestly explained but the risks of the procedure were not, have failed just as Miss Chatterton's claim failed.[35] In *Sidaway v Royal Bethlem Hospital* in the Court of Appeal, Lord Donaldson said:

> It is only if the consent is obtained by fraud or misrepresentation of the *nature* [*emphasis added*] of what is to be done that it can be said that an apparent consent is not a true consent.[36]

---

[31] [1981] 1 All ER 257. The nature and purpose test for battery is cogently criticised by TK Feng, 'Failure of Medical Advice: Trespass or Negligence' [1987] 7 *Legal Studies* 149. And see A Maclean, 'The Doctrine of Informed Consent: Does it Exist and Has it Crossed the Atlantic?' (2004) 24 *Legal Studies* 386 at 398–401.

[32] See *Potts v North West Regional Health Authority* (1983) Guardian, 23 July.

[33] *Appleton v Garrett* [1996] PIQR P1. Contrast this with *R v Richardson (Diana)* (1998) 43 BMLR 21, CA (dentist acquitted of criminal assault even though she failed to inform her patients that she had been struck off the dental register).

[34] *R v Tabassum* [2000] Lloyd's Rep Med 404, CA.

[35] *Hills v Potter (note)* [1984] 1 WLR 641 at 653.

[36] [1984] 1 All ER 1018 at 1026 and *Freeman v Home Office (No 2)* [1984] 1 All ER 1036.

The House of Lords unanimously endorsed his views.[37] Lord Scarman, giving the most patient-oriented opinion, nonetheless declared:

> ... it would be deplorable to base the law in medical cases of this kind on the torts of assault and battery.[38]

The Canadian courts also view battery as an inappropriate remedy for inadequate counselling. The Canadian Chief Justice has said:

> I do not understand how it can be said that the consent was vitiated by failure of disclosure of risks as to make the surgery or other treatment an unprivileged, unconsented to and intentional invasion of the patient's bodily integrity ... unless there has been misrepresentation or fraud to secure consent to the treatment, a failure to disclose the attendant risks, however serious, should go to negligence rather than battery.[39]

It is easy to understand why courts shy away from finding doctors liable in battery. The word itself is emotive. Doctors resent being accused of 'battering' their patients, being equated with '... the mugger who assaults his victim'.[40] However, distinguishing between battery and no battery on the *Chatterton v Gerson* test is not easy. Consider the example of a patient tested for HIV without his consent.[41] He agrees to a blood test preparatory to surgery. He is never told that among the tests to be carried out on his blood is a test for HIV. Did he understand the nature and purpose of the test? He understood what would be done to him and that several tests would be carried out on his blood. Opinion about whether such a practice constitutes battery is divided.[42] Normally, express and detailed information about exactly what tests are proposed when blood is given is rarely sought or offered. Patients agree to tests so that doctors can find out what problems they may encounter and treat them safely. It is difficult to say that such patients, including the patient tested for HIV, do not understand in broad terms what is going on. Were some ruse employed to obtain consent the picture might be different. Imagine that a doctor suspects a patient is HIV positive and wants a test for that sole purpose. Fearing that the patient would refuse consent if asked outright, the doctor uses a pretext, for example, a suspicion of anaemia. Would you argue that the patient falls within the *Chatterton v Gerson* test, that his consent was obtained by fraud or misrepresentation? The difficulty is that what constitutes fraud is complex.

In the context of criminal law, the courts have tended to say that the fraud must deceive the victim about the very nature of what is being done to her.[43] The patient agreeing to the blood test, albeit believing the test is designed to check his red blood count, still understands what is being done. It may be that

37 *Sidaway v Board of Governors of the Bethlem Royal and the Maudsley Hospital* [1985] 1 All ER 643.
38 [1985] 1 All ER 643 at 650.
39 *Reibl v Hughes* (1980) 114 DLR (3d) 1.
40 See Maclean (2004) 24 *Legal Studies* 386 at 399.
41 See the lively discussion in JK Mason and GT Laurie, *Mason and McCall Smith's Law and Medical Ethics* (7th edn, 2006) OUP, pp 386–393.
42 Discussed elegantly in J Keown, 'The Ashes of AIDS and the Phoenix of Informed Consent' (1989) 52 *Modern Law Review* 790.
43 *R v Clarence* (1888) 22 QBD 23.

civil and criminal law adopt different tests of fraud. In the case where a dentist was prosecuted for assault because, unbeknown to her patients, she continued to practise when suspended from the dental register, the Court of Appeal quashed her conviction for criminal assault.[44] The patients were not misled about what was being done to them, or as to the identity of the accused. Nonetheless, Otton LJ condemned the accused's conduct as reprehensible and suggested that a civil claim for damages might well succeed.

A duty to advise

5.5 What is clear is that, where no question of misrepresentation arises, a claim based on failure to give a patient adequate information about proposed treatment lies in negligence. The doctor's duty of care to his patient undoubtedly includes a duty to give him careful advice and sufficient information upon which to reach a rational decision whether to accept or reject treatment. Lord Steyn[45] has emphasised that '... a patient's right to an appropriate warning from a surgeon when faced with surgery ought normatively to be regarded as an important right which must be given effective protection whenever possible'. The problem is, when is the doctor in breach of his duty to warn? In the famous (or infamous) case of *Bolam v Friern Hospital Management Committee*,[46] Mr Bolam agreed to electro-convulsive therapy to help improve his depression. He suffered fractures in the course of the treatment. The risk was known to his doctor, but he did not tell Mr Bolam. Mr Bolam alleged that the failure to warn him of the risk was negligent. The judge found that the amount of information given to Mr Bolam accorded with accepted medical practice in such cases and dismissed his claim. He added that even if Mr Bolam had proved that the doctor's advice was inadequate, he would only have succeeded if he could have further proved that, had he been that given that information, he would have refused consent to the treatment. The test of negligence was the test of responsible medical opinion. Other cases were even more favourable to the doctors. For instance, Lord Denning held it to be entirely for the individual doctor to decide what to tell his patient, even if the doctor went so far as to resort to what his Lordship termed 'a therapeutic lie'.[47]

The underlying trend in the English courts until recently was that 'doctor knew best'. Across the Atlantic, however, matters took a startlingly different turn. The doctrine of 'informed consent' was born. In *Canterbury v Spence*[48] a US court said that the 'prudent patient' test should prevail. Doctors must disclose to their patients any material risk inherent in a proposed line of treatment:

---

[44]   *R v Richardson (Diana)* (1998) 43 BMLR 21, CA.
[45]   *Chester v Afshar* [2004] UKHL 41 at para 17.
[46]   [1957] 2 All ER 118.
[47]   *Hatcher v Black* (1954) Times, 2 July; and see *O'Malley-Williams v Board of Governors of the National Hospital for Nervous Diseases* [1975] *British Medical Journal* 635.
[48]   (1972) 464 F 2D 772, 780.

A risk is material when a reasonable person, in what the physician knows or should know to be the patient's position, would be likely to attach significance to the risk or cluster of risks in deciding whether or not to forgo the proposed therapy.

The Canadian Supreme Court also rejected the 'professional medical standard' for determining how much the doctor must disclose. Emphasis was laid upon 'the patient's right to know what risks are involved in undergoing or forgoing surgery or other treatment'.[49] The Canadian court did allow that a particular patient might waive his right to know, might put himself entirely in the hands of the doctors. And they said that cases might arise where '… a particular patient may, because of emotional factors, be unable to cope with facts relevant to the recommended surgery or treatment and the doctor may, in such a case, be justified in withholding or generalising information as to which he would otherwise be required to be more specific'. The doctor could rely on a defence of therapeutic privilege. The High Court of Australia followed Canada in rejecting the *Bolam* test of professional opinion. In *Rogers v Whittaker*[50] failure to disclose a 1:14,000 chance of blindness in both eyes inherent in surgery was held negligent. The patient had made clear her concerns about risks of losing her sight altogether.

In England, invoking the transatlantic doctrine of informed consent, lawyers tried to breach the walls of medical silence. Miss Chatterton, who as we saw lost in battery, failed in negligence. The doctor, the judge said, did owe her a duty to counsel her as to any real risks inherent in the surgery proposed. He did not have to canvass every risk and in deciding what to tell the patient he could take into account '… the personality of the patient, the likelihood of misfortune and what in the way of warning is for the particular patient's welfare'. This standard Dr Gerson had met.

Sidaway

5.6 So what amounts to a 'real risk of misfortune inherent in the procedure'? The decision of the Law Lords in *Sidaway* remains a key part of the story. For several years, following an accident at work, Mrs Sidaway had endured persistent pain in her right arm and shoulder. Later the pain spread to her left arm. In 1960 she became the patient of Mr Falconer, an eminent neurosurgeon at the Maudsley Hospital. An operation relieved the pain for a while. By 1973, Mrs Sidaway was again in pain. She was admitted to the Maudsley Hospital and Mr Falconer diagnosed pressure on a nerve root as the cause of her pain. He decided to operate to relieve the pressure. Mrs Sidaway gave her consent to surgery. As a result of that operation Mrs Sidaway became severely disabled by partial paralysis.

Mrs Sidaway sued both Mr Falconer and the Maudsley Hospital. She did not suggest that the operation had been performed otherwise than skilfully and

49 *Reibl v Hughes* (1980) 114 DLR (3d) 1.
50 [1993] 4 Med LR 79; discussed in D Chalmers and R Schwartz, 'A Fair Dinkum Duty of Disclosure' (1993) 1 *Medical Law Review* 189.

carefully. Her complaint was as follows. The operation to which she agreed involved two specific risks over and above the risk inherent in any surgery under general anaesthesia. These were (1) damage to a nerve root, assessed as about a 2 per cent risk and (2) damage to the spinal cord, assessed as less than a 1 per cent risk. Alas for Mrs Sidaway, that second risk materialised and she suffered partial paralysis. She maintained that Mr Falconer never warned her of the risk of injury to the spinal cord. Throughout the long and expensive litigation, Mrs Sidaway's greatest handicap was that Mr Falconer died before the action came to trial. The courts were deprived of vital evidence as to exactly what the patient was told by her surgeon and what reasons, if any, he had for withholding information from her. The case had to proceed from the inference drawn by the trial judge that Mr Falconer would have followed his customary practice, that is he would have warned Mrs Sidaway in general terms of the possibility of injury to a nerve root but would have said nothing about any risk of damage to the spinal cord.

Ten years after the operation which left Mrs Sidaway paralysed, and seven years after Mr Falconer's death, the case reached the House of Lords.[51] The paucity of evidence about what actually happened when Mrs Sidaway and Mr Falconer discussed the proposed surgery rendered the case, as Lord Diplock put it, 'a naked question of legal principle'. What principle governed the doctor's obligation to advise patients and to warn of any risks inherent in surgery or treatment he recommended? The majority of their Lordships largely endorsed the traditional test enunciated in the case of Mr Bolam nearly 30 years before. The doctor's obligation to advise and warn his patient was part and parcel of his general duty of care owed to each individual patient. *Prima facie*, providing he conformed to a responsible body of medical opinion in deciding what to tell and what not to tell his patient, he discharged his duty properly. There being evidence that, while some neurosurgeons might warn some patients of the risk to the spinal cord, many chose not to, Mrs Sidaway's case was lost.

The *Sidaway* judgment, some of their Lordships said, should not be seen as endorsing the view that providing a doctor follows current medical practice in deciding what information to give his patients he will be immune from legal attack. The courts retain ultimate control of the scope of the doctor's obligation. First, for Lord Bridge and Lord Templeman, a crucial issue in Mrs Sidaway's case was that the risk of which she was not advised was a less than 1 per cent risk, and all the medical expert witnesses were agreed that it was a risk which many responsible neurosurgeons elected not to warn patients of. Had the risk been of greater statistical significance, their Lordships *might* have held in Mrs Sidaway's favour, even if expert medical witnesses supported non-disclosure. Lord Bridge gave as an example '… an operation involving a substantial risk of grave adverse consequences, for example [a] 10 per cent risk of a stroke from the operation'.[52] He went on to acknowledge that there might be cases where '… disclosure of a particular risk was so obviously

[51] *Sidaway v Board of Governors of the Bethlem Royal and the Maudsley Hospital* [1985] 1 All ER 643. In the High Court, Mrs Sidaway also sued for battery. Both claims were dismissed and she appealed on the issue of negligence alone.
[52] [1985] 1 All ER 643 at 663.

necessary to an informed choice on the part of the patient that no reasonably prudent medical man would fail to make it'. Second, for Lord Diplock and Lord Templeman a vital question in the case was that Mrs Sidaway had not expressly inquired of Mr Falconer what risks the surgery entailed. For Lord Diplock the case concerned solely what information the doctor must volunteer. Lord Templeman said that Mr Falconer could not be faulted for failing to give Mrs Sidaway information for which she did not ask.

What four out of five of the Law Lords in *Sidaway* agreed on was the rejection of the transatlantic test that what the patient should be told should be judged by what a reasonable patient would want to know; they demonstrated little enthusiasm for 'informed consent'.[53] Lord Scarman alone rejected current medical practice as the test of what a patient needed to be told. He dissented, and in a powerful judgment asserted the patient's right to know. The patient's right of self-determination, his right to choose what happens to his body, was the factor which to Lord Scarman made the issue of advice given to the patient distinct from other aspects of medical care. The doctor should be liable '... where the risk is such that in the court's view a prudent person in the patient's situation would have regarded it as significant'.[54] But, although the patient's right of self-determination distinguishes advice given from other stages in medical care, advice before treatment cannot be totally separated from the doctor's general duty to offer proper professional and competent service. Doctors, in Lord Scarman's view, should be to a certain extent protected by 'therapeutic privilege'. This would permit a doctor to withhold information if it could be shown that 'a reasonable medical assessment of the patient would have indicated to the doctor that disclosure would have posed a serious threat of psychological detriment to the patient'.[55] Lord Scarman recognised the right of a patient of sound understanding to be warned of material risks save in exceptional circumstances, yet he too found against Mrs Sidaway on the facts of the case. He held that she failed to establish on the evidence put forward by her counsel that the less than 1 per cent risk was such that a prudent patient would have considered it significant.

After Sidaway

5.7 The decision in *Sidaway* has never been formally overruled. Paradoxically, Lord Scarman's dissent comes closer to expressing the principles that today govern information disclosure than the speeches of the majority. Two judgments of the Court of Appeal[56] shortly after *Sidaway* appeared to entrench the *Bolam* test and endorse the professional standard as the touchstone for information disclosure. Patients were to be told what doctors

---

53   In the Court of Appeal, Dunn LJ declared that, 'The concept of informed consent forms no part of English law': *Sidaway v Board of Governors of the Royal Bethlem and Maudsley Hospital* [1984] 1 All ER 1018 at 1030.

54   [1985] 1 All ER 643 at 654.

55   [1985] 1 All ER 643 at 654.

56   *Blyth v Bloomsbury Health Authority* [1993] 4 Med LR 151; *Gold v Haringey Health Authority* [1987] 2 All ER 888, CA. See also *Moyes v Lothian Health Board* [1990] 1 Med LR 463.

thought they should know.[57] For nearly two decades, informed consent seemed to have no place in English law.[58] *Chester v Afshar*[59] signals that, in theory at least, the judiciary has belatedly acknowledged informed consent. Lord Steyn says simply:

> Surgery performed without the informed consent of the patient is unlawful. The court is the final arbiter of what constitutes informed consent.[60]

The trigger for change towards a more patient-oriented test came initially from the doctors themselves. Professional practice changed markedly. Doctors now endorse much more open disclosure of risks. Guidance from the General Medical Council[61] directed doctors to '... take appropriate steps to find out what patients want to know and ought to know about their condition and its treatment'. The professional standard may, in a number of cases, now demand that professionals provide patients with the information which prudent patients might want.[62]

The courts incrementally became more ready to require a fuller disclosure of information about treatment risks and options for patients. For example, in *Smith v Tunbridge Wells Health Authority*[63] a claim was brought by a 28-year-old man who was not warned of the risk of impotence inherent in rectal surgery. His claim succeeded despite expert evidence that a body of surgeons did not warn patients of that risk. The judge, citing Lord Bridge in *Sidaway,* found that failure to warn a patient of a risk of such importance to him was 'neither reasonable nor responsible'. Mere evidence of a medical practice did not counter allegations of negligence. That practice must be reasonable in the context of providing patients with an informed choice. As we shall see in Chapter 7, in *Bolitho v City Hackney Health Authority*[64] the House of Lords stressed that, in relation to all claims of negligence against doctors, expert evidence advanced to support the defendant's case that he acted without negligence must be shown to be responsible. To rebut negligence a practice must have a 'logical and defensible' basis. In *Bolitho*, Lord Browne-Wilkinson seemed at one stage to suggest that in his clarification of the *Bolam* test he was not concerned with cases about informed consent.[65] That statement was not designed to exempt consent claims from judicial scrutiny,

---

[57] Whether or not they asked questions (see *Blyth v Bloomsbury Health Authority* [1993] 4 Med LR 151) and whether or not the medical intervention was therapeutic or non-therapeutic (see *Gold v Haringey Health Authority* [1987] 2 All ER 888, CA).

[58] See MA Jones, 'Informed Consent and Other Fairy Stories' (1999) 7 *Medical Law Review* 103.

[59] [2004] UKHL 41.

[60] [2004] UKHL 41 at para 14.

[61] GMC, *Seeking Patients' Consent: The Ethical Considerations* (1999).

[62] But see Maclean (2004) 24 *Legal Studies* 386 for a more sceptical view, and one which is shared by E Jackson, 'Informed Consent to Medical Treatment and the Impotence of Tort' in SAM McLean (ed), *First Do No Harm* (2006) Ashgate, p 273.

[63] [1994] 5 Med LR 334; and see *McAllister v Lewisham and North Southwark Health Authority* [1994] 5 Med LR 343; *Newall and Newall v Goldenberg* [1995] 6 Med LR 371; *Williamson v East London & City Health Authority* (1997) 41 BMLR 85; *Lybert v Warrington Health Authority* [1996] 7 Med LR 71, CA.

[64] [1998] AC 232.

[65] [1998] AC 232 at 243.

but simply to acknowledge that case law stretching back to Lord Bridge in *Sidaway* already allowed scrutiny of information disclosure practice.[66]

That the *Bolitho* approach is applicable to informed consent claims is confirmed in *Pearce v United Bristol Healthcare NHS Trust*.[67] Mrs Pearce, who was expecting her sixth child, was two weeks past her due date of delivery. She discussed the possibility of induction with her obstetrician who warned her of the risks of induction and Caesarean surgery, but did not tell her that there was a 0.1–0.2 per cent risk of stillbirth associated with non-intervention. Mrs Pearce's child was stillborn and she alleged that failure to warn her of the risk of stillbirth was negligent. The Court of Appeal held that she had not established negligence. The very slight risk of stillbirth arising from non-intervention, compared to the risks of intervention, was not a risk which the defendants were negligent in failing to disclose, especially in the light of Mrs Pearce's distressed condition at the time of the consultation. What is of interest in *Pearce* is that Lord Woolf's judgment in the doctors' favour departs radically from a simple test of whether the information offered Mrs Pearce conformed to a reasonable body of expert opinion. Relying on both Lord Bridge in *Sidaway* and Lord Browne-Wilkinson in *Bolitho*, Lord Woolf declared that '… if there is a *significant risk which would affect the judgement of a* reasonable patient, then in the normal course it is the responsibility of a doctor to inform the patient of that significant risk, if the information is needed so that the patient can determine for him or herself as to what course she should adopt' (*emphasis added*). Lord Woolf suggests that the reasonable doctor must tell the patient what the reasonable patient would want to know.[68]

There are critics who view Lord Woolf's judgment in *Pearce* rather differently. The view stated above might be one '… seeing the judgment through rose-tinted spectacles'.[69] Does Lord Woolf use 'politically correct' language to conceal continuing deference to medical opinion? In future cases how will significant risk be defined? And, ultimately, Mrs Pearce's claim failed as have so many others. Nonetheless *Pearce* is a step in the right direction.

Causation

5.8 Proving that the doctor failed to give the patient a sufficient warning of some possible adverse risk of side-effect is not of itself enough to ensure that a claim in negligence succeeds. The patient must also establish that, had she received such a warning, she would not have consented to the treatment in question. She must show that the doctor's negligent failure caused the injury of which she complains. Despite the grand statements about principles of

---

[66] See M Brazier and J Miola, 'Bye-Bye Bolam: A Medical Litigation Revolution?' (2000) 8 *Medical Law Review* 85 at 107–110.
[67] [1998] 48 BMLR 118, CA. And see *AB v Leeds Teaching Hospital NHS Trust* [2004] EWHC 644 (QB).
[68] Brazier and Miola (2000) 8 *Medical Law Review* 85 at 110. And see *Wyatt v Curtis* [2003] EWCA Civ 1779.
[69] See Maclean (2004) 24 *Legal Studies* 386 at 408–409.

informed consent, it was a narrow question of causation that directly concerned the Law Lords in *Chester v Afshar*.[70]

Miss Chester, a former journalist, had suffered from lower back pain for many years. She was referred to Mr Afshar, a consultant neurosurgeon, who recommended surgery. Miss Chester, a private patient, consented to the operation. Unfortunately, the operation resulted in cauda equina syndrome. Miss Chester suffered significant nerve damage, and became partially paralysed. Miss Chester's claim that Mr Afshar had not warned her of the 1–2 per cent risk of cauda equina syndrome was accepted by the trial judge. He held that the defendant was negligent in failing to give Miss Chester such a warning.[71] The question before the House of Lords was did Mr Afshar's negligence cause Miss Chester's paralysis? Miss Chester did not argue that, had she received such a warning, she would probably never have gone ahead with the operation. She did not say that a risk of paralysis was just too great and she would put up with the pain. Nor did she try to claim that she would have sought out a different surgeon, or a different form of operation.[72] She said only that, had she been properly warned, she would not have gone ahead with surgery on that day. She would have taken time to reflect, to seek a second opinion and consult her friends. The House of Lords found in her favour by a majority of 3:2.

The dissenting judges, Lord Bingham and Lord Hoffmann, applied the conventional principles of causation. Miss Chester had failed to show that, properly warned, she would have been likely to have refused to have surgery. She would most likely have had the operation, albeit some time later. She would have been subject to just the same risk. Her '… injury would have been as liable to occur whenever the surgery was performed and whoever performed it'.[73] The majority considered that the patient's right to autonomy and dignity, the right to make an informed choice, justified '… a narrow and modest departure from traditional causation principles'.[74] Should Miss Chester lose her claim, in conformity with the normal rules on causation, Lord Hope argued that the duty on doctors to warn patients of risks of surgery would be rendered '… useless in the cases where it may be needed most'.[75] Lord Hope stressed that many patients might find a decision about whether to go ahead with risky treatment difficult. They could not with hindsight say definitively 'I would have said yes or no'. Many people might share Miss Chester's ambivalence. Patients who would find such a decision difficult should not be deprived of a remedy. Hence he agreed with the majority to modify the rules of causation, as he saw it 'modestly'. Lord Bingham saw any departure from those usual rules as 'substantial and unjustified'.[76]

---

[70]   [2004] UKHL 41, HL.
[71]   The Court of Appeal refused leave to challenge the trial judge's findings of fact.
[72]   See *Chappel v Hart* [1999] 2 LRC 341.
[73]   [2004] UKHL 41, HL at para 8.
[74]   [2004] UKHL 41, HL at para 24, per Lord Steyn.
[75]   [2004] UKHL 41, HL at para 86, per Lord Hope.
[76]   [2004] UKHL 41, HL at para 9. And see S Green, 'Coherence of Medical Negligence Cases: A Game of Doctors and Purses' (2006) 14 *Medical Law Review* 1.

What is informed consent and does it really matter?

5.9 Doctors' fears of litigation[77] surrounding 'consent' are understandable. The sheer difficulty of recalling, reviewing and interpreting conversations which took place years ago in a context a million miles from a courtroom should not be underestimated (though none of these factors should be allowed to override the importance of providing patients with comprehensible and comprehensive information). Information is a prerequisite of meaningful choice. The term 'informed consent' informs popular culture as much as law and medical practice. But what does it mean?[78] The term tends to be used to signal how much information must be offered to a patient, yet the two words of themselves do nothing to guide the reader to discern how much is enough. The Human Fertilisation and Embryology Act 1990 opts for the term 'effective consent'. The Human Tissue Act 2004 prefers 'appropriate consent'. Neither phrase helps us. 'Effective' for what or 'appropriate' for what? Perhaps the courts can do no more than set broad parameters to indicate to doctors that they must seek to ensure that their patients know enough about any treatment proposed to be able to choose. Professional practice will kick-start that process: what is the collective experience in relation to what patients want to know and need to be told? But professional practice is only the first stage in a process. The doctor must reflect on how she might regard the proposed treatment if she were the patient. A risk of 1 per cent is statistically small, but if that risk is of paralysis, many people would want to know, so that they, not their doctors, make the crucial risk-benefit assessment. Then, the particular circumstances of the patient must be considered. A less than 1 per cent risk of acquiring a hoarse voice after throat surgery might not concern many of us, particularly if the surgery were to relieve a great deal of pain. An aspiring opera singer might take a different view.

Difficulties in defining informed consent may also have played their role in the long delay in its incorporation into English law. But definition was not the only obstacle to progress. Lord Diplock in *Sidaway*[79] suggested information might be counterproductive:

(1)   Patients, he contended, do not want more information.
(2)   Patients could not understand that information if they were offered it.
(3)   More information would lead to patients 'irrationally' refusing much-needed treatment.

None of these reasons are sound.[80] Surveys show that most patients do want more information. A right to more information does not mean information must be forced on the unwilling patient. If a patient says, 'Doctor, it's up to

---

[77]   It has been argued that informed consent claims are the thin end of the wedge, opening the door for no-fault liability: see A Meisel, 'The Expansion of Liability for Medical Accidents: From Negligence to Strict Liability by Way of Informed Consent' (1977) 56 *Nebraska Law Review* 51.

[78]   For an impressive analysis of the question, see Maclean (2004) 24 *Legal Studies* 386.

[79]   [1985] 1 All ER 643 at 658–659. See M Brazier, 'Patient Autonomy and Consent to Treatment: The Role of the Law? (1987) 7 *Legal Studies* 169.

[80]   See in particular, President's Commission for the study of Ethical Problems in Medicine, *Making Health Care Decisions* (1982) US Govt Printing Office, and '*What Are My Chances Doctor?*': A *Review of Clinical Risks* (1986) Office of Health Economics.

you. I don't want to know any more about this operation,' a prudent patient test does not require that he be held down and forced to listen. Patients do have difficulties understanding medical details. The remedy is to teach doctors how to communicate more effectively. As for 'irrational' treatment refusals, there is no evidence to support the contention that more information leads to more patients refusing treatment. And how is 'irrationality' to be judged? A woman is told that radical mastectomy will maximise her prospects of recovery from breast cancer. She knows that if she loses a breast her husband will leave her and that psychologically she is unable to cope with the necessary mutilation. Who can say she is 'irrational' if she opts for the statistically less 'safe' option of lumpectomy?

Undue emphasis on statistical risk bedevils debate on how much and what sort of information patients should be given about proposed treatment. The likelihood of a risk materialising is just one factor in a decision about what treatment to undergo if you are ill. The impact of the risk on the way that an individual lives her life is equally significant. It might be thought that an elderly man facing rectal surgery of the same sort as the operation involved in *Smith v Tunbridge Wells Health Authority*[81] would contemplate a small risk of impotence with greater equanimity than the 28-year-old Mr Smith. However, who but the gentleman in question can judge that risk to his own remaining hopes in life?

We have argued that the standard determining how much patients should be told about treatment needs to be patient-centred. As English law moves towards a more patient-centred test, we must also ask whether doctors may be able to rely on a defence of therapeutic privilege. Might a defendant surgeon be able to say, in relation to a very elderly patient whom she failed to warn of a small risk of impotence, 'The patient is highly nervous and exaggerates risks. If he does not have the surgery he will be doubly incontinent and have to go into a home. I just don't think he could cope with the information'? It is clear that any such defence must be based on cogent reasons relating to the welfare of that particular patient. In *AB v Leeds Teaching Hospital NHS Trust*,[82] it was argued that giving families information about the retention of organs from their dead children would cause unnecessary distress, and might result in psychiatric harm. Gage J rejected a blanket plea of therapeutic privilege, saying of the defence:

> In so far as it involved the exercise of a therapeutic privilege it was one that does not appear to have been exercised on a case by case basis.

Fiduciary obligations

5.10 The tort of negligence remains a clumsy mechanism for vindicating a patient's right to information. Battery is inappropriate both because of its emotive language and because it may exclude oral drug therapies. In

---

[81] [1994] 5 Med LR 334.
[82] [2004] EWHC 644 (QB).

Canada,[83] courts have sought to reclassify doctor-patient relationships by adapting the legal concept of the fiduciary relationship to embrace the doctor and her patient.[84] Within such a relationship of trust the doctor's duty would be to make available to the patient that information which it seems likely that individual patients would need to make an informed choice on treatment. Such a change is desirable not just to endorse patient's rights but also to enhance patient care.[85] Full participation in treatment by the patient, an alliance between patient and doctor, improves the quality of health care.[86] Interestingly, growing numbers of doctors are moving towards this view. So far English courts have found little to recommend a departure from established torts to a more innovative fiduciary approach.[87]

Does it matter who operates?

5.11 As important to many patients as what the operation entails may be the question of who operates. If a patient agrees to surgery believing eminent Consultant X will operate on him, is his consent invalidated if Registrar Y operates? Where a private patient contracts with Consultant X that he will operate, the consultant is in breach of contract if he substitutes someone else.

Within the NHS the patient would have to show that his consent was conditional on X operating. He would not have agreed to the surgery if anyone else proposed it. In practice, consent forms used within the NHS expressly provide that no assurance is given that any particular doctor will operate. A patient cannot complain if the registrar operates. If the registrar lacked the experience to perform a particular operation, the patient will be able to sue him and the consultant if harm ensues. The patient can sue the registrar for his lack of competence. He can sue the consultant for failure to provide proper supervision and for allowing an inadequately qualified member of the team to operate.

In 1984, it was reported that a vet was allowed by a surgeon friend to remove a patient's gall bladder. A patient operated on by a vet will have a claim in battery against the vet, however competent he may have proved to be. The patient agreed to a qualified doctor operating on him;[88] he no more agreed to surgery by a vet than to surgery by the authors of this book. An operation performed by a medical student will give rise to a claim in negligence if the

---

[83] *McInerney v MacDonald* (1992) 93 DLR (4th) 415; *Norberg v Wynrib* (1992) 92 DLR (4th) 449.

[84] Alas, such a proposition was rejected by both the Court of Appeal and the Law Lords in *Sidaway* and by the Australian High Court in *Breen v Williams* (1996) 70 ALTR 772. See Brazier (1987) 7 *Legal Studies* 169 at 189–191.

[85] See A Grubb, 'The Doctor as Fiduciary' [1994] *Current Legal Problems* 112; P Bartlett, 'Doctors as Fiduciaries' [1997] 5 *Medical Law Review* 193; M Brazier and M Lobjoit, 'Fiduciary Relationship: An Ethical Approach and a Legal Concept' in R Bennett and C Erin (eds), *HIV and AIDS Testing, Screening and Confidentiality* (1999) OUP, p 170.

[86] See H Teff, 'Consent to Medical Procedures, Paternalism, Self-Determination or Therapeutic Alliance' (1985) 101 *Law Quarterly Review* 432.

[87] *Sidaway v Royal Bethlem Hospital* [1985] 1 All ER 643 at 650–651; *R v Mid-Glamorgan FHSA, ex p Martin* [1995] 1 All ER 356, CA.

[88] See *R v Tabassum* [2000] Lloyd's Rep Med 404, CA; discussed further at 5.4 above.

student is not competent. A claim in battery may also lie if the patient was not expressly informed about the proposal to allow a student to operate. He consented to an operation and accepted, if he signed the standard form, that no particular practitioner undertook to operate. He consented to surgery performed by a practitioner, not an 'apprentice'. Teaching hospitals play a vital role and the public interest requires that medical students train on real people. Never the less, any contact with a patient on the part of a medical student requires the patient's consent.

Increasingly, patients are concerned about the record and experience of whoever operates on them, even lofty consultants. How does their surgeon's record of success compare to his peers? Do his mortality rates exceed the norm? Has he been fully trained in this procedure? (As an example, evidence that surgeons began to practise laparascopic procedures ('keyhole surgery') without adequate training was depressingly common.[89]) Should the law oblige each doctor to provide information about his own background and experience? Patients are entitled to competent care. The medical profession has an obligation to monitor the standards attained by doctors launching into, or continuing to perform, procedures that they are not able to carry out with competence. 'Informed consent' is unlikely to be a fruitful means of attaining these ends. If Dr X has a 4 per cent failure rate in relation to procedure A, and Dr Y a 5 per cent rate, those who are able to make choices will opt for X. The less articulate patient in a weaker bargaining position will be treated by Y. Nor is Y necessarily the poorer doctor. If Y works in a deprived area, a 1 per cent difference in outcome may be more than explained by the poorer state of health of his patients before they enter hospital. More and more league tables are now published which will include each surgeon's mortality rate.

Emergencies

5.12 So far in this chapter, we have discussed the patient in a fit state to give consent himself. When the patient is unconscious, treatment may have to be given immediately, before the patient can be revived and consulted. She may have been wheeled into Casualty after an accident. He may have agreed to Operation X, in the course of which the surgeon discovers a rampaging tumour needing immediate excision. Where there is no available evidence of the patient's own wishes in such circumstances, section 5 of the Mental Capacity Act 2005 grants to doctors a general authority to act in the best interests of the patient and do whatever is immediately necessary to preserve life and prevent any deterioration in health.[90] The doctor can invoke the defence of necessity. Such a defence is not exclusive to doctors. The bystanders who rush to the aid of the unconscious accident victim and administer first aid, the ambulance crew who bring him into Casualty, are equally protected from any claim in battery.

---

[89]   See B Mahendra, 'The Practitioner – Doc Brief' (1995) 145 *New Law Journal* 1475.
[90]   See below in Chapter 6.

Once the immediate threat to a patient's life has passed, other decisions may have to be taken before he regains consciousness. In practice, when a patient is unconscious or otherwise incapable of consenting to treatment himself, the response of the hospital staff is to consult, when possible, with the patient's relatives or friends. What legal validity has a consent given by the relatives of an adult? The answer is none. Consulting relatives is courteous, but is legally significant solely in that as a matter of evidence it establishes that the doctor's consideration of the patient's best interests has been adequately informed as required by the Mental Capacity Act 2005.[91]

One difficult problem arises when some (but inconclusive) evidence is forthcoming about the unconscious patient's own wishes. A patient is wheeled into hospital unconscious and needs an immediate blood transfusion. His wife says, truthfully, that he is a Jehovah's Witness and would refuse a transfusion. Can the doctor lawfully give a transfusion? The procedure is necessary, but the doctor knows the patient would be likely to refuse it. In *Malette v Shulman*,[92] a Canadian case, a young woman was brought unconscious into Casualty. She carried with her a card clearly stating that she was a Jehovah's Witness and that she would in no circumstances consent to a blood transfusion – even if her life was in danger. The Canadian court held that the doctor who administered a transfusion committed a battery. There was in that case no room for doubt that the patient had taken pains to ensure that no doctor should be in doubt of her refusal of blood in any contingency. Attempts to argue that a refusal of treatment must be 'informed' by knowledge of the actual circumstances of treatment were rejected.[93] As we have seen in *Re T (Adult: Refusal of Medical Treatment)*,[94] the English Court of Appeal overruled an apparent objection by T to transfusion. The facts of the cases are markedly different. The evidence that T truly and independently objected to transfusion was shaky. Mrs Malette's convictions were beyond doubt.

The validity of such advance directives is now governed by sections 24 and 25 of the Mental Capacity Act 2005. As we shall see at 6.13, the statute may not be much help if the essence of the question is, did the patient voluntarily and with full capacity make the initial advance decision? One matter is clarified. To be effective to refuse life-sustaining treatment, any advance decision must be both in writing and witnessed.[95]

---

91 See s 4(7) of the Mental Capacity Act 2005.
92 (1988) 63 OR (2d) 243 (Ontario High Court).
93 Discussed in (1990) 5 *Professional Negligence* 118.
94 [1992] 4 All ER 649, CA; discussed above at 5.2.
95 Mental Capacity Act 2005, s 24(5) and (6).

Chapter 6

COMPETENCE, CONSENT AND COMPULSION

6.1 In Chapter 5, the principles relating to consent to treatment by competent adults were examined. This chapter looks at two other dimensions of consent to medical treatment. When an adult is incapable of deciding for herself whether or not to agree to treatment, how can treatment be lawfully authorised on her behalf? If an adult refuses to agree to treatment, can that refusal ever be overruled, either on the grounds that the patient 'irrationally' refused treatment which was in her interests or because, untreated, her physical or mental condition threatens the safety of other people?

The law relating to decision-making on behalf of people who lack mental capacity is now to be found in the Mental Capacity Act 2005.[1] This Act endured a lengthy period of gestation. In 1995, the Law Commission made proposals to reform the existing law.[2] It recommended a new statute to provide a 'code' addressing the many complex questions raised by the care of people who cannot care for themselves. This 'code' should encompass all the different needs of patients, not just health care needs. If an elderly person develops dementia, decisions have to be made about where he should live – whether he needs to move to a nursing home, what happens to his house – just as much as what medical treatment he receives. Social care and medical care cannot be divorced from each other. Eleven years later,[3] after further consultation,[4] the Mental Capacity Act finally becomes law in a far from wholly satisfactory state.

Doctors and nurses caring for a patient who lacks capacity to consent to treatment on her own behalf confront an awkward dilemma. What does the law allow and require them to do when a patient is chronologically aged 30,

---

[1] The Act is due to come fully into force by October 2007.
[2] Law Commission Report No 231, *Mental Incapacity* (1995) HMSO is extensively reviewed in a dedicated edition of the *Medical Law Review*: see (1994) 2 *Medical Law Review* 1.
[3] The Scottish Parliament acted more speedily: see the Adults with Incapacity (Scotland) Act 2000; JK Mason and GT Laurie, *Mason and McCall Smith's Law and Medical Ethics* (7th edn, 2006) OUP, pp 367–368.
[4] See Lord Chancellor's Department, *Who Decides? Making Decisions on Behalf of Mentally Incapacitated Adults* (1997) Cm 3803, and the Government's response, *Making Decisions* (1999) Cm 3803.

but has such severe learning disabilities that she is unable to make decisions about her medical care? Once a person reaches 18, the age of majority, no one else, be he next of kin or a professional carer such as a social worker, can consent to treatment on her behalf. The doctor is faced with a patient who cannot herself give the consent required to make treatment lawful, and so not a battery, and there may be no one else who can lawfully act as the patient's proxy. Not to treat the patient at all would be inhumane and a breach of the duty of care owed to every patient. If a patient's physical condition threatens her life, or grave injury to her health, a defence of emergency might justify necessary treatment, just as it does when an otherwise competent patient is wheeled unconscious into Casualty.[5] What if there is no grave emergency? An elderly lady with dementia suffers from cataracts. A middle-aged patient with severe learning disabilities has a hernia. A 19-year-old girl with severe learning disabilities is found to be pregnant. None of these cases are life-threatening emergencies, yet the patients' families and their doctors may agree that the patients would be 'better off' with treatment. It is these kinds of questions that the Mental Capacity Act 2005 now addresses. Much of the controversy surrounding the Act arose from misplaced fears that it could be used to deny vulnerable patients life-sustaining treatment, that it introduced euthanasia 'by the back door'.[6] As we shall see, in most instances, the 2005 Act is concerned with more mundane matters and its major importance is in providing a framework for making decisions on behalf of those who cannot determine their own medical and social care.

In considering how English law should address the dilemmas posed by those who are unable to make their own decisions about health care, proper account must be taken of human rights law. However well intentioned, non-consensual treatment is in a sense still compulsory treatment. In order to treat a patient, especially if she is actively objecting to treatment, some element of restraint or detention may also be necessary.[7] Could such treatment violate Article 3 of the European Convention on Human Rights? The European Court of Human Rights set out some ground rules in *Herczegfalvy v Austria*.[8] The court emphasised the vulnerability and powerlessness of patients lacking mental capacity. Treatment could lawfully be imposed on a patient where he is entirely incapable of deciding for himself and where such treatment was a 'therapeutic necessity'. Where therapeutic necessity was conclusively established, the 'compulsory' treatment should not be regarded as inhumane or degrading.

Article 5 of the Convention protects the right to liberty. While Article 5(4)(e) allows for the detention of 'persons of unsound mind', we shall see that English law was found wanting in the legal protection offered to patients lacking mental capacity who are hospitalised without either their own consent or any appropriate independent authorisation.[9]

---

5   See *F v West Berkshire Health Authority* [1989] 2 All ER 545, HL; and see s 5 of the Mental Capacity Act 2005.
6   D Mason, 'Euthanasia by the Back Door?' (2004) 154 *New Law Journal* 321.
7   Extending in some instances to the use of 'reasonable force': see *Norfolk and Norwich NHS Trust v W* [1996] 2 FLR 613.
8   (1993) 15 EHRR 437, ECtHR.
9   See *HL v United Kingdom* (2004) 40 EHRR 761, discussed below at 6.8.

The Mental Capacity Act 2005 must be distinguished from the Mental Health Act 1983.[10] The 1983 Act regulates treatment for mental illness allowing (*inter alia*) for compulsory treatment and detention. Many people who may be mentally ill do not lack mental capacity. Few of those who lack mental capacity are eligible for compulsory treatment under the Mental Health Act 1983. There is some overlap between the two statutes which we will seek to address later. To make the reader's life more difficult, a third draft of a controversial new Mental Health Bill is now before Parliament.[11] This Bill seeks to amend the 1983 Act introducing, among other measures, provisions to broaden the definition of mental disorder and powers to allow compulsory supervision in the community for a much greater range of patients.

Not altogether new

6.2 Before looking in more detail at the provisions of the Mental Capacity Act 2005, we should note that in many respects the statute codifies existing case law. There are few radical changes in legal principle. The test of mental capacity remains much the same. 'Best interests' continues to be the benchmark against which lawful treatment of a patient lacking capacity is normally to be judged. Earlier case law remains relevant to illustrate how the Act will work. There are important changes in practice. A person can now, via a lasting power of attorney, appoint a proxy to make medical and personal decisions for him should he lose mental capacity. A court can exceptionally appoint a deputy (a kind of guardian) to act for a patient. A new Court of Protection oversees the framework of the Act. Above all, what the 2005 Act should do is offer a uniform and comprehensive framework to help decision-making on behalf of people lacking mental capacity in all aspects of their lives. Further guidance on the interpretation and application of the Act will be found in an extensive Code of Practice.[12] The Code will not add any new legal requirements, but will provide guidance on the Act. Some, including (amongst others) court-appointed deputies, donees of a lasting power of attorney and people working in a professional capacity (such as doctors and social workers), will come under a legal duty to have regard to its provisions.[13] Failure to comply with the Code will be taken into account in any relevant legal proceedings.

The threshold of capacity

6.3 The first question that needs to be addressed is how the law decides whether or not a person has the mental capacity to make his own decisions about medical treatment. Three different sorts of test could be used. A status test could assess intelligence, and determine that all who fell below the

---

[10] See P Bartlett and R Sandland, *Mental Health Law: Policy and Practice* (2nd edn, 2003) OUP; E Jackson, *Medical Law: Text, Cases and Materials* (2006) OUP, Chapter 7.

[11] HL Bill 1, introduced 16 November 2006.

[12] At the time of writing, the final Code has not been approved: see Department for Constitutional Affairs, *Mental Capacity Act 2005 Draft Code of Practice* (CP 05/06).

[13] Mental Capacity Act 2005, s 42(4) and (5).

requisite 'score' were incapable, and all above were capable. A status test would thus designate a person as competent or incompetent for all legal purposes. An outcome test would judge the capacity of the decision-maker by the rationality or wisdom of the decision made. Neither test has ever found favour with English law, which prefers a functional test. The functional test, endorsed in case law, is retained in the Mental Capacity Act 2005. The relevant question becomes whether X enjoys the necessary understanding to embark on the particular enterprise in question – be it entering a contract, making a will, getting married or consenting to medical treatment. Consider the illuminating case of *In the Estate of Park*.[14] Mr Park, an elderly man who had previously suffered a severe stroke, married his second wife one morning and that afternoon he executed a new will. He died soon afterwards. His family challenged the validity of the marriage. His widow challenged the will. He was found to be mentally-competent to marry, but to lack the necessary mental capacity to make a will. His impaired understanding and reasoning power remained sufficient for him to grasp what was entailed in marriage, but his confusion and loss of memory disabled him from having the necessary recollection of his properties and his obligations to make a will.

The application of the functional test to consent to medical treatment was well illustrated in *Re C*.[15] C was detained in a special hospital. He had been diagnosed as suffering from chronic paranoid schizophrenia. In 1993, he developed severe problems with a grossly infected leg. Doctors judged his life might be at risk if they did not amputate the leg below the knee. Conservative treatment had no better than a 15 per cent prospect of success. C refused to consent to surgery. He sought an injunction to prevent doctors amputating the leg without his express consent. There was no doubt C was mentally ill. He suffered from a number of delusions, including a fixed belief that he himself had had a glittering career in medicine. None the less, Thorpe J found that C was competent to make his own decision on the surgery in question, and granted the injunction C sought. The test for mental capacity in medical treatment involved three stages:

(1)   Can the patient take in and retain treatment information?
(2)   Does he believe it?
(3)   Can he weigh that information and make a decision?

Despite his delusions, C remained capable of understanding what he was told about the proposed treatment and, in particular, he comprehended the risk of death consequent on refusing surgery.

Re C indicates that bizarre beliefs or behaviour should not necessarily result in a finding that a person lacks capacity. However, what others perceive as irrational delusions may influence a judge. Consider *NHS Trust v T (Adult Patient: Refusal of Medical Treatment)*.[16] T suffered from borderline personality disorder and frequently self-harmed. She tended to become severely

---

[14]   [1954] P 112.
[15]   [1994] 1 All ER 819. Compare the decision of Thorpe J (that C retained capacity) with that of Kay J in *R v Collins and Ashworth Hospital Authority ex p Brady* [2000] Lloyd's Rep Med 355.
[16]   [2004] EWHC 1279 (Fam).

anaemic. T sought to execute an advance directive prohibiting the administration of blood transfusions. She spoke of her blood as evil, contaminating any new blood transfused into her. The judge said that irrational decisions should not be equated with lack of capacity. None the less he found that Miss T's view of blood as evil constituted such a 'misconception of reality' as to indicate incompetence.

The *Re C* test forms the basis of the test of capacity within the Mental Capacity Act 2005. Section 1 provides that a person must be assumed to have capacity unless proven otherwise. No-one is to be treated as unable to make a decision unless all practical steps have been attempted to help him to do so. A person is not to be treated as lacking capacity because he makes an unwise decision.[17] Inability to make a decision must relate to an impairment of, or a disturbance in the functioning of, the mind or brain, which may be permanent or temporary.[18] Inability to make a decision depends on establishing that the person is unable:[19]

  (a)   to understand the information relevant to the decision,
  (b)   to retain that information,
  (c)   to use or weigh that information as part of the process of making the decision, or
  (d)   to communicate his decision (whether by talking, using sign language, or any other means).[20]

The 2005 Act directs that what must be assessed is essentially the patient's capacity to understand what is at stake and act on that information. The rationality of the decision itself should not determine the capacity of the decision-maker. However, when doctors profoundly disagree with a patient's decision, they may be tempted to suggest that the patient lacks capacity. Butler-Sloss P warned against the dangers of succumbing to such temptation in *B v An NHS Trust*.[21] Ms B was a tetraplegic patient who sought to have the ventilator keeping her alive switched off. Her doctors challenged her capacity to make such a decision, citing alleged ambivalence in her views, her lack of understanding of other options proposed to her, and supposed depression. Butler-Sloss P found that Ms B retained full mental capacity despite her desperate plight. She warned that:

> It is most important that those considering the issue should not confuse the question of mental capacity with the nature of the decision made by the patient, however grave the consequences. The view of the patient may reflect a difference in values rather than an absence of competence.[22]

---

[17]   Section 1(4).
[18]   Section 2(1).
[19]   Section 3.
[20]   See *Re AK (Adult Patient) (Medical Treatment: Consent)* [2001] 1 FLR 129, CA. AK was in the terminal stages of motor neurone disease. He could communicate only by barely blinking an eye to answer yes or no to questions. He indicated that he wished doctors to switch off the ventilator keeping him alive. The court granted a declaration that it was lawful to act on his instructions. AK retained mental capacity and extraordinary means made communication possible.
[21]   [2002] 2 All ER 449; see also above at 5.2.
[22]   [2002] 2 All ER 449 at para 100.

It would be foolish to suggest that outcome plays no role in determining mental capacity. Capacity is unlikely to be disputed unless others disagree with the outcome. Perhaps we should be more concerned about patients of borderline mental capacity who simply acquiesce in the wishes of their doctors or relatives? And judges themselves do not wholly ignore outcomes. Butler-Sloss P herself said in another case, *Re MB (An Adult: Refusal of Medical Treatment)*:

> The graver the consequences of a decision, the commensurately greater the level of competence is required to take the decision.[23]

Note that section 3(2) of the 2005 Act indicates that lack of capacity may be due to temporary as much as permanent factors affecting the patient's mind or brain. The difficulties innate in identifying a temporary lack of capacity are well illustrated in *Re MB*. MB suffered from acute needle phobia. While she was in principle prepared to agree to the Caesarean section which obstetricians thought necessary to deliver her child safely, she refused to agree to any form of anaesthetic involving an injection. The Court of Appeal held that she lacked the requisite capacity to refuse treatment. Her phobia disabled her from *making* a decision.[24] Although she suffered from no mental illness or impairment, temporary factors could erode a patient's capacity. Such temporary factors might include confusion, shock, pain or drugs. 'Fear may also ... paralyse the will and thus destroy the capacity to *make* a decision.'[25] *Re MB* highlights the complexity of the notion of the ability to make a decision. The 'temporary' factors eroding decision-making powers are common to many patients facing surgery. The cynic may wonder if, outside the context of childbirth, doctors or courts will be assiduous in finding evidence of such a temporary lack of capacity. Legal theory declares that English law does not recognise foetal interests as justifying interference with a competent woman's right to autonomy. In practice, may judges – understandably – be more ready to find evidence of a lack of capacity in a woman in labour endangering herself and her future child[26] than in a panic-stricken man of 44 refusing prostate surgery?

Dramatic lawsuits such as *Re MB* sometimes obscure the questions of patient capacity surfacing every day in routine treatment decisions.[27] The importance of effective communication between patients and professionals cannot be underestimated. When a patient is known to be affected by some degree of learning disability or dementia, it may be too easy to assume a lack of capacity. Consider this example. An elderly patient with moderate dementia

---

[23] [1997] 8 Med LR 217 at 224, CA.

[24] The difficulty inherent in the notion of making a decision is also well illustrated in a series of cases authorising forcible treatment of anorexic patients: see *Re W (Minor) (Medical Treatment)* [1992] 4 All ER 627 at 637; *Riverside Mental Health NHS Trust v Fox* [1994] 1 FLR 614; *B v Croydon Health Authority* [1995] 1 All ER 683, CA; *Re C (Detention: Medical Treatment)* [1997] 2 FLR 180. See also Jackson, *Medical Law: Text, Cases and Materials*, pp 200–201.

[25] *Re MB (Adult: Refusal of Medical Treatment)* [1997] 8 Med LR 217 at 224.

[26] See E Cave, 'Drink and Drugs in Pregnancy: Can the Law Prevent Harm to a Future Child?' (2007) 8 *Medical Law International* 165.

[27] See K Keywood, S Fovargue and M Flynn, *Best Practice? Health Care Decision-Making, By, With and For Adults with Learning Disabilities* (1999) NDT.

needs dental treatment for an abscessed tooth. He has little concept of time, sometimes does not recognise his wife and engages in bizarre behaviour. Is he incompetent to consent to dental treatment? What does he need to be told and to understand? His tooth hurts. The tooth can be removed so the hurt will be 'cured'. Despite his dementia, he enjoys capacity to authorise that simple procedure. He meets the test in section 3 of the Mental Capacity Act 2005.

What of the patient whose understanding and reasoning powers fluctuate? At some times he comprehends what is asked of him and can act on information given to him. Days or even hours later his competence deserts him, albeit to return at some later point. Fluctuating competence may be a result of psychotic disorder or, commonly, a consequence of dementia. Prior to the 2005 Act, the courts tended to find that patients with fluctuating capacity lacked capacity.[28] The Act continues to require an ability to understand and retain information, but section 3(2) states:

> The fact that a person is able to retain the information relevant to a decision for a short period only does not prevent him from being regarded as able to make the decision.

In theory, the functional test of capacity endorsed in the 2005 Act enables many patients with some degree of learning disability to retain capacity to authorise their own treatment. It also entails the risk that, although the patient understands enough to authorise their own treatment, he may refuse to do so. The elderly patient with toothache may allow fear of the dentist to overrule his desire to be rid of the toothache. That outcome will be seen by others as undesirable. Those others will be tempted to say the patients are unable to make a decision. Care should be taken before rushing to enforce treatment in the patient's best interests. Several thousand indubitably competent people damage their dental health by staying away from the dentist. Just because a patient is labelled demented or mentally-disabled, should we enforce his visit to the dentist?

Treating adults who lack mental capacity

6.4 When an adult patient does lack capacity to consent to treatment on her own behalf, two closely related questions have to be answered. First, on what basis is proposed treatment lawful, and second, who authorises such treatment? Two principal tests are canvassed: 'best interests' and 'substituted judgment'. A 'best interests' test requires that decision-makers consider what the overall welfare of the patient demands. It is, in theory at least, an objective test. 'Substituted judgment' demands an attempt to discern what the patient would want were she able to decide for herself. It is illustrated in a famous US case, *Re Quinlan*.[29] Karen Quinlan was a young woman who succumbed to sudden illness and lay in a coma supported on a ventilator. Her father applied to the court to be appointed her guardian and sought court approval to switch off the ventilator. The court authorised his decision on the basis of evidence

---

[28] See *Re R (A Minor) (Wardship: Medical Treatment)* [1991] 4 All ER 177 at 187; *Re D (Medical Treatment: Mentally Disabled Person)* [1998] 2 FLR 22 at 24.

[29] *Re Quinlan* 355 A 2d 664 (NJ, 1976); discussed below at 20.8.

that this was what Karen would have wished. The US court (1) endorsed a test of substituted judgment, and (2) granted Karen's father, her next of kin, powers to act on her behalf. In many civil law jurisdictions, as well as some states in the USA, the law allows next of kin to make decisions on behalf of adults who lack mental capacity,[30] just as English law empowers parents to consent to treatment on behalf of their young children. Both in case law and in the Mental Capacity Act 2005, we shall see that English law leans towards a modified version of a best interests test and refuses to endorse any notion that next of kin should automatically enjoy proxy powers of consent.

Prior to the 2005 Act, the law left patients lacking mental capacity and their doctors in something of a legal limbo.[31] No-one had legal authority to act as proxy and consent on behalf of the patient. Even if a patient was compulsorily detained under the Mental Health Act 1983, section 63 of that Act allowing doctors to dispense with the patient's consent applied only to treatment for mental disorder.[32] And, as we noted earlier, most patients who lack mental capacity are not detained under the Mental Health Act 1983.[33] Nor could an adult lacking mental capacity be made a ward of court so that the court could authorise treatment.[34] One of the extraordinary features of the history of this area of law is that not until 1987 did this question trouble the courts.[35] In earlier times, perhaps no-one gave much thought to the legality of treating patients lacking mental capacity? Doctors and families simply went ahead on the basis that 'doctor knows best'? The rise in medical litigation and increased concern for patients' rights began to worry doctors. Health professionals feared litigation if they went ahead with treatment without consent. They also feared litigation if a patient suffered harm because they did nothing.

---

[30] A test controversially employed in extensive litigation in the USA surrounding the proposed withdrawal of artificial hydration and nutrition from Terri Schiavo. The application was supported by her husband and opposed by her parents: see *Respondent Michael Schiavo's Opposition to Application for Injunction* Case No 04A-825, 24 March 2005 (Supreme Court, USA) (discussed in Chapter 20 at 20.8).

[31] See *T v T* [1988] 1 All ER 613; and see the third edition of this work at pp 115–117.

[32] So under the 1983 Act, doctors may require a detained patient to accept medication for schizophrenia but have no power to authorise surgery for a hernia. It should be noted that judges tend to give mental disorder a wide meaning, for example forcible feeding of anorexic patients was found to constitute treatment for mental disorder: see *B v Croydon Health Authority* [1995] 1 All ER 683; *Riverside Mental NHS Trust v Fox* [1994] 1 FLR 614. In *Tameside and Glossop Acute Services Trust v CH (a Patient)* [1996] 1 FLR 762, a Caesarean section was held to be treatment necessary to alleviate a detained woman's schizophrenia. In *R v Collins and Ashworth Health Authority, ex p Brady* [2000] Lloyd's Rep Med 355, forcible feeding to prevent Ian Brady starving himself to death was held to constitute treatment for his mental disorder.

[33] Or are eligible to be so detained. Patients with severe learning disabilities who are treated in hospital are usually voluntary (or informal) patients.

[34] See BM Hoggett, 'The Royal Prerogative in Relation to the Mentally Disordered: Resurrection, Resuscitation or Rejection' in MDA Freeman (ed), *Medicine, Ethics and the Law* (1988) Stevens, London.

[35] See *Re T* (14 May 1987, unreported); *Re V* (1987) Times, 4 June; *T v T* [1988] 1 All ER 613.

F v West Berkshire Health Authority

6.5 The trigger for judicial action to clarify the legality of treatment of mentally-disabled patients came about in the context of the sterilisation of women over 18 who have learning disabilities. If the girl was under 18, she could be made a ward of court, and the court, if it agreed with her parents and her doctors that sterilisation was in her best interests, could authorise that radical surgery.[36] In the first fully reported case relating to an adult, T was 19 years old. Somehow, despite her mother's care, she became pregnant. She was described as having a 'mental age' of two-and-a-half, she could barely communicate and she was doubly incontinent. Her mother and her doctors applied to Wood J for a declaration that to terminate T's pregnancy and then sterilise her would not be unlawful. He granted that declaration, finding that where a patient was suffering from such mental abnormality as *never* to be able to consent to proposed treatment a doctor was justified in 'taking such steps as good medical practice demands'.[37]

In 1989, a similar case, *F v West Berkshire Health Authority*, reached the House of Lords. F was a 36-year-old woman, said to have a mental age of five to six. She was a voluntary patient in a mental hospital and had entered into a sexual relationship with a male fellow patient. The House of Lords granted a declaration stating that F might lawfully be sterilised. Lord Brandon declared:

> ... a doctor can lawfully operate on, or give other treatment to, adult patients who are incapable, for one reason or another, of consenting to his doing so, provided that the operation or other treatment concerned is in the best interests of the patient.[38]

Their Lordships made it clear that mentally-disabled adults could lawfully receive medical care and treatment. The elderly confused lady with cataracts can have those cataracts removed. But F empowered doctors to decide on what treatment a patient received with no formal restrictions imposed on the exercise of that power. Operating on an old lady with cataracts is one thing, sterilising a mentally-disabled woman is an intervention of a different order of magnitude.[39] Disquiet about the decision in *F v West Berkshire Health Authority* arose from a suspicion that the judgment benefited doctors rather more than patients. A declaration from a High Court judge protected him

---

[36] See *Re B (A Minor) (Wardship: Sterilisation)* [1987] 2 All ER 206, HL, discussed further in Chapters 12 and 15.

[37] *T v T* [1988] 1 All ER 613 at 625.

[38] [1989] 2 All ER 545 at 551.

[39] Lord Griffiths dissented. He argued that a grave decision such as sterilisation with all its implications should not be left to doctors alone. He believed that it was open to the House of Lords to develop a common law rule that prior judicial approval was required before an operation as radical as sterilisation could be performed (at 561–562). The Court of Appeal had tried to meet such concerns. If a radical, irreversible intervention such as sterilisation, or use of the patient as an organ donor, was proposed, the Appeal Court said that doctors *must* apply to the High Court for a declaration that the intervention was in the patient's best interests. The House of Lords concluded by a majority of four to one that they had no jurisdiction to require doctors to apply for a declaration before any form of surgery or treatment on mentally-incompetent patients. As a matter of practice, a doctor contemplating radical and/or irreversible treatment should normally choose to make an application to the court.

from subsequent litigation.[40] Particularly if there is some dispute between the patient's relatives, or relatives and carers, the doctor benefits from the court's intervention.

Defining best interests

6.6   The most fundamental problem lay in the way their Lordships defined best interests in *F v West Berkshire Health Authority*.[41] Courts should apply the *Bolam* test. Treatment would be lawful if it conformed with a reasonable and competent body of professional opinion, albeit there might be another reasonable and competent body of professional opinion which would take a contrary view.[42] Gynaecologists have sharply differing views about the circumstances in which non-consensual sterilisation is justified. The application of the *Bolam* test to determine whether a doctor acts lawfully in a patient's 'best interests' could mean that women with exactly the same degree of mental disability would be sterilised in Brighton, but not in Manchester. The Law Commission has criticised the use of *Bolam* in this context. Its Report recommended that it '... should be made clear beyond any shadow of a doubt that acting in a person's best interests amounts to more than not treating a person in a negligent manner'.[43] The Commission proposed that a 'best interests' test should be retained to assess the lawfulness of treatment of mentally-disabled people, but verifiable criteria to determine a person's best interests needed to be spelled out.

After a decade of rubber stamping medical opinion, the courts adopted a much more proactive approach to best interests well before the advent of the Mental Capacity Act 2005. Refusing to authorise a vasectomy on a mentally-disabled man, Thorpe LJ[44] emphasised that the decision about the patient's interests was one which the judge must make. It encompasses 'medical, emotional and other issues'.[45] In assessing the pros and cons of treatment, the judge should embark on a balancing exercise. Before authorising major invasive and irreversible procedures, the judge must be satisfied that the case for such treatment will be significantly in credit. *Re S (Adult Patient: Sterilisation)*[46] concerned an application to carry out a hysterectomy on a 29-year-old woman with severe learning difficulties. Doctors and her mother were concerned about the risk of pregnancy and the woman also suffered from severe menstrual problems. She had a phobia about hospitals. Overturning the trial judge's decision that hysterectomy would be lawful, the Court of Appeal held that other, less invasive alternatives should be tried first. Butler-Sloss P said this:

---

[40]   See J Bridgeman, 'Declared Innocent?' (1995) 3 *Medical Law Review* 117.
[41]   [1989] 2 All ER 545.
[42]   *Bolam v Friern Hospital Management Committee* [1957] 1 WLR 582, discussed fully in Chapter 7. See also MA Jones, 'Justifying Medical Treatment Without Consent' (1989) 5 *Professional Negligence* 178.
[43]   Law Commission Report No 231, *Mental Incapacity*, para 3.27.
[44]   See *Re A (Medical Treatment) (Male Sterilisation)* [2000] 1 FCR 193, CA.
[45]   [2000] 1 FCR 193 at 200, CA.
[46]   [2000] 3 WLR 1288.

The *Bolam* test [is] irrelevant to the judicial decision, once the judge [is] satisfied that the range of options was within the range of acceptable opinion among competent and reasonable practitioners.[47]

Thorpe LJ emphasised that what the medical expert witnesses offered was expert advice on the options for treatment. The court then must exercise the choice the patient was unable to make. The patient's welfare in its broadest sense must be the paramount consideration.[48] In *R (on the application of N) v Doctor M*[49] there was a body of expert opinion testifying that a particular treatment was *not* in the patient's best interests. It was held that expert opinion was relevant, but not conclusive.

'Therapeutic' interventions

6.7 When doctors seek a declaration, at least a public forum is available in which an independent evaluation of what is proposed is possible. Seeking judicial sanction for every intervention involving a mentally-disabled adult is obviously impractical. The High Court issued procedural rules standardising how applications to court should be made.[50] A series of cases, however, ruled that where treatment was essentially *therapeutic* in intent, to relieve the patient from pain or illness, no declaration from a court need be sought. If her doctors and family believed that a woman lacking mental capacity should be sterilised because sterilisation was the only effective means of protecting her from pregnancy, they should seek the court's sanction; if it were proposed to carry out a hysterectomy to alleviate 'menstrual disorder', no independent review of that judgment was called for.[51] Yet hysterectomy is a much more radical operation with exactly the same effects as sterilisation, ie removing the woman's fertility.

What constitutes a therapeutic intervention? Were a mentally-disabled woman of 46 to be suffering from irregular heavy menstrual bleeding and acute pain, conditions which had proved resistant to non-surgical treatment, accepting that hysterectomy might be the best option to protect her welfare is not difficult. What of a younger woman whose 'menstrual disorder' is essentially that her mental state renders her unable to cope with the effects of menstruation leading to problems of hygiene and an added burden on her carers? Just as the courts eventually adopted a more interventionist approach to best interests, so the Court of Appeal made it clear that where there is real dispute about the best means to protect the patient's welfare, an application to court should be made regardless of whether the disputed procedure could arguably be labelled 'therapeutic'. So in *Re S* (discussed earlier), Thorpe LJ[52] made it clear that '... if a particular case lies anywhere near to boundary line it should

---

[47] [2000] 3 WLR 1288 at 1299.
[48] See also *Simms v Simms* [2003] 1 All ER 669; *A v A Health Authority* [2002] 1 FCR 481.
[49] [2003] 1 FLR 667.
[50] *Practice Note (Official Solicitor: Declaration Proceedings Medical and Welfare Decisions for Adults Who Lack Capacity)* [2001] 2 FLR 158.
[51] See *Re GF* [1993] 4 Med LR 77.
[52] In *Re S (Adult Patient: Sterilisation)* [2000] 3 WLR 1288 at 1303 (and see 6.6 above). See also *Re Z (Medical Treatment: Hysterectomy)* [2000] 1 FCR 274.

be referred to the court'. Hysterectomy in a young woman where there is no evidence that her condition poses a serious threat to her physical health is just such a case. The judges sought to offer better safeguards for vulnerable patients.

The Bournewood débacle

6.8 The inadequacy of the common law was dramatically highlighted in *R v Bournewood Community and Mental Health Trust, ex p L*.[53] The House of Lords ruled that the common law powers derived from *F v West Berkshire Health Authority*[54] could be invoked to authorise the *detention* of patients lacking mental capacity. L was 48 years old, autistic and severely mentally-disabled. He could not speak and had very limited understanding. L was incapable of making any of his own decisions about his health or personal care. From 1994, after nearly 30 years in mental hospitals, L lived with paid carers. One day, in 1997, he became extremely agitated at his day centre. His carers could not be contacted. L was taken be ambulance to Bournewood hospital and ultimately admitted as a 'voluntary' informal patient. He was not formally detained under the Mental Health Act 1983. He remained in hospital for several months despite his carers' wish for him to return to their home. An action was brought on L's behalf, accusing the hospital of false imprisonment. The essence of the case was whether or not L had been unlawfully detained. The Court of Appeal ruled in L's favour. He had been detained against his will and no lawful grounds for his detention justified his treatment. The Law Lords, by a bare majority, held that L was not imprisoned in the hospital. He was kept in an unlocked ward and not actually restrained from leaving. The majority considered that evidence that had he attempted to leave he would have been restrained, did not establish that he was detained against his will. All their Lordships agreed, however, that L was 'imprisoned' in the ambulance. All their Lordships ruled that his detention was in any event lawful. Given his inability to consent to admission to hospital himself, any necessary removal and detention in hospital, plus whatever consequent treatment was called for, was lawful in his best interests. L found himself subjected to a regime of compulsory detention without any of the safeguards offered by the Mental Health Act 1983.

L's carers took his case to the European Court of Human Rights and won. L's detention violated Article 5[55] of the European Convention on Human Rights:

> Everyone has the right to liberty and security of person. No one shall be deprived of his liberty, save in the following cases and in accordance with a procedure prescribed by law.

Article 5(1)(e) permits the lawful detention of 'persons of unsound mind', but Article 5(4) requires that anyone so deprived of his liberty must have the lawfulness of his detention decided speedily by a court. In *HL v United*

---

[53]   [1998] 3 All ER 289, HL.
[54]   [1989] 2 All ER 545.
[55]   See *Winterwerp v Netherlands* (1979) 2 EHRR 387; *Herczegfalvy v Austria* (1992) 15 EHRR 437.

Kingdom,[56] the European Court of Human Rights ruled that L had been deprived of his freedom solely on the basis of clinical judgments. Moreover, he was denied the opportunity for a speedy judicial review of his detention. Law reform was long overdue.

'Best interests' survives: the Mental Capacity Act 2005

6.9 The Mental Capacity Act 2005 brings about reform, but only in part. The Act does not close the 'Bournewood gap'; clauses 38 and 39 of the Mental Health Bill seek to do so.[57] The concept of 'best interests' survives the 2005 Act. Section 5 provides a statutory basis, the general authority, for any act done in relation to the care or treatment of a person lacking mental capacity. In brief, section 5 gives statutory force to the test promulgated in *F v West Berkshire Health Authority*.[58] It provides that:

1. If a person ('D') does an act in connection with the care of treatment of another person ('P'), the act is one to which this section applies if –
   (a) before doing the act, D takes reasonable steps to establish whether P lacks capacity in relation to the matter in question, and
   (b) when doing the act, D reasonable believes –
      (i) that P lacks capacity in relation to the matter, and
      (ii) *that it will be in P's best interests for the act to be done.*
      [*Emphasis added.*]
2. D does not incur any liability in relation to the act that he would not have incurred if P –
   (a) had had capacity to consent in relation to the matter, and
   (b) had consented to D's doing the act.

Section 5 has a broad application extending beyond medical treatment. Anyone who intervenes to assist a person lacking mental capacity is protected from liability in battery if he acts in that person's best interests. The passer-by who pulls a distressed elderly person with dementia out of the way of oncoming traffic falls within section 5. The paramedics who lift her into an ambulance, and all the doctors and nurses who tend her in hospital, act lawfully by virtue of section 5. The carers who feed and wash her when she returns to a nursing home act lawfully. Note, however, that section 5 grants only immunity from battery. Should the patient's care be negligent, she retains her rights to redress.

Should Parliament have seized the opportunity to junk the best interests test? Would 'substituted judgment' be a preferable test? The Law Commission rejected a simplistic substitution of 'substituted judgment' for best interests. The difficulty is this. Where a patient once enjoyed mental capacity, his known preferences, and even idiosyncrasies, the views which he has expressed to family and friends of what he would hope for were he ever to lack mental capacity, are useful and crucial factors on which to base treatment decisions. In the majority of cases where a patient has lacked mental capacity all his life,

---

[56] (2004) 40 EHRR 761.
[57] Discussed below at 6.11.
[58] [1989] 2 All ER 545.

'substituted judgment' is a myth. The unfortunate young woman in *T v T* was never capable of communicating her preferences and choices to others – she was never able to make autonomous choices at all. None the less, the Law Commission strove to give force where appropriate to the prior preferences of someone who now lacks mental capacity.

(1) The Commission recommended giving statutory force to advance directives.[59] 'Living wills', whereby a person gives directions about treatment which he should (and should not) receive if he becomes unable to decide such matters for himself, should be enforced. Thus we could today set out our decisions about continuing treatment in circumstances where for us death would become preferable to life.

(2) The Commission recommended that people should be empowered to nominate their own chosen proxy (attorney) to act for them should they lose capacity to act for themselves.

We shall see that both recommendations are implemented at least in part in the Mental Capacity Act 2005. The Act provides for advance refusals of treatment, hedged with multiple restrictions. Section 9 allows the appointment of a lasting power of attorney. However, both advance refusals and lasting powers of attorney will work to reflect the wishes of the individual herself only in limited circumstances. First, the patient must at some point in her life have enjoyed the necessary mental capacity to execute such an instrument. Second, she must actually have done so, contemplated a future loss of capacity and acted to attempt to extend her autonomous choices beyond that sad event. The number of patients making advance refusals, or creating lasting powers of attorney, may well be small.

(3) Most importantly, in its proposed definition of best interests, the Law Commission sought to ensure that any evaluation of best interests took into account any available evidence of what the patient herself might want were she able to articulate her own views. Section 4 of the Mental Capacity Act 2005 adopts (with some additions) the Law Commission's notion of a modified best interests test, a test incorporating at least some element of substituted judgment.

Modified best interests

6.10 In determining best interests, decision-makers are first instructed that in making their decision they should not act merely on the basis of:

(a) the person's age or appearance, or (b) a condition of his, or an aspect of his behaviour, which might lead other to make unjustified assumptions about what might be in his best interests.[60]

Simply because a patient is 94 does not justify assuming that she would be better off dead in some life-threatening emergency.

---

[59] Law Commission Report No 231, *Mental Incapacity*, Part V.
[60] See section 4(1).

Next, when considering best interests, the decision-maker must consider if the patient is ever likely to recover the capacity to make her own decisions and, if so, when this may be.[61] Wherever possible, the patient must be allowed and assisted to participate in decisions as far as she is able.[62] So if X has suffered serious brain injuries in a road accident, only immediately necessary decisions should be taken by others while there remains the possibility that X will recover at least some of his reasoning powers. As X slowly recovers, where feasible, he should at least be consulted. In determining best interests, a decision-maker must consider as far as reasonably possible,

* the person's past and present wishes and feelings (and in particular any relevant written statement made by him when he had capacity).
* the beliefs and values that would be likely to influence his decision if he had capacity.
* the other factors he would be likely to consider if he were able to do so.[63]

In considering these matters, the 2005 Act further requires that a decision-maker seek the views of those people who may be best placed both to offer the views of the patient himself and to judge his welfare. So, where possible, the decision-maker must consult:

(a) anyone named by the person as someone to be consulted on the matter in question or on matter of that kind,

(b) anyone engaged in caring for the person or interested in his welfare,

(c) any donee of a lasting power of attorney granted by the person, and

(d) any deputy appointed for the person by the court.[64]

This modified best interests test requires decision-makers to focus on the individual patient and make a judgment to promote his welfare, a judgment which takes proper account of any prior views that he may have expressed and involves the people most likely to know about his views. Substituted judgment becomes an integral part of best interests where such judgment can practically be discerned. The dignity of every patient, including those who never enjoyed mental capacity, is given due regard. The patient in *T v T* never had the capacity to make judgments. None the less she would have preferences and feelings. Perhaps she may have displayed particular aversions, or especial pleasures. Treatment which transgressed those aversions or removed those pleasures could only be in her interests if strong evidence supported its continuation, despite the distress occasioned to T.

A statutory best interests test no longer conflates best interests with non-negligent care. Prior to the Mental Capacity Act 2005, as we have seen, the courts had already rejected such a conflation. Under the Act, however, doctors remain proxy decision-makers for their patients. The Law Commission's initial proposals, following the Mental Health Act model, called for further safeguards against cavalier or paternalist decision-making. The general

---

[61] See section 4(3).
[62] See section 4(4).
[63] Section 4(6). See *Ashan v University Hospitals Leicester NHS Trust* [2006] EWHC 2624 (importance of religious faith).
[64] Section 4(7).

authority to make decisions in a patient's best interests should be subject to restrictions.[65] Certain controversial radical and/or irreversible treatments would normally demand authorisation by a court. These would include sterilisation, organ or bone marrow donation. Other debatable treatments, including hysterectomy for menstrual management and abortion, would require a certificate from an independent doctor who would review the best interests criteria in each case.

The Government rejected such restrictions on general authority.[66] Doctors carrying out such procedures are not required to seek an independent judgment of the benefits of the procedure to the patient, nor are they obliged to seek court approval in any case. The current practice whereby doctors may choose to seek a declaration of the legality of what they propose to do continues.[67]

Sections 30–34 of the 2005 Act set out special rules relating to the inclusion of people lacking mental capacity in medical research.[68] Section 37 obliges NHS authorities to seek advice from an independent mental capacity advocate, (1) if they are proposing to provide serious medical treatment for a patient lacking mental capacity, and (2) if there is no-one (other than professional carers or advisers) who can be consulted about the patient's best interests. Serious medical treatment is defined as:

> ... treatment which involves providing, withdrawing or withholding treatment in circumstances where –
> (a)   in a case where a single treatment is being proposed, there is a fine balance between its benefits to the patient and the burdens and risks it is likely to entail for him,
> (b)   in a case where there is choice of treatments, a decision as to which one to use is finely balanced, or
> (c)   what is proposed would be likely to involve serious consequences for the patient.[69]

Are the interests of the patient given sufficient weight in this watered down version of the Law Commission's proposal? Envisage a woman of 33 who lacks capacity as a result of a cerebral haemorrhage, and is a voluntary patient in hospital. Her only adult relative is her husband, now living with a new partner. He readily agrees to a proposal to sterilise her and carry out a hysterectomy. The draft Code of Practice[70] seeks to fill any lacuna in the law. The Code strongly advises that any proposal to withdraw artificial nutrition or hydration, to use a person lacking mental capacity as an organ or tissue donor, or to carry out a non-therapeutic sterilisation, should be brought

---

[65]   Law Commission Report No 231, *Mental Incapacity*, Part VI.

[66]   *Making Decisions* (1999) Cm 3803, para 12.

[67]   For fuller advice, see paras 7.9 and 7.17–7.23 of the draft Code of Practice (Department for Constitutional Affairs, *Mental Capacity Act 2005 Draft Code of Practice* (CP 05/06)), detailing situations in which it is good practice to seek a declaration from the Court of Protection. Contravention of the Code by a health professional will be taken into account in proceedings in any court or tribunal: Mental Capacity Act 2005, s 42(4) and (5).

[68]   See Chapter 16 below.

[69]   The Mental Capacity Act 2005 (Independent Mental Capacity Advocate) (General) Regulations 2006, SI 2006/1832, reg 4.

[70]   *Mental Capacity Act 2005 Draft Code of Practice* (CP 05/06), paras 7.17–7.23.

before a court. So should some cases involving termination of pregnancy and 'other cases where there is a doubt or dispute about whether a particular treatment will be in a patient's best interests'.

There is one further protection to be found in the new statutory regime to define best interests. Section 4(5) of the 2005 Act provides:

> Where the determination relates to life-sustaining treatment [the decision-maker] must not in considering whether the treatment is in the best interests of the person concerned, be motivated by a desire to bring about his death.

We discuss this further when we consider end of life decisions in Chapter 20.

Use of restraint and detention[71]

6.11 Many patients who lack mental capacity will simply acquiesce in treatment. What of the patient who forcefully objects – the dentist moves towards him and the patient jumps out of the chair? Section 6 of the Mental Capacity Act 2005 authorises the use of force and restraint, if such measures are necessary, and a proportional response to (1) the likelihood of the patient suffering harm if he is not treated and (2) the seriousness of that harm. Sometimes, continuing treatment may require more than brief restraint. An elderly patient with dementia may need to be confined in her care home. An anorexic patient who is to be fed forcibly will also need to be detained in hospital. Prior to the 2005 Act, judges were prepared to use common law powers to authorise detention in a patient's best interests.[72] And, as we have seen, those powers were invoked to detain Mr L in a mental hospital in breach of Article 5 of the European Convention on Human Rights.[73] The Mental Health Bill contains complex proposals to amend the Mental Capacity Act 2005, regulate any deprivation of liberty and close the 'Bournewood gap'. We can only outline those proposals briefly here, and warn that the Bill may be significantly amended before it reaches the statute book. Two new Schedules will be added to the 2005 Act – Schedules A1 and 1A. Amendment of the Mental Capacity Act 2005 will first make it clear that only in the most limited circumstances may the Act be used to detain a patient. Detention will be lawful only if:

(1)   the patient meets stringent conditions about eligibility;[74] *and*
(2)   the Court of Protection has authorised detention in a matter relating to the patient's personal welfare; *or*
(3)   deprivation of liberty is authorised by a supervisory body (the patient's primary care trust).

If a decision is being sought from the court, anything immediately necessary to preserve the patient's life, or prevent deterioration in his condition, may be done pending an order of the court. Conditions limiting detention under the

---

[71]   For fuller advice, see paras 5.37–5.59 of the draft Code of Practice.
[72]   See *Re C (Detention: Medical Treatment)* [1997] 2 FLR 180.
[73]   See *HL v United Kingdom* (2005) 40 EHRR 32, ECtHR.
[74]   Schedule A1 sets out criteria of eligibility and Schedule 1A defines ineligibility.

Mental Capacity Act 2005 include that the patient is over 18, that he lacks mental capacity, that detention is in his best interests, that he would fall within the categories of persons suffering from mental disorder under the Mental Health Bill (except that the provisions of the Bill excluding learning disability from the definition of mental disorder should be disregarded), and he has not objected to detention. This means, in effect, a patient lacking mental capacity by reason of, for example, learning disability or as a result of brain damage can be detained in a hospital or care home so she can be cared for properly – as long as she does not refuse to accept treatment and detention. The powers to be granted under the 2005 Act cannot, however, be used to treat patients for mental disorder as such. The Bill amendments seek to ensure that where a patient should properly be treated within the Mental Health Act 1983, he is not assigned to an appropriate regime with fewer safeguards of his liberty. The powers to be granted under the 2005 Act do, however, provide for regular review of the patient's detention and authorisation of detention can last no longer than twelve months without a further review of the patient's condition.

Let families decide?

6.12 Why not remove decision-making about patients lacking mental capacity from doctors altogether? Should decisions be entrusted to an appropriate 'guardian', often a family member?[75] Intuitively, many people may feel that if a person cannot make decisions for himself, his family are the best substitute decision-makers. The Law Commission and the Government rejected both granting automatic proxy powers to families and a system whereby people lacking mental capacity are routinely subjected to guardianship.

Laws granting automatic decision-making powers to 'next of kin' would be fraught with difficulty and danger. Identifying *who* the decision-maker should be is not straightforward. Imagine X, a retired school teacher who is suffering from dementia and who, at 84, has lived for 20 years with Y, a longstanding friend. Y is better placed to act as X's 'guardian' than X's only niece Z who may in the strict sense be her next of kin. Envisage A who is a widow with three children. The 'next of kin' do not agree how their mother should be treated. Perhaps A has just one son, but he has visited her no more than once or twice a year in the past five decades. He will not be the ideal 'guardian' of his mother's interests. Her interests and his may conflict. He stands to inherit a substantial sum of money if she dies. If she recovers and enters a nursing home his inheritance may wither away.

Such difficulties might be overcome if the law allowed the express appointment of a guardian. In the case of X, Y (her friend) could be appointed her guardian. Wholesale appointment of guardians for every person unable to make decisions for themselves is simply impracticable. The courts would sink under a flood of applications. Nor is guardianship necessarily beneficial to patients. It imposes a child-like status on an adult. Given that English law

[75] See A Grubb, 'Treatment Decisions, Keeping it in the Family' in A Grubb (ed), *Choices and Decisions in Health Care* (1993) Wiley.

endorses a 'functional' test of capacity, the law's aim is that the person herself should take as many decisions as she is capable of making.

Advance directives[76]

6.13 The use of advance directives, often described as 'living wills', to enhance patient autonomy has been promoted for decades.[77] An advance directive enables a person to set out his own instructions about any future treatment which he should, or should not, receive were he to lose mental capacity to make such decisions for himself. Such decisions need not be restricted to instructions about the continuation of life-sustaining treatment. A woman might, for example, want to give instructions about the management of her pregnancy in advance. A person in the early stages of a neuro-degenerative disease might wish to set out his own care plan. Prior to the Mental Capacity Act 2005, the courts had made it clear that advance refusals of treatment were legally binding as long as there was unequivocal evidence that the patient's decision was voluntary, competent and directly relevant to the factual circumstances in question.[78] So, as we have seen, the instructions given by Ms T not to administer blood transfusions were found to be defective. The threshold for finding an advance refusal to be binding was set high.

Advance requests (or demands), on the other hand, were not legally binding. The Court of Appeal in *R (on the application of Burke) v GMC*[79] made it clear that any advance demand (or request) for treatment has no legal force.

> ... a patient cannot demand that a doctor administer a treatment which the doctor considers is adverse to his clinical needs.

So at common law, advance refusals were binding in theory but exceptionally difficult to execute in practice in order to ensure that the individual's wishes prevailed.[80] The 2005 Act makes the exercise no easier. 'Advance decisions'[81] operate only to prohibit specified treatment being carried out. Only advance refusals have legal force.[82] An advance refusal of life-sustaining treatment must meet stringent conditions. Such a refusal must (*inter alia*):

---

[76] Discussed further below in Chapter 20 at 20.13. See also A Maclean, 'Advance Directives, Future Selves and Decision Making' (2006) 14 *Medical Law Review* 291.

[77] See Centre of Medical Law and Ethics, King's College, *The Living Will* (1988) Edward Arnold.

[78] See *Re T (Adult: Refusal of Medical Treatment)* [1992] 4 All ER 649, CA, discussed above at 5.2.

[79] [2005] EWCA Civ 1003 at para 35.

[80] See, for example, T Thompson, R Barbour, L Schwartz, 'Adherence to Advance Directives in Critical Care Decision Making: Vignette Study' (2003) 327 *British Medical Journal* 1011, demonstrating the divergent attitudes of health care professionals when faced with a patient's mock advance directive.

[81] See ss 24–26 of the Mental Capacity Act 2005.

[82] Under s 26(1) if P has made an advance decision which is (a) valid and (b) applicable to a treatment, the decision has effect as if he had made it, and had had capacity to make it, at the time when the question arises whether the treatment should be carried out or continued.

- be verified by a statement to the effect that it is to apply to treatment even if life is at risk;
- be in writing;
- be signed by the patient or another in his presence and acting on his direction;
- have the signature witnessed.[83]

In other circumstances, there is no formal requirement that the advance decision be in writing, or witnessed. Evidence that such a decision was made when the patient had capacity to make such a decision, and has not been withdrawn, must still be forthcoming.[84] And the decision will not have effect if:

- the treatment in question 'is not the treatment specified in the advance decision';
- 'any circumstances specified in the advance decision are absent' or
- 'there are reasonable grounds for believing that circumstances exist which [the patient] did not anticipate at the time of his advance decision and which would have affected his decision had he anticipated them'.[85]

These stringent conditions set by the 2005 Act illustrate the difficulty of transforming theory into practice. The conditions make the task of executing a fire-proof advance decision nigh on impossible. Imagine this scenario. A is successfully treated for a brain tumour, but warned that there is a 20 per cent risk of recurrence and poor prospects of long-term survival if the cancer recurs. Should the tumour return, it will gradually rob her of her reasoning powers, memory and capacity for independent life. So she sets out an advance decision that, should the cancer recur and she is unable to articulate her own wishes, she should not be resuscitated if she suffers a cardiac arrest, and should not be given antibiotics if she develops an infection. The cancer recurs and advances rapidly. A suffers a cerebral haemorrhage. Her advance decision does not cover the treatment in question and so has no force. Or, the cancer does not recur, but A suffers traumatic brain injuries in a road accident. Her advance decision does not apply because it does not relate to the circumstances that materialise. In an attempt to tackle this dilemma, section 24(2) of the 2005 Act provides that the 'decision may be regarded as specifying a treatment or circumstance even though expressed in layman's terms'. Perhaps, then, the best advice is to express any advance decision in as general a way as possible? But then you may fall foul of section 25(3) because of failure to anticipate circumstances that might have affected your decision. Yet section 25(3) in itself is an important safeguard for patients. Consider A again. She executes her advance decision in 2007, refusing all treatment should her cancer recur. It recurs in 2012 by which time a new highly effective treatment has been developed.

---

[83] See s 25(6).
[84] See s 25(1).
[85] See s 25(4).

Next we must consider withdrawal of any advance decision. People must be free to change their minds. What seemed intolerable at 40 may be acceptable at 70. Changes in personal circumstances will alter one's perspective of quality of life. Section 24(4) of the Mental Capacity Act 2005 provides that a withdrawal (or partial withdrawal) need not be in writing. *HE v NHS Trust*[86] demonstrates the difficulty of establishing informed withdrawal of an advance directive. When HE was a practising Jehovah's Witness, she executed (in writing) an advance directive prohibiting any blood transfusion. Later she renounced the Witness faith and reverted back to her original Muslim faith, becoming engaged to a fellow Muslim. Her advance directive stated that it could only be revoked in writing. She had taken no formal steps to revoke her original directive. None the less, Munby J found that her conduct offered sufficient evidence that her directive no longer represented her wishes. It was implicitly revoked. He went on to say that '... once there is some real reason for doubt, then it is for those who assert the continuing validity and applicability of the advance directive to prove that it is still operative'. In effect, the facts of each case must be assessed. As Munby J goes on to say, '... the longer the time which has elapsed since an advance directive was made, and the greater the apparent change in circumstance since then, the more doubt there is likely to be as to its continuing validity and applicability'.

Lasting powers of attorney

6.14 As we have seen, an inevitable difficulty in any form of advance directive is defining in exactly what sort of circumstances one might lose capacity, and what sorts of disease lie in wait. Appointing a chosen proxy to act for you may be an option welcome to many people. Before the advent of the Mental Capacity Act 2005, it was possible to execute an enduring power of attorney[87] and thus appoint a proxy to take decisions in relation to property and financial affairs. An elderly person, who feared that his mental faculties were declining, could appoint a relative or friend to act as his agent in managing his property and finance. If he subsequently lost mental capacity, the agent could continue to act on his behalf. It was not possible to execute such a power to appoint a proxy decision-maker for health care or personal welfare decisions.

Section 9 of the Mental Capacity Act 2005 introduces a significant reform of the law. A person can now execute a lasting power of attorney (LPA), whereby he nominates the chosen donee (or donees) of the power to make decisions for him both in relation to personal welfare (including decisions about medical treatment), and in relation to his property and financial affairs. One person can be selected to manage your affairs for you. An elderly parent can now authorise a daughter to make any necessary decisions about her intimate welfare and medical care, as much as about her property. The proxy (the donee) may only make decisions about life-sustaining treatment if the donor of the power expressly authorised her to do so. In making any decision on behalf of the donor, the proxy must act in the best interests of the donor and

86 [2003] 2 FLR 408.
87 See the Enduring Powers of Attorney Act 1985.

conform fully to the principles underlying the 2005 Act. The proxy's powers are limited by any advance decision made earlier by the donor. A number of formalities are prescribed.

Some people may choose to grant a LPA to a professional adviser. More may prefer to choose a close friend or relative. So is there a risk of conflict of interest again? We think not. LPAs overcome many of the difficulties inherent in automatically entrusting decisions about health care to 'next of kin'. The patient actively chooses her preferred 'agent'. If, in 30 (or 50) years, we are estranged from our daughters, we will not grant them power of attorney. If we suspect that they are over-anxious to receive their inheritance, we will not give them power over our life and death. As long as the requisite rules about the execution and registration of LPAs ensure that the grant of a LPA is a free and informed decision of the patient, LPAs are an attractive option to people who want to entrust their decisions about future health to relatives, friends or professional advisers chosen by them.

Deputies

6.15   Although guardianship of adults is generally eschewed in the Mental Capacity Act 2005, sections 15–21 make provision for exceptional cases when the new Court of Protection may see fit to appoint a deputy authorised to make personal welfare decisions on behalf of the patient. Such an appointment must be shown to be in the patient's best interests and the court has a wide discretion to determine the scope of the powers conferred on the deputy. Where serious questions arise about the continuing treatment and welfare of a patient lacking mental capacity, a deputy may be appointed who will be authorised within strict limits, and for as short a time as possible, to act on the patient's behalf generally. Their powers would not be limited to medical care, but extend to all questions of personal welfare, health care, property and finance.

Appointment of a deputy might be envisaged in the following example. A 45-year-old barrister, who is the single father of small children, is severely injured in a road accident. He has substantial shareholdings in several companies and owns three properties. Injuries to his brain have deprived him of mental capacity. Other injuries may necessitate several further operations. A number of decisions need to be made over a period of a couple of years. Should he sue? How can his property and money best be used to benefit him and his children? How should decisions be taken about further surgery? Appointing a suitable relative or colleague as a deputy in such a case could make good sense.

The Court of Protection[88]

6.16   Central to the Mental Capacity Act 2005 is the new expanded Court of Protection, which enjoys a wide-ranging jurisdiction to oversee the care of

[88]   See ss 45–61 of the Mental Capacity Act 2005.

adults lacking mental capacity and adjudicate on disputes about what form such care should take. The court is based on the model provided by the old Court of Protection, but embraces in a single jurisdiction all the decision-making processes involving such people, including health care and welfare matters. The court will hear any disputes between the several parties involved in the care of a person lacking mental capacity. It inherits the jurisdiction to issue declarations about the legality of proposed treatment. The court will be supported by a new officer, the public guardian.[89] The court can appoint deputies where appropriate, register and supervise LPAs. But, as we have noted, resort to the court to oversee especially controversial or problematic medical procedures would not be mandatory. Does this matter? Can we not trust the good sense of doctors and families to seek judicial oversight of what they propose to do in cases when, and only when, such oversight is truly needed? Doctors and carers will be guided by the Code of Practice. As we have seen, in its current draft form, the Code advises that certain cases are brought before the court.[90] A failure on the part of a health professional to comply with this guidance will be taken into account in any relevant proceedings in any court or tribunal. It would, for example, be relevant to an assessment of a doctors' fitness to practise before the General Medical Council. One difficulty remains. When doctors and families disagree either with each other or among themselves, an application to court is likely to be made. Where there is either consensus among the several people involved with the patient, or perhaps an absence of involved family or friends, resort to court is less likely. The patient, lacking an advocate, is deprived of any voice to speak on his behalf.

Mental health legislation[91]

6.17 This book does not attempt to deal in any detail with the provisions of the Mental Health Acts. Some reference needs to be made here to the Mental Health Act 1983, the Mental Health (Patients in the Community) Act 1995 and the Mental Health Bill now wending its way through Parliament. The 1983 Act grants statutory authority to dispense with detained patients' consent to certain treatment and treat such patients in their best interests. A patient's refusal of treatment can thus be overridden, even if he meets the test of mental capacity under the Mental Capacity Act 2005.

Part II of the 1983 Act makes provision for the detention in hospital of certain mentally-disordered patients. Only a minority of patients with mental disorder are in fact detained in hospital under the Act. An application for admission for assessment (observation and tests) must be based on the written recommendations of two medical practitioners who testify that the patient (1) is suffering from a mental disorder of a nature warranting his detention in hospital, at least for a limited period, and (2) ought to be so detained in the interests of his

---

[89] See ss 57.

[90] Department for Constitutional Affairs, *Mental Capacity Act 2005 Draft Code of Practice* (CP 05/06), para 7.17. See further, paras 7.18–7.24. See also above, at 6.10.

[91] See *Mason and McCall Smith's Law and Medical Ethics*, Chapter 20; Jackson, *Medical Law: Text, Cases and Materials*, Chapter 7; Bartlett and Sandland, *Mental Health Law: Policy and Practice*; P Fennell, *Treatment Without Consent* (1996) Routledge.

own health or safety, or to protect others.[92] Admission for the assessment authorises the patient's detention for 28 days. If he is to be detained longer an application for admission for treatment must be made.[93] Such an application made under section 3 of the Mental Health Act 1983 must be founded on grounds that the patient:

(a)   ... is suffering from mental illness, severe mental impairment, psychopathic disorder or mental impairment and his mental disorder is of a nature or degree which makes it appropriate for him to receive treatment in a mental hospital; *and*

(b)   in the case of psychopathic disorder or mental impairment, such treatment is likely to alleviate or prevent a deterioration in his condition; *and*

(c)   it is necessary for the health and safety of the patient or for the protection of other persons that he should receive such treatment and it cannot be provided unless he is detained under this section.

'Severe mental impairment' is defined as 'a state of arrested or incomplete development of mind which includes severe impairment of intelligence and social functioning'. 'Mental impairment' is similarly defined, save that impairment need not be severe. Where the grounds for detention are based either on any degree of mental impairment or on psychopathic disorder there must additionally be evidence of 'abnormally aggressive or seriously irresponsible conduct'.

The Mental Health Bill will (if enacted) broaden the definition of mental disorder to include 'any disorder or disability of the mind'.[94] References to 'severe mental impairment', 'psychopathic disorder' and 'mental impairment' will be deleted.[95] The 'treatability' condition will be altered to require only that 'appropriate medical treatment is available for that patient'.[96] 'Learning disability'[97] will not as such be said to constitute mental disorder.[98] A person with a learning disability will be able to be detained only if his 'disability is associated with abnormally aggressive or seriously irresponsible conduct'.[99]

The number of people lacking capacity eligible to be detained under the 1983 Act is small:

(1)   In the case of mental impairment, whether existing since birth or as a result of accident or disease, condition (b) (treatability) is unlikely to be

---

[92]   See s 2 of the Mental Health Act 1983. An emergency application founded on the recommendation of a medical practitioner may be made under s 4 and authorises detention for up to 72 hours.

[93]   A successful application for admission for treatment authorises detention for an initial period of six months.

[94]   See Clause 1(2).

[95]   See Clause 1(3).

[96]   See Clause 5.

[97]   Defined as a 'state of arrested or incomplete development of the mind which includes significant impairment of intelligence and social functioning' (Clause 1(3)).

[98]   See Clause 4. (Except for the purposes of Schedule 1A to the Mental Capacity Act 2005 as amended.)

[99]   Clause 4(2).

met. Being shut up in hospital will not do them any good.[100] The amended definition of 'treatability' in the Mental Health Bill may increase the number of patients with learning disability who meet its conditions.

(2) A person lacking mental capacity can usually be protected from herself by means other than detention, so condition (c) may not be met. And note under the Bill, people with 'learning disability' are only eligible for detention if their disability is associated with aggressive or irresponsible conduct.

(3) Government policy for several years was to promote care in the community, and all over the country long-stay mental hospitals were closed down.

(4) Psychiatrists maintain that there are insufficient beds in mental hospitals even for patients who indubitably meet the criteria set out in the 1983 Act. Only the most dangerously disordered or profoundly disabled patients are detained in hospital under the 1983 Act.

Compulsory treatment under the Mental Health Act 1983

6.18 Part IV of the Mental Health Act 1983 provides for the compulsory treatment of that minority of patients detained under the Act. Section 63 provides that:

> The consent of a patient shall not be required for any medical treatment given to him for the mental disorder from which he is suffering, not being treatment given within section 57 or 58 [of the Act].

Section 63 applies to detained patients only. It cannot be used on voluntary patients, or on an out-patient basis. At one hospital doctors admitted patients under section 3, gave them long-term medication, then released them on licence until their next dose of medication was due. That practice was found to be unlawful.[101] Section 63 could be used to dispense with a patient's consent to treatment only where that patient actually needed to be detained, the conditions laid down in section 3 for admission for treatment were not met and the use of section 3 to enforce treatment was an unlawful fiction. However, the Court of Appeal later held that as long as some element of hospital treatment was required, 'extended leave' could be used to 'enforce' medicating in the community.[102]

Section 63 on its face authorises psychiatric treatment, not treatment for physical illness. It has been interpreted by judges to extend to allow the forcible feeding of anorexic patients and to justify non-consensual Caesarean surgery on a detained patient. The first example of this is perhaps the least

---

[100] Even though the Court of Appeal has developed a fairly broad definition of treatment to include group therapy and nursing care in a structured environment: *R v Canon Park Mental Review Tribunal, ex p A* [1994] 2 All ER 659, CA; *R v Mental Health Review Tribunal, ex p Macdonald* (1998) Crown Office Digest 205.

[101] *R v Hallstrom, ex p W (No 2)* [1986] QB 824.

[102] *B v Barking, Havering and Brentwood Community NHS Trust* [1999] 1 FLR 106.

curious. In *B v Croydon District Health Authority*[103] the Court of Appeal authorised the naso-gastric feeding of a woman of 24. She suffered from a borderline personality disorder, including among its symptoms a compulsion to self-harm. She was dangerously anorexic and was detained in hospital under the 1983 Act. The Appeal Court held that feeding constituted treatment for her mental disorder because such treatment included treatment to alleviate the symptoms of her disorder. Refusing food was such a symptom. Forcible feeding thus constituted a 'cure'.[104] *Tameside and Glossop Acute Services Trust v CH*[105] requires an even more imaginative approach to section 63. CH suffered from paranoid schizophrenia and was detained in a mental hospital. On admission to hospital she was discovered to be pregnant. At 37 weeks, the retarded growth of the foetus caused doctors to suspect placental failure and they wanted to deliver the child swiftly by Caesarean section. Wall J held that such surgery was justified under section 63 as treatment for CH's mental disorder. CH maintained a belief that medical staff were malicious and out to harm her child. She could not be given the medication most appropriate to treat her mental illness while still pregnant. The judge ruled '... a successful outcome of her pregnancy is a necessary part of the overall treatment of her mental disorder'. Whether B or CH should have been compelled to submit to treatment is something reasonable people might disagree on. The extended use of section 63 as a device to compel them to do so is disturbing

Whatever reservations judicial interpretation of section 63 of the Mental Health Act 1983 may provoke, other aspects of the 1983 Act offer safeguards for patients absent from the Mental Capacity Act 2005. Within its original and intended context, section 63 empowers doctors to determine what routine psychiatric treatment detained patients should receive. Sections 57 and 58 provided important safeguards both for patients' welfare and autonomy.

Section 57 is unusual in that it applies to *all* patients and not just those detained in hospital. Any form of psychosurgery,[106] such as lobotomy, and any surgical implantation of hormones to reduce male sexual drive will be unlawful[107] unless (1) the patient consents *and* (2) an independent doctor (appointed by the Mental Health Commission) certifies that (a) the patient is capable of understanding the nature and purpose of the treatment proposed and its likely effects; and (b) the treatment is likely to benefit the patient. The role of the Mental Health Act Commission is crucial. The Commission acts as a watchdog for patients' interests. It has a lay chair and a mixed professional/lay membership. In 2008, it will merge with the Healthcare Commission and

---

[103] [1995] 1 All ER 683, CA; *Re KB (Adult) (Mental Patient: Medical Treatment)* (1994) 19 BMLR 144. See also *R v Collins and Ashworth Hospital Authority, ex p Brady* [2000] Lloyd's Rep Med 355.

[104] See K Keywood, 'Rethinking the Anorexic Body; How English Law and Psychiatry "Think" ' (2003) 26 *International Journal of Law and Psychiatry* 599; P Lewis, 'Feeding Anorexic Patients Who Refuse Food' (1999) 7 *Medical Law Review* 21.

[105] [1996] 1 FCR 753.

[106] See s 57(1).

[107] See s 57(2) and the Mental Health (Hospital Guardianship and Consent in Treatment) Regulations 1983, SI 1983/893, reg 16(2). Section 57(2) of the Mental Health Act 1983 empowers the Secretary of State to bring other treatments within the ambit of the section.

the Commission for Social Care Inspection in order to create a streamlined body with regulatory functions covering both health and social care.

Section 58 applies to detained patients only. Electro-convulsive therapy[108] and any long-term medication (administered for longer than three months[109]) are authorised only if either (1) the patient consents and a doctor certifies that he is competent to do so or (2) an independent doctor certifies that the patient is incapable of giving consent or has refused to do so but that none the less '... having regard to the likelihood of the [treatment] alleviating or preventing a deterioration of his condition the treatment should be given'.[110]

At the time of writing, the 1983 Act only applies to patients actually in hospital. Insufficient hospital beds coupled with a desire to help rehabilitate patients into everyday life means that many patients are discharged from hospital while still ill and needing to continue to take medication. The Mental Health (Patients in the Community) Act 1995 grants powers to supervise patients returned to the community and, if the patient refuses to comply with his supervised aftercare, to return him to hospital. More radical proposals, including powers to impose compulsory supervision in the community, are envisaged in the latest draft of the Mental Health Bill. Clause 26 provides for community treatment orders (CTO). A patient could be discharged from hospital subject to such an order. The responsible clinician will have to be satisfied that such an order is necessary. The CTO may contain a number of conditions, including conditions about where the patient lives, that he makes himself available for treatment at specified times and places, that he 'receive medical treatment in accordance with the responsible clinicians directions' and that he 'abstain from particular conduct'. Patients cannot be forced to accept medication in the community, but a breach of a CTO will result in recall to hospital.

Compulsory treatment: beyond the Mental Health Acts

6.19 We conclude this chapter by considering whether compulsory treatment of a competent patient can ever be legally justifiable, outwith any Mental Health Act. Can an elderly, confused, yet still competent, patient be required to submit to dental treatment in his own 'interests'? Should a patient who refuses to bathe, yet retains mental capacity, be compelled to do so in the interests of those who share a ward with him?

In the UK, unlike the USA,[111] legislation has never enforced sterilisation on those seen as mentally or physically unfit to reproduce. In England, unlike in

---

[108] See s 58(1) and SI 1983/893, reg 16(2). Again, the Secretary of State is empowered to bring further treatments within the ambit of s 58(1).

[109] See s 58(2).

[110] Clause 11 of the Mental Health Bill contains proposals to amend sections 57, 58 and 63 of the Mental Health Act 1983, to ensure that the assessment of whether or not treatment should be given is independent. It is proposed that the role of 'responsible medical officers' is handed over to 'approved clinicians in charge of the treatment in question'.

[111] For a discussion of compulsory sterilisation laws in the USA, see MDA Freeman, 'Sterilising the Mentally Handicapped' in Freeman (ed), *Medicine, Ethics and Law*.

many countries in Europe, childhood vaccination has never been compulsory. Compulsory treatment outside the sphere of mental health law has been confined to the control of infectious disease. The Public Health (Control of Disease) Act 1984 provides that patients suffering from 'notifiable diseases', for example cholera or typhus,[112] lose not only their right to confidential treatment, but may also lose their liberty. Magistrates may order such a patient to be removed to hospital[113] and they may require suspected carriers of the disease, or a patient thought to be incubating the disease, to submit to medical examination.[114] HIV is not a notifiable disease under the 1984 Act.[115] However, the Public Health (Infectious Diseases) Regulations 1985 apply the provisions of the Act, giving magistrates powers to order compulsory detention and testing to people who have, or are suspected of having, AIDS. To our knowledge these powers have only once been invoked in the case of a patient with AIDS.

British laws governing control of communicable diseases have developed in a haphazard manner since the Victorian era. Designed to deal with plague diseases where infection swiftly robbed the victim of both his physical health and mental capacity, the legislation addresses a situation where the patient, deprived of his liberty, is likely either to die or recover in short order. The diseases which were first designated notifiable diseases carried a high risk of potentially deadly infection to others with little possibility, whatever the sufferer did, of protecting others from infection. Diseases such as HIV and hepatitis B (and even tuberculosis) do not fit into that pattern. A person may be seropositive for HIV or hepatitis B, but not ill – and certainly not suffering from any mental impairment of confusion. If he amends his lifestyle in conformity with medical advice the risk he poses to others is minimal. Using public health powers to force his compliance with 'safe living' necessarily involves an invasion of his liberty. For how long could society justifiably detain a person with hepatitis B? She will never cease to be a carrier of that disease.

The legality of the powers to detain people to prevent the spread of infectious diseases was tested in the European Court of Human Rights in 2005. In *Enhorn v Sweden*,[116] a HIV positive man who had unknowingly infected a 19-year-old girl was required under Sweden's Infectious Diseases Act 1988 to attend regular medical appointments. When he failed to do so, he was compulsorily isolated in hospital. Over a period of six years, he spent around 18 months in compulsory isolation. Did the Swedish courts unlawfully deprive Mr Enhorn of his liberty, protected by Article 5, or was the deprivation justified under Article 5(1)(e) for 'the lawful detention of persons for the prevention of spreading of infectious diseases, of persons of unsound mind, alcoholics or drug addicts, or vagrants'? The court held that the isolation was

---

[112] See ss 10, 11, 16.
[113] See s 38.
[114] See s 35.
[115] The AIDS (Control) Act 1987 requires reporting of HIV/AIDS, but on a wholly anonymous basis.
[116] (2005) 41 EHRR 30.

Compulsory treatment: beyond the Mental Health Acts   6.19

a disproportionate response to the threat to the public. Mr Enhorn's Article 5 right to liberty had been breached.[117] Compulsory isolation must be used only as a last resort.

Does a 'patient' who fails to protect other people from herself and recklessly disregards the welfare of others commit a criminal offence?[118] A midwife knows that she is infected by hepatitis B, conceals her condition and infects several patients; is her conduct significantly different from the train driver who, knowing that he is over the alcohol limit, still takes the controls and endangers his passengers? Identifying a pigeonhole in which to fit criminal liability for spreading diseases used to be tricky. If our hypothetical midwife's patients have consented to her ministrations, their consent is unlikely to be vitiated by lack of information about her infection, so no assault is committed.[119] In one case, a surgeon continued to operate, fraudulently concealing that he had hepatitis B. Several of his patients contracted hepatitis. The surgeon was ultimately convicted of the antiquated common law offence of causing a public nuisance.[120]

In *R v Dica*,[121] the Court of Appeal held that reckless transmission of serious disease constituted a criminal offence in English law.[122] Mr Dica was convicted on two counts of inflicting grievous bodily harm, contrary to section 20 of the Offences Against the Person Act 1861, on lovers whom he infected with HIV. The trial judge ruled (*inter alia*) that any consent on the part of the victims to the risk of contracting HIV, thus their knowledge or otherwise of the accused's seropositive status, was irrelevant and provided no defence because the women had no capacity to consent to such serious harm.[123] Following the judge's ruling, the accused chose not to give evidence and the question of whether his lovers knew of his HIV positive condition was not left to the jury. The Court of Appeal quashed the conviction and ordered a retrial. Consensual acts of sexual intercourse do not become unlawful '... merely because there may be a known risk to the health of one or other participant'.[124] As Judge LJ said,[125] '... interference of this kind with personal

[117] See A Mowbray, 'Compulsory Detention to Prevent the Spreading of Infectious Diseases' (2005) 5 *Human Rights Review* 387.
[118] See SH Bronitt, 'Spreading Disease and the Criminal Law' [1994] *Criminal Law Review* 21; KM Smith, 'Sexual Etiquette, Public Interest and the Criminal Law' (1991) 42 *Northern Ireland Legal Quarterly* 309.
[119] *R v Clarence* (1888) 22 QBD 23; *Hegarty v Shine* (1878) 14 Cox CC 124. But note a prosecution for causing grievous bodily harm of a doctor who allegedly infected his lover with herpes: (2002) Times, 12 January.
[120] *R v Gaud* (unreported), analysed in M Mulholland, 'Public Nuisance – A New Use for an Old Tool' (1995) 42 *Professional Negligence* 70.
[121] [2004] 3 All ER 593; see M Brazier, 'Do No Harm – Do Patients Have Responsibilities Too?' (2006) 65(2) *Cambridge Law Journal* 397.
[122] In *HM Advocate v Kelly* (2001) High Court of Judiciary, Glasgow, a Scottish court convicted a man who infected his lover with HIV of culpably and recklessly endangering her health: see J Chalmers, 'The Criminalisation of HIV Transmission' (2002) 28 *Journal of Medical Ethics* 160. See also *R v Konzani* (2005) 2 Cr App Rep 13, discussed in M Weait, 'Knowledge, Autonomy and Consent: *R v Konzani*' [2005] *Criminal Law Review* 673.
[123] Relying on *R v Brown* [1994] 1 AC 212, HL.
[124] [2004] 3 All ER 593 at 605.
[125] [2004] 3 All ER 593 at 606.

autonomy, and its level and extent, may only be made by Parliament'. The key question was had the victims consented to the risk of contracting HIV? To consent they must first be aware of the accused's condition, though knowledge alone would not normally establish consent. Absence of consent to such a risk did not vitiate consent to intercourse. Mr Dica was not guilty of rape. Inflicting serious bodily harm is no longer an offence parasitic on assault.[126] No assault need be proven, simply the imposition on the victim of serious harm to which she has not consented.

The decision in *Dica* goes beyond the proposal in the Draft Offences Against the Person Bill to criminalise intentional transmission of disease. It has met with much criticism.[127] Critics maintain that criminalisation will reinforce stigmatisation of people living with HIV, will deter patients from seeking testing and counselling, and, in its operation, discriminate against minority groups such as gay men and drug users.[128] John Spencer lends his voice to a powerful defence of *Dica*:

> To infect an unsuspecting person with a grave disease you know you have, or may have, by behaviour you know involves a risk of transmission, and that you know you could easily modify to reduce or eliminate the risk, is to harm another in a way that is both needless and callous. For that reason criminal liability is justified unless there are strong countervailing reasons.[129]

There are circumstances where private interests should rightly be subordinated to the public good. This reasoning lies at the heart of public health laws. The basis of enforced treatment under public health legislation is the protection of the public. A person can be removed to hospital if precautions to prevent the infection spreading can be taken but are not being taken and a 'serious risk of infection is thereby caused to other people'. There is no pretence that the compulsory powers are exercised solely in the 'best interests' of the patient. Where someone, albeit through no fault of his own, poses a threat to the health of others, his interest in autonomy cedes to others' interest in health and safety. Is this a doctrine applicable outside the confines of the Public Health Acts?

At common law an individual enjoys a right to self-defence. This is a common law right which almost certainly survives the enactment of a public right to use force to prevent crime in section 3 of the Criminal Law Act 1967. If you are attacked by a person so mentally-disordered that he could not be found guilty of any crime, you are still lawfully entitled to fend off the attacker using whatever degree of force is necessary. Might there then be circumstances in which treatment of a competent but confused or disturbed patient could be justified because of the harm his untreated condition poses to others? Can a patient who refuses to bathe be washed to prevent him becoming a hazard to hygiene? Such a suggestion sounds like heresy. Apart from the provisions in the Public Health Acts, the Mental Health Acts (discussed earlier), and special

---

[126] See *R v Ireland, R v Burstow* [1998] AC 147, HL.
[127] See M Weait, 'Criminal Law and Sexual Transmission of HIV: *R v Dica*' (2005) 68 *Modern Law Review* 121.
[128] Weait (2005) 68 *Modern Law Review* 121 at 134.
[129] JR Spencer, 'Liability for Reckless Infection – Part 2' (2004) 154 *New Law Journal* 448.

provisions in the National Assistance Act 1948 concerning elderly patients,[130] treatment of patients whose mental capacity is disputed is in theory lawful only if in the patient's 'best interests'. Section 47 of the National Assistance Act 1948 survives the Mental Capacity Act 2005, but will be substantially amended if the Mental Health Bill becomes law. The Bill amends the 2005 Act to control any deprivation of liberty of a person lacking mental capacity.[131] Schedules A1 and 1A will be inserted in the 2005 Act. The proposed Schedules set out at length complex rules for restraining hospital and care home residents.

'Best interests' = 'exclusive interests'?

6.20 In practice there can be little doubt that health care professionals are imposing 'treatment' on patients which cannot be shown to be exclusively in patients' interests. We are not suggesting that gynaecologists are sterilising women for eugenic reasons, or that surgeons are experimenting on unfortunate patients. Rather, patients are washed against their will. Patients are sometimes given medication they would rather not have, perhaps disguised in their food. Without such stratagems, nurses struggling to care for wards catering for confused geriatric patients, or working in long-stay institutions for voluntary mental patients, might give up the struggle. Should such miscreants be tracked down and prosecuted for assault?

It is unclear whether it is ever possible to divorce the interests of the individual entirely from the interests of the carer. The example that follows is unpleasant but is an instance of a dilemma that doctors have to face, and parents may have to live with. A young woman lives at home with her father. She is physically adult and normal but has the mind of a two-year-old. She is sexually provocative and fertile. She is incontinent and it is her father who every month has to cope with her periods. None of this distresses her any more than it would a two-year-old child. Sterilisation by hysterectomy could never be said to be in her best interests, even if sterilisation *per se* could. Yet her father may find that he cannot cope much longer. Dealing with menstruation is the straw that breaks the camel's back. Is that young woman better off without a uterus but with her father, or with her uterus intact but in an institution? Her interests and her father's are inextricably intertwined.

The interests of the patient must be the predominant interest to be considered. Perhaps other interests should also be taken into account? Individuals live as part of society. Society has obligations to the individual, especially the vulnerable individual. Individuals, though, have reciprocal obligations to

---

[130] Section 47 of that Act (as amended by the National Assistance (Amendment) Act 1951) empowers community health physicians to remove from their homes and place in a suitable hospital a person 'suffering from chronic disease or being aged, infirm or physically incapacitated' and unable to care for themselves. The community health physician may apply to a magistrates' court for an order removing such a person to hospital either in his own interests or to 'prevent injury to the health of, or serious nuisances to, other persons'. Section 47 is highly controversial and many geriatricians refused to invoke such powers: see *Mason and McCall Smith's Law and Medical Ethics*, pp 449–452.

[131] See Clause 38 of and Schedules 6–8 to the Bill.

society. Moreover, a careful review of all the decided cases on non-consensual treatment may suggest that courts do in fact take note of interests other than the patient's. If 19-year-old T would never have been properly aware of her pregnancy, or the birth and removal of a child, that experience may at any rate not have harmed her. Her mother and the child would certainly suffer. Would it be wrong to consider their interests? If the interests of others will inevitably be considered, would it not be better to do so openly?

Chapter 7

CLINICAL NEGLIGENCE[1]

7.1 The civil law of negligence is designed to provide compensation for one individual injured by another's negligence. A person seeking compensation for negligence has to establish (1) that the defendant owed him a duty to take care, (2) that the defendant was in breach of that duty (ie that he was careless), and (3) that the harm of which the victim complains was caused by that carelessness. He must satisfy all these tests to succeed. A widow succeeded in establishing that a hospital doctor was careless in not coming down to Casualty to examine her husband. He was admitted to hospital in an appalling state which eventually proved to be caused by arsenic poisoning. He died within hours. She failed to recover any compensation from the hospital in respect of her husband's death because the evidence was that, even had he been properly attended, he would still have died.[2]

The bare bones of the law of negligence outlined above are general to everyone, in the conduct of their everyday activities and in carrying out their job. They are not specific to doctors. Certain special factors about clinical negligence claims need to be introduced here. We have already mentioned the factual difficulty of proving negligence where there is a clash of medical opinion, and the effect that the need to prove fault has on the medical profession's reaction to claims against it. Doctors have become defensive. Patients used to be deferential. For a long time, English judges were unwilling to find against a 'medical man'. A brotherly solidarity bound the ancient professions of law and medicine together. Judicial attitudes are changing.[3] Claims against doctors and damages awarded against NHS hospitals have risen dramatically. The medical profession is haunted by the spectre of a malpractice crisis. In the next chapter, we explore whether it is a spectre of any substance.

---

[1]   See generally, V Harpwood, *Negligence and Healthcare: Clinical Claims and Risk* (2001) Informa; MA Jones, *Medical Negligence* (3rd edn, 2003) Sweet and Maxwell; CJ Lewis, *Clinical Negligence: A Practical Guide* (6th edn, 2006) Tottel Publishing.

[2]   *Barnett v Chelsea and Kensington Hospital Management Committee* [1969] 1 QB 428.

[3]   See Lord Woolf, 'Are the Courts Excessively Deferential to the Medical Profession?' (2001) 9 *Medical Law Review* 1.

Gross negligence may be punished by the criminal courts. We consider any possible criminal liability incurred by doctors at the end of this chapter.

Duty of care

7.2 A patient claiming against his doctor, or a hospital, generally has little difficulty in establishing that the defendant owes him a duty of care. A general practitioner accepting a patient on to her list undertakes a duty to him. A hospital and its entire staff owe a duty to patients admitted for treatment. If the patient is an NHS patient, the duty derives from the law of tort, which imposes a duty wherever one person can reasonably foresee that his conduct may cause harm to another. Where the patient is a private patient the duty arises from his contract with the doctor or the hospital. It is the same duty regardless of its origins. We look later at the circumstances in which the private patient is owed duties other than that of care. Difficulty arises where a person has not been accepted as a patient. English law does not oblige anyone to be a Good Samaritan. If someone has a coronary attack on an inter-city express, and a doctor fails to respond to the guard's call of, 'Is there a doctor on the train?', the doctor incurs no liability to the victim who dies for lack of medical treatment.[4] The law almost discourages the Good Samaritan, for if the doctor comes to the sick man's aid she undertakes a duty to him and may be liable if her skill fails her.[5]

A practical problem arises from the increasing practice of centralising Casualty facilities in larger hospitals. More and more hospitals have notices on their gates stating that they do not accept emergencies and accident victims. The notice refers the injured person to another named hospital. An accident victim whose injuries worsened because of the delay in reaching a Casualty department is unlikely to succeed in a claim against the hospital which refused him admission. It never assumed any duty to him. A hospital which operates a Casualty department, by contrast, is responsible for the patients who come within its doors – regardless of whether they have been formally admitted to hospital. By running a Casualty department, an NHS hospital undertakes to treat those who present themselves and will be liable in negligence if any failure on the part of their staff causes the patient to be sent away untreated.[6] Similarly, a GP owes a duty to emergency patients as well as to those on his own list. His contract with the NHS provides that he will treat visitors to his practice area falling suddenly ill. Like the hospital with the Casualty ward, he undertakes to treat the genuine emergency as much as his regular patients.

In *Kent v Griffiths*,[7] the duties owed to patients by the ambulance service came before the courts. The claimant was asthmatic. She was also pregnant.

---

4   Though she may be in breach of her professional code of conduct and may face professional disciplinary proceedings: see General Medical Council, *Good Medical Practice* (2006), para 11.
5   However, the standard of care which she must attain in such a case will take account of the conditions in which she volunteers to offer treatment.
6   *Barnett v Chelsea and Kensington Hospital Management Committee* [1969] 1 QB 428.
7   [2000] 2 All ER 474, CA. See K Williams, 'Litigation Against NHS Ambulance Services and The Rule in *Kent v Griffiths*' (2007) 15 *Medical Law Review* (forthcoming).

She had been exceptionally wheezy on the day in question and called her GP, who telephoned for an ambulance using the 999 service. The ambulance took 40 minutes to arrive despite two further anxious phone calls from the claimant's husband. On the journey to the hospital, the claimant was given oxygen. Shortly before arrival at the hospital she suffered a respiratory arrest resulting in serious brain damage and a miscarriage. The ambulance service denied negligence. They contended that their only duty to the claimant was not by their own actions to cause her any additional injury. They had no duty to come to her aid, to 'rescue' her from the danger her illness placed her in. Earlier cases[8] involving police and fire services had found that (generally) simply failing to respond to, or respond sufficiently promptly to, a 999 call did not render those services liable in negligence. The Court of Appeal was adamant that the ambulance service was different. It is an NHS service owing equivalent responsibility to patients in need of that service to doctors and nurses. Where an identifiable patient needed and summoned the ambulance service, there was a duty to respond. Due care on the part of an ambulance service demands a reasonably prompt response. There might be cases of conflicting priorities. For example, two major road accidents take place in the same city at the same time as a winter influenza epidemic. The elderly 'flu patient, whose call is given lower priority than the crash victims, is still owed a duty by the ambulance service. In the circumstances, there may be no breach of duty because, confronted by competing demands, the ambulance service responds reasonably.

One common scenario poses a tricky question relating to a hospital's duty to a patient. A patient is referred by her GP to an out-patients clinic at the local hospital. The consultant who examines her decides that she needs surgery as soon as possible. Lengthy waiting lists mean that surgery is delayed and the patient's condition deteriorates. Could she sue the hospital for negligence, arguing that she was owed a duty as a patient from the time she was first given an appointment to attend the hospital clinic? The courts have refused to order hospitals to operate on patients, refused to review waiting list priorities, but if she can prove actual damage from delay, might she have a claim in negligence? Determining what constitutes negligence would be awkward.[9]

Another possible avenue of redress for patients whose health deteriorates because treatment is delayed might be to sue their primary care trust (PCT).[10] PCTs are now responsible for arranging secondary care for all NHS patients within their jurisdiction. If a PCT fails to arrange, sufficiently promptly, a cardiac bypass for a patient with clogged arteries and he dies, could his family bring a claim in negligence? We would argue that PCTs, like the ambulance service, owe a duty to all their patients for arranging reasonably prompt and adequate secondary care for those in need of such care. That does not mean a PCT will be liable to compensate every patient who does not obtain the

---

[8] See, for example, *Capital & Counties plc v Hampshire County Council* [1997] QB 1004, CA.

[9] For a thorough survey of problems *re* duties to patients, see I Kennedy and A Grubb, *Medical Law: Text and Materials* (3rd edn, 2000) Butterworths, pp 277–369.

[10] See M Brazier and J Beswick, 'Who's Caring for Me?' (2006) 7 *Medical Law International* 183.

treatment he needs. The demand for secondary care may outstrip what the PCT can supply. The PCT must act reasonably. If the unfortunate cardiac patient did not get his operation quickly enough because the PCT lost his notes, or simply bungled the arrangements, his family should succeed. If difficult decisions about priorities for treatment have to be made, resulting in other sick patients having first call on the PCT budget, proving negligence will be harder.

Psychiatric harm

7.3   Patients may seek to sue, not just in respect of physical harm (such as brain damage in the course of surgery), but also in cases of psychiatric injury. Where additional psychiatric harm ensues directly from bungled treatment of the claimant herself, such claims have a fair chance of success.[11] In *Farrell v Merton, Sutton and Wandsworth Health Authority*,[12] the claimant suffered a horrific childbirth. She remained aware during an emergency Caesarean section, she contracted a post-operative infection and her child was born with serious brain damage. News of her child's condition was communicated inadequately and totally insensitively. She recovered compensation to include the adverse effects on her mental health of all that had happened to her.

Claims where one person alleges that negligent treatment of someone else, a close relative, caused them to suffer mental illness are harder to sustain. The law regards such people as *secondary* victims of psychiatric injury, akin to those who witness some horrific disaster, such as events at Hillsborough Football Stadium when fans were crushed to death as a result of negligence on the part of the police.[13] Just because a relative suffers injury from inadequate treatment and the effects of distress and grief make you ill, you are not owed a duty by the defendant hospital. Only if you actually suffer psychiatric injury from the trauma and shock of witnessing or discovering what has happened to your relative, are you likely to be owed any duty.[14] A husband who was present and watched his wife screaming in agony because she remained awake during Caesarean surgery and saw her haemorrhaging might well succeed. A mother coming to visit her daughter who had had routine surgery, and who, with no warning, is simply and abruptly told that her child is dead and directed to the mortuary might be owed a duty.[15] If, in either case, husband or mother were not in any sense at the scene of the 'accident' to their beloved, but simply learned of their fate or were told of the tragedy insensitively, they

---

[11]   See generally, Harpwood, *Negligence and Healthcare: Clinical Claims and Risk*, pp 14–17, 23–27; Lewis, *Clinical Negligence: A Practical Guide*, pp 268–297; P Case, 'Secondary Iatrogenic Harm: Claims for Psychiatric Damage Following a Death Caused By Medical Error' (2004) 67 *Modern Law Review* 501.

[12]   (2001) 57 BMLR 158; and see *Walters v North Glamorgan NHS Trust* [2002] EWCA Civ 1792.

[13]   On which see *Alcock v Chief Constable of South Yorkshire* [1991] 4 All ER 907, HL.

[14]   See *Sion v Hampstead Health Authority* [1994] 5 Med LR 170, CA.

[15]   Though see *Taylor v Somerset Health Authority* (1993) 16 BMLR 63.

will not recover compensation – even if, not unnaturally, the original injury to wife or daughter drives them into clinical depression.[16]

Medical examinations

7.4 A number of cases consider how far doctors examining patients not for the patient's benefit, but on the instruction of a third party, owe a duty to the patient being examined. For example, you have to have a medical examination before a job offer will be confirmed. Two different scenarios must be addressed.

(1)   The doctor, had he carried out the examination with due care, would have discovered that you had early signs of cancer. Delay in diagnosis means that your cancer is now inoperable. Did the doctor who performed your 'medical' owe you a duty to alert you to your dangerous condition? There is no case directly in point but such a duty may well be found.[17]

(2)   The doctor carries out the 'medical' negligently and wrongly concludes that you are unfit for the job. You lose the chance of the job. Does the doctor owe you a duty to protect you from the financial (economic) loss of not getting the job? One case suggests such a duty is owed.[18] A later judgment of the Court of Appeal is to the contrary.[19] The examining doctor owed no duty to the job applicant to protect him from economic loss: he was not responsible for looking after his job prospects.[20]

The medical standard of care

7.5 The second matter that any claimant in negligence has to prove is that the defendant was careless. The onus of proof is on the claimant. He must show that the defendant fell below the required standard of care. The basic standard is that of the reasonable man in the circumstances of the defendant. A professional person must meet the standard of competence of the reasonable professional doing his job. A woman who went to a jeweller's to have her ear pierced developed an abscess because the jeweller's instruments were not aseptically sterile. The jeweller had taken all the precautions that any jeweller could be expected to take. The woman's claim failed. The defendant had done all a jeweller could reasonably be expected to do.[21] If she wanted the standard of care a surgeon could offer, she should have consulted a surgeon.

---

[16] For an exceptionally generous interpretation of what may constitute trauma and shock of witnessing injury to a wife, see *Frogatt v Chesterfield and North Derbyshire Royal Hospital NHS Trust* [2002] All ER (D) 218 (Dec).

[17] See Harpwood, *Negligence and Healthcare: Clinical Claims and Risk*, pp 18–21; and see DM Kloss, 'Pre-Employment Health Screening' in M Freeman and A Lewis (eds), *Law and Medicine: Current Legal Issues* (2000) OUP, Vol 3.

[18] *Baker v Kaye* (1996) 39 BMLR 12.

[19] *Kapfunde v Abbey National plc* (1998) 46 BMLR 176, CA.

[20] For discussion of other circumstances where a medical examination is carried out on the instructions of a third party, see E Jackson, *Medical Law: Text, Cases and Materials* (2006) OUP, pp 119–121.

[21] *Phillips v William Whiteley Ltd* [1938] 1 All ER 566.

7.5 Clinical Negligence

Before examining the case law in clinical negligence, we should note briefly section 1 of the Compensation Act 2006. The Act was passed as something of a knee-jerk reaction to much publicised claims of a 'compensation culture'. Supposedly, schools were refusing to take children on school trips and local authorities were closing playgrounds to avoid any risk of liability for injury. Section 1 provides:

> A court considering a claim in negligence or breach of statutory duty may, in determining whether the defendant should have taken particular steps to meet a standard of care (whether by taking precautions against a risk or otherwise), have regard to whether a requirement to take those steps might—
>
> (a)   prevent a desirable activity from being undertaken at all, to a particular extent or in a particular way, or
>
> (b)   discourage persons from undertaking functions in connection with a desirable activity.

We doubt that the Act will have any effect on clinical negligence claims. Unless judges decide to accept the wildest claims about defensive medicine, and determine that allowing doctors to be sued damages health care, the Compensation Act 2006 in our context needs only to be noted and not treated as a matter of great concern.

The standard of care demanded of the doctor, then, is the standard of the reasonably skilled and experienced doctor. In *Bolam v Friern Hospital Management Committee*,[22] the judge said:

> The test is the standard of the ordinary skilled man exercising and professing to have that special skill. A man need not possess the highest expert skill, it is well established law that it is sufficient if he exercises the ordinary skill of an ordinary competent man exercising that particular art.

The defendant doctor will be tested against the standard of the doctor in his particular field of medicine: the general practitioner must meet the standard of the competent general practitioner, the consultant gynaecologist the standard of the competent consultant in that specialty. As Lord Scarman, put it: '... a doctor who professes to exercise a special skill must exercise the ordinary skill of his specialty'.[23] A patient who attends her general practitioner complaining of an eye disorder cannot require him to have the skill of a consultant ophthalmologist. She can complain if the GP fails to refer her on to a consultant when her condition should have alerted a reasonable GP to the need for further advice or treatment.

Junior doctors

7.6 No allowance is made for inexperience. The Court of Appeal has consistently rejected arguments that standards of care should vary to allow for the degree of experience possessed by the defendant. They held a L-driver liable where, although she had done the best that could be expected of a learner, she fell short of the standard of the reasonably competent and

---

[22]   [1957] 1 WLR 582 at 586.

[23]   *Maynard v West Midlands Regional Health Authority* [1984] 1 WLR 634 at 638, HL.

experienced motorist.[24] In *Wilsher v Essex Area Health Authority*,[25] the Appeal Court considered the liability of junior hospital staff. Martin Wilsher was born nearly three months prematurely. He was admitted to a neonatal unit managed by the defendants where skilled treatment probably saved his life. He needed extra oxygen to survive. Sadly, junior doctors made an error in monitoring the oxygen levels in Martin's blood and, on two occasions, he received an excess of oxygen. It was argued by Martin's lawyers that excess oxygen caused him to develop retrolental fibroplasia (RLF), a retinal condition which left Martin nearly blind. Ultimately, the House of Lords held that the plaintiff had failed to prove that excess oxygen caused RLF in Martin and ordered a retrial.[26] The importance of the Court of Appeal's judgment lies in their exposition of the rules on negligence by junior staff. Argument by the defendants that staff concerned did their best in view of their inexperience was rejected. The law requires all medical staff in such a unit to meet the standard of competence and experience society expects from those filling such demanding posts. Their Lordships recognised the need for medical staff to train 'on the job'. They stressed that a finding of negligence on one occasion did not imply incompetence or any degree of moral culpability. Legal and moral tests of negligence may differ. Doctors may find the distinction hard to understand. One point must be made clear here. A junior doctor, who, recognising his inexperience, calls in his consultant will have discharged his duty. Responsibility in law will move to the consultant.[27]

Ascertaining the standard of care: Bolam rules?

7.7 How does a court ascertain the standard of skill which the doctor should have met? Let us consider the case of Mr Bolam again. He was given electro-convulsive therapy and sustained fractures. He argued that the doctor was negligent (1) in not giving him relaxant drugs, (2) as drugs were not given, in failing to provide adequate physical restraints, and (3) in not warning him of the risks involved in the treatment. We have seen in Chapter 5 that he failed in his argument that he should have been warned. As to the absence of relaxant drugs or restraints, the evidence was that while some doctors would have thought them necessary, many did not. The judge found the doctor not guilty of negligence for he acted:

> ... in accordance with a practice accepted as proper by a responsible body of medical men skilled in that particular area ... a man is not negligent, if he is acting in accordance with such a practice, merely because there is a body of opinion who would take a contrary view.[28]

The *Bolam* test was destined to become (in)famous. At first sight, it is unexceptional. Courts cannot decide whether a doctor was negligent without

24 *Nettleship v Weston* [1971] 2 QB 691, CA.
25 [1986] 3 All ER 801, CA.
26 [1988] 1 All ER 871; see below at 7.17.
27 See *Jones v Manchester Corpn* [1952] 2 QB 852 at 871. Note that in *Wilsher v Essex Area Health Authority* [1986] 3 All ER 801, CA, Dr Wiles, the house officer, was found not negligent.
28 *Bolam v Friern Hospital Management Committee* [1957] 1 WLR 582 at 587–588.

expert evidence of 'accepted medical practice'.[29] Within any profession, genuine differences of opinion may surface. In obstetrics, doctors have different views about how best to deliver a premature breech baby. Some doctors consider that, in every case, the woman should be strongly advised to agree to an elective Caesarean section. Others believe that a trial of labour should be permitted and surgery should be resorted to only if complications ensue. Both sides of the debate advance logical reasons for their respective judgments. Judges are not well placed to resolve such questions.

The *Bolam* test, focusing on 'accepted practice', came to be applied to all claims for professional negligence. 'Responsible professional opinion' is the litmus test of liability for solicitors, accountants and architects, just as much as for doctors. However, there was a crucial difference. In claims against other professionals, the courts rigorously scrutinised expert evidence to ensure that evidence of professional opinion could be demonstrated to be responsible and reasonable.[30] In claims against doctors, it appeared that as long as suitably qualified expert witnesses endorsed the defendant's conduct, English judges simply deferred to the doctors. Providing the expert testimony was seen to be truthful, the courts assumed that it must be responsible.[31] The key to successfully defending a claim in negligence was to find expert witnesses who would be impressive in the witness box.[32]

Trial judges who took it upon themselves to scrutinise and evaluate medical evidence faced reprimands from above. In *Maynard v West Midlands Regional Health Authority*,[33] the plaintiff had consulted a consultant physician and a surgeon with symptoms indicating tuberculosis, but she also displayed symptoms which might indicate Hodgkin's disease. The doctors decided on a diagnostic operation, mediastinoscopy. It carried a risk of damage to the vocal cords and Mrs Maynard's vocal cords were in fact damaged. She proved to have tuberculosis. She alleged that the defendants were negligent in subjecting her to the operation. Her expert witness argued that the operation should never have been done. He would have regarded her condition as almost certainly a case of tuberculosis. The defendants called a formidable number of experts who testified that the fatality rate for Hodgkin's disease if treatment was delayed justified the defendants in exposing Mrs Maynard to the risk of the mediastinoscopy. The original judge preferred the evidence of the plaintiff's expert witness. The Court of Appeal and the House of Lords overruled him. Lord Scarman said:

> ... a judge's 'preference' for one body of distinguished professional opinion to another also professionally distinguished is not sufficient to establish negligence in a practitioner ...[34]

[29] See *A v Burne* [2006] EWCA Civ 24 at para 10.
[30] See, for example, *Edward Wong Finance Co Ltd v Johnson, Stokes & Master* [1984] AC 296, PC.
[31] See the account of the first instance decision in *Bolitho v City & Hackney Health Authority* [1998] AC 232, HL.
[32] Graphically illustrated in *Whitehouse v Jordan* [1981] 1 All ER 267, HL.
[33] [1984] 1 WLR 634, HL.
[34] [1984] 1 WLR 634 at 639, HL.

In *Maynard*, the defendants had numbers on their side. In *De Freitas v O'Brien*,[35] the expert evidence established that only a tiny minority of neurosurgeons endorsed the defendant's practice, just four or five out of 250 doctors in that specialty. The Court of Appeal ruled that the body of opinion supporting the defendant need not be large. The perception arose that English judges would not cross swords with the doctors, however thin the evidence advanced in defence of a claim.[36]

Individual judges did on occasion attempt to assert judicial authority over medical evidence. Sir John Donaldson MR[37] emphasised that professional opinion must be '... *rightly* accepted as proper by a body of skilled and experienced medical men'. In 1968, the Court of Appeal in *Hucks v Cole*[38] rejected expert evidence in the defendant's favour. Evidence that other doctors would have followed the same practice as the defendant was 'a very weighty matter', but not conclusive. Such challenges to the supremacy of medical evidence tended to be ephemeral, apparently forgotten in the next flurry of cases.

Bolitho: a new dawn?

7.8 In *Bolitho v City & Hackney Health Authority*,[39] Lord Browne-Wilkinson reasserted the proper authority of the courts. *Bolitho* involved questions of causation as much as breach of duty. The facts, briefly, were these. Patrick Bolitho, aged two, was admitted to the defendant's hospital suffering from respiratory difficulties. On the second afternoon of this hospital stay, Patrick was in respiratory distress. A nurse summoned the paediatric registrar. She promised to attend as soon as possible, but did not do so. Patrick appeared to recover. At 2.00pm, Patrick was once again having breathing problems. The registrar was called a second time, but again failed to attend. At 2.30pm, the boy collapsed; he stopped breathing and suffered a cardiac arrest causing catastrophic brain damage. The hospital admitted negligence on the part of the paediatric registrar. She should have come to examine the child, or arranged for a suitable deputy to do so. They denied liability, however, arguing that, even if the doctor had attended Patrick prior to 2.30pm, she would not have intubated him. Intubation offered the only prospect of averting the respiratory distress and cardiac arrest which Patrick suffered at 2.30pm.

The trial judge accepted the doctor's evidence of fact that *she* would *not* have intubated Patrick. The question then became whether or not a competent doctor who had attended Patrick *should* have intubated the child. The *Bolam*

---

35 [1993] 4 Med LR 281, CA.
36 Michael Jones expressed the state of play as a football score. In six medical negligence claims before the House of Lords between 1980 and 1999, the score stood at *Plaintiffs 0 Defendants 6*: see MA Jones, 'The *Bolam* Test and the Responsible Expert' [1999] *Tort Law Review* 226.
37 *Sidaway v Board of Governors of the Royal Bethlem Hospital* [1984] 2 WLR 778 at 752, CA. See also per Lord Bridge [1985] 1 All ER 643 at 663, HL.
38 [1993] 4 Med LR 393, CA.
39 [1998] AC 232, HL.

question became the key to resolving causation. The experts were sharply divided. The plaintiff's five experts testified that Patrick's history of breathing problems was such that responsible practice required that he be intubated to prevent just the sort of catastrophe which materialised. The defendants' three experts argued that, apart from the two episodes of respiratory difficulty, Patrick seemed generally well. Intubation was distressing and not risk free for so young a child. A responsible doctor would not have intubated Patrick prior to 2.30pm. The judge ruled that, as both sets of experts represented a body of professional opinion espoused by distinguished and truthful experts, he was bound to conclude that Patrick's injury did not result from the defendants' admitted negligence. In effect, the judge asserted that he was disqualified from any form of scrutiny of expert medical evidence.

The Court of Appeal upheld the trial judge. The case proceeded to the House of Lords. Two issues fell to be resolved by their Lordships. The first, whether the *Bolam* test ever applies in determining causation, will be addressed later. The second is our present concern: does the *Bolam* test require a judge to accept without question truthful evidence from eminent experts? Their Lordships, speaking with one voice through Lord Browne-Wilkinson, answered that question with a firm and forceful 'no'. Reviewing precedents relating to claims of negligence against other professionals, his Lordship declared that:

> ... the court has to be satisfied that the exponents of the body of opinion relied on can demonstrate that such opinion has a logical basis. In particular, in cases involving as they so often do, the weighing up of risks against benefits, the judge before accepting a body of opinion as being reasonable, responsible or respectable, will need to be satisfied that, in forming their views, the experts have directed their minds to the questions of comparative risks and benefits and have reached a defensible conclusion on the matter.[40]

Expert evidence after *Bolitho* remains of the highest importance to the success or failure of clinical negligence claims. Lord Browne-Wilkinson acknowledged that in '... the vast majority of cases the fact that distinguished experts in the field are of a particular opinion will demonstrate the reasonableness of that opinion'. None the less, he went on to say '... if in a rare case, it can be demonstrated that the professional opinion is not capable of withstanding logical analysis, the judge is entitled to hold that the body of opinion is not reasonable or responsible'.[41]

Bolitho returns *Bolam* to its proper limits.[42] Doctors, like solicitors and all other professionals, are subject to legal scrutiny. The courts, not the medical profession, are the ultimate arbiters of the standard of care in clinical

---

40   [1998] AC 232 at 242, HL.
41   [1998] AC 232 at 243, HL.
42   As Andrew Grubb so nicely put it, '"Eureka!" The courts have got it at last. Expert evidence, whether of professional practice or otherwise is not conclusive in a medical negligence case that the defendant has not been careless!': A Grubb, 'Negligence, Causation and Bolam' (1998) 6 *Medical Law Review* 378 at 380. See also MA Jones, 'The Illogical Expert' (1999) 15 *Professional Negligence* 117.

negligence claims. *Bolitho* has generated a plethora of academic commentary.[43] How influential *Bolitho* is remains difficult to evaluate. Pessimistic commentators point out that Lord Browne-Wilkinson speaks of 'rare' cases and later notes that it will be 'very seldom' that it would be right to conclude that views genuinely held by competent experts were unreasonable. *Bolitho*, they fear, will do little to aid patients.[44] Others are concerned that *Bolitho* might go too far and stifle innovative medicine. Mason and Laurie suggest:

> *Bolam* provides some protection for innovative or minority opinion. If this protection is removed then the opinion which the cautious practitioner will wish to follow will be that which involves least risk. This may have an inhibiting effect on medical progress: after all, many advances in medicine have been made by those who have pursued an unconventional line of therapy.[45]

We hope both fears will prove unfounded. We believe *Bolitho* does herald a new dawn. The proclamation of judicial authority over medical practice in *Bolitho* comes at last from the Law Lords. It comes at a time when several other developments in the manner medical practice is regulated and audited are placing limits on unfettered clinical autonomy.[46] Cases decided after *Bolitho* send somewhat mixed messages.

In *Marriott v West Midlands Health Authority*,[47] the plaintiff had suffered head injuries in a fall. He was discharged from hospital but remained unwell. Eight days after the fall he was visited by the defendant general practitioner. The GP carried out some basic neurological tests, prescribed painkillers and told the plaintiff's wife to telephone him again if her husband's condition got worse. Four days later the plaintiff collapsed and was readmitted to hospital. A large extradural haemotoma was operated on and surgery revealed a skull fracture and internal bleeding. The plaintiff was left paralysed and afflicted by a speech disorder. In the claim against the GP, the crucial question was whether a responsible GP would have judged that a full neurological examination was called for and re-admitted the plaintiff to hospital. The defendant's expert acknowledged that the defendant should have recognised that there was a risk that the plaintiff had a clot on the brain, but contended that the risk was so small that it was not negligent to fail to refer the plaintiff for further tests. The trial judge evaluating that evidence held that, although the risk was small, '... the consequences, if things go wrong are disastrous to the patient. In such circumstances, it is my view that the only reasonable prudent course ... is to re-admit for further testing and observation.' The Court of Appeal upheld the judgment. Beldam LJ endorsed the judge's exercise in risk assessment. Whatever the expert witnesses might say, the devastating nature of the

---

[43] See H Teff, 'The Standard of Care in Medical Negligence – Moving on from *Bolam*' (1998) 18 *Oxford Journal of Legal Studies* 473; J Keown, 'Reining in the Bolam Test' (1998) 57 *Cambridge Law Journal* 248; J Badenoch, 'Brushes With Bolam: Where Will It Lead?' (2005) 72 *Medico-Legal Journal* 127.

[44] See N Glover, 'Bolam in the House of Lords' (1999) 15 *Professional Negligence* 42.

[45] JK Mason and GT Laurie, *Mason and McCall Smith's Law and Medical Ethics* (7th edn, 2006) OUP, p 314.

[46] See M Brazier and J Miola, 'Bye-Bye Bolam: A Medical Litigation Revolution' (2000) 8 *Medical Law Review* 85.

[47] [1999] Lloyd's Rep Med 23.

consequences of a clot on the brain were such that no responsible doctor would have subjected the plaintiff to that risk.[48] In *A v Burne*,[49] Sedley LJ stressed that:

> ... judges are there to exercise judgment, and their judgment cannot be entirely dictated by expert evidence, even where the evidence is unopposed. The question always remains (provided a party raises it) whether the expert evidence makes sense.

Extra-judicially both the then Lord Chancellor[50] and Lord Chief Justice[51] have indicated that judges should no longer blindly defer to medical opinion. Alasdair MacLean takes a less optimistic view.[52] His research into clinical negligence claims shows that out of 64 cases post-*Bolitho*, but before 2001, *Bolitho* was only even mentioned in 29. It has been made clear that *Bolitho* in no sense reverses the burden of proof,[53] but nor was it ever designed to do so. Judges have reinforced the view that it will seldom be right to reject expert opinion as unreasonable.[54] And a tendency to presume that eminent experts will necessarily give logical evidence can be discerned in *Wisniewski v Central Manchester Health Authority*.[55]

If *Bolitho* heralds a new dawn for patient-claimants, will it endanger innovative medicine? Will doctors simply retreat into defensive practice? Will guidelines and protocols replace a sensitive and imaginative approach to the needs of particular patients? This should not happen. *Bolitho* does not seek to usurp judgments which properly rest with doctors. Post-*Bolitho*, judges are not empowered to decide what constitutes good medical practice. What *Bolitho* does is to require expert witnesses to justify and explain the basis of their judgments.[56]

'Responsible practice' means current practice

7.9 It has never been a defence for a doctor to say that a practice was widely accepted when he was at medical school and is therefore accepted practice, once informed medical opinion has rejected the practice.[57] A doctor clearly cannot '... obstinately and pig-headedly carry on with some old technique if it has been proved contrary to what is really substantially the whole of informed medical opinion'.[58] Doctors must keep up to date with new developments. But

---

[48] *Penney v East Kent Area Health Authority* [2000] Lloyd's Rep Med 41; *Reynolds v North Tyneside Health Authority* [2002] Lloyd's Rep Med 453; *Lillywhite v University College London Hospital NHS Trust* [2005] EWCA Civ 1466.
[49] [2006] EWCA Civ 24 at para 10.
[50] Lord Irvine of Lairg, 'The Patient, the Doctor their Lawyers and the Judge: Rights and Duties' (1999) 7 *Medical Law Review* 255.
[51] See Lord Woolf (2001) 9 *Medical Law Review* 1.
[52] A MacLean, 'Beyond Bolam and Bolitho' (2002) 5 *Medical Law International* 205.
[53] *Smith v West Yorkshire Health Authority* [2004] EWHC 1592 (QB).
[54] *Morris v Blackpool Victoria NHS Trust* [2003] EWHC 1744 (QB); *Dunn v South Tyneside Health Care NHS Trust* [2003] EWCA Civ 1878.
[55] [1998] Lloyd's Rep Med 85.
[56] Brazier & Miola (2000) 8 *Medical Law Review* 85 at 106.
[57] *Hunter v Hanley* (1955) SC 200.
[58] *Bolam v Friern Hospital Management Committee* [1957] 1 WLR 582 at 587.

there is an inevitable 'time-lag' between the making of new findings by researchers and the percolation of ideas through to doctors in the field. A doctor will be judged by the standard of awareness and sophistication to be expected of a doctor in his sort of practice. Great emphasis is placed on the professional position and the specialty of the defendant.[59] A patient who suffered from brachial palsy as a result of his arm being extended in a certain position while he was given a blood transfusion in the course of a bladder operation brought a claim against the anaesthetist. Six months before the operation, an article had appeared in the *Lancet* condemning this practice because of the risk of brachial palsy. The claim failed. Failure to read one recent article was not negligent.[60]

The relevant date to judge current practice must be the date of the operation or treatment, not the date the claim comes to trial. In *Roe v Ministry of Health*, a patient had become permanently paralysed after an injection of the spinal anaesthetic Nupercaine, administered in 1947. His claim against the doctors and the hospital came to trial in 1954. Before the operation, the drug had been kept in glass ampoules in a solution of phenol. The accident to the patient occurred because phenol percolated through invisible cracks in the ampoules and contaminated the Nupercaine.

No-one had ever known this to happen. The claim in negligence failed. Lord Denning said:

> We must not look at the 1947 accident with 1954 spectacles.[61]

Once a tragic incident of this nature has occurred and has been attended by publicity then, of course, a further incident would easily be proved to be negligence. Current practice would have been shown to be wanting.

Protocols and guidelines[62]

7.10 The buzzwords in medicine today are evidence-based medicine and clinical governance. Within the NHS, the Government seeks to ensure that treatment provided to patients is soundly based on good practice derived from concrete evidence. The National Institute of Clinical Excellence (NICE) is expressly instructed to investigate medical practice and provide authoritative guidelines on good practice. The Royal Colleges of Medicine, and other doctors' organisations, increasingly draw up protocols for treatment and issue guidelines on good practice.

---

[59] See *Gascoine v Ian Sheridan & Co* [1994] 5 Med LR 437.
[60] *Crawford v Board of Governors of Charing Cross Hospital* (1953) Times, 8 December, CA. See also *Whiteford v Hunter* (1950) 94 Sol Jo 758, HL.
[61] *Roe v Ministry of Health* [1954] 2 QB 66 at 84.
[62] See V Harpwood, 'NHS Reform: Audit Protocols and the Standard of Care in Medical Negligence' (1994) 1 *Medical Law International* 1; V Harpwood, 'The Manipulation of Medical Practice in Law and Medicine' and H Teff, 'Clinical Guidelines, Negligence and Medical Practice', both in M Freeman and A Lewis (eds), *Law and Medicine: Current Legal Issues*; A Samanta *et al*, 'The Role of Clinical Guidelines in Medical Negligence Litigation: A Shift from the Bolam Standard' (2006) 14 *Medical Law Review* 321.

Evidence of good practice as defined by protocol and guidelines will play a role in any claim for clinical negligence. The considered judgment of NICE, or the profession itself, will be evidence of what constitutes responsible practice. Does this mean any doctor departing from official guidelines will be proven negligent? Some doctors fear guidelines enforced by the courts will lead to a 'tick-box' approach to patient care.[63] Doctors will cease to exercise professional judgment based on the needs and circumstances of the individual patient. This should not happen. Where departure from the guidelines can be justified in the interests of the patient, the doctor discharges his duty of care. Blind adherence to guidelines or protocols would itself be negligent. *Bolitho* requires that responsible practice be demonstrably logical and defensible. Guidelines will offer some evidence of what constitutes proper treatment for a patient's condition. Evidence that a patient requires a different mode of care should not be excluded by the presence of such general guidance.[64]

Diagnosis

7.11 A wrong diagnosis is by itself no evidence of negligence on the part of a doctor. As a Scottish judge said:

> In the realm of diagnosis and treatment there is ample scope for a genuine difference of opinion and one man is clearly not negligent merely because his conclusion differs from that of other professional men ...[65]

A patient alleging that a wrong diagnosis was negligent must establish either that the doctor failed to carry out an examination or a test which the patient's symptoms called for, or that his eventual conclusion[66] was one that no competent doctor would have arrived at. While the myth of infallibility of 'clinical judgment' has been exploded, a patient who relies solely on an allegation that the doctor's conclusions were mistaken will rarely succeed. Not surprisingly, a doctor who failed to diagnose a broken knee-cap in a man who had fallen twelve feet on to a concrete floor was found to be negligent.[67] Other examples are hard to find.[68]

The courts are readier to find negligence when a patient and his experts can point to a specific failure on the part of the doctor. A Casualty doctor who failed to examine or X-ray a drunken patient admitted with the information that he had been seen under a moving lorry was found to be negligent when, after the patient's death next day, he was discovered to have 18 fractured ribs and extensive damage to his lungs. It was no defence that the patient never complained of pain: the doctor should have known that alcohol would dull

---

[63]   See J Warden, 'NICE to Sort our Clinical Wheat from Chaff' (1999) 318 *British Medical Journal* 416.
[64]   See Brazier and Miola (2000) 8 *Medical Law Review* 85; but see also B Hurwitz, 'How does evidence based guidance influence determinations of medical negligence?' (2004) 329 *British Medical Journal* 1024.
[65]   *Hunter v Hanley* 1955 SLT 213 at 217.
[66]   See *Lillywhite v University College London Hospitals NHS Trust* [2005] EWCA Civ 1466.
[67]   *Newton v Newton's New Model Laundry* (1959) Times, 3 November.
[68]   For details of a number of unreported more recent cases, see Harpwood, *Negligence and Healthcare: Clinical Claims and Risk*, pp 98–102.

the patient's reaction to pain.[69] The doctor must be alert to the patient's background. A GP who failed to test for, and diagnose, malaria in a patient who had recently returned from East Africa was held liable for the patient's death. The doctor was consulted nine days after the patient's return to this country; a relative suggested malaria, but the doctor diagnosed flu. Six days later malaria was diagnosed in hospital, where the patient died that day.[70] Failure to diagnose diabetes where the symptoms complained of by the patient should have alerted the doctor to this possibility may lead to liability.[71] Too hasty a diagnosis of hysteria or depression will often be negligent.[72] By dismissing the patient as 'neurotic', physical symptoms go uninvestigated.[73]

In all the above examples, the doctor was negligent because he failed to act on information available to him and/or to perform routine tests. Where a diagnostic procedure is not routine, is costly, painful or risky, an additional factor has to be considered. Do the symptoms displayed by the patient justify subjecting him to the procedure? The doctor faces a legal as well as a medical dilemma. If he does not arrange for the test and the patient does suffer from some condition which the test would have revealed, the doctor may be sued for that failure. If he does arrange the test and an inherent risk of the test harms the patient, the patient may sue if the test reveals that the doctor's suspicions were groundless. We saw that that is what happened with Staff Nurse Maynard.[74] The defendants were *not* liable to her because they had followed accepted practice in going ahead with the test, despite its dangers. Doctors argue forcefully that alacrity to pin liability on them for every diagnostic error may cause patients to be submitted to more expensive and potentially risky procedures than may be strictly medically desirable.

Treatment

7.12 A claim in respect of negligent treatment may be based on an allegation that the treatment chosen was inappropriate or that, while the treatment embarked on was correct, it was negligently carried out. Doctors must ensure that they act on, and supply each other with, adequate information. A GP prescribing drugs must check what other medication the patient is on. Doctors must be alert to common drug reactions and actively seek relevant information from patients. A clinic which injected a woman with penicillin was held liable for her death an hour later.[75] Had they inquired of her, or examined her records, they would have been aware of her allergy to penicillin. A GP arranging for the admission of a pregnant patient to hospital, while he was

---

[69] *Wood v Thurston* (1951) Times, 25 May.
[70] *Langley v Campbell* (1975) Times, 6 November; and see *Tuffil v East Surrey Area Health Authority* (1978) Times, 15 March (failure to diagnose amoebic dysentery in a patient who had spent many years in the tropics).
[71] MDU, *Annual Report* (1990), pp 26–27.
[72] *Serre v De Filly* (1975) OR (2d) 490; and see MDU, *Annual Report* (1982), pp 22–23 and (1983), p 24.
[73] See Harpwood, *Negligence and Healthcare: Clinical Claims and Risk.*
[74] *Maynard v West Midlands Regional Health Authority* [1984] 1 WLR 634; see above at 7.7.
[75] *Chin Keow v Govt of Malaysia* [1967] 1 WLR 813.

treating her for a septic finger, was found negligent in not so informing the hospital. She contracted septicaemia. Had the hospital known of the state of her finger they would have put her on antibiotics straight away.[76] Doctors must be wary of relying entirely on information supplied by their colleagues. A patient was admitted for a gynaecological operation. The gynaecologist asked a general surgeon to remove what he said was a ganglion from the patient's wrist. Thus the patient would be spared two separate operations. It was not a ganglion. Surgery of that sort was inappropriate and the patient's hand was permanently paralysed. The Medical Defence Union (MDU) settled because the general surgeon should have made his own pre-operative assessment, and not relied on a colleague from another specialty.[77]

Once a doctor is properly informed and has selected his course of treatment, he must ensure that he carries it out properly. He must check the dosage of any drug. Prescribing an overdose will readily be found to be negligent.[78] He must be sure that his handwriting is legible.[79] Care must also be taken always to read drug labelling properly. In a tragic case,[80] a senior house officer misread a label and administered potassium chloride instead of saline to a newborn infant. The baby died.

Where surgery is called for, the risk of injury is increased. Especially risky is the administration of the anaesthetic. The anaesthetist will be found to be negligent if he failed to make a proper pre-operative assessment of the patient, failed to check his equipment, failed to monitor the patient's blood pressure and/or heartbeat in the course of surgery or if, an inevitable accident having occurred, the anaesthetist fails to invoke adequate resuscitation measures. Some specific failure on the defendant's part must be pinpointed. A disturbing number of claims arise from failure to intubate the patient properly (putting the tube in the wrong place) or attaching tubes to the wrong gas so that the patient fails to receive essential oxygen.[81] Several claims have arisen from failure to anaesthetise the patient completely. Patients are paralysed and unable to communicate, but remain awake and feel pain throughout surgery.[82]

An anaesthetic tragedy of itself is generally not evidence of negligence. An anaesthetist who injected cocaine instead of procaine was found negligent,[83] as was the junior doctor who injected pentothal into an anaesthetised patient, causing his death.[84] If the wrong drug, the wrong dosage or a contaminated drug is used, the patient's claim will generally be made good. The exception will be where the error cannot be laid at the anaesthetist's door. So, as we saw in *Roe v Ministry of Health*,[85] a patient who was paralysed because a then

---

[76]   *Hucks v Cole* (1968) 112 Sol Jo 483.

[77]   MDU, *Annual Report* (1984), p 18.

[78]   *Dwyer v Roderick* (1983) 127 Sol Jo 805; and see J Finch, 'A Costly Oversight for Pharmacists' (1982) 132 *New Law Journal* 176.

[79]   *Prendergast v Sam and Dee* [1989] 1 Med LR 36.

[80]   MDU, *Annual Report* (1989), p 32.

[81]   See MDU, *Annual Report* (1988), pp 28–29 and (1989), pp 20–21.

[82]   For example, *Taylor v Worcester and District Health Authority* [1991] 2 Med LR 215.

[83]   *Collins v Hertfordshire Corporation* [1952] 2 QB 852.

[84]   *Jones v Manchester Corporation* [1952] 2 QB 852.

[85]   [1954] 2 QB 66, CA.

unknown risk of phenol percolating into the ampoules of local anaesthetic materialised, recovered no compensation.

Surgery must be performed with the utmost care. One judge has suggested that the more skilled the surgeon, the higher the standard of care.[86] Some errors advertise negligence. Leaving swabs and equipment inside the patient is a good example. A surgeon must accept responsibility for such matters and not rely on nursing staff.[87] Nor does a surgeon's responsibility end with the careful completion of surgery. He must give his patient proper post-operative care and advice. A surgeon performed a cosmetic operation just below the eye. He told his patient to inform him if bleeding occurred within 48 hours. It did and the patient tried to telephone the surgeon and got no reply. The surgeon was held to be negligent.[88]

Overtired, overworked doctors

7.13 If a doctor makes a mistaken diagnosis because she is intolerably weary, or makes a surgical error because her dexterity fails her, will the patient's rights be in any way affected? No – the courts rightly will not accept any argument that the doctor's duty is fulfilled if he provides an adequate service generally and only occasionally falls below the required standard of competence.[89] Judges sympathise with hard-pressed doctors. A doctor who carries on beyond the point when fatigue and overwork impair her judgement remains liable to an injured patient. The fact that the doctor was required by his employer to work such hours will not affect the patient.

The patient might, though, more appropriately proceed against the doctor's employers, the hospital. He would allege that the hospital undertook to provide him with adequate care.[90] Requiring their doctors to work to the point of utter exhaustion is a breach of that duty. The essence of the patient's claim would become, not that the hospital was vicariously liable for an individual doctor's negligence, but that there was a breach of a primary duty to ensure an adequate and competent service. In *Wilsher v Essex Area Health Authority*,[91] Browne-Wilkinson VC suggested that in many cases this was a more appropriate analysis of clinical negligence claims, avoiding stigmatising overworked doctors for understandable errors. But there is a risk that even fewer patients may obtain compensation if this analysis were accepted. The defendant hospital might plead in its defence the problems it faces arising from lack of resources. If Patient A suffers an injury because the surgeon who operated on him was too tired to perform the surgery properly and no other surgeon was available, the hospital may argue that it could not afford to employ more, or more senior, surgeons. It will be contended that, although far from ideal, the level of service was reasonable in the light of the defendants'

[86]   *Ashcroft v Mersey Regional Health Authority* [1983] 2 All ER 245 at 247. See also *Lillywhite v University College London Hospitals NHS Trust* [2005] EWCA Civ 1466.
[87]   *Urry v Biere* (1955) Times, 15 July.
[88]   *Corder v Banks* (1960) Times, 9 April.
[89]   *Wilsher v Essex Area Health Authority* [1986] 3 All ER 801, CA.
[90]   See *Cassidy v Ministry of Health* [1951] 2 KB 343; see further, Chapter 8.
[91]   [1986] 3 All ER 801 at 833–834.

limited budget. In one judgment, a judge expressly said that lack of resources should be taken into account in medical negligence claims.[92] The 'wrong' inflicted on the overworked junior doctor should not be remedied at the expense of the patient. The doctor must have a remedy against the employer who demands that he work impossible hours. The decision of the Court of Appeal, that young doctors whose health is threatened by the impossible demands made on them may bring their own action in negligence against their employer, was much to be welcomed.[93]

General practice

7.14   At first sight, legal problems concerning general practitioners appear less prevalent than claims against hospital doctors. Patients visit their GP on average four or five times a year and make one or two hospital visits in a lifetime. Malpractice actions against GPs are becoming more common, but still are far less so than lawsuits against hospitals.[94] Historically, there have been several reasons for this. NHS arrangements for general practice and the quality of consistent care offered by the majority of GPs were such that many family doctors still enjoy high esteem. Patients traditionally enjoyed a long-standing personal relationship with their GP. A mistake is more likely to be forgiven and forgotten in the context of a GP's continuing care than in an impersonal hospital atmosphere: the patient is less likely to want to put a man or woman he knows well 'into the dock'. (Changes in general practice, however, may risk jeopardising the more personal relationship between GP and patient.) There are other reasons, too, for fewer claims against GPs. Proving negligence, and that the patient's injury resulted from that negligence, is always difficult. Against a GP the problems multiply. How do you prove that a child's sudden deterioration resulted from the GP not visiting at once? Would immediate treatment have arrested the condition? Added to these difficulties, the common run of complaints about general practice do not tend to be the sort that make litigation, with its expense, pomp and ceremony, worthwhile. Patients object to unhelpful receptionists, difficulty in getting home visits, and often simply sense a lack of sympathy. Rarely do these irritations cause injury serious enough to merit litigation.

Every GP must attain that standard of skill and competence to be expected of the reasonably skilled and experienced GP. It is no defence that he has just entered practice, or that he is elderly and infirm. Nor, as we have seen, can he be expected to have the skills or qualifications of a consultant specialist. He must exercise his judgement about when to refer a patient to a specialist, or admit him to hospital, with due care.[95] Should a GP offer additional services to his patients, for example if he is on the obstetric list and is prepared to attend home confinements, then he must show the skill that he holds himself

[92]   *Knight v Home Office* [1990] 3 All ER 237. But such an argument was firmly rejected in *Brooks v Home Office* (1999) 48 BMLR 109.
[93]   *Johnstone v Bloomsbury Health Authority* [1991] 2 All ER 293.
[94]   See National Health Service Litigation Authority, *Factsheet 3*.
[95]   *Marriott v West Midlands Area Health Authority* [1999] Lloyd's Rep Med 23.

out as possessing. He must attain the standard, not of the consultant obstetrician, but of the specially qualified and experienced GP.

In reported cases where negligence has been proved against GPs, certain danger areas stand out. The maintenance of proper records and ensuring adequate communication with patients,[96] and with hospitals and other doctors sharing the care of a patient, is one. A failure to record and pass on to a hospital information on a patient's allergy to certain drugs is a clear case of negligence.[97] Similarly, a failure to check exactly what treatment has been given by the hospital may result in liability. A GP was found liable for a young man's death in this case.[98] The man had gone to a cottage hospital after a lump of coal had fallen on him and crushed his finger. A nurse dressed the wound and instructed him to go to another, larger hospital. Either because this was not properly explained to him or because he was in shock he did not go. He went later to his own doctor, who did not inquire as to his earlier treatment and simply put on a new dressing. At no stage did the patient receive an anti-tetanus injection and he died of toxaemia. The cottage hospital and the GP were both found to be negligent and responsible for the youth's death. The judge made his views emphatically clear:

> the National Health Service had been developed on the basis that a patient might well be transferred for treatment from one person to another so that the responsibility for the patient shifted ... Any system which failed to provide for effective communication was wrong and negligently wrong.

Prescription errors

7.15 Prescribing medicines is another area where GPs must be ultra-cautious, not just out of professional concern for the patient, but also in order to safeguard themselves. In 1982, a GP prescribed Migril for a Mrs Dwyer. Carelessly, he wrote out a prescription for a massive overdose of the drug. A pharmacist dispensed the drug as prescribed. Mrs Dwyer became ill. A partner in the same practice attended her at home. The Migril was on a table in her bedroom, but the second doctor did not notice the bottle. Mrs Dwyer suffered gangrene as a result of the overdose. She sued both doctors and the pharmacist. All were originally found liable.[99] Mrs Dwyer received £100,000 in damages. Eventually the second doctor was exculpated on appeal. At the end of the day, the GP whose slip caused the over-prescription paid 45 per cent of the damages and the pharmacists 55 per cent. In *Prendergast v Sam and Dee Ltd*,[100] a general practitioner prescribed Amoxil, a common antibiotic, for the plaintiff (who was suffering from a chest infection). The doctor's handwriting was so atrocious that the pharmacist read the prescription as an instruction to dispense Daonil, an anti-diabetic drug. The plaintiff succumbed to hypoglycaemia and brain damage. The Court of Appeal upheld

---

[96] See *Langley v Campbell* (1975) Times, 6 November.
[97] *Chin Keow v Government of Malaysia* [1967] 1 WLR 813.
[98] *Coles v Reading and District Hospital Management Committee* (1963) Times, 30 January.
[99] *Dwyer v Roderick* (1983) 127 Sol Jo 805. (Recounted in Finch (1982) 132 *New Law Journal* 176.)
[100] [1989] 1 Med LR 36.

Auld J's finding that both the doctor and the pharmacist were negligent. The doctor was liable because he should have foreseen that his careless writing of the prescription might mislead the pharmacist into a dangerous error. The pharmacist was liable because the dosage prescribed and other indications on the prescription should have alerted him to the fact that the doctor did not intend to prescribe Daonil. Both judgments operate as timely warnings against sloppy practice. Doctors must exercise great care in writing out prescriptions. Pharmacists must exercise even greater care in checking on the doctors.

Duty to attend

7.16 A frequent complaint about GPs is that patients have difficulty getting appointments or home visits, and that receptionists take it upon themselves to decide when and if someone can see the doctor. What exactly is the GP's duty to attend his patients and who in law are his patients? He must provide medical care during 'core hours' to all 'his' patients. A GP's terms of service[101] provide that 'his' patients are, first, those who are accepted on his list.[102] Provision is made to ensure that no patient is ever without a GP. Most importantly, the doctor's patients include persons accepted as 'temporary residents' and 'persons to whom he may be requested to give treatment which is immediately required owing to an accident or other emergency at any place in his practice area'.[103] The doctor's obligation to the health service is to provide an umbrella of cover. Wherever an NHS patient goes he should be able to see a GP. If he falls ill on holiday and can get to a doctor himself, he can go temporarily on to the local doctor's list. In dire emergency, he or his companions can call on, and count on, any GP practising in the area to come to his aid. Breach of the terms of service could lead to disciplinary sanctions.

Is there any obligation directly to the patient? Could a patient sue if denied treatment so that his condition deteriorated? A doctor on an express train can sit by and watch a fellow passenger die of a coronary. The GP's position is quite different. As far as the patients on his list are concerned, he has a continuing duty to them. A failure to attend such a patient where a competent GP would recognise the need for attendance is as much a breach of duty as giving wrong and careless treatment. Patients accepted as 'temporary residents' by a GP are in the same position for as long as they are registered with that GP.

What about 'emergency cases'? A GP's terms of service oblige her to treat such cases *in her practice area* when she is available to provide medical care. In 1955, lawyers acting for a doctor being sued by a patient on his NHS list conceded that the creation of the NHS had created a legal duty on a doctor to treat any patient in an emergency, whether or not the patient was on his

---

[101] See the National Health Service Act 2006, ss 83–95; the National Health Service (General Medical Services Contracts) Regulations 2004, SI 2004/291; the National Health Service (Primary Care) Act 1997.

[102] National Health Service (General Medical Services Contracts) Regs, reg 15.

[103] National Health Service (General Medical Services Contracts) Regs, reg 15(6).

list.[104] Nathan and Barrowclough doubted the correctness of this concession. They commented that such a duty might reflect '... the standards by which the medical profession regards itself as bound and would wish to be judged [but] from the strictly legal point of view [it was] too wide'.[105] We cannot see why it is 'too wide'. The doctor has undertaken to provide an emergency service. The area and circumstances in which he must act are closely defined. The obligation on him is not unbearably onerous. Emergency patients within his practice area when he is on duty are a foreseeable class of persons to whom, by accepting the position of GP within the NHS, he has undertaken a duty – and a duty which should be legal and not merely moral.

Establishing a duty to treat will rarely be a cause of difficulty, except towards emergency cases. A patient suing a GP will find that his problems start when he seeks to prove, as he must, that the GP's failure to treat him was negligent. Some patients make intolerable demands on their doctors. A doctor is not obliged to respond immediately to every call. He may indeed be in breach of duty to his more patient patients if he always responds to the most insistent call on his services. He has to exercise his judgement. In 1953, a GP was sued when he failed to visit a child whose mother reported (a) that the child had abdominal pains, and (b) that she had previously been examined by a hospital Casualty officer who had sent her home. The child proved to have a burst appendix. The judge found that the Casualty doctor was negligent and the GP was not. He had acted reasonably on the information available to him.[106]

The information available to the doctor is vital in assessing his obligation to the patient. When a patient changed his address without telling his doctor and then summoned the doctor, the doctor was found not negligent when, after an attempt to visit the old address, he left to complete other calls. The judge found that he acted reasonably in assuming that if urgent treatment was needed, he would be contacted again. The doctor could not be expected to mount a search for his missing patient.[107] Similarly, information as to the patient's condition must be full and accurate. A patient may fail in any action for failure to attend if all he said to the doctor was that he felt sick and had a headache, when in fact he was feverish, vomiting and had severe abdominal pains. The courts will condemn the doctor who fails to act on information from his patient, but the patient must give the doctor the information to act on. Often, information about requests for visits and appointments is not given directly to the doctor. It is channelled via the receptionist. This makes not a jot of difference to the doctor's legal obligation. His terms of service will require that he provide treatment during approved hours or, if he operates an appointments scheme, that the patient be offered an appointment within a reasonable time. And if the patient's condition so requires, he must be visited at home. The doctor is responsible for his staff and must ensure that their service, as well as his, is efficient. His liability for them is absolute. Let us imagine a GP whose receptionist, in a burst of temper totally out of character, verbally abuses the mother of a seriously ill toddler and refuses to ask the

[104] *Barnes v Crabtree* (1955) Times, 1 and 2 November.
[105] PC Nathan and AR Barrowclough, *Medical Negligence* (1957) Butterworths, p 38.
[106] *Edler v Greenwich and Deptford HMC* (1953) Times, 7 March.
[107] *Kavanagh v Abrahamson* (1964) 108 Sol Jo 320.

doctor to visit the patient. The child has peritonitis and dies for lack of immediate treatment. The receptionist, not the doctor, is negligent but, as her employer, he is legally responsible for her negligence.[108]

Relating the injury to medical negligence

7.17 So far, the majority of the cases examined involved something going wrong as a result of a medical mistake. The patient's problem has been to prove that what was done, or not done, amounted to actionable negligence. Proving negligence by the doctor does not conclude the case in the patient's favour. He must also show that his injury, his worsened or unimproved condition, was caused by the doctor's negligence. He must prove causation. In practice, proving causation is often the most problematic aspect of a patient's claim. The difficulties of causation in medical malpractice cases fall into two main categories:

(1)   Can the patient convince the court that it was the relevant negligence which caused his injury, rather than the progress of his original disease or condition?

(2)   How should the courts proceed when the essence of a claim is not that clinical negligence caused any fresh or additional injury to the patient, but that that negligence deprived him of a chance of full recovery from his original disease or condition?

In each and every case the patient must advance evidence showing that it is more likely than not that the defendants' negligence caused the injury of which he complains.

In *Kay v Ayrshire and Arran Health Board*,[109] a two-year-old boy, Andrew Kay, was rushed into hospital suffering from pneumococcal meningitis. He was negligently given a massive overdose of penicillin and nearly died as a result. Intensive efforts by hospital staff saved Andrew's life and he recovered from both the toxic overdose and from meningitis. But he was found to be profoundly deaf. His parents, on his behalf, sued the Scottish health board responsible for the hospital where Andrew had been treated. The board admitted negligence, but denied that Andrew's deafness resulted from that negligence. Deafness is often a complication of meningitis even where the disease is correctly treated. Massive overdoses of the sort that Andrew was given are mercifully rare, so there was little available evidence of whether such an overdose materially increased the risk that Andrew would become deaf as a result of his disease. The House of Lords quashed the trial judge's decision, finding in Andrew's favour. Lord Keith commented that the lack of recorded cases demonstrating the effect of overdose of penicillin '... cannot in itself make good the lack of appropriate evidence'.[110]

As we have seen, in *Wilsher v Essex Area Health Authority*[111] junior doctors were found to be negligent in administering excess oxygen to a very premature

[108]   Because of the doctrine of vicarious liability: see below in Chapter 8.
[109]   [1987] 2 All ER 417. See also *Loveday v Renton* [1990] 1 Med LR 117.
[110]   [1987] 2 All ER 417 at 421.
[111]   [1988] 1 All ER 871, HL.

baby, Martin Wilsher. Martin succumbed to retrolental fibroplasia (RLF), an incurable condition of the retina causing gradual blindness. The question that went to the House of Lords was whether Martin's lawyers could prove that RLF resulted from that negligent administration of excess oxygen. The scientific evidence suggested that RLF *may* result from excess oxygen, but there were five other possible causes of RLF in very sick, very premature infants. The trial judge had held that, as negligence had been proved, the burden of disproving that that negligence caused Martin's injuries moved to the defendants. He said that, as the evidence showed that the doctors were in breach of their duty to Martin and failed to take a precaution expressly designed to safeguard Martin from RLF, it was then up to them to prove that Martin's condition resulted from one of the other possible causes. The House of Lords roundly condemned such an approach, and ordered a retrial. The burden of proving causation rests on the claimant alone, and does not move to the defendant even though negligence has been proved or admitted. What is crucial for the claimant is the quality of the expert scientific evidence presented on his behalf. That evidence must, at the very least, demonstrate that it is more likely than not that the defendants' negligence materially contributed to the claimant's condition, or materially increased the risk that the claimant would succumb to such a condition.[112] Where the scientific evidence is ambivalent or suggests a variety of competing causes for the claimant's state, the action for negligence will normally fail.

Uncertainty about causation is likely to be common in many claims that essentially relate to whether the defendants' negligence caused or exacerbated disease. In *Fairchild v Glenhaven Funeral Services Ltd*,[113] claims were brought by workers who had been exposed to asbestos dust or fibres during their working lives and developed the fatal lung disease mesothelioma. The men had worked for several different employers, so pinpointing which defendant employer was responsible for the onset of the disease was nearly impossible. Mesothelioma can result from a single asbestos fibre entering the lung. The greater your exposure to asbestos fibres, the more likely it is that this will occur. The Law Lords allowed the claim, holding all the defendant employers liable, as each of them had materially increased the risk of harm to their employees. The judges overtly invoked policy considerations to support their modified approach to, and departure from, the usual strict rules of causation.[114] Might the harsh decision in *Wilsher* thus be reconsidered? It seems unlikely. Lord Hoffmann not only declares *Wilsher* to be correctly decided in principle, but also suggests that policy reasons to protect NHS budgets could play a part in denying patient-claimants a more favourable approach to causation. He says:

> The political and economic arguments involved in the massive increase in the liability of the National Health Service which would have been a consequence

---

[112] [1988] 1 All ER 871 at 882–883, per Lord Bridge, HL.

[113] [2002] UKHL 22.

[114] Subsequently, in *Barker v Corus UK Ltd* [2006] UKHL 20, the Law Lords ruled that each defendant should be liable only to the extent of their relevant contribution to the claimant's exposure to asbestos dust. In the specific context of claims for contracted mesothelioma, s 3 of the Compensation Act 2006 nullified that decision (discussed fully in J Murphy, *Street on Torts* (12th edn, 2006) OUP, pp 145–151).

of the broad rule favoured by the Court of Appeal in *Wilsher's* case are far more complicated than the reasons ... for imposing liability upon an employer who has failed to take simple precautions.[115]

Modifying the 'strict rules'

7.18 In *Chester v Afshar*,[116] a patient-claimant none the less benefited from judicial willingness to modify strict application of the rules of causation. As we have seen, Mr Afshar failed to warn Miss Chester of the 1–2 per cent risk of nerve damage in the course of spinal surgery. Miss Chester did not contend that, had she been properly warned, she would never had consented to surgery, or that she would have sought a second opinion. All she claimed was that, had she been warned, she would not have gone ahead with surgery that day. The risk of damage on any later occasion would have been just the same. Miss Chester faced the utmost difficulty in proving that, but for Mr Afshar's negligence, she would have avoided injury. The majority (3:2) in the House of Lords invoked policy grounds to assist her. Giving proper legal force to patients' rights to autonomy and dignity justified 'a narrow and modest departure from traditional causation principles'.[117]

Bolitho v City & Hackney Health Authority[118] raised a rather different question of causation. You will recall that Patrick Bolitho stopped breathing and suffered a cardiac arrest resulting in serious brain damage. The hospital admitted negligence in relation to the failure of the paediatric registrar to attend Patrick when she had been summoned to do so earlier. They denied liability because, they said, the registrar would not have intubated Patrick, had she attended him prior to his collapse. Intubation was the only means by which Patrick's respiratory failure and cardiac arrest might have been averted. The plaintiffs argued that, had Patrick been intubated, he would not have suffered injury. The defendants responded that attendance would have made no difference: medical opinion would support not intubating the child. The key question became does the *Bolam* test play a role in causation.

Lord Browne-Wilkinson agreed with counsel for the plaintiff that 'in the generality of cases' *Bolam* plays no role in causation. *Bolitho* exemplifies an unusual problem. How do the courts address causation when the essence of the matter is whether something should have been done which has not been done? The factual inquiry proceeds into the 'realms of hypotheses'. The court has to ask:

(1)   What would the defendant have done if she had attended the boy? This is a purely factual question to which *Bolam* has no relevance.

---

[115] [2002] UKHL 22 at para 69.

[116] [2004] UKHL 41 (discussed fully at 5.8 above).

[117] [2004] UKHL 41 at para 24, per Lord Steyn; but see to the contrary, Lord Bingham at para 9.

[118] [1998] AC 232, HL. See also MA Jones, 'The Bolam Test and the Responsible Expert' [1999] *Tort Law Review* 226; A Grubb, 'Negligence Causation and Bolam' (1998) 5 *Medical Law Review* 378.

(2)   If the answer to that first question is that she would *not* have intubated, would that have been negligent?[119]

In addressing that question, *Bolam* is central. The court had to decide if non-intubation conformed to responsible professional practice, applying their Lordships' *caveat* that responsible practice must be demonstrated 'logical and defensible'. In the event, the evidence of the defendants' experts that intubation of a child of Patrick's age in his circumstances was itself far from risk free, convinced their Lordships.

Loss of a chance

7.19 When the unfortunate claimant complains not of some new injury inflicted by the defendants, but of a lost chance of recovery, his claim is even more difficult to prove. In *Hotson v East Berkshire Health Authority*,[120] the plaintiff (a schoolboy of 13) fell heavily, from a rope on which he had been swinging, to the ground twelve feet below. He was taken to hospital. His knee was X-rayed and revealed no injury. No further examination was made and the plaintiff was sent home. Five days later, the boy was taken back to the same hospital and an injury to his hip joint was diagnosed and subsequently swiftly and correctly treated. The injury had traumatic consequences. The boy suffered a condition known as avascular necrosis. This condition, caused by a restriction of the blood supply in the region of the original injury, leads to misshapenness of the joint, disability and pain, and later in life almost certainly brings on osteoarthritis in the joint. The plaintiff's disability might have ensued from the accident in any case, but there was a 25 per cent chance that given the correct treatment immediately the plaintiff might have avoided disability and made a nearly full recovery.

The defendant hospital admitted negligence in failing to diagnose and treat the plaintiff's injury on his first visit. Both parties agreed that prompt treatment would have offered a 25 per cent chance of avoiding permanent disability. The trial judge awarded the boy 25 per cent of full compensation for his condition, that is a sum of money to compensate him for a 25 per cent lost chance of full recovery.[121] The House of Lords quashed this judgment.[122] Their Lordships held that the plaintiff had failed to prove that it was more likely than not that avascular necrosis resulted from the negligent delay in treatment, because there was a 75 per cent chance he would have suffered from avascular necrosis, even if the treatment had been given promptly. To recover damages for the avascular necrosis, the plaintiff needed to establish at least a 51:49 likelihood that 'but for' the negligent delay in treatment, he would have made an uncomplicated recovery from his original injury. Had he succeeded in so doing, he would have been entitled to 100 per cent compensation for his

---

[119] [1998] AC 232 at 240, HL.
[120] [1987] 2 All ER 909, HL. See T Hill, 'A Lost Chance for Compensation in the Tort of Negligence in the House of Lords' (1991) 54 *Modern Law Review* 111.
[121] [1985] 3 All ER 167.
[122] [1987] 2 All ER 909, HL.

disability. Their Lordships declined to say that loss of a less than 50 per cent chance of full recovery was never recoverable in a medical negligence claim. They left that question open.

The claimant in *Gregg v Scott*[123] may have hoped that his case for loss of a chance was stronger. In November 1994, his GP (the defendant) wrongly diagnosed a lump under Mr Gregg's arm as a benign lipoma. The following August, a different doctor referred him to a consultant, and, in November 1995, a biopsy revealed a malignant lymphoma. The delay in diagnosis reduced Mr Gregg's chance of a 'cure' (defined as ten years in remission) from 42 per cent to 25 per cent. Mr Gregg (unlike the young plaintiff in *Hotson*) could therefore argue that, as a consequence of the defendant' negligence, he had lost a 17 per cent chance of a 'cure'. But, alas, he could not establish that had the defendant done his job properly, he would have had a better than 50 per cent chance of a 'cure'. He was still more likely than not to face an early death – even had his cancer been more promptly diagnosed. The majority of the House of Lords (3:2) applied the rules in causation strictly and found against Mr Gregg. Lord Hoffmann declared:

> [A] wholesale adoption of possible rather than probable causation as the criterion of liability would be so radical a change in our law as to amount to a legislative act. It would have enormous consequences for insurance companies and the National Health Service.[124]

One of the dissenting judges, Lord Nicholls retorted:

> It cannot be right to adopt a procedure having the effect that, in law, a patient's prospects of recovery are treated as non-existent whenever they exist but fall short of 50%. If the law were to proceed in this way it would deserve to be likened to the proverbial ass ...[125]

How may *Gregg v Scott* be distinguished from *Chester v Afshar*[126] and *Fairchild*?[127] Baroness Hale seeks to contend that the latter two decisions were confined to '... problems which could be remedied without altering the principles applicable to the great majority of personal injury cases which give rise to no real injustice or particular problems'.[128] Their Lordships seem deeply divided on causation. Sarah Green argues cogently that distinguishing *Chester* and *Gregg* on grounds of principle cannot be done. Both are hard cases. In her view, it is *Chester* that made bad law.[129]

Private patients

7.20 A patient who pays for treatment enters into a contract with his doctor. They are free to set the terms of that contract, save that the doctor cannot

---

[123] [2005] UKHL 2.
[124] [2005] UKHL 2 at para 90.
[125] [2005] UKHL 2 at para 43.
[126] [2004] UKHL 41.
[127] *Fairchild v Glenhaven Funeral Services Ltd* [2002] UKHL 22.
[128] [2005] UKHL 2 at para 192.
[129] S Green, 'Coherence of Medical Negligence Cases: A Game of Doctors and Purses' (2006) 14 *Medical Law Review* 1.

exempt himself from liability for any injury to his patient arising from his negligence.[130] There is rarely a written contract between them. The terms will be implied from their relationship. This usually means that the doctor undertakes a duty of care to the patient. His duty of care to his private patient is usually indistinguishable from his duty in tort to his NHS patient. The possibility remains of doctors agreeing to undertake a higher standard of care.

In private practice could a doctor be found to have contracted to guarantee the desired result of treatment? This can never happen in the NHS: a doctor can only be liable in tort for a failure in care. Only rarely will a private doctor be found to have guaranteed a result in contract. Where a patient is ill and seeks a cure, unless the doctor foolishly and expressly promises success in his treatment, no court will infer any term other than that the doctor will exercise skill and care. And, so far, claims by patients who have undergone private sterilisation have ultimately failed in attempts to argue that the surgeon guaranteed permanent sterility.[131]

Criminal liability

7.21 Negligence is normally a matter for the civil, not the criminal, law. However gross, however culpable an act of negligence, negligence will generally not be criminal in England unless made so by an Act of Parliament (as in the case of careless driving). The picture changes if the victim dies. Gross negligence causing death can lead to a conviction for manslaughter. Much more than ordinary negligence, of the sort which would found a civil action for negligence, must be proved. Prosecution of doctors used to be rare. In older cases, the negligence will be seen to derive from morally disgraceful conduct – a doctor operating while drunk or under the influence of drugs. In *R v Bateman*,[132] the Court of Appeal overruled a conviction for manslaughter of a doctor whose ignorance and failure to send a woman to hospital resulted in his patient's death. The judge at the trial had failed to direct the jury properly. Criminal liability required more than the degree of negligence needed to establish civil liability. The doctor must be proved to have shown '… such disregard for the life and safety of others as to amount to a crime against the State and conduct deserving of punishment'.

There has recently been a rise in the number of doctors prosecuted for manslaughter – albeit ending, in many cases, in acquittal.[133] In *R v Prentice, R v Adomako and R v Holloway*,[134] the Court of Appeal considered two[135] appeals by doctors against conviction for manslaughter. In the first case, two

---

130 Unfair Contract Terms Act 1977, s 2.

131 *Eyre v Measday* [1986] 1 All ER 488; *Thake v Maurice* [1986] 1 All ER 497, CA.

132 (1925) 41 TLR 557.

133 See R Ferner and S McDowell, 'Doctors Charged with Manslaughter in the Courts of Medical Practice' (2006) 99 *Journal of RSM* 309; O Quick, 'Prosecuting "Gross" Medical Negligence: Manslaughter, Discretion and the Crown Prosecution Service' (2006) 33 *Journal of Law and Society* 421.

134 [1993] 4 All ER 935, CA.

135 The third appeal, *R v Holloway*, involved an electrician whose faulty wiring caused a death.

junior doctors, Drs Prentice and Sulman, were convicted of manslaughter after they had wrongly injected a potent chemotherapeutic drug (vincristine) into the patient's spine, when it should have been administered intravenously. Their 16-year-old patient was suffering from leukaemia. Every month he received an intravenous injection of vincristine. Every other month he received a spinal injection of another powerful drug, methotextrate. The drug came down to the ward on the same trolley. Neither Dr Prentice nor Dr Sulman had ever administered such drugs before, and they were left unsupervised.

The second case involved a Dr Adomako. He was an anaesthetist. During surgery to re-attach a detached retina, Dr Adomako failed to notice, for over four minutes, that the tube administering oxygen to his patient had become disconnected. He neither noted the evidence before his eyes that the tube was no longer in place, nor responded to the alarm raised by the operating theatre's monitoring system. One prosecution expert described his standard of care as abysmal. The Appeal Court reversed the convictions of Drs Prentice and Sulman, but upheld Dr Adomako's conviction.

The Court of Appeal set the following test for gross negligence manslaughter.

(1)   Did the doctor show obvious indifference to the risk of injury to his patient?

(2)   Was he aware of the risk but nonetheless (for no good reason) decided to run the risk?

(3)   Was an attempt to avoid a known risk so grossly negligent to deserve punishment?

(4)   Was there a degree of inattention or failure to have regard to risk, going beyond mere inadvertence?[136]

Only if at least one of these questions could be answered affirmatively should a doctor be convicted of manslaughter. In the case of Dr Prentice and Dr Sulman, there was insufficient evidence of gross negligence deserving punishment. Dr Adomako, the Court of Appeal declared, failed to perform:

> ... his essential and in effect sole duty to see that his patient was breathing satisfactorily and to cope with the breathing emergency ... his failure was more than mere inadvertence and constituted gross negligence of the degree necessary for manslaughter.[137]

Dr Adomako appealed to the House of Lords without success. His conviction was upheld.[138] The Law Lords offered no precise definition of 'medical manslaughter'. Lord Mackay endorsed the trial judge's warning to the jury:

> You should only convict a doctor of causing death by negligence if you think he did something which no reasonably skilled doctor would have done.[139]

The lack of clarity about what degree of negligence constitutes 'gross' medical negligence was challenged in the Court of Appeal in *R v Misra and R v*

---

[136]   *R v Prentice, R v Adomako, R v Holloway* [1993] 4 All ER 935 at 943–944, CA
[137]   At 954.
[138]   *R v Adomako* [1995] 1 AC 171, HL.
[139]   [1995] 1 AC 171 at 188, HL.

Srivastava.[140] Drs Misra and Srivastava were convicted of manslaughter after a patient died because of a failure to treat a post-operative infection. The evidence established that, over a period of 48 hours, the doctors failed to act on information that their patient was critically ill. They did not chase up blood tests, and ignored warnings from nurses and another doctor. Part of the grounds for their appeal was that the ill-defined boundaries of gross negligence manslaughter contravened Article 7 of the European Convention on Human Rights. Article 7 requires that criminal offences must be defined in clear enough terms so that people are aware what constitutes criminal conduct. The appeal failed.[141] The Court of Appeal said that to be convicted of gross negligence manslaughter, the doctor must have failed to avert a risk of death. Other risks of lesser harm were not sufficient. Once a risk of death was established, it was for the jury to determine if the relevant negligence was gross. The citizen seeking to understand his potential criminal liability should be advised that, if he negligently breaches a duty of care so as to endanger life, he may be convicted of manslaughter if a jury is satisfied that his negligence is gross. The Appeal Court judges acknowledged an element of circularity in their own arguments.

When should doctors face criminal prosecution?[142] The increasingly common demand that doctors be punished for tragic mistakes causes anxiety within the profession. Some argue that only if there is evidence of indifference or total disregard for a patient's welfare should a doctor face criminal liability.[143] The civil law should compensate victims of mistakes. Incompetent doctors should be dealt with by the GMC. Patients may lack trust in the GMC and perceive monetary compensation which comes from the NHS, not the doctor's pocket, as inadequate redress for the death of a relative. Doctors are not the only workers who risk prosecution for negligence doing their job; train drivers and electricians, for example, meet the same fate.[144] In 2003, a teacher was jailed when his inadequate supervision of a school trip led to a child's death by drowning.[145] In all these cases, the crux of the difficulty is to determine when is a fatal mistake so bad that an otherwise law-abiding citizen deserves to be branded a criminal.

Two final points need to be made:

(1) Careful reading of virtually all the cases of accusations of medical manslaughter reveal a series of errors, many committed by people other than the doctors in the dock. Inadequate systems existed to minimise

---

[140] [2004] EWCA Crim 2375. Note that subsequently the trust employing the two doctors was convicted of offences contravening health and safety legislation in respect of the same events: *R v Southampton University Hospitals NHS Trust* (11 April 2006, unreported).

[141] Leave to appeal to the House of Lords was refused: *R v Misra* [2004] A11 ER (D) 150 (Oct).

[142] See M Brazier and N Allen, 'Criminalising Medical Malpractice' in C Erin and S Ost (eds), *The Criminal Justice System and Health Care* (2007) OUP (forthcoming).

[143] See A McCall Smith, 'Criminal Negligence and the Incompetent Doctor' (1993) 1 *Medical Law Review* 336.

[144] The fourth appellant in *R v Prentice, R v Adomako, R v Holloway* [1993] 4 All ER 935, CA was an electrician whose faulty rewiring of a house resulted in the death of one of the residents.

[145] (2003) Times, 24 September.

opportunities for errors. In *R v Prentice*, the two young doctors should have been supervised. The packaging of the two drugs should have given much clearer warnings about the consequences of wrongly administering vincristine. Should the hospital, rather than the doctors, have been on trial for corporate manslaughter?[146]

(2) Preventing error is preferable to retrospective punishment. More thought needs to be given to learning from error, and the impact of blame.[147]

---

[146] See M Childs, 'Medical Manslaughter and Corporate Liability' [1999] *Legal Studies* 316; N Allen, 'Medical or Managerial Manslaughter' in Erin and Ost (eds), *The Criminal Justice System and Health Care*.

[147] See A Merry and A McCall Smith, *Errors, Medicine and the Law* (2001) CUP.

Chapter 8
MALPRACTICE LITIGATION[1]

8.1 We have addressed the principles governing liability for clinical negligence. Formidable practical problems confront the patient. How can she fund a lawsuit? Whom should she sue? How quickly must she act? How does she prove negligence? What level of compensation is available? Is it worth it?

There have been radical changes in the process of litigation. The way in which patients fund claims, how the NHS meets the cost of claims and the fundamental rules of civil procedure (the Woolf reforms) have all altered in the last decade. We begin this chapter by examining the litigation process. Then we consider claims that escalating rates of lawsuits against doctors are damaging medicine. The spectre of the malpractice crisis haunts the colleges of medicine, the courts of justice and the corridors of Whitehall. Is it a spectre with any substance?

Funding a lawsuit[2]

8.2 Few people are rich enough to meet the costs of clinical negligence claims out of their own income and savings. The majority of clinical negligence claims in the past were funded by legal aid. The success rate of such claims was low. The cost to the public purse of legal aid in personal injury claims rose rapidly. Unsurprisingly the Government sought to find ways to reduce the legal aid bill. The Access to Justice Act 1999[3] removed legal aid from most personal injury claims but, at least at present, legal aid remains available in clinical negligence claims. However, gaining legal aid is not an easy task: eligible claimants must meet a stringent means test; only adults with a very low income and minimal capital will qualify. Even if the potential claimant

---

[1] For practical advice, see CJ Lewis, *Clinical Negligence: A Practical Guide* (6th edn, 2006) Tottel Publishers. An extremely helpful, but not wholly impartial, account of the impact of malpractice litigation can be found in Chief Medical Officer, *Making Amends: A Consultation Paper Setting Out Proposals for Reforming the Approach to Clinical Negligence in the NHS* (2003) Department of Health.

[2] See Lewis, *Clinical Negligence: A Practical Guide*, Chapter 3.

[3] The Act also replaces the Legal Aid Board with the Legal Service Commission and established a Community Legal Service.

passes the means test, her case must be strong on its merits. Children under 18[4] are assessed on their own, not their parents' income, so child-patients are still likely to qualify for legal aid.

The state will only fund claims likely to succeed. Solicitors able to act for legally-aided clients must be approved by the Legal Services Commission. Only firms who hold a franchise to do legally-aided clinical negligence work can act. The franchise system has advantages for aggrieved patients. Clients can be assured that their case is in the hands of a solicitor judged competent to handle such cases. They are receiving specialist 'care'. However the numbers of franchised solicitors may not meet demand. Lewis[5] expresses concern that fewer and fewer firms are undertaking this work. Patients may have to travel long distances, and not enough young solicitors are being trained to manage clinical negligence claims.

Whether legal aid for clinical negligence claims will survive is another pressing question. Conditional fees have become the norm in other personal injury claims. Under a conditional fee agreement (CFA)[6] the solicitor agrees to provide legal services on the basis that unless the claim is successful the client will pay nothing for her services. If the case is won, legislation allows the solicitor to charge up to twice the normal fee, up to a limit of 25 per cent of any damages recovered.[7] In practice, lawyers are not normally expected to take more than a 25 per cent uplift in their fees. Unsuccessful defendants may be required to meet that 'success fee'.[8] Conditional fees are often styled 'no-win no-fee' agreements. The major problems for clinical negligence claimants are two-fold. (1) Conditional fees involve risk to the lawyers. They will only take on claims if satisfied that the majority of the claims on their books will succeed. Otherwise, the firm will lose money. (2) The 'no-win no-fee' provision only covers the patient's own solicitors' costs. If the case fails, he becomes liable for the defendant hospital's, or doctor's, costs. These may be crippling. In most personal injury claims, claimants can buy insurance to cover them against the risk of liability for the defendants' costs, about £60,000 at least for anything other than a modest claim.[9] The complexity and expense of clinical negligence claims is such that insurers have been wary about entering this field. However, if the claimant wins her case, she can recover the cost of insurance premiums from the defendant, the losing party, providing the premium is set at a reasonable rate.[10]

Defending claims

8.3 Until 1990, the medical defence organisations, principally the Medical Defence Union and the Medical Protection Society, indemnified individual doctors against personal liability for clinical negligence. Each hospital, health

---

4   Access to Justice Act, s 7.
5   See Lewis, *Clinical Negligence: A Practical Guide*, p 35.
6   Lewis, *Clinical Negligence: A Practical Guide*, pp 41–49.
7   Lewis, *Clinical Negligence: A Practical Guide*, p 46.
8   Lewis, *Clinical Negligence: A Practical Guide*, p 46.
9   Lewis, *Clinical Negligence: A Practical Guide*, p 46.
10   *Callery v Gray* [2001] EWCA Civ 1246, [2002] UKHL 28.

authority or other NHS organisation met its own costs. NHS Indemnity, introduced in 1990,[11] now provides that hospital trusts indemnify hospital doctors against liability; trusts have taken over the cost of attending all claims and the management of claims. The medical defence organisations continue to meet claims against GPs and claims arising in the private sector. From 1990 to 1995, individual hospital trusts, health authorities and the defence organisations dominated defence of NHS claims. Different sets of legal advisers might adopt different policies about settling claims and how aggressively a claim was defended. Where a case succeeded, the cost fell on an individual hospital. A large compensation award could force a hospital to make budget cuts, immediately affecting patient care in that hospital. In 1995, the Clinical Negligence Scheme for Trusts (CNST) was established.[12] NHS trusts could choose to join the CNST and it created a pooling arrangement to meet liabilities arising out of patient claims. 'Premiums' for trusts are worked out depending on the type of trust, the specialties offered and their scale of operations. Membership of the CNST is voluntary but, at 31 March 2005, all foundation trusts, NHS trusts and primary care trusts (PCTs) were members. Membership is conditional on trusts complying with risk management procedures prescribed by the CNST. It offers a mutual assurance system so that no individual trust risks devastation of its service because of a clutch of unfortunate losses in the courts.

The National Health Service Litigation Authority[13] (NHSLA) now administers the CNST.[14] Since April 2002, the NHSLA has dealt with all CNST claims regardless of value. The NHSLA is the driving force behind defence of claims against the NHS today. It exercises significant control over all claims, seeking to ensure swift resolution of indefensible claims and to minimise the cost to the NHS. Greater efficiency and uniformity should benefit patients as much as hospitals. The NHSLA plays an active role, not just in advising on defence of individual claims but also in seeking to ensure that the whole litigation system is regularly kept under review. The medical defence organisations and NHS trusts were often accused of persisting in defending 'indefensible' cases. The NHSLA claims that it seeks to avoid litigation, encourage apologies and explanations, and settle appropriate claims swiftly.[15] Lawyers who act for claimants take a less rosy view of the NHSLA.[16]

---

[11]   HC (89) 34 'Claims of Medical Negligence Against NHS Hospitals and Community Doctors and Dentists' as amended by HGG (96) 48; see M Brazier, 'NHS Indemnity: The Implications for Medical Litigation' (1990) 6 *Professional Negligence* 88; CMO, *Making Amends*, pp 53–55.

[12]   See CMO, *Making Amends*, p 55.

[13]   See CMO, *Making Amends*, pp 55–57.

[14]   For the first three years of its life, the CNST was administered by the Medical Protection Society. The NHSLA also runs the Existing Liabilities Scheme, dealing with claims prior to April 1999.

[15]   See NHSLA, *Report and Accounts 2006* (HC 1179), pp 4–5. See also the Compensation Act 2006, s 2.

[16]   See Lewis, *Clinical Negligence: A Practical Guide*, pp 17–18.

Whom should the patient sue?

8.4 Once funding is assured, one of the first practical matters which the patient and his legal advisers must consider is whom they should sue. The legal doctrine of vicarious liability provides that when a person who is an employee commits a tort in the course of his employment, his employer is also responsible to the victim. The employer will often be better able to pay compensation than an individual employee. Let us look first at a claim by a patient who alleges that he suffered injury in the course of treatment as an NHS patient in an NHS hospital. If he can identify a particular individual as negligent he may, of course, proceed against him – be he consultant, anaesthetist, house officer, nurse, physiotherapist or hospital porter. However, the patient may also sue the person's employer (in the case of an NHS trust, or foundation, hospital, the hospital itself). Where a hospital doctor is a defendant in the action, payment of any award of compensation made against her is guaranteed. NHS Indemnity ensures that any liability incurred by an NHS hospital doctor will be met by her employer. NHS trusts indemnify doctors directly, just as they have always done for nurses and other hospital employees. There is no practical need to bring a claim against the doctor personally. Patients who bring a claim based on the alleged negligence of a nurse rarely bother to name the nurse personally as a defendant. Patients and their lawyers should ponder the wisdom of suing a doctor personally. As her employer will meet any award of compensation in full, there is little to gain from naming the doctor in the claim. However, suing a doctor individually may be designed not to obtain compensation, but to ensure accountability. As long as complaints and review procedures in health care are perceived by patients as inadequate, patients may go on using clinical negligence claims and naming individuals as a means to ensure accountability.[17]

The employer to sue, as vicariously liable, in the case of NHS hospital treatment will normally be the NHS trust, or foundation, hospital. As privatisation creeps into the health service, this must be examined carefully. Take this example: an elderly, confused patient slips and falls on a highly polished floor. Who, if anyone, is responsible? The relevant negligence may be that a nurse failed to supervise the patient, or it may be that cleaners were careless. The nurse will be employed by the hospital. The cleaner may be the employee of a private contractor. If the patient can rely only on the doctrine of vicarious liability to make someone other than the individual nurse or cleaner liable, he may have difficulty in selecting the correct defendant. Hospital and contractor may each blame the other's employee.[18] What we now need to examine is the direct liability of the hospital to an NHS patient, what is often described as a non-delegable duty. First, the hospital will be liable for any failure of its own. A patient may suffer injury not because any particular doctor or nurse is careless, but because the system provided by the authority is inadequate. There may be insufficient medical staff to cope swiftly enough with injured patients admitted to the Casualty ward. Lack of experienced staff on night duty may cause injury to a patient whose condition deteriorates

---

[17] Membership of a defence organisation is no longer required of hospital doctors. Most doctors retain membership of such a body to ensure access to individual legal advice.

[18] Consider also the problem of agency nurses. They are not employed by the hospital.

rapidly, and whom the staff on duty cannot, with the best will in the world, treat sufficiently promptly. For such 'systems errors' an action will lie directly against the hospital.[19] The Court of Appeal has confirmed that hospitals have an 'organisational duty'. An NHS hospital must '... ensure that the hospital staff, facilities and organisation provided are those appropriate to provide a safe and satisfactory service for the patient'.[20]

May direct responsibility to NHS patients go further? When a patient is admitted for hospital treatment under the NHS, the NHS trust undertakes to provide him with reasonably careful, competent and skilled care. Should his treatment fall below that standard, the hospital is directly, not just vicariously, responsible to the patient.[21] So, if an elderly patient falls on a slippery floor, and had proper care been taken that would not have happened, the hospital is liable. It matters not whether a nurse employed by the hospital or a cleaner employed by a contractor was the individual personally at fault. The hospital undertook to care for the patient. It failed and is directly liable. In *X (Minors) v Bedfordshire County Council*, Lord Browne-Wilkinson said this:

> It is established that those conducting a hospital are under a direct duty of care to those admitted as patients to the hospital.[22]

What of a patient offered a hip-replacement on the NHS whose operation is contracted out to a private hospital or independent treatment centre?

In *M v Calderdale Health Authority*,[23] M became pregnant and consulted an NHS doctor at an NHS community health centre. He arranged an abortion at a private hospital, but it was negligently performed and the woman went on to give birth to a baby boy. The health authority was found liable in negligence to M. Although no NHS employee was negligent, nor was the health authority negligent in selecting the private clinic to which they contracted out abortions, they were in breach of a direct non-delegable duty to their patient. The judge summed up the position.

> [M] never left the care of the first defendant. She was its patient. She never had an opportunity to divert from the route of treatment arranged on her behalf. In these circumstances she is entitled in my view to remain in the same position as a patient who remains in house relying upon the expectation of an effective provision of services.[24]

M would suggest that an NHS patient suffering injury in the private sector could sue the PCT who contracted out her care. *Child A v Ministry of Defence*[25] is dismissive of *M*, stating that the decision does '... not represent the current state of English law'.[26] Very briefly, Child A was born in 1998, in

---

[19] See *Bull v Devon Area Health Authority* [1993] 4 Med LR 117, CA; *Robertson v East Kent Health Authority* [1999] Lloyd's Rep Med 123.
[20] *Child A v Ministry of Defence* [2004] EWCA Civ 641 at para 32.
[21] See *Cassidy v Ministry of Health* [1951] 2 KB 343 at 359–360, per Lord Denning; *Roe v Ministry of Health* [1954] 2 QB 66 at 82.
[22] [1995] 2 AC 633 at 740.
[23] [1998] Lloyd's Rep Med 157.
[24] [1998] Lloyd's Rep Med 157 at 161.
[25] [2004] EWCA Civ 641.
[26] [2004] EWCA Civ 641 at para 52.

a German hospital while his father was serving with the British Army. Until 1996, the Ministry of Defence had run its own military hospitals in Germany. From 1996, the Ministry (via a complicated set of contracts) contracted out health care for service personnel and their families to German hospitals. A suffered brain damage in the course of his delivery. It was not disputed that his injuries were as a result of negligence. A could claim damages in Germany under German law, but his lawyers sought to sue in England and make the Ministry of Defence liable for A's injury, just as Calderdale Health Authority had been liable to M. The Court of Appeal found against him. The Ministry owed a duty to use reasonable care to provide access to suitable hospital care for service personnel and their families.[27] They had a responsibility (an organisational duty) to act reasonably to ensure care provided was on the basis of an adequate system, ie properly equipped hospitals were selected to provide care.[28] There was no 'duty to ensure that the treatment administered ... is administered with reasonable care and skill'. There was no duty '... broken if one of the hospital staff, however competent, commits an isolated act of negligence in the treatment of the patient'. Such a duty (described in *A* as a non-delegable duty) would generally only lie 'in an environment over which the defendant is in control'.[29] An NHS trust hospital might well owe such a duty to all patients being treated in their hospital. The Ministry of Defence had no control over its German contractors. Does that mean that PCTs can similarly never be liable for treatment contracted out to the private sector? Not necessarily. Lord Phillips says that, even if PCTs did owe such a duty, it would not follow that a similar duty is incumbent on the Ministry of Defence.[30] Moreover, Department of Health guidance expressly suggests that PCTs sending patients abroad for treatment owe those patients a duty of care that cannot be delegated.[31] One of us argues elsewhere that PCTs should owe a direct non-delegable duty to those patients for whose care they are responsible.[32]

Private patients

8.5 Our next concern is the private patient. A private patient who engages a private bed in an NHS hospital contracts individually with the surgeon and anaesthetist for the surgery and the administration of the anaesthetic, and contracts separately with the hospital trust for nursing and ancillary care. Even if the surgeon and the anaesthetist are employed by the trust when caring for NHS patients, when they act for a private patient they are acting on their own behalf, and not in the course of their NHS employment. If an error by surgeon or anaesthetist causes the patient injury, he can sue only the responsible individual. If the carelessness is that of nursing or other medical staff, he may sue the trust. As we shall see, this may cause problems of proof

---

27 [2004] EWCA Civ 641 at para 32.
28 [2004] EWCA Civ 641 at para 32.
29 [2004] EWCA Civ 641 at para 47.
30 [2004] EWCA Civ 641 at para 54.
31 Department of Health, *Treating More Patients and Extending Choice: Overseas Treatment for NHS Patients* (November 2002).
32 M Brazier and J Beswick, 'Who's Caring For Me?' (2006) 7 *Medical Law International* 183.

of negligence. Identifying who was the responsible individual may be virtually impossible, leaving surgeon and hospital to blame each other, and the patient to go uncompensated.

A patient entering a private hospital needs to consider carefully the nature and scope of his contract. The usual arrangement is similar to that entered into by a private patient taking a private bed within the NHS. The patient engages his own surgeon and anaesthetist, who will not be employees of the private hospital. The hospital contracts to provide other medical and nursing care. Like the private patient within the NHS, the patient must proceed against the surgeon for any error of his, and against the hospital for any error by their staff. Some private hospitals and clinics will contract to provide a whole 'package' of care and treatment. When the hospital undertakes to provide total care (the operation, anaesthetic, post-operative care, etc), any failure to meet the required standard of care means it is in breach of contract and is liable.[33] It is irrelevant that the surgeon, anaesthetist – or anyone else – is not an employee of the hospital. The hospital is not vicariously liable for any fault of a particular person. It is directly responsible for its own breach of contract.

General practitioners

8.6 What of claims against general practitioners? First of all, most general practitioners are not employees of a PCT. A claim relating to negligence by a GP operating a single-doctor practice lies usually against that GP alone.[34] Where a GP is a member of a partnership, his partners may be sued as jointly responsible for any negligence. If it is not the doctor himself who is at fault, but a receptionist or nurse employed by the practice, the GP and his partners are vicariously liable as employers. If a receptionist refuses to allow a home visit, refuses to allow the patient to speak to a doctor or fails to pass information on to the doctor with the result that a seriously ill patient becomes sicker or even dies, the doctor, while she may be personally blameless, will be vicariously at fault and liable to the patient or his family.

When must proceedings be started?[35]

8.7 A patient contemplating an action for clinical negligence must act relatively promptly. The general rule is that all actions for personal injuries must be brought within three years of the infliction of the relevant injury. This is known as the limitation period and is laid down in the Limitation Act 1980. A claim form must be served no later than three years from the date of the alleged negligence. But sections 11 and 14 of the 1980 Act provide that where

---

[33] Note the Supply of Goods and Services Act 1982, s 13 (implied term that service will be carried out with care and skill) and Part I of that Act (imposing conditions as to goods supplied in the course of a contract for services): see AP Bell, 'The Doctor and the Supply of Goods and Service Act 1982' (1984) 4 *Legal Studies* 175.

[34] But a PCT might be liable if they should have known and acted on information that a GP was not providing appropriate care: see *Godden v Kent & Medway Strategic Health Authority* [2004] Lloyd's Rep Med 521.

[35] See Lewis, *Clinical Negligence: A Practical Guide*, Chapter 26.

the patient originally either (1) was unaware that he had suffered significant injury,[36] or (2) did not know about the negligence which could have caused his injury, the three-year period begins to run only from the time when he did discover, or reasonably should have discovered, the relevant facts. Where the patient knew all the relevant facts, but was ignorant of his legal remedy, the three-year limitation period runs from the time when he was, or should have been, aware of the facts.

All is not quite lost for the patient who delays beyond three years, or who is ignorant of the law. Section 33 of the 1980 Act gives the courts a discretion to override the three-year limitation period where, in all the circumstances, it is fair to all parties to do so. The courts will examine the effect of allowing the action to go forward on both parties, taking into account, amongst other things, the effect of delay on the cogency of the evidence, the conduct of the parties and the advice sought by, and given to, the patient by his lawyers and medical advisers.[37] The three-year (or longer) limitation period applies only to starting legal proceedings. Once started, an action may drag on for years before it is settled or finally decided.

One further aspect of the rules on limitation must be noted. Where the injured patient is under a legal disability at the time he suffers injury, that is to say he is under age (under 18) or lacks mental capacity, the limitation period does not begin to run until he reaches the age of majority or ceases to lack mental capacity. This means that, for example, a baby might be injured at birth and the obstetrician could face an action in respect of the injury up to 21 years after the event. Until 1990, legal aid rules provided that if parents claimed earlier on their child's behalf, their income would be taken into account in assessing their child's eligibility for legal aid. Now that the child's income alone (if any) is relevant, parents no longer face a financial deterrent to taking action at the earliest possible stage.

Civil justice reform: the Woolf Report

8.8 Cost, complexity and delay bedevilled not just clinical negligence claims, but all actions for compensation in the latter part of the twentieth century. The civil justice system was perceived as inadequate. One of England's most senior judges, Lord Woolf, was commissioned to conduct a comprehensive review of the civil justice system and to recommend radical reform. He issued his Final Report in 1996.[38] Lord Woolf set out a number of admirable objectives for the civil justice system. It should be just in its results, and the operation of the system should be fair to all parties. Costs should be proportionate to the nature of the case. Claims must be dealt with reasonably swiftly. The process should be understandable to everyone using it, including any litigant who chooses not to engage a lawyer but to sue in person. The

---

[36] For example, he did not know for some years that he had been given blood infected by CJD: *N v UK Medical Research Council* [1996] BMLR 83.

[37] See, for example, *Smith v Leicestershire Health Authority* (1996) 36 BMLR 23.

[38] *Access to Justice: Final Report to the Lord Chancellor on the Civil Justice System in England and Wales* (1996). See also CMO, *Making Amends*, pp 86–87.

system should be responsive to the needs of litigants. There should be certainty in the way the process works. Civil justice should be adequately resourced and reasonably funded.

Four features of the Woolf reforms are central to malpractice litigation:

(1) The Pre-Action Protocol for the Resolution of Clinical Disputes[39] (the Clinical Negligence Protocol) seeks to find less adversarial and more cost-effective ways of resolving disputes about health care.

(2) In April 1999, the Civil Procedure Rules 1998 (CPR)[40] came into force. These Rules introduced a unified set of procedures for claims regardless of whether a claim is heard in the county court or the High Court.

(3) Integral to the Rules is the concept of case management. Judges are given infinitely greater powers to manage cases.

(4) The rules governing expert witnesses are altered, seeking to limit the misuse of expert evidence.

The Clinical Negligence Protocol

8.9 The Clinical Negligence Protocol sets out '... "ground rules" for handling disputes at their "early stages" '. It seeks to encourage a greater climate of openness, to provide guidance how this more open culture can be achieved, and recommends a timed sequence of events when disputes do arise. The Protocol aims to maintain or restore the relationship between the aggrieved patient and health care professionals and providers, and to resolve as many disputes as possible without litigation. Communication between the parties lies at the heart of the Protocol. Cases should be investigated swiftly, and records volunteered to the claimant for a reasonable period of time. Full consideration needs to be given to early settlement and, whether, if agreement between the parties cannot be reached, resort might be had to mediation or some other form of alternative dispute resolution.[41] The Protocol promotes a 'cards on the table' approach. Ideally, when a patient believes that she has a case in clinical negligence, in a matter of months she will be able to judge whether her belief is well founded. The defendant doctor or hospital will be in a position to settle any sustainable claim quickly. Means other than litigation of resolving genuine disputes will be reviewed. Only the truly intractable case will go to court. Once in the court system, the case will be resolved efficiently.

The Clinical Negligence Protocol focuses on pre-action events, before any claim form is issued and formal litigation begins. Requests for health records should be met within 40 days at a cost no greater than if the patient requested her records under the Data Protection Act 1998. The request must provide sufficient information for the doctor or hospital to know if the injury of which the patient complains is serious and has serious consequences, and the request must be as specific as possible about which records are required. Just as the potential defendant must not keep the claimant in the dark, so the Protocol

---

[39] See Lewis, *Clinical Negligence: A Practical Guide*, Chapter 10.
[40] Civil Procedure Rules 1998, SI 1998/3132.
[41] See CMO, *Making Amends*, pp 95–96.

aims to ensure that claimants and their lawyers are open and frank and do not set traps for unwary defendants. Where appropriate, on receipt of a request for records, the hospital should start to investigate the case fully.

A patient who is considering initiating litigation should send a letter of claim identifying any alleged negligence, her injuries and any consequential financial losses. The letter or claim must identify relevant documents and give sufficient information to enable the defendant to commence investigations and evaluate the claim. The patient may choose to include an offer to settle the case, stating his valuation of what would constitute satisfactory compensation. No formal legal proceedings should be issued until three months after the letter of claim. The potential defendant must acknowledge the letter of claim within 14 days, and within three months must provide a reasoned answer. That letter of response must make it clear if the claim or part of the claim is admitted, and if admissions are binding. If the claim is denied, specific answers must be given to the patient's allegations. If additional documents are relied on, they must be disclosed. Where the patient makes an offer to settle, the doctor or hospital must respond to that offer. Every opportunity to resolve the case without going to court must be explored.

The Clinical Negligence Protocol aims to ensure that NHS hospitals, and their staff, understand the law. It encourages proper risk management, prompt action when adverse outcomes occur, and good communication with patients. When the Protocol works, patients should have no incentive to rush into litigation and both sides have every incentive to work together. What happens, however, if parties do not co-operate and comply with the Protocol? Breaches of the Protocol can result in sanctions against the parties and their solicitors. Parties may be refused extension of time to serve claim forms or take various other steps in litigation (ie they will not be allowed to delay proceedings). Costs may be disallowed for unnecessary proceedings, eg if a patient rushes off to start formal proceedings before the three-month period has elapsed and before receiving a response from the defendants. Opinions vary on how effective sanctions are,[42] but one matter is clear: if the defendant refuses, or fails, to provide records, the patient still has to resort to formal proceedings to force disclosure of records; he must seek an order for pre-action disclosure.

Compulsory disclosure of records

8.10 The patient seeking to compel disclosure of records will rely on section 33[43] of the Supreme Court Act 1981. She can apply for a court order requiring the doctor or hospital that she plans to sue to disclose any records or notes likely to be relevant in forthcoming proceedings. Section 34[44] goes further. The court may order a person not a party to proceedings to produce relevant documents. So, if the patient has started proceedings against a GP, or a private medical practitioner, but believes that the hospital or clinic holds

---

[42] See MA Shaw, 'Pre-action protocol for the resolution of clinical disputes' [1999] *New Law Journal* 252.
[43] CPR 31.16. See Lewis, *Clinical Negligence: A Practical Guide*, Chapter 8.
[44] See also CPR 31.7.

notes of value to his claim, the hospital or clinic can be made to hand over the notes. This will help the private patient in a dilemma over whether he should properly proceed against doctor or hospital. It may also lead to the clinic being brought into the proceedings.

Three important matters on disclosure need to be mentioned. First, the intention to bring proceedings and the likelihood that they will go ahead must be real before a court will order disclosure. The patient must have some solid ground for thinking he has a claim. He cannot use an application for disclosure as a 'fishing expedition' on the off-chance that some evidence of negligence will come to light.[45] Resort to compulsory disclosure ought now to be rare. Documents truly relevant to a sustainable claim should have been volunteered under the Clinical Negligence Protocol. Other avenues to discover records and information may also be pursued. A patient wondering if he has a claim, but who is not yet ready to approach a solicitor, may apply to see his records under the Data Protection Act 1998.[46] He may also use the complaints procedure to explore whether he has any legal entitlement to pursue a compensation claim.[47]

Second, will the patient be able to see notes of any inquiry ordered by the hospital into his misadventure? The position is complex. If the inquiry was held mainly to provide the basis of information on which legal advice about the authority's legal liability is based, the records are protected by legal professional privilege. If the dominant purpose of the inquiry was otherwise – for example to improve hospital procedures or to provide the basis of disciplinary proceedings against staff, then the patient may be allowed access to the notes.[48] That is the legal position. The Court of Appeal has expressed its disquiet about the effect such claims of legal professional privilege may have on the patient's claim. Claims of privilege can be used to frustrate the patient's attempt to find out what happened, what went wrong. In *Lee v South West Thames Regional Health Authority*,[49] a little boy, Marlon Lee, suffered a severe scald at home but he should have recovered completely. He was taken to a hospital run by Health Authority A and then transferred to a burns unit controlled by Health Authority B. The next day he developed breathing problems, was put on a respirator and, still on the respirator, was sent back to A in an ambulance provided by Health Authority C, the South West Thames Regional Health Authority. When, three days later, the boy was taken off the respirator, he was found to have suffered severe brain damage, probably due to lack of oxygen. In her attempts to find out what went wrong, the child's mother sought disclosure of records and notes on her son prepared by staff of all three authorities. Health authority A asked South West Thames Regional Health Authority to obtain a report from their ambulance crew. South West Thames Regional Health Authority complied and forwarded the report to A. It was this report which the plaintiffs went to court to obtain access to. South West Thames Regional Health Authority had revealed its existence, but

[45] *Dunning v United Liverpool Hospitals' Board of Governors* [1973] 2 All ER 454.
[46] See above at 4.13.
[47] See below, Chapter 9.
[48] *Waugh v British Railways Board* [1980] AC 521.
[49] *Lee v South West Thames Regional Health Authority* [1985] 2 All ER 385.

refused to hand it over to the family. They claimed it had been prepared in contemplation of litigation, and to enable legal advice to be given in connection with that litigation. So it had – but it had been prepared on the request of Health Authority A to obtain advice as to A's liability to the child. Reluctantly, the Court of Appeal held that the privilege attaching to the document was enjoyed by Health Authority A. South West Thames could not be ordered to disclose the report. Even had they been prepared to do so, they could not have handed over the report without A's agreement. The principle was that defendants or potential defendants should be '... free to seek evidence without being obliged to disclose the result of his researches to his opponent'.[50] So a child was damaged for life in circumstances pointing to negligence on someone's part, and the law was powerless to help his mother find out what exactly caused his brain damage. The Court of Appeal expressed their disquiet and called for reform of the law. Within the doctor-patient relationship, Sir John Donaldson MR said there was a duty to answer questions put, before treatment was agreed to. Why should the duty to be frank with the patient be different once treatment was completed? In 1987,[51] he again emphasised the importance he placed on what he termed 'a duty of candour'.

Third, the court retains the power to refuse to order disclosure where to do so would be injurious to the public interest.[52] This is unlikely to be the case where what is asked for is the patient's own medical notes. An attempt by the Secretary of State for Health to plead public interest immunity to avoid disclosure of records in actions brought by several haemophiliac patients who had contracted HIV from contaminated blood products failed.[53]

Going to court: case management

8.11 If attempts to resolve the claim fail, and the patient starts formal proceedings, the conduct of the case will now be strictly controlled, with an emphasis on enforcing strict time-limits and keeping costs down. The claim will be allocated to a *track*. A clinical negligence claim worth less than £1,000 would theoretically be allocated to the *small claims track*. Most such claims ought never to result in proceedings, but rather be resolved within complaints procedures. Claims worth between £1,000 and £15,000 are allocated to the *fast track*. This means that the case should be resolved within 30 weeks. The actual hearing should take one day or less and oral expert evidence is limited. Claims worth more than £15,000, or where the issues are especially complex, go onto the *multi-track*. Judges control the allocation process. Most clinical negligence claims will be multi-track. None the less, the process should be speedier than before the Woolf reforms. At every point, opportunities to resolve the case without further proceedings must be seized. Time-wasting and unnecessary manoeuvres by lawyers will be penalised.

---

[50] At 389.
[51] *Naylor v Preston Area Health Authority* [1987] 2 All ER 353.
[52] Supreme Court Act 1981, s 35.
[53] *Re HIV Haemophilia Litigation* (1990) 41 BMLR 171, CA.

Proving negligence: the role of the expert[54]

8.12 We come now to the heart of the problem: how does the patient prove negligence? The onus lies on him. Mrs Ashcroft underwent an operation on her left ear. In the course of the operation, she suffered damage to the facial nerve and her face was left permanently partly paralysed. The judge found the evidence finely balanced. There was formidable evidence that this should not have happened if proper care was taken, but equally formidable evidence that, in such delicate surgery, damage to the nerve might occur even where the utmost skill and care were used. The judge held that the patient must fail.[55]

How does the claimant discharge the onus of proof laid on him? He will be heavily reliant on expert testimony. He will need to put forward medical evidence to demonstrate (1) that there was negligence on the part of the defendant, or a person for whom the defendant was responsible, and (2) that the relevant negligence caused the harm of which he complains. Obtaining expert evidence used to be very difficult for patients: doctors are naturally unhappy about voicing public criticism of a colleague; doctors in the same hospital may remain unwilling to testify against each other. However, greater openness today does mean that most patients should be able to obtain legal advice fairly locally. The organisation Action against Medical Accidents (AvMA) maintains a comprehensive list of reliable expert witnesses.

Until the Civil Procedure Rules 1998 came into force, unrestricted freedom for each side to call its own experts sometimes made a mockery of justice.[56] Reform of the rules governing expert evidence is fundamental to the Woolf reforms. The CPR are explicit and emphatic: the expert's primary duty is owed to the court to assist the court in matters involving his expertise, and this duty to the court '... overrides any obligation to the person from whom instructions were received or by whom the expert is paid'.[57] The CPR also impose limits on the use of expert evidence. Expert testimony must be restricted to what is reasonably required to resolve the case.[58] The court has power to direct the appointment of a single joint expert rather than each party choosing their own experts.[59] Obviously, if a single expert is to be appointed, it makes sense for the parties themselves to agree on such an expert. Lord Woolf saw no reason why, in a straightforward clinical negligence claim up to a value of £10,000, parties should not be able to agree on a single expert. Such cases may necessarily not be all that common. They are likely to be limited to cases where there is no substantial medical dispute about causation or prognosis, and perhaps all that is in issue is the appropriate measure of compensation. Many clinical negligence cases will involve disputes about whether there was negligence at all, whether the negligence caused the injuries of which the claimant complains and what the likely prognosis for the claimant will be. Such issues may well require separate experts. Imagine a claim that a child was

---

[54] See Lewis, *Clinical Negligence: A Practical Guide*, Chapter 9.
[55] *Ashcroft v Mersey Regional Health Authority* [1983] 2 All ER 245.
[56] See, for example, *Whitehouse v Jordan* [1981] 1 All ER 267, HL.
[57] CPR 35.3.
[58] CPR 35.1.
[59] CPR 35.7.

brain-damaged because of a mismanaged delivery. Obstetric evidence will be needed to establish if the obstetrician was negligent. Neurologists may have to be called to testify to the likely cause of the brain damage. Paediatricians and rehabilitation experts will be required to assess how the child can best be cared for into adulthood. Multiple experts may be unavoidable. None the less, control of proliferation of expert evidence will be asserted by the court. Where practical, a single joint expert must be agreed in relation to any particular issue. So, if there is a real and substantive dispute about whether the obstetrician was negligent, each party will probably be allowed to call its own obstetric expert, but – save in the most exceptional case – not more than one expert each. If there is no especial complexity about causation, a single expert should be agreed to address that issue. As much of the expert evidence as possible should be in writing. Oral testimony is allowable only with the permission of the court.

Where there are multiple experts, all letters, documents and instructions must be disclosed to the experts and there must be mutual disclosure of all experts' reports. Experts' meetings are encouraged. The hope may be that, at such a meeting, the experts will resolve the differences between them and promote resolution of the case without proceeding to a hearing. Initially it was envisaged that experts would meet alone and conduct a quasi-scientific seminar. Lawyers and their clients were uncomfortable with such a process, which could be seen as surrendering the judicial process to doctors. Additionally, the objective of resolving proceedings more speedily might well be frustrated. The parties would not accept the experts' conclusions as binding. Consequently, it is now agreed that the parties' lawyers may be present at experts' meetings.

May the burden of proof shift to the doctor?

8.13 While in the majority of cases the patient must prove negligence and the doctor is not called on to prove her 'innocence', are there ever occasions when that burden shifts to the doctor? There is a general rule of the law of negligence that where the defendant is in complete control of the relevant events, and an accident happens which does not ordinarily happen if proper care is taken, then the accident itself affords reasonable evidence of negligence. The defendant will be held liable unless he can advance an explanation of the accident consistent with the exercise of proper care. This rule is known as *res ipsa loquitur* ('the thing speaks for itself').[60] *Res ipsa loquitur* can be applied in clinical negligence cases, but the courts are reluctant to do so. At first, it was argued that *res ipsa loquitur* applied only where everyone of reasonable intelligence would know that that sort of accident did not ordinarily happen without negligence. As most people are not medically qualified, how could they know whether the accident to the patient was one which could, or could not, happen if proper care was taken? The Court of Appeal said that expert medical evidence was admissible to establish what should and should not occur if ordinary care was exercised.[61] *Res ipsa loquitur* proved to be a boon

---

[60] See J Murphy (ed), *Street on Torts* (12th edn, 2007) OUP, pp 127–133.
[61] *Mahon v Osborne* [1939] 2 KB 14.

in the following kind of case. Sometimes after an abdominal operation, a swab, or even a pair of forceps, is discovered in the patient's body. Without evidence of a quite exceptional nature, it is clear someone has been careless. *Res ipsa loquitur* may also help the NHS patient who has undoubtedly suffered because someone was negligent, either in the theatre or in the course of post-operative care, but she cannot identify that someone. If every member of the staff who might be responsible is employed by the hospital, then an inference of negligence is raised against the hospital, which is necessarily vicariously liable for whoever may be the culprit.[62] So in *Cassidy v Ministry of Health*,[63] a patient was operated on for Dupuytren's contraction affecting two of his fingers. After the operation, the patient's hand and lower arm had to be kept rigid in a splint for up to 14 days. When the splints were removed, the plaintiff's whole hand was paralysed. Upon finding that all the staff involved in Mr Cassidy's care were NHS employees, the court held that there was evidence of negligence against their common employer. The onus shifted to the hospital to explain how this disaster might have struck without any of its employees being negligent.

Beyond this kind of obvious bungling, *res ipsa loquitur* has limited use in clinical negligence claims. In many operations, the source of greatest danger for the patient lies not in the surgery itself, but in the anaesthetic. An anaesthetic mishap will not usually be of itself evidence of negligence, although *res ipsa loquitur* was applied in *Saunders v Leeds Western Health Authority*.[64] In that case, the patient was a four-year-old girl in otherwise perfect health who underwent surgery to correct a congenitally displaced hip. She suffered a cardiac arrest and consequent brain damage. Mann J said:

It is plain from evidence called on her [the child's] behalf that the heart of a fit child does not arrest under anaesthesia if proper care is taken in the anaesthetic and surgical processes.

The Court of Appeal[65] has however made it clear that *res ipsa loquitur* will rarely be applicable in such cases and criticises the phrase itself. It can arise only when either what happened simply cannot normally happen with negligence (for example, the patient went into theatre for surgery on his left foot and comes out with unnecessary surgery having been performed on the right foot) or where expert evidence agrees that, without negligence, such an adverse outcome is highly unlikely. An unexpected outcome in itself will not raise any inference of negligence.

Even in those cases of apparently obvious negligence (such as the forceps left in the abdomen) where the facts give rise to an inference of negligence, problems surface if one of the staff caring for the patient is not an employee of the hospital. For example, the theatre sister may be an agency nurse. Can the hospital say, 'No inference of negligence is raised against *us* because the

62 *Roe v Ministry of Health* [1954] 2 QB 66.
63 [1951] 2 KB 343.
64 (1985) 82 *Law Society Gazette* 1491.
65 *Ratcliffe v Plymouth & Torbay Health Authority* [1998] Lloyd's Rep Med 162, CA. See also *Lillywhite v University College London Hospitals NHS Trust* [2005] EWCA Civ 1466.

negligent actor may well have been that nurse for whom we are not responsible'? Once again it depends on whether the hospital's liability is solely vicarious or whether the hospital is (as we argued earlier) directly liable for any failure to measure up to the required standard of skill and care. If the hospital is directly liable, it matters not to the patient who actually employs the negligent individual. The private patient may be less fortunate. Whether he enters an NHS or a private hospital, he will usually contract separately with the surgeon and the anaesthetist for surgery and anaesthetic. The surgeon and the anaesthetist will not be acting as employees of the hospital. If something goes wrong in the operating theatre or post-operatively and it is not clear who is to blame, *res ipsa loquitur* probably cannot be invoked. The hospital is not liable for any negligence on the part of the surgeon or anaesthetist. He can raise an inference of negligence against the hospital only if he can trace the relevant negligence to one of their staff. He can raise an inference of negligence against the surgeon or anaesthetist only if he can pin the relevant act on one of them personally.

If the surgeon, anaesthetist and hospital are all sued, none of them can be compelled to testify against each other. The patient will not be able to identify who was negligent. However, hope lies in the following statement made long ago by Lord Denning:

> ... I do not think that the hospital and [the doctor] can both avoid giving an explanation by the simple expedient of throwing responsibility on to the other. If an injured person shows that one or other or both of two persons injured him, but cannot say which of them it was, then he is not defeated altogether. He can call on each of them for an explanation.[66]

Thus robust common sense would force open any 'conspiracy of silence'.

Awards of compensation[67]

8.14   Once a patient has established that there has been negligence by the defendant as a result of which she suffered harm, what damages will she receive? There are no special rules governing clinical negligence awards. The patient's damages will be assessed to compensate her for any actual, or prospective, loss of earnings, and for the pain, suffering and disability which she has endured, and will endure. Her compensation for loss of earnings will include a sum representing any period in which she would have expected to be alive and earning but, because of her injuries, she will be prematurely dead.[68] Additionally, for these sums to represent what she has lost, the patient will be awarded an amount to cover extra expenses which she and her family will incur. If she requires intensive nursing care, her house needs adapting to her invalid needs or she requires constant attendance so that her husband gives up his job, all these expenses will be reflected in the award of damages. If the patient herself is dead, the damages awarded to her family will reflect the loss

---

[66]   *Roe v Ministry of Health* [1954] 2 QB 66 at 82.
[67]   See CMO, *Making Amends*, pp 65–76.
[68]   This is known as compensation for the 'lost years': see *Pickett v British Rail Engineering Ltd* [1980] AC 136, HL; s 3 of the Damages Act 1996.

to them of the moneys she regularly expended on them. They recover for their loss of dependency.[69] It takes little imagination to see that if the patient dies, the burden of compensation may be reduced. Dead she suffers no pain, dead she incurs no expenses.

Returning to the living patient, thorny problems bedevil the question of damages. The first is as follows. The patient must usually sue within three years. At that stage, a prognosis about future health is speculative. All his medical advisers may be able to say is, the patient has a degree of brain damage; he is mildly disabled now. There is a 20 per cent chance he may deteriorate to become paralysed, and totally unable to do anything for himself, in ten years' time. The court now has power to make an award of provisional damages based on the assumption that the prospect of further damage or deterioration will *not* materialise. Should it do so at some later date, the patient may return to court to ask for a further award to compensate him for the consequences of that damage or deterioration.[70]

Until recently, courts had to struggle to assess damages on a once and forever basis. The exercise was particularly difficult when estimating claims for future expenses – especially where the patient was so badly injured as to be unable to manage his own affairs. Large sums of money can be claimed to cover the cost of future care in expensive nursing homes, but there is no guarantee that that money will be so spent: the patient may be consigned to the NHS and the money deposited to grow with interest and eventually, when the patient dies, form a 'windfall' for relatives. The courts are alert to this danger. They will seek to ensure that the sum awarded is such as will be wholly exhausted by care of the patient, aiming to provide no surplus as a bonus for relatives. Plans for care must be realistic, and section 5 of the Administration of Justice Act 1982 provides that 'any saving to the injured person which is attributable to his maintenance at public expense … in a hospital … or other institution shall be set off against any income lost …'. A further anomaly in the law is that the claimant may be able to claim for the full cost of *any* private medical care regardless of whether such facilities are available free on the NHS.[71] Even where exactly identical surgery to alleviate the patient's condition could have been performed without charge, the claimant may demand the full cost of private care.

Once the patient's monetary losses have been quantified, consideration must then be given to how to compensate pain and suffering. Levels of compensation for those non-monetary losses have traditionally been much lower in this country than in the USA. In 1986, the Court of Appeal ruled that £75,000 was the 'tariff' to compensate the suffering of a young woman left tetraplegic (paralysed from the neck down).[72] Incrementally, that sum crept up to about £100,000. Claimants felt that £100,000 for a lifetime of suffering was ludicrously low. The Law Commission conducted a review of compensation for pain and suffering and recommended that such compensation should be

---

[69] Fatal Accidents Act 1976 as amended by the Administration of Justice Act 1982.
[70] See s 32A of the Supreme Court Act 1981.
[71] Law Reform (Personal Injuries) Act 1948, s 2(4).
[72] *Housecroft v Burnett* [1986] 1 All ER 332, CA.

increased dramatically, in some instances of catastrophic injury by as much as 100 per cent.[73] In *Heil v Rankin*,[74] the Court of Appeal considered the Law Commission's proposals. An especially enlarged court agreed that more generous compensation for suffering and disability was justified. They settled on a lesser increase than that envisaged by the Law Commission. No increase should be offered in claims of less than £10,000. Graduated increases would be allowed thereafter to a maximum of about 50 per cent above prior levels of awards. Their Lordships acknowledged that the impact on the NHS of increased levels of damages played a role in motivating their caution.[75]

Other changes in the law relating to damages have also contributed to the increase in compensation payable in negligence claims against the NHS.[76] Medical skills mean patients who suffer injury as a consequence of medical mistakes live much longer. Greater opportunities exist to improve their quality of life. Such benefits escalate costs. The concern generated by spiralling awards of damages is exacerbated by the fact that compensating people for injury can never be an exact science.

Claimants and defendants are often unhappy with the level of compensation awarded. For example, when negligence results in a patient's death, compensation for bereavement is only available to parents of children under 18 or to spouses. The level of compensation is set at £10,000. The child left desolate at the loss of her father receives no compensation for her emotional loss. The parent losing a child is told her child is worth £10,000. This amount can be seen as an insulting assessment, but can any sum compensate bereavement? Was the old rule that bereavement damages were never available preferable? When a patient survives paralysed from the waist down, will £150,000 heal her pain? Defendants also feel badly done to. Who the patient is may be crucial to the extent of their liability. Should one of the authors be left paralysed by an anaesthetist's mistake, the defendant hospital will have to cover the cost of future care and of equipment we will need, such as wheelchairs and alterations to our home. Providing that we can still go on lecturing, even if seated, our loss of income will be minimal. Should England's football captain suffer an identical mishap at the height of his career, his claim for loss of income could easily exceed £20m. The lottery element in compensation awards was graphically illustrated by the case of Hollie Calladine.[77] Nine-year-old Hollie was awarded £700,000 in respect of brain damage caused by negligence during her birth. Much of this sum was to cover the expense of her future care. Days after the award was made, Hollie died. The hospital tried unsuccessfully to recover their damages. This sad case must suggest lump sum payments are not accurate or fair. The only equity of the system is that both sides suffer. For every case like Hollie Calladine's, there is another where claimants go grossly under-compensated by any lump sum payment. Take the example of a young man of 23 who is injured in the course

---

[73]   Law Commission Report No 257, *Damages for Personal Injury: Non-Pecuniary Loss* (1999).
[74]   [2000] 3 All ER 138.
[75]   [2000] 3 All ER 138 at 150.
[76]   See *Wells v Wells* [1999] 1 AC 345, HL; and see the Damages Act 1996.
[77]   See 'Legal Moves' (2001) 138 *Liability Risk and Insurance* 19.

of surgery. Doctors estimate he will live a further ten years. He survives for 25 years. His compensation will be less than half of what he required.

Periodical payments: structured settlements[78]

8.15 Some of the uncertainties generated by having to assess compensation as a lump sum are avoidable by resort to periodical payments or, as they used to be described, structured settlements. The claimant receives an initial capital sum to cover actual losses already quantifiable and such matters as compensation for pain and suffering. The remainder of the money is used by the defendant to purchase an annuity for the claimant's benefit. The annuity will be flexible, to adapt to the changing circumstances of the patient. The income received by the patient is not taxable. The money paid out will be what he requires and no more. Should he die earlier than anticipated, payments stop. Periodical payments avoid cases like that of Hollie Calladine. In certain cases, the periodical payments agreed or ordered can be reviewed at a later date. In ordinary personal injury claims, the defendant's insurer arranges the settlement and negotiates the purchase of annuities. As we have seen, the NHS does not insure against liability for clinical negligence on the commercial market. NHS structured settlements are usually self-financed.[79] The NHS uses its own income to arrange periodical payments, building the settlement into budgets. Tax concessions aid this process. Periodical payments in large claims may save the NHS some money. Recent reforms in the law allow the courts to impose an order for periodical payments.[80] Until 2005, structured settlements could only be established with the agreement of both parties.

Periodical payments may be efficient and fairer. The overall size of some awards for catastrophic injury is unlikely to drop. In 2002, the maximum award was £12m, compared to £16,500 in the mid 1970s.[81]

Malpractice crisis: reality or illusion?[82]

8.16 It will by now be apparent that, though the Woolf reforms improved the system, bringing a claim for compensation in any but the most straightforward of cases is rarely easy. Yet despite the obvious difficulties associated with funding a claim and proving negligence, critics of the civil justice system argue that England has succumbed to a 'compensation culture'. Personal injury claims, it has been said, are stifling ordinary life. 'Gold-diggers' make spurious claims. Schools are afraid to let children engage in any sort of risky activity. Children are barred from conker fights without wearing goggles.[83] Lord Hobhouse has said:

---

[78]   See *Street on Torts*, pp 664–666. See also A Sands, 'Periodical Payments – The Development of a Pragmatic Approach' (2006) 74 *Medico-Legal Journal* 69.
[79]   See CMO, *Making Amends*, p 74.
[80]   See the Damages Act 1996, ss 2–2B (as inserted by the Courts Act 2005 and the Damages (Variation of Periodical Payments) Order 2005, SI 2005/841).
[81]   See CMO, *Making Amends*, p 65.
[82]   The problems of the medical litigation process are further explored above at 8.2–8.14.
[83]   See (2006) Times, 18 September.

The pursuit of an unrestrained culture of blame and compensation has many evil consequences and one is certain interference with the liberty of the citizen.[84]

In the context of clinical negligence claims, this alleged compensation culture, it is argued, results in a malpractice crisis. It has been claimed that doctors practice 'defensive medicine', that is to say a doctor will choose the treatment for the patient most likely to be 'legally safe' to ensure that he will not be sued by the patient. That treatment may not necessarily be medically best for the patient, and may be unnecessarily expensive and time-consuming. A common example of alleged defensive medicine is a decision to carry out a Caesarean section as soon as there is any sign of difficulty in the course of labour, rather than to run the legal risk of continuing to attempt a natural delivery. It is also contended that the NHS is drained of resources because so many people sue.

Defensive medicine

8.17 The prospect of doctors basing decisions concerning treatment not on their professional judgment of what is best for the patient but on what is 'legally safest' for the doctor does sound appalling. But is there hard evidence that doctors are being forced to practise defensive medicine?[85] The classic example often given of defensive medicine – the rise in the rate of Caesarean sections – has often been found to be explicable by many other factors. Caesarean rates have risen in several countries, not all of which have experienced rising litigation rates.[86] None the less, obstetricians have voiced a subjective belief that fear of litigation makes them more ready to move swiftly to surgery rather than allow a difficult labour to proceed.[87]

Then there is the question of what is meant by 'defensive medicine'. In the House of Lords 20 years ago, Lord Pitt argued that the rising tide of litigation meant that doctors ordered unnecessary and sometimes painful tests, and he predicted '... an increase in defensive medicine with an alarming waste of resources'.[88] The difficulty is to decide when further tests and cross-checks cease to be a sensible precaution in the interests of the patient and become a waste of resources.[89]

Some of the concerns felt by doctors about defensive medicine may stem from anxiety that this country will see the excesses of malpractice litigation in the USA cross the Atlantic.[90] However, before concluding that England will necessarily follow the US pattern to its extreme, differences between the two

---

[84]   *Tomlinson v Congleton Borough Council* [2003] UKHL 47 at para 81.

[85]   See MA Jones and AE Morris, 'Defensive Medicine: Myths and Facts' (1989) 5 *Journal of the Medical Defence Union* 40; in relation to defensive medicine in the USA, see DM Studdert, MM Mello and TA Brennan, 'Medical Malpractice' (2004) 350 *New England Journal of Medicine* 283.

[86]   See C Ham *et al*, *Medical Negligence, Compensation and Accountability* (1998) King's Fund Institute/Centre for Socio-Legal Studies, pp 14–15, and note in particular Fig 6.

[87]   Royal College of Gynaecologists, *National Sentinel Caesarean Section Audit* (2001) (www.rcog.org.uk).

[88]   HL Official Report, 10 November 1987, cols 1350–1351.

[89]   See generally, P Danzon, *Medical Malpractice* (1985) Harvard University Press.

[90]   See CMO, *Making Amends*, pp 26–27.

countries must be noted.[91] In the USA, most medical care is provided by the private sector. If your treatment goes wrong and you suffer a medical accident, you will have to pay out more money for corrective treatment. Naturally an aggrieved patient is going to be looking to the doctor whom she perceives as responsible for the accident for the money to pay for any necessary corrective treatment. Most US patients will carry private health insurance. Their insurers will be as keen as the patient to ensure that any costs, arising from medical negligence, are recovered from the doctor and his insurers. In a private health system such as that of the USA, health care is charged on a fee-for-service basis. The more tests a doctor carries out, the more money he makes. Perhaps some of the apparent evidence for 'defensive medicine' is better explained as 'expensive medicine'?

Lawyers acting for the clients in the USA act on a *contingency* fee basis. If the case fails, the client pays nothing; if the claim succeeds, the lawyer takes a percentage of the damages (normally about one-third). Such a system makes it much easier for patients to litigate, and gives lawyers a direct interest in the level of damages awarded. As we have seen, English lawyers are now allowed to take on clinical negligence claims on a *conditional* fee basis.[92] Solicitors can agree to provide legal services on the basis that they charge no fee if the claim fails, but are permitted to increase their fee if the claim succeeds. The reward for the lawyer of an enhanced fee remains less alluring than the full-blown contingency fee system of the USA. The number of lawyers campaigning to allow contingency fees in England is growing. Awards of damages in the USA are decided not by the judge, as is the case in England, but by the jury. Even though the Court of Appeal[93] recently raised the tariff for compensation for pain and suffering in this country, levels of such compensation remain infinitely more generous in the USA. Moreover, damages in this country are currently awarded solely for the purpose of compensating the patient for what he has lost as a result of the defendant doctor's negligence. A US jury is empowered in certain circumstances to double, or even treble, compensatory damages by making a further award of punitive damages, to punish the defendant for negligence.[94] All these factors mean that while malpractice litigation consumes 0.2 per cent of Gross Domestic Product in the USA, that figure is only 0.04 per cent in the UK.[95]

Financial costs to the NHS

8.18 However, the financial effects of litigation on the NHS have generated serious concern. In the 1980s and 90s, rises in the numbers of claims painted

---

[91]   See generally, Ham *et al*, *Medical Negligence, Compensation and Accountability*, pp 19–20. Note, too, suggestions that any US malpractice crisis is at least in part a creation of the medical insurers seeking to protect their profits: see N Terry, 'The Malpractice Crisis in the United States: A Dispatch from the Trenches' (1986) 2 *Professional Negligence* 145.

[92]   See above at 8.2.

[93]   *Heil v Rankin* [2000] 2 WLR 1173, CA (see above at 8.14).

[94]   Although Law Commission Report No 247, *Aggravated, Exemplary and Restitutionary Damages* (1997) did propose that, in exceptional cases, punitive damages should be awarded in England.

[95]   See CMO, *Making Amends*, p 26.

a grave picture. A comprehensive study of medical litigation[96] published in 1988 demonstrated that numbers of claims against doctors doubled between 1983 and 1987.[97] In 1999–2000, the National Audit Office[98] reported that 10,000 new claims were initiated against the NHS (of which 76 per cent failed). The cost to the NHS escalated. Between 1983 and 1987, the average cost of compensation doubled. Overall, in 1996, litigation cost the NHS £300m.[99] In March 2000, £2.6 billion was set aside to meet the cost of claims, and £1.3 billion was estimated as needed to meet claims not yet reported. Since 1995–96, the cost of litigation to the NHS had increased seven-fold. In claims worth less than £50,000 in 1999–2000, costs exceeded compensation in 65 per cent of cases. One Health Minister was provoked to declare, 'The only place for a lawyer in the NHS is on the operating table'.[100]

But are numbers of claims beginning to level out? In 2004/05, the number of claims fell to 5,609 (from 6,251 in 2003/04). The following year showed a small rise in numbers to 5,697. However, the cost to the NHS remains large: £560.3m in 2005/06. The NHSLA estimates that its total liability (the 'theoretical cost' of paying all outstanding claims, including the incidents not yet reported to the NHSLA) amounts to £8.22 billion. How efficiently are claims dealt with? In claims of above £10,000 which were closed in 1999–2000, the time from making the claim to settlement or an award of damages was on average five-and-a-half years.[101] The average time to deal with a claim is said now to be just under one-and-a-half years.[102] How do claims fare? In relation to claims handled by the NHSLA in the past decade, 38 per cent were abandoned by the claimant, 43 per cent were settled out of court, and 15 per cent remain outstanding. Some of the worst problems of dealing with claims seem to be being addressed.[103]

Any judgment about whether the number of clinical negligence claims brought is excessive must be made in the context of estimates of the numbers of medical errors causing harm to patients. In one survey, 2,081 deaths were attributed to error.[104] It has been estimated that 10 per cent of 'in patient episodes' result in some injury to patients and that half of these 'adverse events' may be preventable.[105] Just over 6,000 claims in a year for clinical negligence suggests that many patients or families who could sue do not do so.

Never the less, where a claim is made by an NHS patient, money to compensate an injured patient – and money to defend claims brought in

[96]   Ham *et al*, *Medical Negligence, Compensation and Accountability*.
[97]   Ham *et al*, *Medical Negligence, Compensation and Accountability*, p 26.
[98]   National Audit Office, *Handling Clinical Negligence Claims in England* (2001). However, see the criticism of the NAO Report in P Fenn, A Gray and N Rickman, 'The Economics of Clinical Negligence Reform in England' (2004) 114 *The Economic Journal* 272.
[99]   See *Hansard* (24 March 1998), cols 165–166.
[100] See (1998) Guardian, 30 April.
[101] House of Commons Public Accounts Committee, *Handling Clinical Negligence Claims in England* (2002) HC 280, p 6.
[102] Research Paper 06/29, *NHS Redress Bill HL 137* (2006), p 11.
[103] See NHSLA, *Factsheet 1* and *3*; NHSLA, *Report and Accounts 2006* (HC 1179).
[104] See National Audit Office, *A Safer Place for Patients: Learning to Improve Patient Safety* (2005).
[105] See CMO, *Making Amends*, pp 31–41.

respect of alleged negligence – must come out of NHS funds which might otherwise have been used to employ an extra surgeon, pay for a new neonatal unit or support a programme of preventive medicine.[106] When that money is used to compensate an injured patient, at least some benefit to society can be discerned. When 76 per cent of claims failed, the disproportion between costs and compensation was extremely disturbing. Current statistics suggest a lesser degree of 'wasted resource'. None the less, John Harris[107] has argued that claimants in clinical negligence should compete for scarce resources with patients in urgent need of treatment. If resources for treatment are rationed, so compensation for medical accidents should be too. Costs arguments too must be kept in proportion. In absolute terms, just under 1 per cent of the NHS budget is expended on malpractice litigation.[108]

Wider costs to the NHS

8.19 Financial costs to the NHS are not the only cause for concern. Critics of the medical litigation process argue that it is unfair to doctors and damaging to the doctor-patient relationship. Are doctors unfairly treated? The evidence does not substantiate such a claim. When the rise in the number of claims was at it most dramatic, 76 per cent of legally-aided claims failed. 38 per cent of claims are still abandoned,[109] and among the 43 per cent of claims settled out of court, many will result in limited compensation to the claimant. Claimants do not seem to be 'winning' disproportionate numbers of cases. The recent reduction in numbers of claims may indicate that lawyers are less willing to take on 'weak' cases, and that patients struggle today to fund any claim. Nor does an argument that doctors are unjustly judged by lawyers stand up to scrutiny. For in deciding whether a doctor is negligent, in the majority of cases the court relies on expert professional opinion.[110] A doctor can normally only be found to be negligent if his peers testify to his negligence. The House of Lords in *Bolitho v City & Hackney Health Authority*[111] has endorsed judicial power to disregard expert testimony in exceptional cases. Evidence of adequate practice to rebut a claim of negligence must be shown to be 'logical and defensible'. Doctors cannot really complain if courts refuse to accept evidence of 'illogical or indefensible' practice.

What is true is that many doctors have become so frightened by the spectre of a malpractice crisis that doctor-patient relationships may be damaged.[112] Evidence of defensive medicine may be disputable, but defensiveness in

---

[106] See A Merry and A McCall Smith, *Errors, Medicine and the Law* (2001) CUP, p 212.
[107] J Harris, 'The Injustice of Compensation for Medical Accidents' (1997) 314 *British Medical Journal* 182.
[108] See CMO, *Making Amends*, p 26.
[109] NHSLA, *Factsheet* 1 and 3; NHSLA, *Report and Accounts 2006*.
[110] *Bolam v Friern HMC* [1957] 1 WLR 582 (see above at 7.7).
[111] [1998] AC 232, HL (see above at 7.8).
[112] See CMO, *Making Amends*, p 76.

medicine is a sad fact.[113] Doctors in 'high-risk' specialties such as obstetrics and anaesthetics are the worst affected among the profession. Doctors who are sued are concerned about:

> ... the damage to their professional reputation, whether they were found negligent or not: the fact of the case was sufficient for the damage to reputation and morale.[114]

The Chief Medical Officer noted:

> Legal proceedings for medical injury frequently progress in an atmosphere of confrontation, acrimony, misunderstanding and bitterness.[115]

Medical litigation is difficult and unfair for patients, expensive for the NHS and damaging to the morale of doctors. In 2006, two Acts of Parliament sought to address the problems.

Addressing the compensation culture

8.20 Evidence of any compensation culture[116] and, more specifically, a malpractice crisis, is mixed. What is clear is that the current litigation system satisfies neither doctors' nor patients' needs.[117] The Government, while denying the existence of a compensation culture, none the less assert that the *cost* of such a belief, in terms of risk aversion, is real.[118] Two new statutes, the Compensation Act and the NHS Redress Act, reached the statute book in 2006.

As we note in Chapter 7,[119] unless judges decide that doctors should not be sued because of the detrimental effects it will have on health care, the

---

[113] Hence Ian Kennedy argued that what is required to defuse any 'crisis' is better information about the law for doctors so that they will not feel constrained to practise 'defensive medicine': see I Kennedy, 'Review of the Year 2. Confidentiality, Competence and Malpractice' in P Byrne (ed), *Medicine in Contemporary Society* (1987) King's Fund, London.

[114] See CMO, *Making Amends*, p 76. Note also that it has been estimated that 38 per cent of doctors who have been sued suffer clinical depression: *Making Amends*, p 43.

[115] See CMO, *Making Amends*, p 7.

[116] Better Regulation Taskforce, *Better Routes to Redress* (May 2004) (available online at http://www.brc.gov.uk/downloads/pdf/betterroutes.pdf); House of Commons Constitutional Affairs Committee, *Compensation Culture* Third Report of Session 2005–06, HC 754–1 (2006) (http://www.publications.parliament.uk/pa/cm200506/cmselect/cmconst/754/754i.pdf); House of Commons Constitutional Affairs Committee, *Compensation Culture: NHS Redress Bill* Fifth Report of Session 2005–06, HC 1009 (2006) (1009http://www.publications.parliament.uk/pa/cm200506/cmselect/cmconst/1009/1009.pdf); R Lewis, A Morris and K Oliphant, 'Tort Personal Injury Claims Statistics: Is There a Compensation Culture in the United Kingdom?' (2006) 14 *Torts Law Journal* 158; K Williams, 'State of Fear: Britain's "Compensation Culture" Reviewed' (2005) 25 *Legal Studies* 499.

[117] See CMO, *Making Amends*.

[118] House of Commons Constitutional Affairs Committee, *Compensation Culture* Third Report of Session 2005–06, HC 754–1, para 111.

[119] See above at 7.5. See also A Samuels, 'The Compensation Act 2006: Helpful Or Unhelpful to Doctors?' (2006) 71 *Medico-Legal Journal* 171.

Compensation Act 2006 is likely to have minimal impact on clinical negligence claims. The NHS Redress Act 2006, which received Royal Assent on 8 November 2006, will have greater effect. It gives the Secretary of State power to implement a new redress scheme for patients which will combine investigation, explanation and financial redress without the need to go to court. The scheme is likely to run from 2008 and will most probably apply, initially at least, only to the provision of hospital services and to claims under £20,000.[120] Ultimately, the aim of the legislation is to reduce costs. A no-fault scheme such as the one which operates in New Zealand might have had a greater impact on doctors' morale and patients' access to compensation, but the CMO and others before him advised against it,[121] largely on the basis of cost. Instead, the new scheme will be fault-based and is likely to be run by the NHSLA. Patients do not need to accept an offer made under the scheme. They can reject it and sue. The possibility of litigation still hangs like the sword of Damocles above the doctor's head. A critique of the NHS Redress Act 2006 is central to the next chapter of this book.

---

[120] Department of Health, *NHS Redress: Statement of Policy* (2005).
[121] See *Learning from Bristol: The Report of the Public Inquiry into Children's Heart Surgery at the Bristol Royal Infirmary 1984–1995* (2001) Cm 5207(1); Report of the Royal Commission on Civil Liability and Compensation for Personal Injury (1978) Cmnd 7054 (the Pearson Report).

Chapter 9

COMPLAINTS AND REDRESS

9.1 When injury results from medical treatment, patients or their relatives seek accountability. This can take a number of forms. Some may wish the responsible health professionals to be disciplined, and we examined in Chapter 1 ways in which that might be achieved. Some seek financial compensation and bring a clinical negligence claim (examined in Chapters 7 and 8). Others simply want an explanation and an assurance that the same mistake will not be repeated. In particularly serious cases of repeated error or bad practice, patients often demand a formal public inquiry. In other cases, the individual affected may make a formal complaint. But, as we shall see, the NHS complaints procedure has come under fire in recent years. Evidence mounted that it was failing patients, especially in terms of providing explanations for mistakes. In New Zealand, where patients are compensated without proving fault through the Accident Compensation Corporation, doctors have a legal duty of candour and adverse events are usually admitted.[1] Here, doctors fear the complaints process might lead to patients seeking compensation in the courts and so they may be reluctant to admit errors. Many patients have lost confidence in the UK's inadequate complaints system, and choose to bring proceedings in court. A survey in 2000 showed that, when patients first pursued medical litigation, over 50 per cent of them primarily sought an admission of fault, action to prevent what happened to them happening to others and an investigation of their complaint. Only 30–39 per cent of aggrieved patients initially wanted monetary compensation.[2] Some patients sue simply to find out what really happened.[3]

The complaints system was reformed in 1996, and again in 2003 and 2006. The NHS Redress Act 2006 acts on some of the Chief Medical Officer's

---

[1]   P Davis *et al*, 'Acknowledgement of "No-Fault" Medical Injury: Review of Patients' Hospital Records in New Zealand' (2003) 326 *British Medical Journal* 79.
[2]   See L Mulcahy, *Mediating Medical Negligence Claims: An Option for the Future* (2000) HMSO. See also C Vincent *et al*, 'Why do People Sue Doctors? A Study of Patients and Relatives Taking Legal Action' (1994) 343 *Lancet* 1609.
[3]   See M Bismark, EA Dauer, 'Motivations for Medico-Legal Action' (2006) 27 *The Journal of Legal Medicine* 55.

recommendations in *Making Amends*[4] and will, in 2008, introduce a new system which will combine investigation, explanation and compensation in relation to small claims (probably below £20,000) without recourse to medical litigation. We examine this new legislation in the second half of this chapter. The NHS Redress Act will complement, rather than replace, the existing complaints procedure which, though capable of generating lessons for the wider NHS, more often focuses on the failures of local NHS organisations. We will turn to this system having first outlined the ways in which services or individuals may be made the subject of a health service public inquiry in order that the NHS as a whole can benefit from the outcome of the investigation.

Health service public inquiries[5]

9.2 Dissatisfaction with the outcome of complaints procedures in a number of high profile cases fuelled a growing demand for public inquiries. Such inquiries colour popular perceptions of the NHS as a whole, even if they address the exceptional, rather than the routine, grievance. Patients and patients' organisations want a comprehensive and independent review, either of an inadequate service in general, or of the misconduct of particular individuals. They want to see the whole picture and receive assurance that action is being taken to remedy the shortcomings of the NHS and/or call to account staff whose wrongdoing caused serious harm. A number of different procedures within the NHS provide for further investigation of such NHS 'scandals'. An NHS inquiry may be established under section 2 of the new National Health Service Act 2006,[6] whereby the Health Minister has a general power to do anything calculated to facilitate the discharge of his duty. In serious cases, an independent team will be drafted in to conduct the investigation. Such an inquiry will be conducted by a small committee, usually consisting of a legally-qualified chairman and two medical practitioners (one from the same specialty as the person whose competence is in issue). All inquiry members will be unconnected with the hospital where the complaint originated. Copies of all documents are circulated to all parties. The complainant and the subjects of the complaint may be legally represented, and cross-examination of witnesses is allowed. The committee's findings of fact are then submitted to the staff concerned for further comment. Finally, the committee reports its findings and recommendations. The inquiry procedure can be effective, but if hospital staff refuse co-operation the procedure may break down altogether. No-one can be compelled to attend the inquiry. NHS inquiries of this kind are relatively informal and lack coercive powers.

At the other end of the spectrum, the Department of Health may set up a formal, independent inquiry under the Inquiries Act 2005, where the matter is

---

4 Chief Medical Officer, *Making Amends: A Consultation Paper Setting Out Proposals for Reforming the Approach to Clinical Negligence in the NHS* (2003) Department of Health (hereafter CMO, *Making Amends*).
5 See K Walshe, 'The Use and Impact of Inquiries in the NHS' (2002) 325 *British Medical Journal* 895.
6 Formerly s 2 of the National Health Service Act 1977.

of sufficient public concern. The findings of such an inquiry are not determinative of liability.[7] Instead the aim is to restore public confidence and ensure that mistakes are not repeated. The Act also gives Ministers the power to convert other types of inquiry, both statutory and non-statutory, into an Inquiry Act inquiry[8] at which point the Minister can change the terms of reference. Previously, formal statutory NHS inquiries of this kind were conducted under section 84 of the National Health Service Act 1977. At a section 84 inquiry, all those involved were compelled to attend, and to produce documents, and, if the person appointed to hold the inquiry saw fit, all evidence had to be given under oath. Ministers used to invoke their coercive powers rarely. The most famous example of a section 84 inquiry was the public inquiry into children's heart surgery at the Bristol Royal Infirmary.[9] The Bristol Inquiry led to many other dissatisfied patient groups demanding similar public inquiries.[10] Section 84 inquiries could be public or partially private.[11] So too under section 19(4)(d) of the Inquiries Act 2005, where wide-ranging restrictions on public access may be applied according to the requirements of the particular inquiry. In 2000, the Secretary of State announced a private inquiry into the murders committed by Harold Shipman. There was uproar from patients and media. A public inquiry was duly ordered in September 2000 under the Tribunals of Inquiry (Evidence) Act 1921.

Patients involved in the many grievances caused by the conduct of Drs Neale and Ayling pressed the Secretary of State for Health for public inquiries. Richard Neale had been struck off the register in Canada in 1985, but continued to practise in Yorkshire long after that event. He was arrogant, overly optimistic about patients' prognoses and undertook clinical procedures that were beyond his expertise. Clifford Ayling was convicted on twelve counts of indecent assaults on former patients in 2000. The Secretary of State refused a public inquiry in both cases. His decision was unsuccessfully challenged in the courts. The resulting inquiries were private.[12] Patients will have less confidence in inquiries held behind closed doors. Government fears the cost of public inquiries, both in cash and to the reputation of the NHS. The Bristol Report[13] points out that private inquiries may be counterproductive. Holding the inquiry in private may be '... more likely to inflame than protect the feelings of those affected by the Inquiry'. The Report emphasises the need for transparent, clear criteria determining when a public inquiry should be established. These warnings fell on deaf ears.

---

[7] Section 2 of the Inquiries Act 2005.

[8] Section 15.

[9] See *Learning from Bristol: The Report of the Public Inquiry into Children's Heart Surgery at the Bristol Royal Infirmary 1984–1995* (2001) Cm 5207(1) (hereafter the Bristol Inquiry).

[10] Note that the Alder Hey Inquiry was not a public inquiry but an independent confidential inquiry set up under s 2 of the National Health Service Act 1977: see *The Royal Liverpool Children's Inquiry Report* (2001) HC 12–11.

[11] With relatives and participants admitted, but not the general public.

[12] Department of Health (hereafter DH), *Report of the Committee of Inquiry into how the NHS Handled Allegations about the Conduct of Richard Neale* (2004) Cm 6315. DH, *Committee of Inquiry – Independent Investigation into How the NHS Handled Allegations about the Conduct of Clifford Ayling* (2004) Cm 6298.

[13] At page 31.

Aligning complaints and redress

9.3   If an individual wants a swifter, more personalised investigation of his particular case, he may make a complaint. If he seeks financial redress he may initiate legal proceedings. Things are set to change. The whole system of clinical negligence litigation has come under sustained attack in recent years. In particular, the blame culture has been perceived as adverse to the promotion of patient safety and proper accountability for error.[14] The Bristol Inquiry[15] called for the 'abolition of clinical negligence litigation, taking clinical error out of the courts and the tort system'. Litigation should be replaced by effective systems for identifying and addressing errors and new no-fault-based provisions for compensation.

Responding to such criticisms, the Chief Medical Officer (CMO) circulated a Consultation Paper, *Making Amends*[16] setting out proposals to unify the approaches to complaints and redress within the NHS. Making a complaint would no longer disqualify an individual from making a claim for compensation. The Report focused on changing the culture of the NHS to one of openness and learning and restoring public trust. The Report rejected the possibility of a comprehensive no-fault compensation scheme for medical accidents,[17] in favour of a limited NHS Redress scheme which remains, for the most part, wedded to the law of tort.

The NHS Redress Act 2006 will apply in England and Wales. Scotland is currently considering a more radical no-fault scheme.[18] The 2006 Act gives the Secretary of State power to introduce a new scheme for torts claims relating to NHS hospital services. The scheme will combine investigation and, where appropriate, explanation, apology and financial redress. Eligible applicants will have the opportunity to bypass the expensive and convoluted legal system. The Government hopes that the scheme will benefit patients and health care professionals alike, leading to better redress and to a new culture of openness within the NHS. However, NHS Redress will only deal with low value claims. The Secretary of State has the power to place an upper limit on claims and, at the outset, this is likely to be set at £20,000,[19] so clinical negligence will continue to play an important role where monetary compensation is expected to exceed this limit. Though legal firms might have taken on claims below £20,000 where the claimant was publicly-funded through the legal aid scheme, the case would have to be very strong to take on such a low value claim on a conditional basis. The 2006 Act should therefore provide redress for some patients who would otherwise have found it impractical to claim in negligence. This leads some to question the economic viability of the

---

[14]   See A Merry and A McCall Smith, *Errors, Medicine and the Law* (2001) CUP, p 217.
[15]   The Bristol Inquiry, Chapter 26; and see DH Expert Group, *An Organisation with a Memory* (2000).
[16]   CMO, *Making Amends*.
[17]   The option of a no-fault scheme had been canvassed in the CMO's initial position paper: see *Clinical Negligence: What are the Issues and Options for Reform* (2001) DH.
[18]   SNP, *NHS No Fault Compensation Consultation* (19 June 2006).
[19]   DH, *NHS Redress: Statement of Policy* (2005), para 37.

scheme.[20] The Act determines which cases can be brought under the scheme and the organisations which can be members of the scheme, but the detail will be provided in secondary legislation which is not available at the time of writing. Subject to this, we will later examine the reforms more fully, and evaluate the extent to which they meet the stated goals of the Government. If many patients simply want explanations and apologies, effective complaints systems should meet their needs. So far they have not done so. Whilst the new NHS Redress scheme will combine investigation, explanation and redress, it will not apply comprehensively. It will run in conjunction with medical litigation and the existing NHS complaints procedure, to which we now turn.

Complaints procedures: a troubled history

9.4 A formal NHS complaints system was introduced in 1966. There were three separate schemes, relating to primary care, clinical care and non-clinical care respectively. In 1996,[21] new procedures were introduced:

(1) One single complaints procedure became applicable throughout the NHS. Hospital doctors, GPs and other community-based health professionals were dealt with within a unified complaints system.

(2) A three-step process was established so that complaints were first subject to 'local resolution' which could be followed by an 'independent review' of the case, with an ultimate right to resort to the Health Service Commissioner (popularly known as the NHS Ombudsman).

(3) The NHS Ombudsman was finally empowered to investigate complaints about clinical judgment and his jurisdiction was extended to cover GPs.

The revised NHS complaints system had a number of laudable objectives. Procedures should be responsive to complainants and seek to answer their grievances. They should enhance the quality of care and be cost-effective. All processes should be accessible, be seen to be impartial, be simple and swift. Complainants need to be assured of confidentiality. NHS authorities must be accountable for the operation of complaints procedures. No-one would dissent from these sentiments. Putting principle into practice proved a harder

---

[20] See BMA, *NHS Redress Bill – England and Wales* (2005), accessible at http://www.bma.org.uk/ap.nsf/COntent/NHSRedressBill; B Capstick, 'The Future of Clinical Negligence Litigation?' (2004) 328 *British Medical Journal* 457. However, note that the Government does not 'expect people to come forward' but that, due to the ease of making a claim, claims may rise by 'anything from 2,200 to 19,500 a year.' The HC(CAC) responds that the figures seem to have been 'plucked form the air': House of Commons Constitutional Affairs Committee, *Compensation Culture: NHS Redress Bill* Fifth Report of Session, 2005–06, HC 1009 (2006), para 11.

[21] See NHSE, *Complaints – Listening – Acting – Improving: Guidance on Implementation of the NHS Complaints Procedures* (1996) DH; *Being Heard – The Report of a Review Committee on NHS Complaints Procedures* (1994) DH.

task. Dissatisfaction with NHS complaints systems endured.[22] Patients complained that the second stage was not truly independent and that the process was complex, time-consuming and inefficient. Doctors were perceived as defensive, and mistakes were repeated.

So, in 2003, the Department of Health proposed further reform.[23] Section 113 of the Health and Social Care (Community Health and Standards) Act 2003 empowered the Secretary of State to make provision for the consideration of NHS complaints. Phased implementation began in 2004. The National Health Service (Complaints) Regulations 2004[24] entrust independent review to the Healthcare Commission. A number of major inquiries necessitated further reform. The Shipman Inquiry and the Neale and the Ayling Inquiries considered the raising of complaints and concerns in the NHS. The Fifth Report of the Shipman Inquiry,[25] to which we shall return, made recommendations for improvements to the system, especially in relation to general practitioners.

As a result, in 2006 the Regulations were amended again. The National Health Service (Complaints) Amendment Regulations 2006[26] (hereafter, the 2006 Regulations) seek to improve local resolution and to align the NHS and social care complaints systems. Whilst complaints may relate to a single isolated incident, they more frequently concern the package of care received. The ultimate aim is to merge the NHS and social care complaints system. Regulations 3A and 3B go some way towards that goal by requiring the two organisations to co-operate and provide a co-ordinated response where the complainant requests it.

Raising a concern

9.5 The reformed NHS complaints procedure draws a distinction between concerns and complaints. A concerned individual can talk informally to the designated complaints manager, or Patient Advice and Liaison Service (PALS) staff in each trust.[27] PALS are concerned with wider patient safety issues. They will attempt to resolve the situation without the need for a formal complaint. Otherwise, they can provide details of how to complain formally and refer complainants to an independent service – the Independent Complaints Advisory Service (ICAS),[28] which replaces the Community Health Councils.

---

[22] Select Committee on Health Sixth Report, *Procedures Related to Adverse Clinical Incidents and Outcomes in Medical Care*, HC 549 (1999); and see D Longley, 'Complaints After Wilson: Another Case of Too Little Too Late?' (1997) 5 *Medical Law Review* 172.

[23] DH, *NHS Complaints Reform – Making Things Right* (2003).

[24] SI 2004/1768.

[25] *Safeguarding Patients: Lessons from the Past – Proposals for the Future* (2004) Cm 6394. See also Citizens Advice Bureau, *The Pain of Complaining* (2005), recommending measures to raise standards, improve access, ensure timeliness and learn from complaints.

[26] SI 2006/2084.

[27] See http://www.pals.nhs.uk/

[28] Established under s 12 of the Health and Social Care Act 2001, replaced by s 248 of the National Health Service Act 2006.

ICAS

9.6 ICAS is a free, independent and confidential service designed to help patients and relatives make a complaint. It has come under fire in recent years. Launched in 2003, it originally comprised four voluntary organisations – the Citizens Advice Bureau (CAB), South East Advocacy Partnership, POhWER and the Carers Federation. None of these organisations had any experience of handling NHS complaints. In its first year, ICAS floundered. It handled 27,000 calls and provided advocacy support in 10,422 complaints,[29] but there were long delays. The Kerr and Haslam Inquiry,[30] a public inquiry which centred on psychiatrists who sexually abused their patients during the 1970s and 1980s, called for special support and assistance for the more vulnerable complainants, such as mental health patients. Following a listening exercise, the Department of Health decided not to renew CAB's contract. New contracts were awarded to the other three providers, which ostensibly offered better value for money, and a new two-tier system was introduced in April 2006. The new 'supported advocacy model' provides greater support for the most vulnerable, including self-help guides, telephone contacts and 'third party professional support'. Others will proceed under the second tier; the 'self-advocacy model'. For them, face-to-face contact with ICAS representatives will be a rare occurrence. Section 248 of the National Health Service Act 2006 places a duty on the Secretary of State for Health to make arrangements to provide independent advocacy services to assist individuals making complaints against the NHS. It is questionable whether, in its current form, ICAS achieves that goal. Dissatisfaction will ensure that complaints endure.

Local resolution

9.7 The first stage of the formal complaints process is to make a complaint at a local level, a process known as 'local resolution'. The scheme applies to all NHS organisations, but the 2004 and 2006 Regulations do not apply to the handling of complaints by NHS foundation trusts or primary care practitioners at local resolution. Parallel arrangements apply in those cases.[31] A complaint may be made to any member of the relevant NHS organisation.[32] Alternatively, it can be put directly to the complaints manager – a designated person in each NHS body responsible for managing the procedures for handling and considering complaints.[33] A complaint can be made orally or in writing,[34] by a patient or any person affected by actions, omissions or decisions made by an NHS organisation.[35] Complaints can be made on behalf

---

[29] DH, *Independent Complaints Advisory Service: The First Year of ICAS* (2005), p 4.
[30] *The Kerr/Haslam Inquiry* (2005) Cm 6640.
[31] Primary care practitioners: see SI 2004/291, SI 2004/627 and SI 2004/865. Foundation trusts have their own local resolution services but the second and third stages of the complaints system (the Healthcare Commission and the Health Service Ombudsman) apply to all NHS organisations.
[32] NHS (Complaints) Regulations 2004, reg 9(1).
[33] See NHS (Complaints) Regulations 2004, reg 5, as amended by SI 2006/2084, reg 5.
[34] NHS (Complaints) Regulations 2004, reg 9(2).
[35] NHS (Complaints) Regulations 2004, reg 8(1).

of a person where that person so requests, or who has died, is a child or cannot make a complaint himself due to a lack of mental capacity.[36] The complaints manager may, however, decide that the representative is unsuitable if she believes that the representative does not have a sufficient interest in the person's welfare.

At local resolution, the complaint is investigated, and conciliation or mediation arranged as appropriate.[37] Until the 2006 Regulations came into force in September 2006, the local NHS organisation had only 20 days to respond to the complainant. Substantial delays were common. In one case,[38] Mr B complained to the trust in July 2001. He received a partial response in September, and the Healthcare Commission referred the remaining matters back for local resolution in December. Mr B sent several reminders, but not having received a response (or a reason for the delay) by March 2003, referred the matter to the Ombudsman who upheld the complaint that the trust's attempts at local resolution were inadequate.

Improvements were made. In 2005–06, 75 per cent of complaints were resolved locally, within the (then) 20-day target time.[39] The 2006 Regulations increase the target to 25 days. This period can be further extended with the complainant's agreement.[40] The aims are to give local resolution a better chance and to reduce the number of complaints proceeding to the next stage (the independent Healthcare Commission). It is also hoped that the number of complaints referred back to local resolution by the Healthcare Commission will be reduced.

The 2006 Regulations amend Regulation 14 of the National Health Service (Complaints) Regulations 2004 so that complainants now have the right to refer their cases to the Healthcare Commission within six months of the end of local resolution. The complaints manager has discretion to extend this period if there are good reasons for the delay and the complaint may still be effectively investigated.[41] Otherwise, the complainant can go straight to the third and final stage, the NHS Ombudsman, missing the independent review stage altogether.

The Healthcare Commission

9.8 The revised complaints procedure seeks to ensure that the vast majority of complaints are dealt with locally. If a complainant does not feel that her grievance is resolved, or the matter is serious in nature, then she has a right to take it to the next stage: the Healthcare Commission. The Commission is an independent body set up under the Health and Social Care (Community Health and Standards) Act 2003 to promote improvements in health care. It

---

[36] NHS (Complaints) Regulations 2004, reg 8(2).
[37] NHS (Complaints) Regulations 2004, reg 12.
[38] Parliamentary and Health Service Ombudsman Case No E 3762/02–03.
[39] NHS Information Centre Press Release, 'Latest Statistics on NHS Written Complaints' (November 2006) (accessible at http://www.ic.nhs.uk/news/press/pr151106).
[40] NHS (Complaints) Regulations 2004, reg 13(3), as amended by SI 2006/2084, reg 7.
[41] Regulation 10(2).

will review each case and determine the appropriate course of action. The remit of the Healthcare Commission is subject to a number of limitations. The complaints procedure is not intended to deal with disciplinary matters. Sometimes a disciplinary process will need to be initiated separately. Any evidence of a criminal offence must be referred to the police. Both these sort of cases may delay the complaints process. Most importantly, the Commission cannot consider a complaint where the complainant has stated in writing that he intends to take legal proceedings.[42] There is nothing to stop the complainant suing once he has an explanation and apology. Traditionally this has resulted in defensive reactions to the possibility of lawsuits. One of the aims of the NHS Redress Act 2006 is to reduce defensiveness amongst health care professionals by combining investigation, explanation and financial redress in a new, fast-track, non-adversarial procedure. Whether or not the reforms are likely to achieve this worthy goal is examined in the second half of this chapter.

The Commission may decide to take no further action on a case, or it may recommend that the NHS body apologise or provide feedback, recommend procedural changes, refer the case to the Ombudsman or investigate the complaint further (for example by establishing a panel).[43] Written recommendations are produced and distributed. The Commission is in a position to look at the whole of a patient's experience and to make recommendations for the improvement of services. In 2005, complaints focused on:

> Poor communication with patients and relatives, poor clinical practice, unsatisfactory patient experience, poor staff attitude and poor complaints handling.[44]

The latter is particularly worrying. The Commission is not meeting its targets. It was expected that the Commission would receive around 3,000 complaints a year. Nearly 7,000 requests were received in the first ten months alone. The Commission was so severely stretched that its role in promulgating wider lessons was seriously curtailed – a vital role if mistakes are not to be repeated.[45] In one report, Mrs Johns' husband died in 2001 from lung cancer. By 2005, she had been waiting for two years for a report from the Commission.[46] In September 2006, it emerged that the Healthcare Commission had a backlog of nearly 3,000 cases of which nearly 900 had spent over a year awaiting review.[47] The amended complaints Regulations, which came into force in September 2006, aim to reduce the burden on the Commission by improving local resolution. But will the improvements prove effective? In the short term it is doubtful. Whilst a culture of blame[48] endures, NHS staff will remain guarded and patients suspicious.

---

[42] Regulation 15(3)(a).
[43] Regulation 16, as amended by SI 2006/2084, reg 10.
[44] National Audit Office, *A Safer Place for Patients: Learning to Improve Patient Safety* HC 456 (2005).
[45] NAO, *A Safer Place for Patients*, para 3.15.
[46] J Dreaper, 'NHS "Complaints" Body Criticised' (2005) BBC News, 31 October (accessible at http://news.bbc.co.uk).
[47] D Batty, 'Waiting Lists Grow for Patient Gripes' (2006) Guardian, 4 September.
[48] To use the term favoured by the Bristol Inquiry (at p 442).

The Ombudsman

9.9 The Healthcare Commission will not always resolve the situation to the satisfaction of the patient. The complainant must then be informed of his right to take his complaint to the Health Service Commissioner, better known as the Ombudsman. The Health Service Ombudsman is independent of both the NHS and Government, and unaffected by the new Regulations. For complex or unresolved cases, she is the 'court of last resort'. The post was established in 1973.[49] The Ombudsman is empowered to investigate any complaint where it is alleged that a failure in the health service or maladministration in the service resulted in injustice or hardship. She may not pursue a complaint where the person concerned may have a remedy in the courts unless she is satisfied that it is not reasonable to expect the complainant to invoke that remedy.[50] Most crucially, since 1996, the Ombudsman is empowered to investigate action taken as a result of the exercise of the professional, clinical judgment of doctors or nurses.[51] What, then, is the extent of the Ombudsman's power and influence today?

Complaints to the Ombudsman must be made in writing, normally within one year of the incident giving rise to the complaint.[52] The complaint may be made by a patient or by some responsible person acting on his behalf. Health service organisations may also refer written complaints to the Ombudsman.[53] Her powers of inquiry are extensive. She and her staff investigate in private. They will contact all hospital or primary care staff involved in complaints and seek their comments. The Ombudsman has complete control of the investigation. If co-operation from hospital staff or administrators is not forthcoming, the production of records and documents may be ordered and staff may be compelled to testify to the Ombudsman.[54] The Ombudsman only investigates complaints where the patient can show that he has 'sustained injustice or hardship'[55] as a result of maladministration or a failure in the service (except in the case of complaints about clinical judgment, where this restriction does not apply). She will only investigate a complaint if all local remedies to resolve the complaint have first been exhausted. Investigations take considerable time and resources. The Ombudsman has to select the most pressing complaints to follow up. On completion of an investigation the Ombudsman reports to the complainant, the relevant NHS organisation and any individual against whom

---

[49] National Health Service Reorganisation Act 1973. The Ombudsman's powers are set out in the Health Commissioners Act 1993, as amended by the Health Service Commissioners (Amendment) Act 1996, the National Health Service (Primary Care) Act 1997, the Health Act 1999 and the Health Services Commissioners (Amendment) Act 2000. In theory there are three separate NHS ombudsmen. In practice, to date, the post has been held by one person who is also the Parliamentary Commissioner for Administration (the general national ombudsman). The Ombudsman is supported in her NHS post by a Deputy Commissioner with experience of NHS management.

[50] Health Service Commissioners Act 1993, s 4(1)(b).

[51] See V Harpwood, 'The Health Service Commissioner: The Extended Role in the New NHS' (1996) 3 *European Journal of Health Law* 207.

[52] Health Service Commissioners Act 1993, s 3. The Ombudsman has discretion to extend this time-limit.

[53] Health Service Commissioners Act 1993, s 10.

[54] See Health Service Commissioners Act 1993, ss 11, 12.

[55] Health Service Commissioners Act 1993, s 3(1).

allegations were made. The report will contain a decision about whether the complaint was justified and recommend a remedy.

Each year the Ombudsman makes an Annual Report to Parliament, which is published by HMSO and available to the public. Additionally, in the course of each year, she publishes three reports summarising selected investigations with all the parties involved kept anonymous. Her activities are monitored by a Select Committee of MPs which encourage her in her work and spur her on to greater efforts on behalf of NHS patients. There have been a record number of complaints in recent years.[56] The Ombudsman reported on 904 health complaints in 2005/06, of which 56 per cent were upheld in full or in part.[57] Overall, there were 95,047 written complaints about NHS hospital and community health services in 2005/06 compared with 90,413 the previous year.[58]

The Ombudsman and clinical judgment

9.10 The exclusion of clinical judgment from review by the Ombudsman was once a most serious limitation on her effectiveness. In 1989–90, out of 470 complaints rejected as outside the Health Service Commissioner's jurisdiction, 204 related to clinical judgment.[59] The Health Service Commissioners (Amendment) Act 1996 extended the Ombudsman's jurisdiction to embrace clinical judgment. By 2000–01, 77 per cent of completed investigations concerned clinical judgment.[60] The nature of these complaints is varied. Quite a number deal with the level of care provided by junior doctors, and the adequacy of supervision and support provided for junior staff. In one case,[61] a man was diagnosed with food poisoning at presentation at the A&E. He was admitted for further tests but, despite negative test results, junior doctors continued to treat him for food poisoning for the following ten days, during which the patient suffered unremitting pain. At last a second opinion was sought and a serious complication of ulcerative colitis known as toxic dilation was diagnosed. Tragically, he died three weeks later. The Ombudsman found that a more timely diagnosis would probably have saved his life, and was critical of the consultant's lack of leadership. Dealing with complaints about clinical matters is not easy. Identifying if a complaint has substance is

---

[56] See D Sing, 'Ombudsman Reports Record Number of Complaints' (2004) 329 *British Medical Journal* 192.

[57] Parliamentary and Health Service Ombudsman, *Making a Difference: Annual Report 2005–6* HL 1363 (2006), figure 7.

[58] NHS Information Centre, 'Data on Written Complaints in the NHS' (November 2006) (accessible at www.ic.nhs.uk). According to an NHS Information Centre Press Release ('Latest Statistics on NHS Written Complaints' (November 2006), accessible at http://www.ic.nhs.uk/news/press/pr151106), '… just over 36,000 complaints about all aspects of clinical care, just under 11,500 complaints about delays and cancellations of outpatient appointments and nearly 11,500 regarding the attitude of staff. The number of complaints about family health services, (such as GPs, general dental practitioners), has remained level at around 43,000 for the past three years.'

[59] See the tables at page 23 of the *Annual Report for 1989–90*.

[60] *Annual Report for 2000–2001*, p 1.

[61] Case No E 82/02–03. Accessible at: http://www.ombudsman.org.uk/improving_services/selected_cases/HSC/index.html.

time-consuming. Records must be obtained with the complainant's consent. Clinical advice is required and often has to be sought from specialists outside the Ombudsman's office.

The Ombudsman and the courts

9.11 Many of the complaints dealt with by the Ombudsman would not be the subject of court action for a variety of reasons. For example, a baby was born prematurely and placed on a ventilator. Staff sought to wean him off the ventilator but soon judged that the child would not survive. A week after his birth he collapsed and died. NHS doctors were not in any sense responsible for his death; they were not negligent in their care of the infant. However, staff did not explain to the child's mother what was happening. When the consultant finally spoke to her, he said 'he had decided to let [the child] go'. His parents' felt excluded from his care and lack of communication left them unprepared for his sudden death.[62]

Other investigations undertaken by the Commissioner are more likely subjects of a claim for compensation. One notorious example concerned a woman of 23. She sought an abortion in 1970 and attended the hospital with her mother. The woman held a job but suffered from temporal lobe epilepsy and a degree of personality disorder. After discussion with the parents, the consultant sterilised the woman with their consent. The first the woman herself learned of the operation was when, some years later and married, she was trying to have a baby. The Ombudsman found no evidence that sterilisation was necessary for the woman's health. He judged that the consultant, acting in breach of DHSS guidance (which he had never read), was at fault.[63] Other, more routine cases, where a claim for clinical negligence looks more straightforward, come before the Ombudsman. A Caesarean section resulted in injury to a patient who had had problems with anaesthesia in earlier surgery. The complainant alleged that records of her previous difficulties were not transferred to her obstetric records, that her own warnings were ignored and that her complaint was badly and unsympathetically dealt with. Her first two allegations were of simple negligence. The Ombudsman never the less agreed to investigate the case in return for an undertaking that the complainant would not take legal proceedings.[64] This became common practice. However, such an undertaking is not legally binding and there is nothing to stop a complainant assuring the Commissioner he will not sue and then launching proceedings on the basis of evidence uncovered by the Ombudsman.

Complaints about complaints

9.12 The phased reforms which began in 2004 improved the system, but did not address the fragmentary nature of the complaints system. The NHS is not the only focus of concern: the private patient has limited options in pursuing

[62] Case No E 1095/99–99.
[63] Case W 236/75–6, HC 160 (1976–77), p 23.
[64] Case W 241/79–80, HC 51 (1982–83).

any grievance.[65] Where private treatment was paid for by the NHS, the new NHS complaints procedure applied, but where private treatment was conducted in an NHS hospital, it did not (unless it concerned the facilities or NHS staff). Concern led to the creation of the National Care Standards Commission, established by the Care Standards Act 2000, to regulate independent care services. Part of the National Care Standards Commission's remit was to investigate complaints and concerns. Its work is now covered by the Healthcare Commission and the Commission for Social Care Inspection.

Difficulties arise within the NHS too, particularly where a patient's care crosses the boundaries between health and social care. In 2005, the Ombudsman's report *Making Things Better?*[66] recommended the integration of health and social care complaints, which the Government accepted in its White Paper *Our Health, Our Care, Our Say.*[67] The Healthcare Commission and the Commission for Social Care Inspection are due to merge in 2008. The Ombudsman's report also called for stronger leadership from the Department of Health, and suggested that the Healthcare Commission should take on an inspectorate role assessing the performance of each trust. The NHS, the Ombudsman opined, should be more responsive and less defensive to complaints and feedback provided. In 2005, the Department of Health and the Healthcare Commission developed an NHS Complaints Standard to improve local services.[68]

The Fifth Report of the Shipman Inquiry presented an opportunity for further change. The CMO reviewed the medical regulation system in the wake of the report. The complaints system was not strictly speaking within his remit. His 2006 report *Good Doctors, Safer Patients*[69] considers the system none the less.[70] The consultation revealed the following criticisms:

1.   The current complaints system is not well publicised and is complex for the public to use.
2.   It is particularly difficult for the public to understand the role of many different bodies (e.g. Foundation Trusts, NHS Trusts, Primary Care Trusts, the General Medical Council, the police, the Healthcare Commission, the Ombudsman) in dealing with complaints.

---

[65]   See Fifth Report of the House of Commons Health Committee, *The Regulation of Private and Other Independent Healthcare* HC 281–1 (1998–99), and note measures to introduce complaints procedures in the private sector in the Care Standards Act 2000 and Health and Social Care Act 2001.

[66]   Parliamentary and Health Service Ombudsman, *Making Things Better? A Report on Reform of the NHS Complaints Procedure in England* HC 413 (March 2005).

[67]   (2006) Cm 3767. Implemented in part in the National Health Service (Complaints) Amendment Regulations 2006, amending the NHS (Complaints) Regulations 2004, regs 3A and 3B.

[68]   DH, *NHS Core Standard C14* (2005). This led to the production of Healthcare Commission, *Effective Responses to Complaints About Health Services   A Protocol* (January 2006).

[69]   DH, *The CMO's Report: Good Doctors, Safer Patients* (2006) .

[70]   DH, *The CMO's Report: Good Doctors, Safer Patients*, Chapter 8, paras 33–34 and Chapter 10, paras 70–76. NAO, *Handling Clinical Negligence Claims in England* HC 403 (2001).

3.   It is often difficult and inappropriate to separate out elements of a complaint into administrative, clinical and organisational because they are often interlinked and require a single rather than separate investigative process.

4.   There is little evidence of systemic learning from complaints either to improve the quality of clinical practice or of NHS services.

The criticism is reiterated that where complaints relate to a number of elements of care and cross organisational boundaries, as they most often do, the system fails. Interestingly, the CMO did not join others in a call for a single complaints portal. He recognised the 'surface attraction' of this option, but did not see it as a solution. Like the Ombudsman, he called for a change in outlook: complaints must be valued and utilised as a learning tool. The National Audit Office also notes that, 'Information from complaints and litigation is still greatly under-exploited as a learning resource'. It recommends that the Healthcare Commission liaise more closely with the NHS Litigation Authority (NHSLA) and the National Patient Safety Agency to identify key lessons and feedback information to trusts.[71]

Redress

9.13 As we have seen, a significant problem endemic in the complaints procedure is the defensiveness of doctors. If doctors were more open, faith might gradually be restored in the complaints process. Lack of patient confidence in the complaints system, as well as a requirement for financial compensation, leads some patients to litigate – and fear of litigation prompts more defensiveness on the part of doctors. It is a vicious circle, of little benefit to doctors, patients or the public. The Bristol Inquiry Report[72] eloquently implored the Government to abolish clinical negligence litigation:

> The system of clinical negligence litigation is now ripe to review ... [W]e take the view that it will not be possible to achieve an environment of full, open reporting within the NHS when, outside it, there exists a litigation system the incentives of which press in the opposite direction. We believe that the way forward lies in the abolition of clinical negligence litigation, taking clinical error out of the courts and the tort system. It should be replaced by effective systems for identifying, analysing, learning from and preventing errors, along with all other sentinel events. There must also be a new approach to compensating those patients harmed through such events ... [W]e recognise that such a radical change is likely to have wide implications not least in terms of any new system of compensation ...

So in September 2001, the Chief Medical Officer[73] initiated a comprehensive consultation process to explore potential options for reform of clinical negligence claims. Two years later the Department of Health's consultation paper *Making Amends* rejected a comprehensive no-fault system of compensation on the grounds of financial costs, problems of causation and the scheme's perceived inability to deal with wider learning issues. The NHS

---

[71] NAO, *Handling Clinical Negligence Claims in England*, p 10, para I.
[72] See the Bristol Inquiry, p 367.
[73] DH, *Clinical Negligence: What are the Issues and Options for Reform* (2001).

Redress Act was given Royal Assent in 2006. As we shall see, whilst the legislation gives the claimant the opportunity to take 'clinical error out of the courts', as suggested in the Bristol Inquiry Report, it does not remove it from the tort system. Should the Government have gone further and abolished clinical negligence litigation?

An attack on tort

9.14 Criticism of the tort of negligence as a means of compensating for personal injury however caused, whether by medical error or in a road accident or any other area of human activity, is far from new.[74] The tort system has been condemned as unpredictable, expensive and unfair.[75] The injured claimant, on whom the burden of proving negligence falls, cannot know in advance whether he will receive any monetary compensation. He cannot plan his personal finances and put his life in order. For example, a person rendered paraplegic in an accident cannot know whether he will be able to afford to convert his house to meet the limitations imposed by his new disability. Uncertainty and delay[76] may even impede his recovery.

The tort system remains expensive because of the cost of litigation. Where the claimant is still publicly-funded, the state funds his claim, perhaps with nothing to show for it in the end. The expense hits the NHS particularly hard. Resources spent fighting costly legal battles could be better spent on improving the quality of care, so reducing the number of accidents that occur in the first place. The NHS will bear the cost of defending the claim and any costs or damages payable. In 2005/06, the NHSLA paid out £591.59m. The legal costs in connection with claims closed that year were £145.2m.[77]

Patients suffer in equal measure. The prohibitive cost of litigation may deter claimants with a genuine case from pursuing it if they are not wealthy but are sufficiently well off to fall outside provision for public funding and are not a good enough gamble for a conditional fee arrangement. The Chief Medical Officer in *Making Amends* stated that in England:

> The legal and administrative costs of settling claims exceeded the money actually paid to the claimant in the majority of claims under £45,000 and took up an even higher proportion of the total amount paid out in the smaller claims.[78]

---

[74] See, in particular, P Cane, PS Atiyah, *Atiyah's Accidents, Compensation and the Law* (7th edn, 2006) CUP.

[75] The Pearson Report (Report of the Royal Commission on Civil Liability and Compensation for Personal Injury (1978) Cmnd 7054), Vol 1, paras 246–263.

[76] For claims closed 1999–2000, with settlement costs exceeding £10,000, the average time from claim to payment of damages was five-and-a-half years: House of Commons Public Accounts Committee, *Handling Clinical Negligence Claims in England* HC 280 (2002), p 6. In 2004/05 the average was reduced to 1.44 years: *NHS Redress Bill* HL 137, Research Paper 06/29 (2006), p 11.

[77] NHS Litigation Authority, *Factsheet 2: Financial Information* (2006), accessible at http://www.nhsla.com.

[78] See CMO, *Making Amends*, p 69.

Most of all, the tort system is not fair. First, the difficulties and cost of litigation place enormous pressure on a claimant to settle for less than full compensation. Second, the dividing line between negligence and no-negligence is paper thin. In *Ashcroft v Mersey Regional Health Authority*,[79] Kilner Brown J reluctantly dismissed the plaintiff's claim for compensation after an operation on her ear left her with a degree of facial paralysis. He found the expert evidence on whether such damage could occur without negligence equally balanced and so the plaintiff failed to discharge the burden of proof. He commented:

> Where an injury is caused which never should have been caused common sense and natural justice indicate that some degree of compensation ought to be paid by someone.[80]

Finally, the tort system has been attacked as unfair on the grounds that it lacks any proper moral basis. What is the justification for giving X, who can attribute his injury to human error, full compensation and leaving Y, whose injury has some other cause, to struggle on state benefits?

The litigation system has generated blame, distrust and dissatisfaction on the part of patients and defensiveness, concealment and low morale on the part of doctors. Solicitors and claims management companies tout for business, inviting claims with advertising campaigns. The Constitutional Affairs Committee reported in 2006 that the compensation culture is a myth, but that the *cost* of the belief, in terms of risk aversion, is real.[81] Although the media has exaggerated the rise in the number of clinical negligence claims, the *size* of clinical negligence awards is increasing. Unsurprisingly, there have been several proposals for reform.[82]

Alternatives to tort

9.15 So should we abolish clinical negligence litigation? Tort is not the only means of providing compensation to victims of misadventure. Private insurance is one option.[83] Another is no-fault liability. In the UK, there are various no-fault schemes – including the Industrial Injuries Scheme, the Criminal Injuries Compensation Scheme and the Vaccine Damage Payment Scheme – but they are piecemeal and incomprehensive. The case for a no-fault scheme is made out in part by the manifest deficiencies of the present system. It is beyond the scope of this book to consider whether a comprehensive no-fault scheme for all types of accidents should be introduced. In a perfect society, any

---

[79] [1983] 2 All ER 245. See also *Nash v Richmond Health Authority* (1996) 36 BMLR 123.
[80] [1983] 2 All ER 245 at 246. See also *Wilsher v Essex AHA* (1986) 3 All ER 801 at 810, per Mustill LJ.
[81] House of Commons Constitutional Affairs Committee, *Compensation Culture* Third Report of Session, 2005–06, HC 754–1, para 111.
[82] See, for example, the Pearson Report 1978; the Kennedy Report, *The Report of the Inquiry into the Care and Management of Children Receiving Complex Heart Treatment Between 1984 and 1995* (2001); NAO, *Handling Clinical Negligence Claims in England* HC 403 (2001); House of Commons Public Accounts Committee, *Handling Clinical Negligence Claims in England*; CMO, *Making Amends*.
[83] See *Atiyah's Accidents, Compensation and the Law*.

person suffering from disability – from whatever cause – would receive appropriate financial support. A person paralysed by a stroke has identical needs to a person paralysed by a fall from a ladder or a bungled operation. That ideal would require not an accident compensation scheme, but provision of a general disability income.[84] Radical reform can never be expected to happen instantly. It must be approached incrementally. Previous editions of this book have put forward a scheme of no-fault compensation embracing two categories of medical injury:

(1)   Injury or illness arising from an absence of, or delay in, appropriate medical treatment[85] provided that
        (i)   treatment would have prevented that injury or illness, and
        (ii)   a reasonable request for medical care from a person or authority under an obligation to provide care has been made by the patient or some other person acting on his behalf.
(2)   Injury or illness resulting from medical treatment provided that
        (i)   the injury or illness is not caused by the natural progression of disease or the ageing process, and
        (ii)   the injury or illness in not the consequence of an unavoidable risk inherent in the treatment, of which the patient has received proper warning.

Category 1 would cover injury arising from failure to treat, both in circumstances where the present tort of negligence would operate and where it would not. For example, a request for treatment might be made and not acted on by a GP because at the time he acted reasonably in thinking an immediate visit was not necessary. Events prove him wrong. They do not render him negligent. Under this proposed no-fault scheme the patient would recover because he did in fact suffer as a result of lack of treatment, albeit no-one was to blame.

Category 2 is more difficult to define. The intention of Category 2 is that it should extend to any damage to the patient which is neither the result of the natural progression of his original disease or condition nor a consequence inherent in its treatment and unavoidable if that treatment is to be successful. Under that last limitation, the side-effects of certain surgery and therapy would be excluded. At one level, the patient could obviously not recover compensation for pain and suffering ordinarily attendant on surgery. At another level, unpleasant and dangerous side-effects, for example, the patient's hair falling out during chemotherapy, or the risk of a stroke in some forms of brain surgery, would have to be excluded if they were inescapable in the pursuit of proper treatment. One important proviso is attached to the exclusion of unavoidable side-effects from compensation: the patient must have been properly warned. Failure to give proper warning, which results in injury unexpected and unconsidered by the patient, would remain a ground for compensation.

---

[84] See C Ham *et al*, *Medical Negligence. Compensation and Accountability* (1988) King's Fund Institute/Centre for Socio-Legal Studies.

[85] Treatment would be defined to include treatment given to the pregnant woman and injuring the child. Consideration of the implications of ante-natal treatment would be required. For example, would treatment necessary for the mother but injuring the child be excluded?

Avoiding definitions and drafting points may well be criticised as cowardice. The scheme above operates in a presumption of entitlement when injury follows medical treatment and ensues from lack of treatment. It seeks to avoid the linguistic complications of concepts of error or mishap. Ken Oliphant[86] has argued that experience from New Zealand should make us cautious. Initially at least, a compensation scheme should be based on evidence of 'medical error'. Where investigation and hindsight indicate that the patient received less than the optimum treatment and with such treatment her injury could have been avoided, she would receive compensation. Simple evidence of an unexpected outcome of treatment would not suffice, however serious that outcome. If a previously healthy patient suffers a cardiac arrest in the course of minor surgery, he will recover compensation if, for example, a defect is found in the anaesthetic equipment or some error was made by the anaesthetist. He will not have to show blameworthiness. If no reason for the sudden heart failure can be discovered, he has no claim in relation to that mishap.

The 'Oliphant solution' would, as Ken Oliphant says, provide 'consistency and ease of application'. It might provoke awkward questions of causation and make it difficult to cast off the shackles of negligence. It is a notable attempt to put substance into the defining of 'medical misadventure'. A root cause of the inadequacy of two attempts to introduce legislation to implement no-fault compensation in the UK was their failure to define medical mishap. Harriet Harman's Compensation for Medical Injury Bill contained this partial definition only: mishap did not occur if resulting from '... a reasonable diagnostic error, having regard for the state of medical knowledge and best medical practice'. Rosie Barnes's National Health Service (Compensation) Bill left the definition of mishap open. Her Bill provided that '... "Mishap" includes but is not restricted to, any act or omission which gives rise to an action at common law'.

No-fault compensation abroad[87]

9.16 A growing number of no-fault compensation schemes operate abroad. We briefly outline only two, the New Zealand Accident Compensation Scheme (which covers medical injury within comprehensive provision for compensation for personal injury from all causes) and the Swedish Patients' Insurance Scheme (designed specifically for medical injuries). Review of New Zealand's and Sweden's experience will highlight certain problems of no-fault liability. They are problems which should be treated as an education in mistakes to avoid, rather than an indication that the concept of no-fault liability should be abandoned. In this brief review of both schemes, we concentrate on how the basic principle of no-fault liability works. Space does not allow consideration in detail of the funding and administration of either

---

[86] K Oliphant, 'Defining "Medical Misadventure": Lessons from New Zealand' (1996) 1 *Medical Law Review* 1 at 30–31.

[87] For a comparative analysis of five general no-fault schemes and two schemes relating specifically to birth-related neurological injuries, see CMO, *Making Amends*, Chapter 6, pp 97–109.

scheme. It will swiftly become apparent that defining the criteria governing eligibility to compensation is the litmus test of whether no-fault compensation can be made to work.

The New Zealand scheme was first set up in 1974, to award compensation to anyone who suffered 'personal injury by accident'. It was reformed in 2002, but links to fault-based compensation were retained as concepts of 'medical error' and 'medical mishap' were introduced. Further reform in 2005 finally broke those links.[88] In 2005, eligibility for compensation was significantly expanded to cover all 'treatment injuries'. The scheme now covers most personal injuries suffered while receiving treatment from health professionals. It is a true no-fault compensation system. Claims are expected to rise by 50 per cent. Whilst the scheme has been commended for providing timely compensation and effective complaints resolution, there remain concerns surrounding patient safety.[89] Moreover, the provision of a no-fault scheme does not necessarily render doctors unaccountable. A new Patient Safety Team was introduced in order to address systemic problems and an independent health ombudsman, the Health and Disability Commissioner,[90] mediates, resolves complaints and promulgates lessons for the health service.

The Swedish Patients' Insurance Scheme[91] is expressly designed to provide compensation for medical injuries. Compensation is payable in respect of any injury or illness resulting from any procedure related to health care. Injury arising from any diagnostic procedure, inappropriate medication, medical treatment or surgery falls within the ambit of the Swedish scheme. However, compensation for such injury is subject to three important provisos. First, the injury must be proved to result from the procedure in issue, and not from the original disease. Second, injury resulting from a risk taken by a doctor to save life or prevent permanent disability is excluded. Third, and most crucially, the claimant has to show that the procedure causing his injury was not medically justified. The test of whether the procedure was medically justified often re-introduces the question of negligence. Never the less, certain claimants who lose in England would obtain compensation in Sweden. Mrs Ashcroft, who suffered injury to a facial nerve when the surgeon accidentally cut the nerve, would recover in Sweden. The surgeon was not to blame, but cutting the nerve was not medically indicated.[92]

---

[88] Injury Prevention, Rehabilitation, and Compensation Act 2001, s 32 (as amended by the Injury Prevention, Rehabilitation, and Compensation Amendment Act (No 2) 2005).

[89] See M Bismark and R Paterson, 'No-fault Compensation in New Zealand: Harmonizing Injury Compensation, Provider Accountability and Patient Safety' (2006) 25(1) *Health Affairs* 278.

[90] Created by the Health and Disability Commissioner Act 1994 (NZ). The Act was passed to implement the recommendations of Cartwright J in *The Report of the Committee of Inquiry into Allegations Concerning the Treatment of Cervical Cancer at National Women's Hospital and Into Other Related Matters* (1988) Auckland, Government Printing Office.

[91] Patient Injury Act 1996 (Sweden). See C Oldertz, 'The Swedish Patient Insurance Scheme: Eight Years of Experience' (1984) 52 *Medico-Legal Journal* 43 at 43–59; C Oldertz, 'Security Insurance, Patient Insurance and Pharmaceutical Insurance in Sweden' (1986) 34 Am J Comp Law 635.

[92] *Ashcroft v Mersey Regional Health Authority* [1983] 2 All ER 245.

Examination of the problems encountered in New Zealand and Sweden must not obscure the benefits of no-fault schemes. Patients uncompensated by a tort-based system benefit in those countries. In Sweden the investigation of the cause of a medical injury may still involve questions akin to negligence. It is an investigation. The patient will discover what happened. Never the less, the opportunities for scoring points, and the advantages to be gained from having the best advocate rather than the best case, do not exist.

The rejection of no-fault compensation in England

9.17 As long ago as 1978 the Pearson Commission[93] advised against abolition of tort as a means of compensating personal injuries. They made a number of specific proposals for more limited reforms. We concentrate on the proposals which relate to medical injuries. The Commission decided against recommending a no-fault scheme for all medical injuries.[94] Following its recommendations, the Vaccine Damage Payment Scheme was introduced. Strict liability for defective drugs was introduced by the Consumer Protection Act 1987. That reform came not as a result of the Pearson Report, but because of pressure from Europe. The Commission's Report gathered dust. Many of its proposals went unheeded.

The Bristol Inquiry Report[95] renewed the attack on tort and in *Making Amends*, the Chief Medical Officer also condemned the torts system in terms of both its financial and emotional ramifications, especially in relation to low value claims:

> Legal proceedings for medical injury progress in an atmosphere of confrontational acrimony, misunderstanding and bitterness. The process is anathema to the spirit of openness, trust, and partnership which should characterise the modern relationship between doctor and patient. Moreover, the whole nature of a legal dispute between two parties works against the wider interests of patients. The emphasis is on revealing as little as possible about what went wrong, defending clinical decisions that were taken and only reluctantly releasing information.[96]

Yet, once again, the problems associated with causation, deterrence and accountability, as well as the financial implications, led to the rejection of a comprehensive no-fault system. Let us examine these criticisms more carefully.

Causation

9.18 The CMO, like the Pearson Commission before him, felt that distinguishing between an injury arising from treatment given and the natural progression of disease or inescapable side-effects of treatment was too difficult. This is a valid concern. But is it enough to rule out a change to

---

[93] The Pearson Report, Vols 1–3.
[94] The Pearson Report, paras 1304–1371.
[95] See the Bristol Inquiry, p 367.
[96] CMO, *Making Amends*, at p 7.

no-fault compensation? Causation presents just as much of a problem within the present system. Reform of the law introducing a no-fault principle would have the following benefits. A greater number of claimants would obtain compensation to help them adapt their lives to their disabilities, or to meet financial loss resulting from death of a breadwinner. The damage done to relations between the medical profession and the public by bitter and protracted litigation would be removed. The patient would obtain compensation because he suffered injury as a result of treatment going wrong. The issue of *why* it went wrong and the doctor's competence would be for completely separate investigatory procedures. The problem of causation would still be present. Distinguishing between injury and the progression of disease (or whatever) would be made easier. The issue of causation would be investigated. It would not be part of a battle between the patient and the NHS, with the NHS having a vested interest in finding experts to deny that the patient's condition was caused by the treatment. Consideration could be given to whether the burden of proof of causation might be alleviated by requiring only proof of a reasonable possibility of causation.

Deterrence and accountability

9.19 Arguably tort serves a valuable purpose in emphasising the accountability and responsibility of individual medical staff. It may be costly and inefficient, may be inequitable in whom it compensates, but if it deters medical malpractice, can we afford to abandon it? The authors remain unconvinced that the tort system has much systematic deterrent effect in health care in so far as individual doctors are concerned. Moreover, the alleged deterrent impact of tort often obscures the crucial question of accountability.

(1) The tort system is capricious in its operation. Obstetricians are at high risk of a law suit. The highest payment relating to cerebral palsy in infants after an allegedly negligent delivery is £5.5m.[97] Geriatricians are hardly ever sued. This is not because obstetricians are more likely to be negligent than their colleagues in geriatrics. It is because if Granny dies as a result of a negligent overdose so little could be claimed by way of damages that it is not worth suing the responsible doctor. Remember the Legal Services Commission will not fund claims of less than £10,000; nor would such a claim be a good risk for a conditional fee agreement.

(2) Even where doctors are sued, the deterrent effect of tort is not direct. The damages will not come out of the doctor's pocket nor will his 'premiums' be increased. The deterrent function of tort normally operates via the insurance system. Poor drivers are deterred from carelessness and encouraged to improve because 'carelessness costs money'. NHS Indemnity means that NHS doctors do not pay any sort of insurance or indemnity. There *is* the emotional impact of litigation. Does the worry of being sued deter the incompetent doctor? We doubt it. Where negligence is gross and obvious, claims are settled swiftly to avoid adverse publicity. It is the cases where there truly is doubt about

[97] CMO, *Making Amends*, p 50.

whether an error is negligent that drag on in the public eye. We suspect 'good' doctors worry about litigation and 'bad' doctors rarely give the possibility much thought.

(3)   Finally, there are a number of cases where, albeit there was actionable negligence, there is no moral culpability. Doctors who make mistakes after hours without sleep in under-resourced hospitals should not be blamed for their error. The tort system could operate to deter such 'negligence' only by encouraging a doctor to refuse to treat patients at all once he suspected he could not do so entirely competently. Such an outcome would prompt more, not less, patient suffering.

One *caveat* must be issued before dismissing the impact of deterrence via the tort system. primary care trusts (PCTs) and NHS hospital trusts are encouraged to be cost-conscious. Is there a risk that a hospital trust anxious to offer the lowest-cost appendectomy will cut corners and offer less than safe appendectomies? The fear of litigation might operate on the collective mind of the trust to deter economy measures that prejudice patients' safety. The impact of tort on PCTs and hospital trusts must not be overlooked in the no-fault debate. Evaluating the extent to which PCTs and hospital trusts may be influenced by the deterrent function of tort is difficult. Risk management has a high profile within the NHS now. That is good. Hospitals review their practice and investigate adverse outcomes to try and prevent medical accidents. Currently a key player in risk- management is the Clinical Negligence Scheme for Trusts (CNST), which is run by the NHSLA. Membership of the CNST is voluntary, but currently all NHS trusts and PCTs are members. Failure to implement adequate risk management strategies can lead to expulsion from the CNST. That will mean a hospital is left to bear all its own litigation costs. The CNST is the enforcer of risk management. It operates a strategy embedded in the tort system. Put simply, NHS hospitals and other bodies are obliged to comply with risk management or face financial disaster. Risk management could and should survive a no-fault compensation scheme. But what would replace CNST and would it have the same 'teeth'?

Returning to accountability, does the tort system ensure that health professionals and NHS trusts are made to account for their conduct? Tort's role in ensuring accountability is minimal. The nature of adversarial litigation militates against such an outcome. If an operation goes wrong and a patient is injured, what went wrong and why it went wrong needs investigation. The professional or professionals involved should be required to explain all they can to the patient, and their conduct should be evaluated to discover whether it fell below a standard of good practice and to consider what measures might be taken to avoid such an accident in future. It may well be that even though there is no negligence in the tort sense, doctors and nurses can learn from the accident and amend standard procedures in the light of that knowledge. Adversarial litigation does not encourage such an investigation of the incident. Even after the Woolf reforms, little opportunity exists in litigation to evaluate disputed practices. Doctors and nurses in the shadow of litigation clam up; they are naturally wary of admitting any doubts they may have as to what they did or did not do. If the patient fails to prove negligence, within the tort system that is the end of the matter. Accountability is crucial. The tort system provides only token accountability. It is organisations such as the Healthcare Commission and the National Patient Safety Agency which will help ensure the NHS learns from its mistakes.

Cost

9.20 For Mason and Laurie, cost is a major reason for the rejection of no-fault compensation in England.[98] The overall cost of a no-fault scheme is difficult to judge. It is not a cheap option. They estimate a total cost of £4 billion annually. One article suggests that the operation of a no-fault scheme in England along the lines of the Swedish system would cost several times the cost of the current system due largely to the increase in claimants.[99] No-fault is, however, cost-effective. In New Zealand, administrative costs in 2000/01 ran to around 7 per cent of the cost of the system,[100] ie at least 90p in every pound was paid out to victims.

The ultimate cost of a no-fault scheme will depend on the level of payments made to victims. Several hard questions need to be addressed. It would seem obvious that the payment of compensation for loss of income and cost of care should generally be by way of periodical payments rather than as a lump sum. Payments can then be adjusted to meet the claimant's current needs. Should there be a ceiling on payments? Under the tort system, a high-earning solicitor rendered unable to work obtains money to make up her actual loss of income. Should no-fault compensation be limited to being sufficient to provide for the claimant's needs arising from her disability up to the 'average' standard of living?[101] What about compensation for pain and suffering? The harder a no-fault scheme tries to offer generous compensation, the harder it is to fund a scheme to meet the needs of the widest possible range of claimants. An affordable no-fault scheme will necessarily have to limit compensation payments. Typically, no-fault compensation schemes do not compensate non-pecuniary loss. Previously wealthy victims of medical accidents will not receive full compensation for their monetary loss. Their loss of income will be capped. Medical and rehabilitation costs which could be met from other sources will not be included in compensation payments.

Consider this scenario. X and Y are both paralysed in a medical accident. X, a PE teacher who might have got nothing from the tort system because he could not prove negligence, will benefit from no-fault whatever his prior circumstances. He will gain a reasonable income (shall we say £500 a week) if he can no longer work. He will obtain money to pay for care at home over and above what the social security system may provide, and money to adapt his house to the demands of his disability. Y, who could win damages under the tort system, may lose. Assume that prior to his accident, Y was a wealthy young

[98] JK Mason and GT Laurie, *Mason and McCall Smith's Law and Medical Ethics* (7th edn, 2006) OUP, p 299. See also CMO, *Making Amends*, p 15.
[99] P Fenn, A Gray and N Rickman, 'The Economics of Clinical Negligence Reform in England' (2005) 114 *The Economic Journal* 272 at 290.
[100] See CMO, *Making Amends*, p 98.
[101] In New Zealand, a maximum limit of 80 per cent of actual earnings: CMO, *Making Amends*, p 98.

football star. Now he is paralysed. £500 a week could be about 5 per cent of his previous income. He will get nothing for pain and suffering. A no-fault scheme will not pay for him to have costly private care in the USA.

Proponents of social justice will argue that it is better to offer some recompense to more people than award lottery-type damages to winners in the tort system. The problem is this. If a no-fault compensation scheme exists side by side with access to the tort system, patients such as Y will still opt for the tort system. Two options could be explored:

(1)   Claimants who opt to sue in tort do so at their peril. If their claim fails they are excluded from the no-fault scheme. That might radically lower the cost of tort claims because only the most clear-cut claims will be brought and they should be swiftly settled.

(2)   As in New Zealand, where a claimant is entitled to claim under the no-fault scheme a tort claim is barred altogether. No-fault becomes the exclusive route to compensation for medical accidents.

Financially, and to achieve the objective of a no-fault scheme, the second option makes most sense. But in barring access to the courts, would it violate Article 6 of the European Convention on Human Rights entitling everyone to a fair trial in determination of his civil rights and obligations?

Reforming the torts system

9.21 In *Making Amends*, the CMO rejected a no-fault medical injury scheme. Instead the report proposed reform of the existing negligence system, incorporating four main elements:

- an investigation of the incident which is alleged to have caused harm and of the harm that has resulted;
- provision of an explanation to the patient and of the action proposed to prevent repetition;
- development and delivery of a package of care providing remedial treatment, therapy and arrangements for continuing care where needed;
- payments for pain and suffering, out of pocket expenses and care or treatment which the NHS could provide.[102]

The report provided the basis for the NHS Redress Act 2006. The Bill, introduced in 2005, was contentious. Many felt that tinkering with the torts system would not make the problems go away. Some of the measures proposed in *Making Amends* and designed to increase openness and reduce the blame culture were excluded. We stand on the cusp of an experiment, paradoxically made more risky by its conservative aspirations. Though the scheme aims to save money by cutting out the lawyer it will, at least initially, prove expensive to a financially-crippled NHS. If it fails to engender the support of the public and health care professionals it will not have succeeded in its goals.

---

[102] CMO, *Making Amends*, p 16.

The NHS Redress Act 2006

9.22 The NHS Redress Act received Royal Assent in November 2006. The Redress scheme is likely to be implemented in April 2008.[103] It applies in England and gives regulation-making powers to the National Assembly for Wales.

> The Act provides for the establishment of a scheme to enable the settlement, without the need to commence court proceedings, of certain claims which arise in connection with hospital services provided to patients as part of the health service in England, wherever those services are provided.[104]

It is an enabling Act and much of the detail will be contained in secondary legislation which is unavailable at the time of writing. During the passage of the Bill, this fuelled criticism. *NHS Redress: Statement of Policy*,[105] published in 2005, gives limited assistance. There is little detail as to how the scheme will work in practice. 'It is surprising that the Department of Health has brought forward an ambitious Redress scheme, without setting out in detail how it will be run.'[106]

The scheme is non-adversarial, but is not a no-fault scheme. It is tort-based and will primarily cover cases of clinical negligence. Initially the scheme will apply only to cases involving liability in tort arising from hospital services provided by the NHS in England. It will apply even if the services are carried out elsewhere in the UK or abroad. Primary care services are, for now, excluded.[107] The scheme is open only to those who have not, and are not, bringing civil proceedings in court.[108] There is no appeal mechanism. Provided they do not accept an offer made by the NHS, there is nothing to prevent dissatisfied claimants from suing afterwards. It is likely that eligibility for public funding for medical litigation will depend upon the claimant having first used the scheme and failed to reach a settlement.[109] Alternatively, a dissatisfied claimant may complain.[110] Secondary legislation will give details of a new complaints procedure which will deal with complaints relating to maladministration under the new Redress scheme. The Ombudsman will be the final arbiter.[111] All other complaints will go through the existing complaints procedure outlined in the first half of this chapter.

According to *NHS Redress: Statement of Policy*, all providers of NHS hospital services in England, including NHS trusts, NHS foundation trusts and independent providers, will be compulsory scheme members. A trust will identify a case which may be eligible, either because it has received an application, has identified an eligible case or has had a case referred from the

---

[103] DH, *Full Regulatory Impact Assessment* (2006), accessible at: http://www.dh.gov.uk/assetRoot/04 /12/09/24/04120924.pdf.
[104] Explanatory notes to the NHS Redress Act 2006, para 5.
[105] DH, *NHS Redress: Statement of Policy*.
[106] HC(CAC), *Compensation Culture* Third Report, para 94.
[107] The exclusion will be reviewed in three years.
[108] NHS Redress Act 2006, s 2(2).
[109] DH, *NHS Redress: Statement of Policy*, p 11.
[110] NHS Redress Act 2006, s 14.
[111] NHS Redress Act 2006, s 15.

Healthcare Commission.[112] It will then inform the patient and investigate the incident. Section 11 of the 2006 Act requires that a 'scheme authority' is appointed. The NHSLA is likely to fill this role. Claims which fall outside the scheme, because they exceed the £20,000 limit, will continue to be dealt with by the Clinical Negligence Scheme for Trusts. As we shall see, questions arise as to the impartiality of the NHSLA, which is traditionally the defender of the NHS's interests. The trust will inform the NHSLA of the results and then provide an explanation and, where appropriate, an apology to the patient. The NHSLA will then, where appropriate, make an offer of financial settlement. If accepted, the offer prevents the claimant from bringing court proceedings relating to that particular incident. Redress is expected to roughly to mirror the level of compensation awarded in an equivalent successful court claim. It will include pain and suffering, loss of earnings and potentially remedial care. A contract for health care may be offered, which will cover clinical but not social care.

The Secretary of State is required to arrange assistance to individuals seeking redress.[113] This is likely to include free independent legal advice relating to the offer and any settlement agreement,[114] and the provision of the services of jointly instructed medical experts.[115] It is likely that the Legal Services Commission will maintain a list of independent providers of legal advice for this purpose, paid at a flat rate. It is unclear whether doctors and lawyers will be willing to work for the flat rate.[116] Moreover, it is unclear what additional assistance will be provided. Under section 8(1) of the 2006 Act free legal advice could be extended to cover initial advice regarding the strength of a particular claim, but this is unlikely. It seems that PALS and ICAS must fulfil this role. This is worrying. ICAS are equipped (though, as we have seen, already overstretched) to deal with complaints. Their current role is to guide the patient through the various stages of the complaints procedure. They are not equipped to advise on matters of duty, breach and causation. They are not lawyers. They will be able to guide applicants through the process but less able to tell them whether their claim is likely to fall above or below the proposed £20,000 cut-off point and, on that basis, whether a complaint, application under the Redress scheme or action in negligence is appropriate.

There is some overlap with the complaints system, as the scheme for redress incorporates the giving of an apology and the provision of an explanation. It is impossible at this stage to accurately predict the interface between the two procedures. Under section 5(2) of the 2006 Act, the Healthcare Commission will be placed under a duty to consider the potential application of the Redress scheme when considering complaints. This means that an investigation into a complaint will no longer be halted on the basis that the claimant is

---

[112] DH, *NHS Redress: Statement of Policy*, para 43.
[113] NHS Redress Act 2006, s 9.
[114] NHS Redress Act 2006, s 8(2).
[115] NHS Redress Act 2006, s 8(1)(b).
[116] HC(CAC), *Compensation Culture* Third Report, para 10; and see HC(CAC), *Compensation Culture: NHS Redress Bill* Fifth Report, paras 4–8.

seeking compensation under the scheme. Duplication will be avoided. On the other hand, determining eligibility will be as difficult for the Healthcare Commission as it will be for ICAS.

The NHS Redress scheme will not replace clinical negligence litigation. It will not, initially at least, apply to primary care trusts or to claims from before the Act was passed. At the outset at least, it will cover only claims of a low monetary value. On the other hand, it is likely to result in new claims being brought into the system. The combination of these factors means that costs are likely to rise. But ultimately the aim of the NHS Redress Act 2006 is to cut costs by vastly reducing legal expenses. If, as expected, there is a £20,000 limit under the scheme, it is estimated that it would, in the first year, result in anything between a £7m saving and a cost of £48m. After ten years, it is predicted that the scheme would range between a saving of £15m and a cost of £80m.[117] Arguably, by increasing the £20,000 limit incrementally to incorporate many of the claims attractive to law firms on a contingency basis, the scheme could, in time, produce further savings.

Around two thirds of the total liability for clinical negligence in 2004/05 resided in a small number of large claims where up to 75 per cent of damages were awarded for future care.[118] In a large part, this is a result of section 2(4) of the Law Reform (Personal Injuries) Act 1948, under which claimants are permitted to claim compensation for the cost of future care in the private sector, even though the NHS could adequately provide for their needs. In *Making Amends* the CMO questioned whether section 2(4) ought to be repealed. The Department of Constitutional Affairs is currently considering the issue.[119] Under the new NHS Redress scheme, immediate clinical care is likely to be provided by the NHS and long-term remedial care may be provided by the NHS or commissioned as part of the offer of redress. The £20,000 limit on redress does not include the cost of remedial care, which will be paid for in addition to the formal offer of redress. Outside the Redress scheme, section 2(4) will continue to represent a substantial drain on NHS resources.

Criticism of the NHS Redress scheme

9.23 The new NHS Redress scheme addresses some of the faults in the tort system. It provides an alternative to litigation, removing many of the delays, risks and costs. Proponents of no-fault compensation argue that the new Redress scheme does not go far enough. It does little more than formalise what already happens. While the authority managing the scheme is part of the NHS itself, public confidence will remain elusive. For health professionals the scheme limits, but does not remove, the disincentives to openness. Disgruntled

---

[117] NHS Redress Bill Explanatory Notes, Bill 137-EN, para 52. But see above, at footnote 20.
[118] According to the written submission by the Medical Defence Union Ev 121, para 8.
[119] See P Goodenham, 'Proposed Further Tort Reform After the NHS Redress Act: A Trojan Horse from Making Amends' (2007) 13 *Clinical Risk* 25.

patients retain the option of suing. Until an offer of compensation is accepted, the threat of litigation persists and, with it, an interest on the part of health professionals in maintaining silence.

Supporters of the CMO's original proposals in *Making Amends*, which recommended a fast-tracked procedure for small claims, are also concerned. One article estimated that the CMO's scheme would have cost around £42m per year. It recommended that the cost was 'relatively modest' when compared with the alternatives.[120] A no-fault scheme would be considerably more expensive, but doing nothing would continue to compromise safety and might engender defensive medicine. Even this proved too much. The beleaguered NHS could not afford it.

There are four significant departures from the CMO's recommendations. First, the CMO recommended a separate, no-fault *NHS Redress Scheme for Severely Neurologically Impaired Babies*[121] where it could be shown that the injury was birth-related. Currently only around one third of cerebral palsy births result in a claim in clinical negligence. Of these, only one third receive damages, averaging since 1995 at around £650,000. The claims are costly in terms of both the emotional effects on the parents and health professionals, and the financial effects on the NHS. The CMO was impressed by no-fault schemes for birth-related neurological injuries run in Virginia and Florida, USA. Although the government has not ruled out such a scheme, it forms no part of the NHS Redress Act 2006. The substantial damages awarded in successful birth-related injury cases would usually fall outside the ambit of the scheme. The Government indicated that any plans for a birth-related injuries scheme would be taken forward under the National Service Framework for Children, Young People and Maternity Services, which was published in 2004. To our knowledge, no such plan has yet emerged.

Second, the CMO recommended a 'duty of candour' to encourage openness in the reporting of adverse events.[122] This would be accompanied by an exemption from disciplinary action where incidents are reported. In relation to doctors, for example, the duty of candour is already incorporated in the General Medical Council's *Good Medical Practice* guidelines for doctors. Government declined to give it statutory force. A doctor admitting to error will therefore be subject to disciplinary proceedings by the GMC: a potential disincentive to honesty?

Third, the CMO's thirteenth recommendation was that 'documents and information collected for identifying adverse events should be protected from disclosure in court'. The aim was to limit disincentives to reporting of adverse events. This too was rejected by the Government. The balance between the public interest in encouraging reporting and the individual interest in access to information was, it felt, not properly reflected in a protection from disclosure. The NHS is patient-focused; such defensiveness is contrary to public policy.

---

[120] Fenn, Gray and Rickman (2005) 114 *The Economic Journal* 272 at 291.
[121] CMO, *Making Amends*, recommendation 2.
[122] CMO, *Making Amends*, recommendation 12.

Finally, one of the most contentious aspects of the legislation is the perceived and actual independence of the scheme. The 2006 Act does not refer to the organisation which will run the scheme, but Government policy statements indicate that it will be the NHSLA.[123] It will be an internal process. Fact finding will be conducted by the scheme member (the hospital) that made the mistake. Liability will be defined by the NHSLA, which is responsible for maximising the resources available for patient care. During the passage of the Bill, the Opposition sought to impose amendments separating fact finding and fault finding on the basis that the NHSLA would lack independence and impartiality. Fault finding, they suggested, would be conducted by independent patient redress investigators, overseen by the Healthcare Commission. In the House of Lords, the amendment was won by one vote. The Bill progressed through Parliament, and the amendment on independence was reversed. The Government did not want to duplicate the complaints procedure which, as we have seen, has an independent second and third stage. Nor did it want to replicate an independent legal process. The new Redress scheme governs the way the NHS investigates *itself*. It is about the NHS responding appropriately to complaints at the first level:

> To be effective in driving culture change, scheme members will need to take ownership both of how their own risk management systems work and of the solutions to any shortfalls.[124]

If the trust in question wants to avert a costly legal battle, it will move mountains to explain, apologise and provide redress to the applicant. Or so the argument goes. If the applicant has no faith in the trust, and health professionals remain tight-lipped due to the potential for legal action, applicants will remain dissatisfied. Trusts may indeed move mountains but will the patients appreciate it? There is a culture of distrust and in order to prove successful, the scheme needs to rebuild bridges. The Ombudsman will find her workload increasing if patients feel let down.

Public confidence will depend to a large degree on the practical measures contained in secondary legislation. First, it seems unlikely that the applicant will receive free and independent legal advice as to whether a complaint, an application for redress under the scheme or a clinical negligence claim is suitable. Without such advice the scheme will add to existing confusion. Second, how will the interface between complaints and redress be managed? The indications are that, though the scheme is largely applicant-based, there will be a duty on NHS staff and the Healthcare Commission to consider whether incidents or complaints give rise to a potential application under the scheme and to duly notify the relevant trust.[125] The Redress scheme incorporates elements of explanation and apology. The complaints procedure is separate. But what if the applicant wants to complain and does not want financial compensation? Whilst the redress system incorporates explanation and apology, it does not contain a right to appeal to the independent

---

[123] In *Making Amends*, at p 122, the CMO proposed that a new organisation which builds on the work of the NHS Litigation Authority should manage the Redress scheme, that it should have a widened remit and be given a new name to reflect its wider role.

[124] DH, *NHS Redress: Statement of Policy*, para 65.

[125] DH, *NHS Redress: Statement of Policy*, para 49.

Healthcare Commission. Will this right be lost to all those who are eligible under the scheme, whether they like it or not?

Chapter 10

MEDICAL PRODUCTS LIABILITY[1]

10.1 The pharmaceutical industry once basked in the warm glow of public acclaim. The development of antibiotics, of drugs to combat high blood pressure and heart disease, of medicines to alleviate the pain of rheumatism, and later the invention of the contraceptive Pill, brought benefits to many and life itself for some.[2] Events were to change the drug companies' image. Starting with the thalidomide tragedy, a series of disasters taught us the painful lesson that drugs can be dangerous and their use must be paid for. The list of drugs enthusiastically promoted in the first place and withdrawn from the market a few years later, amid bitter allegations that the drug in question caused injury and even death, is long.[3] Opren,[4] the benzodiazepine tranquillisers such as Valium,[5] human growth hormone,[6] the Pill itself,[7] and most recently the painkiller Vioxx,[8] are but a random sample of the better-known cases. Allegations of gross profit-making by multinational drug companies have proliferated.[9] Pharmaceutical companies have been criticised for testing

---

[1]   See generally CJ Miller, R Goldberg, *Product Liability* (2004) OUP; D Fairgrieve (ed), *Product Liability in Comparative Perspective* (2005) CUP.

[2]   Though J Blech and GW Hajjer, *Inventing Disease and Pushing Pills* (2006) Routledge suggests that the pharmaceutical industry is guilty of medicalising normal life processes such as birth, unhappiness and sexuality to create new markets. Arguably, the recent emphasis on prioritising prevention over cure within the NHS extenuates this process: I Heath, 'In Defence of a National Sickness Service' (2007) 334 *British Medical Journal* 19. See also MA Santaro, TM Gorrie (eds), *Ethics and the Pharmaceutical Industry* (2005) CUP for an excellent examination of the growing tension between the pharmaceutical industry and the public.

[3]   See PR Ferguson, *Drug Injuries and the Pursuit of Compensation* (1996) Sweet & Maxwell, pp 1–20.

[4]   See below at 10.11.

[5]   See *AB v John Wyeth & Bro Ltd* (1996) 7 Med LR 267.

[6]   *The CJD Litigation, Newman v Secretary of State for Health* (2000) 54 BMLR 85.

[7]   See *XYZ v Schering Health Care Limited* [2002] EWHC 1420 (QB). See below at 10.11.

[8]   J Robins, 'Stars and Gripes' (2006) 46 *Litigation Funding* 4 at 4–6, discussing a New Jersey court decision to reject a UK class action for alleged injuries suffered as a result of using the anti-arthritic drug Vioxx.

[9]   M Goozner, *The $800 Million Pill: The Truth Behind the Cost of New Drugs* (2004) University of California Press; L Eaton, 'Drug Companies are Defrauding Healthcare Systems, Conference Hears' (2004) 329 *British Medical Journal* 940.

products destined for the West on patients in developing countries.[10] Concern about the safety of drugs has extended today to anxiety about the safety of vaccinations, medical devices (such as breast implants) and, most worrying of all, to the risks posed by contaminated blood supplies[11] and other body parts.

Thalidomide was developed originally by West German manufacturers, Chemie Grunenthal. A British company, Distillers, bought the formula and manufactured and marketed the drug here under licence from Chemie Grunenthal. The drug was promoted as a safer alternative to existing sedatives and was expressly claimed to be suitable for pregnant and nursing mothers. Thalidomide was alleged to be the cause of gross foetal deformity. All over Europe, wherever thalidomide had been available, babies began to be born suffering from startlingly similar deformities, notably phocomelia (flipper limbs). After a bitter campaign, Distillers and the children's parents reached a settlement to provide compensation for children recognised as damaged by thalidomide.[12]

The anti-rheumatic drug Opren, withdrawn in the UK in 1982, is alleged to have caused kidney and liver damage, and even death, in some of its elderly users. Patients who suffered injury took legal action on both sides of the Atlantic. In the USA, Opren sufferers secured substantial compensation payments. British victims found themselves entangled in lengthy and complex litigation. They won some preliminary skirmishes,[13] but ultimately the cost of litigation forced many of them to accept an out-of-court settlement offering only meagre compensation.[14] Other Opren victims fought on in the courts. The defendant drug company successfully contended that they took legal action too late and were barred from either benefiting from the settlement or pursuing their case further in the courts.[15] Costly litigation ending in minimal compensation payments was for decades the pattern for virtually all claims for drug-induced injury in England.[16]

In 1987, Parliament enacted the Consumer Protection Act, imposing on all producers of goods strict liability for unsafe products. This Act was based on a European Community Directive[17] which required all Member States to introduce such strict liability for products. In part the intention of the

---

[10] See S Shah, *The Body Hunters: How the Drug Industry Tests its Products on the World's Poorest Patients* (2006) The New Press.

[11] See *Re HIV Haemophiliac Litigation* (1990) 41 BMLR 171, CA; *N v Medical Research Council* [1996] 7 Med LR 309; *The Creutzfeldt-Jakob Disease Litigation* (1997) 41 BMLR 157; *A v National Blood Authority* [2001] Lloyd's Rep Med 187.

[12] For a full and lively history of the events surrounding the thalidomide tragedy, see H Teff and C Munro, *Thalidomide: The Legal Aftermath* (1976) Saxon House.

[13] See, for example, *Davies v Eli Lilly and Co* [1987] 1 All ER 801, CA.

[14] In *Davies v Eli Lilly and Co* [1987] 1 All ER 801, CA it was held that the costs of litigation must be borne proportionately by all claimants. Legally-aided claims could not be used to provide 'lead' cases so that the costs would be borne by the legal aid fund.

[15] *Nash v Eli Lilly and Co* (1991) Times, 13 February. For a full analysis of the Opren litigation, see Ferguson, *Drug Injuries and the Pursuit of Compensation*, p 14.

[16] Indeed, no reported English case of an award of damages for personal injury for drug-induced injury can be discovered: see H Teff, 'Regulation under Medicines Act 1968' (1984) 47 *Modern Law Review* 303 at 320–322.

[17] Council Directive (EEC) 85/374 of 25 July 1985 on Products Liability.

Directive was to ensure fair competition between businesses in the Community: if France required French producers to meet more stringent safety laws than other Member States, French businesses competed at a disadvantage when compared to their rivals. However, much of the impetus for strict liability for unsafe goods in Europe[18] and the UK arose from a desire to give more effective protection and remedies to people who suffered injury as a result of defects in goods.

The Consumer Protection Act 1987 might be thought to make the law on drug-induced injury straightforward. A drug which causes kidney damage or foetal abnormality would be perceived by most lay observers as 'unsafe'. However, defining 'defective' under the Act will be seen to be more problematical. The damage caused by some drugs takes years to manifest itself. No action under the 1987 Act is allowed more than ten years after the drug in question was put on the market.[19] Nor is a drug company's liability under the Act wholly strict, for the Act permits producers to plead a 'development risks' defence and so escape liability. Victims of drug-induced injury often still resort to prior common law remedies in contract and the tort of negligence. And negligence liability for drug-induced injury needs to be understood to evaluate how far strict liability under the Act is a real advance on the bad old rules which thalidomide and Opren victims had to play under. For well over a decade the 1987 Act seemed almost irrelevant. A trio of judgments in 2000 and 2001 breathed life into strict liability. None the less applying the Consumer Protection Act 1987 to drugs is far from straightforward.[20]

Product liability and drugs

10.2 Whatever scheme for compensation is in operation there are problems relating to drug-induced injury which will not go away. English law purports to treat drugs as just another product.[21] For legal purposes a defective drug is (in theory) little different from a defective electric blanket or kettle. In practice there are vital distinctions affecting both user and manufacturer if litigation is started. Defects in products can be of two sorts: in *design*, which means that every example of the product will prove defective, or in *construction*, which means that some but not all of the eventual products will be faulty simply because they have not been put together properly.[22] Faults in electric blankets, kettles, or even aircraft, are usually construction faults. Defects in drugs are mostly design defects. That means that a drug company facing a claim alleging

---

18   For a disparaging view of the impact of the Products Liability Directive, see J Stapleton, 'Products Liability in the United Kingdom: The Myths of Reform' (1999) 34 *Texas International Law Journal* 45.

19   For definition of 'put into circulation' see Case C127/0 *O'Byrne v Sanofi Pasteur MSD Ltd (formerly Aventis Pasteur MSD Ltd)* [2006] ECJ. See H Preston, 'Liable to Change' 156 (2006) *New Law Journal* 538.

20   *Richardson v LRC Products Ltd* [2000] Lloyd's Rep Med 280; *Abouzaid v Mothercare (UK) Ltd* (2001) Times, 20 February; *A v National Blood Authority* [2001] Lloyd's Rep Med 187.

21   In contrast to West Germany, which after the thalidomide disaster enacted a special regime of liability for injury caused by drugs.

22   In *A v National Blood Authority* [2001] Lloyd's Rep Med 187, Burton J preferred the terminology *standard* and *non-standard* products.

their product to be defective is facing a disaster. There are going to be not just one or two claimants but a host of embittered and injured users. The cost to the company may put it out of business. The company fights back with equal vigour.

From the user's viewpoint, the greatest difficulty in any claim against the drug company is proving that the drug caused her injury. Should a new brand of electric blanket suffer a design defect, and within a week of purchase 5 per cent of users suffer an electric shock, the link between cause and effect is clear. With a new drug the process will be nothing like as swift or sure. Consider the case of diethylstilboestrol, a drug prescribed over 50 years ago to women threatening to miscarry. Evidence has emerged that women, *in utero* when their mothers took the drug, were affected in disproportionate numbers by vaginal and cervical cancer.[23] Delay in effect is only one of the problems. There may be uncertainty whether injury resulted from the drug taken, the original disease or some other natural cause. When a drug is alleged to cause foetal deformity this is a particular difficulty. Was the child's disability the result of the drug, of some inherited disorder or disease in the mother, or one of a number of other possible causes? Then in all claims there is the problem of proving that the drug was taken by the patient in the proper dosage and, as the same drug is often manufactured under different brand names, it must be shown which brand the patient actually used.[24] Medical records are often far from perfect; memory is fallible. Finally, there is the intractable difficulty of personal idiosyncrasy. A drug beneficial to 99.9 per cent of us may be lethal to 0.1 per cent. Is that drug defective? Should the company, or anyone else, compensate the 0.1 per cent who suffers injury?

The pharmaceutical industry argues that laws which weigh too onerously on it may inhibit research.[25] Medicine would be held back and British companies would suffer loss of competitiveness. Some view this claim sceptically. Much of the competition appears aimed at producing new brands of the same basic drugs. The pace of innovation has slowed down.[26] Doctors are moving away from prescribing as freely as in the past. Any decline in the pharmaceutical industry is as likely to be due to these factors as it is to be the result of law reform to help drug-injured patients.

---

[23] A particular difficulty here has been establishing which manufacturer made the actual drug taken by the mother. There were several brands of the same drug on the market: see *Sindell v Abbott Laboratories* (1980) 26 Cal 3d 588; *Mindy Hymowitz v Eli Lilly & Co* (1989) 541 NYS 2d 941 (NY CA); and, generally, Ferguson, *Drug Injuries and the Pursuit of Compensation*, pp 135–147. See also the discussion of *Fairchild v Glenhaven Funeral Services Ltd* [2002] UKHL 22, *Barker v Corus* [2006] UKHL 20 and the Compensation Act 2006 below at 10.9.

[24] See *Sindell v Abbott Laboratories* (1980) 26 Cal 3d 588.

[25] See, for example, J Abraham, G Lewis, *Regulating Medicines in Europe: Competition, Expertise and Public Health* (2000) Routledge; RA Epstein, *Overdose: How Excessive Government Regulation Stifles Pharmaceutical Innovation* (2006) Yale University Press.

[26] J Abraham, 'Regulating the Drug Industry Transparently' (2005) 331 *British Medical Journal* 528.

Consumer-buyers: most favoured claimants

10.3 A victim of drug-induced injury who bought the offending drug himself, or acquired the drug in the course of a contract, has a more effective remedy than any of his fellow sufferers. Despite the Consumer Protection Act 1987, consumer-buyers remain the most favoured claimants in England.

Two conditions are implied in every contract for the sale of goods. First, the goods must be of satisfactory quality.[27] This means they must meet the standard that a reasonable person would regard as satisfactory. Second, the goods must be reasonably fit for the purpose for which they are sold.[28] When drugs are bought over the counter they must meet these conditions just like any other goods. To take a simple example, a patient buying a bottle of cough mixture suffers internal injury because the medicine is contaminated by powdered glass. That patient recovers full compensation for his injuries from the pharmacist who sold him the medicine. The pharmacist may be entirely without fault. The medicine may have been supplied by the manufacturer in a sealed, opaque container. That does not matter; the medicine is neither of satisfactory quality nor fit to be sold, and the pharmacist is in breach of contract. This simple and effective remedy has a defect, however. It is normally available only when the person suffering injury from the defective drug bought it himself. Had the contaminated medicine in our example been purchased by a husband and taken by his wife, she may well have had no remedy in contract.[29] She cannot benefit from a contract to which she is not a party.

How useful is the contractual remedy in practice? A growing range of medicines are no longer available by prescription only. They have been re-classified to allow sale in pharmacies or, in many cases, in ordinary shops.[30] Antihistamines to alleviate hay fever, similar drugs to aid sleep, antibiotic eye drops and a host of medicines to help digestive problems can now be bought over the counter. These 'deregulated' drugs are more likely to carry inherent risks of harm than the sort of cough and cold remedies available over the counter not long ago. More patients may look to their pharmacist or local supermarket for redress. Patients prescribed their medicines on the NHS remain less favoured. Such medicines will not attract conditions of satisfactory quality and fitness for purpose because there is no contract between the pharmacist and the patient into which such conditions can be implied, even though the patient will often pay for his prescription.[31] The pharmacist dispenses the drug as part of his obligation under his contract with the local

---

[27] Sale of Goods Act 1979, s 14(2) (as amended by the Sale and Supply of Goods Act 1999). See WCH Ervine, 'Satisfactory Quality: What does it Mean?' (2004) *Journal of Business Law* 684.

[28] Sale of Goods Act 1979, s 14(3). See C Twigg-Flesner, 'The Relationship between Satisfactory Quality and Fitness for Purpose' (2004) 63 *Cambridge Law Journal* 22.

[29] Unless she can show that her husband bought the medicine for her as her agent.

[30] See RR Fenichel, 'Which Drugs Should be Available Over the Counter? (2004) 329 *British Medical Journal* 182.

[31] *Pfizer Corpn v Ministry of Health* [1965] AC 512; *Appleby v Sleep* [1968] 1 WLR 948.

primary care trust to provide pharmaceutical services in the area. The patient pays a statutory charge. He does not buy the drug; he pays a tax for NHS services.

By contrast, when drugs are dispensed under a private prescription a contract does exist between the pharmacist and the patient. The patient pays the full cost of the drug directly to the pharmacist. It matters not whether the contract is one of simple sale or a contract of service under which the pharmacist provides a skilled service and incidentally supplies the drug. Quality conditions are imposed in identical terms regardless of whether goods are supplied in the course of a service or in an ordinary sale transaction.[32] The number of private prescriptions is rising. The pharmacist is exposed on the front line of liability for defective drugs. When more potent drugs become the subject of conditions of fitness, whether by prescription or an over the counter sale, problems of applying those conditions are likely. The question may arise as to whether a drug perfectly safe for all but pregnant women is fit to be supplied. If it is specifically aimed at pregnant women – for example a morning sickness preparation – clearly, if it damages the woman or her baby, it is not fit for the purpose for which it is supplied. If it is a general medicine, such as a hay fever remedy, it could be argued that if it carries risk to a substantial section of the community – pregnant women – then it is not of satisfactory quality, nor fit to be on general sale. This immediately raises further questions. Did the manufacturer warn of the risk to pregnant women? Is such a warning sufficient? Should the woman herself be aware of the dangers of taking drugs and avoid drugs while pregnant?

These sorts of problems inevitably plague questions of liability for defective drugs. Where a remedy lies in contract, once a court finds the drug unsafe, the claim for compensation is established. It is no defence for the retailer of the drug, or the pharmacist dispensing the drug, to argue that he personally was blameless. Nor is it any answer to the patient's claim that the state of scientific and technical knowledge at the time when the drug was produced was such that the defect could not have been discovered. There is no 'development risks' defence against a claim in contract. The liability imposed on the retailer or supplier is truly strict.

The remedy in negligence

10.4 Patients who suffer injury as a result of drugs prescribed within the NHS must look outside contract for a remedy. Prior to the Consumer Protection Act 1987 that remedy would have been found in the tort of negligence,[33] and even today, gaps in the 1987 Act mean that victims of drug-induced injury cannot ignore this tort.

---

[32] See the Supply of Goods and Service Act 1982; AP Bell, 'The Doctor and the Supply of Goods and Service Act' [1984] *Legal Studies* 175.

[33] The Consumer Protection Act 1987 applies only to products marketed *after* 1 March 1988, so any claim arising out of a drug put on the market *before* that date (albeit taken by the patient at some later date) will still lie exclusively in negligence.

An action in negligence arises where one person suffers injury as a result of the breach of a duty of care owed him by another. His doctor may be the first person to whom the patient turns for a remedy when he believes a drug prescribed by that doctor has harmed him. The doctor will be liable for drug-induced injury if the drug caused damage because she prescribed an incorrect dosage, because she ought to have appreciated that that drug posed a risk to a particular patient in the light of his medical history, or where drugs have been prescribed in inappropriate and harmful combination. Similarly, if the injury to the patient resulted from a negligent error by the pharmacist in, for example, dispensing the wrong drug or indicating the wrong dosage, an action in negligence lies against the pharmacist. In a number of cases, it is the cumulative negligence of both doctor and pharmacist which causes injury, as where a doctor's atrocious handwriting misled the pharmacist into dispensing entirely the wrong drug.[34] The problem for the patient is that all he knows is that he is ill and he believes the drug to be the cause. He will have no means of knowing whether an inherently 'safe' drug was prescribed for him in an unsafe and careless fashion, or whether the drug is inherently defective and harmful, however careful his doctor may be. Hence patients contemplating litigation for drug-induced injury often have to start by considering suing the doctor, the pharmacist *and* the manufacturer, and hope that evidence of who was actually to blame will emerge in the course of the litigation.

Turning now to the liability in negligence of drug companies manufacturing drugs, the manufacturer of any product

> ... which he sells in such a form as to show that he intends them to reach the ultimate consumer in the form in which they left him with no reasonable possibility of intermediate examination, and with the knowledge that the absence of care in the preparation or putting up of the products will result in injury to the consumer's life or property, owes a duty to the consumer to take that reasonable care.[35]

There is no doubt that this duty to take care attaches as much to the manufacturer of drugs as to the manufacturer of ginger beer or any other product. The duty covers the design and formulation of the drug as well as its construction. Nor is the duty limited to the original manufacturer. Thalidomide was initially developed by a West German company and manufactured under licence here by Distillers. Distillers still owed a duty to British patients to take steps to check on the safety of the drug by testing and monitoring the formula before putting the product on the UK market.[36]

Establishing a duty to avoid negligence is not the problem. Determining what amounts to negligence is a formidable task. The potential harm caused by a defective drug is such that a very high standard of care will be imposed on the manufacturer. This is generally acknowledged. However, in England no action for personal injuries against a drug company has yet resulted in an award of

34 *Prendergast v Sam and Dee* [1989] 1 Med LR 36. See also *Dwyer v Roderick* (1988) 127 Solicitors' Journal 805.
35 *Donoghue v Stevenson* [1932] AC 562 at 599.
36 *Watson v Buckley and Osborne, Garrett & Co Ltd* [1940] 1 All ER 174 (duty imposed on distributors of hair dye).

damages by a court (although a claim against the National Blood Authority has, as we shall see, succeeded[37]). What are the obstacles confronting claimants? First, the drug company must be judged by the standards for drug safety pertaining at the date when the drug was put on the market, not at the date proceedings are taken against them. Drug companies, like doctors, must not be judged negligent on hindsight alone. Today the risk to the developing foetus of drugs taken by the mother is well known to all lay women. When thalidomide was first on the market it is far from clear that the dangers of drugs to the foetus were widely appreciated, even by gynaecologists and scientists.

Consideration of the history of the thalidomide claim[38] leads us to the second difficulty for litigants. How does a claimant obtain the evidence he will need to prove the company careless? The thalidomide story is instructive, albeit depressing. The charge against Distillers was that they should have foreseen that the drug might harm the foetus and therefore should have conducted adequate tests before promoting it as safe for use in pregnancy and/or, once adverse reports on the drug reached them, they should have withdrawn it at once. In retrospect, the available evidence that Distillers was negligent falls into three categories. First, there was material available from 1934 onwards to suggest that drugs could pass through the placenta and damage the foetus. Second, in the 1950s a number of drug companies marketing new products had carried out tests to check the effect on the foetus mainly by way of animal experiments. Such evidence would need to have been given by experts and might not have been conclusive. The burden of proof lies on the claimant. The defendant's experts would have argued that when thalidomide was developed it was by no means universally accepted that drugs could damage the foetus, the efficacy of animal tests would have been disputed and it would have been strongly submitted that in any case such tests were not then current general practice.

The third and final category of evidence might have been more damning if the claimants could have got hold of it. Reports of the original testing of thalidomide in West Germany by Chemie Grumenthal suggest that it may have been a pretty hit and miss affair. Fairly early on, adverse reports on the drug and concern over risk to foetuses were in the hands of Chemie Grumenthal. Some considerable time elapsed before they withdrew the drug. Distillers acted faster, taking the drug out of circulation soon after adverse reactions were reported to them. The contents of adverse reports on a drug, the sequence and exact dates on which those reports are received, are of crucial importance to a claimant. No drug company is going to hand the reports over voluntarily. The process of discovery, of compelling a defendant to hand over documents, can be complex enough in a malpractice claim against an individual doctor. In claims against a drug company the process often becomes an insuperable obstacle race.

One general point on the law of negligence as it affects drug claims can be made by way of illustration from the thalidomide case. It may ultimately

[37] See below at 10.6.
[38] Teff and Munro, *Thalidomide: The Legal Aftermath*, Chapters 1 and 2.

prove to be the case that there is insufficient evidence that the company was negligent when it originally marketed the drug. There may be evidence, however hard to come by, that it was negligent in failing to act on adverse reports and recall the drug. Is that a breach of the manufacturer's duty? Two separate situations must be examined. Had it been proved that a child was injured by thalidomide when the drug taken was put on the market by Distillers *after* a date by which they should have known it to be dangerous, there is no problem. The drug that injured that child was negligently put into circulation. Difficulty would arise where the drug taken by the mother had been put into circulation before Distillers should have known it was danger-ous but was actually prescribed to her and taken by her after that date. There is a strong case that a manufacturer owes a further duty to monitor his product and to take reasonable steps to withdraw it if it proves unsafe.[39] Proving breach of the duty could be a nightmare. Stories of doctors continuing to prescribe, and pharmacists retaining stocks of, withdrawn drugs recur. The patient bringing such a claim may falter and sink in a sea of allegation and counter-allegation between drug company, doctor and pharmacist.

The inadequacy of negligence as an effective means of compensating victims of drug-induced injury has been demonstrated time and time again. Successive reviews of negligence as a means of remedying personal injuries resulting from any unsafe product concluded that the reform of product liability laws was essential.[40] What must now be evaluated is how effective reform by way of the Consumer Protection Act 1987 has proved to be.[41]

Strict liability: the Consumer Protection Act 1987[42]

10.5 The concept of strict liability is simple. A claimant seeking compensa-tion from the manufacturer of a product need prove only (1) that the product was defective *and* (2) that the defect in the product caused his injury. Strict liability is fairer to claimants because it establishes that responsibility for an injury caused by a defective product is borne by the person creating the risk and benefiting financially from the product (that is, the manufacturer). The manufacturer is in the best position to exercise control over the safety and quality of the product, and can more conveniently insure against the risk of injury posed by the product. Prolonged, expensive and complex litigation should be less common with a strict liability regime.

---

[39] *Wright v Dunlop Rubber Co Ltd* [1972] 13 KIR 255; *Hollis v Dow Corning Corporation* (1995) 129 DLR (4th) 609 (Canada); and see Forte, 'Medical Products Liability' in SAM McLean (ed), *Legal Issues in Medicine* (1981) Gower, Aldershot, p 67.
[40] Notably the Law Commission in its Report No 82, *Liability for Defective Products* (1977) Cmnd 6831, and the Report of the Royal Commission on Civil Liability and Compensa-tion for Personal Injury (1978) Cmnd 7054 (the Pearson Report).
[41] See C Newdick, 'Strict Liability for Defective Drugs in the Pharmaceutical Industry' (1985) 101 *Law Quarterly Review* 405.
[42] The pharmaceutical industry repeatedly argued that drugs should remain exempt from any regime of strict liability, mainly on the grounds that: (1) scientific research and innovation would be adversely affected; (2) the nature of drug disasters means that strict liability could have catastrophic results for the industry; and (3) it is difficult to define 'defect' in a drug. These arguments have been consistently rejected: see Law Commission Report No 82, pp 19–21 and the Pearson Report, para 1274.

10.5 Medical Products Liability

The 1987 Act imposes liability for personal injury arising from defective products on all *producers* of goods. 'Producers' embraces a wider category of businesses involved in the marketing of drugs than simply the companies manufacturing the finished products.[43] Manufacturers of components are liable for any defect in the components. Companies importing drugs into the European Union are liable under the Act as if they manufactured the drug in England. If the drug in question was manufactured in Japan, the aggrieved patient need not concern himself with the potential difficulties of suing the Japanese company abroad; he can bring his claim in England[44] against the European Union company who brought the drug into the EU. A company that brand-names a drug is a producer within the Act. Companies cannot use their name to claim the credit and the profit for a drug and, when something goes badly wrong, disclaim any responsibility for that drug. Finally, any supplier[45] of a drug will be deemed to be a producer unless he identifies the source of his supply. This provision is crucial for patients. The patient may well receive his prescription or injection in a form such that he cannot possibly identify the original producer of the drug. The community pharmacist or hospital pharmacy supplying the drug must identify the producer or bear liability for the patient's injuries themselves. The intention of the European Directive,[46] on which the Consumer Protection Act 1987 is based, and of the Act itself, is that there should, as far as humanly possible, always be an identifiable producer on whom liability must rest. No company can hide behind a smokescreen.

So far so good, but how do you establish that a drug is defective? Section 3(1) provides that:

... there is a defect in a product ... if the safety of the product is not such as persons generally are entitled to expect;

Section 3(2) goes on to direct the judge to take into account all relevant circumstances pertaining to the safety of a product including:

(a)   the manner in which, and purposes for which, the product has been marketed, its get-up, the use of any mark in relation to the product and any instructions for, or warnings with respect to, the doing of anything with or in relation to the product;

(b)   what might reasonably be expected to be done with or in relation to the product; and

(c)   the time when the product was supplied by its producer to another; and nothing in this section shall require a defect to be inferred from the fact alone that the safety of a product which is supplied after that time is greater than the safety of the product in question.

---

[43]   See sections 1–2 of the Consumer Protection Act 1987.

[44]   Even if the importer is not an English company, but a company based in another EU or EFTA state, the victim will usually be able to sue here in England if he suffered injury here: see the Civil Jurisdiction and Judgments Acts 1982 and 1991 and the Civil Jurisdiction and Judgments Order 2001, SI 2001/3929 (which gave courts jurisdiction under Council Regulation (EC) 44/2001).

[45]   This includes pharmacists dispensing NHS drugs even though they do not sell NHS drugs to patients.

[46]   Council Directive (EEC) 85/374 on Products Liability.

Determining when a drug falls within the definition is far from easy.[47] Drugs are by their nature dangerous. They are designed to do damage to the bacteria or diseased cell or whatever caused the original disease. How much safety are persons generally entitled to expect? Side-effects are often unavoidable. The courts have to try to balance the potential benefit against the risk when deciding if an unwanted side-effect renders a drug defective. Distinctions may be drawn based on the condition that the drug was designed to combat. A minor tranquilliser which carried an unforeseen 5 per cent risk of liver damage could be deemed defective when an anti-cancer drug carrying identical risk would not. Relief of moderate anxiety may be seen as insufficient to warrant the risk, whereas the battle against cancer may justify that degree of inherent danger. Anticipated risks raise different issues. An anticipated risk must be warned against. Will the tranquilliser be deemed not defective if its potential danger is outlined to doctors and patients, leaving the choice to them? Clearly the warning must be taken into account. An antibiotic harmful only to the foetus will almost certainly not be defective if a warning of its risk is clearly given. Less essential drugs may remain defective even if risks are detailed in the literature supplied to doctors. The patient may never have the warning passed on to him. In such a case, though, a heavy share of liability would rest with the doctor prescribing the drug, for contravening or ignoring warnings from the producer.

Other problems in applying the Consumer Protection Act 1987's definition of defective beset the patient. What of the patient who suffers injury because of an allergic reaction to the drug? The drug could be perfectly safe and effective for us, but lethal to him. So, might it be argued that the drug is safe for 'persons generally'? Such an argument will fail. Society, 'persons generally', demands that regard be had to the safety of all where, as in the case of drugs, allergic and idiosyncratic reactions are a well-known risk of the product. If risk to an individual or group is foreseeable and *not* warned of in the presentation of the product, the product is defective. An individual is entitled to expect that the manufacturer will not simply ignore an identified danger to however small a group. When the risk is not foreseeable, the size and predictability of the affected group will be crucial. A sedative which causes damage to the foetus or causes liver damage in 10 per cent of over-70s will be defective. Pregnant women and the elderly are large groups of potential consumers known to be vulnerable to drug-induced injury. But what if the sedative injures only a handful of users out of millions?

Guidance on defining 'defective' is to be found in three relevant judgments. In *Abouzaid v Mothercare Ltd*[48] a twelve-year-old boy was trying to attach a fleece-lined sleeping bag to his baby brother's pushchair. The sleeping bag had to be clipped on to the pushchair by passing elasticated straps round the back of the chair joined by a metal buckle. There were no instructions provided. As the boy struggled to fasten the sleeping bag to the chair, one of the straps slipped from his grasp and the metal buckle flew up and hit him in his left eye. The injury caused him to lose significant vision in that eye. The Court of

---

[47] See the thorough and excellent discussion of this problem in Newdick (1985) 101 *Law Quarterly Review* 405 at 409–420.
[48] (2001) Times, 20 February, CA.

Appeal found that the product was defective. There was a failure to provide instructions and the design of the product was unsafe because it could not be secured without risk. Consumers would properly expect that such a product could be used without that degree of risk. Relatively minor alterations in design would eliminate that risk.

The *Mothercare* judgment can be applied to make two key points about liability for drugs. First, instructions about use and warnings concerning possible adverse effects of drugs are crucial. Failure to warn of a known risk will, as argued earlier, render a drug defective. Second, common sense will play its part in determining what 'people generally' may expect from a product. That latter point is reinforced in *Richardson v LRC Products Ltd.*[49] The plaintiff became pregnant after a condom split. She sued the manufacturers, arguing that the condom failure demonstrated that the product was defective. She was unable to identify any particular construction defect in the condom or point to a risk of damage which the manufacturers should have avoided. The judge found no evidence of unsatisfactory testing of the product. The evidence was simply that, in actual use, an inexplicable number of condoms fail. Dismissing the plaintiff's claim, the judge held that the manufacturers made no claims that their (or any method) of contraception was 100 per cent safe. The fallibility of contraception is well known.

Returning to drug-induced harm, consider the following examples in the light of the above cases. You purchase ibuprofen in a supermarket. The packet clearly warns you *not* to take the medicine if you suffer from asthma. You ignore that warning and despite your asthma, take several tablets. An acute attack of asthma lands you in hospital. Is that pack of ibuprofen defective? You are prescribed a cream to cure acne. No warning accompanies the product. The cream causes the eruption of a rash all over your body. Evidence emerges that that product will produce just such an allergic reaction in about 2 per cent of female users if they use the cream during pregnancy. Neither you nor your GP was aware you were pregnant at the time. Is the product defective?

A v National Blood Authority[50]

10.6 The judgment in *A v National Blood Authority* is by far the most important case yet to interpret the Consumer Protection Act 1987. It breathed new life into strict liability. The case addressed claims by patients infected with hepatitis C from blood and blood products through blood transfusions after March 1 1988. Two important points must be made. First, the defendants (rightly) conceded that blood and body parts fell within the regime of strict liability imposed by the Consumer Protection Act. Second, the judge ruled that the provisions of the British legislation (the 1987 Act) must be interpreted in the light of the European Product Liability Directive. Where there were

---

49   [2000] Lloyd's Rep 280. And see *Worsely v Tambrands* [2000] PIQR P 95; *Foster v Biosil* (2000) 59 BMLR 178.
50   [2001] Lloyd's Rep Med 187. See R Goldberg, 'Paying for Bad Blood: Strict Product Liability after the Hepatitis C Litigation' (2002) 10 *Medical Law Review* 165.

apparent inconsistencies between the two, the Directive should be preferred. The importance of this will be highlighted later.

Moving to the substance of the claims, the judge held that, in determining whether the contaminated blood products were defective, what must be decided is what the *legitimate expectations* of the public were in relation to that product. People expected blood to be 100 per cent clean. Whether the relevant 'defect' in the product was *avoidable* was not the issue. The defendants had tried to argue that the public could only expect they would have done what was possible to screen blood and avoid contamination. In more diplomatic language, the judge effectively declared this to be nonsense. He said

> ... it is as inappropriate to propose that the public should not 'expect the unattainable' – in the sense of tests and precautions which are impossible – at least unless it is informed as to what is unattainable or impossible as it is to reformulate the expectation as one that the producer will not have been negligent or will have taken all reasonable steps.[51]

The judge marked a clear boundary between negligence and strict liability. He went on to say a distinction needs to be made between *standard* and *non-standard* products, a distinction analogous to design and construction defects. Establishing that a standard product was defective would continue to be difficult. The infected batches of blood were non-standard. They could only not be defective if it could be shown the public were made aware of the risks. In this instance, this was not the case. Unlike condoms, which most people know do and can split for no apparent reason, most of us assume that a blood transfusion will not cause us to succumb to serious, even fatal, disease.

Development risks

10.7 In *A v National Blood Authority*,[52] the Blood Authority had another weapon. If the contaminated blood was defective, they argued they were not liable because they could invoke the 'development risks' defence.[53] A development risks defence amounts to this: the manufacturer will not be liable if he can prove that the state of scientific and technical knowledge at the time when he put the product into circulation was not such as to enable the existence of the defect to be discovered.[54]

The scope of the development risks defence in the UK looks broad. The European Directive on Products Liability framed the defence in terms of the scientific and technical knowledge generally available. Section 4(1)(e) of the Consumer Protection Act 1987 provides '... *the state of scientific and technical knowledge was not such that a producer of products of the same*

---

51 [2001] Lloyd's Rep Med 187 at 216.
52 [2001] Lloyd's Rep Med 187.
53 See section 4(1)(e) of the Consumer Protection Act 1987. The remainder of section 4 outlines a number of defences which will only rarely be relevant in claims for drug-related injuries.
54 Article 7(e) of Council Directive (EC) 85/374 on Products Liability permitted states to incorporate a development risks defence.

description as the product in question might be expected to have discovered the defect.' The test in the 1987 Act appears to be what was the knowledge and practice of the pharmaceutical industry at the time. The European Commission challenged the English Act, alleging that the UK had improperly sought to broaden the defence allowed by the Directive. The challenge failed and[55] the European Court of Justice allowed the British interpretation of the Directive. The result might have been depressing.[56] Academic research may reveal significant concerns about the safety of a novel drug. If that research has not permeated industry, the 'development risks' defence could still avail the drug companies creating a test little different from 'old' negligence rules. So, in *A v National Blood Authority* the defendants argued (1) that as at the relevant time there was no effective test to screen blood for hepatitis C the development risks defence applied, and, (2) that the 1987 Act provided that producers of analogous products must at the relevant time have been aware of and able to eliminate the relevant risk. Construing the Act in the light of the Directive, the judge dismissed both arguments. The defence applies only where the very existence of the defect was unknown and undiscoverable.[57] Authorities responsible for blood supplies at the relevant time were aware of the risks of contamination. That no method of screening for hepatitis C had yet been developed was irrelevant. The wording of section 4(1)(e) of the 1987 Act was inappropriate. The Directive made it clear that once knowledge of a risk was accessible to manufacturers, the risk was known. A single article in an obscure Chinese journal ('the Manchurian exception') might not suffice.[58] General knowledge accessible to the academic and commercial communities would.[59]

If *A v National Blood Authority* is followed in the higher courts, the Consumer Protection Act 1987 may make a difference.[60] A producer invoking the development risks defence will have to establish that the defect in the drug, device or bodily product was undiscoverable – and the onus will lie on him to prove this.

vCJD contaminated blood products

10.8 When bovine spongiform encephalopathy (BSE) was linked to new variant Creutzfeldt-Jakob Disease (vCJD), a class action was mounted against the Government.[61] It petered out when a no-fault compensation scheme, run by the national CJD Surveillance Unit, was put in place in 2001 in the wake of

---

[55] Case C-300/95 *Commission v United Kingdom* [1997] All ER (EC) 481.
[56] Discussed in C Hodges, 'Developing Risks: Unanswered Questions' (1998) 61 *Modern Law Review* 560; M Mildred and G Howells, 'Comment on Development Risks: "Unanswered Questions" ' (1998) 61 *Modern Law Review* 570.
[57] See also *Richardson v LRC Products Ltd* [2000] Lloyd's Rep Med 280.
[58] [2001] Lloyd's Rep Med 187 at 220–221.
[59] See G Howells and M Mildred, 'Infected Blood: Defect and Discoverability: A First Exposition of the EC Product Liability Directive' (2002) 65 *Modern Law Review* 95.
[60] For a contrary view, see J Stapleton (1999) 34 *Texas International Law Journal* 45 and J Stapleton, 'Bugs in the Anglo-American Products Liability' (2002) 53 *South Carolina Law Review* 1225.
[61] See, for example, 'Families of CJD Victims Will Sue for Millions' (2001) Telegraph, 19 June.

the BSE Inquiry.[62] In 2004, the Secretary of State announced a similar *ex-gratia* compensation scheme for people infected with hepatitis C from NHS blood or blood products.[63]

More recently, fears have arisen surrounding the contamination of blood products with vCJD. In 2003, it was found that a blood donor may have transmitted vCJD to a patient who underwent a blood transfusion.[64] By 2004, it was estimated that nine donors had developed vCJD after giving blood.[65] What are the implications? If A donates blood and goes on to develop vCJD then those at risk include 'B' (who receives a blood donation from 'A'), 'C' (who donated blood to 'A') and 'D' (who received blood from 'C' who donated blood to 'A'). Blood products include blood components, which are derived from a pool of up to six donations, and plasma products (which until 1999 emanated from plasma pools containing thousands of blood donations). It is theoretically possible, though there has been no proven link to date, that plasma pools were contaminated with vCJD. The potential class of persons 'at risk' in the UK is immense.

The National Blood Service[66] has responded cautiously. It asks anyone who has received blood products since 1980 not to donate blood. A donor history is taken from potential or definite vCJD cases, and their blood products recalled. Plasma is imported from countries with few or no cases of BSE. All children born after 1996 who require plasma are given the imported product. Since 2005, donors and donees who are identified as being 'at risk' for public health purposes are informed of the public health precautions they and their health care staff should take. Around six thousand patients, many of them haemophiliacs, have been told they are 'at risk'. For them the uncertainly has the potential to blight their lives. There is no test and no cure for this fatal disease, although researchers are getting closer to developing a test for vCJD. But if blood is screened should donors be made aware of the results? Will anyone consent to give blood any more?

For those who go on to develop vCJD, the compensation fund will provide for those victims who, on the balance of probabilities:

> ... contracted vCJD as a result of (i) exposure to bovine product(s) purchased in the UK which came from cattle reared and slaughtered in the UK or (ii) otherwise as a result of exposure in the UK to BSE or vCJD ...[67]

---

[62]   See http://www.bseinquiry.gov.uk/.
[63]   Department of Health, 'Details of Hepatitis C Ex-Gratia Payment Scheme Announced' 2004/0025.
[64]   See, for example, CA Llewelyn, PE Hewitt, RS Knight, K Amar, S Cousens, J Mackenzie, RG Will, 'Possible Transmission of Variant Creutzfeldt-Jakob Disease by Blood Transfusion' (2004) 363 Lancet 417.
[65]   'Thousands Warned over CJD Risk' (2004) BBC News, 21 September. Available online at http://news.bbc.co.uk/1/hi/health/3675470.stm.
[66]   Part of the NHS Blood and Transplant Authority, a Special Health Authority established by SI 2005/2529.
[67]   *vCJD Main Trust Deed* (2002), para. 1.12.2. (See http://www.cjdtrust.co.uk/cjdtrustdeeddoc02. pdf.)

Acceptance of compensation does not preclude legal action.[68] For those infected, a possible class action exists if it can be demonstrated that the Government was aware of the potential risk but took no action because of the cost of alternative synthetic products.[69]

The UK also sold blood products abroad.[70] The wording of the Trust Deed clearly encompasses cases where infected meat products are exported, but it seems that transmission of vCJD from blood products contaminated in the UK will not result in *ex-gratia* compensation unless *exposure* occurred 'in the UK'. Whilst the compensation fund may deter UK citizens from pursuing legal action, there is no such luxury for someone infected by exported blood products.

Causation

10.9 The claimants in *A v National Blood Authority*[71] were lucky in one respect. They knew who had supplied the 'defective' blood. Where a claim relates to a drug, a potential claimant may well have taken the drug over several years and not be able to trace which of several drug companies manufactured the drug that caused his injury. An analogous problem arose in *Fairchild v Glenhaven Funeral Services Ltd*,[72] facing workers who contracted the industrial disease mesothelioma. They could show that their illness was caused by exposure to asbestos dust or fibres. They established that their employers were negligent in exposing them to asbestos. However, as they had worked for several companies during their working lives, they could not pinpoint which employer was actually responsible for their disease, which can be caused by a single fibre entering the lung. The Law Lords ruled that as each defendant employer had increased the risk to the affected workers, causation was established against all of them. In the USA, in *Sindell v Abbott Laboratories*,[73] it has been held that where patients are exposed to risk from a defective drug manufactured by several different companies, each company is held liable in proportion to its market share. Lord Hoffmann in *Fairchild* did not consider that the industrial disease claims before the Law Lords and claims against drug companies were the same. He said that the risk from consuming a drug bought in one shop is not increased by the fact that it can be bought in another shop. With respect, he overlooks the possibility of drug-induced injury caused by prolonged or incremental use of a medicine. However, more importantly, he signalled that, even if *Fairchild* does not conclusively determine that the *Sindell* rule prevails in England, he looked at

[68] *vCJD Main Trust Deed* (2002), para B.
[69] For an examination of products liability for pathogenically-infected products, see Stapleton (2002) 53 *South Carolina Law Review* 1225. For tortious liability arising from public health initiatives, see R Martin, 'Public Health and the Scope of Potential Liability in Tort' (2005) 21 *Professional Negligence* 39.
[70] J Meikle, R Evans, 'British Blood Products May Pose vCJD Risk in 14 Countries' (2006) Guardian, 14 May.
[71] [2001] Lloyd's Rep Med 187.
[72] [2002] UKHL 22. See also *Gregg v Scott* [2005] UKHL 2. These cases are discussed in Chapter 7.
[73] (1980) 607 P 2d 924.

256

the possibility with some favour. He described the market share approach against several drug companies as 'imaginative' and suggested that such a possibility would be looked at if a claim came before the House of Lords.'[74]

Lord Hoffmann implemented this approach in *Barker v Corus*,[75] which also involved a mesothelioma victim employed by a number of employers who had breached their duty of care and exposed the employee to asbestos. Lord Hoffmann stated:

> In my opinion, the attribution of liability according to the relative degree of contribution to the chance of the disease being contracted would smooth the roughness of the justice which a rule of joint and several liability creates. The defendant was a wrongdoer, it is true, and should not be allowed to escape liability altogether, but he should not be liable for more than the damage which he caused and, since this is a case in which science can deal only in probabilities, the law should accept that position and attribute liability according to probabilities.[76]

Consequently Corus were liable according to the probability of risk they created. They were not liable for the probability of risk created by the first, insolvent employer. This meant that Mr. Barker went under-compensated. Those employed by a single solvent employer, however, could be assured of 100 per cent compensation. The Government responded with the Compensation Act 2006, section 3 of which reverses the effect of *Barker* for mesothelioma victims and provides that compensation will be joint and several. Victims of mesothelioma can seek full compensation from any solvent negligent employer. The negligent employer will then be able to claim back contributions from other responsible persons under the Civil Liability (Contribution) Act 1978. *Barker* remains an authoritative decision in non-mesothelioma cases, though the ambit of the decision was restricted. In cases where the damage results from a single agent, and multiple factors have increased the damage or the risk of damage, it remains to be seen how widely the decision will be construed.[77] The *Sindell* rule might still find favour in a case involving prolonged or incremental use of a medical product.

In Chapter 5, we examined a case which has potentially wider implications for product liability. In *Chester v Afshar*[78] Miss Chester underwent surgery on the advice of Mr Afshar, her surgeon, during which she suffered nerve damage to her legs. The operation was performed with due care but even so, there was a 1–2 per cent risk of nerve damage. Miss Chester was not warned of the risk. Had she been so warned, she would have deferred the operation but, on the balance of probabilities, it could not be said that she would have withheld consent. Did the lack of causation defeat her claim? The majority held that it did not. Lord Hope stated:

[74] [2002] UKHL 22 at para 74.
[75] [2006] UKHL 20. Examined in Chapter 7.
[76] [2006] UKHL 20 at para 43.
[77] See M Jones, 'Proving Causation – Beyond the "But For" Test' (2006) 22 *Professional Negligence* 251.
[78] [2004] UKHL 41.

To leave the patient who would find the decision difficult without a remedy, as the normal approach to causation would indicate, would render the duty useless in the cases where it may be needed most. This would discriminate against those who cannot honestly say that they would have declined the operation once and for all if they had been warned. I would find that result unacceptable. The function of the law is to enable rights to be vindicated and to provide remedies when duties have been breached.[79]

Once again, it remains to be seen whether this approach will be applied in wider contexts.[80] If the same practical justice is applied to product liability it seems that a failure by a manufacturer or supplier to warn a patient of side-effects or adverse reactions may result in liability, even if the claimant cannot prove that he would not have used the product if he had been properly warned.[81]

Prevention better than cure?[82]

10.10 The thalidomide tragedy prompted new laws to vet drugs before they could be marketed in the UK. The Medicines Act 1968 provided for the licensing and monitoring of drugs. In 1998 a similar system was set up to regulate medical devices. The two systems were amalgamated into one single agency, the Medicines and Healthcare Products Regulatory Agency (MHRA), in 2003. The licensing process (described below) has evolved to take into consideration the increasing relevance of European regulations.

No medicine[83] may be manufactured, imported or marketed without a licence. The Clinical Trials Directive[84] requires three different types of licence in the development of an investigational medicinal product. First, the companies manufacturing and distributing the medicines are required to have 'manufacturer's and wholesale dealer's licences'; second, 'clinical trial authorisations' are required in order to develop new products; and third, a 'marketing authorisation' is required before the product can be marketed. Marketing authorisations are granted for periods of up to five years (after which they must be renewed).

The pharmaceutical industry is the UK's third most profitable market after tourism and finance. It is an international business. Since 1998 all medical devices (for example diagnostic tests or intra-uterine devices) have been

---

79   [2004] UKHL 41 at para 87.
80   *Chester* was distinguished in a claim for negligent financial advice: *Beary v Pall Mall Investments* [2005] EWCA Civ 415. See J Stapleton, 'Occam's Razor Reveals an Orthodox Basis for *Chester v Afshar*' (2006) 122 *Law Quarterly Review* 426.
81   See L Jones, '*Chester v Afshar*: Effect of Product Liability' (2005) 5(1) *Health and Safety Law* 12 at 12–14.
82   For a fuller account, see G Appelbe and J Wingfield, *Dale and Appelbe's Pharmacy, Law and Ethics* (8th edn, 2005) Pharmaceutical Press; J Merrills and J Fisher, *Pharmacy Law and Practice* (4th edn, 2006) Elsevier; JL Valverde and P Weissenberg, *The Challenges of the New EU Pharmaceutical Legislation* (2005) IOS Press.
83   As to what constitutes a medicine, see MHRA Guidance Note 8, *A Guide to What is a Medicinal Product* (2003).
84   Directive (EC) 2001/20, implemented in the UK by the Medicines for Human Use (Clinical Trials) Regulations 2004.

regulated in a manner broadly similar to medicines.[85] And an increasing range of medicines have been deregulated to be available in pharmacies or ordinary shops. There are two licensing routes in the UK – via the European Medicines Agency and via the Medicines and Healthcare Products Regulatory Agency.

The European Medicines Evaluation Agency (EMEA) was established in 1995 to harmonise and streamline licensing across Europe. It was renamed the European Medicines Agency (EMA) in 2004. One of its committees is called the Committee for Proprietary Medicinal Products (CPMP), which licenses human medicinal products for distribution across the EU. Two delegates from each Member State sit on the Committee. There are two systems by which an EU-licence might be granted:

(1)   Under the EU *centralised* system, the pharmaceutical company nominates the representatives of one Member State and another is chosen by the CPMP. The CPMP gives an opinion within 210 days of receipt of the application. If negative, the company must respond, and, if satisfactory, the application can then proceed. If positive, the Member States have 28 days to give comments before a final decision is made by the CPMP. Under the EU centralised system, drugs will have a ten-year period of exclusivity.

(2)   Alternatively, the *decentralised* system provides an eight-year period of exclusivity. The CPMP passes the application to a Member State chosen by the company. In the UK, this forms a large part of the MHRA's role. It has 210 days to consider the application, after which the other Member States have 90 days to express their mutual recognition. Where objections are raised, the CPMP has a further 30 days to make a decision.

The second route, by which the product is licensed in the UK only, is via the UK's Medicines and Healthcare Products Regulatory Agency, an Executive Agency of the Department of Health which was created from a merger of the Medicines Control Agency and the Medical Devices Agency in 2003. The MHRA has a staff of around 700. In addition to licensing health care products, the MHRA regulates clinical trials, operates post-marketing surveillance, monitors compliance with legal obligations and promotes good practice in the safe use of medicines and devices. It also supports expert advisory bodies, such as the Committee on the Safety of Devices and the Commission on Human Medicines (CHM), which replaced the Committee on the Safety of Medicines in 2005. The CHM reviews licensing applications and produces an independent assessment. It will review the safety, quality and efficacy of the health care product but will not consider its efficacy in comparison with any existing product. The CHM does not exist to prevent expensive copies, sometimes referred to as 'me-too' drugs.

The CHM must also 'promote the collection and investigation of information relating to adverse reactions for human medicines'.[86] Post-marketing surveillance systems include the 'yellow card scheme' which concerns adverse

---

[85]   See D Longley, 'Who is Calling the Piper? Is there a Tune? The New Regulatory Systems for Medical Devices in the United Kingdom and Canada' (1998) 3 *Medical Law International* 319.

[86]   See http://www.mhra.gov.uk.

reactions to medicines and Adverse Incidence Reports regarding devices. On the basis of these systems the CHM makes recommendations regarding safety issues and the minimisation of risk and less urgent issues are communicated via a regular bulletin.

Section 28 of the Medicines Act 1968 empowers the Secretary of State for Health to revoke an existing licence. Several grounds for revocation are established, of which the most important is where:

> ... medicinal products of any description to which the licence relates can no longer be regarded as products which can safely be administered for the purposes indicated in the licence, or can no longer be regarded as efficacious for those purposes ...

The decision to withdraw a drug from the market is no longer solely a matter for the manufacturer. A manufacturer aggrieved by the refusal or revocation of a product licence may seek a review by the CHM.[87] No product licence can be refused or revoked without consultation with the Commission. A manufacturer whose product has been approved by the CHM, but who is refused a licence by the Secretary of State has a right to a further hearing. If he chooses, as he may, to reject their advice, he must set up an independent inquiry before which the manufacturer may state his case.[88]

The MHRA authorises, inspects, surveys and enforces the use of medicines and devices, aiming to protect, promote and improve public health. But does the reformed system adequately represent patient's interests? Critics fear that drug regulators lack transparency and favour efficacy over patient safety. As long as drug companies evaluate their own products the public interest will not be served. The MHRA, they complain, is 'unaccountable, slow, and lacking the necessary expertise'.[89] The House of Commons Select Report on the Pharmaceutical Industry[90] is critical of the MHRA's close proximity to industry, its over-reliance on trust and its failure to properly scrutinise licensing data,[91] concluding:

> In view of the failings of the MHRA, we recommend a fundamental review of the organisation in order to ensure that safe and effective medicines, with necessary prescribing constraints, are licensed.[92]

Further criticism resulted from the MHRA's handling of the drug trial debacle at Northwick Park hospital in 2006 when six volunteers suffered multiple organ failure after an adverse drug reaction to TG1412.[93] The injured participants sought compensation, from both TeGenero, the German manufacturer (who went insolvent shortly after the incident with liability insurance of only £2m) and Parexel, USA who managed the trial. The MHRA's report

---

87   Established under section 2 of the Medicines Act 1968. The terms of reference are set out in section 3 of the 1968 Act as amended by the Medicines (Advisory Bodies) Regulations 2005.
88   Medicines Act 1968, s 21(5).
89   F Godlee, 'Can we Tame the Monster?' (2006) 333 *British Medical Journal* 0.
90   HC 42-I (2005).
91   HC 42-I (2005), p 4.
92   HC 42-I (2005), p 5.
93   See further, Chapter 16 at 16.1.

concluded that the reaction was an 'unprecedented biological reaction'; they found a number of departures from protocol, but no errors in the formulation or administration of the drug. Never the less, it recommended a 'precautionary approach' in future drug trials where the risk to participants is as high as it was in the TG1412 trial. Claims of 'whitewash'[94] were followed by an independent review by an expert scientific group under Professor Duff.[95] One recommendation, which relates to high-risk drugs involving monoclonal antibodies, proposes a tightening of the regulatory rules and better dialogue between the developer and regulator.

Claims against the regulators

10.11 The possibility of governmental liability for drug-induced injury was aired even in the thalidomide days. The Health Minister of the day, Sir Keith Joseph, dismissed suggestions that the Government could be liable. He argued further that, even when the elaborate licensing provisions of the 1968 Act were in force, the legal liability for any defect in the drug rested on the manufacturers alone.[96] The patients injured by the anti-arthritic drug Opren sought compensation from the Health Minister and the erstwhile Committee on Safety in Medicines as well as from the drug company.[97] They contended that the Government and the CSM had been negligent both in originally licensing the drug and for continuing to allow it to be marketed after its dangers should have become apparent to the Ministry and the CSM. The Opren case against the Government was ultimately abandoned.

Another claim against the CSM was mounted in *Smith v Secretary of State for Health (on behalf of the Committee for Safety of Medicines).*[98] In May 1986, seven-year-old Amanda Smith caught chickenpox and was given one aspirin tablet on two consecutive days by her mother, who followed the advice on the label. Amanda's condition worsened. She developed spastic tetraplegia and was eventually diagnosed with Reye's syndrome. In June 1986, the CSM issued a warning that aspirin should not be given to children under the age of twelve except on medical advice because it could trigger Reye's syndrome. They had met in March 1986, but delayed the warning so as to co-operate with the drug companies. No interim warning was made. Was the CSM negligent? Morland J held that it was not. There was no breach of statutory duty or common law duty of care. The decision by the CSM was a discretionary policy decision which is not, Morland J held, justiciable in private law, even if there was fault in the timetabling of the warning.[99]

In *XYZ and others v Schering Health Care Ltd,*[100] the CSM was once again under fire, but this time from the drug companies. The case involved a group

---

94 See, for example, 'Lessons from TG1412' *Science in Society*, Autumn 2006 (http://www.i-sis.org.uk/isisnews/sis31.php).

95 See Department of Health, *Expert Scientific Group on Phase One Clinical Trials: Final Report* (2006) HMSO.

96 HC Deb Vol 847 Col 440–441, 29 November 1972.

97 The claim against the CSM was dropped.

98 [2002] EWHC 200 (QB).

99 [2002] EWHC 200 (QB) at para 93, per Morland J.

100 [2002] EWHC 1420 (QB).

action by claimants alleged to have suffered cardio-vascular injuries as a result of taking the certain brands of the combined oral contraceptive (the Pill). In 1995, the CSM circulated a warning to prescribers of the Pill that three as yet unpublished articles indicated a two-fold increase in risk of venous-thromboembolism. The defendants argued that the letter was ill-considered and that the ensuing 'Pill scare' was a public health disaster. Mackay J held that there was not in fact a two-fold increase in risk and on that basis the claimants lost their case. Nor was the advisability of the CSM's letter under review in this case. Regulators have the unenviable task of deciding when it is appropriate to 'act as though a given association were causal rather than to continue to assume that it is not.'[101]

Could a claim against the new Commission on Human Medicines, in effect for negligently monitoring drugs and/or blood products, succeed? In *Smith*, Morland J did not rule out the possibility. Neither the Secretary of State nor the CHM enjoys blanket immunity from a common law suit.[102] Improper exercise of duty, such as the postponing of a meeting 'because it clashed with the Epsom Derby meeting'[103] would clearly be considered negligent. Beyond that, claimants would have to persuade the court that it was 'just, fair and reasonable' for the CHM to be subjected to a duty of care to individual patients and that the decision was not discretionary or policy-based. Two particular questions will pose problems for claimants. The court will seek to ask whether the scheme of regulation established by the Medicines Act 1968, and now heavily influenced by European legislation, was designed to provide a right to compensation to those injured by unsafe drugs. And given that the primary responsibility for the medicine still rests with the drug company, should the Government be liable for the company's wrongdoing?

Claims brought abroad

10.12 The majority of drug companies are multinationals. Drugs are not confined within national borders. British women who suffered injury as a result of using the Dalkon Shield IUD sued the manufacturers in the USA and recovered compensation from a settlement fund set up when the company went bankrupt.[104] When can an injured patient resort to a foreign court and why should he want to?

When a claim has a foreign element a set of rules known as private international law, or conflict of laws, comes into play. These are excessively complex and we give only the barest outline of the relevant law. Essentially, when a claim for negligence is brought the claimant can sue in any country where a relevant act of negligence occurred, or in the country where the drug company is based.[105] There may be more than one such country. So in the case

---

[101] [2002] EWHC 1420 (QB) at para 19, per Mackay J.
[102] *Stovin v Wise* [1996] AC 923 at 937–941, per Lord Nicholls.
[103] *Smith v Secretary of State for Health* [2002] EWHC 200 (QB) at para 95.
[104] See Ferguson, *Drug Injuries and the Pursuit of Compensation*, pp 6–8.
[105] See Article 5(3) of the Brussels I Regulation 44/2001; the Civil Jurisdiction and Judgments Act 1982; the Civil Jurisdiction and Judgments Act 1991; the Civil Jurisdiction and Judgments Order 2001, SI 2001/3929; the Civil Procedure Rules (CPR 6.20). These

of a defective drug, negligence may have occurred both in the country where it was carelessly manufactured and in the country where it was carelessly marketed as safe[106] and injured the claimant. It is on the basis of the careless manufacture of the device in the USA that the women suing over the Dalkon Shield were able to go to court in the USA. Where there is a dispute over whether an action should be allowed to go ahead, the law of the country where the claimant is trying to sue determines whether it should do so.

Why should anyone want to sue abroad? After all, if they took the drug here and were injured here they can bring their claim in their homeland on the basis of that it was here that the drug caused them harm. There are two reasons why claimants may opt for a foreign lawsuit. First, the procedural rules in the foreign courts may be more favourable to claimants. They may be able to conduct a 'class action' more effectively than in England. That is to say, the group of claimants will be able to bring their action co-operatively, sharing expenses and expertise. Second, there remain financial incentives to sue in the USA. Not only is liability for drugs strict, but awards of damages are made by juries and are generally much higher than English judge-made awards. The contingency fee system may offer more favourable access to the courts than conditional fees do here. And, finally, a threat to sue in the USA may prompt the defendants into offering a more generous settlement than would otherwise have been the case.

Vaccine damage: a special case?

10.13 Vaccine damage has received special treatment because of the distinction in social effect between vaccines and other drugs.[107] Generally the benefit and risk of taking a drug rests with the individual patient alone. No one else suffers directly if he does not take the drug. No one else benefits directly if he does. With a vaccine the position is different. If a child is immunised, the child himself benefits from the immunity conferred and his friends and schoolfellows benefit from the elimination of the risk that he will pass that disease on to them. Consequently, vaccination of young children against diseases such as tetanus, diphtheria, polio, measles, meningitis C and whooping cough is actively promoted by the Department of Health. The whooping cough vaccine caused outcry and distress, and concerns about the MMR vaccine generated similar controversy. A number of children healthy before vaccination have, their parents claim, suffered severe and lasting brain damage as a consequence of receiving the vaccine. More recently, however, the scientific claims that MMR vaccine had such an effect have been largely discredited and the doctor who led the case for such a link faces disciplinary proceedings before the GMC.[108]

complex rules are neatly summarised in A Saggerson, 'PI Litigation Across Jurisdictions: Summary of Service Regimes' (2002) 6 *Personal Injury* 3.

[106] *Distillers Co (Biochemicals) Ltd v Thompson* [1971] AC 458 (New Zealand mother allowed to sue the British company Distillers in New Zealand over thalidomide manufactured in the UK; the essence of the negligence alleged was failure to warn her, in New Zealand, of the danger to her baby).

[107] See, in particular, the Pearson Report, Chapter 25.

[108] B Deer, 'MMR Doctor Given Legal Aid Thousands' (2006) Sunday Times, 31 December.

What remedies have the parents of a vaccine-damaged child? First, they may, as a number of parents of children allegedly damaged by whooping cough vaccine have done, seek to use the tort of negligence to obtain compensation. The advantage of this course is that, if the claim was successful, their children would receive full compensation for any disability caused by the vaccine. One problem is whom to sue. The crux of the question is often whether the risk of the vaccine to a child is greater than the risks posed by contracting the disease itself. An action against a doctor for negligently using a reputable vaccine is likely to fail because, even if some doctors and experts condemn its use, a substantial body of informed opinion still backs the vaccine. A negligence action is usually only viable if some special feature of the child's history should have ruled out routine vaccination or if symptoms at a first vaccination, indicating that further vaccination was unwise, were missed. Suing the manufacturers will run into the problem of the risk/benefit ratio of the product. The manufacturers dispute the level of risk from the vaccine and will argue that the overwhelming benefit to the community of vaccination outweighs any risk to a very few. They will contend that, properly used, the vaccine is not defective. In relation to the whooping cough vaccine the companies deny that the vaccine does indeed cause brain damage. In *Loveday v Renton*[109] a judge held that the claimants failed to prove that the pertussis (whooping cough) vaccine caused the child's brain damage. Attempts to recover compensation for vaccine injuries through claims in negligence have generally proved unsuccessful in England.[110] The MMR litigation has cost in the region of £15m. In 2004, the High Court rejected an application for a judicial review of an earlier decision to withdraw legal aid on the basis that the claims were unlikely to succeed and would cost the public a further £10m. The Legal Services Commission is clamping down on funding. Unless there is a good chance that the case will succeed – unless the claim is based on solid research – group actions such as the MMR Vaccine Group Litigation and for Gulf War syndrome are less likely to receive funding in the future.[111]

The problems of litigation deter many parents from going to court. Successive reviews of the issue of compensation for vaccine damage recognise that it is an example of injury where compensation via the tort of negligence, or the Consumer Protection Act 1987, may be inappropriate. There may prove to be no negligence on anyone's part because the benefit to the majority is held to justify the risk to a small minority. Yet it is scarcely fair that those who suffer damage should bear the whole burden of disability alone. On the recommendation of the Pearson Commission, Parliament enacted the Vaccine Damage Payments Act 1979 to provide for a no-fault compensation scheme for vaccine-damaged individuals. In June 2000, the amount payable was raised to £100,000 and the former requirement of 80 per cent disability was reduced to 60 per cent.[112] Claims for payments under the 1979 Act are made initially to the Department of Health. If the Department official responsible is not

---

[109] [1990] 1 Med LR 117.

[110] Though parents in Ireland succeeded: see *Best v Wellcome Foundation* [1993] 2 IR 421.

[111] See G Langdon Down, 'Practice Area: Product Liability: Productive Work' (2004) April *Law Society Gazette* 22.

[112] The Vaccine Damage Payments Act 1979 Statutory Sum Order 2000, SI 2000/1983. See also the Regulatory Reform (Vaccine Damage Payments Act 1979) Order 2002, SI 2002/1592.

satisfied that the claim is made out, the claimant may ask for the decision to be reviewed by an independent medical tribunal. The decision of the tribunal is final. The making of a payment under the 1979 Act does not debar a claimant from also suing for negligence in respect of the vaccination.

The Vaccine Damage Payments Act 1979 Act remains a target of criticism.[113] Successful cases are rare.[114] £100,000 may sound a substantial amount, but if a child is so damaged that he will never be able to care for himself and earn his own living, it falls far short of his needs. A successful tort claim would result in a multi-million pound award. The Act remains a compromise. It has not replaced tort with an adequate compensation mechanism. Critics complain that the ever-present problem of causation of drug-induced injury is simply ignored in the Act. The claimant must establish on the balance of probability that his disablement resulted from the vaccine.

---

[113] See S Pywell, 'The Vaccine Damage Payment Scheme – A Proposal for Radical Reform' (2002) 9 *Journal of Social Security Law* 73.

[114] See 'Vaccine Damage Payments' (2004) 27 *Consumer Law Today* 4(5)(1): in 2000, of 171 claims, one was successful; in 2001, of 176 claims, two were successful; in 2002, of 4,061 claims, eight were successful.

Part III

MATTERS OF LIFE AND DEATH

Chapter 11

FAMILY PLANNING

11.1 In 1924, Marie Stopes sued for libel after her work had been described as a 'monstrous campaign of birth control', with the rider that 'Bradlaugh was condemned to jail for a less serious crime'. Viscount Finlay said of the practice of birth control:

> ... it is impossible to hold that the bounds of fair comment are exceeded by the expression of an opinion that such practices are revolting to the healthy instincts of human nature. There is an old and widespread aversion to such methods on this ground.[1]

In 1954, Lord Denning MR said of vasectomy:

> Take a case where a sterilisation operation is done so as to enable a man to have the pleasure of sexual intercourse without shouldering the responsibilities attached to it. The operation is plainly injurious to the public interest. It is degrading to the man himself. It is injurious to his wife and any woman who he may marry, to say nothing of the way it opens to licentiousness, and unlike other contraceptives, it allows no room for a change of mind on either side. It is illegal, even though the man consents to it ...[2]

Attitudes have changed radically. In 2002, Munby J[3] resoundingly declared that contraception was a matter for personal choice and conscience, and no business of the law. The judge declared that it was:

> ... not any part of the responsibilities of public authorities – let alone of the criminal law – to be telling adult people whether they can or cannot use contraceptive devices of the kind which I have been considering.

Can contraception be criminal?

11.2 Contraceptives were never banned in England, as they were in Ireland and France. Not until 1967 was formal provision made for contraceptive

---

[1] *Sutherland v Stopes* [1925] AC 47 at 68.
[2] *Bravery v Bravery* [1954] 3 All ER 59 at 67–68.
[3] *R (on the application of Smeaton) v Secretary of State for Health* [2002] 2 FLR 146.

advice and treatment to be offered within the NHS.[4] The boundary between prevention of pregnancy and early abortion will be examined in Chapter 14. In *Gillick*,[5] prescribing contraceptives to girls under 16 was unsuccessfully argued to be aiding and abetting unlawful sexual intercourse (see Chapter 15). After post-coital contraception was made available over the counter in pharmacies, pro-life groups unsuccessfully went to court to overturn the relevant regulations allowing such sales, expressing outrage that young girls might be able to gain easy access to a controversial form of contraception.[6]

What of sterilisation? Is there any substance in Lord Denning MR's argument in *Bravery* that performing a sterilisation could entail criminal liability for the surgeon? That cannot now be the law. His argument was based on the principle that a victim's agreement cannot make lawful an inherently criminal act. A man who sadistically beat a 17-year-old girl was convicted of a criminal assault upon her despite her consent to be beaten. Inflicting violence on another person for sexual gratification is unacceptable to society.[7] Lord Denning MR argued that sterilisation without medical cause was mutilation of the patient, and unacceptable because of its potential for risk-free immorality. Several thousands Britons undergo sterilisation every year. It is an acceptable option for birth control.[8] No judge would categorise sterilisation as inherently unlawful and put the surgeon on a par with the sadist. Today, the principal controversy surrounding sterilisation is how readily the courts will impose sterilisation on young women with learning disabilities.

Contraception, sterilisation and marriage

11.3 Two questions arise. Can the use of contraception by, or the prior sterilisation of, one of the spouses affect the validity of a marriage? Does a refusal to have children give rise to grounds for divorce?

English law provides that a marriage which remains unconsummated because of the lack of capacity or wilful refusal of one party to consummate the marriage is voidable and may be annulled.[9] The earlier sterilisation of one of the spouses, or the use of mechanical or chemical contraception, does not prevent consummation taking place.[10] Consummation means full sexual intercourse regardless of whether or not the act is open to the procreation of children. Refusal by one spouse to have intercourse unless contraceptives are used will not amount to wilful refusal to consummate. This can create a knotty problem. If one party is entirely prepared to engage in normal sexual intercourse only if contraceptives are used and the other, for religious reasons perhaps, only if they are not, the marriage remains unconsummated but

---

4 See the National Health Service (Family Planning) Act 1967 as amended by the National Health Service (Family Planning) Amendment Act 1972.
5 *Gillick v West Norfolk and Wisbeck Area Health Authority* [1985] 3 All ER 402, HL.
6 See *R (on the application of Smeaton) v Secretary of State for Health* [2002] 2 FLR 146.
7 *R v Donovan* [1934] 2 KB 498; and see *R v Brown* [1993] 2 All ER 75, HL.
8 See the discussion on this matter in SAM McLean and TD Campbell, 'Sterilisation' in SAM McLean (ed), *Legal Issues in Medicine* (1981) Gower.
9 Matrimonial Causes Act 1973, s 12(b).
10 *Baxter v Baxter* [1948] AC 274.

neither spouse is guilty of wilful refusal to consummate and the marriage cannot be annulled.[11] Their remedy lies in divorce. Any hardship in having to await a divorce is alleviated by the Matrimonial and Family Proceedings Act 1984, which permits divorce in normal circumstances after one year of marriage only.

A divorce will be granted if the petitioner can establish that the marriage has irretrievably broken down. One means of establishing the breakdown is to show that the respondent has behaved in such a way that the petitioner cannot reasonably be expected to live with him or her. This test of 'unreasonable behaviour' is liberally interpreted by the courts. Undergoing a vasectomy after the marriage[12] or insisting on using contraceptives[13] was held in the past to be cruelty on the part of the husband if the effect was damaging to the wife's health. Today a wife would probably succeed in establishing unreasonable behaviour without having to show evidence of damage to her health. Equally, a husband could *prima facie* show it to be unreasonable for his wife to refuse, without good reason, to have children. One difficulty can be outlined. In *Archard v Archard*[14] the parties were both Roman Catholics. The wife was advised on medical grounds not to conceive, and refused to have intercourse without the use of contraceptives. Her devout husband refused to have intercourse if contraceptives were used. She failed to establish that his behaviour was unreasonable, as she was aware of his faith and his views. Equally, he would have failed to establish her behaviour to be unreasonable on the grounds of her medical condition. The reasons for one party's refusal to have children must be examined in determining whether this conduct is such that the petitioner can no longer be expected to go on with the marriage, and today may well not be limited to cases where the wife (or the husband) is medically advised against contraception, but embrace the whole of the parties' lifestyle and aspirations.

Finally, there is one anomaly in the law. What if one spouse has been sterilised before the marriage and never tells the other? We have seen that that is no ground for nullity. Nor is it evidence of unreasonable behaviour so as to support a petition for divorce. The relevant conduct, undergoing sterilisation, takes place before the marriage. A divorce can be granted only on the basis of conduct after the marriage.[15] The unhappy spouse will have to establish the breakdown of the marriage on other grounds. A divorce may be granted after two years' separation where the other party consents. Should the contesting party be obdurate, a divorce can be granted without consent after five years' separation. Five years may be enough to end an older woman's hope of children within a future marriage. Had the Family Law Act 1996 been fully implemented allowing 'no-fault' divorce after a waiting period of one year, the law's role in disputes over a spouse's 'right' to a child would be ended. If the other party's refusal to have children in effect destroys a marriage, no longer

---

[11] See N Lowe and G Douglas, *Bromley's Family Law* (10th edn, 2006) LexisNexis Butterworths, p 91.
[12] *Bravery v Bravery* [1954] 3 All ER 59 at 62.
[13] *Baxter v Baxter* [1948] AC 274.
[14] (1972) Times, 19 April.
[15] *Sullivan v Sullivan* [1970] 2 All ER 168, CA.

would that refusal have to be fitted uncomfortably into the strait-jacket of unreasonable behaviour? We are still bedevilled by outdated concepts of marital 'behaviour'.

Contraceptives: patients' rights

11.4 An infallible contraceptive has yet to be invented. The more sophisticated and convenient contraceptives, such as the Pill and the IUD, carry a price tag in that they pose some risk to women's health. Contraception is very much a medical as well as a social issue. And it largely concerns women for, except for the experimental 'male Pill', the more sophisticated contraceptives which pose medical risk are used by women. Women seek two sorts of protection from the law. First, they require definition of the doctor's obligation to assist them to avoid pregnancy at the least possible risk to health. Second, they demand information, and greater control of their reproductive and sexual lives. The law is fairly well equipped for the first task, and almost entirely a futile weapon in the second.

A doctor advising a woman on contraception owes her the same duties as in any other area of medicine. He must offer her competent and careful advice. He must perform any technical procedure, for example inserting an IUD, skilfully. He must obtain her consent to any invasive procedure. When a woman consults her GP his obligation to her is part and parcel of his ordinary care of her. He will be aware of her medical history, prescribe in the light of that history, and take note of any symptoms of general ill health that are revealed by any examination he undertakes. Many women prefer to consult specialist family planning clinics. They feel that clinics have greater experience. Some prefer not to discuss their sexual lives with the family doctor. Clinics must beware. Their obligation is not limited to providing competent advice on how to avoid conception. Contraception cannot be divorced from general health care. The clinic must act on any indication that the woman's general health is at risk, whether from the prescription of a particular contraceptive, or otherwise. In *Sutton v Population Services Family Planning Ltd*,[16] Mrs Sutton visited the defendant's clinic and was examined by a nurse preparatory to being given contraceptive advice. The nurse either failed to note, or failed to act on, evidence of early signs of cancer. The cancer was diagnosed much later, with the result that far more drastic treatment was called for and the disease was likely to recur at least four years earlier than would have been the case had it been promptly treated. Mrs Sutton was awarded damages for her additional suffering. Clinics must ensure that women receive treatment when signs of disease are present. This will usually be done by advising the patient to contact her GP. While the clinic staff may not wish to alarm a patient with what may be a tentative diagnosis, she must be given sufficient information on which to act and, if she agrees, her GP be directly notified. The clinic must respect her confidence and should a woman refuse permission to contact her GP, say where a sexually transmitted disease

---

[16]   (1981) Times, 7 November. See M Latham, 'Emergency Contraception' (1999) 149 *New Law Journal* 366.

is suspected, they must not breach her confidence. In such a case a clinic must take steps to advise the woman on alternative sources of treatment.

Litigation and contraception

11.5 Modern contraceptive treatments have not just generated moral controversy. They have resulted in litigation where use of contraceptive methods has resulted in adverse effects for women. Several million dollars in compensation were paid out to women who suffered injury through use of the Dalkon Shield, an IUD which caused substantial pelvic injuries to patients.[17] The injectable contraceptive Depo-Provera led to a number of lawsuits in the UK. The use of Depo-Provera in its early years offers a classic example of how not to approach contraceptive advice and treatment.

Depo-Provera is a synthetic form of a natural hormone, which acts like most brands of the Pill to prevent eggs developing and makes the womb hostile to any fertilised embryo. One injection is effective for at least three months. Doctors may advise the use of the drug for women for whom the Pill is a health risk, women who are considered too unreliable to be trusted to use other means of contraception and where pregnancy should be completely ruled out, for example when a woman has just been vaccinated against rubella. Increasingly women choose Depo-Provera for its convenience. Depo-Provera can produce unpredictable and unpleasant side-effects, including severe and irregular bleeding. Complaints were made that (1) some women were injected with the drug without ever being told of its nature, and (2) even where Depo-Provera was expressly prescribed and described as a contraceptive, inadequate explanation of its potential side-effects was given. Fears were voiced that Depo-Provera might be 'forced' on inarticulate, or not particularly intelligent, women.[18]

A Salford woman, Mrs Potts, won £3,000 damages[19] after she was injected with Depo-Provera concurrently with a vaccination against rubella. She suffered severe bleeding. The injection was given days after the delivery of her third child, and she thought that it was a routine post-natal 'jab'. The aim of her doctor was laudable, to protect her from pregnancy while the vaccine might harm any unborn child. He had no right to deprive her of her choice of whether or not to accept or decline a controversial drug. Women must be told the nature of the drug offered to them, and if their right to choose is to be effective they must have its advantages and disadvantages explained to them. The judge awarding Mrs Potts's compensation said: 'She should have been given the choice, and she was entitled to know beforehand what the decision entailed'. The same holds true of any contraceptive treatment.

---

[17] See above at 10.12.
[18] When Depo-Provera and Norplant (a slow release capsule injected into the arm) were first licensed in the USA, they were used as sentencing alternatives as a pregnancy restriction for drug and alcohol addicts and child abusers, though most cases were overturned on appeal: see J Mertus, S Heller, 'Norplant Meets the New Eugenicists: The Impermissibility of Coerced Contraception' (1992) 11 *St Louis University Public Law Review* 359.
[19] See (1983) *Guardian*, 27 July, p 4.

Scare stories about the Pill and risks of cancer, heart disease or thrombosis hit the headlines with monotonous regularity. Growing awareness of the potential risks has led women to demand more information about a substance that so many of us swallow every day. What can the law do for them? A doctor prescribing the Pill must be properly informed about the current stage of research and knowledge about brands of Pill and their risks to particular patients. A GP is not required to have the experience of a consultant gynaecologist specialising and researching into the control of fertility, but he must be adequately informed if he elects to offer advice personally rather than referring women to a specialist clinic. His terms of service do not oblige him to offer contraceptive services. He must take care to ensure that the Pill is 'safe' for the patient consulting him. If there are special risk factors relating to the woman's medical history, or weight, or smoking habit, he must seek to ensure that she is protected as far as is possible from those risks. The most crucial question is what information is the woman entitled to? Information leaflets accompanying prescriptions of the Pill have lengthened considerably in recent years in their description of side-effects and contra-indications to taking that brand. Clearly both her doctor and the drug company manufacturing the Pill are required to give the woman sufficient information to enable her to make an informed choice about whether to use, or continue to use, that method of contraception. We would argue that in the light of *Bolitho v City & Hackney Health Authority*[20] and *Pearce v United Bristol Healthcare NHS Trust*,[21] women must be advised of any risk that the Pill poses to them which a sensible woman would consider material to a reasonable decision about what sort of contraception to use.[22]

The doctor's duty to warn his patient about the risks of the Pill does not relieve the drug company of its responsibility to provide adequate information and warning about its product to both the prescribing doctor and the patient. A Canadian court expressed the manufacturer's duty in this way:

> ... the manufacturer's duty is to provide to the consumer written warnings conveying reasonable notice of the nature, gravity and likelihood of known or knowable side-effects and advising the consumer to seek fuller explanation from the prescribing physician or other doctor of any such information of concern to the consumer.[23]

In respect of any product put on the market in the UK after 1 March 1988, the drug company will be subject to strict liability under the Consumer Protection Act 1987 for injury arising from a defect in that product. Unfortunately strict liability does not make the task of suing in respect of drug-induced injury much easier. This is especially the case with the Pill – and what is said about the Pill applies too to certain mechanical methods of contraception such as the IUD. Risks associated with the Pill are well known, particularly the risk of succumbing to a stroke. Hence all manufacturers expressly warn patients of those risks and seek to ensure that women especially vulnerable to that risk,

20 [1997] 4 All ER 771.
21 [1999] PIQR P 53; see above at 5.7.
22 But see *Vadera v Shaw* (1998) 45 BMLR 162.
23 *Buchan v Ortho-Pharmaceuticals (Canada) Ltd* (1986) 54 OR (2d) 92, 100.

for example older women or women who smoke, avoid the Pill. None the less 'at-risk' women continue to take the Pill. The Pill is a lesser evil than unwanted pregnancy.

Occasionally a woman with no identifiable risk factor falls seriously ill. The legal questions become:

(1)   Were the manufacturers' warnings adequate?
(2)   Bearing in mind the innate risk posed by the Pill balanced against its benefit as an effective contraceptive, is the Pill defective?
(3)   Can the woman prove that her injury was caused by taking the Pill?[24]

The analysis of these questions is unlikely to be different whether the woman's claim is framed in negligence or under the Consumer Protection Act 1987. Strict liability under the 1987 Act may help a patient injured by some construction defect in a contraceptive, such as a negligently constructed IUD which damages the cervix. It will do little for the patient claiming that the inherent design of a contraceptive drug or device is defective. For such an action to succeed, there will need to be overwhelming evidence that the manufacturer failed to note, and act on, evidence of clear risk to women's health, a risk not justified by the contraceptive benefit of the product. It should be stressed that the manufacturer's duty is a continuing duty. It is no answer for the manufacturer to contend that his product was safe by, say, 2001 standards if evidence of its dangers has emerged from its use and that same product is still being marketed in 2007.

What about contraceptives which simply fail? We shall see later that the House of Lords has ruled that parents cannot recover compensation for the cost of bringing up a normal, healthy child.[25] In *Richardson v LRC Products Ltd*[26] it was held that evidence a condom split was not by itself sufficient to prove that product defective. The fallibility of condoms was well known. The manufacturer never guaranteed 100 per cent success.

Voluntary sterilisation

11.6 When a further pregnancy or the burden of caring for more children may endanger a woman's health, therapeutic sterilisation may be advised. Non-therapeutic sterilisation is increasingly sought as a method of permanent birth control, both by older couples who feel that their family is complete and by younger childless women adamant that they never wish to reproduce. Both sorts of prospective patients express disquiet about present practice. Too many doctors regard the decision to sterilise as theirs and not their patients'.[27] They are over-inclined to sterilise women whom they regard as unfit for childbearing, or childrearing. They are disinclined to help the fit but unwilling. The

[21]   See *XYZ v Schering Health Care Ltd* [2002] EWHC 144420 (QB); *Vadera v Shaw* (1998) 45 BMLR 162.
[25]   See *McFarlane v Tayside Health Board* [1999] 4 All ER 961, HL. See below at 11.7.
[26]   [2000] Lloyd's Rep 280.
[27]   See H Draper, 'Women and Sterilisation Abuse' in M Brazier and M Lobjoit (eds), *Protecting the Vulnerable* (1991) Routledge, Chapter 6.

latter struggle to find a legal remedy. A plethora of private clinics has grown up offering female sterilisation and vasectomy at a price. Patients refused sterilisation within the NHS must resort to that private sector if they can meet the cost.

A doctor undertaking sterilisation must ensure that the patient understands and agrees to what is to be done. Operating without any consent is obviously a battery. Nor should sterilisation be automatically performed concurrently with some other gynaecological operation to which the patient has consented. The doctor may correctly judge, in the course of some other form of surgery, that a woman should not risk pregnancy again. He cannot act 'in her best interests' without her agreement. In *Devi v West Midlands Area Health Authority*,[28] a married woman of 33 who already had four children entered hospital for a minor gynaecological operation. Her religion outlawed sterilisation or contraception. In the course of the operation the surgeon discovered her womb to be ruptured and sterilised her there and then. She received £4,000 damages for the loss of her ability to conceive again and £2,700 damages for the 'neurosis' caused by the knowledge of what had been done to her. The choice whether to accept sterilisation is the patient's. It may be more convenient to sterilise the patient on the spot. It is never so immediately necessary as to justify acting in an emergency without consent.

A doctor who has obtained consent may still be liable for negligence if he fails to discuss properly with the patient the implications of the operation in a manner consistent with good medical practice. The doctor must not only give the patient sufficient information on which to make up her mind, but do so at a time when she is in a fit state to make a reasoned decision. A Roman Catholic woman of 35 was awarded £3,000 damages in negligence when she was sterilised in the course of a Caesarean operation to deliver her second child. She signed the consent form just as she was about to be wheeled into the operating theatre. The judge said that, although she consented to the additional surgery and understood what would physically be done to her, she had been inadequately counselled about its implications for her.[29] Sterilising a woman in the course of an abortion or Caesarean saves time and money for the NHS and cuts down on pain and suffering for the patient. It is a course of action fraught with legal hazard unless the patient has been properly advised about the physical and emotional consequences of electing to be sterilised. The doctor must assess not just his patient's physical condition, but also her religious and moral attitudes to enable him and her to take into account the possible emotional impact of sterilisation. Moreover, if sterilisation is proposed on therapeutic grounds the patient's consent must necessarily be based on adequate and careful advice as to the medical need for sterilisation. In *Biles v Barking Health Authority*[30] a woman was advised to undergo sterilisation on the grounds that she was suffering from a severe and probably fatal kidney complaint. That diagnosis was proved later to be mistaken and negligent. Mrs Biles recovered damages of £45,000, which included the cost of a failed

---

[28] [1980] 7 *Current Law* 44.
[29] *Wells v Surrey Area Health Authority* (1978) Times, 29 July.
[30] See M Puxon, A Buchan, 'Damages for Sterility' (1988) 138 *New Law Journal* 80.

attempt to reverse the sterilisation and the cost of IVF treatment to try to enable her to have a child of her own, despite her surgically-blocked Fallopian tubes.

Who pays for the unplanned child?

11.7 Contraception and sterilisation are fallible. No doctor guarantees avoidance of conception. He undertakes to use his skill to maximise the chances of preventing pregnancy. Sterilisation is often expected and intended to be final. What if it fails? This can happen if the surgeon is negligent. There is also a small but real risk inherent in both vasectomy and female sterilisation that tissues will rejoin naturally and conception will once again be possible. Who foots the bill for the unexpected infant?

When the surgeon admits that sterilisation failed because he was negligent the only issue is the amount of damages he should pay. Should damages be limited to compensation for the mother's pain and discomfort arising from the useless operation and from the subsequent pregnancy? Or should parents be able to recover the cost of bringing up their unplanned child?[31] In *Udale v Bloomsbury Area Health Authority*[32] Jupp J held that the birth of a healthy child could not be allowed to create a claim in damages. He argued that the child, when he came to know of the award, might feel unwanted and the family's relationship be disrupted. Doctors might put pressure on women to have abortions. Children were a blessing, and any financial loss was offset by the joy of their birth.

A series of judgments from the Court of Appeal firmly rejected Jupp J's invocation of policy to refuse parents compensation in such a case.[33] Damages amounting to the cost to the family of raising an unplanned child appeared to be readily endorsed in claims for wrongful conception. Two decisions of the House of Lords restored English and Scottish law to the position declared by Jupp J in *Udale*, albeit on different grounds. It was held in *McFarlane v Tayside Health Board*[34] that compensation for the cost of bringing up a healthy child will not be awarded. Such a loss is categorised now as irrecoverable economic loss. *McFarlane* is difficult to analyse.[35] Five Law Lords rejected the parents' claim. Five sets of very different reasons are advanced by their Lordships.

The facts of the case are straightforward. Mr and Mrs McFarlane had four children. Mr McFarlane had a vasectomy. Six months after his operation, the surgeon told him that his sperm count was negative and he and his wife could

---

[31] See A Mullis, 'Wrongful Conception Unravelled' (1993) 1 *Medical Law Review* 320.

[32] [1983] 2 All ER 522.

[33] See *Thake v Maurice* [1984] 2 All ER 513, CA; *Emeh v Kensington & Chelsea Health Authority* [1993] 1 All ER 651.

[34] [1999] 4 All ER 961, HL. See also *Greenfield v Irwin (A Firm)* [2001] 1 FLR 899.

[35] Se JK Mason, 'Unwanted Pregnancy: A Case of Retroversion?' (2000) 4 *Edinburgh Law Journal* 191; J Weir, 'The Unwanted Child' (2000) 59 *Cambridge Law Journal* 238; L Hogano, 'Misconceptions about Wrongful Conception' (2002) 65 *Modern Law Review* 883.

dispense with contraception. The couple relied on that advice. Mrs McFarlane became pregnant. They alleged that the surgeon was negligent and sought compensation, (1) for Mrs McFarlane's pain and distress in pregnancy and labour and (2) for the costs of bringing up their healthy daughter, Catherine. Four out of the five Law Lords[36] held that Mrs McFarlane could recover damages for the pain and discomfort of pregnancy and any immediately consequential financial loss to her. All agreed that the more substantial claim for the cost of raising Catherine should fail. All tried to avoid Jupp J's forthright reliance on policy to categorise such claims as repugnant to the public interest.

Lord Slynn appeared to accept that the blessings conferred by healthy children come in tandem with substantial burdens. He rejected the argument that courts should regard the financial costs of raising a child as offset by the joys of parenting. He claimed not to be concerned by possible psychological consequences to a child of learning that she is unwanted because her parents received damages for her wrongful conception. His speech focused on his finding that doctors are not responsible for the economic loss entailed in child rearing. Doctors owe a duty of care to prevent pregnancy and the consequential physical effects on the mother. It is not fair, just or reasonable to extend that responsibility to the costs of rearing the child.[37] Lord Hope took a somewhat similar approach. He appeared exercised by the potential scale of claims for wrongful conception. If such a claim is allowable it would relate to the actual costs to particular parents of raising that child. Thus a claim by wealthy aristocrats might extend to the cost of nannies, ponies, public school and so on. The extent of liability would be disproportionate to the negligence.[38]

Lord Hope and Lord Steyn both, unlike Lord Slynn, adverted to the benefits of parenthood. Lord Hope declared:

> ... it would not be fair, just or reasonable, in any assessment of the loss caused by the birth of a child, to leave these benefits out of account. Otherwise the [claimant] would be paid far too much. They would be relieved of the costs of rearing the child. They would not be giving anything back to the wrongdoer for the benefits. But the value attached to their benefits is incalculable. The costs can be calculated but the benefit, which must in fairness be set against them, cannot. The logical conclusion, as a matter of law, is that the cost to the [claimant] of meeting their obligations to their child during her childhood are not recoverable as damages.[39]

Lord Steyn contended that his rejection of the parents' claim was not on policy grounds. He '... would avoid those quicksands'.[40] He saw the question as one of distributive justice. He stated that he was 'firmly of the view that an overwhelming number of ordinary men and women' would reject claims such as the McFarlanes. He argued that if claims by a child for wrongful life should be rejected as repugnant to the value of human life, so should a claim by

---

[36] Lord Millett dissented on this point.
[37] [1999] 4 All ER 961 at 978, HL.
[38] At 985.
[39] At 985.
[40] At 998.

parents for its wrongful conception.[41] Lord Steyn may have sought to avoid the quicksands of public policy but became immersed in them none the less.

Lord Clyde treated the claim as one of *quantum* of damages. Like Lord Hope, he was exercised by questions of proportionality. There could be significant differences in the level of awards depending on parental lifestyle. The expense of bringing up the child would be disproportionate to any wrongdoing and go beyond reasonable restitution.[42] Lord Millett, uniquely, sought to reject both claims by the parents, the claim for the mother's pain and suffering in pregnancy, as well as the claim for the cost of raising Catherine. Lord Millett was forthright in his views:

> In my opinion, the law must take the birth of a normal healthy baby to be a blessing, not a detriment. In truth it is a mixed blessing. It brings joy and sorrow, blessing and responsibility. The advantages and disadvantages are inseparable. Individuals may choose to regard the balance as unfavourable and take steps to forego the pleasures as well as the responsibilities of parenthood. They are entitled to decide for themselves where their own interests lie. But society itself must regard the balance as beneficial. It would be repugnant to its own sense of values to do otherwise. It is morally offensive to regard a normal, healthy baby as more trouble and expense than it is worth.[43]

The only damages Lord Millett would allow was a nominal sum to represent the loss of the parental freedom to limit the size of their family. He proposed £5,000. Lord Millett stands alone in the openness of his opinion that it is unacceptable to society to compensate parents for having a child, however hard they had tried to avoid further pregnancies. His honesty should be commended. The reasons advanced by his colleagues are not convincing.

The judges in *McFarlane* expressly confined their ruling to cases where a healthy child is born.[44] Subsequent judgments held that where a disabled child is born, his parents may recover the additional costs ensuing from their child's disability. The rationale is difficult to comprehend. Unless the defendants' negligence related to advice or treatment expressly to help parents avoid the birth of a disabled child, how does the child's disability result from negligent advice about, or performance of, sterilisation? As we shall see, the House of Lords decision in *Rees v Darlington Memorial Hospital NHS Trust*[45] throws serious doubt on the validity of any principle of compensation for the birth of a child.

In *Parkinson v St James and Seacroft University NHS Hospital Trust*[46] the parents' claim related to the birth of their fifth child. Sadly the baby proved to have substantial disabilities, possibly related to autism. Mrs Parkinson was sterilised after the birth of her fourth child but the operation was performed negligently. The surgeon failed to secure effectively a clip to Mrs Parkinson's left Fallopian tube. She conceived again ten months after the operation. The

---

[41]   At 998.
[42]   At 998.
[43]   At 1005.
[44]   At 979, per Lord Steyn.
[45]   [2002] 2 All ER 177, CA.
[46]   [2001] EWCA Civ 530.

Court of Appeal ruled that, *McFarlane* notwithstanding, the parents could recover the special costs of raising a child with their son's disabilities.[47] A doctor who performs a sterilisation negligently should reasonably foresee the birth of a disabled child as a possible consequence of his breach of duty. Only a limited group of people (parents whose children were unfortunately born disabled) could bring a claim and Brooke LJ saw no difficulty with the proposition that the doctor assumed responsibility for the disastrous economic consequences of the birth of such a child: '[O]rdinary people would consider that it would be fair for the law to make an award in such a case provided that it is limited to the extra expenses associated with the child's disability'.[48] Both Brooke and Hale LJJ[49] constructed elegant examples to distinguish the case of the disabled child from *McFarlane*. Hale LJ proposed a model of 'deemed equilibrium' whereby the costs and benefits of a healthy child balance each other out. The reader may ponder whether the Appeal Court did not in reality simply regard *McFarlane* as wrongly decided.[50] Unable to say so forthrightly, the judges sought to mitigate its worst effects.

Subsequently the Court of Appeal went further in its attempt to limit the effects of *McFarlane*. In *Rees v Darlington Memorial Hospital NHS Trust*,[51] they held that a seriously disabled woman could recover the additional costs to her of raising her healthy son born after a negligently performed sterilisation. The claimant suffered from retinitis pigmentosa. She had only very limited vision in one eye. She elected to be sterilised because she did not want children and judged that her virtual blindness would prevent her looking after a child. Hale LJ[52] distinguished *McFarlane* on a number of grounds, relying on the pragmatic 'deemed equilibrium' model she first set down in *Parkinson*. Unlike the healthy parent of a healthy child, but like the parent of any disabled child, the claimant incurred extra costs in bringing up a child. The compensation awarded to her was not compensation for the cost of the child *per se*, but the costs occasioned by her own disability.

When *Rees* reached the House of Lords,[53] the Law Lords had an opportunity to revisit their judgment in *McFarlane*. They refused to do so, and unanimously reaffirmed it. By a 4:3 majority, it was held that Mrs Rees could *not*

---

47 For guidance on what constitutes 'disability', see [2001] EWCA Civ 530 at para 91, per Hale LJ.

48 [2001] EWCA Civ 530 at para 50; and see Hale LJ at para 82.

49 Note Hale LJ's analysis of the nature of the loss and injury. Are the costs consequent on the birth of an unplanned child, disabled or not; truly pure economic loss?

50 The Australian High Court rejected *McFarlane* in *Cattanach v Melchior* [2003] HCA 38. Queensland and New South Wales have legislated to counteract the effects of this case.

51 [2002] 2 All ER 177, CA. Note, though, that there must be a real financial burden imposed on the claimant as a result of struggling to bring up a child and cope with her own disabilities: see *AD v East Kent Community NHS Trust* [2002] Lloyd's Rep Med 424.

52 Note the difference in reasoning between Hale and Robert Walker LJJ. Consider whether poverty is a 'disability' deserving at least some compensation for an unplanned child. Waller LJ dissented, comparing a hypothetical woman driven to 'crisis in health terms' by the birth of a fifth child following a negligent sterilisation with a similar crisis on the part of a disabled parent. For both, the recovery of the costs of caring for the healthy child might alleviate the crisis. Why should the law treat the two differently?

53 [2003] UKHL 52. See A Morris, 'Another Fine Mess ... the Aftermath of *McFarlane* and the Decision in *Rees v Darlington Memorial Hospital NHS Trust*' (2004) 20 *Professional Negligence* 2; N Priaulx, 'Damages for the 'Unwanted' Child: Time for a Rethink?' (2005) 73 *Medico-Legal Journal* 152.

recover the costs of raising and maintaining a healthy child. However, the Law Lords added a 'gloss' to the *McFarlane* ruling. Though, for reasons of public policy it is unacceptable to view a healthy child as a financial liability, Lord Millett's (then rejected) suggestion in *McFarlane* that an award of general damages was appropriate to mark the injury and loss was taken up. Loss of autonomy suffered by the parents resulted from a legal wrong. Lord Bingham proposed a conventional figure of £15,000 which should be awarded in addition to the award for pregnancy and birth. The majority agreed.

Hale LJ's 'deemed equilibrium' was rejected on the basis that the costs and benefits associated with the birth of a child were unquantifiable and consequently impossible to balance. Alasdair Maclean argues that, though correct, this leaves no legal basis for the 'gloss' on *McFarlane*.[54] Whilst there may be public policy grounds for the avoidance of general negligence principles in wrongful birth cases, even after two House of Lords decisions, sound legal reasoning remains elusive. Perhaps, as Emily Jackson suggests,[55] the Law Lords in *Rees* were simply creating their own novel scheme of compensation to acknowledge the legal wrong whilst limiting the pay out. On the other hand the 'gloss' may be viewed, as Lord Steyn suggested in his dissenting judgment, as 'a radical and most important development which should only be embarked on after rigorous examination of competing arguments'.[56] On this view, the majority in *Rees* overstepped the limits of judicial discretion.

Rees has implications for the status of *Parkinson*.[57] Though Lord Hutton approved of the decision,[58] Lord Bingham was critical of it.[59] Further, the refusal of the majority to make a calculation of costs based on benefits and detriments in the case of a healthy child is arguably equally applicable to the disabled child.[60] It remains to be seen whether general damages or additional costs associated with the child's disability will be awarded in future.

---

[54] A Maclean, 'An Alexandrian Approach to the Knotty Problem of Wrongful Pregnancy: *Rees v Darlington Memorial Trust* in the House of Lords' [2004] 3 *Web Journal of Current Legal Issues*. See also P Cane, 'Another Failed Sterilisation' (2004) 120 *Law Quarterly Review* 181.

[55] E Jackson, *Medical Law: Texts, Cases and Materials* (2006) OUP, p 681.

[56] *Rees v Darlington Memorial Hospital NHS Trust* [2003] UKHL 53 at para 43, per Lord Steyn (dissenting). See also Lord Hope's judgement.

[57] *Parkinson v St James and Seacraft University NHS Hospital Trust* [2001] EWCA Civ 530.

[58] [2003] UKHL 53 at para 96.

[59] [2003] UKHL 53 at para 9.

[60] See Maclean [2004] 3 *Web Journal of Current Legal Issues*: 'Unless one is prepared to argue that having a disabled child is not – as a matter of policy – a blessing, which might be interpreted as devaluing the disabled, then the calculation is no more possible for the birth of a disabled child than it is for the birth of a healthy child. ... [I]f x cannot be balanced against y then nor can x be balanced against y + x.' See also JK Mason and GT Laurie, *Mason and McCall Smith's Law and Medical Ethics* (7th edn, 2006) OUP, p 179.

What constitutes negligent sterilisation?

11.8 It might be that a factor motivating the decisions in *McFarlane* and *Rees*[61] was an explosion in unmeritorious claims.[62] Where a surgeon bungles the operation by only clipping one Fallopian tube, imposing responsibility for the consequences of his carelessness seems instinctively right. Pre-*McFarlane* liability for failed sterilisation extended beyond such examples of crass negligence. Consider cases where conception occurs because tissues heal naturally. The operation has been performed impeccably. Nature reverses the operation. At first sight it might appear that the surgeon is in no way responsible. What could he have done? The practice of most surgeons has long been to warn patients of the risk when discussing the proposed operation with them. In *Thake v Maurice*, Mr and Mrs Thake had five children and little money. They wanted no more children. Mr Thake decided to have a vasectomy and paid £20 for the operation. The judge found that the defendant never warned Mr and Mrs Thake of the small but real risk that nature would reverse the surgery. Mrs Thake did not discover her pregnancy until it was nearly five months advanced. The couple sought compensation from the defendant surgeon. As Mr Thake had paid for his vasectomy, unlike an NHS patient he had a contract with the surgeon. The trial judge held[63] that Mr Thake had agreed to an operation that he understood would render him irreversibly infertile. That is what he contracted for. The defendant was in breach of contract if he failed to achieve that aim. By failing to warn Mr Thake of the risk of natural reversal of the vasectomy, the defendant *guaranteed* to make him sterile. The defendant was responsible for the financial loss to the family occasioned by the birth of the unplanned infant. The Court of Appeal[64] held by a majority that the surgeon never guaranteed to make Mr Thake sterile. Neill LJ found that no reasonable person would have understood the defendant as giving a binding promise that the operation would achieve its purpose. They nevertheless unanimously found for Mr Thake on grounds enabling NHS patients as well as private patients to sue if they are not warned of the risk of nature reversing sterilisation of either sex. They held that failure to warn of this risk was negligent. That negligence resulted in Mrs Thake being unaware of her pregnancy until abortion was no longer a safe option. The defendant was responsible for that state of affairs and thus for the birth of the child. He was liable in contract to his private patient. He would have been liable in negligence to an NHS patient.

In *Thake v Maurice*, the defendant conceded that failure to warn the patient of the risk of reversal in vasectomy was negligent. In other cases the crux of the dispute became the question of when such a failure was negligent. Practice among doctors used to differ quite substantially. Professional opinion today is clear. Patients must be told about the risks of reversal of male and female sterilisation. Guidance[65] from the Royal College of Obstetricians and Gynaecologists on consent to sterilisation – male and female – stresses that such

[61]   *McFarlane v Tayside Health Board* [1999] 4 All ER 961, HL; *Rees v Darlington Memorial Hospital NHS Trust* [2002] 2 All ER 177, CA.
[62]   See, for example, *Danns v Department of Health* [1998] PIQR P 226.
[63]   [1984] 2 All ER 513.
[64]   [1986] 1 All ER 497; and see *Eyre v Measday* [1986] 1 All ER 488.
[65]   Royal College of Obstetricians and Gynaecologists, *Male and Female Sterilisation* (1999, revised 2004).

information should routinely be given. The RCOG's advice should be enough to render any failure to warn a maverick, not a responsible, opinion.

A claim by an NHS patient based on failure to warn of the risks of reversal will succeed. Where a healthy child is born, damages will be limited to the losses pregnancy occasions to the mother, and a notional sum of compensation for loss of autonomy.[66] It remains open to question whether a private patient suing in contract can evade the bar on recovery of child-rearing costs imposed in *McFarlane*. Could it be argued that what one pays for in arranging a private vasectomy is, at the least, care to avoid the imposition of the financial burden of further offspring? The question of whether it is 'fair, just and reasonable' to impose a duty of care in tort is irrelevant in contract.

Who is entitled to sue in respect of failed sterilisation? When vasectomy fails, the man's wife or an established partner enjoys a claim in respect of the loss pregnancy occasions her.[67] She is within the scope of the duty undertaken by the doctor operating on her man. In the reverse case, given that costs of childrearing are excluded from such claims now, a man whose female partner's sterilisation failed would find it difficult to identify a recoverable injury to him. Subsequent partners are beyond the scope of any duty owed by the surgeon. In *Goodwill v BPAS*[68] a woman became pregnant by a man who had had a vasectomy three years before they met and started a sexual relationship. She claimed that she relied on the expertise of the defendant's clinic that had performed her lover's vasectomy. The Court of Appeal threw out the claim with some disdain. Thorpe LJ said:

> It cannot be said that [the doctor] knows or ought to know that he also advises any future sexual partner of his patient who chance to receive his advice at second-hand. Presented with such a set of facts, a doctor is entitled to scorn the suggestion that he owes a duty of care to such a band so uncertain in nature and extent and over such an indefinite future span.[69]

Involuntary sterilisation

11.9 No statute in England ever provided for the compulsory sterilisation of mentally-disabled patients. None the less, in 1987 the House of Lords in *Re B*[70] authorised the involuntary sterilisation of a girl under 18, referred to as Jeanette. In 1989, in *F v West Berkshire Health Authority*,[71] their Lordships ruled that sterilisation of an adult woman with mental disability was not unlawful if that operation was in her 'best interests'. In theory, a woman may not be sterilised in the interests of society, of her potential children or on

---

[66] In *Rees v Darlington Memorial Hospital NHS Trust* [2003] UKHL 52 at para 8, Lord Bingham awarded £15,000 general damages to the disabled mother. This will apply in 'all cases', though it remains to be seen whether a parent who is compensated for the excess costs of bringing up a disabled child will qualify for the £15,000. See above at 11.7.
[67] As was the case in *McFarlane v Tayside Health Board* [1999] 4 All ER 961, HL.
[68] [1996] 2 All ER 161, CA.
[69] [1996] 2 All ER 161 at 170, CA.
[70] [1987] 2 All ER 206, HL.
[71] [1989] 2 All ER 545, HL.

eugenic grounds. She may be sterilised only where she lacks the capacity to make decisions on childbearing for herself, and to protect her health and welfare.

The Mental Capacity Act 2005, which is expected to come into force in October 2007, governs the law surrounding adults and young persons[72] who lack mental capacity. It is examined in detail in Chapter 6. Much of the Act and the accompanying Code of Practice, in draft form at the time of writing, enshrine principles developed by the common law. In *F v West Berkshire Health Authority* protection from liability to carers and health professionals was granted through the application of the doctrine of necessity. Section 5 of the Mental Capacity Act 2005 performs a similar role, granting a 'general authority' to act in the best interests of a patient lacking mental capacity and setting conditions that must be satisfied before liability can be avoided. The 2005 Act defines what constitutes a lack of capacity in section 2(1):

> ... [A] person lacks capacity in relation to a matter if at the material time he is unable to make a decision for himself in relation to the matter because of an impairment of, or a disturbance in the functioning of, the mind or brain.

The draft Code of Practice gives guidance on how to make that judgment.[73] The requirement of an 'impairment or disturbance' sets the 'diagnostic threshold' for lack of capacity. In addition to this, it must be demonstrated that the person is 'unable to make a decision'; the test is decision-specific. The protection of the incapacitated person's health or welfare is more complex. The 2005 Act endorses the common law position that the 'act done, or decision made ... must be done, or made, in his best interests'.[74] Best interests do not necessarily mean best *clinical* interests. As the Act retains the test developed by the common law, previous case law remains relevant to illustrate how 'best interests' should be interpreted in the context of sterilisation.

In *Re B*, Lord Oliver said of the argument that sterilising Jeanette violated her right to reproduce: '[A] right to reproduce is of value only if accompanied by the ability to make a choice ...'.[75] Where a woman lacks the ability to choose, and pregnancy may be harmful to her, any right to reproduce may be taken from her. But does it logically follow that just because the woman is incapable of making a rational decision on whether to embark on childbearing, it is in her interest to be sterilised?[76] A number of questions arise.

---

[72] The Mental Capacity Act 2005 applies largely to persons of age 16 and over who lack capacity (see section 2(5)). For those under 16, persons with parental responsibility can consent on their behalf. Disputes are resolved under the Children Act 1989, the Mental Health Act 1983 or under the jurisdiction of the High Court. In the case of young persons between the ages of 16 and 18, there is overlap between the Mental Capacity Act 2005 and the Children Act 1989.

[73] Department for Constitutional Affairs, *Mental Capacity Act 2005 Draft Code of Practice* (CP 05/06), para 3.10.

[74] Mental Capacity Act 2005, s 1(5). See also section 4 of the 2005 Act, which lists factors relevant to the determination of an individual's best interests. See above at 6.10.

[75] [1987] 2 All ER 206 at 219, HL.

[76] See MDA Freeman, 'Sterilising the Mentally Handicapped' in MDA Freeman (ed), *Medicine, Ethics and Law* (1998) Stevens, London.

First, sterilising a mentally-disabled woman 'protects' her from one evil which might befall her if she is enticed or coerced into sexual intercourse. It in no way safeguards her from exploitation by men taking advantage of her, from perversion or sexually transmitted disease. Knowing she cannot become pregnant, those caring for her may be less vigilant in attempts to prevent her from being enticed into exploitative sexual relations.

Second, one reason advanced for sterilising severely mentally-disabled women is that they can be allowed more freedom. Free from the risk of pregnancy, the woman, although deprived of a right to reproduce, can exercise a 'right' to sexuality. Two difficulties confront this superficially attractive proposition:

(a) Has the woman capacity to consent to sexual intercourse? T[77] was said to have a mental age of two. Sexual intercourse with T would constitute rape. It may well be that other women in cases involving non-consensual sterilisation, such as Jeanette,[78] understood enough of what was entailed in sexual intimacy to give consent to intercourse and seemed to invite such contact. Yet intercourse with Jeanette would still be a criminal offence under sections 30–33 of the Sexual Offences Act 2003.

(b) If the rationale for sterilising mentally-disabled women is to enable them to enjoy sexual pleasure, sterilisation on its own is not enough. For a right to sexuality to have any meaning, positive steps need to be taken to ensure circumstances where such women could enjoy such pleasure safely and without risk of harm or disease.

The most troubling question remains how to decide who should be sterilised. Sir Brian Rix of MENCAP greeted *Re B* with horror, claiming that sterilising mentally-disabled girls was to reduce them to the status of pets to be neutered at will. Some decisions soon after *Re B* seemed to offer *post facto* justification for Sir Brian's outrage.

Consider the case of *Re P*.[79] At 17, P was said to have a mental age of six, but unlike M and Jeanette, she had good communication skills and could cope with her own bodily needs. P seemed to have some maternal feelings; she understood what was involved in sexual intercourse and said she thought it sounded horrid and painful. Her mother feared that as she was of an attractive 'normal' appearance she would be vulnerable to seduction, and that if she became pregnant she might well refuse to have an abortion. The judge acknowledged that P was a borderline case and even accepted that she might well have capacity to marry, yet he still authorised her sterilisation. In *Re B* Lord Oliver had agreed with Dillon LJ in the Court of Appeal that '... jurisdiction in Wardship proceedings to authorise such an operation is one which should be exercised only in the last resort ...'.[80] Was P really a case of this magnitude? The judge said that it no longer need be proved that sterilisation was the 'last resort': Professor Robert Winston had testified that

77 See *T v T* [1988] 1 All ER 613.
78 See *Re B (A Minor) (Wardship: Sterilisation)* [1987] 2 All ER 211, HL.
79 *Re P (A Minor) (Wardship: Sterilisation)* [1989] 1 FLR 182. And see *Re M (a minor) (a wardship: sterilisation)* [1988] 2 FLR 497.
80 [1987] 2 All ER 211 at 218, HL.

reversal of sterilisation carried out by clips on the Fallopian tubes achieved a 95 per cent success rate. However, the House of Lords in *Re B* had regarded sterilisation as irreversible. If that were not so, judges could properly accept less draconian criteria for authorising 'reversible' surgery. Unfortunately not many gynaecologists do think that they could attain a 95% success rate for reversal of sterilisation – and how realistic is it to expect that even a mildly learning-disabled woman will be offered reversal surgery? P understood enough about childbearing for her mother to fear that she would oppose any proposal for an abortion if she became pregnant. True, pregnancy might well be a disaster for P and her child, but if that is the criterion for involuntary sterilisation are we sliding down a slippery slope?

The Mental Capacity Act 2005 requires that consideration is given to the least restrictive means by which the best interests of an individual lacking capacity can be met.[81] There is evidence that, even before the Act comes into force, judges are endorsing this principle. In *Re S (Medical Treatment: Adult Sterilisation)* (1998),[82] a 22-year-old woman lived with her parents. She was meticulously cared for and well supervised. The arrangements for her care at home, at the day centre which she attended and when she was in respite care, meant that the risk of her engaging in sexual intercourse or being subject to sexual assault was exceptionally low. Her mother feared that S might be a victim of a sexual assault, and that especially as her parents grew older and less able to care for her, some care worker might take advantage of her. Johnson J refused to authorise sterilisation. Citing Thorpe J in *Re LC (Medical Treatment: Sterilisation)*,[83] he held that the risk of pregnancy must be balanced against the risks and distress of surgery. That risk in S's case was, at the time of the hearing, no more than speculative. The case that S's interests and welfare demanded immediate surgery was not made out.

In *Re S (Adult Patient: Sterilisation)* (2000),[84] the Court of Appeal firmly endorsed a proactive approach to applications to sterilise mentally-disabled women. The patient in this case was 29 and had severe learning disabilities. She was cared for by her mother but at some point as her mother aged she would have to move into local authority accommodation. She might be at risk of pregnancy. S also suffered from menstrual problems involving heavy periods, which she did not understand and which distressed her. Her mother sought a declaration that S could lawfully be sterilised and/or a hysterectomy be performed. Medical experts offered a range of views. One option was to fit S with a Mirena coil, an intra-uterine device which would both prevent pregnancy and alleviate menstrual bleeding. The Court of Appeal refused to authorise sterilisation or hysterectomy. Medical opinion was crucial to identify the responsible options for treating the woman. The choice of which option best met the woman's needs was one for the court. The *Bolam* test is relevant to the first stage of a process of assessing the patient's interests to ensure that

---

[81] Mental Capacity Act 2005, s 1(6).
[82] [1998] 1 FLR 944.
[83] [1997] 2 FLR 258.
[84] [2000] 3 WLR 1288, CA. See also *Trust A and Trust B v H (An Adult Patient by her Litigation Friend, the Official Solicitor)* [2006] EWHC 1230 (Fam). See above, Chapter 6 at 6.6.

any option for treatment proposed conforms to responsible medical opinion. It has no relevance to the second stage of assessing what is best for this patient. The patient's welfare must be the paramount consideration. 'That embraces issues far wider than the medical. Indeed it would be undesirable and probably impossible to set borders on what is relevant to a welfare determination.'[85]

Could a mentally-disabled man be subjected to a non-consensual vasectomy? In *F v Berkshire Health Authority*,[86] a woman patient in a hospital was, as we saw, sterilised in her 'best interests' after she embarked on a sexual relationship with a fellow (male) patient. Evidence emerged later that suggested that the male patient had a number of other 'girlfriends' in the hospital. Some of these other women were also sterilised in 'their own interests'. Could the man have been sterilised instead? The question never reached the courts at that time. In *Re A (Medical Treatment: Male Sterilisation)*,[87] A had Down's syndrome and suffered from significant learning disabilities. He lived with his elderly mother. He had no understanding of the link between sexual intercourse and pregnancy. While at home he had shown no interest in sex, nor was there much chance of him establishing sexual relationships. His mother feared that when she could no longer care for him and he moved into local authority care, he might form a sexual relationship and father a child. He would be unable to understand the concept of paternity, and unable to undertake any sort of responsibility as a father. Thus an application was made to sterilise A. The heart of the problem before the court was whether vasectomy could be said to be 'necessary' for A's welfare. He would not become pregnant, or face the risks and discomfort a woman with similar disabilities confronts as a possible consequence of sexual intercourse. The Court of Appeal refused to authorise a vasectomy for A. They did not rule out the possibility that a case might be made out to justify non-consensual sterilisation of a man with mental disabilities. In A's case the risk of his entering into a sexual relationship was assessed as low. Like S he was carefully supervised. Dame Elizabeth Butler-Sloss P wisely noted:

> If sterilisation did take place, it would not save A from the possibility of exploitation nor help him cope with the emotional implications of any closer relationships that he might form.[88]

The Court of Appeal rightly rejected any notion that sexual 'equality' required that if women could be sterilised in their 'best interests', men must be treated 'the same'. They focused on the welfare of A himself. In recognising that preventing pregnancy does not protect men from potentially adverse consequences or sexual relationships, do the courts open the way to an equivalent view of cases involving women?

---

[85]   [2000] 3 WLR 1288, CA at 1302, per Thorpe LJ.
[86]   [1989] 2 All ER 545, HL.
[87]   [2000] 1 FCR 193, CA.
[88]   [2000] 1 FCR 193 at 203, CA.

Involving the courts

11.10 Disquiet about involuntary sterilisation in England becomes even greater where the woman concerned is over 18, for, as we saw in Chapter 6, the House of Lords in *F v West Berkshire Health Authority*[89] found that there was no jurisdiction enabling them to require doctors to seek a declaration before sterilising an adult woman. No declaration is required provided that two practitioners are of the opinion that the operation is a therapeutic necessity.[90]

What constitutes a therapeutic necessity? The Appeal Court in *Re S*[91] made it clear that only where it was plain that hysterectomy was necessary, for example to deal with uterine cancer or inoperable fibroids, should doctors go ahead without the sanction of the court. 'Borderline' cases should be subject to independent review.[92] One of the expert witnesses in *Re S* considered that her heavy periods were not outside normal limits and in 'a woman of normal intelligence no doctor would contemplate a hysterectomy as a means of treating the condition'.[93]

What if there is no 'necessity'? In 2001, a Practice Note of the High Court[94] advised that it was good practice to seek a declaration from the court.[95] In *D v An NHS Trust (Medical Treatment: Consent: Termination)*[96] Coleridge J considered the circumstances in which prior judicial sanction is required for the proposed abortion of a pregnant woman lacking capacity.

> In my view, where the issues of capacity and best interests are clear and beyond doubt, an application to the court is not necessary. However, there will be other circumstances in which the authorisation of the court is required in order to avoid any doubt as to the legitimacy of the Article 8 [of the European Convention on Human Rights] interference.[97]

Though it is unlikely that Coleridge J intended to 'transform the requirement to seek the approval of the court from a matter of good practice into a legal requirement',[98] section 8 of the Human Rights Act 1998 gives more force to the privacy rights of individuals lacking capacity.

In common law, the distinction between therapeutic and non-therapeutic interventions is crucial. In non-therapeutic cases, it is good practice to obtain a

---

[89] [1989] 2 All ER 545, HL.
[90] See *Pembrey v The General Medical Council* [2003] UKPC 60.
[91] [1998] 1 FLR 944.
[92] And see *Re Z (Medical Treatment) Hysterectomy* [2000] 1 FCR 274.
[93] [1998] 1 FLR 944 at 1294.
[94] *Practice Note (Official Solicitor: Declaratory Proceedings: Medical and Welfare Decisions for Adults who Lack Capacity)* [2001] 2 FLR 158.
[95] Approved in *Burke v United Kingdom* [2006] App 19807/06. In *R. (on the application of Burke) v The General Medical Council* [2005] EWCA Civ 1003 (explored fully in Chapter 20), the Court of Appeal held that courts do not *authorise* medical actions, they merely declare whether or not an action is lawful.
[96] [2003] EWHC 2793 (Fam).
[97] [2003] EWHC 2793 (Fam) at paras 32–33.
[98] *R. (on the application of Burke) v GMC* [2005] EWCA Civ 1003, per Lord Phillips MR at para 74.

declaration from the court that the intervention is lawful. However, provided the intervention is a therapeutic necessity, a court declaration is not required, but, as we have seen, the threshold for therapeutic necessity is extremely contentious.[99]

Does the Mental Capacity Act 2005 clarify the situation? At the extremes of the spectrum, the Act is clear. The draft Code of Practice on the Mental Capacity Act 2005[100] advises that a court order[101] be sought in all cases of non-therapeutic sterilisation. The Act also gives authority to the decision-maker to act when there is a therapeutic necessity. Thus, the draft Code of Practice acknowledges that there may be situations when treatment should be given without delay[102] and the duties incumbent on the decision-maker under section 4(6) and (7) to consult others when determining whether treatment is in the best interests of the person lacking capacity exist only 'if it is practicable and appropriate'. Where the procedure is therapeutic but not urgent, the waters remain murky. As we saw in Chapter 6, the definition of best interests under the Act is not synonymous with non-negligent care. The decision-maker is required to look beyond the clinical need of the person lacking capacity, to her wider welfare issues. Consequently, it is likely that when the 2005 Act comes into force, doctors and carers will seek reassurance from the Court of Protection that any therapeutic (but not urgent) sterilisation they propose for an adult lacking capacity is in her best interests.

[99] See also Chapter 6 at 6.1.
[100] *Mental Capacity Act 2005 Draft Code of Practice* (CP 05/06), para 3.10. s 5.18, 7.17 and 7.12. And see the Mental Capacity Act 2005 (Independent Mental Capacity Advocates) (General) Regulations 2006, SI 2006/1832.
[101] Section 45 of the Mental Capacity Act 2005 establishes a new Court of Protection which can make declarations regarding the person's capacity and the lawfulness of an act done, or yet to be done, and can make decisions on the person's behalf or appoint deputies to do so.
[102] Mental Capacity Act 2005 Draft Code of Practice (CP 05/06), para 5.32.

Chapter 12

PREGNANCY AND CHILDBIRTH

Conception to birth

12.1 Medical care begins long before a baby is born. Research into the growth of the foetus in the womb has established the crucial importance of good ante-natal care, while the likes of the thalidomide tragedy have highlighted the vulnerability of the developing foetus. The drug thalidomide was prescribed to a number of pregnant women to help them sleep. It was described as non-toxic and safe for use by pregnant and nursing mothers, but it was not safe. Many children were born without limbs and with other awful disabilities. The drug company denied negligence. A settlement was eventually reached, but not all children received compensation because of dispute as to whether their disabilities did relate to their mothers taking the drug.[1] A further difficulty for the children was that, at the time of the birth of children disabled by the drug thalidomide, the English courts had not decided whether doctors or drug companies (or anyone at all) could be sued by children for injuries suffered by them before their birth.[2] Parliament enacted the Congenital Disabilities (Civil Liability) Act 1976 to govern claims by children born after 1976. The Act governs the child's rights only.

Can parents sue?

12.2 The parents of a child injured before birth may be able to recover for their loss at common law. The doctor caring for the mother in pregnancy owes her a duty in relation to her own health and in respect of the health of the developing foetus. The damage which she will suffer if she bears a disabled child, the emotional trauma[3] *and* the financial burden of the extra expense

---

[1]   For a thorough discussion of the legal implications of the thalidomide tragedy, see H Teff and C Munro, *Thalidomide: The Legal Aftermath* (1976) Saxon House. See also Chapter 10.

[2]   Sixteen years after the 1976 Act, the Court of Appeal held that a duty was owed at common law to a child born in 1967: *Burton v Islington Health Authority* [1992] 3 All ER 833; see A Whitfield, 'Common Law Duties to Unborn Children' (1993) 1 *Medical Law Review* 28.

[3]   *S v Distillers Co* [1970] 1 WLR 114.

such a child entails are readily foreseeable and recoverable. But will she be able (1) to prove negligence and (2) to prove that the child's disability resulted from that negligence?

Proving negligence is, as we have seen, no easy task in any malpractice claim.[4] A claim in relation to the birth of a disabled child has two special problems of its own. First, if the claim lies against the doctor, it has to be established that he should have been aware of the risk posed to the foetus by drugs he prescribed or treatment he gave. Second, where a mother becomes ill in pregnancy, or the pregnancy itself is complicated, the interests of mother and child may conflict. An ill or injured pregnant woman may need treatment known to carry risk to the child. For example, a woman injured in an accident may need surgery which can only be carried out under general anaesthetic. The anaesthetic may harm the baby. The doctor's duty to the mother, his patient, is this: he must consult and advise her, giving her sufficient information about her needs and the risk to her baby. If she chooses to reject a particular course of treatment for the sake of the baby he cannot impose that treatment. The doctor must in any case aim at a course of action which will benefit the mother with minimum risk to the child.

Even if it can be shown that the doctor has failed in his duty to the mother, that he was negligent, establishing that the infant's disability resulted from that negligence is likely to be even more difficult.[5] Despite immense advances in knowledge concerning the development of the embryo, pinpointing the exact cause of the birth defect remains extremely difficult. Success in a claim for negligence depends on proof that it is more likely than not that the relevant negligence caused the injury. All a claimant with a damaged child is likely to be able to prove is that a drug she took or treatment she received may have caused the defect in the baby. However, the cause may be inherited disease, a problem that the mother suffered in pregnancy, or some other, unknown cause. The parents may well fail to satisfy the burden of proof.

The Congenital Disabilities (Civil Liability) Act 1976

12.3   The Congenital Disabilities (Civil Liability) Act 1976, passed to give rights and a remedy to children born disabled as a result of human fault, is ambitious, complex and largely irrelevant. It is ambitious in that it sought to provide a scheme to protect children, not just against injury in the womb, but against any act at any stage of either parent's life which might ultimately result in a disability affecting a child. Its complexity we outline in succeeding sections. It is irrelevant because it fails to address the central problem in this type of claim: how do you prove that the disability resulted from an identified act of negligence? Just as his mother's claim is likely to founder for lack of proof of the cause of the disability, so is the child's. If Parliament intends and

---

4   See above at 7.17.
5   On the difficulties in proving causation of birth defects, see the Report of the Royal Commission on Civil Liability and Compensation for Personal Injury (1978) Cmnd 7054, paras 1441–1452 (the Pearson Report), and see SAM McLean, 'Ante-Natal Injuries' in SAM McLean (ed), *Legal Issues in Medicine* (1981) Gower.

desires to give children disabled by human act a remedy, it must consider whether retaining the normal burden of proof in actions by mother and child is practical.

The Act applies to all births after 1976 – but only after 1976[6] – and purports to provide a comprehensive code of liability for disabled children in respect of damage caused to them before birth. Under the 1976 Act, the child's mother[7] is generally exempt from any liability to her child. The father is offered no such immunity. The Act entirely replaces the common law and it would not be possible for a child unable to recover under the Act to argue that liability exists at common law. So, for example, a child seeking to sue his mother, exempt under the Act, must fail – however reckless her conduct in pregnancy and however clear it might be that she caused him to be born disabled.

The scheme of the Act is this. The child must be born alive.[8] He must establish that his disabilities resulted from an 'occurrence' which:

(1) affected the mother or father in her or his ability to have a normal healthy child (a 'pre-conception event');
(2) affected the mother during her pregnancy; or
(3) affected mother or child in the course of his birth.

At this first hurdle, proving the cause of the disability, many claims will fail. Where proof of cause is forthcoming the child faces further obstacles. It is not enough to show that the person responsible for the occurrence was negligent. The child must prove that the person responsible for the occurrence was liable to the affected parent. The child's rights are derivative only. The likelihood is that the occurrence at the time caused the parent no harm. Thalidomide's original effect was to sedate anxious mothers-to-be. Section 1(3) of the 1976 Act provides that it is no answer that the parent affected suffered no visible injury at the time of the occurrence providing there was '… a breach of legal duty which, accompanied by injury, would have given rise to the liability'. The breach of duty is the negligence of the defendant in relation to the affected parent's reproductive capacity. For instance, Sandra Roberts recovered £334,769 in compensation for catastrophic damage she suffered during her mother's pregnancy.[9] A blood transfusion administered to her mother seven years before her birth rendered her parents rhesus incompatible, creating danger for any child of theirs. The hospital knew of Mrs Roberts's condition. They failed to act to prevent or minimise the risk to Sandra. This was negligent care for the mother and thus created a right to compensation for mother and, via her, for Sandra. Other cases are less straightforward.

---

[6] But a child born before 1976 could sue at common law: see *Burton v Islington Health Authority* [1992] 3 All ER 833.

[7] Under section 2, she is liable for injuries caused through negligent driving of a vehicle on the road.

[8] Where the child is not born alive, the mother may be able to claim for the pain and suffering of miscarriage or stillbirth.

[9] (1986) Times, 26 July. The hospital conceded liability.

Drugs and damage to the foetus

12.4 Let us take first what appears to be a simple case, the sort of case the Congenital Disabilities (Civil Liability) Act 1976 was intended to remedy. A pregnant woman takes a drug prescribed for her by her GP that damages her baby so that he is born disabled.

The child can prove that his disability results from the effect of the drug on the foetus. He will have to show that the doctor was negligent towards his mother. It must be proven that (1) the doctor knew or ought to have known that the mother was pregnant, and therefore was in breach of duty to her in prescribing a drug which might damage her baby, and (2) that the doctor ought to have been aware of the risk posed by the drug. It will be no defence for the doctor to answer that, far from injuring the mother, the primary effect of the drug benefited her by ameliorating the symptoms of some common ailment, or by helping her to relax or sleep. The doctor's responsibility to the mother embraces taking care to avoid harm to the child she carries. Two difficulties arise. First, a general practitioner is judged by the standard of the reasonable, average GP. He is not expected to be an expert on embryology or drug-related damage. Proving that he ought to have been aware of the risk of the drug may be awkward. Second, the doctor may be aware of the risk to the baby, but argue that the risk to mother and child in not prescribing the drug is greater. Perhaps the mother might argue that given the uncertainty surrounding the effect of medicines on foetal development, only in exceptional cases should *any* drug be prescribed to a pregnant woman by her GP. Advice should be sought from the specialist obstetrician. However, is it reasonable to deny pregnant women basic medicine for minor ailments and is the cost to the NHS of multiple referrals to obstetricians justifiable? The focus ought to lie on ensuring that all doctors give women adequate advice about the potential risks of drugs in pregnancy.

Doctors are not the only potential source of compensation for a drug-damaged child. Could the child sue the drug company? Providing the relevant drug was marketed after 1 March 1988, the company's liability would be governed by the Consumer Protection Act 1987 (see above, Chapter 10). The crucial questions will be, is the drug defective and did it cause the relevant injury to the foetus? There can be little doubt that if the company can be shown to be aware of a risk of foetal damage, yet still marketed the drug with *no* warning of that risk, the drug is defective. The unborn baby is most vulnerable to harm in the earliest stages of pregnancy. The mother may not know that she is pregnant. Warnings about the use of many non-prescription medicines in pregnancy are routine, but futile if a woman is unaware of her pregnancy. Might a drug be defective simply because it poses a risk of foetal harm? Clearly that cannot generally be the case with many prescription drugs. The benefit such drugs offer when properly prescribed outweigh the remote chance of unwitting foetal harm. Over-the-counter, non-prescription medicines might be looked at differently. If a cough remedy poses a substantial risk of harm, greater than other similar products, for relatively small benefit, that product might be found to be defective. A further difficulty in establishing liability under the 1987 Act arises where the company can show that it was unaware of any risk of foetal harm. The 1987 Act allows the defendant to rely on the development risks defence, and it is at least arguable that such a defence would have enabled the manufacturers of thalidomide to escape liability.

Suing a doctor

12.5 We have already mentioned the potential liability of a mother's GP in prescribing drugs for her. She will meet other doctors during ante-natal visits. One special feature of suing a doctor under the Congenital Disabilities (Civil Liability) Act 1976 needs note: section 1(5) of the Act (the so-called 'doctors' defence') provides:

> The defendant is not answerable to the child, for anything he did or omitted to do when responsible in a professional capacity for treating or advising the parent, if he took reasonable care having due regard to the then received professional opinion applicable to the particular class of case; but this does not mean that he is answerable only because he departed from received opinion.

The aims of those who sought the inclusion of those words 'then received professional opinion' were probably twofold. First, they quite reasonably wanted it made clear that hindsight as to the effect of a drug or course of treatment should not prejudice a doctor's case. As the defendant's standard of care will always be tested by what was expected of the competent practitioner at the time of the alleged breach of duty, that first objective was met at common law. Second, perhaps doctors sought to ensure courts would not seek to evaluate 'received professional opinion'. In 1976, it is likely that no court would have done so. However, the judgment of the House of Lords in *Bolitho v City & Hackney Health Authority*[10] now requires that responsible professional opinion be demonstrably 'logical and defensible'. We see no reason why section 1(5) of the 1976 Act should not be susceptible to similar judicial scrutiny.

Ante-natal screening[11]

12.6 Ante-natal screening to diagnose foetal abnormalities has become routine. Just some of the more common procedures are looked at here.[12] In amniocentesis a needle is inserted, through the mother's abdomen and the uterine wall, into the sac surrounding the foetus. A small amount of the amniotic fluid surrounding the baby is removed. Tests on the fluid will indicate whether a number of abnormalities are present, including spina bifida and Down's syndrome. Cultures from the fluid may be grown which will disclose the child's sex. A mother who underwent amniocentesis and was told

---

[10]   [1997] 4 All ER 771.

[11]   For a more comprehensive account of ante-natal screening and genetic counselling, see JK Mason and GT Laurie, *Mason and McCall Smith's Law and Medical Ethics* (7th edn, 2006) OUP, Chapter 7.

[12]   See Royal College of Obstetricians and Gynaecologists, *Amniocentesis and Chorionic Villus Sampling* (2005).

that she carried a spina bifida or Down's syndrome baby could then opt for an abortion. A mother who knew she was a carrier of haemophilia and learned that she carried a male child might similarly seek a termination. There are medical problems with amniocentesis. It cannot be performed before the 14th week of pregnancy and is often delayed until the 16th week. It carries about a 1 per cent risk of causing a miscarriage. It sometimes causes the mother acute discomfort. It is expensive, reserved largely for mothers at special risk of producing a disabled infant, in particular those over 35 or where blood tests suggest some abnormality in the baby. Chorionic villus testing, whereby early placental cells are removed and analysed, is possible earlier in pregnancy, at about ten to twelve weeks. But there is a slightly greater risk of miscarriage and chorionic villus testing does not detect neural tube defects (such as spina bifida). Increasingly doctors are seeking to limit the number of women who need to undergo invasive tests of this sort by using simple blood tests to identify high-risk pregnancies. A blood test to discover raised alpha-protein levels, an indication of possible spina bifida, has been available for several years. A blood test identifying increased risk of Down's syndrome is available. Only women whose blood tests indicate possible foetal abnormalities will then have to undergo the invasive procedures of amniocentesis or chorionic villus testing. Finally, ultrasound scans are now routinely used to check on the growth and development of the foetus and will in certain cases reveal the presence of such deformities as spina bifida without the need to submit the pregnant woman to risky or invasive tests.[13]

What are the legal implications of amniocentesis and chorionic villus testing? First, they involve an invasion of the mother's body. Her consent is essential and should be obtained expressly and in writing. Second, the risk that a healthy baby may be lost should be communicated to the parents. The duty of the obstetrician caring for the mother must embrace offering her the information on which to make such a crucial decision. Tests should be carried out and analysed with due care. Negligence in offering or carrying out ante-natal screening may result in claims by both mother and child. They will contend that had adequate care been provided for the mother in pregnancy, she would have elected to terminate the pregnancy. The mother would have avoided the burden of a disabled child.[14] The child would have avoided the harm of its disabled existence. In neither case is the essence of the claim a claim for wrongful disability. Unlike the examples discussed earlier in this chapter, the defendants' negligence is not responsible for causing disability to a foetus normal at conception. The defendants' negligence is responsible for the birth of a child who, but for his negligence, would not have been born. The mother seeks compensation for a wrongful birth, a birth which – if properly advised –

---

[13] For example, in *P v Leeds Teaching Hospital NHS Trust* [2004] EWHC 1392, a routine scan revealed a foetal bladder anomaly. P was referred for a specialist scan and was told that the foetus had a minor, correctable condition. On birth, P's son had a major bladder and bowel deformity. P was awarded damages due to the high standard owed by the specialist on the basis that P would, on the balance of probabilities, have opted for a termination has she known the real extent of her son's condition.

[14] See, for example, *Farraj v King's Healthcare NHS Trust* [2006] EWHC 1228, where a private laboratory responsible for culturing a chorionic villus sample and the trust responsible for carrying out DNA testing were held liable when a hereditary condition was missed.

she would have chosen to avoid. The child sues in respect of wrongful life, a life (its counsel argues) it would have chosen not to endure.

Wrongful life

12.7 A classic claim for wrongful life is recounted in *McKay v Essex AHA*.[15] The plaintiffs in *McKay* were a little girl, born disabled as a result of the effect of rubella suffered by her mother early in pregnancy, and her mother. When Mrs McKay suspected that she had contracted rubella in the early weeks of her pregnancy, her doctor arranged for blood tests to establish whether she had been infected. As a result of negligence by either her doctor or by laboratory staff, Mrs McKay was wrongly informed that she had not been infected by rubella. She continued with the pregnancy. Had she known the truth she would, as her doctor was well aware, have requested an abortion under the Abortion Act 1967. The little girl was born in 1975, before the Congenital Disabilities (Civil Liability) Act 1976 was passed. The Court of Appeal had to decide the position at common law. They said that no action lay where the essence of the child's claim was that, but for the negligence of the defendant, she would never have been born at all. The child's claim was thrown out, although her mother's claim was allowed to proceed. The case is not solely of historical interest. The judges further said that under the 1976 Act no child born after its passing could pursue such a claim.

In the view of the Court of Appeal, the 1976 Act[16] can never give rise to a claim for 'wrongful life'. Ackner LJ, considering section 1(2)(b) of the Act, said that the relevant 'occurrence' has to be one that affected the mother in pregnancy 'so that the child *is born* with disabilities which would not otherwise have been present'. Clearly under the 1976 Act, then, where the breach of duty consists of carelessness in the conduct of the pregnancy or the birth, the claim must relate to disabilities inflicted as a result of the breach of duty by the defendants. Where the essence of the claim is that the child should never have been born at all, it lies outside the scope of section 1(2)(b). A claim by the child that amniocentesis should have been performed, or that subsequent tests were negligently conducted so that the pregnancy continued and he was born disabled, will fail.

The effect of the judgment in *McKay* is that in England a child injured before birth may claim only compensation for *wrongful disability*, that is against a defendant whose conduct actually caused his disability. He cannot sue for *wrongful life*. The Court of Appeal gave three main reasons for ruling out such claims:

---

[15]   [1982] 2 All ER 771.
[16]   It has been argued that the 1976 Act does not apply to a 'wrongful life' claim. The Act provides a scheme to compensate for disability inflicted by human error, not to a claim for allowing a disabled foetus to be born at all. See J Fortin, 'Is the "Wrongful Life" Action Really Dead?' [1987] *Journal of Social Welfare Law* 306.

(1)   It was not possible to arrive at a proper measure of damages representing the difference between the child's disabled existence and non-existence.[17]

(2)   The law should not impose a duty on doctors to abort, to terminate life *in utero*.[18]

(3)   To impose any duty to abort would be to violate the sanctity of life and to devalue the life of handicapped persons.[19]

The second and third reasons are difficult to sustain in the light of the fact that the court did allow Mrs McKay to pursue her *wrongful birth* action.

Wrongful birth

12.8 Until the controversial decision of the House of Lords in *McFarlane v Tayside Health Board*,[20] it appeared that in English law parents of a child born in circumstances akin to those in *McKay* could (like Mrs McKay) sue for the wrongful birth of a disabled child.[21] The Law Lords in *McFarlane* rejected a claim for wrongful conception, in so far as that claim sought damages for the cost of bringing up an unplanned and healthy child. Negligent advice following the husband's vasectomy resulted in the unwanted and unexpected conception of the couple's fifth child. As we saw in Chapter 11, Mrs McFarlane was awarded compensation for her pain and suffering in pregnancy and immediately consequential financial losses. The more substantive part of the claim for damages, the cost of rearing her child, was ruled inadmissible as irrecoverable economic loss. The reasons advanced by their Lordships for their ruling were diverse. They sought to avoid categorising the question as one of policy but, as we argue in Chapter 11, it is difficult to make any sense of their decision except in terms of judicial repugnance against compensating parents for the birth of a healthy infant. Will *McFarlane* affect a claim by parents of a disabled child who can establish that, had the child's disability been diagnosed *in utero*, the mother would have terminated the pregnancy? The Law Lords in *McFarlane* expressly restrict their decision to claims concerning normal, healthy infants. Yet consider the approval Lord Steyn bestows on the following statement from an Australian textbook:

> … it might seem inconsistent to allow a claim by the parents, while that of the child, whether *healthy or disabled*, is rejected [*emphasis added*]. Surely the parents' claim is equally repugnant to ideas of the sanctity and value of human life and rests, like that of the child, on a comparison between a situation where a human being exists and one where it does not.[22]

---

[17]   [1982] 2 All ER 771 at 782, 787 and 790. See the American judgments in I Kennedy and A Grubb, *Medical Law: Text and Materials* (2000) Butterworths, pp 1537–1547.

[18]   [1982] 2 All ER 771 at 787.

[19]   [1982] 2 All ER 771 at 781.

[20]   [1999] 4 All ER 961. See also *Greenfield v Irwin (a firm)* [2001] 1 WLR 1279 (where loss of earnings in caring for an unwanted baby were not recoverable; *McFarlane* applied).

[21]   See, for example, *Salih v Enfield Health Authority* [1991] 3 All ER 400 (where only the amount of compensation was disputed).

[22]   F Trindade and P Cane, *The Law of Torts in Australia* (2nd edn, 1993) OUP, p 434.

Lord Steyn comments '... the reasoning is sound. Coherence and rationality demand that the claim by the parents should also be rejected'.[23]

So, can a distinction between a claim for wrongful birth of a healthy child and wrongful birth of a disabled child be sustained? The Court of Appeal endorsed such a distinction in *Parkinson v St James and Seacroft NHS Hospital Trust*,[24] ruling that where a disabled child is born as a consequence of clinical negligence his parents may recover the additional costs occasioned by his disability. The relevant negligence in *Parkinson* ensued from a bungled operation to sterilise the mother. The case for compensation covering the costs resulting from a child's disability when the alleged 'wrong' is a failure to prevent the birth of a disabled infant looks stronger. Doctors expressly advising potential parents about the risks of conception, and screening women in pregnancy, undertake that responsibility expressly to avoid the birth of a disabled child. The 'harm' to the parents of the birth of a child with spina bifida, or damaged by rubella,[25] is just what the doctors seek to prevent. The distress of the parents when their expectations of a healthy child are confounded, combined with the financial cost of raising a disabled child, are directly related to the relevant negligence. The parents' damages however will be limited to the additional costs of raising a child with his particular disability. Before *McFarlane*, English courts awarded such parents the whole cost of childrearing.[26] Compensation in such cases of wrongful birth will now relate only to the additional cost of caring for the disabled child.[27] Compensation may still be considerable. It can and should include cost of care beyond the child's minority.[28] 'Good' parents will seek to provide for their disabled children into adulthood.

The tangled web of case law following *McFarlane* may be morally disturbing to some people. Refusing to compensate parents for the unplanned birth of a healthy child, Lord Millett said:

> There is something distasteful, if not morally offensive, in treating the birth of a normal healthy child as a matter of compensation.[29]

He regarded childbirth as akin to a balance sheet. The joys of parenthood offset financial costs. Mutual support of parent and child, the support perhaps of the parent in old age offset the burdens of parenting. Distinguishing the healthy and disabled child might seem to suggest the latter is a 'curse' not a 'blessing'. In *Parkinson*, Hale LJ took a pragmatic approach. She said of the disabled child that:

---

23 [1999] 4 All ER 961 at 978.
24 [2001] Lloyd's Rep Med 309, CA.
25 As in *Hardman v Amin* [2000] Lloyd's Rep Med 498.
26 *Salih v Enfield Health Authority* [1991] 3 All ER 400 (though note that, if the parents would in any case have gone on to have a healthy child, the damage would be restricted to the costs incurred by the child's disability).
27 *Rand v East Dorset HA* [2000] Lloyd's Rep Med 181; and see *Anderson v Forth Valley Health Board* (1997) 44 BMLR 108 (Scotland).
28 *Nunnerley v Warrington Health Authority* [2000] Lloyd's Rep Med 170; and see R Glancy, 'Damages for Wrongful Birth: Where Do They End?' (2006) 3 *Journal of Personal Injury Law* 271–279.
29 [1999] 4 All ER 961 at 1003, HL.

This analysis treats a disabled child as having exactly the same worth as a non-disabled child. It affords him to same dignity and status. It simply acknowledges that he costs more.[30]

If cost is key, then what of the wrongful birth of a healthy baby to a disabled parent? In Chapter 11 we examined the case of *Rees v Darlington Memorial Hospital NHS Trust*,[31] in which the Court of Appeal allowed the claim of a visually-impaired woman whose negligent sterilisation led to the birth of a healthy child. *McFarlane*, it was held, applied only to healthy parents. The case proceeded to the House of Lords,[32] where the seven Law Lords unanimously reaffirmed *McFarlane*. By a 4:3 majority, they overturned the decision of the Court of Appeal and held that Mrs Rees could not recover costs relating to the upbringing and maintenance of her healthy child. However, by virtue of a 'gloss' on the *McFarlane* ruling, she was able to recover £15,000 in general damages. Hale LJ's pragmatic approach, which she first set down in *Parkinson* and relied on in the Court of Appeal decision in *Rees*, was rejected by the House of Lords on the basis that the costs and benefits are unquantifiable and therefore impossible to balance. No reasonable alternative was proposed beyond the explanation that general damages should reflect the fact that negligence was a legal wrong which caused the parents to suffer a loss of autonomy. It remains to be seen whether the *Rees* ruling will be limited to cases involving wrongful birth to disabled parents, or if it will be extended to other wrongful birth cases. What is clear is that the law distinguishes between a claim for wrongful birth of a healthy child and wrongful birth of a disabled child. Compensation will only be awarded to the latter. Elevated costs of rearing a healthy child as a result of parental disability are not recoverable. 'General damages' are all such parents can hope for.

Children damaged by pre-conception events

12.9 The Congenital Disabilities (Civil Liability) Act 1976 purports to protect children against pre-conception injury,[33] not just injury *in utero*. This could happen where the father or mother is affected by radiation or drugs so that the sperm or egg carries a serious defect. Or the child may be damaged if doctors mismanage a previous pregnancy, for example if they fail to take note of and treat Rhesus incompatibility in the mother and the second child is born

---

[30] *Parkinson v St James and Seacroft NHS Hospital Trust* [2001] Lloyd's Rep Med 309 at 325, CA. It should be noted that Hale LJ seems less than convinced of Lord Millett's general reasoning that the joys of a healthy child outweigh the costs. See also *Hardman v Amin* [2000] Lloyd's Rep Med 498. *Mason and McCall Smith's Law and Medical Ethics* argues at p 179 that Lady Hale's opinion, which is based on bodily integrity, can be applied equally to the disabled and healthy child: 'The feeling remains that one or other decision [*McFarlane* or *Parkinson*] must be wrong.'

[31] [2002] 2 All ER 177.

[32] [2003] UKHL 52; discussed fully at 11.7.

[33] Including injury caused by infertility treatment: see section 1A of the Congenital Diasbilities (Civil Liability) Act 1976 as amended by section 44(1) of the Human Fertilisation and Emrbyology Act 1990.

brain-damaged.[34] The 1976 Act intended to cover such cases, providing as it does that the relevant occurrence may be one which affected either parent in his or her ability to have a healthy child. But it may be argued that, if the claim is that the child was born disabled because one of his parents is incapable of creating a healthy infant, his claim is essentially that he should never have been born at all – and that it is an action for 'wrongful life' and is barred under the 1976 Act. We think this is a mistaken view of the Act. The child's claim in the case of a pre-conception occurrence rests on the hypothesis that *but for* that occurrence he would have been born normal and healthy, and that his actionable injury is therefore the difference between the life he might have had and the life he must now perforce endure. In *McKay*,[35] the child sought to maintain that her actionable injury was life itself, and as such her claim was not and would not be sustainable. What *McKay* does clarify in cases of *pre-conception* injury is that, when not responsible for that original injury, a doctor cannot be liable under the 1976 Act if he fails to diagnose the child's disabilities in pregnancy and fails to perform an abortion in such circumstances.

What if a parent realises the risk?

12.10 Alas, further problems confront the child whose claim is based on pre-conception injury. Section 1(4) of the Congenital Disabilities (Civil Liability) Act 1976 provides that in such cases if the affected parent is aware of the risk of the child being born disabled the defendant is not liable to that child. Responsibility for knowingly running the risk of creating a disabled baby rests with the parents, and whatever the degree of fault, the original creator of the risk is relieved of liability to the child. There is one exception to this rule. Where the child sues his father, the fact that the father is aware of the risk of begetting an abnormal child will not defeat the child's claim as long as his mother is ignorant of the danger. This raises a nice question. A young man suffers contamination by toxic chemicals at work through the negligence of his employers. He is warned that his reproductive capacity has been damaged, that he is likely to beget abnormal offspring and is advised never to have children. He ignores the warning, marries and tells his wife nothing. A disabled child is born. The child cannot sue his father's original employers. Even if they were in breach of duty to his father, 'the affected parent', the father's knowledge of the risk is a defence. Can the child sue his father? The answer has to be no. This child, like the plaintiff in *McKay*,[36] can only claim against his father that he should never have been born at all. The father's condition at the time of the relevant 'negligence', begetting the child, was such that he could not beget a normal child. The father's 'negligence' was in creating the child, not in inflicting a disability which but for some act or

---

[34] See American cases *Yeager v Bloomington Obstetrics and Gynaecology, Inc* 585 NW2d 696 (Ind, 1992) and *Lazenvnick v General Hospital of Munro City Inc* F Supp 146 (Md, 1980).

[35] *McKay v Essex Area Health Authority* [1982] 2 All ER 771.

[36] *McKay v Essex Area Health Authority* [1982] 2 All ER 771.

omission on his part would not have been present. We will consider a little later if fathers can ever be liable for causing pre-natal injury to their own children.

Must a mother consider abortion?

12.11 Section 1(7) of the Congenital Disabilities (Civil Liability) Act 1976 offers a partial defence, whereby if the affected parent shared responsibility for the child being born disabled, the child's damages may be reduced. For example, the child's disabilities may be diagnosed when the mother has an ultrasound scan or amniocentesis before his birth. Once the mother knows of the potential damage to her child, she will be entitled under the Abortion Act 1967 to an abortion on the grounds that there is substantial risk that the child if born would be seriously handicapped. Assuming that it is the mother who is the affected parent, does she share responsibility for the child being born disabled if she refuses an abortion? In *McKay v Essex Area Health Authority*, refusing to allow the child's claim that she should have been aborted, Ackner LJ said that he could not accept:

> ... that the common law duty of care to a person can involve, without specific legislation to achieve this end, the legal obligation to that person, whether or not *in utero*, to terminate his existence. Such a proposition runs wholly contrary to the concept of the sanctity of human life.[37]

Applying Ackner LJ's proposition to a submission that a mother should have accepted abortion advanced by the defendant responsible for inflicting the disabilities suffered by the child, such a submission must fail. To impose an *obligation* on a mother to undergo an abortion is more repugnant to the concept of the sanctity of human life than to impose an obligation to abort on a doctor.

In *Emeh v Kensington, Chelsea and Fulham Area Health Authority*,[38] the plaintiff brought a wrongful conception claim, long before *McFarlane*.[39] An operation to sterilise her was carried out negligently by the first defendant and she became pregnant again. She was offered, but refused, an abortion. The trial judge held that once the plaintiff elected to continue the pregnancy, the pregnancy ceased to be unwanted and that the birth of the child was the result of her own actions and not a consequence of the defendant's negligence. The plaintiff's refusal to consider an abortion was so unreasonable as to eclipse the defendant's wrongdoing. The Court of Appeal overruled him.[40] Mrs Emeh did not become aware of her pregnancy until it was about 17 to 18 weeks advanced. Refusing an abortion at that stage in pregnancy could not be considered unreasonable. Whether the court would have taken a different view had the pregnancy been less advanced remains open to question. Waller LJ laid great stress on the increased risk, discomfort and hospitalisation

---

[37] [1982] 2 All ER 771 at 787.

[38] (1983) Times, 3 January.

[39] *McFarlane v Tayside Health Board* [1999] 4 All ER 961, HL.

[40] [1984] 3 All ER 1044.

entailed in abortion at twelve weeks plus.[41] Slade LJ was emphatic that abortion should generally never be forced upon a woman. He said:

> Save in the most exceptional circumstances, I cannot think it right that the court should ever declare it unreasonable for a woman to decline to have an abortion in a case where there is no evidence that there were any medical or psychiatric grounds for terminating the particular pregnancy.[42]

Slade LJ's condemnation of judicially-enforced abortion is endorsed in *McFarlane* by Lords Slynn,[43] Steyn[44] and Millett. Lord Millett declares[45] that it is morally repugnant to suggest that it is unreasonable not to have an abortion.

Some slight doubt, however, lurks in the kind of cases we are currently considering. If a foetal abnormality is diagnosed in pregnancy, and caused by the defendants' prior negligence, does this constitute *medical* grounds to terminate the pregnancy, and constitute the sort of exceptional circumstances Slade LJ refers to in *Emeh*? Certainly the foetal injury would entitle the mother to choose to abort the child. We cannot see that it could require her to do so or risk a reduction to her child's compensation for the disability he suffers. Section 1(7) of the Congenital Disabilities (Civil Liability) Act 1976 envisages the sort of case where a pregnant woman ignores medical advice and exacerbates her child's disability by drinking, smoking or failing to take precautions advised by her doctors. The mother actively contributes to the disability. That is very different from refusing abortion. Assume a court was prepared to entertain this defence, how will they assess the mother's decision? Is it some totally objective test? Or must the woman's own moral views and religious affiliation be considered? Given that the Court of Appeal has finally confirmed that no women can be forced to undergo a Caesarean section to protect the life or health of the foetus, to 'force' a woman to 'kill' her foetus would be illogical.[46] Maternal autonomy demands that pregnant women's choices in this delicate arena of moral controversy should be respected.

Maternal immunity: discriminating against fathers?[47]

12.12 We noted earlier that, save in respect of road accidents on public roads, mothers remain immune from claims under the Congenital Disabilities (Civil Liability) Act 1976. Fathers enjoy no such formal immunity. A pregnant woman who drinks so heavily that her child is born with foetal alcohol syndrome or whose drug habit is such that her baby is born addicted to crack cannot be sued by her child. The Law Commission,[48] recommending that

---

[41] [1984] 3 All ER 1044 at 1048.
[42] [1984] 3 All ER 1044 at 1053.
[43] [1999] 4 All ER 961 at 970, HL.
[44] [1999] 4 All ER 961 at 976, HL.
[45] [1999] 4 All ER 961 at 1004, HL.
[46] *St George's Healthcare NHS Trust v S* [1998] 3 All ER 673, CA.
[47] See generally, R Scott, Rights, *Duties and the Body: Law and Ethics of Maternal-Fetal Conflict* (2002) Hart Publishing; E Jackson, *Regulating Reproduction: Law Technology and Autonomy* (2001) Hart Publishing, pp 140–160.
[48] Discussed fully in P Pace, 'Civil Liability for Pre-Natal Injuries' (1977) 40 *Modern Law Review* 193.

mothers be exempted from claims for pre-natal injury, offered a number of reasons for maternal privilege. It considered that a claim against the mother would have little practical utility. She, unlike the father, was unlikely to have funds to meet an award of damages. Suing 'mum' would disturb the parental bond and in practice would only happen where a father used his child's claim as a weapon in parental dispute. The first of these two reasons looks rather outdated now, when many more women have independent means. The second applies equally to fathers. Other reasons remain more compelling.[49]

How could an equitable standard of reasonable pregnancy conduct be set? Women are beset by contradictory advice about what they should and should not eat, drink or do when pregnant. Though, objectively, one might agree that the reasonable mother-to-be should give up smoking, achieving that standard is more difficult for some than others. The harassed mother of four struggling alone in poverty may know that she ought to quit smoking but struggles to do so. Most importantly, potential liability for foetal injury would in practice constitute a significant invasion of pregnant women's liberty and privacy. The threat of possible redress by the child could be used by partners and doctors to impose their judgment of foetal welfare. Given evidence of the foetus's vulnerability in early pregnancy – when a woman may not know she is pregnant – the law, as Sheila McLean has said, would in effect demand that '... fertile, sexually active women of childbearing age should act at all times as if they were pregnant'.[50] Finally, pragmatically, we should remind ourselves that a claim under the 1976 Act can only arise if a child is born alive. Maternal liability under the 1976 Act could simply provide an incentive to abort. A woman fearing, perhaps for little reason, that she has harmed her child could ensure that he was never born at all.

If there remains a case for maternal immunity, consideration must at least be given to paternal immunity. In 1976, the kind of harms men might do their unborn children were perceived as crude and obvious wrongdoing. A father who beats his partner so badly that he injures both her and the child in the womb elicits little sympathy. What science can now tell us about how lifestyle from an early age may affect human gametes is cause for concern. Studies have shown that heavy smoking in teenage years could increase the risk of a man's child born years later succumbing to certain cancers. Whether fathers ought to be constrained by law in their pre-conception conduct must be questionable. Paternal liability unearths a further quirk of the Congenital Disabilities (Civil Liability) Act 1976. Even absent maternal immunity, in what sort of circumstances could either parent be liable for pre-conception injury? Liability under the 1976 Act is derivative only. The defendant must be liable in tort to the affected parent. Consider this example. A man is a heavy drug user in his youth in an era when such drug use is known to damage sperm. Later he begets a child born disabled because of his damaged gametes. To be liable to the child, he must be liable to her mother. To be liable to the mother, the courts would have to find that men have a duty of care to their future partners to ensure that they protect those partners' reproductive health. Imagine the

[49] See M Brazier, 'Parental Responsibilities, Foetal Welfare and Children's Health' in C Bridge (ed), *Family Law: Towards the Millennium* (1997) Butterworths, p 263.
[50] See SAM McLean, *Old Law, New Medicine* (1999) Pandora Press, p 66.

outcry if the law declared that women must order their lives to safeguard their husbands' right to have healthy children.

Criminal liability[51]

12.13 Before concluding that pregnancy conduct can never be subjected to legal redress, the decision of the House of Lords in *Attorney General's Reference (No 3 of 1994)*[52] must be considered. A father attacked his pregnant girlfriend and injured his child in the womb. The baby was born alive but subsequently died of her pre-natal injuries. The father was charged with his daughter's murder. Following his acquittal, the Attorney-General referred the case to the Court of Appeal to determine whether murder or manslaughter can be committed where a foetus is injured *in utero* but is subsequently born alive only to die later of pre-natal injuries. In a convoluted judgment, the Court of Appeal answered yes to both questions.[53] The House of Lords partially upheld their judgment on very different grounds. The Law Lords endorsed earlier judgments[54] that a charge of murder or manslaughter can be sustained where a foetus injured *in utero* is born alive and later dies as a consequence of those injuries. On the facts of this case, their Lordships held that a charge of murder could not be sustained, but that a charge of manslaughter could. Murder could not be committed in this case because there was no express design to harm the foetus 'or the human person which it would become'.[55] However, manslaughter could be established in this instance. In his assault on the mother, the father committed an unlawful and dangerous act likely to cause harm to the child, and the event resulting in her death. Such conduct constituted unlawful act type manslaughter. The implications of *Attorney-General's Reference (No 3 of 1994)* are that:

(1) a person whose unlawful and dangerous conduct results in foetal injury followed by the birth of a child 'doomed to die' commits manslaughter;

(2) gross and culpable negligence in relation to the foetus may similarly, where the child is born alive and subsequently dies, constitute manslaughter; and

(3) a deliberate attempt to harm or kill the foetus directly could in such cases amount to murder.

Finally, Lord Mustill[56] suggests any violence against the foetus resulting in harm short of death may engage criminal responsibility.

At no point do any of the Law Lords consider maternal criminal responsibility. Their reasoning leaves pregnant women open to such liability in a range of

51 See E Cave, *The Mother of All Crimes* (2004) Ashgate.
52 [1997] 3 All ER 936. See S Fovargue and J Miola, 'Policing Pregnancy: Implications of the Attorney-General's Reference (No 3 of 1994)' (1998) 6 *Medical Law Review* 265 and Cave, *The Mother of All Crimes*.
53 [1996] 2 All ER 10, CA, discussed in M Seneviratne, 'Pre-Natal Injury and Transferred Malice: The Invented Other' (1996) 59 *Modern Law Review* 884.
54 *R v West* (1848) 175 ER 329; *R v Senior* (1832) 168 ER 1298.
55 [1997] 3 All ER 936 at 949, per Lord Mustill.
56 [1997] 3 All ER 936 at 942.

scenarios. The pregnant woman who continues to abuse illegal drugs so that her child is born damaged by those substances and dies of their effect could be said to commit unlawful act type manslaughter. The woman whose heavy abuse of alcohol results in a child so dreadfully harmed by foetal alcohol syndrome that he lives only a short while, could be seen as criminally negligent. If Lord Mustill's statement about harm short of death is right, even if her child does not die the mother could be charged with causing him grievous bodily harm.

The sorts of illegal or reckless behaviour which might engage criminal liability might seem to create a case for endorsing criminal responsibility for egregiously bad behaviour in pregnancy. The moral obligation to have due regard for the welfare of a child whom a mother elects to bring to term is incontrovertible. Whether the invocation of the criminal law would in practice enhance foetal welfare or simply offer means of coercing pregnant women and stigmatising unfortunate mothers is to be doubted.[57]

Pre-pregnancy advice and genetic counselling

12.14 Women planning a child often seek advice before allowing themselves to conceive. For a healthy woman, this may be simply a check that she is immune from rubella. Another may seek reassurance that pregnancy will not damage her own health, for example, if she has a history of cardiac disease. Couples in whose family genetic disease is prevalent, or couples who already have a child with a genetic disease, may need specialised genetic counselling.

In all these cases, those counselling the woman undertake a duty to her in relation not only to her own health and welfare, but also in relation to the birth of a healthy child. If she is given the green light to go ahead with a pregnancy and suffers at the end of it the trauma and additional financial burden of a damaged child, she may have a claim in negligence.[58] She and the child's father will be able to claim the additional cost to them of caring for a disabled child. Proving negligence may not be easy. Not only must she show that the doctor failed to take into account factors relating to her medical history or genetic background, or failed to conduct tests that would have alerted him to the danger, she must show that a reasonably competent doctor would have discovered the risk. If a woman requests a test for immunity from rubella, is brushed aside and subsequently contracts the disease in pregnancy, her claim should succeed. The enormous publicity given to the Department of Health campaign to eradicate the risk to the unborn child posed by rubella is such that any GP must be aware of and guard against the risk. If the sister of a haemophiliac consults her doctor and explains her brother's condition, and the doctor fails to refer her for counselling with the result that she bears a

---

[57] See Fovargue and Miola (1998) 6 *Medical Law Review* 265; M Brazier 'Parental Responsibilities, Foetal Welfare and Children's Health'; Cave, *The Mother of All Crimes*; M Brazier 'Liberty Responsibility and Maternity' (1999) 52 *Current Legal Problems* 359.

[58] See *Parkinson v St James and Seacroft University Hospital NHS Trust* [2001] EWCA Civ 530, CA; *Hardman v Amin* [2000] Lloyd's Rep Med 458; *Enright v Blackpool Victoria Hospital NHS Trust* [2003] EWHC 100 (QB); *Farraj v King's Healthcare NHS Trust* [2006] EWHC 1228.

haemophiliac son, she too should succeed.[59] Beyond these obvious examples of want of competence the medical profession is much divided on the value of pre-conception advice. Some doctors run special clinics and advise special diets and total abstinence from alcohol when attempting to conceive. Significant evidence of the relationship of such regimes to the reduction of risk to the child, and their acceptance by the profession at large, will be needed before a claim based on the lack of such detailed guidance could succeed. Finally, the claimant must also establish that had she received proper advice she would not have allowed herself to become pregnant when she did.

Has the disabled child a remedy? We must distinguish three types of cases where negligent pre-pregnancy advice results in the birth of a disabled child. In the first case, the relevant negligence may be that the woman was encouraged to become pregnant when, had proper care been taken, she could have been advised never to contemplate pregnancy because of the risk to *any* child she might bear. The child's action in such a case will fail because the essence of his claim is that he should never have been born at all. It is a claim for 'wrongful life'.

In the second instance, the negligence may have been in failing to counsel the mother properly on precautions to take, or the timing of pregnancy. Such a claim raises an awkward problem. For example, a woman is not tested for immunity to rubella or the test is negligently conducted. She is wrongly told that she has immunity. She becomes pregnant, contracts the disease and the child is born disabled. Had she been properly advised, she would have been vaccinated against the disease and advised in the strongest of terms to delay pregnancy for three months after the vaccination. The actual child born would never have been born. The particular set of genes in the egg and sperm that went to create him would never have met. A literal interpretation of *McKay*[60] would deny the child a remedy on the ground that that unique individual would never have been born had his mother had proper advice. It would seem a harsh result, but the conclusion that it follows from the interpretation of the Congenital Disabilities (Civil Liability) Act 1976 by the Court of Appeal in *McKay* is difficult to resist. Examples of this sort could be multiplied endlessly. A parent might be undergoing treatment for venereal disease. He or she is carelessly advised that pregnancy is now safe. It is not. Treatment was not complete. The particular child born disabled would not have been born, had proper advice been given. A woman knows a little of a family history of genetic disease affecting the males in her family. She seeks counselling. She should have been advised of the risks to male children and been offered pre-implantation genetic diagnosis (PGD) so that she could if she wished have ensured she did not give birth to a male child. A disabled male child cannot sue under the 1976 Act, for had PGD or amniocentesis been offered and accepted, that boy would not exist.

Finally, there is one limited class of case where the child's action based on allegedly careless pre-pregnancy advice may succeed. That is where adequate counselling advice would have enabled that very child to be born hale and

[59] See *Anderson v Forth Valley Health Board* (1998) 44 BMLR 108.
[60] *McKay v Essex AHA* [1982] 2 All ER 771.

hearty. Realistic examples are difficult to think of. Perhaps one example concerns the relationship between maternal diet before conception and spina bifida. There is evidence that folic acid supplements may reduce the likelihood of spina bifida. The child could contend that, had his mother been advised to follow that regime, his disability would not have developed. He would have been born, but not born disabled. Such a child claims for his disabilities, not wrongful life. He overcomes the first problem in his claim against medical staff, but will he be able to prove that the treatment, if given, would have prevented his disability?

Genetic counselling and confidentiality[61]

12.15 The genetic counsellor's legal problems are not confined to his obligations to the woman seeking his advice. For example, if he discovers that she is, or is likely to be, the carrier of a sex-linked disease, he will be aware that her sisters are also at risk as carriers (and so to a lesser degree are other female relatives). Obviously he will ask her permission to inform her sister or her sister's doctor. What if the woman refuses permission? She will argue that the counsellor owes her an obligation of confidence. If the sister later bears a damaged child, the consequences to her are dreadful and she might sue the counsellor. The sister could contend that the risk to her was readily foreseeable and the counsellor had a duty to warn her. We would suggest that in such circumstances the counsellor exceptionally may be justified in breaking his obligation of confidence. The Court of Appeal[62] has held that information obtained in a confidential relationship may be disclosed if disclosure is in the public interest. Is the interest in preventing the birth of damaged children sufficient to merit disclosure? Does it depend on the degree of disability afflicting the child?[63]

Childbirth: how much choice?

12.16 Our great-grandmothers gave thanks if they survived the perils of childbirth. Today medical technology offers a whole range of sophisticated devices to monitor mother and baby and ensure safe delivery. Increasingly, many women reject the panoply of machinery found in many hospital labour wards. Accepting the necessity of 'high-tech' birth for a minority of difficult cases, the natural childbirth movement has campaigned for the medical profession to be more willing to let nature take its course. For a number of women the ideal is delivery at home in the comfort of familiar surroundings.

---

[61] Legal questions relating to genetics are dealt with fully in *Mason and McCall Smith's Law and Medical Ethics*, Chapter 7.

[62] *W v Egdell* [1990] 1 All ER 835; *Lion Laboratories Ltd v Evans* [1984] 2 All ER 417. Consider also the implications of the Data Protection Act 1998 and Article 8 of the European Convention on Human Rights.

[63] The Human Genetics Commission, *Inside Information* (2002), para 19 states: 'Disclosure of sensitive personal genetic information without consent may be justified in rare cases where a patient refuses to consent ot such disclosure but the benefit to other family members or the wider public substantially outweighs the need to respect confidentiality. We would expect this to remain an exceptional situation.'

The debate around childbirth is largely medical and social. Obstetricians in many areas of the country have accepted the ideas propounded. Hospital birth in 2007 is usually less interventionist and impersonal than in 1977. Home delivery remains difficult to obtain. Few general practitioners deliver babies at home. There are insufficient NHS community midwives to meet demand. Progress is being made, but the overall impression to a laywoman is that, while doctors make efforts to meet women's demands for more natural childbirth in hospital, all but a few in the profession are opposed to home delivery.

What role does the law play? Childbirth remains a professional monopoly. The law denies a woman, unable to persuade a doctor or midwife to attend her at home or a hospital to comply with her wishes concerning the birth, the choice of seeking alternative help.[64] For it is a criminal offence for a person, other than a registered midwife or a registered medical practitioner, to attend a woman in childbirth. And any person means any person. In 1982, a husband was convicted of delivering his own wife and fined £100.[65] Nor is the unqualified attendant the only potential 'criminal'. The mother herself, if she procures the other's services – in ordinary English, if she asks for help – may be guilty of counselling and procuring a criminal offence. So her choice is to accept the medical help available or give birth alone. Giving birth alone is not an attractive option and one not free of legal hazard, not to speak of medical risk. For if the baby dies, the mother may face prosecution for manslaughter.[66] Gross negligence by attendants in the delivery of a baby has resulted in criminal conviction where the baby died.[67] The issue where an unattended mother was on trial would be whether refusing medical attendance was sufficiently culpable negligence in relation to the safety of her child.

The rationale for legislation which makes professional attendance at childbirth compulsory may appear self-evident. If a person refuses to seek medical help for any other life-threatening condition he physically harms himself alone. A woman refusing medical attention in childbirth puts her baby at risk. Yet she can lawfully refuse attention for the nine months up to delivery. Proposals that maternity grants and benefits should be made dependent on ante-natal visits have been made. Nobody has yet suggested that it should be a criminal offence to fail to attend the ante-natal clinic. There is no express and considered policy on the respective rights and liberties of mother and baby. The legislation originally enacted to require professional attendance at childbirth was intended to outlaw the 'Sarah Gamps', elderly and often dirty local women who made their living as unqualified midwives.[68] Today's legislation has moved a long way from that point. It may by chance be correct, but it

---

[64] Nurses, Midwives and Health Visitors Act 1979, s 17. An exception is made for emergencies to protect family, policemen and ambulance crew from liability for helping in emergencies. For thorough discussion of the monopoly on childbirth, see JM Eekelaar and RWJ Dingwall, 'Some Legal Issues of Obstetric Practice' (1984) *Journal of Social Welfare Law* 258, and J Finch, 'Paternalism and Professionalism in Childbirth' (1982) 132 *New Law Journal* 995 at 995 and 1011.

[65] For further discussion of this case, see Finch (1982) 132 *New Law Journal* 995.

[66] See *Attorney-General's Reference (No 3 of 1994)* [1997] 3 All ER 936.

[67] *R v Senior* (1832) 1 Mood CC 346; and see *R v Bateman* (1925) 19 Cr App Rep 8.

[68] See Finch (1982) 132 *New Law Journal* 995 at 995–996.

needs proper consideration whether a husband delivering his wife, or a mother her daughter, should be branded as criminal when all goes well and mother and baby thrive.

Hospital birth

12.17 How far does a woman retain control of her labour? Save in an emergency, explicit consent is required for any invasive examination or procedure in labour.[69] That does not mean that the midwife must obtain a written consent for every vaginal examination, or that explicit consent to wiping the woman's brow is called for. Any significant procedure must where possible proceed with the woman's agreement. Most midwives regard treating mothers as partners in labour as simply good practice. One of the most controversial issues of hospital birth is the use of episiotomy. A small cut is made in the vagina to assist delivery and prevent tearing. One of its advantages is said to be that the deliberate cut will heal better than a random tear. In some hospitals, episiotomy became routine. It was performed regardless of any necessity for it. Many women will enter the labour ward confused and a little overwhelmed. They will have given no express instructions. Episiotomy without express consent is unlawful. It is not an inevitably necessary invasion of the mother's body, as are the contacts by the midwife when she feels the abdomen and assists the baby's exit. Episiotomy is a greater invasion of the body than any contacts implicitly authorised simply by seeking professional aid. The skin is cut and a wound, however small, is made. The law should uphold the mother's right to control what happens to her. More recently, the number of episiotomies has fallen.

Childbirth can be an unpredictable process. Midwives and obstetricians sometimes have to respond swiftly to an unforeseen emergency. The woman may be in acute pain, perhaps a little panicky, or significantly affected by doses of painkilling drugs which cause some mental confusion. Doubts may surface about her decision-making capability and/or the time to seek consent may truly be limited. The Court of Appeal[70] has suggested that if the woman is temporarily incompetent to make decisions for herself, health professionals may do whatever is required in her best interests. Defining the borderline between capacity and mental incapacity in such cases is tricky. It is too easy to assume women are incompetent. 'Birth plans' offer a partial solution to such dilemmas. Women, ideally in consultation with their midwives, outline how they wish to be treated if certain emergencies materialise. 'Advance decisions'[71] should have just as great force and authority at childbirth as in the life-threatening circumstances in which they are more usually invoked. The controversy over whether the law should compel medical attendance in childbirth would be much less substantial if the woman's rights in hospital were fully protected.

---

[69] Though see the contrary view expressed by Eekelaar and Dingwall (1984) *Journal of Social Welfare Law* 258.
[70] *Re MB (An Adult) (Medical Treatment)* [1997] 2 FCR 541, CA.
[71] See Chapter 6.

It goes without saying that a mother suffering injury as a result of carelessness in the management of childbirth is entitled to compensation for negligence. She will recover compensation for her pain and suffering and for the shock and grief consequent on the death of a baby or birth of a disabled child. Her damages may also include any effect of the mismanaged delivery on her prospects of future childbearing.[72] Where obstetric negligence results in the birth of a disabled infant, the child too has a claim. The most common case centres on allegations that the baby suffered brain damage as a consequence of oxygen starvation during delivery. The parents argue that the obstetric team failed to act on signs of foetal distress and perform a Caesarean section as swiftly as the circumstances required. The child is born with cerebral palsy. Very often the core of the dispute is not whether clinical negligence can be proven, but whether causation can be established. Such cases are expensive, slow and worryingly common. A survey by the National Audit Office[73] demonstrates that cerebral palsy and birth injury claims account for 80 per cent of outstanding claims against the NHS in terms of value and 26 per cent in crude numbers. Little wonder the Chief Medical Officer gave serious thought to a special no-fault scheme to compensate birth injuries.[74]

Maternal autonomy/foetal welfare

12.18 The child injured by obstetric negligence will have a claim against the doctors and midwives who failed him. What are his rights if his mother refuses a course of action that will benefit him and thus causes him injury? In theory the child's rights are governed by the Congenital Disabilities (Civil Liability) Act 1976, although the Act appears to go unnoticed in the relevant case law. The 1976 Act covers not just injury to the child in the womb but also any occurrence which *affected mother or child in the course of its birth*. It has been argued that the 1976 Act reduces the child's rights.[75] Liability under the Act arises only where the defendant would have been liable in tort to the affected parent. Where a failure by the defendant caring for the mother, for example failure to proceed quickly enough to Caesarean section, is in no way the responsibility of the mother, no problem is caused to the child. The duty to the mother embraces care of her child. A breach of duty to her which injures the child creates rights for both her and her child.

The thrust of the argument that the 1976 Act reduces the child's rights lies in these sorts of circumstances. The child is believed to be at risk. Doctors recommend Caesarean section. The mother refuses and the child is born suffering brain damage. The child will not be able to sue the doctor. The doctor is not liable to the mother. The child cannot sue his mother, for the Act grants immunity to mothers.[76] If there is no duty directly to the child, a doctor

[72] *Kralj v McGrath* [1986] 1 All ER 54.
[73] National Audit Office, *Handling Clinical Negligence Claims* (2001)
[74] CMO, *Making Amends – Clinical Negligence Reform* (2003), Recommendation 2. However, the redress scheme for neurologically-impaired babies does not form part of the NHS Redress Act 2006. Instead it is likely to be taken forward separately under the National Service Framework for Children, Young People and Maternity Services (2004).
[75] Eekelaar and Dingwall (1984) *Journal of Social Welfare Law* 258 at 265.
[76] Section 1(2).

cannot, after the 1976 Act, advance his duty to the child as a defence to acts done to the mother.[77] Where there still a direct duty to the child, the doctor might contend that in exceptional circumstances, he could, for example, proceed to Caesarean section without consent in order to save the baby. That begs the fundamental question of whether doctors ought ever to be allowed to prioritise the child's welfare above the mother's right to autonomy, to make her own choices about her childbirth.

In 1998, the Court of Appeal in *St George's Healthcare NHS Trust v S*[78] finally ruled that in English law no mentally-competent woman could be required to submit to a Caesarean section or any other form of obstetric intervention to which she objected. Neither pregnancy nor labour diminished the woman's rights of self-determination. Judge LJ put the position succinctly:

> ... while pregnancy increases the personal responsibilities of the pregnant woman it does not diminish her entitlement to decide whether or not to undergo medical treatment.[79]

Six years of uncertainty were ended. In 1992, in *Re S*,[80] the then President of the Family Division had ruled that doctors could carry out a Caesarean section on a woman whose own life and that of her child were imminently imperilled by an obstructed labour. Several other cases[81] followed where courts, often in hurried hearings in circumstances of dire emergency, ordered Caesarean surgery despite maternal objections. In a number, but not all, of these cases the mother's mental capacity was questionable. In 1997, in *Re MB (Adult: Medical Treatment)*[82] the Court of Appeal said that if a woman retained mental capacity she retained the right to make decisions about surgery for herself but found on the facts that MB's needle phobia rendered her temporarily incompetent.

The theory of the law is this. Unless a woman lacks the mental capacity to make her own decisions about labour, her freedom to determine what is and is not done to her is unimpaired. In practice, the temptation to seek grounds to find her capacity to be impaired is great.[83] Judge LJ in *St George's* is emphatic in his endorsement of maternal autonomy. The mother's wishes should be respected even if her thinking process is '... apparently bizarre and irrational and contrary to the views of the overwhelming majority of the community at large'. Yet in *Re MB*, Butler-Sloss LJ suggested a woman might suffer temporary incapacity induced by confusion, shock, pain or drugs. Or fear might paralyse the will. Finding any of these factors in childbirth will not be hard.

---

[77] Eekelaar and Dingwall (1984) *Journal of Social Welfare Law* 258 at 265.
[78] [1998] 3 All ER 673.
[79] [1998] 3 All ER 673 at 692.
[80] [1992] 4 All ER 671.
[81] *Rochdale Healthcare NHS Trust v C* [1997] 1 FCR 274; *Norfolk and Norwich (NHS) Trust v W* [1996] 2 FLR 613; *Re L (An Adult: Non Consensual Treatment)* [1997] 1 FCR 609; *Tameside & Glossop Acute Services Trust v CH* [1996] 1 FLRC 762.
[82] [1997] 2 FLR 426.
[83] See *Bolton Hospitals NHS Trust v O* [2003] 1 FLR 824.

The situation is altered little by the Mental Capacity Act 2005.[84] The Act codifies the test for capacity in section 2. Capacity is judged at the 'relevant time'. Its temporary nature is irrelevant. However, neither a condition (such as pregnancy) nor an aspect of the person's behaviour (such as irrationality) can establish a lack of capacity under the Act.[85] It must be demonstrated that the pregnant woman is unable to make the particular decision as a result of an impairment or disturbance of the mind. The Code of Practice on the Mental Capacity Act 2005 (in draft form at the time of writing) recognises a wide range of factors which can lead to such impairment, including drugs and delirium.[86] Consequently, it will remain the case that doctors may have little difficulty in demonstrating a temporary lack of capacity during labour.

Is the theory right? Or should the foetus at the point of birth to be more highly valued? The difficulty of using law to enforce a duty to the foetus is well illustrated in *Re F (In Utero)*,[87] where a local authority unsuccessfully tried to make a foetus a ward of court. The mother was a 36-year-old woman who suffered from severe mental disturbance but who was not 'sectionable' under the Mental Health Act 1983. She refused ante-natal care and had disappeared by the time the local authority started proceedings to make the foetus a ward of court. There was concern for the child's welfare. Refusing to extend the wardship jurisdiction to unborn children, the court advanced the following reasons for their decision:

(1)   In English law the foetus has no legal personality until it is born and has an existence independent of the mother.
(2)   To extend the wardship jurisdiction to the foetus, with its predominant principle that the interests of the ward are paramount, would create inevitable conflict between the existing legal interests of the mother and her child. Is the mother to be 'sacrificed' for the child?
(3)   There are immense practical difficulties in enforcing any order against the mother. If she is, for example, refusing to consent to an elective Caesarean section and is not already in hospital, will the police be called on to go and arrest her?
(4)   There would be problems with the limit of such a jurisdiction. Mothers can do most harm to their unborn children early in pregnancy, for example through alcohol or drug abuse. Yet up to 24 weeks in pregnancy a mother may well be able to obtain a legal abortion. Would a woman who wants her baby be subject to coercive measures in the baby's interests, yet free to destroy it should she change her mind?

May LJ concluded that in the light of these problems any such radical extension of the wardship jurisdiction was a matter for Parliament and not for the courts. In the event, and unbeknownst to the court, while they were hearing the action the mother had already safely given birth to a healthy child.

---

[84]   See Chapter 6.
[85]   Mental Capacity Act 2005, s 2(3)(b).
[86]   Department for Constitutional Affairs, *Mental Capacity Act 2005 – Draft Code of Practice* (9 March 2006), para 3.11.
[87]   [1989] 2 All ER 193.

Parliament should reject any proposal to extend the wardship jurisdiction to unborn children or to endorse non-consensual obstetric interventions.[88] Over and above those reasons given by the Court of Appeal in *Re F (In Utero)*, such a proposal should be thrown out on the grounds of the damage it would do to ante-natal care generally. Obstetricians, knowing that they could in the end coerce their patients, would become less willing to inform and persuade, to rely on patience rather than compulsion. Women, knowing that they could be forced against their will to submit to blood transfusion or surgery, may opt out of formal obstetric care and far more babies could be born damaged as a result. The law must continue to recognise the pregnant woman's autonomy and her sovereignty over her own body. In no other circumstances can one person be required to submit to any medical procedure to benefit another's welfare. Once a child is born neither of his parents could be forced to donate even a drop of blood to him however trivial the discomfort to them or great the child's need. Caesarean surgery remains major invasive surgery with significant risks and pain for the patient.[89]

[88]   As the Royal College of Obstetricians and Gynaecologists itself has done: see RCOG, *A Consideration of the Law and Ethics in Relation to Court-Ordered Obstetric Intervention* (1994, revised 1996).

[89]   See L Miller, 'Two Patients or One? A Problem of Consent in Obstetrics' (1993) *Medical Law International* 97.

Chapter 13

ASSISTED CONCEPTION[1]

13.1 It has been estimated that one in seven couples have difficulty conceiving naturally and seek medical help.[2] The development of *in vitro* fertilisation (IVF) and the birth of the first 'test-tube baby', Louise Brown,[3] in 1978 gave hope to childless couples. Nearly 30 years later, the pace of development in the reproductive technologies has been relentless. Reproductive medicine no longer focuses exclusively on the management of infertility. Single women can be assisted to have a child without resort to sexual intercourse. Couples who are fertile, but know that they are, or one of them is, a carrier of a genetic disease can be helped to have a healthy child. This may be simply by way of pre-implantation genetic diagnosis (PGD), whereby embryos are screened to avoid implanting any embryos with the defective gene. Or couples who already have one sick child can seek PGD together with tissue typing, to attempt to create a 'saviour sibling' for their sick child. Each and every development in the reproductive technologies attracts controversy. For everyone who rejoices at what doctors can now do, there are those who condemn these advances in medicine as unnatural, contrary to the will of God or destructive of 'normal family life'.

Louise Brown's birth did not only generate moral controversy. Concerns arose about the safety of the 'new' technologies. Fears grew about the competence of practitioners and basic issues, such as hygienic storage of human gametes.[4] In response, the Government established a Committee under Dame Mary Warnock (now Baroness Warnock) to consider:

> ... recent and potential developments in medicine and science related to human fertilisation and embryology; to consider what policies and safeguards should be applied, including consideration of the social, ethical and legal implications of these developments; and to make recommendations.

---

[1] See, generally, R Lee and D Morgan, *Human Fertilisation & Embryology: Regulating the Reproductive Revolution* (2000) Blackstone; E Jackson, *Regulating Reproduction: Law Technology and Autonomy* (2001) Hart

[2] Human Fertilisation and Embryology Authority, *Facts and figures* (2007); and see Human Fertilisation and Embryology Authority, *Guide to Infertility – Treatment and Success Data Based on Treatment Carried Out Between 1 April 2003 and 31 March 2004.*

[3] Who gave birth to her own first child without fertility treatment in 2006.

[4] There is a (possibly apocryphal) story about one clinic storing sperm in the same fridge as milk for staff coffee breaks.

The Warnock Report was published in 1984.[5] The central focus of the Report was its insistence that the burgeoning business of reproductive medicine should be regulated, and that the status of children born as a result of the new and various forms of assisted conception needed to be clarified. Dame Mary Warnock's recommendations remained in abeyance until enacted in a modified form in the Human Fertilisation and Embryology Act 1990.[6] That Act entrusts the primary responsibility for regulating the reproductive technologies in the UK to the Human Fertilisation and Embryology Authority (HFEA).

The 1990 Act and the HFEA were once seen as the model for effective regulation of assisted conception and embryo research. In recent years, the Act and the HFEA have been subjected to increasingly intense criticism.[7] It is scarcely surprising that a statute enacted in 1990 no longer meets the needs of scientific developments that were undreamed of 17 years ago. Thus the Act has generated prolific litigation.[8] Its paternalistic structure of regulation is perceived as outdated and incompatible with a human rights culture, especially section 13(5) of the Act which requires that consideration be given to a child's 'need for a father'. Deep divisions about the legitimacy of the creation and use of human embryos endure. Liberal critics of the 1990 Act attack it as insufficiently responsive to reproductive autonomy.[9] Conservative critics charge that the Act permits the degradation of human embryos and children, reducing them to mere means to an end.[10] In 2005, the Department of Health launched a review of the Act.[11] A White Paper[12] proposing substantial reforms was published in December 2006. Some fertility specialists have argued that there was no longer any need for special regulation of reproductive medicine. This argument for wholesale deregulation was rejected by the Government. The White Paper proposes that the '... current model of regulation, whereby Parliament sets the prohibitions and parameters within which a statutory authority licenses activities should continue'.[13] Moreover, '... activities involving the creation, keeping, or use of embryos outside the body, or the use of donated gametes, should continue to be subject to licensing by an independent

---

5   Report of the Committee of Inquiry into Human Fertilisation and Embryology (1984) Cmnd 9314 (the Warnock Report).
6   The Act reached the statute book only after vitriolic debate in Parliament and the publication of two further reports by the Government, a general consultation document early in 1987 and a White Paper later that year: see *Legislation on Human Infertility Services and Embryology* (1987) Cm 46; *Human Fertilisation and Embryology: A Framework for Legislation* (1987) Cm 259.
7   See, in particular, the House of Commons Science and Technology Committee Fifth Report of Session 2004–5, *Human Reproductive Technologies and the Law* Vol 1 HC 7–1.
8   See, for example, *R (Quintavalle) v Human Fertilisation and Embryology Authority* [2003] 2 All ER 105; *R (Quintavalle) v Human Fertilisation and Embryology Authority* [2005] 2 All ER 555, HL (discussed below at 13.12).
9   See Jackson, *Regulating Reproduction: Law Technology and Autonomy*.
10 See J Laing and DA Oderberg, 'Artificial Reproduction, the "Welfare Principle" and the Common Good' (2005) 13 *Medical Law Review* 328.
11 Department of Health, *Review of the Human Fertilisation and Embryology Act – A Public Consultation* (2005); Department of Health, *Report on the Consultation on the Review of the Human Fertilisation and Embryology Act 1990* (2006).
12 *Review of the Human Fertilisation and Embryology Act – Proposals for Revised Legislation (including the Establishment of the Regulatory Authority for Tissue and Embryos)* (2006) Cm 6989.
13 *Review of the Human Fertilisation and Embryology Act* (2006) Cm 6989, para 2.4.

regulator'.[14] The basic structure of the 1990 Act, whereby most forms of assisted conception are subject to licensing and control by a regulator, will continue. The HFEA itself will be abolished. The HFEA will be merged with the Human Tissue Authority[15] (HTA) to form the Regulatory Authority for Tissue and Embryos (RATE). RATE will have an amazingly broad remit. This one authority will become responsible for the regulation and monitoring of embryo research, assisted conception, organ transplants, organ retention and the donation of whole bodies to medical schools. The White Paper sets out its functions in deceptively simple terms:

- To provide general oversight of the area of donation, procurement, storage, use and disposal of human blood, organs, tissue and cells – including tissue and cells donated for reproductive use.
- To license, inspect and regulate specific activities including the creation and use of embryos *in vitro* for treatment and research, human tissue banking, *post-mortem* practice, anatomical examination and public display.
- To advise Ministers on developments in society, science or medicine that might significantly affect the practice of regulated activities.
- To provide to the public and to persons carrying on activities within its remit, such information and advice as it considers appropriate about the nature and purpose of such activities.[16]

While the common denominator in all RATE's diverse jobs is the regulation of human bodily products, the diverse sources of such tissue, from gametes to corpses, means that, within RATE itself, neither all the requisite expertise – nor lay opinion – can be adequately represented. Moreover, the Government envisages that RATE will have a smaller membership than the present HFEA (21). Hence it is suggested that a key part of the structure of the new Authority will be expert advisory panels (EAPs).[17] One such EAP will cover assisted reproduction and embryology. That EAP may become the successor to many of the HFEA's current functions. One other significant change proposed is this. RATE, unlike the HFEA, will not necessarily act as the licensing authority for embryo research or fertility clinics. The White Paper says merely that, 'The Government believes that RATE will operate most effectively with a flexible system whereby it is able to establish its own licensing procedures ...'.[18] Appeals and reviews of decisions would fall to RATE. The White Paper sets out proposals for reform in general terms. The full picture will emerge only when a Bill is presented to Parliament. So, in this chapter we describe the system at the time of writing and seek to indicate what form new legislation may take.

---

[14] *Review of the Human Fertilisation and Embryology Act* (2006) Cm 6989, para 2.9.
[15] See below, Chapters 18 and 19.
[16] See *Review of the Human Fertilisation and Embryology Act* (2006) Cm 6989, para 3.7.
[17] *Review of the Human Fertilisation and Embryology Act* (2006) Cm 6989, paras 3.13–3.15.
[18] *Review of the Human Fertilisation and Embryology Act* (2006) Cm 6989, para 3.17.

The Human Fertilisation and Embryology Authority

13.2 The primary responsibility for regulating the reproductive technologies in the UK remains at present with the Human Fertilisation and Embryology Authority, operating as a statutory licensing authority and established by section 5 of the Human Fertilisation and Embryology Act 1990. Schedule 1 to the Act prescribes the authority's membership. Neither the chairman nor the deputy chairman may be a medical practitioner, or professionally involved in embryo research or assisted conception. At least one third, but fewer than half, of the members must be persons so involved in research or infertility treatment. The requirement for a lay chair and a majority of lay members will continue when the HFEA is replaced by RATE. The Secretary of State for Health, who appoints members of the HFEA, is directed to '... have regard to the desirability of ensuring that the proceedings of the Authority, and the discharge of its functions are informed by the views of both men and women'. This has resulted in a substantial number of female members of the HFEA.

The HFEA was granted impressive powers. Section 3 of the 1990 Act makes it a criminal offence to bring about the creation of an embryo outside the human body, or keep or use such an embryo,[19] except in pursuance of a licence granted by the HFEA. Any infertility treatment requiring the creation of an embryo by means of *in vitro* fertilisation, that is the creation of a 'test-tube' embryo, must be licensed, and, as we have noted, new legislation will retain such a requirement. Section 4 prohibits any storage of gametes (sperm or eggs), and the use of donor sperm or eggs, without a licence from the HFEA. Any infertility treatment involving artificial insemination by donor (DI)[20] or egg donation is generally unlawful unless licensed by the HFEA. Sections 3 and 4 also outlaw a number of specific procedures, for example creating human/animal hybrids. Those issues are dealt with further in the next chapter. This chapter concentrates on regulation in relation to, and the legal principles governing, assisted conception.

Licensing fertility treatment

13.3 Any clinic that offers IVF or artificial insemination (DI) is subject to the control of the HFEA. It cannot operate lawfully without a licence and its staff and procedures are strictly monitored and controlled. Failure to comply with HFEA guidelines about, for example, safety procedures, numbers of embryos to be implanted,[21] selection of donors or assessment of patients may lead to forfeiture of that licence. However, one area of reproductive medicine remains beyond the ambit of the 1990 Act and the control of the HFEA. Gametes intra-Fallopian transfer (GIFT) is a procedure whereby eggs are taken from an infertile woman and sperm from her partner. The eggs and sperm are mixed

---

[19]   See *Attorney-General's Reference (No 2 of 2003)* [2004] EWCA Crim 785.

[20]   Though note that, if self-insemination using fresh sperm is practised by a couple, the Act does not apply: see below at 13.14. The White Paper will seek to introduce regulation in relation to artificial gametes. The use of fresh gametes will be regulated to some extent via implementation of the EU Tissue Directive (Directive (EC) 2004/23).

[21]   See *R (on the application of the Assisted Reproduction and Gynaecology Centre) v Human Fertilisation and Embryology Authority* [2002] EWCA Civ 20.

together in the laboratory and returned to the woman's body before the process of fertilisation begins. There is no creation of an embryo outside the body of a woman which would require to be licensed. There are arguments that a provision in section 1, the section defining embryo (section 1(2)(a)), which provides that the Act does apply to an embryo created partly *in vitro* and partly in the body, may 'catch' GIFT. But this is unlikely as, in GIFT, fertilisation does not even begin until the eggs and sperm are returned to the woman's body. Section 1(2)(a) is designed to cover a procedure whereby if a woman undergoes IVF at a clinic with no facilities to store embryos, the 'surplus' embryos are collected in a minute glass tube which is then placed in the woman's vagina. She acts as an 'incubator', and goes to a clinic with storage facilities. There 'her' embryos are removed and frozen. Attempts in Parliament to include GIFT expressly within the 1990 Act failed. This is despite evidence that GIFT is more likely than IVF to result in multiple pregnancies, with attendant risk to mother and children, and so to over-stretched neonatal facilities.[22]

The 1990 Act only provided a basic framework of rules governing assisted conception in the UK. The Act entrusted to the HFEA extensive powers to fill in the details of those rules and to regulate both the ethical and practical problems of assisted conception – powers RATE will inherit. The HFEA has to operate within the framework set by Parliament, but many crucial decisions are left to the Authority. So, as we shall see, the HFEA has had to consider questions like, should ovarian tissue be harvested from foetuses, should sister-to-sister egg donation be banned, should egg sharing be permitted? (And these are examples of the HFEA's less contentious business.) Developments in techniques of assisted conception continually pose novel problems for the HFEA. The ethics of sex selection constantly troubles the HFEA. The controversy relating to pre-implantation genetic diagnosis (PGD) exposed the HFEA to attack on several fronts. Other ethical dilemmas facing the HFEA fade almost into insignificance in comparison to the debate surrounding human cloning. The HFEA found itself making policy in relation to deeply divisive social questions generated by rapid developments in reproductive medicine. It had had little choice but to do so, given the inadequacy of primary legislation in certain respects. The reward for its efforts were charges that the unelected Authority has usurped the role of Parliament.[23] The unpopularity of some of its decisions won the HFEA few defenders.

Grand ethical issues face the HFEA. Their everyday difficulties are apparently more mundane. How often should gametes from one donor be used? The more often sperm from one donor is used, the higher the risk of unwitting incest. No single donor is to be used for more than ten inseminations.[24] The HFEA limits the number of embryos which may be replaced in the woman.

---

[22] For a discussion of the political horsetrading that resulted in GIFT being omitted from the 1990 Act, see Lee and Morgan, *Human Fertilisation & Embryology: Regulating the Reproductive Revolution*, pp 142–145.

[23] See in particular, the Report of the House of Commons Science and Technology Committee, *Human Reproductive Technologies and the Law*.

[24] See Human Fertilisation and Embryology Authority, *Code of Practice* (6th edn, 2003), paras 8.20–8.21.

The current limit is two[25] in relation to women under 40. In a woman over 40, three embryos may exceptionally be implanted if the woman's own eggs are being used. There is pressure to move to a single embryo transplant for most women. The more embryos replaced in the woman, the greater the risk of multiple pregnancies. Such pregnancies increase the risk of premature labour, with adverse consequences for mother, babies and overstretched neonatal units within the NHS. Some fertility specialists vehemently oppose what they see as paternalistic interference with clinical freedom. If a woman considers that increased chances of pregnancy outweigh the risk of multiple pregnancy, those doctors argue that the number of embryos replaced is none of the HFEA's business. An attempt to strike down this policy by way of judicial review failed.[26]

Another dilemma for the HFEA surrounded clinics with poor success rates. Live birth rates per cycle using fresh eggs remain on average about 28.2 per cent for women under 35, falling to 10.6 per cent for women aged between 40 and 42.[27] Small, less well-equipped centres achieve much less success. All clinics are regularly inspected. The HFEA publishes information enabling patients to know about the track record of each clinic. Ensuring patients receive information designed to help them to determine whether and where to seek treatment might seem uncontroversial. Alas for the HFEA, this is not the case. Clinics complain about the criteria used to grade them. It is claimed that some clinics turn away older women, or couples with complex fertility problems, to inflate their success rates.[28]

The HFEA became a target for attack. The ethical decisions entrusted to it go to the heart of differences in our society. The role of the HFEA as a regulator of fertility practice is sometimes overlooked. The HFEA received little credit for the job it did in ensuring 'quality control' of reproductive medicine at a time when in some other European countries assisted conception was wholly unregulated. British patients, lucky enough to gain access to treatment, could be reasonably assured that they would be treated by competent practitioners and protected by standards enforced by the HFEA.[29] A series of serious errors, however, contributed to the HFEA coming under attack for incompetence, as much as for its policy-making role. In one incident, evidence emerged that an embryologist who was working for two clinics had engaged in a range of malpractice. A number of frozen embryos had been allowed to thaw. The embryologist knew this, but did not disclose this disaster to his colleagues. Several women underwent procedures which they believed involved implanting 'their' embryos. In fact, no embryo was within the substances inserted in the women. The embryologist was convicted of assault as well as several

[25] HFEA, *Code of Practice*, paras 8.20–8.21.
[26] See R *(on the application of the Assisted Reproduction and Gynaecology Centre) v Human Fertilisation and Embryology Authority* [2002] EWCA Civ 20.
[27] See HFEA, *Facts and figures* (2007); HFEA, *Guide to Infertility – Treatment and Success Data Based on Treatment Carried Out Between 1 April 2003 and 31 March 2004.*
[28] See Human Fertilisation and Embryology Authority, *Understanding Clinic Success Rates* (2006), accessible at www.hfea.gov.uk/cps/rde/xchg/SID-3F57079.
[29] See M Brazier, 'Regulating the Reproduction Business?' (1999) 7 *Medical Law Review* 166.

charges of fraud.[30] Another mistake came to light in *Leeds Teaching Hospital NHS Trust v A*.[31] A white couple, Mr and Mrs A, were receiving IVF treatment; when Mrs A gave birth to mixed-race twins, it emerged that failure to monitor the sperm used to create the embryos implanted in Mrs A had led to the use of sperm from Mr B, who was black. Mr and Mrs B were also undergoing treatment at the same clinic.

Donor insemination (DI)

13.4 Where it is the man who is infertile, a couple may be offered the opportunity to have a child using sperm from another man, by artificial insemination by donor (DI). As a procedure, DI is so simple that it can be, and often is, performed without medical assistance. The problems are legal and ethical, not medical. Let us look first at DI in its simplest setting. A couple are married. The husband fully and freely consents to DI.[32] Sections 28 and 29 of the Human Fertilisation and Embryology Act 1990 apply not just to DI, but to any treatment involving the use of donor sperm. So if a couple undergo IVF using donor sperm, not the man's own gametes, section 28 governs his, and the donor's relationship, with the child. Section 28(2) re-enacts the earlier provision relating to DI children born within marriage, deeming the child to be the husband's child[33] and giving the husband all the usual privileges of fatherhood, including an entitlement to contact with his child should the marriage break down.[34]

Section 28(3) extends that provision to children born to unmarried couples seeking DI together. Whenever DI is provided for a woman and a man together by a person to whom a licence applies, the man is to be treated as the father of the child. That means he is subject to the same rights and obligations as any other natural father not married to the mother of his child.[35] The intent of section 28(2) and (3) is to bestow the legal rights and responsibilities of fatherhood on the social father, the man who seeks a child with his wife or partner. The apparent simplicity of these provisions about legal paternity is misleading. Evidence that at the time the mother received DI she was living with a male partner is not sufficient. The social father himself is unlikely to

30 See (2003) Guardian, 16 January. See also *Attorney-General's Reference (No 2 of 2003)* [2004] EWCA Crim 785.
31 [2003] 1 FLR 1091; see below at 13.8.
32 Until 1987, a child born as a result of DI was born into a legal limbo. Even if his mother was a married woman whose husband, the 'social' father, had agreed to DI, the child was in law the illegitimate child of his mother and the donor. The first attempt to clarify the status of DI children came in the Family Law Reform Act 1987. Section 27 of that Act provided that where a married woman received DI with her husband's consent, the child was in law the child of the woman and her husband.
33 In cases where the husband's consent is disputed, it would be for him to prove that he did not consent.
34 *Re CH (Contact: Parentage)* [1996] 1 FCR 768.
35 This means that if he and the mother register the birth of the child together, they share parental responsibility for the child. Should they not do so, to gain parental responsibility for the child, the 'social' father must either enter into a formal agreement with the mother to do so, or seek a court order to share parental responsibility with the mother: see s 4 of the Children Act 1989 as amended by the Adoption and Children Act 2002.

receive any treatment, though he will have undergone fertility tests at an earlier date.[36] Wilson J proposed a simple test in *U v W (Attorney-General Intervening).*[37] Was the treatment provided in response to a request '... made by the woman and man as a couple, notwithstanding the absence in the man of any physical role in the treatment'? What many clinics sought to do was to ensure that the man acknowledged his role and intentions in writing, assuring the clinic that the request was, in truth, a joint enterprise whereby he undertook the responsibility of fatherhood to any child who might be born. In *Re R (A Child) (IVF: Paternity of Child)*, a new twist to the tale emerged. An unmarried couple (D and R) were treated with IVF using donor sperm, and several embryos were created. An unsuccessful attempt of implantation took place and the remaining embryos were frozen. Subsequently, the couple parted and shortly afterwards the woman embarked on a new relationship. She returned to the clinic and was successfully treated with embryos taken from storage. Her former partner, R, sought a parental responsibility order and contact with the child. The judge at first instance upheld his claim.[38] He emphasised the importance of certainty and stressed that the assurances whereby both partners stated that they were being treated together had never been withdrawn. The clinic's perception that they were a couple being treated together endured.[39] The Court of Appeal reversed his judgment,[40] and the House of Lords upheld the Court of Appeal. The Law Lords[41] ruled that the relevant time when it must be established that a couple are being treated together is the time when the relevant embryos are placed in the mother. By that time, D and R were in no sense any longer together. Further complexities relating to section 28(3) will become apparent later when we examine the law relating to surrogacy.

Section 28(4) of the 1990 Act goes on to provide that wherever the woman's husband or partner is to be treated as the child's legal father, no other person is in any sense the legal father of the child – that is, all links between the donor and the child are severed. Even when no husband or partner is to be deemed to be the child's father, where a donor donates sperm and gives the appropriate consent to donation required by the Act in Schedule 3, he is not to be treated as the child's father.[42] Whenever DI is provided in a licensed clinic, in accordance with the rules laid down in the Act, the donor has no legal relationship to the child. The child has no claim on the donor. The donor can never assert any parental rights.

However, section 28(3) and (4) grant paternity to the male partner[43] and severing the link between the sperm donor and his genetic offspring applies

---

36 *Re B (Parentage)* [1996] 2 FLR 15; *Re Q. (parental order)* [1996] 1 FLR 369.
37 [1998] Fam 29 at 40.
38 Reported as *B v R* [2002] 2 FLR 843.
39 See C Lind, '*In Re R (Paternity of IVF Baby)* – Unmarried Paternity under the Human Fertilisation and Embryology Act 1990' (2003) 15 *Child and Family Law Quarterly* 327.
40 *Re R (A Child) (IVF: Paternity of a Child)* [2003] Fam 129, CA.
41 *Re R (A Child) (IVF: Paternity of a Child)* [2005] 2 AC 621, HL.
42 See s 28(6).
43 Note s 29(4), which provides that the rules on paternity will not apply where inheritance of fines or honours is in question. Thus, if a Duchess underwent DI with the Duke's consent, the ensuing son could not inherit the title!

only when insemination takes place under medical supervision in a licensed clinic. Should a woman find a willing sperm donor prepared to donate fresh sperm and then inseminates herself, the donor remains in law the child's father. Should a couple seek medically supervised DI abroad, the 'social' father has no obligations to, or claims to, the child.[44] A couple (U and W) sought treatment in Rome using donor sperm as part of IVF. The woman (U) gave birth to twins. The relationship between the couple broke down. When the mother sought support for the children under the Child Support Act 1991, her former partner (W) denied any responsibility for children who he contended were not his. The court reluctantly found in his favour. Section 28(3) applied only to treatment in clinics licensed in this country.

The limited application of section 28(3) and (4) provoke a number of questions. In so far as the principles clarifying the child's relationship to his 'social' father – the man who jointly with his mother sought his birth – are territorially limited, is this justifiable? Should W have been able to reject his children? The provisions of section 28 also force us to consider why self-insemination remains totally unregulated. Where DI is provided in a licensed clinic, stored sperm are used and subjected to rigorous testing, including HIV screening. Using fresh sperm is a risky business. But could laws outlaw the simple process of self-insemination when, obviously, no restrictions surround sexual intercourse? Women and couples may prefer the privacy of self-insemination, bypassing intrusive assessment of their personal circumstances and parental fitness. Could it be argued that Article 8 of the European Convention on Human Rights, protecting the right to respect for private and family life, would be incompatible with attempts to police self-insemination? On a practical level, it is difficult to see how any rules banning self-insemination could ever be enforced. One proposal in the White Paper may encourage one group to seek licensed treatment and avoid the risks of self-insemination: at present, if one partner in a lesbian couple conceives via DI, the other partner enjoys no automatic parental responsibility in relation to the couple's child. The White Paper proposes[45] that provisions relating to status and legal parenthood should confer the same status in relation to same sex couples as that enjoyed by heterosexual couples. Presumably civil partners[46] will be treated as husband and wife, and other partners treated together will be able to share parental responsibility as would a heterosexual unmarried couple.

DI and single mothers

13.5 An increasing number of women who have no male partner want to have a child. Such women may reject as distasteful the prospect of a 'one-night stand' to get pregnant, and not want a transient partner to have any legal claim on 'her' child. They may prefer not to engage in heterosexual intercourse. During the passage of the Human Fertilisation and Embryology Act 1990, attempts were made in Parliament to outlaw DI for women without

---

[44]   *U v W (Attorney-General Intervening)* [1997] 2 FLR 282.
[45]   At paras 2.65–2.69.
[46]   See the Civil Partnership Act 2004.

a male partner. A compromise was embodied in section 13(5) of the Act, which provided, apparently innocuously, that a licence holder treating a woman must take into account the welfare of any child who may be born as a result of treatment, *including the need of that child for a father*.[47] Today, the notion that doctors should impose any sort of conditions about the form of family structure a child should be born into is seen by many people as outdated.[48] The House of Commons Select Committee on Science and Technology concluded that the requirement to consider the need for a father was '... unjustifiably offensive to many' and constitutes 'unjustified discrimination against unconventional families'.[49] The Select Committee went further and recommended abolition of this welfare principle in its current form. The Government White Paper[50] none the less proposes the retention of a modified welfare principle, but agrees that provisions insisting on consideration of the need for a father should be abolished. The HFEA always sought to attenuate the effect of that provision, looking more to the mother's capacity to raise a child alone, and evidence of male role models in the child's life. After extensive consultation of its own, the HFEA[51] revised its guidance. Clinics should operate on a presumption of providing treatment to those seeking help to conceive whether they be heterosexual couples, lesbian couples or single women. Only if there is evidence of risk of serious harm to a future child should treatment be refused.

There remain those who argue that it is not right to provide DI to help a woman have a child who will have no father.[52] The effect of section 28(6), severing all links between a DI donor and child, is that a child born to a woman with no partner is literally fatherless. It is argued that society should not allow fatherless children to be born by assisted conception because children need a parent of either sex to develop properly. Yet countless children are born by natural means to women alone, and countless more lose contact with their 'legal' father. If it is asserted that a woman unable to have children by the usual means must be denied help via assisted conception unless she has a male partner, a case must be made out that her child's welfare is likely to be imperilled by fatherlessness. Perhaps never having a father is less traumatic than losing one? A woman who sets out to have a child alone is not misled into thinking she can always rely on a man for support. Finally, whenever arguments are advanced to ban assisted conception for women without a male partner, those arguments should be analysed carefully. Is the essence of the argument that *any* woman without a male partner should not be helped, or

---

[47] A number of MPs and peers (in 1990) hoped that the HFEA would ban DI, and other forms of assisted conception, for all single women, save in the most exceptional circumstances.

[48] See, for example, E Jackson, 'Conception and the Irrelevance of the Welfare Principle' (2002) 65 *Modern Law Review* 176.

[49] See the Report of the House of Commons Science and Technology Committee, *Human Reproductive Technologies and the Law*, para 101.

[50] See *Review of the Human Fertilisation and Embryology Act* (2006) Cm 6989, paras 2.20–2.26.

[51] See Human Fertilisation and Embryology Authority, *Tomorrow's Children* (2005); Human Fertilisation and Embryology Authority, *Welfare of the Child and the Assessment of Those Seeking Treatment Guidance* (2005), accessible at www.hfea.gov.uk/cps/rde/xbcc/SID-3F7D79B-BF1E1172/hfea/Revised_Guidance.pdf.

[52] See Laing and Oderberg (2005) 13 *Medical Law Review* 328.

that lesbians must not be allowed to use DI to have children? We suspect that it is often the latter.[53] And we should not forget, banning women from licensed clinics does not prevent them practising self-insemination: it simply bars access to assisted conception in safer, supervised conditions.

Artificial insemination by husband (AIH) or partner (AIP)

13.6 There are rare cases where, although a woman's husband or partner is fertile, he cannot beget a child because he is incapable of normal intercourse. His sperm may be used to impregnate his wife or partner by artificial means. Or the man may produce some sperm, but not sufficient healthy and mobile sperm to achieve fertilisation in the usual way. Such a couple may be helped by intra cytoplasmic sperm injection (ICSI), where a single sperm is injected into the cytoplasm (outer casing) of the woman's egg. IVF is combined with AIH. Concerns have been expressed about the safety of ICSI.[54] A child's legal status will be just the same as if she were conceived naturally. Where normal intercourse was not possible so that a marriage has never been consummated, AIH will not prevent the wife from petitioning the court to annul the marriage,[55] although, on policy grounds, the court may refuse a decree if they consider that in having the child the wife approbated the marriage. The child will remain legitimate even if his parents' marriage is later annulled, for they were married when he was conceived and non-consummation only renders a marriage voidable. It does not mean that the marriage was never valid.

The facility to store sperm by freezing may cause problems if a man banks sperm. He may choose to do so before undergoing vasectomy, treatment that might damage his fertility or treatment which might pose a risk to children later conceived. Chemotherapy for cancer is an obvious example. To whom do the sperm 'belong' if the man dies? May the wife ask for insemination then, and if so, what is the child's status? As long ago as 1984, a court in France ordered a sperm bank to release a deceased husband's sperm to his widow.[56] The Warnock Report recommended that posthumous AIH should be actively discouraged.[57] No express provision banning posthumous AIH is to be found in the Human Fertilisation and Embryology Act 1990, but section 28(6)(b) provides that where the sperm of any man, or an embryo created from his sperm, is used after his death, he (the deceased man) is not to be treated as the father of the child. If a widow is inseminated with her dead husband's sperm, a child resulting from AIH has no claim on his genetic father's estate. Again, he becomes a child who is legally fatherless.

---

[53]   See E Sutherland, 'Man Not Included: Single Women, Female Couples and Procreative Freedom in the UK' (2003) 15 *Child and Family Quarterly* 155.

[54]   Do resulting children face a greater risk of genetic disease? Will some born via ICSI be themselves infertile? See S Mayor, 'Technique for Treating Infertility May Be Risky' (1996) 313 *British Medical Journal* 248.

[55]   *L v L* [1949] P 211.

[56]   *Parpalaix v CECOS* (1984) Gazette du Palais, 15 September, Court de Cassation. See generally, R Atherton, '*En Ventre Sa Frigidaire*: Posthumous Children in the Succession Context' (1999) 19 *Legal Studies* 139.

[57]   At p 55.

Diane Blood

13.7   The issue of whether a wife has a 'right' to posthumous AIH arose in the poignant case of Diane Blood. Diane and Stephen Blood had been married for four years before Mr Blood was struck down with meningitis. He lapsed into a coma and died. Shortly before his death, at Mrs Blood's request, doctors used electro-ejaculation to take sperm from her dying husband which was then stored at a licensed fertility clinic. The HFEA instructed the clinic not to treat Mrs Blood, nor to release her husband's sperm to her so that she could seek treatment abroad. The HFEA ruled that the recovery and storage of Stephen Blood's sperm was unlawful. The taking of sperm did not comply with Schedule 3 to the Human Fertilisation and Embryology Act 1990, which imposes a mandatory requirement for written 'effective' consent. No such written consent had ever been given by Mr Blood, although his widow argued that they had planned to start a family, and that Stephen had told her that in the kind of tragic circumstances which ultimately overtook him she should do just as she did.

Mrs Blood challenged the HFEA by way of an application for judicial review, alleging that it was the HFEA who was acting unlawfully. The High Court upheld the HFEA, but Mrs Blood succeeded in the Court of Appeal.[58] While the Appeal Court agreed that the taking of sperm without Mr Blood's written consent was unlawful, that it contravened the 1990 Act and constituted a common law assault, the court expressed sympathy with Mrs Blood. She had acted in good faith and there should be no question of prosecution. None the less, treatment in the UK would be unlawful. However, the Court of Appeal held that the HFEA had failed to give sufficient consideration to European Union Law.[59] Section 24(4) of the 1990 Act permits the HFEA to issue directions authorising the export of sperm. Articles 59 and 60 of the Treaty of Rome guarantee certain fundamental freedoms, which include a right to receive services. Such a right is not absolute, but any limitations on that right must be justified. Given that the court's ruling that taking sperm without written consent was unlawful, the circumstances of Mrs Blood's case would not be repeated. The Court of Appeal directed the HFEA to reconsider Mrs Blood's request to export sperm. They did so and granted her permission to take her husband's sperm to Belgium where she finally received treatment and gave birth to a healthy son, Liam, followed some years later by a second son.

The narrow grounds of the Appeal Court's ruling in Mrs Blood's favour left domestic law unchanged. No woman in a similar position would benefit. The law was clear. Unless the deceased had given formal written consent to storing and use of his sperm,[60] no British clinic could treat his widow or former partner. Lord Winston introduced a Bill to allow for exceptional cases where

---

[58]   [1997] 2 All ER 687, CA. See D Morgan and R Lee, 'In the Name of the Father? *Ex parte* Blood Dealing with Novelty and Anomaly' (1997) 60 *Modern Law Review* 84.

[59]   See T Hervey, 'Buy Baby: The European Union and Regulation of Human Reproduction' (1998) 18 *Oxford Journal of Legal Studies* 207.

[60]   A number of children have been born after posthumous AIH where the requisite written consent had been given.

written consent could be dispensed with. The Bill did not proceed. Professor Sheila McLean conducted an extensive review of the law on consent and removal of gametes, but recommended only limited changes in the law.[61] One change did however result from the review and Mrs Blood's campaign to have her dead husband recognised as her sons' father. The Human Fertilisation and Embryology (Deceased Father) Act 2003 amends section 28(6) of the 1990 Act to allow the name of the deceased (genetic) father to be entered on the child's birth certificate.

The *Blood* case leaves more questions unanswered that it resolves. If Stephen Blood's sperm had been lawfully stored, would Diane Blood have been able to demand treatment? It seems unlikely – the ultimate decision remains with the clinician. In the context of private treatment a widow might seek to argue that she has a contractual right to AIH. The possibility remains of attempts to contend that frozen sperm forms part of a deceased husband's estate. Should a court accept that sperm can be classified as 'property' and 'inherited' by the wife, it would logically follow that she could demand 'her' sperm, but she could still not require the DI clinic to inseminate her.[62] In the light of the underlying philosophy of the 1990 Act, it seems unlikely that such a 'property' argument would succeed.

The White Paper[63] proposes one further limited change relating to the storage of gametes. It should be lawful to store gametes without written consent when a person lacks capacity to give such consent, but storage is deemed to be in his or her best interests and medical opinion indicates that the person is likely to regain capacity at some point. Any later use of those gametes would require the 'donor's' consent. For example, if a man is seriously injured in an accident and surgery threatening his fertility is necessary to preserve his life, then, in consultation with his wife or partner, sperm might be stored – even though at the relevant time the man is incapable of giving any consent, written[64] or oral. This proposal will not affect women in a similar position to Diane Blood. Her husband was dying, never likely to regain capacity and self-evidently not able to give consent to use of his sperm after his death.

In vitro fertilisation

13.8 A woman who ovulates normally, but whose Fallopian tubes are absent or damaged, will not conceive naturally because the eggs that she produces cannot travel to meet sperm and be fertilised. The test-tube baby procedure (*in vitro* fertilisation or IVF) offers such women the chance of their own child. Eggs are removed from the woman and fertilised in the laboratory with sperm taken from her husband or partner. The embryo, or embryos, thus created are

61 *Review of Common Law Provision Relating to the Removal of Gametes and of the Consent Provision in the Human Fertilisation and Embryology Act 1990* (July 1998).
62 See the discussion in I Kennedy and A Grubb, *Medical Law: Text and Materials* (3rd edn, 2000) Butterworths, pp 1308–1315.
63 See *Review of the Human Fertilisation and Embryology Act* (2006) Cm 6989, para 2.31.
64 A new Act would also permit a person physically unable to give written consent (eg due to spinal injury) to direct another person to sign on his behalf: *Review of the Human Fertilisation and Embryology Act* (2006) Cm 6989, para 2.32.

carefully tested and then implanted in the mother's womb. IVF is used in a number of other instances, including cases of 'unexplained infertility'. The woman ovulates, her Fallopian tubes are clear and her partner provides healthy sperm, yet no pregnancy results. No questions of family law normally arise from IVF. The child has the same relationship to her parents as if she were naturally conceived.

What happens if a mistake is made, as occurred in *Leeds Teaching Hospital NHS Trust v A*?[65] As we noted earlier, sperm from Mr B (intended for treatment of his wife, Mrs B) was in error used to fertilise eggs from Mrs A (who was undergoing treatment with her husband, Mr A). The mistake became apparent only when Mrs A gave birth to mixed-race twins.[66] Who was the twins' father? Which couple should bring up the children? Section 28(2) was of no help to Mr A as he patently did not consent to donor insemination of his wife. Section 28(3) relating to treatment together could not apply to Mr and Mrs A because they were married. Nothing in the Human Fertilisation and Embryology Act 1990 assisted Mr A in his claim to become the legal father of his wife's children. Mr B was their genetic father. Dame Elizabeth Butler-Sloss P ruled that, as he had not consented to the use of his sperm to fertilise Mrs A's eggs, Mr B, as the genetic father, should be treated as the legal father of the twins. None the less, she ruled that Mr and Mrs A should retain 'custody' of the children. The twins should stay with the 'parents' who had settled them in a loving home. Mr A could apply for a parental responsibility order or the couple could apply to adopt the twins. At some point when they were older, their origins should be explained to them and contact with Mr B arranged.

More usually, it is the possible variations of IVF, where eggs or sperm (or both) are provided by a third party, which raise questions of family law. A woman may be infertile because of blocked Fallopian tubes and have an infertile male partner. Donor sperm can be used to fertilise her eggs, again returning the resulting embryo or embryos to her womb. As we have seen, a child born as a result of this combination of IVF and DI is to be treated in law just like any other DI child. If the woman is married, and her husband consents to IVF and DI, the child is a child of the marriage. The husband, not the donor, is the legal father. If the couple are unmarried but seek treatment together, again the male partner, the 'social' father, is the legal father of the child.[67]

Egg donation and embryo transplants

13.9 Some women do not ovulate and so cannot conceive naturally. They can be helped by egg donation. Egg donation may also be used where the woman

---

[65] [2003] 1 FLR 1091; and see above at 13.3. See also A Bainham, 'Whose Sperm Is It Anyway?' [2003] *Cambridge Law Journal* 566.

[66] It is suggested that this is not a unique error, but one which became apparent because the couples involved had different racial origins: see (2002) Guardian, 8 July.

[67] See s 28 and note in particular, *Re R (A Child) (IVF: Paternity of Child)* [2005] 2 AC 621, HL (discussed above at 13.4).

carries a genetic disease, to avoid transmitting that disease to her children. Eggs can be taken from a donor, fertilised in the laboratory with the recipient's partner's sperm, and the resulting embryo or embryos implanted in the recipient's womb. Should both partners be infertile, or both be carriers of genetic disease, egg and sperm donors may be used, resulting in an embryo created and implanted in the woman's womb that is genetically unrelated to either partner.

The first question arising from egg donation is: who is the legal mother of the child? Section 27(1) of the Human Fertilisation and Embryology Act 1990 gives a clear answer:

> The woman who is carrying or has carried a child as a result of the placing in her of an embryo or of sperm and eggs, *and no other woman* [*emphasis added*], is to be treated as the mother of the child.

The woman who gives birth to the child is the mother. The genetic 'mother' has no legal claim on the child, nor has the child any claim on her. When the recipient's partner provides the sperm, the legal status of the child is identical to a child naturally conceived by the couple. If donor sperm are used, the same rules deeming the male partner to be the legal father apply, as apply to any use of DI in a licensed clinic.

Unlike sperm donation, egg donation is attended by some risk to the donor. Egg donation requires a surgical procedure, an invasion of the donor's body. Her consent is essential if her doctor is to avoid liability for battery. Often the woman will be given drugs to induce her to supra-ovulate, to produce several eggs at once. A number of eggs are fertilised, the best embryos are implanted, defective embryos are disposed of and 'spare' embryos are frozen for future use. Supra-ovulation carries risks to the health and in a very, very few cases to the life of the woman. A woman undergoing IVF runs identical risks. She does so to have 'her' baby. Egg donors are asked to risk harm with no prospect of benefit to themselves. Healthy volunteers who agree to participate in medical research are invited to act in a similarly altruistic manner. Egg donors remain in short supply.[68] What could be done to recruit more egg donors?

(1)   In its submission to the Warnock Committee, the Royal College of Obstetricians and Gynaecologists (RCOG) suggested that eggs might 'conveniently' be collected from patients undergoing sterilisation or hysterectomy. Such action might be seen as avoiding unnecessary surgical interference by using women already scheduled for surgery. The procedure for collecting eggs is relatively simple and risk-free. The risks centre on supra-ovulation. A woman asked to donate eggs concurrently with other surgery is in effect asked to agree to a further risky and, for her, unnecessary procedure. Will she be in a proper state of mind to give a full and free consent? Will she feel constrained to 'help out' the doctor treating her? The practice has been condemned by the International

---

[68]   See A Plomer and N Martin-Clement, 'The Limits of Beneficence: Egg Donation Under the Human Fertilisation and Embryology Act 1990' (1995) 15 *Legal Studies* 434.

Federation of Obstetrics and Gynaecology.[69] Of particular concern has been the practice of offering free sterilisation to women who agree to be donors. Waiting lists for NHS sterilisations can be lengthy. For a woman to be offered a private sterilisation free of charge is a powerful inducement to agree to donate eggs.

(2) Payments for gametes are limited in the UK. Any payment is unlawful unless authorised by the HFEA.[70] The HFEA used to allow a 'fee' for eggs or sperm up to £15. In response to requirements in the EU Tissue Directive[71] to promote wholly altruistic tissue donation, the HFEA now limits recompense to gamete donors to expenses and loss of income. £15 may have persuaded some impecunious students to donate sperm; it did little to lure egg donors into such an unlucrative market. To encourage a greater pool of vendors, the reward would need to run into thousands of pounds: in the USA, payments of $50,000 are not unknown to attract tall, healthy, highly intelligent college students to sell their eggs.[72]

If an open 'egg market' is not allowed in the UK, does 'egg sharing' operate as a covert market? Women who are undergoing egg collection as part of their own IVF treatment agree to donate a proportion of their eggs to others. In return, they receive free IVF. 'Egg sharing' avoids subjecting the donor to risks unrelated to her own treatment.[73] But does the invitation to 'egg sharing' operate as a questionable inducement to women who could never afford private fertility treatment? Unless they agree to 'egg sharing' some women have no chance of treatment by IVF. How might a donor feel if she learns that the recipient of her eggs had a successful pregnancy, when she did not?

(3) It is now possible for women to store their own eggs (or a portion of ovarian tissue) for future use. A woman about to undergo chemotherapy could store eggs to preserve her fertility, avoiding the need for an egg donor. A woman at the peak of her fertility who does not yet want to embark on childbearing might choose to store eggs for future use. Freezing eggs proves more difficult than freezing sperm.[74] More damage is caused when the eggs are thawed, and there are fears of causing abnormalities in children born from frozen eggs. It is likely that freezing sections of ovarian tissue will be more successful. When the woman wishes to contemplate pregnancy the ovarian tissue (with eggs intact) is simply re-implanted.

Most of the problems surrounding storing eggs and ovarian tissue taken from the intending mother herself are generated by questions about the safety of the procedure. For example, if ovarian tissue is taken from a woman about to undergo chemotherapy for cancer, is there a risk of re-implanting cancer cells in her? Legal and ethical dilemmas are not

---

[69] See JK Mason and GT Laurie, *Mason and McCall Smith's Law and Medical Ethics* (7th edn, 2006) OUP, p 91.

[70] See s 12(e) of the Human Fertilisation and Embryology Act 1990.

[71] Council Directive (EC) 2004/23 on Setting Standards of Quality and Safety for the Donation, Testing, Processing, Preservation, Storage and Distribution of Human Tissues and Cells. See E Jackson, *Medical Law: Text and Materials* (2006) OUP, pp 829–830.

[72] See Jackson, *Medical Law: Text and Materials*, p 830.

[73] See HFEA *Code of Practice*, Appendix H.

[74] Though note that children have been born using frozen eggs.

absent. If a child of seven is about to undergo chemotherapy, can her parents authorise surgical removal of ovarian tissue in case their daughter, when an adult, wants to have children? Is such a procedure in the child's interests? Perhaps that will depend on the depths of immediate risk and distress posed to the child by additional surgery. The prospect of adult women choosing to 'bank' eggs for future use appals some people. Nothing in the 1990 Act forbids such a procedure, and storing eggs avoids some of the practical and moral problems that arise if embryos are stored.[75]

(4) It is technically possible to collect immature eggs from foetuses.[76] Aborted female foetuses could be collected, 'their' eggs harvested and subjected to a process of maturation. A plentiful supply of eggs would be secured. Controversy over such a possibility led to the amendment of the Human Fertilisation and Embryology Act 1990. Section 3A now bans treatment using eggs derived from foetuses. Research can still lawfully continue.

(5) Ovarian tissue might be taken from dead women, just as kidneys and other organs are taken from cadaver donors. Such a process would need to meet the legal conditions currently provided for by both the Human Tissue Act 2004 *and* Schedule 3 to the 1990 Act.

Storing gametes and embryos

13.10 The capacity to freeze and store gametes and embryos has been crucial to the improvement of success rates in fertility treatment.[77] Storage of gametes and embryos is lawful only if licensed by the HFEA.[78] Storage has generated its own ethical and legal conundrums. The Human Fertilisation and Embryology Act 1990 originally prescribed a maximum statutory storage period of ten years for gametes and five years for embryos.[79] In opting for these maximum storage periods, the Act sought to impose limits recognised as safe in 1990. Freezing inevitably means that at the end of the storage period there will be embryos left unused. The 1990 Act requires that such embryos be 'allowed to perish'.[80] In 1996, the first five-year storage period came to an end, and thousands of embryos were to be disposed of. In many cases, clinics had lost all contact with the gamete donors (or parents). A public outcry greeted the fate of what the media styled the 'orphan embryos'. Finally, the Government used powers under the 1990 Act to extend the storage period for embryos from five to ten years in certain cases.[81] The White Paper proposes that new legislation should extend the storage period for embryos in all cases to ten

---

75 No question of destroying embryos arises if a woman decides later that she does not wish to have children. A woman who stores her eggs avoids the fate that overtook Natalie Evans (see *Evans v United Kingdom* [2006] 1 FCR 585, ECHR, discussed below at 13.10).

76 See Human Fertilisation and Embryology Authority, *Donated Ovarian Tissue in Embryo Research and Assisted Conception* (July 1994).

77 The first British baby to 'start life' as a frozen embryo was born in Manchester in 1985.

78 Section 4 of the Human Fertilisation and Embryology Act 1990.

79 See s 14(4)(5). Section 14(5) allows for reduction or extension of these periods by regulations.

80 Section 14(1)(c).

81 Human Fertilisation and Embryology (Statutory Storage Period for Embryos) Regulations 1996, SI 1996/375.

years.[82] The furore around orphan embryos remains instructive. If embryos can be equated to orphan children, they should not be created doomed to die. If children, these 'orphans' should have been offered to other infertile couples for adoption. If embryos are morally insignificant, they should be put to some good use, whether to help other infertile couples or forward research.

As to the fate of embryos in storage prior to their expiry date, the 1990 Act requires anyone storing gametes or embryos to decide what may or may not be done with those embryos before any treatment begins. The donors of the genetic material jointly decide its fate in foreseeable circumstances. But what if they disagree? In *Evans v Amicus Healthcare Ltd*,[83] Natalie Evans wanted to be able to have 'her' frozen embryos implanted to establish a pregnancy. Her former partner, Howard Johnson, refused to agree and sought to have the embryos destroyed. Some years earlier, Ms Evans had been diagnosed with pre-cancerous tumours in both ovaries. She was advised to have her ovaries removed. As the cancer was growing slowly, there was time for her and her partner to undergo IVF and freeze embryos for future use. Ms Evans enquired about the possibility of freezing her eggs and was told that success rates using frozen eggs were much lower than where frozen embryos were used. Her partner reassured her that they would not split up, and would go on to have children together when she was fully recovered and clear of cancer. Both partners signed the necessary forms consenting to storage of the embryos. A year later, the relationship broke down, and Mr Johnson notified the clinic that he withdrew his consent to storage of the embryos and asked that they be destroyed. Ms Evans was prepared to undertake that she would never make a financial claim for child support and argued that the stored embryos offered her her only chance to have a child genetically related to her.

The obstacle confronting Ms Evans, when persuasion failed to change her former partner's mind, lay in Schedule 3 to the 1990 Act. To summarise, any continuing storage of the embryos and any use (ie implantation) of the embryos required the 'effective consent' of both the parties who had contributed the gametes creating the embryos. 'Effective consent' means a consent 'which has not been withdrawn'. Mr Johnson had withdrawn his consent to continued storage of the embryos and never gave any consent to Ms Evans to use the embryos on her own. In the High Court, Wall J held that Schedule 3 made it clear that the continuing consent of both parties was required and that either party was free to withdraw that consent. The Court of Appeal upheld his judgment.[84] Throughout the litigation in England, Ms Evans argued that if Schedule 3 was interpreted to require Mr Johnson's continuing consent, the 1990 Act was incompatible with Ms Evans' rights under Articles 8, 12 and 14 of the European Convention on Human Rights. Her rights to family life and to found a family were violated by an absolute rule that denied her her only chance to have a genetically related child. The Court of Appeal held (*inter alia*) that any interference with Ms Evans' right to private and family life

---

[82] *Review of the Human Fertilisation and Embryology Act* (2006) Cm 6989, paras 2.35–2.37.

[83] [2003] EWHC 2161 (Fam).

[84] [2004] EWCA (Civ) 727; see A Alghrani, 'Deciding the Fate of Frozen Embryos' (2005) 15 *Medical Law Review* 244.

under Article 8(1) was justifiable within the terms of Article 8(2). Permitting implantation without Mr Johnson's consent would violate his Article 8 rights. Justification for violating the father's right to self-determination and autonomy could not be based on any claim that violation was necessary to protect Ms Evans' right:

> The need, as perceived by Parliament, is for bilateral consent to implantation ... To dilute this requirement in the interests of proportionality, in order to meet Ms Evans' otherwise intractable biological handicap, would create new and even more intractable difficulties of arbitrariness and inconsistency.[85]

Ms Evans took her case to the European Court of Human Rights. She lost again.[86] The court noted that there is no consensus among Convention states, or internationally, as to how to regulate consent to implantation of embryos. A number of states conform to the UK model allowing consent to be withdrawn up to the time of implantation. Others limit the male partner's right of veto. Ms Evans sought to argue that her circumstances were exceptional and precluded the court from deciding that this vexed question of consent fell within the margin of appreciation allowed to Member States. Destruction of the embryos destroyed her right to reproduce. Permitting the consent regime in the 1990 Act to stand was not necessary or proportionate. The position of women and men could not be equated. Mr Johnson might suffer some violation of his right to determine his reproductive fate. Ms Evans' right was obliterated. Despite sympathy from the European judges, the court held that the UK regime was based on a clear and principled rule and fell within the margin of appreciation. Ms Evans fights on and her case has been heard by the Grand Chamber of the European Court. Domestically, Schedule 3 to the 1990 Act came under review. The White Paper recommends a minor change in the law: if one party withdraws consent to storage of embryos, a one-year 'cooling off' period should be introduced before the embryos have to be destroyed.[87] Within that year, the hope is that the parties can reach some agreement about the future of the embryos.

Post-menopausal motherhood[88]

13.11 Egg donation offers women the opportunity to extend their reproductive lives. Several babies have been born to women who have undergone the menopause. Eggs are collected from a donor and implanted in the post-menopausal woman whose womb has been restored to a pre-menopausal state by hormone treatment. Success rates are low; none the less, in July 2006, a British woman of 62 gave birth as a result of such treatment in Russia. In

---

[85] [2004] EWCA (Civ) 727 at para 69, per Thorpe LJ.
[86] [2006] 1 FCR 585, ECtHR. (The House of Lords declined to hear Ms Evans' appeal.) See T Annett, 'Balancing Competing Interests Over Frozen Embryos: The Judgment of Solomon' (2006) 14 *Medical Law Review* 425; C Lind, 'Evans v United Kingdom – Judgments of Solomon: Power, Gender and Procreation' (2006) 18 *Child and Family Law Quarterly* 576.
[87] *Review of the Human Fertilisation and Embryology Act* (2006) Cm 6989, para 2.34.
[88] See F Fisher and A Somerville, 'To Everything there is Season? Are There Medical Grounds for Refusing Treatment to Older Women?' in J Harris and S Holm (eds), *The Future of Reproduction* (1998) Clarendon Press, p 203.

Spain, a woman of 67 had twins. The crux of the question should not be the post-menopausal state of the woman. Some women suffer a premature menopause in their twenties. Few argue that they should be denied help. The question is whether women over 50, or 55, or 60 should be assisted to have a child. France prohibits treatment of women past the normal age of childbearing. Those opposed to treating older women focus on the child. If a woman gives birth at 62, she will be 80 before her child is legally an adult. It is more likely that her health may decline, or the child will face the death of his mother, than if she were merely 40. Others point out that men fairly often beget children in their fifties and later. Is it discriminatory to prohibit helping women to do what nature permits men to do? Perhaps what we should ask is whether to create a child at an age when the chances are your ability to care for that child are diminishing is morally responsible – for either men or women? Then we need to consider if it is ethical to assist another person to do something irresponsible.[89]

Pre-implantation genetic diagnosis

13.12 Advances in reproductive medicine have helped not only infertile couples, but also couples who risk transmitting a genetic disease to their children. A woman who is a haemophilia carrier could avoid giving birth to an affected son by opting for egg donation. PGD offers such a woman the chance to have her own genetic child. Embryos are created by IVF, and PGD is used to screen out embryos affected by the relevant genetic disease. Only healthy embryos are selected for implantation. In some cases, PGD involves sex selection for medical reasons, for example screening out male embryos potentially susceptible to haemophilia. As PGD develops, doctors become more able to refine the screening process and identify affected, and unaffected, embryos. One particular development has created especial controversy – around what are popularly described as 'saviour siblings'. Parents who have a child already afflicted by a potentially fatal genetic disorder can seek to have another baby whose stem cells, taken from her umbilical cord, could 'cure' her brother or sister. PGD is combined with tissue typing of the embryos via human antigen tissue typing (HLA). By this means, a baby is created who is both unaffected by the genetic disorder in question, and an exact tissue match for the sick sibling. Opponents of PGD/HLA argue that it is wrong to create a baby purely as a means to an end. But desperate parents often make several attempts to have a baby naturally to achieve just that end – a tissue match for a sick child. The HFEA has struggled to deal with the dilemma posed by 'saviour siblings'. The Authority gave a clinic permission to treat Zain Hashmi. Zain suffered from beta thallasaemia (BT), a genetic disease. His family could provide no compatible stem cell donor, so his parents sought PGD with HLA. Charlie Whitaker suffered from Diamond Blackfan Anaemia (DBA). His parents also wanted to use PGD with HLA to create a 'saviour sibling' for Charlie. The HFEA said no. The Hashmi embryo was itself at risk of BT. DBA is not thought to be a genetic disease, so the HFEA initially argued

---

[89] See M Brazier, 'Liberty, Responsibility, Maternity' (1999) 52 *Current Legal Problems* 359.

that Whitaker embryos could not be screened as they would obtain no benefit. The distinction between the two cases met vigorous criticism.[90] The HFEA changed its mind.

Meanwhile, pro-life groups challenged the legality of the HFEA decision to allow PGD with HLA in the Hashmi case. Ultimately, the House of Lords[91] ruled in favour of the HFEA, confining themselves to an exercise in statutory interpretation and seeking to side-step moral controversy. The White Paper[92] seeks to give statutory force to the Law Lords' ruling. A new Act will set out explicit criteria to allow screening out of genetic or chromosomal abnormalities which may lead to serious medical conditions[93] or disabilities, or miscarriage, and will also enable identification of a tissue match for a sibling suffering from a life-threatening illness. 'Saviour siblings' will be expressly legitimised.

PGD raises other questions, though. Should it be used to allow sex selection for non-medical reasons? A couple with three sons want a daughter to 'balance' their family. A single woman wants only female children. The HFEA prohibits sex selection, using PGD, for non-medical reasons. Another technique, sperm sorting, is outside the remit of the HFEA. Using fresh sperm, some doctors argue that they can, with reasonable accuracy, separate out X and Y sperm. Those wanting only daughters discard all Y sperm. Sex selection is perennially controversial. In parts of the world, ante-natal testing and infanticide are used to abort or kill female foetuses and babies. Opinion in the UK is divided.[94] The White Paper,[95] however, proposes an absolute ban on sex selection for non-medical reasons, including for the purposes of 'family balancing'.[96] This will apply as much to sperm sorting as to PGD.

One final possibility arising out of PGD needs to be noted. PGD is currently used to screen out certain sorts of disease or disability. What if a couple sort to screen in a particular condition, for example a deaf couple wanted to ensure that their child was also deaf?[97] The White Paper says, categorically, 'Deliberately screening-in a disease or disorder will be prohibited'.[98]

---

[90] See S Sheldon and S Wilkinson, 'Hashmi and Whitaker: An Unjustifiable and Misguided Distinction' (2004) 12 *Medical Law Review* 137.

[91] *R (on the application of Quintavalle) v Human Fertilisation and Embryology Authority* [2005] 2 All ER 555, HL.

[92] *Review of the Human Fertilisation and Embryology Act* (2006) Cm 6989, para 2.43.

[93] What counts as serious? Should PGD to rule out genetic susceptibility to diseases not manifesting themselves until adulthood be allowed? See Jackson, *Medical Law: Text and Materials*, pp 842–885.

[94] See Human Fertilisation and Embryology Authority, *Sex Selection: Options for Regulation* (2003).

[95] *Review of the Human Fertilisation and Embryology Act* (2006) Cm 6989, paras 2.45–2.47.

[96] The House of Commons Science and Technology Committee endorsed sex selection for 'family balancing' in their Report, *Human Reproductive Technologies and the Law*.

[97] See J Savulescu, 'Deaf Lesbians, "Designer Disability" and the Future of Medicine' (2002) 325 *British Medical Journal* 771.

[98] See *Review of the Human Fertilisation and Embryology Act* (2006) Cm 6989, para. 2.43.

What should the child be told?

13.13 Does a child born after the use of donor gametes have a right to know the identity of his genetic parents? An adopted child has, at 18, a right of access to his original birth certificate and so has the opportunity to trace his natural parents.[99] If an adopted child may trace his birth mother and genetic father, should children born from gamete donation be afforded a similar right? Until August 2005, anonymity protected all gamete donors, while affording some limited rights to children born as a result of donation. The Human Fertilisation and Embryology Act 1990 adopted a compromise. Section 31 provides that the HFEA shall keep a register detailing the provision of treatment services and the use of gametes. At the age of 18 a person could, after proper counselling, request information from that register. Section 31(4)(b) provides that information *must* include information about whether or not the applicant and a person whom he proposes to marry are related. Section 31(4)(a) provides that such other information relating to the applicant 'as the Authority is required by regulations to give' shall be made available to him. The wording of section 31(4)(a) is such that the HFEA would be free to decide whether the information should include the *identity* of the child's genetic parents, the gamete donors.

Section 31(5), however, ensures that any removal of anonymity cannot be retrospective. If anonymity prevailed when sperm was donated, a later change in the rules will not give children access to the identity of the donor. The rules have now changed. Regulations now provide that from April 2005,[100] a child will, at the age of 18, acquire the right to information about the identity of donor parents. As the new rules cannot apply retrospectively, no pre-existing donor risks losing his or her anonymity until 2023. Clinics fear that loss of prospective anonymity will exacerbate the acute shortage of gamete donors. Some children will acquire the right to know the identity of a genetic parent at the expense of couples who remain childless for lack of donors. The removal of anonymity to donors was prompted by powerful arguments that the child's interests in private and family life require that she has access to such information. A person's psychological well-being is, it is claimed, intimately connected to a sense of identity and heritage. If donation is seen as an ethical, altruistic act why must it be kept secret? If adopted children need to know the identity of their genetic parents, why are the needs of children born from gamete or embryo donation less pressing?[101] Granting a young man who had spent a miserable childhood in care access to all the files held on him, the European Court of Human Rights declared that '… everyone should be able to establish details of their identity as individual human beings'.[102] In *R (on the application of Rose) v Secretary of State for Health*,[103] Scott Baker J held

---

[99]   Adoption Act 1976, s 51(2).
[100]   Human Fertilisation and Embryology Authority (Disclosure of Donor Information) Regulations 2004, SI 2004/1511.
[101]   But see K O'Donovan, 'What Shall We Tell the Children? Reflections on Children's Perspectives and the Reproduction Revolution' in R Lee and D Morgan (eds), *Birthrights: Law and Ethics and the Beginning of Life* (1989) Routledge.
[102]   *Gaskin v United Kingdom* [1990] 1 FLR 167.
[103]   [2002] EWHC 1593 (Admin).

that Article 8 of the European Convention on Human Rights was relevant to the question of what access to information children born via assisted conception should enjoy.

Access to assisted conception

13.14 The liberal interpretation of section 13(5) of the Human Fertilisation and Embryology Act 1990 adopted by the HFEA, and in particular their new guidance that only evidence of risk of significant harm[104] to a potential child should 'disqualify' a woman or a couple from receiving treatment, grants clinics a broad discretion about whom to treat. It has been argued that section 13(5) never made much difference in practice to the range of patients private clinics will treat.[105] IVF treatment is largely provided in the private sector, with limited NHS facilities for those who cannot pay for treatment. NHS clinics have to make hard choices. Practice varies, but many clinics operate criteria based on the likelihood that patients would be good parents.[106] Some follow adoption guidelines used by local services departments. Most offer treatment only where neither partner has any existing children. Many operate upper age limits as low as 35 for women. Courts have been reluctant to interfere. As an example, Mrs Harriott was refused IVF because of a criminal record for prostitution offences and because she and her husband had been rejected as prospective adoptive or foster parents by Manchester social services department. Clinicians referred her case to the hospital's informal ethical advisory committee, who endorsed their decision. She sought judicial review of that decision, alleging that the grounds for refusing her treatment were unreasonable and unlawful. The judge held that decisions on IVF treatment could be reviewed by a court. If a patient was refused treatment on grounds, say, of religion or ethnic origin, that could be clearly unlawful. Public bodies and officials, including clinicians taking decisions within the NHS, must act reasonably and not on the basis of irrational prejudices. In Mrs Harriott's case, however, the judge found that the grounds for regarding her to be an unsuitable parent were reasonable.[107] In another case, Mrs Seale and her husband were refused NHS treatment because, at 37, she was 'too old'. Her health authority argued that 35 was a sensible cut-off point because the older the woman, the less the chances of establishing a successful pregnancy. Given a tight budget, the NHS should concentrate on treating women most likely to benefit from treatment. The judge agreed.[108] Conditions set by NHS clinics vary widely. Criteria by which PCTs decide to fund fertility treatment also vary. Where you live might determine whether you are 'too old' to be treated or whether you are 'unsuitable'. In 2003, NICE recommended

---

[104] See Human Fertilisation and Embryology Authority, *Tomorrow's Children* (2005); Human Fertilisation and Embryology Authority, *Welfare of the Child and the Assessment of Those Seeking Treatment Guidance* (2005), accessible at www.hfea.gov.uk/cps/rde/xbcc/SID-3F7D79B BF1E1172/hfea/Revised_Guidance.pdf.

[105] G Douglas, 'Assisted Reproduction and the Welfare of the Child' (1993) *Current Legal Problems* 46.

[106] See D Savas and S Treece, 'Fertility Clinics: One Code of Practice?' (1998) 3 *Medical Law International* 243.

[107] *R. v Ethical Advisory Committee of St Mary's Hospital, ex p Harriott* [1988] 1 FLR 512.

[108] *R v Sheffield Area Health Authority, ex p Seale* [1994] 25 BMLR 1.

that every infertile couple should be offered three cycles of IVF within the NHS.[109] The Government reduced that to one cycle. Some PCTs still refuse to fund fertility treatment at all. British couples may look with envy at France. France provides generous public funding for fertility treatment. Couples of childbearing age are unlikely to be turned away.[110] However, treatment is limited to heterosexual couples of reproductive age. Single women, lesbian couples or post-menopausal mothers are excluded. British patients have considerable 'freedom' if they can pay. Income is not an impediment in France.

A right to reproduce?

13.15 The practical questions raised by assisted conception are many and varied. At the heart of those questions lies the intractable problem of whether individuals enjoy a right to reproduce, and just what such a right entails. Articles, 8, 12 and 14 of the European Convention on Human Rights all touch on this problem. The European Court of Human Rights in *Evans*[111] acknowledged that Article 8 rights to private life were engaged in laws regulating reproductive medicine, and access to treatment. Article 12 speaks of a 'right to marry and found a family'. Article 14 prohibits unjustifiable discrimination, so a woman denied fertility treatment might argue that barriers to treatment discriminate against her just because she is infertile. The first difficulty of a rights-based argument in the context of fertility treatment is this. As Wall J noted in his first instance judgment in *Evans*:

> The right to found a family through IVF can only, put at its highest, amount to a right to have IVF treatment. Self-evidently it cannot be a right to be treated successfully.[112]

Two cases involving prisoners seeking access to DI so their wives could conceive while they remained in prison further highlight the complexity of rights arguments. In *R v Secretary of State for the Home Department, ex p Mellor*,[113] Mr Mellor was serving a life sentence. His wife would be 31 when his tariff expired, and he would be eligible for parole. They wanted to start a family, but the Home Office refused their request to make arrangements for semen collection from Mr Mellor. Mr Mellor challenged the decision, citing his right to 'marry and to found a family'. Note that, unlike Article 8, Article 12 appears to be an unqualified right. The Court of Appeal dismissed his case. Imprisonment necessarily involved an interference with family life justifiable under Article 8(2), and also constitutes a justifiable interference with Article 12. A prisoner could claim no right to beget children. In the *Mellor* case, if access to artificial insemination was refused, but Mr Mellor gained parole when his tariff expired, founding a family was merely delayed, not wholly prevented. Mr and Mrs Dickson faced a graver

[109] Accessible at www.nice.org.uk/pdf/CS011niceguidelines.pdf.
[110] See M Latham, 'Regulating the New Reproductive Technologies: A Cross-Channel Comparison' (1998) *Medical Law International* 89.
[111] [2004] EWCA (Civ) 727. For a highly critical account of the analysis of the European Court of Human Rights in *Evans*, see Lind (2006) 18 *Child and Family Law Quarterly* 576.
[112] [2003] EWHC 2161 (Fam) at para 263.
[113] [2001] 3 WLR 533.

dilemma. Mr Dickson was also serving a life sentence. By the time he was to be eligible to be freed from prison, his wife would be 51. Their chances of having a family together would be slim without immediate access to fertility treatment. But the couple had met via a pen-friend scheme when both were in prison. They married in prison and had never lived together. Mrs Dickson had three children by other relationships. The Home Office refused access to artificial insemination on a number of grounds, including that the marriage had never been tested in a normal environment, there was a lack of provision to ensure the welfare of any child, and there would be public concern that the legitimate punitive element of Mr Dickson's sentence would be circumvented by permitting him to father a child by artificial insemination while serving his life sentence. The Court of Appeal dismissed Mr Dickson's application for judicial review, and the couple took their case to the European Court of Human Rights. Note that Mrs Dickson's right to found a family was also at stake. None the less, the court found against them, by a majority of four to three.[114] The majority held that imprisonment necessarily involved limitations on Convention rights. The Home Office had given careful consideration to the case. One judge said that merely forwarding sperm did not constitute founding a family. At the time of writing, the Dicksons' case is under review by the Grand Chamber of the European Court. Perhaps that judgment will offer some further clarification about rights and reproduction.

Liability for disability

13.16 What if fertility treatment results in the birth of a disabled infant? This could happen for several reasons. In DI, the donor may turn out to be the carrier of some disease or genetic disorder. Babies have been born abroad suffering from HIV contracted from donor sperm. An error may be made in the laboratory, damaging an IVF embryo. Or treatment, such as ICSI, might in years to come be shown to produce abnormalities manifesting themselves only when the children reach maturity, or try to have children themselves.

Parents will be able to maintain an action against doctors and clinics if mother or child is injured by negligence. Clearly, if the mother herself suffers any injury (for example, in the course of collecting eggs), she may recover compensation for that injury. The woman accepted for treatment expects care, not only in relation to herself but also in the 'production' of a healthy infant. If, by negligence, the child is born disabled, damage to the parents is readily foreseeable. Both mother and father will suffer emotional trauma and face the added expense of bringing up a disabled child.[115] Is there a problem if the parents cannot pinpoint exactly who was negligent? It may be impossible for them to know if the embryo was damaged by the gynaecologist removing the eggs and implanting the embryo, or by the scientists in the laboratory. In NHS clinics, the NHS trust owes a direct duty to the parents and is responsible for

---

[114] Case 44362/04 *Dickson v United Kingdom*; see H Codd, 'The Slippery Slope to Sperm Smuggling: Prisoners, Artificial Insemination and Human Rights' (2007) 15 *Medical Law Review* (forthcoming).

[115] See *Parkinson v St James and Seacroft University Hospital NHS Trust* [2001] 3 All ER 97, CA.

negligently failing to discharge that duty. In the private sector, patients should ensure that the clinic similarly undertakes a contractual duty to provide and underwrite the whole course of treatment. Exactly what the contractual terms agreed with a private clinic entail may be crucial. A couple successfully sued a private clinic who implanted three embryos in the woman after she had specifically stated that no more than two embryos should be replaced. The clinic was held liable for breach of contract and responsible for the birth of a third child.[116] One final point relating to actions by parents is that, while they may have legal redress if a damaged baby is born, there will be no legal remedy if no baby is born. Success rates for IVF remain low, neither NHS nor private clinics undertake more than to attempt to assist conception using all due skill and care.

What of an action by the child? He will need to rely on the right of action in respect of pre-natal injuries enacted in the Congenital Disabilities (Civil Liability) Act 1976. The Human Fertilisation and Embryology Act 1990 expressly amends the 1976 Act to allow for an action arising out of negligence in the process of assisted conception. Section 44 inserts into the 1976 Act a section 1A which provides for an action if a child carried by a woman as a result of the placing in her of an embryo, sperm and eggs, or DI is born disabled, and the disability results from negligence in the selection, or keeping or use outside the body, of the relevant embryo or gametes. Providing the defendant is answerable in tort to one or both parents, he is liable to the child. The sorts of cases envisaged by this new section 1A are just the sort of examples mentioned earlier – the child born HIV positive because doctors failed to screen donors adequately, the child born damaged by some technical error in his creation, the child born disabled because a defective embryo was negligently implanted in the mother. A further extension to the rights of the child is made in section 35(4) of the 1990 Act, again amending the 1976 Act, to provide that injury to the reproductive capacity of the genetic parent gives rise to a derivative action under the 1976 Act for the child. Section 34 and 35 of the 1990 Act make extensive provision for disclosure of information necessary to any action by parent or child for damages occasioned by assisted conception.

One difficulty facing an action by the child remains. Is the essence of his action for 'wrongful life' or 'wrongful disability'? If the former, no action can lie.[117] Much will then turn on how it is alleged the child came to suffer injury. If it is claimed that gametes and embryo were originally healthy, but damaged by some act of the doctors or scientists treating the mother, the claim is for 'wrongful disability'. It is on a par with a claim that a healthy foetus was damaged *in utero* by drugs given to the mother. But what if the alleged negligence is that infected sperm was used to inseminate the mother or a defective embryo implanted in her? Such a claim must logically be classified as a 'wrongful life' claim. Assume these facts. A DI clinic negligently fails to check donors for HIV. Baby X is born with HIV from contaminated sperm. Had the clinic exercised due care in the collection of sperm, that individual,

---

[116] *Thompson v Sheffield Fertility Centre* (24 November 2000, unreported), QBD; and see (2000) Guardian, 4 December.
[117] See *McKay v Essex Area Authority* [1982] 2 All ER 771, CA (discussed above at 12.7).

Baby X, would never have been born at all. Similarly, if a defective embryo is not screened and discarded in the laboratory, any action the child brings is for 'wrongful life'. His parents could, 'but for' the relevant negligence, have had a healthy child. He would not have been that child.

Both parents and children seeking compensation for disability will face problems proving negligence where it is difficult to isolate the cause of the damage to the child. A baby resulting from DI born HIV positive, or afflicted by a genetic disease carried by the donor father, poses no legal problem in a claim by his parents. Competent screening should have discovered the disease or defect and that sperm should never have been used to inseminate the mother. Linking a defect to an error in the laboratory will be less easy. An action based on abnormalities manifesting themselves later in life is almost bound to fail. If in 2015 it is shown that freezing embryos produces cancer in the late teens and early twenties, the defence to any claim in negligence will be that responsible professional opinion, endorsed by countless official reports, believed freezing to be safe in 1995, when the child was born.

Finally, if parent or child has a right to sue and proves negligence, are there defences open to the doctor based on the parents having agreed to run the risk of a damaged child? Section 44(3) of the 1990 Act provides that an action by the child shall fail if either or both parents knew of the risk of their child being born disabled, '... that is to say, the particular risk created by the act of omission'. So if the mother is known to carry a genetic disease herself and is counselled that it would be better to use donor eggs for an IVF pregnancy, yet insists on a child who is genetically hers, she cannot turn round and sue the doctors who carried out her wishes, if her genetic problem is inherited by her child. However, it would be no defence for a defendant simply to say, 'Well, parents know that this is a relatively new and risky process, so I am not liable.' The parents must be aware of the particular risk of harming their child. Often the risk of harm to an IVF or GIFT baby arises from the increased danger of a multiple pregnancy. A parent who was not fully counselled on this risk might argue that not warning of that particular risk was negligent. To succeed in an action she would then have to prove that, had she been warned, she would not have gone ahead with the treatment.

Reproductive cloning

13.17 When Parliament enacted the Human Fertilisation and Embryology Act 1990, the assumption was made that section 3(1)(d) outlawed any form of human cloning. Replacing the nucleus of an embryo with the nucleus of a cell taken from any other person or embryo was prohibited. The development of cell nuclear replacement (CNR), heralded by the birth of Dolly the Sheep, highlighted the inadequacy of section 3(1)(d). Placing a donated nucleus into an emptied egg still fell outside the prohibition. As we shall see in the next chapter, the Government sought to permit the HFEA to license the use of CNR in developing stem cell therapies (often referred to as therapeutic cloning).[118]

---

[118] See the Human Fertilisation and Embryology (Research Purposes) Regulations 2001, SI 2001/188 (discussed fully below at 14.8).

Reproductive cloning was condemned.[119] Pro-life groups, however, challenged the Regulations, arguing that CNR embryos fell outside the 1990 Act altogether because the embryos were not created by fertilisation. Their victory at first instance[120] led to the Human Reproductive Cloning Act 2001 prohibiting the implantation in a woman of an embryo 'created otherwise than by fertilisation'. Ultimately, the House of Lords[121] ruled that all embryos *in vitro*, however created, fell within the 1990 Act. New legislation will make it absolutely clear that all embryos, however created, fall within the scope of regulation.[122] In the immediate future, it seems impossible to envisage the HFEA or RATE even sanctioning research into reproductive cloning.

Several arguments are advanced for,[123] and against, reproductive cloning.[124] Safety is a concern that all parties in the debate share. Mammalian cloning has shown a high rate of birth defects and miscarriage. But research might overcome this hurdle to permitting cloning. Other arguments centre on the impact on the cloned child of her means of production. She will (it is said) lack a unique identity, but so does any identical twin. If she is a clone of her mother, she will see her genetic future mapped out from birth. Moreover, she may be condemned to live more generally in her creator's shadow – a copy, not a daughter. If she is a clone of a dead sibling, her parent(s) may not value her, but rather the ghost of her sister. Yet environment shapes us as much as our DNA. A clone of either of the authors would grow up in different times and with different parents. Confusion about relationships is another problem for a clone. Would a clone of Emma Cave have Emma for her mother? Or would Emma's mother be mother to the clone? The Emma clone would be truly fatherless. The debate goes on. Yet Mason and Laurie[125] 'suspect that the days of the outright prohibition on reproductive cloning are numbered'.

Surrogacy

13.18 Where a woman is unable to carry a child herself, perhaps because she has undergone a hysterectomy or has endured several miscarriages, surrogacy may be her only hope for a child. Surrogacy can take a number of forms. In partial surrogacy, a surrogate agrees with the commissioning couple to undergo artificial insemination with the man's sperm. She agrees to carry any resulting child, and to hand the child over to the genetic father and his wife or partner as soon as she is born. The surrogate may well practise self-insemination privately.[126] IVF offers a couple where the woman ovulates, but cannot safely carry a child to term, the chance of a baby who is genetically

---

[119] HFEA/HGAC, *Cloning Issues in Reproduction, Science and Medicine* (1998).

[120] *R (on the application of Quintavalle) v Secretary of State for Health* [2001] 4 All ER 1013.

[121] *R (on the application of Quintavalle) v Secretary of State for Health* [2003] 2 All ER 113, HL.

[122] See *Review of the Human Fertilisation and Embryology Act* (2006) Cm 6989, para 2.11.

[123] See, notably, J Harris, *On Cloning* (2004) Routledge.

[124] Summed up in Jackson, *Medical Law: Text and Materials*, pp 858–869.

[125] *Mason and McCall Smith's Law and Medical Ethics*, p 252.

[126] See M Brazier, A Campbell and S Golombok, *Surrogacy: Review for Health Ministers of Current Arrangements for Payments and Regulation* (1998) Cm 4068 (hereafter the *Surrogacy Review*).

theirs. Eggs are taken from the woman, fertilised in the laboratory with sperm from the man, and the embryo implanted in the surrogate. The surrogate once again carries the child and agrees to hand her over at birth. The surrogate is literally a 'hostess' for the couple's embryo. This practice may be styled 'full surrogacy'. Surrogacy, while still rare, attracts controversy. After the Warnock Report the only swift response from Government was to ban commercial surrogacy.[127] The Warnock Report went further, and would have prohibited any third party, commercial agency or doctor, from assisting a couple to arrange a surrogate pregnancy, regardless of whether what was envisaged was full or partial surrogacy.[128]

What are the legal issues arising out of surrogacy? Can it ever amount to a crime to arrange a surrogate pregnancy? What happens if the surrogate changes her mind and refuses to hand the baby over? Where the baby is genetically that of the wife and implanted in the surrogate via IVF, what are the rights of the genetic parents? What rights can the father assert? Should surrogacy be better regulated?

Prohibiting 'commercial' surrogacy

13.19 Surrogacy where no money changes hands is lawful in the sense that no crime is committed. If payment is made to an agency, however, an offence is committed. The Surrogacy Arrangements Act 1985 makes it a criminal offence for anyone to play any part in setting up a surrogacy arrangement on a commercial basis. Advertising or compiling information to promote or assist surrogacy arrangements are also made criminal. Offenders face a punishment of a fine and/or up to three months in prison. Under the Act, no offence is committed by a woman herself seeking to become, or becoming, a surrogate, nor is any offence committed by the man or the couple who persuade her to carry a child. The Act is limited to banning the activities of any commercial agencies or individuals aiming to make a profit out of surrogate motherhood. A fertility specialist who helps in establishing a full surrogacy incurs no criminal liability so long as he does not involve himself in arranging the introduction of couple and surrogate. The Warnock Report's proposal that any third-party intervention, including professional help from a doctor, which was intended to set up a surrogacy arrangement should be made illegal was not acted on. The 1985 Act does, however, embrace all forms of surrogacy, be they 'partial' or 'full' surrogacy.[129]

Although the surrogate and the couple engaging her services do not commit any offence under the 1985 Act, even if she is paid for what she does, all three parties may be guilty of an offence under section 95 of the Adoption Act 2002 if the surrogate is offered an overt payment for her services. For it is a criminal offence to give or receive any payment in relation to the adoption of a child,

---

[127] The Surrogacy Arrangements Act 1985. The Act was also prompted by controversy about 'Baby Cotton': see *Re C (A minor) (Wardship: Surrogacy)* [1985] FLR 846.
[128] At p 46.
[129] The 1985 Act will apply however the embryo came to be created, be it by GIFT or IVF: see s 36 of the Human Fertilisation and Embryology Act 1990.

the grant of consent to adoption, or the handing over of a child with a view to its adoption, unless that payment is authorised by a court. In order to make the baby born to the surrogate legally theirs, the commissioning couple must ultimately obtain a 'parental order' or adopt the child. In theory, any payment beyond 'reasonable expenses' will debar the couple from obtaining a parental order. If they try to adopt the child and money paid to the surrogate is found to include a sum in payment for her agreement to the adoption and handing over the child, the surrogate and the couple may face prosecution. Moreover, the Adoption Act 2002 further provides that the court may order the infant to be removed to a place of safety 'until he can be restored to his parents or guardians or until other arrangements can be made for him'. A child could in theory be removed from all those involved in the surrogacy arrangement. Would such drastic action make any sort of sense if that surrogate was happy to hand over the baby, and there was no reason to believe that the commissioning couple were unfit to care for the child? How to respond to such a surrogacy case was a dilemma which confronted Barnet Social Services in 1985. A baby girl was born in their area amid great publicity. Her mother (Kim Cotton) had agreed to carry her for a childless couple from abroad. She was artificially inseminated with the husband's sperm. The arrangements were made through an agency who were paid £13,000 by the father, of which the surrogate received £6,500. At the relevant time, the Surrogacy Arrangements Act had not yet been enacted. The baby was born and the mother prepared to hand her over. Barnet Social Services stepped in. The child was made a ward of court. Latey J[130] had to decide on her fate. He said that the crucial issue before him was what was best for this baby. The methods used to create the child and the commercial aspects of the case raised delicate problems of ethics, morality and social desirability. They were not for him to decide. Careful inquiries showed that the father and his wife were eminently suitable to be parents. The judge granted them custody of the baby and permission to take her abroad with them to their home. The question of adoption, and so the illegality of any payment under the Adoption Act 1976, did not arise in that case.

Two years later, Latey J was called on again to adjudicate on the consequences of a surrogacy arrangement where all the parties desired to abide by that arrangement.[131] Mr and Mrs A arranged for Mrs B to carry a child for them. The child was conceived by natural sexual intercourse between Mr A and Mrs B. Mrs B was to be paid £10,000.[132] A baby was born and handed over to Mr and Mrs A after birth. They sought to adopt the child, as they then had to do to acquire parental rights. Were they in breach of the Adoption Act 1976 and so at risk of losing their child? Latey J found they were not. He held that the payments were *not* to procure Mrs B's consent to adoption. At the time of the agreement this was not in the parties' minds. The payments were in the nature of expenses for Mrs B, recompense for her time and inconvenience. Furthermore, the judge held that, even if he were wrong and

---

[130] *Re C (A Minor) (Wardship: Surrogacy)* [1985] FLR 846.
[131] *Re an Adoption Application (Surrogacy)* [1987] 2 All ER 826. See also *Re Q (Parental Order)* [1996] 1 FLR 369.
[132] In the event, Mrs B accepted only £5,000 of the agreed fee, having co-authored a book on her experience of surrogacy.

the payments *were* illegal payments, he had power to ratify those payments retrospectively. Payments authorised by the court are not unlawful. As a matter of pure legal reasoning Latey J's grounds for finding the payments made by Mr and Mrs A to Mrs B to be lawful may well be faulty. What is clear is that the judge saw no reason to upset an arrangement which had worked, or to remove the child, now two, from the only parents it had known. What else could he do? If Parliament wanted to ban surrogacy, it should have done so outright.

If the surrogate is content to hand the baby over, the courts will help the commissioning couple to keep the baby. What if she changes her mind? First, it is absolutely clear in England that surrogacy agreements are not enforceable as contracts. The commissioning couple cannot sue the surrogate for breach of contract, or ask a court to order performance of a contract. Nor can the surrogate sue if she does not receive any agreed payments. Section 36(1) of the 1990 Act inserts a new section 1A in the Surrogacy Arrangements Act 1985, providing quite simply that:

> No surrogacy arrangement is enforceable by or against any of the persons making it.

It does not matter by what means the child was created, be it sexual intercourse, DI or IVF – the arrangement is not an enforceable contract.

'Custody' of the baby

13.20 That still leaves open the question of what happens if the surrogate wants to keep the baby. In England, if the surrogate changes her mind and refuses to surrender the child, she will usually be allowed to keep the child. In *A v C*,[133] as long ago as 1978, a young woman agreed to have a baby by DI and hand over the child to the wealthy father and his partner. She was to be paid £3,000. When the child was born she refused to give him up. The father sought care and control. The trial judge found that the mother should be allowed to keep the child, but granted the father limited access. The Court of Appeal removed his rights of access, condemning the whole arrangement as 'irresponsible, bizarre and unnatural'. Nor does it seem that a greater tolerance of surrogacy has altered judicial policy where surrogates change their minds. In *Re P (Minors) (Wardship: Surrogacy)*,[134] Sir John Arnold P refused to order a surrogate mother to hand over twins born as a result of her artificial insemination by the father. It would seem that in England, a surrogate would be deprived of her baby only if she were an unfit mother who would not be allowed to keep the child however it had come to be conceived. Surrogacy is an arrangement couples enter into at their peril. If all goes to plan, they will get 'their' baby. If the arrangement breaks down, the law will not assist them in a battle with the surrogate, save in one exceptional situation. If the surrogate hands over the child, who is settled into the couple's home, but later changes her mind about consent to adoption or a parental

---

[133] [1985] FLR 445, FD and CA.
[134] *Re P (Minors) (Wardship: Surrogacy)* [1987] 2 FLR 421.

order, the court has on two occasions at least overruled the surrogate's refusal of consent.[135] The welfare of the child once he or she is established in a 'new' family will override any claims of the surrogate.

Is the position any different where the surrogate is not the genetic mother, where the child was created by IVF from the eggs and sperm of the commissioning couple? Prior to the Human Fertilisation and Embryology Act 1990, the genetic mother might have argued thus: 'I am this baby's mother. I do not need to adopt my own child. She (the surrogate) has no right to keep my child from me.' That argument is killed stone dead by section 27 of the Act. Section 27 provides, as we have seen, that it is the woman who carries the child *and no other woman* who is to be treated as the mother of the child.

Parental orders

13.21 Late in passage of the Human Fertilisation and Embryology Act 1990 through Parliament, section 30 was inserted to help some commissioning couples in surrogacy cases.[136] It provides for a procedure, other than adoption, by which some couples will be able to acquire parental rights over 'their' child. Section 30 gives the court power to order that the commissioning couple be treated in law as the parents of the child, but *only* in a limited number of circumstances:

(1)   The couple must be married.
(2)   The child must have been conceived from either the placing of the embryo (IVF) or sperm and eggs (GIFT) in the woman, or by DI. And the eggs or sperm or both must come from the couple. Children conceived by natural intercourse between the surrogate and the husband are not within the ambit of section 30.[137]
(3)   At the time of the making of the order, the child must be living with the couple and the surrogate (and the 'legal father')[138] must have given full and free consent not less than six weeks after the birth. Section 30 is of no relevance if the surrogate changes her mind and is not willing to hand over the child. Nor is it a backdoor route to enforcing a surrogacy contract.
(4)   No payments (other than for expenses reasonably incurred)[139] must have been made to the surrogate unless authorised by the court.

In effect, section 30 is a statutory embodiment of what might be called the 'Latey approach' to surrogacy: if it has worked out and a child is settled with 'her parents', the law should give legal effect to the actual family circumstances prevailing.

---

[135] *Re MW (Adoption: Surrogacy)* [1995] 2 FLR 759; *C v S* (1996) SLT 1387.
[136] See *Re W (Minors Surrogacy)* [1991] 1 FLR 385.
[137] As was the case in *Re an Adoption Application (Surrogacy)* [1987] 2 All ER 826.
[138] On which see *Re Q (Parental Order)* [1996] 2 FCR 345.
[139] But note that £12,000 has been deemed reasonable expenses: *Re C (Application by Mr and Mrs X under s 30 of the Human Fertilisation and Embryology Act)* [2002] EWHC 157.

Section 30 is limited in scope. Could the male partner in the commissioning couple assert paternal rights by other means? How do the provisions of the 1990 Act defining paternity affect surrogacy? Section 28 deems the husband of a woman treated with donor sperm to be the father of the child and designates any man treated together with the woman as the father if the couple are not married. Its impact on surrogacy is complicated. If the surrogate is married, her husband will be treated as the child's father! Section 30 will then require his consent to the grant of a parental order to the commissioning couple. If the surrogate is not married, and is treated in a licensed clinic, could it be argued that she and the commissioning father are treated together? If so, could the surrogate and the child's genetic father agree to share parental responsibility, with the father seeking a residence order? It seems not.[140] If partial surrogacy is established by self-insemination, however, the commissioning father is the legal father of the child. He could, with the surrogate's concurrence, simply seek a residence order. The couple could have the child in their home, yet the commissioning mother would have no legal relationship with the child.

Surrogacy developed pragmatically after Warnock – keep commercial agencies at bay and otherwise deal with each case as it arose seemed to be the policy. Difficult questions remained unanswered. What happens if the baby was born disabled and no-one wanted her? What if the commissioning couple split up?

The number of surrogacy arrangements is impossible to ascertain accurately. In 1998,[141] it was estimated that there were about 50–80 births in the UK arising from surrogacy arrangements. Surrogacy had not, as the Warnock Report had hoped, 'withered on the vine'.[142] 'Partial surrogacy' remains the most 'popular' form of surrogacy. Payments are rising, with evidence that payments of up to and beyond £12,000[143] are (sometimes reluctantly) sanctioned as *expenses* by courts authorising parental or adoption orders. At least two voluntary agencies provide services for couples seeking surrogates. It is relatively common for surrogates to act as such on a number of occasions. Concerns about surrogacy resurfaced in the final years of the twentieth century. In one well publicised case, a young woman agreed to carry a child for a Dutch couple in return for £12,000 expenses. She changed her mind and first she told them that she had had an abortion. Later she said that she was still pregnant but planned to keep the baby.[144] Around the same time, one of the leading US surrogacy agents arrived in Britain advertising his commercial surrogacy service. The Government set up a review[145] of payments for and regulation of surrogacy.

The *Surrogacy Review* made a number of recommendations for law reform. The most controversial proposal was that the prohibition on paying surro-gates for their services should be maintained, and given teeth. A new

---

[140] *Re Q (Parental Order)* [1996] 2 FCR 345.
[141] See the *Surrogacy Review*.
[142] The *Surrogacy Review*, para 2.23.
[143] *Re C (Application by Mr and Mrs X under s 30 of the Human Fertilisation and Embryology Act)* [2002] EWHC 157 (Fam).
[144] See the *Surrogacy Review*, para 1.9.
[145] The Surrogacy Review.

Surrogacy Act should define expenses to exclude covert payments. Unless pregnancy causes the surrogate to give up work, it is difficult to see how genuine expenses resulting from pregnancy can add up to more than a couple of thousand pounds. Any agency which introduced couples and surrogates or offered advice on surrogacy would have to be registered with the Department of Health. A Code of Practice would be developed which agencies must abide by and which sets out a model of good practice for couples and surrogates. The Code would seek to ensure frank exchanges of information and offer independent counselling to all involved. Multiple surrogacy would be discouraged. Parties who complied with the Code would be able to obtain a parental order swiftly. Where the Code was not followed, the lengthier process of adoption would be required, with provision for a full investigation of the circumstances of the arrangement. The proposed Surrogacy Act would reinforce a philosophy of surrogacy as a gift relationship, and set in place regulations which would seek to safeguard the interests of all parties.

Prohibition on payments was vigorously opposed by the major surrogacy agency COTS (Childlessness Overcome Through Surrogacy) and a number of eminent scholars. The most telling criticism of the *Surrogacy Review* came from Michael Freeman[146] who argued, first, that surrogates are entitled to payment and, second, that a ban on payment will drive surrogacy underground, increasing risks of exploitation and harm to the children.

There is, however, agreement that some sort of regulation of surrogacy is needed. The form of regulation will never be settled, however, unless the vexed question of payment is resolved. The arguments are finely balanced. We expect and receive payment for the use of our brains. Why should a surrogate not be paid for the use of her uterus? But should bodily services or body parts be traded? Can you buy children?[147] Proponents of payment argue that paying a surrogate for reproductive labour is not buying a child. Yet what couple would pay if the child is not surrendered? Most pro-payment campaigners argue that surrogacy contracts should remain unenforceable.[148] Is that logical? If the use of the uterus is no different from manual or intellectual labour, why should the surrogate not be obliged to honour her contract?

No immediate action followed the Report of the *Surrogacy Review*. Nearly ten years later, the White Paper on reform of the Human Fertilisation and Embryology Act 1990 suggests some minor changes in the current law. The White Paper notes that 'over time, professional opinion has shifted to a position where surrogacy is recognised as an appropriate response to infertility in some circumstances ...'. The Government proposes to 'clarify' the extent to which non-commercial agencies could facilitate surrogacy arrangements,

---

[146] M Freeman, 'Does Surrogacy Have a Future after Brazier?' (1999) 7 *Medical Law Review* 1.

[147] See M Brazier, 'Can You Buy Children?' (1999) 11 *Child and Family Law Quarterly* 345.

[148] With the honourable exception of COTS. See also Jackson, *Medical Law: Text and Materials*, pp 903–906.

including being allowed to advertise.[149] The provisions of section 30 of the 1990 Act will also be amended to allow heterosexual and same sex couples to apply for a parental order.[150]

[149] *Review of the Human Fertilisation and Embryology Act* (2006) Cm 6989, para 2.64.
[150] *Review of the Human Fertilisation and Embryology Act* (2006) Cm 6989, para 2.69.

Chapter 14

ABORTION AND EMBRYO RESEARCH

14.1 Few medico-legal issues continue to provoke as much controversy as the status of the human embryo. For, if a life given by God begins at conception, the deliberate destruction of an embryo, be it in the course of embryo research or by abortion, is the equivalent of murder. The destruction of the embryo can only be justifiable, if at all, where the mother's life is at risk. If the human embryo has, as others contend, no greater moral status than a mouse embryo, neither research nor abortion is morally wrong. 'Gradualists' argue that the embryo acquires increasing moral claims as it develops in the womb. For many feminists, a right to abortion is part and parcel of a woman's rights over her own body.

The present law[1] on abortion represents an attempt to reach a compromise in a debate in which there is no consensus. In 1990, Parliament, in the Human Fertilisation and Embryology Act, sanctioned embryo research up to 14 days from the day when the gametes are mixed, and permitted abortion in certain cases up to the moment of birth. 'Pro-life' campaigners continue to fight to ban research and restrict abortion. In recent years, the principal thrust of the campaign to restrict abortion in the UK has centred on attempts to reduce the time-limit for legal abortions. In December 2006, as we have seen, the Government put forward a range of proposals to amend existing law relating to assisted conception and embryo research.[2] The Human Fertilisation and Embryology Authority (HFEA) will be replaced by the Regulatory Authority for Tissue and Embryos (RATE). We will discuss the proposals relating to embryo research later in this chapter. The Government proposals expressly disclaim any intent to make changes in the law governing abortion.[3]

---

[1] On the history of abortion law in England, see J Keown, *Abortion, Doctors and the Law* (1988) CUP.

[2] *Review of the Human Fertilisation and Embryology Act: Proposals for Revised Legislation (Including Establishment of the Regulatory Authority for Tissue and Embryos)* (2006) Cm 6989; see above at 13.1.

[3] *Review of the Human Fertilisation and Embryology Act* (2006) Cm 6989, para 2.1, Note 1.

Criminal abortion[4]

14.2 The law relating to criminal abortion is still to be found in section 58 of the Offences Against the Person Act 1861. Strictly speaking, all that the Abortion Act 1967 does is create defences to charges under the 1861 Act. Section 58 of the Offences Against the Person Act makes it a criminal offence punishable by a maximum of life imprisonment (1) for any woman, being with child, unlawfully to do any act with intent to procure a miscarriage, and (2) for any other person unlawfully to do an act with intent to procure the miscarriage of any woman. Self-induced abortion by the woman herself is criminal only if the woman is in fact pregnant. Any act by a third party is criminal regardless of whether or not the woman can be proved to be pregnant. This limited protection afforded to the woman extends only to cases where she acts entirely alone. If she seeks help from a doctor, or any other person, she may be charged with aiding and abetting that person to commit the offence of criminal abortion[5] or of conspiracy with him to commit that offence.[6] The rigour of the law was tempered by a defence to a charge of criminal abortion by a doctor that he acted to preserve the life or health of the mother.[7] At no time in England was abortion absolutely prohibited so as to require the mother to be sacrificed for her unborn child.

In *R v Bourne*,[8] acquitting a doctor of a charge of criminal abortion, the judge suggested that there might be a *duty* to abort to save the 'yet more precious' life of the mother. The extent of the defence available to doctors was unclear. Some doctors interpreted this defence liberally to include the mother's mental health and even happiness. Others would intervene only to prevent a life-threatening complication of pregnancy endangering the woman. Abortion on the ground that the foetus suffered from some serious disability was not lawful. Illegal abortion flourished. Several thousand women were admitted to hospital for treatment after backstreet abortions. The Abortion Act 1967 was introduced to bring uniformity to the law, to clarify the law for doctors, and to stem the misery and injury resulting from unhygienic, risky, illegal abortions.

The Abortion Act 1967

14.3 The Abortion Act 1967 provides that abortion may be lawfully performed under certain conditions.[9] A pregnancy may be terminated by a registered medical practitioner if two registered medical practitioners are of the opinion, formed in good faith, that one of four grounds specified in the Act are met. They are:

---

[4]   See, generally, S Sheldon, *Beyond Control: Medical Power and Abortion Law* (1997) Pluto; E Lee (ed), *Abortion: Whose Right?* (2002) Hodder and Stoughton.

[5]   *R v Sockett* (1908) 72 JP 428. In 1927, a girl of 13 was prosecuted for attempting to induce an abortion on herself by taking laxative tablets and sitting in a hot bath.

[6]   *R v Whitchurch* (1890) 24 QBD 420.

[7]   *R v Bourne* [1939] 1 KB 687.

[8]   *R v Bourne* [1939] 1 KB 687 at 693.

[9]   See section 1 as amended by section 37 of the Human Fertilisation and Embryology Act 1990. The Abortion Act 1967 does not apply in Northern Ireland.

(1) The pregnancy has not exceeded its 24th week and the continuance of the pregnancy would involve risk to the life of the pregnant woman, or of injury to her physical or mental health, or that of the existing children of her family, greater than if the pregnancy were terminated. This is sometimes described as the 'social' ground for abortion.

(2) The termination is necessary to prevent grave permanent injury to the physical or mental health of the woman.

(3) The continuance of the pregnancy would involve risk to the life of the pregnant woman, greater than if the pregnancy were terminated.

(4) There is a substantial risk that if the child were born it would suffer such physical or mental abnormalities as to be seriously handicapped.

No time-limit restricts termination of pregnancy on any of these latter three grounds. In assessing any risk to the health of the woman or her children, account may be taken of the woman's actual or reasonably foreseeable environment. Exceptionally, one registered medical practitioner may act alone when he is of the opinion that an abortion is immediately necessary to save the life of the woman, or to prevent grave permanent injury to her physical or mental health. Section 4 of the 1967 Act provides that no person shall be under any duty to participate in the performance of an abortion if he has a conscientious objection to abortion, save where immediate treatment is necessary to save the life of the woman or to prevent grave permanent damage to her health.[10]

Forty years later, the furore surrounding the 1967 Act has not abated. Critics argue that women can obtain an abortion on request; too many abortions are performed on trivial grounds. On the other hand, counter-claims are made that there remain areas of the country where the Act is restrictively interpreted, denying women the choice to terminate a pregnancy.

Abortion on demand or request?

14.4 The overwhelming majority of abortions[11] are carried out in the first 13 weeks of pregnancy. Critics claim that abortion is available on demand, and that the Abortion Act 1967 is not being properly applied. Gynaecologists prepared to perform an abortion on the request of the pregnant woman rely on statistics which appear to show that statistically the risk of abortion in the first twelve weeks of pregnancy is always less than the risk of childbirth. Therefore, any abortion performed in that period meets the requirement of the 1967 Act that the continuance of the pregnancy poses a greater risk to the health of the woman than does termination. Such statistics include women for whom pregnancy poses exceptional risk, such as very young girls or older women. The individual patient's risk will often be much less than any statistical 'average'. The issue has never been tested in court.

---

[10] See *Janaway v Salford Area Health Authority* [1988] 3 All ER 1059, HL; discussed below at 14.13.

[11] 88 per cent of abortions in 2004: *Abortion Statistics England and Wales 2004 – Government Statistical Services Bulletin* (2005).

Doctors performing abortions have to make a return to the Department of Health stating the grounds for the operation. The Department changed its forms in 1982 in an attempt to tighten up on the rules for legal abortions. A new form demanded to know the main *medical* condition justifying abortion. 'Pro-choice' doctors continued to return 'pregnancy' as the grounds justifying an operation. No prosecutions were brought. A successful prosecution against a doctor performing an abortion on demand would have to establish (1) that the statistics indicating that abortion posed less risk than childbirth were invalid, and (2) that the doctor on trial did not believe them to be valid and so failed to act in good faith. In view of the fact that only one successful prosecution has ever been brought against a doctor for performing an abortion (purportedly under the 1967 Act) in bad faith,[12] such a course would appear to be a clumsy means of regulating or eliminating abortion on demand or request. Frequent attempts to amend the 1967 Act, to require the risk of pregnancy to be substantially greater than that of abortion, have also failed. However, the Abortion Act 1967 confers on women no right to abortion. By making doctors the 'gatekeepers' for the Act, abortion in England is a privilege granted or withheld at the doctor's discretion.[13]

Post-coital birth control

14.5 The Abortion Act 1967 envisaged that once a diagnosis of pregnancy had been made, the doctor faced with a request for an abortion would consider and weigh any risk to the woman or the child. Post-coital contraceptive drugs (emergency hormonal contraception), if taken by a woman within 72 hours of intercourse, ensure that any fertilised egg will not implant in the womb. This, inaptly named, 'morning-after' pill is not the only means by which a fertilised egg may be disposed of at a stage before pregnancy can be confirmed. An intra-uterine device (IUD) fitted within a similar time after intercourse will have the same effect.[14]

Post-coital contraception raised the question of where the line is drawn between contraception and abortion. Post-coital contraception works before the fertilised egg can implant in the womb. The crucial legal issue, in relation to the use of the post-coital contraception, is whether a drug or a procedure which prevents implantation is an act done to procure a miscarriage.[15] Is there a carriage of a child by a woman before implantation takes place? If not, to prevent that event occurring cannot be an act done to procure a miscarriage. Many fertilised eggs fail to implant naturally and no one suggests that a

---

[12] *R v Smith (John)* [1973] 1 WLR 1510, CA.

[13] The history of abortion in England from well before the 1967 Act is marked by 'medicalisation': see Keown, *Abortion, Doctors and the Law*.

[14] In *R v Price* [1969] 1 QB 541, a prosecution for criminal abortion was brought against a doctor who inserted an IUD into a woman who was some months pregnant. The prosecution failed because it was not proved that he knew her to be pregnant.

[15] As long ago as 1983, the Attorney-General expressed his opinion that prior to implantation there is no pregnancy, and so means used to prevent implantation do *not* constitute procuring miscarriage: HC Official Report, 10 May 1983, Col 238–9. In 1991, a judge dismissed a prosecution for criminal abortion based on the insertion of an IUD, agreeing with the Attorney-General that until implantation there is no pregnancy: *R v Dhingra* (1991) unreported.

miscarriage has occurred. The opponents of post-coital birth control reply that the fertilised egg is present within the body of the woman; thus she carries it within her. Therefore there is a carriage of a child, and any act removing that child from the womb is an act done to procure a miscarriage.[16] As at least 40 per cent of implanted embryos abort spontaneously; the arguments based on spontaneous loss of fertilised eggs are irrelevant.

In 2000, a version of the 'morning after' pill (Levonelle) was deregulated to allow sale over the counter in pharmacies. Women no longer need a prescription to obtain post-coital birth control.[17] The Pro-Life Alliance unsuccessfully sought judicial review arguing that the free availability of such a drug contravened the Offences Against the Person Act 1861 because the drug procures miscarriage. Munby J poured scorn on their case, and forcefully held that no pregnancy is established until the fertilised egg implanted in the uterus.[18] 'Miscarriage' today means the termination of an established pregnancy, whatever it may have meant in 1861.

Emergency hormonal contraception must not be confused with medical abortion and the 'abortion pill'. Mifepristone (RU-486) is a drug which is administered orally in the first twelve weeks of pregnancy, and will, in most women, induce a complete miscarriage within 48 hours or so. A small percentage of women require a surgical abortion to complete the evacuation of the uterus.[19] The use of mifepristone is lawful only within the conditions laid down in the Abortion Act 1967. The development of the drug does not liberalise the law on abortion. Section 37(3) of the Human Fertilisation and Embryology Act 1990 permits its routine use in England by authorising the Secretary of State for Health to approve clinics prescribing the drug. 'Pro-life' campaigners argue that the 'abortion pill' is the ultimate development of abortion – 'anti-life' mentality. The practice of some clinics to allow women to take the final dose of mifepristone and return home so they can 'miscarry' in privacy has been attacked as both dangerous to women and a further liberalisation of abortion practice.

Mason and Laurie, who for the most part support lawful abortion, express concerns that link emergency hormonal contraception and the 'abortion pill'. They fear both 'will inevitably come to be regarded as a safe form of contraceptive back-up', blurring the distinction between preventing new life and taking life.[20] We are less pessimistic. What mifepristone does do is to place responsibility for ending her pregnancy on the woman taking the drug.

[16] See J Keown, 'Miscarriage: A Medico Legal Analysis' [1984] *Criminal Law Review* 604.
[17] See the Prescription Only Medicines (Human Use) Amendment (No 3) Order 2000, SI 2000/3231.
[18] *R (on the application of Smeaton) v Secretary of State for Health* [2002] 2 FLR 146. See J Keown, 'Morning After Pills, Miscarriage and Muddle' (2005) 25 *Legal Studies* 302.
[19] Should the drug fail to work, the woman will be asked to agree to undergo surgical abortion before being offered mifepristone. She cannot be forced to go through with the surgical procedure should she later change her mind. But, providing she has been properly warned of the risk of failure and possible adverse effect on the embryo, neither she nor any child damaged by the drug could sue in respect of their injuries. See RP Jansen, 'Unfinished Feticide' (1990) 16 *Journal of Medical Ethics* 61.
[20] JK Mason and GT Laurie, *Mason and McCall Smith's Law and Medical Ethics* (7th edn, 2006) OUP, p 156.

She cannot evade responsibility by seeing the abortion as something done to her. The procedure involves experiencing the pain and distress of a miscarriage. The loss of the embryo will be very evident to her. It is no more likely to be used lightly than recourse to surgical abortion.

The status of the embryo and embryo research: the debate[21]

14.6 The development of *in vitro* fertilisation (IVF) offered not just new means to overcome infertility, but also the capacity to develop medicine in several directions via research on embryos in the laboratory. The possibilities opened up by embryo research prompted renewed controversy about the nature and status of early human embryos, whether the embryo is located in a Petri dish or a woman's uterus. John Harris argues that it cannot:

> ... be morally preferable to end the life of an embryo *in vivo* than it is to do *in vitro*.[22]

The law regulating abortion in England sanctions the killing of nearly two hundred thousand embryos every year. Advocates of embryo research ask how society can logically accept abortion yet ban research. If an embryo can be destroyed at its mother's request, how can it be unethical to destroy it in the course of beneficial scientific research? Both camps in the debate on embryo experiments link the questions of abortion and research.[23]

At the heart of the debate lies the question of the moral status of the developing embryo. When does it acquire the same right to protection as we enjoy? Is it at fertilisation, when a new unique genetic entity comes into being?[24] Or is it at some later stage in embryonic development? This might be at 14 days, when the primitive streak forms,[25] or when brain activity, brain life, is first discernible at eight to ten weeks.[26] Or is it much, much later – after birth? One school of philosophy argues thus.[27] Humanity is just another species of animal and as such has no greater moral status than any other animal. What gives rise to moral rights is not being a human animal, but being a *person*. It is the capacity to value your own existence which gives a person rights, including the right to life. Embryos, and newborn infants, lack that capacity and so are *not* persons. So at no stage of embryonic or foetal development, inside or outside the womb, does the embryo or foetus have moral status.

---

[21] See generally, A Dyson and J Harris (eds), *Experiments on Embryos* (1989) Routledge.

[22] JM Harris, *The Value of Life* (1985) Routledge & Kegan Paul, p 117.

[23] See M Brazier, 'Embryos' "Rights": Abortion and Research' in MDA Freeman (ed), *Medicine, Ethics and Law* (1988) Stevens, pp 9–23.

[24] See O O'Donovan, *Begotten Not Made* (1984) OUP; A Holland, 'A Fortnight of My Life is Missing: A Discussion of the Status of the Pre-embryo' (1990) 7 *Journal of Applied Philosophy* 25.

[25] As the Warnock Report concluded (see *Report of the Committee of Inquiry into Human Fertilisation and Embryology*, pp 63–64; discussed above at 13.1.)

[26] See, in particular, M Lockwood, 'When Does a Life Begin?' in M Lockwood (ed), *Moral Dilemmas in Medicine* (1988) OUP.

[27] See Harris, *The Value of Life*, pp 18–25; JM Harris, 'Embryos and Hedgehogs: on the Moral Status of the Embryo' in Dyson and Harris (eds), *Experiments on Embryos*, p 65; and see J Glover, *Causing Death and Saving Lives* (1977) Penguin.

Each ethical school of thought marshals impressive arguments in support of its thesis. Argument that the embryo enjoys full human status from fertilisation is an argument often resting on theological grounds. If you believe that human life is divinely created in the image of God, and that human beings possess an immortal, immaterial soul, you are unlikely to find any argument based on personhood acceptable. The crucial moment when the embryo acquires humanity becomes ensoulment. Traditionally, that moment might be seen as fertilisation, but a number of eminent Christian theologians have argued for a later date – either the appearance of the primitive streak as marking clear individuality, or the beginning of brain life.[28] Any concept of human life as special *per se* is irrelevant to those who support the personhood thesis. JK Mason advances a rather different argument, one which allows a clearer demarcation between abortion and embryo research. Mason contends that the crucial factor that brings an embryo within the moral community of human-kind, and so entitles it to protection, is implantation.[29] Implantation in the womb connects the embryo to its mother and grants it capacity for meaningful development. The embryo in the Petri dish is no more than a 'laboratory artefact'.[30]

How should the law respond to such a divergence of moral opinion? Consensus is impossible to attain. Proponents of embryo research argue that no one is compelled to participate in research. A liberal democracy should respect divergent moral views. But that is anathema to 'pro-life' groups. It is rather like saying that if a sufficient number of people decide redheads are not human and have no moral claim on society, anyone who holds that belief may kill off any redhead he meets. Of course, no 'pro-redhead' will be required to join in the slaughter! So what is the difference between redheaded adults and embryos? On any analysis, the redhead enjoys moral and legal rights. She is without doubt a person. The embryo's true nature is unprovable. One of the authors of this work happens to believe that from fertilisation the embryo is *very probably* of the same moral value as herself. It is a unique being created in the image of God, in whom she believes. She cannot prove that belief. But then nor can those who maintain that humanity is just another animal species prove their contention. The verdict on the nature of the embryo must be 'not proven'.

What consequences should the 'not-proven' nature of the embryo have for its legal status? It must be accorded recognition and respect. If its claims to rights conflict with the claims of an entity whose status is beyond doubt, its claims may be subordinated to that entity's. Thus if there is a conflict between the claims of the embryo and the rights of the mother, indubitably a legal person, the mother's rights take precedence. A belief that the embryo must be respected as fully human from fertilisation requires that a woman rejects abortion as an option for herself. As that belief is unprovable, she cannot

---

[28] See GR Dunstan, 'The Moral Status of the Human embryo: A Tradition Recalled' (1984) 10 *Journal of Medical Ethics* 38; K Ward, 'An Irresolvable Debate?' in Dyson and Harris (eds), *Experiments on Embryos*, p 106.

[29] JK Mason, *Medico-Legal Aspects of Reproduction and Parenthood* (2nd edn, 1998), p 234; *Mason and McCall Smith's Law and Medical Ethics*, p 99.

[30] JK Mason, *Human Life and Medical Practice* (1988) Edinburgh University Press, p 94.

legitimately enforce it on other women.[31] Embryo research, by contrast, gives rise to no such direct conflict of rights. The question becomes whether society can legitimately destroy an entity which may be fully human in nature and status. The embryo should be given the benefit of the doubt. Justifications have always been advanced for permitting the killing of indubitably human persons in certain cases. It might be argued that the public 'good' expected from embryo research justifies destruction of these 'maybe' human persons. The onus of proof lies on those who advocate research.

What are the goods which, it is argued, flow from research? They include improvement in fertility treatments (particularly IVF), the development of more effective means of contraception, the detection and 'cure' of genetic defects and disease, and, with the development of stem cell therapies, 'therapeutic cloning' (the use of early embryonic tissue to transplant into sick adults and children). How much could be achieved without research on live human embryos is hotly disputed. It is difficult for a lay person to evaluate the scientific debate, partly because scientific opinion on the merits of research seems to depend on what stance the scientist takes on the ethics of research. However, if the 'pro-research' camp confront some difficulty establishing that the manifest benefit of research justifies the destruction of arguably human embryos, the 'anti-research' camp has a fundamental problem of its own. If an embryo is arguably human, it is wrong to destroy it, to experiment on it for a purpose not designed to benefit it, so that it must ultimately perish. If it is wrong to destroy embryos for research purposes, it must also be wrong to destroy them in the course of infertility treatments using IVF. As long as 'spare' embryos are created, the surplus is doomed to die. To return to a practice of harvesting only one egg from the woman, and so creating and implanting just one embryo, was thought to be a fatal blow to IVF.[32] It is difficult to argue that it is ethical to destroy embryos to alleviate infertility and yet unethical to destroy embryos in order to improve our knowledge and treatment of genetic disease.[33] Those who opposed research should logically also have opposed IVF.[34]

Embryo research: the Human Fertilisation and Embryology Act 1990

14.7 The Human Fertilisation and Embryology Act 1990 permits licensed research up to 14 days from the day when the gametes are mixed. It is a criminal offence punishable by up to two years' imprisonment to bring about the creation of an embryo (outside the human body) or to keep or use an

---

[31] For a powerful argument that even if the embryo is presumed to enjoy full human status, abortion remains defensible, see J Jarvis Thompson, 'A Defence of Abortion' in RM Dworkin (ed), *The Philosophy of Law* (1977), p 112. But note the response by JM Finnis, 'The Rights and Wrongs of Abortion' in the same book, p 129.

[32] Though clinicians are now suggesting that modern treatment may achieve much greater success with single embryos at less risk to the woman.

[33] So if President Bush wished to prevent destruction of embryos, he should have banned IVF as well as vetoing the Stem Cell Research Bill.

[34] See M Brazier, 'The Challenge for Parliament: A Critique of the White Paper on Human Fertilisation and Embryology' in Dyson and Harris (eds), *Experiments on Embryos*, p 142.

embryo except in pursuance of a licence.[35] No embryo may be kept or used after the appearance of the primitive streak, that is 14 days from the day the gametes were mixed, '... not counting any time during which the embryo was stored'.[36] Certain activities are expressly prohibited. Human embryos or gametes may not be implanted in animals, nor may animal embryos be inserted in humans.[37] Replacing the nucleus of a cell *of an embryo* with a cell taken from any person or embryo is outlawed.[38] This was intended to outlaw cloning. Trans-species fertilisation, the attempt to create human/animal hybrids, is forbidden save for the 'hamster' test to establish the fertility or normality of sperm, when any resulting embryo must be destroyed at the two-cell stage.[39] The genetic structure of an embryo may not be altered '... except in such circumstances (if any) as may be specified in ...' regulations to be made by the Human Fertilisation and Embryology Authority (HFEA).[40]

The original rules governing embryo research in the Human Fertilisation and Embryology Act 1990 centred on two principles:

(1)   The Act implicitly accepts that respect is due to the embryo from fertilisation, but that up until the development of the primitive streak, the 'goods' to be expected from research outweigh the interests of the embryo. The Act grants full protection to the embryo only from 14 days.

(2)   The Act sought to allay fears of a science-fiction nightmare in which scientists freely create all sorts of clones, hybrids and other monsters. It should be noted that until the enactment of the Human Fertilisation and Embryology Act 1990 embryos *in vitro* enjoyed no legal protection at all. The wording of abortion legislation prohibiting 'procurement of miscarriage' meant that in theory 'test-tube' embryos could then be grown and destroyed at will.

Subject to these express prohibitions, researchers are given a remarkably free hand by the 1990 Act. It allows embryos to be created solely for research purposes. Schedule 2 outlines what a research licence may authorise. Five specific purposes are set out:

(1)   promoting advances in the treatment of infertility;
(2)   increasing knowledge about the causes of congenital disease;
(3)   increasing knowledge about the causes of miscarriage;
(4)   developing more effective techniques of contraception; and
(5)   developing methods for detecting the presence of gene or chromosomal abnormalities in embryos before implantation.[41]

---

[35]   See section 3(1). Any prosecution under the Human Fertilisation and Embryology Act 1990 will require the consent of the DPP: s 42.

[36]   Human Fertilisation and Embryology Act 1990, s 3(3)(a).

[37]   See section 3(2) and (3)(b) of the Human Fertilisation and Embryology Act 1990.

[38]   Human Fertilisation and Embryology Act 1990, s 3(3)(d).

[39]   Human Fertilisation and Embryology Act 1990, s 4(1), Sch 2, para 3(5).

[40]   Human Fertilisation and Embryology Act 1990, Sch 2, para 3(4).

[41]   Human Fertilisation and Embryology Act 1990, Sch 2, para 2.

These five specific purposes may be regarded as justification for the destruction of embryos, aimed at improving medicine and increasing human happiness, designed to re-assure those who are doubtful about, but not adamantly opposed to, research. To those named purposes is added an apparently innocuous phrase 'or for such other purposes as may be specified in regulations'.

Embryo research and cloning

14.8 From 1990 to about 1998 the fury of the embryo research debate abated. The birth of Dolly, the cloned sheep, changed all that. Dolly was created by a process of cell nucleus replacement (CNR). The nucleus of an adult cell was inserted into an emptied egg cell. The egg cell was then subjected to an electrical impulse so it began to divide and develop as an embryo. The embryo was implanted in a surrogate 'mother'. There is no scientific reason why this process could not (in theory) be replicated in humans. Two principal purposes could drive the development of CNR in humans, albeit mammalian cloning has often proved an uncertain process. First, obviously attempts could be made to create a child, a copy of its lone parent sharing most of his or her DNA. Many British scientists abhor the notion of 'reproductive cloning'. A number of eminent ethicists argue that no case has been made out sufficient to justify banning 'reproductive cloning'.[42] Second, stem cells could be collected from the cloned embryo. Embryonic stem cells retain their pluripotency. That means they can be cultured to develop into different sorts of tissue, or even potentially grown into organs. 'Therapeutic cloning', or stem cell therapy, offers the following scientific benefits. Assume that a patient has a neurological disease. An embryo could be created by CNR using DNA from one of the patient's own cells. Stem cells taken from the resulting embryo could be used to create tissue to repair her damaged brain.

The HFEA joined the Human Genetic Advisory Commission (HEAC) to consider the ethics of cloning. Their Report[43] recommended that Regulations under the Human Fertilisation and Embryology Act 1990 should be extended to allow the HFEA to authorise procedures:

(a)   to extract embryonic stem cells for research on the possible treatment benefits in a wide range of disorders by replacing cells which have become damaged or diseased; and

(b)   to conduct research into the treatment of some rare but serious inherited disorders carried in maternal mitochondria.

A further consultation led by the Chief Medical Officer[44] endorsed the recommendations of the HFEA and HGAC. Both ruled out reproductive

---

[42]   See, for example, J Harris, 'Goodbye Dolly? – The Ethics of Human Cloning' (1997) 23 *Journal of Medical Ethics* 353; and see I Kennedy and A Grubb, *Medical Law: Text and Materials* (3rd edn, 2000) Butterworths, pp 1239–1268.

[43]   HFEA/HGAC, *Cloning Issues in Reproduction, Science and Medicine* (1998). See also J Harris, *Clones, Genes and Immortality* (1998) OUP.

[44]   Expert Group of the CMO, *Stem Cell Research: Medical Progress and Responsibility* (2000) Department of Health. See also House of Lords, *Stem Cell Research* (2002) HL 83(i); Nuffield Council on Bioethics, *Stem Cell Therapy: A Discussion* (2000).

cloning as beyond the pale. 'Good' cloning would be allowed. 'Bad' cloning would be banned. Regulations to permit stem cell therapy were approved by Parliament in January 2001.[45] These regulations purported to authorise the following additional research purposes:

- increasing knowledge about development of embryos;
- increasing knowledge about serious disease; and
- enabling such knowledge to be applied in developing treatment for serious disease.

The Regulations were made on an assumption that CNR fell within the 1990 Act. But it is not covered by section 3(3)(d), which had been intended to ban cloning. Section 3(3)(a) only bars replacing a nucleus of a cell taken from an embryo with a nucleus taken from any person or an embryo. CNR removes the nucleus from an egg cell, not an embryo. The Government argued that, none the less, reproductive cloning was effectively outlawed because the HFEA would never license any attempt at reproductive cloning. So to do so would be a crime, because creating an embryo without an HFEA licence is a crime. 'Embryo' for the purpose of the 1990 Act is defined as follows:

embryo means a live human embryo where fertilisation is complete.[46]

If CNR is used to create the embryo, *fertilisation* never takes place.[47] CNR involves propagation not fertilisation. Did it fall outside the 1990 Act, meaning CNR 'cloning' (of either kind – therapeutic or reproductive) could take place without a licence?

The All-Party Pro-Life Alliance challenged the Regulations allowing stem cell therapy. They argued that the Regulations were *ultra vires* because an embryo created by CNR was not an embryo within the definition provided in the Human Fertilisation and Embryology Act 1990. Crane J agreed that an embryo created otherwise than by fertilisation fell outside the 1990 Act.[48] The Government rushed through the Human Reproductive Cloning Act 2001. That Act made implanting a CNR embryo in a woman a criminal offence. Creating such an embryo and implanting it abroad would not fall within the 2001 Act. The status of the Regulations governing stem cell therapy remained in limbo. The Court of Appeal came to the Government's rescue. They ruled that, whatever the literal wording of the 1990 Act, had Parliament foreseen the development of CNR, it would have intended such embryos to be within the 'genus covered by the legislation' and 'the clear purpose of the legislation would be defeated if the extension were not made'.[49] The House of Lords

---

45 The Human Fertilisation and Embryology (Research Purposes) Regulations 2001, SI 2001/188. Such was the public concern about the Regulations that they were immediately reviewed (and in the event approved) by a Select Committee of the House of Lords (see above, House of Lords, *Stem Cell Research*).
46 Human Fertilisation and Embryology Act 1990, s 1(1)(a).
47 See M Brazier, 'Regulating the Reproduction Business?' (1999) 8 *Medical Law Review* 166.
48 *R (Quintavalle) v Secretary of State for Health* [2001] 4 All ER 1019.
49 *R (Quintaville) v Secretary of State for Health* [2002] 2 All ER 625, CA.

upheld the Court of Appeal.[50] Moral controversy was translated into an exercise in statutory interpretation. Lord Bingham declared[51] that the '... basic task of the court is to ascertain and give effect to the true meaning of what Parliament has said in the enactment to be construed'. The 1990 Act must '... be read in the historical context of the situation which led to its enactment'. Parliament, their Lordships concluded, never intended to distinguish between live embryos produced by fertilisation and embryos produced without fertilisation. Parliament, in 1990, would have been unaware that the latter process was possible. The fundamental purpose of section 3(1)(a) of the 1990 Act was to provide protection for embryos created outside the human body:

> The protective purpose was plainly not intended to be tied to the particular way in which an embryo might be created.[52]

What of the moral arguments? Does it follow that anyone who in 1990 was sceptical about the legitimacy of embryo research should be outraged by developments allowing stem cell therapies, 'therapeutic cloning'? It is no more than a logical outcome of permitting research at all. If the 'goods' of more successful fertility treatments justified destroying embryos, it is difficult to say that the 'good' of helping seriously ill patients does not. The argument may be raised that the use of embryos is not essential to achieve that end. Adult stem cells could be treated to recover pluripotency. It might just take longer to do the research. CNR forces some reconsideration of the basis of opposition for embryo research. Embryos created from fertilisation of eggs by sperm result (normally) in the creation of unique new genetic entities. What is the nature of an embryo created by CNR using our nuclei, our DNA? If used solely for stem cell therapy, is it different from taking a skin graft from a leg to treat burns on an arm?

Revised legislation on embryo research

14.9 The controversy relating to stem cell therapies highlighted how far the Human Fertilisation and Embryology Act 1990 now lagged behind developments in science. Further developments reinforced that view. The HFEA granted licences to allow the use of embryos to develop stem cell therapies. Scientists immediately faced a resource problem. Developing CNR embryos needs a plentiful supply of eggs to be 'emptied' so that nuclei can be inserted to create embryos, from which embryonic stem cells can then be cultured. Human eggs for the purposes of egg donation in fertility treatment are in short supply, never mind human eggs for research such as this. However, human eggs are not necessary for the purpose. A cow or rabbit egg will do just as well. The resulting hybrid embryo remains more than 99.9 per cent 'human'.

---

[50] [2003] 2 All ER 113. The House of Lords, however, also confirmed that section 3(3)(a) of the Human Fertilisation and Embryology Act 1990 did not impose an absolute prohibition on CNR.

[51] [2003] 2 All ER 113 at 118.

[52] [2003] 2 All ER 113 at 126, per Lord Steyn.

Other scientists began to work on the development of artificial gametes. Criticism of how the 1990 Act worked in relation to fertility treatment[53] also became vigorous. Some doctors and scientists argued for a large measure of deregulation – the abolition of the HFEA. A review of the 1990 Act[54] was conducted by the Department of Health, in its White Paper containing proposals for revised legislation to replace or at least radically amend the 1990 Act.[55]

The White Paper rejects the case for deregulation, insisting that all activities involving the creation, keeping or use of embryos outside the body and the use of donated gametes should continue to require licensing by an independent regulator.[56] The time-limit for the development of embryos *in vitro* should remain at 14 days.[57] New legislation must ensure that all human embryos outside the human body should fall within the scope of regulation, whatever the manner of their creation.[58] Any form of artificial gametes should be brought within the legislation.[59] Research on such gametes would need to be licensed and, for the time being, the use of artificial gametes in fertility treatment should be prohibited.[60] Some extension of the lawful purposes of embryo research is proposed to allow research into serious injury (for example to the spinal cord), as it is currently allowed into serious disease.[61] Training embryologists using embryos *in vitro* will be expressly allowed.[62]

The most controversial proposal in relation to embryo research in the White Paper is restrictive: 'The Government will propose that the creation of hybrid or chimera embryos *in vitro* should not be allowed ...'.[63] Scientists criticised the Government's proposal to ban the procedure, arguing it was based solely on unreasoned expressions of pubic revulsion and the opinions of certain religious groups.[64] They have a case. The use of rabbit eggs to develop human embryonic cells will not create a creature half-rabbit, half-human. The cloned embryo will never develop into a living animal of any species. The embryo

---

[53] See House of Commons Science and Technology Committee Fifth Report of Session 2004–5, *Human Reproductive Technologies and the Law* Vol 1 HC 7–1 (www.parliament-.gov.uk). See above at 13.1.

[54] *Review of the Human Fertilisation and Embryology Act – A Public Consultation* (2005 Ref 269640) Department of Health; *Report on the consultation on the Review of the Human Fertilisation and Embryology Act 1990* (2006) (www.dh.gov.uk).

[55] *Review of the Human Fertilisation and Embryology Act* (2006) Cm 6989.

[56] *Review of the Human Fertilisation and Embryology Act* (2006) Cm 6989, para 2.9.

[57] *Review of the Human Fertilisation and Embryology Act* (2006) Cm 6989, para 2.72.

[58] *Review of the Human Fertilisation and Embryology Act* (2006) Cm 6989, para 2.11. Note that 'eggs in the process of fertilisation' will continue to be regulated as though they were embryos: para 2.12.

[59] *Review of the Human Fertilisation and Embryology Act* (2006) Cm 6989, paras 2.13–2.14.

[60] *Review of the Human Fertilisation and Embryology Act* (2006) Cm 6989, paras 2.15–2.16. The White Paper leaves open the question whether new legislation would allow for such a ban to be lifted by secondary legislation.

[61] *Review of the Human Fertilisation and Embryology Act* (2006) Cm 6989, para 2.74.

[62] *Review of the Human Fertilisation and Embryology Act* (2006) Cm 6989, para 2.78.

[63] *Review of the Human Fertilisation and Embryology Act* (2006) Cm 6989, para 2.85. However, a new Act will provide that this position could be modified by secondary legislation. Applications currently before the HFEA to license the use on non-human eggs are unlikely to succeed in the light of Government proposals.

[64] See (2007) Times, January 5.

from which cell lines are developed will contain only the tiniest amount of non-human DNA. The HFEA has launched a consultation on the matter and ministers are re-considering the proposed ban.

The Government's support of continued regulation does not extend to support for the HFEA itself. It will be replaced by the Regulatory Authority for Tissue and Embryology[65] (RATE). RATE will face a formidable task, regulating embryo research, fertility treatment and all the matters that currently fall within the remit of the Human Tissue Authority. Its membership is designed to be smaller than that of the HFEA (21 members). The use of expert advisory panels (EAPs) looks like becoming the principal focus for regulation in the future. A flexible system to allow RATE to develop its own licensing system is proposed. RATE members will review decisions and hear appeals from its constituent bodies. Altering the structure of regulation and changing a name will not make RATE's job any less controversial than that of its predecessor.

Embryo to foetus: foetus to baby

14.10 The White Paper confirms that an embryo *in vitro* should not be allowed to develop beyond 14 days from fertilisation. What of the embryo *in vivo*, growing and developing in his mother's womb? By twelve weeks, the embryo will, if seen on an ultrasound scan, bear a distinct resemblance to a baby[66] and from then on will usually be termed a foetus. In many legal systems, the protection given to the embryo/foetus is extended as the pregnancy progresses and the foetus develops. Thus, in France abortion is allowed on demand up to ten weeks' gestation, and from then is permissible only on the ground of risk to the mother's health. In the USA, the Supreme Court in *Roe v Wade*[67] declared that any restriction on abortion in the first twelve weeks of pregnancy was unconstitutional, as a violation of the pregnant woman's right to privacy. States may regulate abortion to protect maternal health from twelve to 24 weeks, and from viability (between 24 and 28 weeks) the interests of the foetus take precedence over the interests of the mother. *Roe v Wade* adopts a gradualist approach to the conflict of rights between the mother and her unborn child.

In England, the Abortion Act 1967 originally set no limit to the time when an abortion might lawfully be performed. Section 5(1) provided instead that nothing in the Act should affect the provisions of the Infant Life (Preservation) Act 1929 protecting the viable foetus. Under that Act any person who, with intent to destroy the life of a child capable of being born alive, causes the child to die before it has an existence independent of the mother is guilty of child destruction. The foetus was deemed to be capable of being born alive at 28

---

[65] See *Review of the Human Fertilisation and Embryology Act* (2006) Cm 6989, paras 3.1–3.21, and 13.1 above and 18.3 below.

[66] On which, see D Kirklin, 'The Role of Medical Imaging in the Abortion Debate' (2004) 30 *Journal of Medical Ethics* 426.

[67] (1973) 93 S Ct 705. Though since *Roe v Wade*, anti-abortion campaigners have ceaselessly sought to reverse the decision or limit its impact: see *Mason and McCall Smith's Law and Medical Ethics*, pp 150–152.

weeks.[68] The objective of the 1929 Act was to protect the foetus in the course of delivery,[69] and to safeguard any foetus who, but for improper intervention, could have been born alive.

But what was meant by 'capable of being born alive'. In *C v S*,[70] a young man, seeking to stop his girlfriend aborting their child at 18 weeks, argued that at 18 weeks a foetus was 'capable of being born alive'. It is fully formed and its heart may beat for a second or so after expulsion from the mother. At 18 weeks there is no prospect of a baby breathing independently of its mother even with the aid of a ventilator. The Court of Appeal found that to be 'capable of being born alive' a foetus must be able, on delivery, to breathe either naturally or with mechanical aid. The fight to limit late abortions returned to Parliament. Anti-abortion campaigners persuaded the Government to agree to the introduction of an amendment to the Human Fertilisation and Embryology Bill designed to reduce the time-limit for abortions. Their attempt misfired, and after a night of confusion, section 37 of the Human Fertilisation and Embryology Act 1990 emerged. Section 37 produced a liberalisation, rather than restriction, of abortion laws in England; a result now under attack.

Section 37 of the 1990 Act amended the Abortion Act 1967 to provide that the time-limit for lawful abortions carried out on grounds of risk to the physical or mental health of the woman of her existing children (so-called 'social abortions') is 24 weeks. In other cases, there is *no* time-limit, ie an abortion may be performed right up to the end of the pregnancy. Abortion up to birth is lawful when:

(1)   termination is necessary to prevent grave permanent injury to the physical or mental health of the mother;
(2)   continuance of the pregnancy threatens the life of the mother; or
(3)   there is a substantial risk that if the child is born it would suffer from such physical or mental abnormalities as to be seriously handicapped.

It is the third of these cases which has proved most controversial. The Infant Life (Preservation) Act 1929 permitted action necessary to save the life of the mother, even if doing so inevitably entailed the destruction of the child; preventing grave permanent injury to the mother's health was also almost certainly permissible.[71] Such cases of a stark choice between mother and child are few and far between in modern medicine. Permitting abortion up to 40 weeks on grounds of foetal handicap was not lawful prior to the 1990 Act. In debate in Parliament, that provision seemed to be regarded as covering only the most grave of disabilities, perhaps where a woman was found late in pregnancy to be carrying an anencephalic child incapable of surviving more than a few hours after birth. However, the wording of section 37 of the

---

[68]   Although at 28 weeks the foetus was deemed to be capable of being born alive, that did *not* mean an earlier abortion was necessarily lawful. It would be for the prosecution to prove *that* foetus was capable of being born alive.
[69]   Thus closing a lacuna in the abortion laws.
[70]   [1987] 1 All ER 1230. A somewhat different interpretation was offered in *Rance v Mid-Downs Health Authority* [1991] 1 All ER 801.
[71]   See *R v Bourne* [1939] 1 KB 687.

Human Fertilisation and Embryology Act 1990 is identical to the general foetal handicap ground provided for in the Abortion Act 1967. So, if Down's syndrome or spina bifida are diagnosed, however late into pregnancy, may the foetus lawfully be destroyed? The wording of the 1990 Act is vague.[72] The Royal College of Obstetricians and Gynaecologists (RCOG) offer doctors further guidance.[73] They shy away from prescription, emphasising the need for the parents and the doctor to weigh the potential suffering of the child, the suffering of the mother, the burden on the family and the severity of the handicap affecting the foetus. The RCOG acknowledges that in applying these criteria to actual cases, foetal medicine specialists take different moral views.

In 2004, the Reverend Joanna Jepson challenged the decision by West Mercia Police not to investigate a complaint that doctors had authorised the termination of a pregnancy at 28 weeks of a foetus with bilateral cleft lip and palate. She obtained leave to apply for judicial review.[74] The hearing was postponed while police conducted further investigations. The Crown Prosecution Service reviewed the evidence and decided not to pursue a prosecution. It appears that Reverend Jepson will take no further action.[75] The CPS found that doctors acted in good faith on the basis of appropriate expert opinion. Much was made of the importance of consultation in the absence of a precise definition of serious foetal handicap.[76] It seems that, in effect, serious handicap may come to be defined subjectively – do the parents and the doctors consider the relevant handicap to be serious? The impact of section 37 of the Human Fertilisation and Embryology Act 1990 is that in England children capable of being born alive may be killed, providing they are disabled. The protection afforded to the viable foetus by the Infant Life (Preservation) Act 1929 is withdrawn from the disabled foetus. A medical practitioner acting within the provisions of the amended and extended Abortion Act 1967 cannot be convicted of child destruction. The 1929 Act remains in force, but applicable only to *unlawful* late abortions and those cases where a violent attack on a pregnant woman kills the child within her.

Late abortions on grounds of foetal handicap are not the only source of controversy in relation to time-limits to termination of pregnancy. As we shall see in the next chapter, developments in the care of extremely premature babies mean that a small number of babies born before 24 weeks' gestation survive. The 24-week limit for 'social abortions' is under attack. It is argued

---

[72] See E Wicks, M Wyldes and M Kilby, 'Late Termination of Pregnancy for Fetal Abnormality: Medical and Legal Perspectives' (2004) 12 *Medical Law Review* 285; S Sheldon and S Wilkinson, 'Termination of Pregnancy for Reasons of Foetal Disability: Are there Grounds for a Special Exception in Law?' (2001) 9 *Medical Law Review* 85.

[73] Royal College of Obstetricians and Gynaecologists, *Termination of Pregnancy for Fetal Abnormality* (1996); Royal College of Obstetricians and Gynaecologists, *A Consideration of the Law and Ethics in Relation to Late Termination of Pregnancy for Fetal Abnormality* (1998).

[74] *Jepson v The Chief Constable of West Mercia Police Constabulary* [2003] EWHC 3318.

[75] C Dyer, 'Doctor Who Performed Late Abortion will Not be Prosecuted' (2005) 330 *British Medical Journal* 668.

[76] See R Scott, 'The Uncertain Scope of Reproductive Autonomy in Pre-implantation Genetic Diagnosis and Selective Abortion' (2005) 13 *Medical Law Review* 291; R Scott, 'Interpreting the Disability Ground of the Abortion Act' (2005) 64 *Cambridge Law Journal* 388.

that it is not ethically justifiable to destroy a foetus which may have the capacity to survive independently outside its mother's womb. A 'viable' foetus should acquire a right to survive.

The issue of foeticide brings the debate on late abortions into sharp focus. Doctors aborting a foetus late on in pregnancy will seek to ensure that they use means that will destroy the foetus before it emerges from the mother. For if a child is born alive, nothing in the Abortion Act 1967 authorises its destruction. Accounts are given of premature infants left to die in the sluice room adjacent to the operating theatre where an abortion was attempted.[77] What are the legal rules applicable when an attempted abortion results not in a dead foetus, but a living, albeit sick infant? The child, once born alive, is protected by the law of murder. Any positive act to destroy it is murder. Failure to offer the child proper care *with the intention that it shall die* on the part of persons with an obligation to care for the child is equally murder.[78] Failure to offer the child proper care out of incompetence or carelessness is manslaughter. The theory is clear. Reality is more problematical. A doctor who embarks on an abortion undertakes the care of the mother, and to relieve her of her unwanted child. Yet the criminal law imposes on him an obligation to the child. His position none the less is clearly distinct from that of the doctor undertaking safely to deliver a mother of a desired child. And what of the child born disabled? The doctor sets out to abort on the grounds of the substantial disability affecting the child, but if the child survives must he then use all his efforts to save her? This leads us into the question of medical care of the disabled newborn baby, his rights and those of his parents, a minefield we enter in Chapter 15.

Unsurprisingly, obstetricians try to avoid entering that minefield. Advice from the RCOG recommends that in all terminations of pregnancy at a gestational age of more than 21 weeks and 6 days '… the method chosen should ensure that the foetus is born dead'.[79] In practice, this means that foetal medicine specialists administer a fatal injection of potassium chloride into the foetal heart before beginning the process of terminating the pregnancy. Foeticide has become a routine part of late termination of pregnancy. It is performed not only to ensure that the foetus is born dead, but also to ensure that the foetus suffers no pain in the course of the termination.[80] Not all women agreeing to

---

[77] See SK Templeton and L Rogers, 'Babies that Live after Abortions are Left to Die' (2004) Sunday Times, June 20.

[78] *R v Hamilton* (1983) Times, 16 September. In 1983, a consultant gynaecologist was charged with attempted murder. Police had been informed that a baby had been left on a slab to die for some time before being transferred to a paediatric unit. The allegation against the doctor was that he performed an abortion on the basis of an estimate of 23 weeks' pregnancy and, when the baby proved to be of 34 weeks' gestation, left it without attention intending it to die. The prosecution was dismissed by magistrates for lack of evidence.

[79] Royal College of Obstetricians and Gynaecologists, *Further Issues Relating to Late Abortions, Fetal Viability and Registrations at Births and Deaths* (2001).

[80] See Royal College of Obstetricians and Gynaecologists, *Fetal Awareness: Report of a Working Party* (1997); Royal College of Obstetricians and Gynaecologists, *Report of the MRC Expert Group on Fetal Pain* (2001).

termination of pregnancy for a serious abnormality want to agree to foeticide. The RCOG recognises that in cases where a lethal abnormality is present, foeticide may not be appropriate.[81]

Selective reduction: selective foeticide

14.11 So far, discussion of the legality of abortion has proceeded on the basis that the procedure used terminates the woman's pregnancy completely. There are cases where only selected foetuses in a multiple pregnancy are destroyed, and the pregnancy continues to term when the woman delivers her surviving children. Selective reduction, or selective foeticide, may be advised either when a woman has a multiple pregnancy and is unlikely to carry all the foetuses safely to term, or when one of two or more foetuses is disabled. The 'surplus' or disabled foetuses will, using fetoscopically directed procedures, be killed. The dead foetuses are not expelled from the uterus, but become 'foetus papyraceous', and emerge on delivery of their healthy brothers and sisters. Selective reduction to destroy a disabled twin was quietly practised for years. The development of IVF and consequent increase in multiple pregnancies brought the procedure to public attention. Until recently, in a number of fertility clinics, several embryos were implanted to maximise the woman's chances of pregnancy. If the woman conceived quadruplets or more, the risk was that the babies would be delivered prematurely and in the worst case scenario *all* might fail to survive. Selective reduction offered the prospect of one or two healthy children being born safely.

The deliberate destruction of selected foetuses raised ethical and legal problems. Legal debate focused on whether selective reduction was lawful.[82] Section 37(5) of the Human Fertilisation and Embryology Act 1990 legalises selective reduction, if performed for one of the grounds on which termination of the whole pregnancy is lawful. Thus, if foetuses are destroyed on grounds of foetal handicap, or because a multiple pregnancy poses a risk to the mother's health, selective reduction is as lawful as ending the pregnancy altogether would be. The anomalous situation is this. Where multiple pregnancy occurs, the underlying reason for wanting to destroy Foetuses A and B is to maximise the prospects of a healthy birth for Foetuses C and D. The ground that would need to be invoked is that permitting abortion to safeguard the health of any 'existing children' of the pregnant woman. Can Foetuses C and D be regarded as 'existing children'? The whole philosophy of English law relating to the status of the foetus is that a foetus is not for legal purposes a child.

Section 37(5) of the 1990 Act grants legal recognition to a much-disputed procedure.[83] If foetuses can be selected and destroyed in effect as part and

---

[81] See Royal College of Obstetricians and Gynaecologists, *Further Issues Relating to Late Abortions, Fetal Viability and Registrations at Births and Deaths.*

[82] See J Keown, 'Selective Reduction of Multiple Pregnancy' (1987) 137 *New Law Journal* 1165; DPT Price, 'Selective Reduction and Feticide: The Parameters of Abortion' [1988] *Criminal Law Review* 199.

[83] See R Lee and D Morgan, *Human Fertilisation and Embryology: Regulating the Reproductive Revolution* (2000) Blackstone, pp 252–256.

parcel of infertility treatment, the message from Parliament seems to be that unborn life is little more than a means to an end. The foetus itself counts for little. The parents' desire for children justifies its destruction. Selective killing of disabled foetuses with legal blessing reinforces the second-class status of the disabled foetus.

Nurses and abortion

14.12 Nurses are increasingly involved in the process of termination of pregnancy. A particular concern for nurses relates to second-trimester terminations, abortions in the middle months of pregnancy. The Abortion Act 1967 provides for circumstances when a pregnancy may lawfully be terminated by a registered medical practitioner, a doctor. In 1967, all lawful abortions were carried out by surgical means. The surgeon removed the foetus and ended the pregnancy. By 1972, medical induction of abortion was introduced as the standard method of terminating pregnancies in the second trimester. A doctor inserts a catheter into the woman's womb. Later, a nurse attaches the catheter via a flexible tube to a pump, which feeds the hormone prostaglandin through the catheter and induces premature labour. The nurse administers another drug via a drip in the woman's arm to stimulate her contractions. The immature foetus is born dead. The substances that cause the abortion are administered by the nurse. The nurse in effect terminates the pregnancy.

The Royal College of Nursing was doubtful whether a pregnancy terminated by a nurse was lawfully terminated. Might nurses face prosecution for conducting criminal abortions? The Department of Health and Social Security issued a circular upholding the legality of medical inductions of abortion. The Royal College of Nursing went to court for a declaration that the circular was wrong in law. The College lost in the High Court, won in the Court of Appeal and finally lost by three to two in the House of Lords.[84] The majority of their Lordships held that the Abortion Act 1967 must be construed in the light of its social purposes – first, to broaden the ground on which abortions may lawfully be obtained, and second, to secure safe and hygienic conditions for women undergoing abortion. The 1967 Act contemplated the participation of a team of hospital staff involved in the overall treatment of the woman, and exonerated them all from criminal liability if the abortion was carried out within the terms of the Act. It was not necessary for a doctor to perform every physical act leading to the termination of the pregnancy. Provided a doctor accepts full responsibility for every stage in the treatment, a nurse acting under his instructions and in conformity with accepted medical practice does not act unlawfully when she administers the drugs which terminate the pregnancy in an induced abortion.

Conscientious objection

14.13 A vital component of the compromise on which the Abortion Act 1967 was based was the right of conscientious objection. Section 4 of the Act

84 *Royal College of Nursing v DHSS* [1981] AC 800.

provides that no person shall be under any duty 'to participate in any treatment authorised by this Act to which he has a conscientious objection'.[85] It is for the person objecting to prove that their objection rests on grounds of conscience. And, in the case of abortion, the professional's conscience does not relieve him of any duty to intervene to save the life of the mother or to prevent grave permanent injury to her health.

In *Janaway v Salford Area Health Authority*,[86] the House of Lords was asked to determine *who* was entitled to rely on the right of conscientious objection. Mrs Janaway was a devout Roman Catholic employed as a secretary. She refused to type abortion referral letters and the authority dismissed her. She challenged her dismissal as unlawful because, she argued, she was entitled to rely on the right of conscientious objection provided for by section 4 of the 1967 Act. Her action failed. The Law Lords ruled that the term 'participate' in section 4 meant actually taking part in treatment designed to terminate a pregnancy. Mrs Janaway was not asked to do anything that involved her personally in the process of abortion. Yet she was an essential cog in the wheel. Abortion was as repugnant to her as murder. For Mrs Janaway, however irrational others might perceive her views to be, her employers were asking her to type out a death warrant.

The House of Lords' restrictive interpretation of the right to conscientious objection has other consequences too. A health care professional may legitimately refuse to carry out, or assist at, an abortion. He cannot withdraw from any contact with abortion advice. Consider this example. A woman of over 35 receives her ante-natal care from an obstetrician adamantly opposed to abortion. He never discusses with her whether, in view of her age, she should undergo amniocentesis to test for Down's syndrome. The prevalence of Down's syndrome increases in mothers over 35. If she gives birth to a Down's baby, the mother may sue the obstetrician for negligence.[87] If, as we strongly suspect, the overwhelming body of responsible professional opinion regards amniocentesis (or other available tests for Down's) as routine for pregnant women over 35, the obstetrician's right to conscientious objection will be of no avail to him. If his duty of care (as defined by his peers) extends to advice on amniocentesis, then even though that advice on amniocentesis is almost inevitably an act preparatory to abortion, he must fulfil that duty (for it involves no active participation in the process of ending a pregnancy).[88]

The right to conscientious objection is limited in scope and in practice difficult to exercise. Hospitals are wary of staff who will not participate in what has become a fairly common operation. It is said that nurses face greater risk to their career prospects if they declare their conscientious objection to abortion.[89] Paradoxically, there remain areas of England where abortion within the

---

[85] Section 38 of the Human Fertilisation and Embryology Act 1990 confers a similar right to refuse to participate in embryo research or any of the infertility treatments regulated by that Act.

[86] [1988] 3 All ER 1079, HL.

[87] See above at 12.6.

[88] And doctors opposed to abortion should at least refer the patient to another doctor: see *Barr v Matthews* (2000) 52 BMLR 217.

[89] See *Mason and McCall Smith's Law and Medical Ethics*, p 162.

NHS is difficult to obtain. Is that a violation of women's rights caused by giving undue precedence to the professional's right to his conscience? The irony is that consultants and general practitioners can avoid involvement in abortion without having to invoke the right to conscientious objection. The doctor simply refuses to certify that a ground specified in the Abortion Act 1967 is made out. The woman can then only try to find another, more sympathetically inclined doctor. Her only remedy against the first practitioner would lie if she could prove that to refuse her an abortion was a breach of the duty of care owed to her. If the doctor is a consultant or a GP, no one can order him to participate in an abortion.

Fathers and abortion[90]

14.14 Has the father of the unborn child any say in whether or not the child be aborted? In 1978, in *Paton v British Pregnancy Advisory Service*,[91] a husband tried to prevent his wife having an abortion. She had been concerned about her pregnancy and consulted her doctor, but did not consult her husband. She obtained a certificate from two registered medical practitioners that the continuance of the pregnancy would involve risk to her health, so an abortion could lawfully proceed. Her husband intervened. He went to court to ask for an injunction (an order) to prevent the abortion from being carried out without his consent. The court refused an injunction. The judge said that the Abortion Act 1967 gave no right to the husband to be consulted. In the absence of such a right under the Act, the husband had 'no legal right enforceable at law or in equity to stop his wife having this abortion or to stop the doctors from carrying out the abortion'.

The abortion went ahead. The husband went to the European Commission on Human Rights, arguing that the 1967 Act and the judge's decision infringed the European Convention on Human Rights. He argued that his right to family life and the unborn child's right to life had been infringed. The Commission dismissed his claim.[92] It said that where an abortion was carried out on medical grounds, the husband's right to family life must necessarily be subordinated to the need to protect the rights and health of the mother. The unborn child's right to life was similarly subordinate to the rights of its mother, at least in the initial months of pregnancy. In *C v S*,[93] the Court of Appeal, having held that the abortion of a foetus at 18 weeks did not contravene the Infant Life (Prevention) Act 1929, refused the father any right *qua* father or a guardian of the unborn child to challenge the proposed abortion. In England, husbands have no standing to oppose an abortion agreed to by their wife. A father has no right to intervene to 'save' the foetus, nor can anyone argue that the foetus itself has legal personality so enabling him to act as its 'guardian' and stop an abortion.

90 See M Fox, 'Abortion Decision-Making – Taking Men's Needs Seriously' in E Lee (ed), *Abortion Law and Politics Today* (1998) Macmillan, p 198; S Sheldon, 'Unwilling Fathers and Abortion: Terminating Men's Child Support Obligations' (2003) 66 *Modern Law Review* 175.
91 [1979] QB 276.
92 [1980] 3 EHRR 409.
93 [1987] 1 All ER 1230. And see the Scottish case, *Kelly v Kelly* 1997 SLT 896.

One issue remains open. The father in *Paton* reluctantly accepted that the doctors' certificate as to the need for the abortion was issued in good faith. Had he challenged the certificate, could he have asked for an injunction to prevent an unlawful abortion taking place? The judge in *Paton* did not have to decide this point. He expressed the view that an injunction would not be granted. The supervision of abortion and the issue of the doctors' good faith is left to the criminal law and a jury. The Court of Appeal in *C v S* endorsed that opinion.[94]

Foetal status and Vo v France

14.15 The vexed question of foetal status, and whether the unborn child can assert a right to life, came before the European Court of Human Rights once again in *Vo v France*.[95] The applicant, Mme Vo, attended hospital in France for an ante-natal appointment in the sixth month of her pregnancy. Mme Vo was originally from Vietnam and spoke little French. A terrible error led to a doctor mistakenly supposing her to be another woman with a similar name. This other patient was scheduled to have a contraceptive coil removed. The doctor then proceeded to attempt to remove a non-existent coil from the pregnant Mme Vo. He pierced the amniotic sac and a week or so later the pregnancy had to be terminated on health grounds. The foetus was found to be between 20 and 21 weeks' gestation.

Mme Vo began a number of civil and criminal proceedings against the doctor and the hospital. For our purposes, the crucial process was an attempt to bring a criminal prosecution against the doctor for involuntary homicide, what in this country would be styled gross negligence manslaughter. The French courts held a non-viable foetus could not be the subject of homicide. Mme Vo argued that French law violated Article 2 of the European Convention on Human Rights by failing to protect the life of her unborn child.

The majority of the European Court of Human Rights dodged the central question of foetal status.[96] They held that the question of when a right of life accrued fell within the margin of appreciation allowed to contracting states. This was a question unresolved among European countries, and there was no European consensus on scientific and legal definitions of the beginning of life. Additionally, even if the foetus in *Vo* was entitled to such protection under Article 2, its rights were sufficiently protected by the rights the mother enjoyed to protection from assault and injury. It was not desirable to address in the abstract the question of whether an unborn child was a person for the purposes of Article 2. Reading the dissenting opinions within the court will show that the human rights judges in Strasbourg are as divided in their judgments on foetal status as society in general.

---

[94] [1987] 1 All ER 1230 at 1243.
[95] [2004] 2 FCR 577; see JK Mason, 'What's in a Name?: The Vagaries of *Vo v France*' [2005] *Child and Family Law Quarterly* 97.
[96] See K O'Donovan, 'Taking a Neutral Stance on the Legal Protection of the Fetus' (2006) 14 *Medical Law Review* 115.

Girls under 16

14.16 The Abortion Act 1967 made no special provision for abortion involving girls under 16. In 1981, a 15-year-old girl who already had one child became pregnant again while in local authority care. She wanted an abortion. Her doctors believed that the birth of a second child would damage her mental health and endanger her existing child. The girl's father objected. Abortion was contrary to his religion. The local authority applied to have the girl made a ward of court and thereby seek the consent of the court to the operation. Butler-Sloss J authorised the abortion.[97] She said that while she took into account the feelings of the parents she was satisfied that the girl's best interests required that her pregnancy be ended. Her decision was approved by the House of Lords in *Gillick v West Norfolk and Wisbeck Area Health Authority*.[98] *Gillick* would suggest that as long as the girl is mature enough to understand what abortion entails physically and emotionally, the doctor may go ahead on the basis of her consent alone. Nor are doctors under any obligation to inform her parents. The *Gillick competent* girl is as entitled to confidential treatment as the adult woman.[99] If the girl is insufficiently mature to make a decision for herself, the doctor must act in her best interests. Should her parents refuse consent to abortion, doctors and social workers may seek to go to court[100] and ask a judge to decide on the conflict between medical and parental opinion. The girl's wishes will be considered, but not treated as decisive. A doctor who ignores parental views will not be guilty of an offence of criminal abortion. He may face legal action by the girl's parents in the civil courts, or, in an extreme case, prosecution for an assault on her.

What of a case where parents want their daughter to have an abortion but she refuses? The Court of Appeal in *Re W (a minor) (medical treatment)*[101] ruled that a doctor may lawfully proceed with treatment of any young person under 18 with parental consent. He simply needs a valid consent either from his young patient herself, or from her parents. *Gillick competent* children and minors under 18 can authorise their own treatment, but not veto treatment. In theory, a gynaecologist could elect to override his patient's refusal to terminate her pregnancy as long as her parents endorsed the abortion. However, one must question whether doctors or parents who force an abortion on a girl act in her interests. Lord Donaldson in *Re W* considered it unthinkable that doctors would use the law to coerce young girls into abortion.[102]

Mentally-disabled women

14.17 In *T v T*,[103] a woman of 19 became pregnant. She was said to have a mental age of two, was doubly incontinent and incapable of any comprehensible speech. The problem for her mother and her doctors was that T was

[97] *Re P (A Minor)* (1981) 80 LGR 301.
[98] [1985] 3 All ER 402, HL.
[99] *Axon v Secretary of State for Health* [2006] EWHC 37 (Admin).
[100] See *Re B (a minor) (wardship: abortion)* [1991] 2 FLR 426 (Hollis J authorised abortion for a 12-year-old girl).
[101] [1992] 4 All ER 627, discussed below at 15.21.
[102] [1992] 4 All ER 627 at 635.
[103] [1988] 1 All ER 613.

quite incapable of giving her consent to the proposed abortion and, as she was an adult, no one else could authorise treatment on her behalf. Wood J granted a declaration that performing an abortion on T was not unlawful if that operation was considered to be in her best interests and in conformity with good medical practice. Termination of pregnancy in such a case will now be governed by the Mental Capacity Act 2005, discussed earlier in Chapter 6. The fundamental test will continue to be whether, in all the circumstances, abortion is in the best interests of the woman. In determining her best interests, regard must be had for any views or feelings the woman herself expresses, or has expressed, in the past. The impact on her must be fully evaluated. The timing of the proposed abortion may be crucial. In 2002, a judge refused to authorise an abortion close to the 24-week limit for 'social abortions'.[104]

A moral mess?

14.18 The debate on the morality of abortion continues. Consensus on the moral claims of the human embryo remains unattainable. The law in England is clear on one matter: the embryo/foetus has no legal personality or rights of its own until birth. It is recognised as an entity whose status deserves protection, but not as a legal person with rights equal to yours or mine. The question thus becomes how much protection should the embryo/foetus be afforded and at what cost to maternal rights and interests? And should that protection increase with gestational age? Today the law recognises two classes of foetus. Disabled foetuses are denied any protection from destruction even once capable of surviving birth. 'Normal' foetuses acquire a qualified right to birth at 24 weeks, dependent on their survival posing no grave risk to the mother. Up to 24 weeks, the fate of the 'normal' foetus rests in the hands of its mother's doctors. Whatever the intentions of the Abortion Act 1967, in practice it has conferred the authority to grant or withhold abortion to the medical profession. If the fate of the embryo/foetus cannot in our community be decided on the basis of consensus as to its moral status, would it be better to leave women to make the decision on abortion? Can it be right on any analysis that a woman's entitlement to abortion and her child's claim to life should depend on where in the country a woman happens to live?

---

[104] *Re SS (an adult: Late Termination)* [2002] 1 FLR 445. Contrast with *D v NHS Trust (Medical Treatment: Consent: Termination)* [2003] EWHC 2793 (Fam).

Chapter 15

DOCTORS AND CHILDREN

15.1 In this chapter, we examine the law governing doctors' relationships with child patients. The courts are often asked to determine the fate of sick children when doctors and parents disagree about how best to care for a child. Two recent cases have attracted much publicity. Charlotte Wyatt's parents sought assurances that, if their very sick baby daughter stopped breathing, she would be re-ventilated. Charlotte's case has been considered by the courts on no less than six occasions.[1] Doctors caring for a baby known as MB wanted to switch off his ventilator and let him die peacefully. His parents objected and the judge refused to authorise removing MB from respiratory support.[2] The courts continue to struggle with the question of blood transfusions for the children of Jehovah's Witnesses. May a doctor insist on administering a transfusion against the parents' wishes? Some cases involve not disagreement between doctors and parents, but disputes between parents themselves. Should a little boy be circumcised as his Muslim father wishes, when his mother vehemently opposes circumcision? On the opposite side of the coin, are there limits to treatment to which a parent may agree on behalf of the child? For instance, may a mother, learning that her four-year-old daughter is a likely carrier of haemophilia, have the child subjected to genetic testing for carrier status or even sterilised? As a child matures, common sense dictates that she be allowed to make more decisions for herself. *Gillick*[3] appeared to establish a right to adolescent autonomy, but it proved to be an odd sort of 'right', a right to say 'yes' but not to say 'no'.[4]

We begin by looking at the legal position where everyone would agree that the child is too young to make any sort of decision about medical treatment for herself. Then we explore the vexed issues surrounding adolescents.

---

1   *Re Wyatt* [2004] EWHC 2247, [2005] EWHC 117, [2005] EWHC 693, [2005] EWHC 2902, [2006] EWHC 319; *Wyatt v Portsmouth NHS Trust* [2005] EWCA Civ 1181.
2   *An NHS Trust v B* [2006] EWHC 507 (Fam).
3   *Gillick v West Norfolk and Wisbech Area Health Authority* [1985] 3 All ER 402, HL.
4   See *Re R (A Minor)* [1991] 4 All ER 177, CA; *Re W (A Minor)* [1992] 4 All ER 627, CA.

15.2 Doctors and Children

At the threshold of viability[5]

15.2 The birth of a very sick baby is a tragedy. The joy of normal childbirth is replaced by fear for the baby's and the family's future. Until relatively recently, the parents' dilemma was to some extent mitigated because little could be done for the baby. Most extremely premature babies died at birth. Many severely disabled infants survived only a few weeks or months after birth. Their parents suffered the pain of bereavement, but were spared anxiety about the child's future. In any case, whether the child lived or died, the decision was made by 'God or nature'. The parents could do nothing about it. Developments in neonatal intensive care enable doctors to prolong the lives of babies born at ever earlier stages of gestation. And babies born later in pregnancy, but affected by severe abnormalities, can also be 'saved'. The evidence, however, suggests that although these babies' lives are prolonged, many babies will not survive to leave the neonatal intensive care unit and go home. A proportion of those who do survive will be affected by severe impairments. A recent study has shown that just 16 per cent of babies born at 23 weeks, and only 44 per cent of those born at 24 weeks, survive.[6] An earlier, larger study[7] showed that of those babies born at 23 weeks who survived to their sixth birthday, 25 per cent or so were affected by severe disability. At 22 weeks, just two babies survived at all. Babies born nearer to the usual term of pregnancy, or at term, may also suffer from severe abnormalities, for example a baby's brain may not have developed properly or she may be born with virtually no bowel. Some congenital conditions, such as Edwards syndrome, mean that a baby can survive only with intensive care and is unlikely, whatever is done for them, to live for more than a short time. Parents may be faced with agonising decisions about the treatment of their baby within minutes of her birth.

The dilemma of how to care for a very sick person, whether prolonging life is always the right course of action, is not exclusive to babies. The problem arises equally acutely in relation to the terminally or chronically ill adult, or an older child irreversibly injured in an accident. None the less, there are special features surrounding any discussion of the care of sick babies. The conscious adult patient can speak for himself. The decision about any continuation of treatment may be his. Even if unconscious, he may earlier have expressed his wishes should the question arise. The baby cannot express any preference. Her parents may give their views. Should parental wishes be decisive? Parents' views are crucial, but children have interests too. The baby's plight is different from that of a newly-disabled adult. She does not move from full health to disability. She does not experience a dramatic drop in her expectations of life. A life of disability is all that she can know. Nor will her parents be as able to speak for her as for an older child. The older child (even at three or four years old) will have indicated what gives her pleasure and what causes her pain. So, for over a quarter of a century now, a number of doctors, lawyers and philosophers have argued that questions about how to

---

5   See generally, Nuffield Council on Bioethics, *Critical Care Decisions in Fetal and Neonatal Medicine* (2006) (hereafter NCOB Report).
6   See T Markestad *et al*, 'Early Death, Morbidity, and Need of Treatment Among Extremely Premature Infants' (2005) 115 *Pediatrics* 1289.
7   See the discussion of the EPICure study in the NCOB Report.

treat newborn babies raise somewhat different issues to the more general questions about when to give priority to prolonging life.

For doctors, one critical factor has been the evidence that certain kinds of intervention have poor long-term results. Just because we can resuscitate a baby born at 22 weeks and 3 days, does not necessarily mean that we should. If the baby is unlikely ever to leave intensive care and, if he does so, may be so severely disabled that he will never be able to lead an independent life, should he be resuscitated? If a baby has no bowel, he could be resuscitated but will have to be fed intravenously all his life. Neonatal intensive care is highly invasive. The baby is isolated in his incubator with tubes in every orifice. Doctors ask whether it is always in the baby's interests to strive to prolong his life.

While some parents will want doctors to do everything possible to keep their baby alive, others who discover at birth that their baby is severely disabled may be perplexed by suggestions that their newborn baby must now be subjected to aggressive measures to keep him alive. The Abortion Act 1967 permits the termination of pregnancy when there is a substantial risk that the child, if born, will be severely disabled. Amniocentesis is increasingly used to test mothers whose babies are at risk of cystic fibrosis or Down's syndrome. The Abortion Act allows the abortion of such a child right up to the end of the pregnancy. As we have seen in Chapter 14, foetuses have been aborted on evidence of much less serious conditions. Some people ask why a child who could have been actively destroyed if his disability had been diagnosed in pregnancy must be the subject of intensive life-saving measures if his disability goes unnoticed until birth. Some philosophers argue that it is irrational that the law should allow the killing of a foetus at 38 weeks into pregnancy, but insist on saving the baby prematurely delivered at 24 weeks. What moral difference does the journey though the birth canal make?

The concept of the sanctity of each and every human life is under attack. Forceful arguments are advanced[8] that the value of life lies in its quality and its contribution to society, rather than in any intrinsic merit in life itself. The newborn baby is no more a 'person' than the embryo or the foetus. Such arguments are equally forcefully rebutted.[9]

Proposals for reforms of law and practice

15.3 Debate about whether the law should make special provision in relation to newborn babies is not new. The prosecution of Dr Leonard Arthur for murder prompted calls for new legislation as long ago as 1981. Legislation, it was suggested, would clarify the law and more readily allow doctors (with parental consent) to withhold or withdraw life-sustaining treatment from babies whose objective quality of life was low. A draft 'Limitation of

---

8   See J Glover, *Causing Death and Saving Lives* (1977) Penguin, Chapter 12. See also Chapter 2 of this book.

9   See, in particular, JK Mason, *Human Life and Medical Practice* (1988) Edinburgh University Press, Chapter 6.

Treatment Bill'[10] proposed that no criminal offence would be committed where a doctor refused or ceased treatment of an infant under 28 days of age, provided that (1) the parents gave their written consent, and (2) two doctors, both of at least seven years' standing and one of them being a paediatrician, certified in writing that the infant suffered from severe physical or mental handicap which was either irreversible or of such gravity that, after receiving all reasonably available treatment, the child would enjoy no worthwhile quality of life.[11] Broadly similar proposals were made by Mason and McCall Smith in the first edition of *Law and Medical Ethics*,[12] and survived with amendments to the sixth edition of that work.[13] Mason and Laurie now argue that any legal provision relating to newborn babies needs to be addressed in broader legislation relating to the law concerning withholding and withdrawing life-sustaining treatment more generally.[14] Legislation aimed solely at clarifying the law concerning withholding and withdrawing treatment may be of limited utility. What is meant by 'worthwhile quality of life'? What degree of pain and suffering renders life unbearable?

Another question in relation to changing the law to try to clarify when doctors may lawfully withhold or withdraw treatment is this. If it is lawful to withhold life-support from a baby, 'allowing her to die', should it also be lawful to take active steps to end her life swiftly and painlessly? Is there any moral difference between the two?[15] What of the baby whose condition is agonising and likely to be fatal but who hangs on to life? In the Netherlands, the Groeningen Protocol[16] was developed to permit doctors to act to end the life of a baby in the most exceptional circumstances. To put it crudely, the Protocol allows neonatal euthanasia. It is not formally part of Dutch law. A team of physicians, including a doctor who is not directly involved in the care of the baby, must confirm that the baby's condition is such that he is subjected to unbearable suffering, and that his condition is untreatable. If the parents consent, high doses of opiates such as morphine are used to induce the death of the baby gently over one to two days. Immediately lethal injections of substances such as potassium chloride are not used. After the baby's death, a report is made to the coroner, and a committee of five members, including an ethicist and a lawyer, scrutinise the decision to check that the treatment of the

---

[10] D Brahams (1981) 78 *Law Society Gazette* 1342.
[11] The Bill directed doctors to consider a number of factors in assessing the child's likely quality of life. They should consider (*inter alia*) the degree of pain and suffering likely to be endured, the child's potential to communicate, and also the willingness of the parents to care for him and the effect that that may have on their physical and mental health.
[12] JK Mason and RA McCall Smith, *Law and Medical Ethics* (1985) Butterworths, p 89.
[13] At p 390.
[14] JK Mason and GT Laurie, *Mason and McCall Smith's Law and Medical Ethics* (7th edn, 2006) OUP, pp 562–565.
[15] *Mason and McCall Smith's Law and Medical Ethics*, pp 566–568.
[16] See E Verhagen and PJJ Saver, 'The Groeningen Protocol – Euthanasia in Severely Ill Newborns' (2005) 352 *New England Journal of Medicine* 959.

baby met the conditions set out in the Protocol. The 'killing' of the baby remains a criminal offence but, if the Protocol is followed, doctors will not be prosecuted.[17]

If legislation allowing active neonatal euthanasia were to be enacted in the UK, a series of difficult decisions would need to be taken. Do we accept some distinction in the value of the life of the newborn baby, and the older child or adult? If so, where is the line to be drawn? Is it 72 hours or 28 days, or later? The Abortion Act 1967 may have altered perceptions of the sanctity of life. Debate has ebbed and flowed for centuries as to the status and humanity of the unborn. Abortion, although severely punished, was never equated with murder in England. Birth is a relatively clear dividing line. No other distinction can be as clear. So how (if at all) can legislation expressly and exclusively designed to allow the ending of the lives of newborn babies be justified? Do we regard the parents as standing proxy for their child in any decision as to treatment? If so, why draw the line at 28 days? Older children develop chronic disease, are disabled in accidents, or are discovered to suffer from severe disabilities later in childhood.

One other possibility to be considered is whether, without changing the law, clearer guidelines relating to the resuscitation of extremely premature babies would be helpful.[18] When a baby is born below 24 weeks' gestation, practice in the UK varies considerably. Some neonatal units will try and discuss what to do with the parents before the birth where this is possible. Others resuscitate all babies born after 23 weeks, admit the baby to neonatal intensive care and then review his prospects. A few units will seek to resuscitate a baby born at 22 weeks, or even below. The extent of parents' involvement in such decisions also varies. Resuscitation of such a very premature baby raises questions of the ethics of attempting to resuscitate a baby who is highly likely to die whatever is done for her. And when a baby does survive on a ventilator, but the long-term prognosis is dire, decisions to withdraw intensive care may be even more painful than decisions to institute care.

Finally, the question of use of resources raises it ugly head. It is a question of two parts:

(1)   Should money spent on intensive care of babies unlikely to survive be spent elsewhere, say on treatment for early breast cancer?

(2)   Would money spent on Baby A, born at 22 weeks, be better spent on B, born a little later? The limited number of places in neonatal units means that doctors sometimes have to arrange for a baby to be transported hundreds of miles to a neonatal unit far away because there is no capacity to care for him nearer the family home.

---

[17]   Though note that the process of establishing a Protocol, allowing decisions to be made not to prosecute cases of neonatal euthanasia within that Protocol, exactly mirrors the process in relation to active voluntary euthanasia in adults that resulted in the Termination of Life on Request and Assisted Suicide (Review Procedures) Act 2000 (discussed below at 20.19).

[18]   See the NCOB Report.

In the Netherlands,[19] professional guidelines advise against the resuscitation of a baby born before 25 weeks unless the parents press very strongly for resuscitation and doctors have grounds to judge that the particular baby has an exceptional chance of survival. The Nuffield Council on Bioethics[20] examined ethical, social and legal issues arising in relation to critical care decisions in neonatal medicine. Among a number of recommendations, the report proposed guidelines for deciding whether to institute neonatal intensive care. The guidelines suggest that below 22 weeks no baby should be resuscitated, except within an approved clinical research study. Between 22 and 23 weeks, the general practice would be not to institute intensive care unless the parents, fully informed, reiterate requests for resuscitation. Between 23 and 24 weeks, precedence should be given to parental wishes and, from 24 weeks, the presumption should be that full intensive care for the baby should be instituted.

The courts and sick infants

15.4   For the present, legal principles governing the medical care of newborn babies and small children must be discerned from the judgments of the courts. The focus in any case referred to court is the individual baby. This allows judges to adopt a flexible approach tailored to the needs of the case before them. In *An NHS Trust v B*,[21] Holman J said expressly:

> ... this is a very fact specific decision taken in the actual circumstances as they are for this child and today.

> Others may analyse this judgment for its 'implications'. It is not a policy-based judgment at all and is not designed to have 'implications' ... My sole and intense focus has been on this child alone ...

Flexibility has advantages, but may result in some parents feeling that judgments are too subjective and governed by the moral and personal viewpoints of the chosen judge. Doctors worry about lack of certainty. They are concerned that decisions to withhold or withdraw treatment (even when agreed with parents) could subject them to possible criminal liability for murder or manslaughter.

The fundamental principle governing withholding life-saving treatment from young children was settled in *Re B* in 1981. It concerned an infant girl, Alexandra, born suffering from Down's syndrome and an intestinal obstruction. In a normal child, simple surgery would have been carried out swiftly with minimal risk to the baby. Without surgery, the baby would die within a few days. Her parents refused to authorise the operation. They argued that God or nature had given their child a way out. The doctors contacted the local authority and the child was made a ward of court. A judge was asked to

[19]   See Dutch Pediatric Association, *To Treat or Not to Treat? Limits for Life-Sustaining Treatment in Neonatology* (1992) Utrecht, Netherlands; FJ Walther, 'Withholding Treatment: Withdrawing Treatment and Palliative Care in the Neonatal Intensive Care Unit' (2005) 81 *Early Human Development* 905. See also the NCOB Report, p 135.
[20]   NCOB Report.
[21]   [2006] EWHC 507 (Fam) at paras 106–107.

authorise the operation. He refused to do so. The authority appealed, and the Court of Appeal[22] ordered that the operation go ahead. Counsel for the parents submitted that, in this kind of decision, the views of responsible and caring parents must be respected and that their decision should decide the issue. The Court of Appeal rejected the submission, holding that the decision must be made in the best interests of the child.

Templeman LJ said:

> ... it devolves on this court in this particular instance to decide whether the life of this child is demonstrably going to be so awful that in effect the child must be condemned to die, or whether the life of this child is still so imponderable that it would be wrong for her to be condemned to die. There may be cases, I know not, of severe proved damage where the future is so certain and where the life of the child is so bound to be full of pain and suffering that the court might be driven to a different conclusion, but in the present case the choice which lies before the court is this: whether to allow an operation to take place which may result in the child living for 20 or 30 years as a mongoloid (*sic*) or whether (and I think this brutally must be the result) to terminate the life of a mongoloid child because she also has an intestinal complaint. Faced with that choice I have no doubt that it is the duty of this court to decide that the child must live.

In the same year that the Court of Appeal held that Alexandra must be treated and live, Dr Leonard Arthur faced trial for murder.[23] A baby was born in the hospital where Dr Arthur was consultant paediatrician. The baby suffered from Down's syndrome. His parents did not wish him to survive. He died 69 hours after his birth. The prosecution alleged that Dr Arthur ordered nursing care only and prescribed a drug to suppress the baby's appetite and so starve him to death. They claimed that, apart from Down's syndrome, the baby was otherwise healthy, and that his death resulted from starvation and the effect of the drug causing him to succumb to bronchopneumonia. Defence evidence established that (1) the baby suffered from severe brain and lung damage, (2) Dr Arthur followed established practice in the management of such an infant, and (3) that in the first three days of life, normal babies take in little or no sustenance and usually lose weight (which the dead baby had not done). The baby patently did not starve to death. The judge directed that the charge be altered to attempted murder. Summing up, the judge stressed that there is '... no special law in this country that places doctors in a separate category and gives them special protection over the rest of us.' He emphasised that, however severely disabled a child may be, if the doctor gives it drugs in an excessive amount so that the drugs will cause death, then the doctor commits murder. He highlighted the distinction between doing something active to kill the child and electing not to follow a particular course of treatment which might have saved the infant. Considering the ethical arguments on terminating newborn life, the judge reminded the jury that if ethics and the law conflict, the law must prevail. None the less his Lordship concluded:

---

[22] *Re B (A Minor) (Wardship: Medical Treatment)* [1981] 1 WLR 1421, CA.
[23] (1981) 12 BMLR 1. See also 'Dr Leonard Arthur: His Trial and Its Implications' (1981) 283 *British Medical Journal* 1340; H Benyon, 'Doctors as Murderers' [1982] *Criminal Law Review* 17; M Gunn and JC Smith, 'Arthur's Case and the Right to Life of a Down's Syndrome Child' [1985] *Criminal Law Review* 705.

... I imagine that you [the jury] will think long and hard before deciding that doctors of the eminence we have heard in representing to you what medical ethics are and apparently have been over a period of time, you would think long and hard before concluding that they in that great profession have evolved standards which amount to committing crime.

The jury acquitted Dr Arthur.

A confused picture emerges. A baby with Down's syndrome was ordered to be saved, yet Dr Arthur was not guilty of a crime in relation to his treatment of a severely damaged Down's infant. The acquittal of Dr Arthur tells us little about the law. The confusion over the pathological evidence may have irretrievably prejudiced the jury against the prosecution's case. The baby's multiple abnormalities should have been irrelevant to the reduced charge of attempted murder. When Dr Arthur ordered nursing care only, he thought that he was dealing with a Down's baby as entitled to survive as Alexandra. Did the jury see it that way? As Mason puts it: 'Murder, in the popular sense of the word, was the one thing of which Dr Arthur was certainly innocent.'[24]

Deliberate killing

15.5 In all but one exceptional instance, illustrated by the case of the Manchester conjoined twins Jodie and Mary (see below), it is indisputable that neither doctor, parents nor anyone else may do any *act* intended *solely* to hasten the death of a disabled baby. The deliberate killing of any human being is murder. The moment that the child has an existence separate from his mother,[25] the moment he has independent circulation – even though the afterbirth may not yet fully have been expelled from the mother's body – he is protected by the law of homicide. It has on occasion been faintly argued that a grossly malformed child, 'a monstrous birth', should not be regarded in law as human. We shall see that this argument was advanced unsuccessfully in the conjoined twins case.[26] Defining humanity, other than by virtue of human parentage, is an impossible and unacceptable task. Does 'monstrous' refer to appearance, in which case an intelligent infant of appalling mien could legitimately be destroyed? Does it cover lack of intelligence, or lack of a brain?[27] Both are almost impossible to measure at birth.

None the less, in *Re A (Minors) (Conjoined Twins: Separation)*,[28] the Court of Appeal authorised the killing of the weaker of two conjoined twins. Jodie and Mary were born in Manchester after a scan in their native Malta revealed their condition. Their parents came to this country in the hope of surgery to

---

24 Mason, *Human Life and Medical Practice*, p 63.
25 Some dispute exists as to the moment in childbirth when this occurs. Apparently, the child need not have breathed: see *R v Poulton* (1832) 5 C & P 329; *R v Brain* (1834) 6 C & P 349; *Attorney-General's Reference (No 3 of 1994)* [1997] 3 All ER 936, HL. See also the NCOB Report.
26 *Re A (Minors) (Conjoined twins: separation)* [2000] Lloyd's Rep Med 425 at 464–465.
27 How would you classify the status of a baby born with anencephaly?
28 [2000] Lloyd's Rep Med 425. The names were given to the girls to preserve their anonymity, but the ban on identifying the family was later lifted.

separate and save both children. The girls were joined at the pelvis. Each had her own arms and legs as well as a brain, heart and lungs. Mary's brain was said to be 'primitive', her heart was defective and she had no functioning lung tissue. Mary remained alive only because a common artery allowed Jodie's heart to circulate oxygenated blood to both infants. Left conjoined, the strain on Jodie's organs would result in the death of both children within three to six months. Surgery to separate the girls would result in Mary's death within minutes of separation. Surgery would kill Mary,[29] but doing nothing would result in the death of both girls. The parents were devout Roman Catholics. They refused to consent to surgery because they believe that it would be a sin to 'murder' Mary and that their children's fate must be subject to God's will. The hospital applied to the court for authority to overrule the parents' objections.

The Court of Appeal ruled that surgery should go ahead. What follows can only be a summary of their Lordship's complex, and not always unanimous, reasoning. Let us deal first with the question of how it could be said to be lawful to kill Mary. Mary, the judges agreed, was in law a person whose right to life was entitled to respect. She was not to be regarded as non-human, a monster or, as some had suggested, a 'tumour' attached to Jodie's body.[30] Ward and Brooke LJJ[31] accepted that surgery to separate the twins constituted killing Mary. However much their doctors wished the case to be different, in cutting off Mary's blood supply by clamping the common artery, they 'intended' Mary's death. Unless some lawful excuse justified their conduct, the doctors were exposed to liability for murder. The court found such excuse in the doctrine of necessity.[32] Brooke LJ cited the analogy of the captain of a ship about to capsize: he had to choose who entered the lifeboats. The judge continued:

> He would not be guilty even though he kept some of the passengers back from the boat at revolver-point and he would not be guilty even though he had to fire the revolver.[33]

Doctors caring for the conjoined twins had duties to both girls. Surgery would involve an assault, a fatal assault, on Mary. To save Jodie, it was justifiable. It was necessary to avoid an inevitable and irreparable evil. It was no more than what was necessary to preserve Jodie's life. Given Mary too would die without surgery, the evil of her inevitable death was not disproportionate. A finding that surgery did not constitute murder did not conclude the question of the twins' fate. The more important question revolved around who had the right to make the crucial decision. Doctors wanted to operate. The parents objected. Before going on to look at the question of who decides, we must first

---

[29] For an eloquent discussion of the issues raised by surgery to separate conjoined twins prior to *Re A*, see S Sheldon and S Wilkinson, 'Conjoined Twins: The Legality and Ethics of Sacrifice' (1997) 2 *Medical Law Review* 149.

[30] Though note Mason's interesting argument that as Mary had no independent lung function, she should have been classified as stillborn: JK Mason, 'Conjoined Twins: A Diagnostic Conundrum' (2001) 5 *Edinburgh Law Review* 226.

[31] [2000] Lloyd's Rep Med 425 at 456 and 466–467. Robert Walker LJ sought to argue that Mary's death resulted not from surgery but her own inability to sustain life (at 510).

[32] Ward LJ advanced, and preferred, a doctrine of quasi-self-defence.

[33] [2000] Lloyd's Rep Med 425 at 474.

consider the more common case – where what is at stake is not actively killing a child, but withholding treatment from her.

Withholding and withdrawing treatment

15.6 To what extent does the law require parents and doctors to provide treatment to prolong a baby's life? Before any failure to treat a child can engage *criminal* liability, it must be established that a duty to act was imposed on the accused. Parents are under a duty to care and provide for their dependent children. Failing to provide proper care, including medical aid where necessary, will result in a conviction for wilful neglect of the child (provided that the parent was aware of the risk to the child's health).[34] Should the child die, the parents may be convicted of manslaughter.[35] Parents who are aware of the danger to a child's health, but who do not seek medical aid because of religious or other conscientious objection to conventional medicine, have no defence to criminal prosecutions for neglect or manslaughter.[36] Parents who deliberately withhold sustenance and care from a child intending him to die may be guilty of murder.[37] Finally, a range of other legal remedies is available to local authority social services departments: failure to provide medical aid, risking significant harm to the child, is a ground for taking a child into care.[38]

What of the doctor? If he is under a duty to treat a baby then, like the parent, should the child die, he could be prosecuted for manslaughter (if his omission resulted from neglect) or for murder (if he intended the infant to die). Once the doctor accepts the baby as a patient, he assumes a duty to that baby to give him proper medical care. It is unlikely that a paediatrician could, should anyone ever want to, evade responsibility by refusing to accept a child as a patient after his birth. His contract with the NHS imposes on him an obligation towards the children born in his hospital, giving rise to a duty to the individual infant.[39]

Parents and doctors have a duty to provide medical aid, but what is the scope of that duty? Where a child is suffering from severe abnormalities, may proper medical care be defined as keeping her comfortable whilst withholding life-prolonging treatment? Two factors play a vital role in the decision as to whether to treat an acutely ill child. What do her parents desire? What is the practice of the medical profession in the management of her kind of illness or disability? The answer to the second question is that, in many instances, doctors will explain the treatment available, give a prognosis as to the child's future and accept the decision taken by the parents. Yet, as we have seen, the Court of Appeal, in the case of *Re B*,[40] ordered surgery to remove an intestinal blockage against the parents' wishes. Baby Alexandra would be affected by

---

[34] Children and Young Persons Act 1933, s 1(1).
[35] *R v Lowe* [1973] QB 702.
[36] *R v Senior* [1899] 1 QB 283.
[37] *R v Gibbons and Proctor* (1918) 13 Cr App Rep 134.
[38] Children Act 1989, s 31(2).
[39] See Beynon [1982] *Criminal Law Review* 17 at 27–28.
[40] *Re B (A Minor) (Wardship: Medical Treatment)* [1981] 1 WLR 1421, CA.

the mental and physical disabilities attendant on Down's syndrome. If treated, she could expect the same quality of life as any one of the many other Down's babies born each year. She would suffer no pain from her disability, and the evidence suggests that properly cared for Down's children lead happy lives. The surgery needed to save Alexandra was simple and without risk. Her proposed treatment had a purpose, the baby was not inevitably dying and the treatment was in no way unduly burdensome. *Re B* signalled that the legality of withholding treatment is dependent on the degree of a child's disability and the degree of suffering continued life may cause her. Some sort of balance between the pain of prolonged life and the finality of death has to be struck. In striking that balance, the law, in appropriate cases, allows doctors and parents to conclude that it is not in the interests of the baby to intervene to prolong her life.

What, though, of withdrawing treatment already instituted? A baby may be resuscitated at birth, or an older child put on a ventilator after a traumatic injury, but tests later show that the child is never likely to leave hospital or even to survive off the ventilator. It is thought his best interests are best served by allowing him to die peacefully in his parents' arms. Can doctors lawfully switch off the ventilator? Or is that an act hastening death and, so, murder? We shall see later that the House of Lords[41] has ruled that switching off a ventilator, or withdrawing life-sustaining treatment from a patient of any age, does not constitute an act hastening death. Discontinuing life-support is 'no different from not initiating it in the first place'.[42] More recently, in a case directly concerned with the care of a baby in intensive care, the judge stressed that '... there is no legal distinction between withholding or withdrawing life-support ... the best interests test applies equally to both situations.'[43]

'Best interests': a balancing exercise

15.7 In *Re C (A Minor) (Wardship: Medical Treatment)*,[44] a baby had been made a ward of court shortly after birth on grounds of her parents' inability to care for her. C suffered from an exceptionally severe degree of hydrocephalus, and the brain itself was poorly formed. She appeared to be blind and virtually deaf. At 16 weeks she was, apart from her enlarged head, the size of a four-week-old baby. It was said to be inevitable that she would die in a matter of months at most. The issues put before the court were these. If it became impossible to go on feeding her by syringe, must she be fed naso-gastrically or intravenously? If she developed an infection, must she be treated by antibiotics? The judge asked the Official Solicitor to intervene and sought the advice of an eminent professor of paediatrics, who examined C. He advised that those caring for C should not be obliged to resort to artificial feeding, or to treat C with antibiotics, simply to prolong her life. A judgment about how to treat C should depend primarily on relieving her suffering. The judge made an order that leave be given to 'treat the ward to die'. This infelicitous phrase

41 *Airedale NHS Trust v Bland* [1993] AC 789. See below at Chapter 20.
42 *Airedale NHS Trust v Bland* [1993] AC 789 at 866, per Lord Goff.
43 *An NHS Trust v B* [2006] EWHC 507 (Fam) at para 20.
44 [1989] 2 All ER 782, CA.

caused an outcry, being wrongly interpreted by some of the media as sanction for active euthanasia. The Court of Appeal affirmed the judgment, but deleted the unfortunate phrase. Lord Donaldson MR saw C's case as very different from that of *Re B*. C was inevitably dying. Her life appeared to offer her no pleasures. The court ordered: 'The hospital authority be at liberty to treat the minor to allow her life to come to an end peacefully and with dignity ...'. Seventeen years later another case, also confusingly called *Re C*,[45] concerned a baby who became blind and deaf as a result of meningitis. She survived only with the support of a ventilator, suffered repeated convulsions and was likely to die in the next two years, or perhaps sooner. She had a 'very low awareness of anything'. Her parents and doctors both wished to withdraw life-support and let C die. The judge authorised removing the baby from life-support.

Re J (A Minor) (Wardship: Medical Treatment)[46] is a more difficult case. J was born 13 weeks prematurely at a birth weight of 1.1 kg. He nearly died several times, but was saved by medical skill. He was found to have severe brain damage: 'A large area of fluid filled cavities where there ought to have been brain tissue.' J was said to be likely to develop paralysis, blindness and probable deafness. Unlike either baby C, his life expectancy might extend to his late teens. If he developed an infection, must he be treated? If he suffered a further episode of cyanosis and collapse, must he be resuscitated? The Court of Appeal found that he need not. Lord Donaldson regarded *Re B* as near to binding authority that a balancing exercise should be performed in assessing the course to be adopted in the best interests of the child. The exercise must seek to reflect the 'assumed' view of the child. In deciding whether the prolonged life of the child will be 'demonstrably awful', the child's perspective on life is the crucial test. He will know no other life, and the amazing adaptability and courage of disabled people must be considered.

> But in the end there will be cases in which the answer must be that it is not in the interests of the child to subject it to treatment which will cause increased suffering and produce no commensurate benefit, giving the fullest possible weight to the child's, and mankind's, desire to survive.[47]

Note that in *Re J* (as in *Re C* (1996)), there was no disagreement between J's parents and doctors. The application to court was undertaken to ensure that any decision to withhold treatment was lawful so neither parents nor doctors would risk prosecution.

English judges have shown themselves prepared to accept that appropriate care for a terribly sick child is not always to prolong his life. Does the Human Rights Act 1998 make any difference, enforcing as it does the right to life enshrined in Article 2 of the European Convention on Human Rights? In *A National Health Service Trust v D*,[48] a baby was born with irreversible lung disease and multi-organ failure. D was in the process of dying and the Trust sought a declaration that it would be lawful not to resuscitate him if he stopped breathing. The judge held that as long as any decision not to

---

[45] *Re C (A Baby)* [1996] 2 FLR 43.
[46] [1990] 3 All ER 930, CA.
[47] [1990] 3 All ER 930 at 938, CA.
[48] [2000] 2 FLR 677.

resuscitate D was made in his best interests, there was no violation of Article 2. Article 3, which prohibits cruel or inhuman treatment, entails a right to be allowed to die with dignity.

Disputing best interests

15.8 The most difficult cases arise when parents and doctors disagree about the best interests of a baby. As we have seen in the case of the conjoined twins, *Re A*,[49] such disagreement was present. Having decided that ending Mary's life was not unlawful, the court had to address whose judgment on the interests of the two little girls should determine their fate. Their Lordships stressed that while the decisions of devoted and responsible parents should be treated with respect, the court retained power to intervene to protect the paramount welfare of the child. The conjoined twins case was unique because Jodie's welfare depended on Mary's demise. The parents, however, had other separate concerns about Jodie. They feared[50] that she would be profoundly disabled, unable to walk, likely to have to undergo several more operations during her infancy and possibly be doubly incontinent. Their view was that it was not in the interests of either child to operate. The Court of Appeal disagreed. There was a reasonable prospect that Jodie could lead a relatively normal life. Mary, Ward LJ said, was 'beyond help'. Surgery might shorten her brief life. Without surgery she would still die. The '... least detrimental choice, balancing the interests of Mary against Jodie and Jodie against Mary permit the operation to be performed.'[51]

Jodie's prospects, it might be said, were not 'demonstrably awful'. Will the courts always rule in favour of continuing a child's life unless it is either likely to involve unbearable suffering or be such that the child will have virtually no ability to enjoy any of her senses, or use any of her abilities? In *Re T*[52] (1997), T was born with biliary atresia, a life threatening liver disease. Without a liver transplant, he would die at about two-and-a-half years of age. Earlier surgery when he was three-and-a-half weeks old had failed, and the baby suffered great pain and distress. His parents, both health professionals, adamantly opposed transplant surgery. Fearing intervention by social services, the parents fled abroad. The local authority intervened, seeking a court order requiring the family's return to England and that the transplant go ahead. The parents argued that if their son had the transplant, even if the operation was successful, he would be subjected to further pain and distress, would have to take anti-rejection drugs for the rest of his life and might face repeated surgery. They thought that his best interests were better served by a short, happy life and a peaceful death. The Court of Appeal ruled that the parental views should prevail. The parents in *Re T* were entitled to withhold life-saving treatment from their child. The essence of the court's ruling in *Re T* was that,

---

[49] [2000] Lloyd's Rep Med 425 (discussed above at 15.5).

[50] These fears have not materialised. Surgeons expect 'Jodie' to be able to walk, to avoid incontinency and even to be able to bear children.

[51] [2000] Lloyd's Rep Med 425 at 455.

[52] *Re T (A Minor) (Wardship: Medical Treatment)* [1997] 1 All ER 906, CA (discussed in M Fox and J McHale, 'In Whose Best Interests?' (1997) 60 *Modern Law Review* 600).

on the 'unusual facts' of the case, any presumption that the best interests of the child are to prolong his life was rebutted. The trial judge, ordering the transplant, had given insufficient weight to the mother's views. If the operation was ordered against her will, her son's welfare would be compromised. Her commitment to his care was an integral part of any successful recovery post-transplant. Deprived of her care (ie taken into care) he would suffer. If she reluctantly complied with the court order, family problems would beset child and parents. The mother would have to return reluctantly to, and remain in, England. It was not clear whether the father would give up his job and return with her. If not, problems would arise in terms of financial and emotional support for mother and son. Butler-Sloss LJ, finding that the mother's view could not be considered unreasonable, said this:

> The mother and child are one for the purposes of this unusual case and the decision of the court to consent to the operation jointly affects the mother and it also affects the father. The welfare of the child depends on his mother. The practical considerations of her ability to cope with supporting the child in the face of her belief that this course is not right for him, the requirement to return probably for a long time to this country, either to leave the father behind and lose his support or to require him to give up his present job and seek one in England were not put by the judge into the balance when he made his decision.[53]

Is *Re T* an aberration? Consider Butler-Sloss LJ's language. She says 'mother and child are one' and that the child's welfare depends on his mother. Where the child remains with loving parents, is this not usual rather than unusual? A sick child always requires extra parental commitment. Why, you might ask, did a similar analysis not apply to Jodie, the stronger of the conjoined twins? Are there other singular features of *Re T*? All the judges emphasise that the parents were themselves health professionals. Did this give their views extra weight? More importantly, and what is truly unusual about *Re T*, is that any court order would also have needed to drag the family back from the other side of the world. Would *Re T* have had the same outcome if the parents had never left England?[54]

Scruple or dogma?[55]

15.9 *Re T* is an unusual case where parents refuse to consent to life-saving treatment for their infant because of their judgment about the medical outcome for the baby. More common are cases where parents who are Jehovah's Witnesses refuse to consent to blood transfusions. Transfusions violate a fundamental tenet of Witnesses' faith.[56] The kinds of case which

---

53   [1997] 1 All ER 906 at 914–915, CA .
54   This seems to be the tenor of Roch LJ's judgment.
55   See C Bridge, 'Religion, Culture and Conviction – the Medical Treatment of Young Children' (1999) 11 *Child and Family Law Quarterly* 1, and 'Religion, Culture and the Body of the Child' in A Bainham, SD Slater and M Richards (eds), *Body Lore and Laws* (2002) OUP, p 265.
56   Although the Council of Elders does seem to have softened slightly its opposition to transfusions, leaving the matter more to the conscience of the believer.

reach the courts are well illustrated by *Re S* (1993).[57] S was four-and-a-half and suffering from T-cell leukaemia. His parents agreed to intensive chemotherapy. Doctors argued that transfusion of blood products was essential to maximise the prospects of successful treatment and saving S's life. Without resort to blood, the chances of successful treatment were significantly reduced. His parents objected not just on religious grounds. They raised concerns about the safety of blood products. Their lawyers argued that S's relationship with his family might suffer, for his parents would believe that his life had been prolonged by an 'ungodly act'. Thorpe J dismissed the parental objection. The child's welfare required he be given the best chance of prolonged life and Thorpe J was unimpressed by talk of problems in the family later in life. Reconciling *Re S* and *Re T* is virtually impossible. In a series of cases, while judges now show some understanding of the dilemma confronting Jehovah's Witness parents, in the end the courts endorse the child's interest in survival and overrule parental objections.[58]

Perhaps part of the key to apparently contradictory decisions about parents' rights to determine the treatment of their young children can be found in the judgment of Waite LJ in *Re T* (1997).[59] He contrasts cases where parental opposition to treatment is '... prompted by scruple or dogma of a kind which is patently irreconcilable with principles of health and welfare widely accepted by the generality of mankind' and '... highly problematic cases where there is a genuine scope for a difference of opinion'. Ward LJ, in the conjoined twins' case, says[60] that that was not a case where the parents' opposition to surgery to separate the girls was 'prompted by scruple or dogma'. How much weight should parents' religious beliefs carry? Parents will argue that Article 8 of the European Convention on Human Rights (endorsing their right to family life) and Article 9 (guaranteeing religious freedom) mean that their views should be conclusive. Both Articles are qualified. The parents' 'rights' must be balanced against the children's interests. Caroline Bridge has argued that in delaying treatment, so prolonging a child's suffering, in attempts to meet parents' convictions, the child's interests are undervalued.[61]

Responsibilities not rights?

15.10 One consistent message can be elicited from English case law about the medical treatment of young children. The common law only confers on parents those rights they need to fulfil their responsibilities to provide adequate medical care for their children. Lord Templeman summed up the position in *Gillick v West Norfolk and Wisbeck Area Health Authority*.

---

[57] *Re S (A Minor) (Medical Treatment)* [1993] 1 FLR 376.
[58] *Re E (A Minor)* (1990) 9 BMLR 1; *Re O (A Minor) (Medical Treatment)* (1993) 4 Med LR 272; *Re R (A Minor)* [1993] 2 FLR 757.
[59] *Re T (A Minor) (Wardship: Medical Treatment)* [1997] 1 All ER 906.
[60] *Re A* [2000] Lloyd's Rep Med 425 at 454; and see *Re C (A Minor) (Medical Treatment)* [1998] 1 FLR 384.
[61] See C Bridge, 'Parental Powers and the Medical Treatment of Children' in C Bridge (ed), *Family Law: Towards the Millennium* (1997) Butterworths, p 321. Note that in *An NHS Trust v B* (discussed below at 15.11), Holman J accords some weight to the parents' Muslim beliefs.

Where the patient is an infant, the medical profession accepts that a parent having custody and being responsible for the infant is entitled on behalf of the infant to consent or to reject treatment if the parent considers that the best interests of the infant so require. Where doctor and parent disagree, the court can decide and is not slow to act, I accept that if there is no time to obtain a decision from the court, a doctor may safely carry out treatment in an emergency if the doctor believes the treatment to be vital to the survival or health of the infant and notwithstanding the opposition of a parent or the impossibility of alerting the parent before the treatment is carried out.[62]

In a genuine emergency,[63] doctors may proceed without parental consent or court authority. So if a child is brought into Casualty bleeding to death after a road accident and his Jehovah's Witness parents refuse to agree to a blood transfusion, the hospital can overrule them if delay threatens the child's life. Dire necessity justifies the action.

The decision of the European Court of Human Rights in *Glass v United Kingdom*[64] issues a warning to doctors not to stretch the definition of emergency, and places a strong emphasis on a presumption of the parents' right to make decisions about the treatment of their young children. David Glass had multiple disabilities. In 1998, he suffered a series of infections after a tonsillectomy. Doctors believed that David had little awareness of, or pleasure in, his surroundings, and that he was dying. They decided that if David stopped breathing he would not be resuscitated, and administered diamorphine to relieve any distress. His mother vehemently objected both to the administration of diamorphine and the doctors' decision not to resuscitate David. On one occasion she successfully resuscitated David herself. The relationship between David's family and doctors deteriorated into acrimony and violence. Mrs Glass unsuccessfully challenged her son's treatment in the English courts.[65] She eventually took his case to the European Court of Human Rights in Strasbourg and won. The court ruled that administering diamorphine to David against the wishes of his mother violated Article 8 of the European Convention on Human Rights. Doctors violated David's right to respect for his privacy, notably his bodily integrity. Where children are too young, or otherwise unable, to make their own decisions about medical treatment, doctors must normally seek consent from the parents who speak on their child's behalf. Where doctors consider that parents are not acting in the child's interests, they must seek authority from a court before overruling the parents – except where intervention is immediately necessary to save the child's life.

---

[62] [1985] 3 All ER 402 at 432.
[63] As Lord Scarman put it in *Gillick v West Norfolk and Wisbech Area Health Authority* [1985] 3 All ER 402 at 410, HL, 'Emergency, parental neglect abandonment of the child or inability to find the parent are examples of exceptional situations justifying the doctor proceeding to treat the child without parental knowledge or consent'.
[64] [2004] 1 FLR 1019, ECtHR.
[65] *R v Portsmouth Hospitals NHS Trust v Glass* (1999) 50 BMLR 269, CA.

Disputing best interests: parental demands

15.11 *Glass v United Kingdom*[66] reiterated that doctors may not unilaterally override the wishes of a child's parents. Courts retain the authority to do so. We have seen that courts will rarely endorse a parental refusal of treatment offering to a child a realistic prospect of continued life. More recent cases present the reverse scenario. Parents want doctors to continue treating a child for whom the doctors judge there is little (if any) hope of meaningful survival.

In *Re C (A Minor) (Medical Treatment)*,[67] Orthodox Jewish parents argued that their 16-month-old daughter with spinal muscular atrophy should continue to be ventilated. Doctors argued that continued ventilation was futile. The child was dying and ventilation would only prolong her life by a few days. The parents' faith dictated that every effort be made to preserve the spark of life. The court declined to interfere with the doctors' clinical judgment. *Re C* can be explained in several ways. English courts have on several occasions refused to order doctors to carry out treatment which, in their clinical judgment, they consider inappropriate.[68] It can persuasively be argued that prolonging a child's suffering cannot be in her interests.[69] Is *Re C*, however, another case where judges may have been tempted to dismiss the parents' case as 'scruple and dogma'?

Charlotte Wyatt's parents' received a more sympathetic hearing from Hedley J. Their religious faith and determination to prolong their daughter's life were given careful consideration. Charlotte was born at 26 weeks' gestation. She needed to be ventilated for most of her first three months of life. She suffered severe infections and both her breathing and brain functions had steadily deteriorated. The damage was probably irreparable. She was believed at the first hearing to be blind and deaf and incapable of voluntary movement. On five occasions, Hedley J was asked to adjudicate in disputes between her parents and her doctors,[70] and, on one occasion, the case went to the Court of Appeal.[71] The dispute concerned not the current care of the child, but a contingency that might arise: should Charlotte stop breathing, must she be re-ventilated? Her fundamentalist Christian parents were adamant that everything be done to prolong her life. They sought a miracle. Her doctors considered that the pain and distress likely to ensue from ventilation would only prolong the process of her dying. The Trust sought a declaration that doctors were not obliged to re-ventilate Charlotte. At the original hearing in 2004, experts suggested that Charlotte had no more than a 5 per cent chance of surviving the winter of 2004–05. Charlotte defied the odds. Her parents' and her doctors' perception of what sort of life Charlotte could enjoy differed (and differs) radically. The doctors saw a baby with severe brain damage,

---

[66] [2004] 1 FLR 1019, ECtHR.
[67] [1998] 1 FLR 384. See also *Royal Wolverhampton Hospitals NHS Trusts v B* [2000] 2 FLR 953; *A National Health Service Trust v D* [2000] 2 FCR 577; *Re MM (Medical Treatment)* [2000] 1 FLR 224.
[68] *R (on the application of Burke) v General Medical Council* [2005] EWCA Civ 1003.
[69] See *Superintendent of Family and Child Services and Dawson* (1983) 145 DLR (3d) 610.
[70] *Re Wyatt* [2004] EWHC 2247, [2005] EWHC 117, [2005] EWHC 693, [2005] EWHC Civ 1181, [2005] EWHC 2902, [2006] EWHC 319.
[71] *Wyatt v Portsmouth NHS Trust* [2005] EWCA Civ 1181.

unable to respond to stimulation other than pain. Her parents believed (and believe) that she responds to them, that she feels pleasure.

Hedley J emphasised the presumption in favour of prolonging life, but acknowledged that, in assessing the best interests of a sick child, there is this balancing exercise to be performed. He quoted Taylor LJ in *Re J (A Minor) (Wardship: Medical Treatment)*,[72] asking would '... the child in question, if capable of exercising sound judgment ... consider the life to be intolerable'? Hedley J expressly declined to utilise 'intolerability' as a supplementary test, or a replacement test, for best interests. Examining the nature of her current existence and the risks and distress entailed in a tracheotomy, the judge concluded (in October 2004) that further aggressive treatment, even if necessary to prolong Charlotte's life, was not in her best interests. Rejecting her parents' views, Hedley J acknowledged that her parents knew her best. He had to regard their 'intuitive feelings', but he reminded himself '... they may project those on Charlotte'. So, in three hearings, the judge granted and continued the declaration sought by the Trust.

Charlotte survived and, in October 2005, the judge lifted his declaration.[73] The judge found that, given Charlotte's improved condition, it could no longer be said that ventilation would inevitably be futile or wholly inappropriate. Whether ventilation was in Charlotte's best interests would depend on her condition at the relevant time when a decision must be made. Charlotte's improved condition was such that one would expect that decisions about her care would fall to be determined by normal principles of law and clinical practice. However, the relationship between her parents and the hospital had been, at times, openly hostile. Professionals feared retribution if they made a decision opposed by the Wyatts. The Trust sought a declaration that, in the event of irreconcilable disagreement, the professionals' decision would be lawful and final. Hedley J refused to grant this wide declaration. Instead, he sought to reinforce that the usual principles relating to the medical care of infants must apply. If a decision whether or not to intubate (or provide other treatment) arose, Charlotte's parents and doctors must seek to agree on what constitutes her best interests – they must seek to work in partnership. No doctor was compelled to administer treatment he considered not to be in the child's best interests or an affront to his conscience, though he should not prevent other clinicians from so doing. Hedley J concluded by urging the parties to work together. In 2006, the case returned to court. Charlotte developed an infection and her condition had worsened again. The judge reaffirmed that doctors have no obligation to intubate or ventilate her, should she stop breathing.

The protracted litigation relating to Charlotte Wyatt highlights two rather different questions about the role of the law:

---

[72] [1990] 3 All ER 930 at 945.
[73] *Portsmouth NHS Trust v Wyatt* [2005] EWHC 2293 (Fam).

(1)   Hedley J declined to replace the best interests test with any test of 'intolerability' or 'significant harm' that might give more force to parental judgments. He preferred to retain the traditional 'balancing exercise' of best interests.

(2)   The length and bitterness of the litigation spelled out a cruel lesson concerning the consequences of a breakdown in trust between families and professionals.

In *An NHS Trust v B*[74] however, Holman J refused to authorise doctors to withdraw life-support from a baby, MB, against the strongly voiced objections of his parents. MB was 18 months old, he had the most severe form of spinal muscular atrophy and breathed only with the aid of a ventilator. He would inevitably die within the next twelve months or so. His parents refused to consent to switching off the ventilator except as a test to see if he could breathe independently. They also wanted MB to have a tracheotomy to allow the baby to be ventilated outside hospital. The doctors sought to withdraw the endo-tracheal tube and, with the aid of sedatives, allow MB a pain-free, dignified death. Medical evidence unanimously supported this course of action, as did the guardian appointed by the court to represent the baby. His parents gave evidence that MB responded to them, that he enjoyed stories, songs and his favourite television programmes. The Muslim father believed that the decision about when, or if, his son dies must be left to God. The judge refused the parents' request for an order for further invasive treatment to prolong MB's life. He also refused the doctors' request to withdraw ventilation. He attempted a balancing exercise in which the crucial feature was that MB retained some significant cognitive function. He was (or might be) still able to function at some level like any other infant, recognising his mother and taking simple pleasures from touch, light and sound. The suffering he might endure as a consequence of all the invasive, intrusive treatments keeping him alive was in the judge's view balanced by these benefits.

The judgment in *An NHS Trust v B* poses difficult questions. If MB's cognitive function is the *key* factor tipping the balance in favour of continuing to ventilate him, those questions include the following. MB's parents fought to keep him alive. What of a baby whose medical condition is identical to MB, but whose parents want him to be allowed to die – does that tip the balancing exercise the other way? If MB does have the cognitive function to distinguish him from earlier cases where ventilation was withdrawn, is his suffering maybe all the greater? What weight do we put on cognitive function? Does mental disability make a life less worth living than even grave physical abnormalities? Why was this case decided differently from that of Baby C, who was also dying of spinal muscular atrophy?[75]

Not just life or death

15.12 Difficult decisions about the medical care of young children are not exclusively confined to decisions relating to life-sustaining treatment. In *Re C*

[74]   [2006] EWHC 507.
[75]   [1998] 1 FLR 384.

(HIV test),[76] a baby was born to an HIV positive mother. She had declined conventional treatment for HIV, rejected treatment in pregnancy which might have diminished the risk of transmitting HIV to the child and intended to breastfeed. Both parents refused to agree to an HIV test for their baby. They argued that any possible treatment for the child (were she HIV positive) could be more toxic than beneficial, and that sero-positive status would stigmatise the child. The local authority, applying for an order to test the child, relied on medical opinion that the child was at a 25 per cent risk of having contracted HIV and that effective medical care of the child required knowledge of her HIV status. The Court of Appeal upheld the trial judge's view that the child's interests should allow the HIV test. The parents sought to assert their right to respect for family life enshrined in Article 8 of the European Convention on Human Rights. As the trial judge noted, such a claim is swiftly countered by consideration of the child's own rights and the needs of his health and welfare as expressly recognised in Article 8(2).[77]

Resolving 'conflicts of rights' is not easy. Disputes between parents can be just as complex as disagreements between doctors and parents. In *Re J (Child's Religious Upbringing and Circumcision)*,[78] a devout Muslim father sought a court order to circumcise his five-year-old son. The child's non-Muslim mother objected. The couple were estranged. The father argued that circumcision would identify child with father and establish the boy within the Muslim community. He invoked his right under Article 9 of the European Convention on Human Rights to freedom of religion. The mother's religious adherence to Christianity was said to be notional only. There were no medical grounds for circumcision. The courts found for the mother, influenced by the pain and distress circumcision might cause the boy. In *Re C (Welfare of the Child: Immunisation)*,[79] two fathers applied for court orders that their daughters should receive the MMR vaccine. Both girls lived with their mothers who considered the MMR vaccine to be unsafe. The Court of Appeal upheld the trial judge's ruling that vaccination was in the girls' best interests. The judges considered that the medical evidence of both the efficacy and safety of the MMR vaccine was overwhelming. They dismissed the contrary evidence out of hand.

Re J (1999) and *Re C* (2003) came to court because the parents disagreed about the interests of their children. It illustrates one of the anomalies of the law: if the principle is that treatment necessary for the welfare of the child should be carried out and nothing contrary to his interest should be done, is circumcision – even with both parents' agreement – lawful?

The limits of parental consent

15.13 As parental rights to determine medical treatment of their child derive from the parental duty to obtain adequate medical care for them, those rights

---

[76] [2000] Fam 48, CA.
[77] See L Haggar, 'Some Implications of the Human Rights Act 1998 for the Medical Treatment of Children' (2003) 6 *Medical Law International* 25.
[78] [2000] 1 FCR 307.
[79] [2003] 2 FLR 1095, CA.

cannot be unfettered. In Skegg's words, a parent may give '… a legally effective consent to a procedure which is likely to be for the benefit of the child, in the sense of being in the child's best interests'.[80] Routine treatment or surgery for an existing physical condition, diagnostic procedures or preventative measures such as vaccination pose no problem. The benefit is there for all to see. More intricate and even risky procedures cause little difficulty: not all parents might agree to complex heart surgery on a baby but, if doctors and parents weigh risk and benefit and conclude in favour of going ahead, they have exercised their respective duties properly. Problems surface in relation to medical or surgical procedures not immediately called for to treat or prevent ill health. Two classic issues are dealt with later – whether a child can donate organs or tissue (in Chapter 18), and when children can be used for medical research purposes (in Chapter 16). Sterilising minors raises interesting questions about the limits of parental and judicial authority.

Re D[81] concerned a girl aged eleven. She suffered from Soto's syndrome and was afflicted by epilepsy and a number of other physical problems. The girl also had some degree of learning disability. Her mother was anxious about her future and considered that she would never be capable of caring for a child, that having a child would damage her, that she might all too easily be seduced and would be incapable of practising any form of contraception. Accordingly, she sought to have her sterilised before these risks should materialise. The girl's paediatrician agreed, and a gynaecologist was found who was ready to perform the operation. An educational psychologist involved with the child disagreed and applied to have the child made a ward of court. Heilbron J ordered that proposals for the operation be abandoned. Her function, she said, was to act as the 'judicial reasonable parent', with the welfare of the child as her paramount consideration. She found that medical opinion was overwhelmingly against sterilisation of such a child at eleven. The irrevocable nature of sterilisation, the emotional impact on the girl when she discovered what had been done to her and her present inability to understand what was proposed, coupled with evidence that her mental development was such that she would one day be able to make an informed choice for herself on childbearing, all led the judge to conclude that the operation was '… neither medically indicated nor necessary. And that it would not be in [the girl's] best interests for it to be performed'.[82]

None the less, in *Re B*[83] (1987), the House of Lords sanctioned the sterilisation of 17-year-old Jeanette. Jeanette was more profoundly disabled than D. She was said to have a mental age of five or six, with a more limited capacity to communicate. She had no understanding of the link between sexual intercourse and pregnancy. Those caring for her testified that, apart from sterilisation, no means of reliable contraception would be suitable for Jeanette. If she became pregnant, delivery might well have to be by Caesarean section, and the girl had an unbreakable habit of picking and tearing at any

---

80 See PDG Skegg, 'Consent to Medical Procedures on Minors' (1973) 36 *Modern Law Review* 370 at 377.
81 [1986] 1 All ER 326.
82 [1986] 1 All ER 326 at 335.
83 [1987] 2 All ER 206.

wounds. Despite her profound disability, Jeanette was sexually mature. The Law Lords held that the legality of the proposal to sterilise Jeanette must depend only on whether sterilisation would '... promote the welfare and serve the best interests of the ward'.[84] Consideration of eugenics and whether sterilising Jeanette would ease the burden on those caring for her were irrelevant.[85] Their Lordships concluded that as Jeanette (1) would never be capable of making any choice for herself on whether to have a child, (2) would never even appreciate what was happening to her, and (3) would suffer damage to her health if she ever became pregnant, she could lawfully be sterilised by occlusion of her Fallopian tubes (not hysterectomy). Lord Templeman, however, suggested that the radical nature of sterilisation was such that a girl of 18 should never be sterilised without the consent of a High Court judge:

> A doctor performing a sterilisation operation with the consent of the parents might still be liable to criminal, civil or professional proceedings. A court exercising the wardship jurisdiction emanating from the Crown is the only authority which is empowered to authorise such a drastic step as sterilisation after a full and informed investigation.[86]

Following *Re B* a number of subsequent cases appeared to evidence judicial willingness to authorise sterilisation of young girls fairly readily. Recent decisions relating to the proposed sterilisation of adult women indicate that (1) judges are more ready to scrutinise any proposal to sterilise a woman more rigorously and (2) that where other surgery, such as hysterectomy, will result in infertility, cases where reasonable people might disagree on what was best for the patient ought to go before a judge.[87]

What *Re B* reaffirms in the context of children's treatment generally is that parental powers are limited. Even when parents honestly believe they are acting in their child's interests, if they propose to authorise some irreversible or drastic measure, their authorisation alone will not make that measure lawful. It must be shown to be in the child's interests. No mother could authorise the sterilisation of her four-year-old daughter because that daughter was a haemophilia carrier. She has no right to deprive her child of the right to make that decision herself. The child's best interests include her potential right to autonomy. It seems unlikely that parents could authorise a vasectomy on even the most severely mentally-disabled son;[88] such an operation would not be in his interests, even if it benefited society. Similarly, no parent, however strong or genuine his commitment to medical research might be, could lawfully authorise the entry of his healthy child into a research trial posing real and substantial risk to that child's health.

Other examples could be debated endlessly. Just one more will be considered here – cosmetic surgery. May a mother put her son through painful surgery to

[84] [1987] 2 All ER 206 at 213, per Lord Bridge.
[85] Per Lord Oliver at 219.
[86] At 214.
[87] See *Re S (Adult Patient: Sterilisation)* [2000] 3 WLR 1288, discussed above at 6.6 and 11.9.
[88] See *Re A (Medical Treatment: Male Sterilisation)* [2000] 1 FCR 193, CA, discussed above at 6.6 and 11.9.

396

advance his career as a male model? Certainly not. That cannot be said to be in the interests of the child, rather the mother's vicarious ambition. Yet surgery on boys with 'bat ears' is common and lawful. The pain of surgery is balanced by the child's misery at being taunted for his deformity. Parents are allowed to judge the outcome of the 'balancing exercise'. Difficult questions are posed by cosmetic surgery on Down's children. Cosmetic surgery may make the child more socially acceptable. Is that in the interests of the child?

Procedures to protect children

15.14 We do not examine in any detail the procedural means by which disputes about the care or treatment of a child come before the courts. One or two brief points about parental responsibility and family law procedures are noted here. When a child's parents are married, both parents share parental responsibility for her.

When the parents are unmarried, they share parental responsibility if either they jointly register the child's birth or they subsequently enter into a formal agreement to share parental responsibility. A father may seek a court order conferring parental responsibility on him where the mother is not voluntarily prepared to share legal responsibility for the child.[89] Normally, in relation to medical treatment, the consent of one parent to the treatment of their young child suffices. If a mother takes her five-year-old for a booster vaccination, the doctor does not need to delay matters by ensuring that the father also agrees to vaccination. The courts have, however, made it clear that where some major or irreversible decision needs to be made about a child's treatment, or where there is disagreement between the parents sharing parental responsibility, both parents' consent is required and/or the case must be referred to the court.[90]

Should a father without parental responsibility, other relatives (such as grandparents), local social services or any other third party have concerns about a child's medical treatment, a number of means exist by which a dispute concerning the child's welfare can be adjudicated by a court. The child could be taken into care or made a ward of court,[91] but that is rare these days. The inherent jurisdiction of the court can be invoked, or an order sought under section 8 of the Children Act 1989. Section 8 orders are diverse in kind. Of particular relevance here are 'specific issue orders' and 'prohibited steps orders'. If an unmarried father (who does not have parental responsibility) strongly believes that surgery to correct a hideous birthmark is in his child's interests and her mother opposes surgery solely because she believes that her child's deformity was 'God's will – a punishment for being born out of wedlock', he may seek a 'specific issue order'.[92] Should he seek to prevent the

---

[89] See s 4 of the Children Act 1989 as amended by the Adoption and Children Act 2002.
[90] See *Re J (Child's Religious Upbringing and Circumcision)* [2000] 1 FCR 307, CA.
[91] In which case the court will acquire control over all aspects of the child's life and upbringing.
[92] As the fathers did in *Re C (Welfare of the Child: Immunisation)* [2003] EWCA Civ 1148.

performance of purely cosmetic surgery which his child's mother wants because she wants the child to be a model, he could apply for a 'prohibited steps order' to prevent surgery.

Sometimes the machinery to protect children from inappropriate 'treatment' operates fairly randomly. In the course of the judgment in *Re D* (above), it emerged that two similar sterilisation operations on mentally-disabled girls had already been performed in Sheffield. D was lucky: her psychologist was persistent and chance took her dilemma to the High Court. Despite judicial pronouncements that sterilisation of girls under 18 must always be a matter for the courts, girls have been sterilised by hysterectomy for 'hygienic' reasons, without judicial approval. These cases involve girls who cannot in any sense cope with menstruation. They may refuse to wear their sanitary towels (or, in extreme cases, eat them). It is not clear beyond doubt that such an operation is in the girl's interests, though it is certainly in her carers' interests. The Court of Appeal considers such 'borderline' cases should always go before a judge.[93] However, the problem in protecting such girls is, who will know what happened? Only if some interested third party intervenes will the matter reach the light of day in time to prevent the procedure going ahead.

Consider female circumcision, mutilation of a girl child's genitalia to comply with cultural norms. Parliament intervened to ban the practice in the UK in the Prohibition of Female Circumcision Act 1985, now repealed and replaced by the Female Genital Mutilation Act 2003. One might have thought that such mutilation of a child was indubitably an assault on her. In Parliamentary debates on prohibition of female circumcision in 1985, Lord Hailsham rightly argued that genital mutilation of a child was already a crime, assault occasioning actual bodily harm. But who would tell the authorities, who will prosecute? Besides which, had the common law been faced with the question of female circumcision, difficult questions would arise in answering the question of the girl's best interests. What if she agreed, wishing to fall in with the custom of her community? What of arguments that the girl's mental well-being required that she meet the customs of her people? If ritual male circumcision is permissible, why not female circumcision, if carried out by surgeons in aseptic conditions?

The views of the child

15.15 What of a child's own wishes? Once a child can communicate, she will in many cases have an opinion of her own. Most four-year-olds object robustly to injections, dental treatment and anything likely to cause them discomfort. At four, the case that the child cannot form any sensible judgment about the pros and cons of treatment may well be made out. At eight, ten and twelve the child acquires greater maturity, albeit most doctors and parents would be reluctant to bow to the child's judgment. What must be remembered, however, is that the balance of the child's best interests will be (radically) affected by his willingness or otherwise to participate in treatment.

---

[93] *Re S (Adult Patient: Sterilisation)* [2000] 3 WLR 1288, CA.

Obtaining assent even from very young children is good practice.[94] Forcible treatment which may involve restraining, even detaining, the child requires strong justification. And as the child reaches her teens, becomes what is rather pompously called a 'mature minor', the legal picture changes.

The Family Law Reform Act 1969

15.16 The Family Law Reform Act 1969 reduced the age of majority from 21 to 18. When the 1969 Act was before Parliament it was unclear what effect, if any, a consent to medical treatment given by a minor might have. Many 16- and 17-year-olds live, or spend considerable periods of time, away from their parents. Some are married and parents themselves. Section 8 of the 1969 Act clarified the law concerning 16- to 18-year-olds and empowered them to consent to their own medical treatment. Sub-sections (1) and (2) of section 8 provide:

(1)   The consent of a minor who has attained the age of 16 years to any surgical, medical or dental treatment which, in the absence of consent, would constitute a trespass to his person shall be as effective as it would be if he were of full age: and where a minor has by virtue of this section given an effective consent it shall not be necessary to obtain any consent for it from his parent or guardian.

(2)   In this section 'surgical, medical or dental treatment' includes any procedure undertaken for the purposes of diagnosis, and this section applies to any procedure (including, in particular, the administration of an anaesthetic) which is ancillary to any treatment as it applies to that treatment.

So far, so good: once a person is 16 he can consent to treatment himself. That does not mean that any parental consent relating to their children under 18 is always ineffective. If the child of 16 or 17 is incapable of giving consent, for example because he lacks mental capacity, his parents may still act on his behalf until he comes of age. Section 8 goes on in sub-section (3) to provide:

(3)   Nothing in this section shall be construed as making ineffective any consent which would have been effective if this section had not been enacted.

The majority of lawyers and doctors interpreted section 8(3) in this way. The common law had never directly determined when, if at all, a child could give effective consent to medical treatment. The assumption was that the law gave effect to consent by a minor provided she or he was sufficiently mature to understand the proposed treatment or surgery.[95] Sixteen was the average age at which doctors judged patients to be old enough to give consent without consulting parents on every occasion. Never the less, many doctors regarded themselves as free to treat children under 16 without parental approval, if the individual child appeared sufficiently intelligent and grown up to take the decision on treatment alone. Before 1969, every case turned on the doctor's assessment of the particular minor in her surgery. The 1969 Act freed the

94   See P Alderson, *Children's Consent to Surgery* (1995) Open University Press.
95   See Skegg (1973) 36 *Modern Law Review* 370 at 370–375.

doctor from doubt and risk where the patient was over 16. She no longer had to consider the maturity of a patient over 16. She could assume adult status and capability. Sub-section (3), it was argued, simply preserved the *status quo* for the under-16s. Doctors could continue to treat a child under 16 as long as that child was mature enough to make his own judgment. This assumption, that there had always been a limited freedom to treat children under 16 without parental consent, and that what sub-section (3) did was preserve that freedom, was at the heart of the *Gillick* saga and its sequels *Re R*[96] and *Re W*.[97]

The Gillick Case

15.17 The *Gillick* saga has its origins in a circular issued by the DHSS in 1974, outlining arrangements for a comprehensive family planning service within the NHS. Statistics on the number of births and induced abortions among girls under 16 led the DHSS to conclude that contraceptive services should be made more readily available to that age group. The essence of their advice was that the decision to provide contraception to a girl under 16 was one for the doctor. He might lawfully treat, and prescribe for, the girl without contacting her parents. He should not contact parents without the girl's agreement. In 1980, the DHSS revised its advice. The revised version stressed that every effort should be made to involve parents. If the girl was adamant that her parents should not know of her request for contraception, the principle of confidentiality between doctor and patient should be preserved. This amended advice from the DHSS did not satisfy critics. Victoria Gillick sought assurances that none of her daughters would be given contraceptive or abortion advice (or treatment) without her prior knowledge and consent until they were 16. Those assurances were refused, and Mrs Gillick went to court seeking declarations (1) against her health authority and the DHSS to the effect that their advice that children under 16 could be treated without parental consent was unlawful and wrong, and (2) against her health authority to the effect that medical personnel employed by them should not give contraceptive and/or abortion advice and/or treatment to any child of Mrs Gillick's under 16 without her prior knowledge and consent. Mrs Gillick's concern was with contraception and abortion for under-16s. She had no axe to grind in respect of other forms of medical treatment. The trouble is that contraception cannot be isolated from more general questions. Mrs Gillick's counsel challenged the assumption that the common law permitted medical treatment of children under 16 in the absence of parental consent.

Children under 16 and consent to treatment: Gillick competence

15.18 At first instance, Woolf J[98] endorsed the view that once a child was able to understand what was entailed in proposed treatment, he or she could consent to such treatment. Any physical contact involved in treatment would

---

96 *Re R (A Minor)* [1991] 4 All ER 177, CA.
97 [1992] 4 All ER 627.
98 [1984] 1 All ER 365.

not constitute battery. Mrs Gillick appealed and, in a complex judgment, the Court of Appeal[99] found for her. Not only was any treatment of a child under 16 potentially battery unless authorised by a parent, giving children advice or information about contraception without parental knowledge could constitute an infringement of parental rights. After the Court of Appeal decision, no doctor could (save in emergency) safely see a child under 16 in her clinic or surgery without parental knowledge. The DHSS appealed to the House of Lords. By a majority, the House of Lords held that the original advice circulated by the DHSS was not unlawful and that a child under 16 can, in certain circumstances, give a valid consent to medical treatment (including contraception or abortion treatment), without parental knowledge or agreement.[100]

The general problem of consent

15.19 In *Gillick*, the majority of their Lordships rejected the Court of Appeal's finding that consent given by a child under 16 was of no effect. Like Woolf J, they accepted the view that the Family Law Reform Act 1969 had left that question open. The matter was for the common law to determine. The common law was not static, fossilised in eighteenth-century notions of the inviolable rights of the *paterfamilias*. Judge-made law must meet the needs of the times. Parental rights derived from parental duties to protect the person and property of the child. Modern legislation qualified and limited parental rights by placing the welfare of the child as its first priority. Parental rights being dependent on the duty of care for – and maintenance of – the child, they endured only so long as necessary to achieve their end. As Lord Scarman put it: '... the parental right yields to the child's right to make his own decisions when he reaches a sufficient understanding and intelligence to be capable of making up his own mind on the matter requiring decision'.[101]

Their Lordships argued that the common law had never regarded the consent of a child as a complete nullity. Were that the case, intercourse with a girl under 16 would inevitably be rape. That is not so. Provided the girl is old enough to understand what she is agreeing to, intercourse with her consent will not be rape. Parliament, to protect girls under 16 from the consequences of their own folly, enacted a separate offence of unlawful sexual intercourse with girls under 16 in the commission of which the girl's consent is irrelevant. If the girl validly consented, that is the only offence committed – and not the more serious crime of rape.[102]

---

[99] [1985] 1 All ER 533.
[100] [1985] 3 All ER 402.
[101] [1985] 3 All ER 402 at 422.
[102] In another context, just a year before the *Gillick* hearing, the House of Lords had considered the crime of kidnapping as it related to children under 16. They held that the central issue was the agreement of the child, not either parent, to being taken away by the accused. In the case of a young child absence of consent could be presumed. With an older child the question was whether he or she had sufficient understanding and intelligence to give consent: see *R v D* [1984] 2 All ER 449.

Moving from the general issue of consent by children to the problem of consent to medical treatment, the House of Lords saw no reason to depart from the general rule. Lord Fraser thought it would be ludicrous to say that a boy or girl of 15 could not agree to examination or treatment for a trivial injury. Importantly, Lord Templeman, who dissented on the specific issue of contraceptive treatment, agreed that there were circumstances where a doctor could properly treat a child under 16 without parental agreement. He concurred that the effect of the consent of the child depended on the nature of the treatment and the age and understanding of the child. A doctor, he thought, could safely remove tonsils or a troublesome appendix from a boy or girl of 15 without express parental agreement. *Gillick* establishes that a child below 16 may lawfully be given general medical advice and treatment without parental agreement, provided that child has achieved sufficient maturity to understand fully what is proposed. The doctor treating such a child on the basis of her consent alone will not be at risk of either a civil action for battery or criminal prosecution

The special problems of contraception and abortion

15.20 Lord Templeman, however, dissented on the specific issue of contraception. He did not accept that a girl under 16 has sufficient maturity and understanding of the emotional and physical consequences of sexual intercourse to consent to contraceptive treatment. His Lordship put it thus:

> I doubt whether a girl under the age of 16 is capable of a balanced judgement to embark on frequent, regular or casual sexual intercourse fortified by the illusion that medical science can protect her in mind and body and ignoring the danger of leaping from childhood to adulthood without the difficult formative transitional experiences of adolescence. There are many things a girl under 16 needs to practise but sex is not one of them.[103]

The majority of his colleagues disagreed. They conceded that a request by a girl under 16 for contraception, coupled with an insistence that her parents not be told, posed a problem for the doctor. Assessing whether she is mature enough to consider the emotional and physical consequences of the course she has embarked on is not easy. But that question should be left to the clinical judgment of the doctor. Lord Fraser set out five matters the doctor should satisfy himself on before giving contraceptive treatment to a girl below 16 without parental agreement. They are:

> ... (1) that the girl ... will understand his advice; (2) that he cannot persuade her to inform her parents ...; (3) that she is very likely to begin or continue having sexual intercourse with or without contraceptive treatment; (4) that unless she receives contraceptive advice or treatment her physical or mental health or both are likely to suffer; (5) that her best interests require him to give her contraceptive advice or treatment or both without the parental consent.[104]

Lord Fraser's formula failed to satisfy Mrs Gillick. She regarded it as inadequate in two respects. First, in a busy surgery or clinic, has any doctor

103 [1985] 3 All ER 402 at 432.
104 [1985] 3 All ER 402 at 413.

sufficient time to embark on the investigation and counselling of the girl necessary to fulfil the criteria laid down? Second, underlying the judgments of the majority is acceptance of the view that, as significant numbers of young girls under 16 are going to continue having sexual intercourse regardless of whether they have lawful access to contraception, it may be in their best interests to protect them from pregnancy by contraceptive treatment. Mrs Gillick disagreed. She contended that if access to contraception without parental agreement were stopped, at least the majority of young girls would (1) be deterred from starting to have intercourse so young by fear of pregnancy and/or parental disapproval, and (2) would have a defence against pressure from their peers to 'grow up' and sleep with someone. Both sides in the debate on 'under-age' contraception agree that early sexual intercourse increases the danger of disease to the child, be it cervical cancer or venereal disease. Most agree about the emotional damage the child risks. They are no nearer agreement how girls under 16 may best be protected than on the day Mrs Gillick first went to court. The decision to allow emergency contraception (the 'morning after pill') to be sold over the counter in local pharmacies reignited controversy.

What about abortion? The greater part of the Law Lords' decision concentrated on contraception. The rules for abortion on girls under 16 are the same: if a girl is intelligent and mature enough to understand what is involved in the operation, the doctor, if the girl insists on not telling her parents or if they refuse to agree to an abortion, may go ahead on the basis of the girl's consent alone. The House of Lords endorsed the approach of Butler-Sloss J in an earlier case.[105] A 15-year-old girl, with one child already, became pregnant again while in the care of the local authority. She wanted an abortion. Doctors considered that the birth of a second child would endanger the mental health of the girl and her existing child. Her father objected. Abortion was contrary to his religion. The local authority applied to have the girl made a ward of court and so seek the court's consent to the operation. The judge authorised the operation. She said the decision must be made in the light of the girl's best interests. She took into account the parents' feelings, but held that they could not outweigh the needs of the girl.

Mrs Gillick had, however, a second line of attack. The Sexual Offences Act 1956 made it a criminal offence 'to cause or encourage ... the commission of unlawful sexual intercourse with ... a girl for whom [the] accused is responsible'. So Mrs Gillick argued that providing contraception for a girl under 16 amounted to 'encouraging' that crime. The Law Lords dismissed this second claim too. The Sexual Offences Act 2003 replaces the 1956 Act. It creates a raft of new criminal offences and toughens up the law relating to unlawful sexual relations with people under 16. But sections 14 and 73 of the Act provide express protection for doctors and nurses providing contraceptive advice or treatment, abortions or – indeed – any health care relating to the young person's sexual health. No offence of facilitating a child sex offence, of aiding and abetting unlawful sexual intercourse is committed if the person acts either (1) to protect the child from sexually transmitted diseases, (2) to protect

---

[105] *Re P (A Minor)* (1982) 80 LGR 301.

the child's physical safety or (3) to prevent a girl becoming pregnant or to promote the child's emotional well-being.

A right to say no?

15.21 For several years, *Gillick* was assumed to have established that once young people acquired the necessary maturity to consent to treatment, what Lord Donaldson was later to style *Gillick competence*,[106] they acquired a right to determine what medical treatment they received. They had a right to say 'no', as much as a right to say 'yes'. Recall Lord Scarman's words in *Gillick*:[107] '... the parental right yields to the child's right to make his own decision when he reaches a sufficient understanding and intelligence to be capable of making up his own mind on the matter requiring a decision'. Subsequent judgments of the Court of Appeal rejected that apparently logical conclusion. Adolescent autonomy is little more than myth, for no young person under 18 – no minor – has a right to refuse treatment.[108] Parental powers to authorise treatment against their offspring's will endure, concurrent with extensive judicial powers to order minors to submit to treatment others deem necessary for their welfare.

In *Re R*,[109] R was a 15-year-old girl suffering from acute psychiatric problems. Her condition fluctuated. At times she appeared rational and lucid. However, she lacked insight into her illness. During her lucid phases she refused medication and became psychotic once again. R was in care, and the local authority responsible for her sought judicial guidance seeking authority to administer anti-psychotic drugs without R's consent. The Court of Appeal agreed with the trial judge that R was not *Gillick competent*: her illness prevented her from fully understanding the need for drugs to control her condition. R could lawfully be treated against her will. In this particular case, the court authorised treatment via its wardship jurisdiction. But the local authority, as her legal guardian, could equally have provided a proxy consent on R's behalf. The interest of *Re R* lies in Lord Donaldson's *dicta*. He went on to say that even were R *Gillick competent*, she would still have no power to veto treatment. A *Gillick competent* minor could consent to, but not refuse, treatment. Consent was akin to a key which 'unlocked the door to treatment' making the doctor's action lawful, but was not obligatory. Once a young person became *Gillick competent* she became a keyholder. Her parents remained keyholders until she reached 18. They could still authorise treatment on her behalf. Doctors faced with willing parents but unwilling children were not obliged to treat the child, indeed might choose not to. They could lawfully elect to act on the basis of the parents' consent alone. The problem was one of ethical and clinical judgment for the physician.[110]

---

[106] See *Re R (A Minor)* [1991] 4 All ER 177, CA.
[107] [1985] 3 All ER 402 at 422.
[108] See C Bridge and M Brazier, 'Coercion or Caring: Analysing Adolescent Autonomy' (1996) 15 *Legal Studies* 84.
[109] *Re R (A Minor)* [1991] 4 All ER 177, CA.
[110] See *Re R (A Minor)* [1991] 4 All ER 177 at 184, CA.

Re R was not well received.[111] In *Re W*,[112] Lord Donaldson was unphased by his critics. W was a 16-year-old girl. She was critically ill with anorexia nervosa and had had a tragic childhood. The local authority sought guidance whether W could, if it proved necessary, be moved to a specialist unit and force-fed. As W was 16, she was empowered to consent to treatment by virtue of section 8 of the Family Law Reform Act 1969. The Court of Appeal ruled that section 8 on its wording solely empowered a minor over 16 to give an 'effective consent' to treatment. Section 8(3)[113] preserved the concurrent parental power to authorise treatment and the inherent powers of the courts to act to protect a minor's welfare. Lord Donaldson regretted only one part of his *dicta* in *Re R*, his use of the keyholder metaphor. For, as he acknowledged, keys can lock as readily as unlock. In *Re W* he preferred to compare consent to a flak jacket, saying pithily:

> ... I now prefer the analogy of the legal 'flak jacket' which protects from claims by the litigious whether [the doctor] acquires it from his patient who may be a minor over the age of 16, or a *'Gillick competent'* child under that age or from another person having parental responsibilities which include a right to consent to treatment of the minor. Anyone who gives him a flak jacket (ie consent) may take it back, but the doctor only needs one and so long as he continues to have one he has the legal right to proceed.[114]

Re R and *Re W* make a nonsense of *Gillick*. They are explicable on their facts. There are powerful grounds to argue that both R and W lacked mental capacity regardless of their age. Their illness deprived them of the understanding and capacity to make a decision about treatment. Were they adults, they would be found to lack capacity under sections 1 and 2 of the Mental Capacity Act 2005.[115] The same is true of the young people involved in a number of similar cases where judges ruled that an adolescent could not veto treatment.[116]

Consider *Re E*.[117] E was 15 and shared his parents' Jehovah's Witness faith. He was seriously ill with leukaemia. Doctors advised that to maximise the prospects of successful chemotherapy, E should receive transfusions of blood products. E, like his parents, refused to agree to transfusions. The boy was made a ward of court. The judge authorised transfusion. He acknowledged that E was highly intelligent, mature for his age and well informed about his illness. None the less, he held that E was not *Gillick competent*. He lacked insight into the process of dying. He could not turn his mind to the effect of the manner of his death or its effect on his family. How many adults enjoy such insight? Understandably, courts seek to protect young people from decisions that may endanger their life. In E's case, the outcome was tragic.

---

[111] See, for example, A Bainham, 'The Judge and the Competent Minor' (1992) 108 *Law Quarterly Review* 104.

[112] [1992] 4 All ER 627.

[113] See Balcombe LJ at 639.

[114] At 635.

[115] See above at Chapter 6.

[116] For example, *South Glamorgan County Council v B & W* [1993] 1 FLR 574; *Re S(A Minor) (Consent to medical treatment)* [1994] 2 FLR 1065; and see Bridge and Brazier (1996) 15 Legal Studies 84.

[117] *Re E (A Minor)* (1990) 9 BMLR 1.

Treatment at 15 resulted in a temporary remission. At 18 he relapsed, refused treatment and died believing that he had participated in an ungodly act. Then in *Re M (Child: Refusal of Medical Treatment)*,[118] a girl of fifteen-and-a-half refused to consent to a heart transplant. Her refusal was overridden by Johnson J. One of M's reasons for refusing surgery was said to be the prospect of life-long medication. Were her reasons for refusing a transplant much different from those of T's parents in *Re T (A Minor) (Wardship: Medical Treatment)*?[119]

The courts have distorted common sense and ethics in attempts to avoid the implications of *Gillick*. Judges have even gone so far as authorising restraint and detention of young people to ensure that they comply with treatment.[120] All this can be done without resort to the Mental Health Act 1983 (or the amended provisions of the Mental Capacity Act 2005), which at least build in some safeguards for adult patients.[121]

Confidentiality and children under 16

15.22 Do young people seeking treatment independently of their parents have any right to confidentiality? A young girl, embarking on a sexual relationship and considering seeking contraception, probably does not think so much about her capacity to give consent to treatment as 'Will the doctor tell my mum?' The thought that a doctor may be free to give contraceptive advice to a child without the parents even knowing of what is proposed was perhaps at the heart of Mrs Gillick's concern. The disruption of family life, and the danger that the girl might omit to give the doctor information on other drugs she might be taking, worried many caring parents. The Law Lords' decision in *Gillick* did not expressly address confidentiality. The assumption on which most doctors[122] and lawyers proceeded was that a *Gillick competent* minor had as much of a claim to a right of confidentiality as he had a right to grant an independent consent to any treatment proposed by his doctor. Twenty years after *Gillick*, Mrs Axon challenged this assumption.[123] She argued that a parent of children under 16 had a right to be notified if a health professional proposed to offer advice or treatment relating to abortion or contraception to any of their children under 16. The parent's responsibility for the welfare of their child justified a limited exception to the usual duty of confidentiality to patients. The parent's right to respect for their privacy and family life under Article 8 of the European Convention on Human Rights granted them a right to such information about their child. Silber J[124] rejected Mrs Axon's case: a

[118] [1999] 2 FLR 1097.
[119] [1997] 1 All ER 906, CA.
[120] See *Re C (Detention: Medical Treatment)* [1997] 2 FLR 180.
[121] See C Bridge, 'Adolescents, and Mental Disorder: Who Consents to Treatment' (1997) 3 *Medical Law International* 51.
[122] General Medical Council, Confidentiality: Protecting and Providing Information (2000), para 38.
[123] She sought judicial review of Department of Health guidance (Best Practice Guidance for Doctors and Other Health Professionals on the Provision of Advice and Treatment to Young People under Sixteen on Contraception, Sexual and Reproductive Health).
[124] *R (on the application of Axon) v Secretary of State for Health* [2006] EWHC 37 (Admin).

Gillick competent minor has the same right to confidentiality as any adult patient. If a doctor considers that his young patient is not *Gillick competent*, the GMC advises that he first seek to persuade her to involve her family, but ultimately he may disclose information to an appropriate person (usually the girl's parents). Could a doctor justify disclosure without consent in relation to a *Gillick competent* young patient? A difficult dilemma arises if the doctor suspects that the girl is being subjected to sexual abuse. Might public interest justify his action, especially if he suspected that other children might also be at risk from abuse?

Chapter 16

MEDICAL RESEARCH[1]

16.1 In 2006, six healthy volunteers at Northwick Park Hospital were rushed to Critical Care after suffering an adverse reaction in a Phase 1 clinical trial.[2] At least four of them suffered multiple organ failure, and it is feared that they may have suffered permanent damage to their immune systems. The drug, TGN1412, was a monoclonal antibody designed to treat leukaemia and rheumatoid arthritis. The volunteers were paid £2,000 each. The Medicines and Healthcare Products Regulatory Agency (MHRA) concluded that the reaction resulted from an 'unpredicted biological action' of the drug in humans. It found no deficiencies in the manufacturers' work, the formulation of the drug or its administration to the participants.[3] An independent expert scientific review, chaired by Professor Duff, was less sympathetic:[4]

> Our conclusion is that the pre-clinical development studies that were performed with TGN1412 did not predict a safe dose for use in humans, even though current regulatory requirements were met.

The system was at fault. The expert group made 22 recommendations to improve the safety of first-in-man clinical trials.

The shocking incident at Northwick Park continued a trend of diminishing confidence in the regulation of research. In 1981, an elderly widow, Mrs Wigley, died from the effects of an experimental drug she had been given subsequent to an operation for bowel cancer. She died, not from bowel cancer, but from bone marrow depression induced by the drug. Without her knowledge or consent she had been entered in a clinical trial of the new drug. In 2000, inquiries were held into allegations that research was carried out on

---

[1] For an international perspective on medical research see A Plomer, *The Law and Ethics of Medical Research: International Bioethics and Human Rights* (2005) Cavendish. See also E Jackson, *Medical Law: Texts, Cases and Materials* (2006) OUP, pp 469–478.

[2] Department of Health, *Expert Scientific Group on Phase One Clinical Trials* Final Report (2006) HMSO.

[3] MHRA, *Investigations into Adverse Incidents During Clinical Trials of TGN1412* Final Report (May 2006), para 6.

[4] *Expert Scientific Group on Phase One Clinical Trials* Final Report, p 2.

newborn babies without parental consent in a hospital in North Stafford-shire.[5] In 2001, a 24-year-old volunteer died in the course of a clinical trial in Washington.[6] Scandals surrounding retention of body parts originated in Bristol and Liverpool, with evidence of children's body parts being retained for research without their parents' consent or knowledge.[7] And in 2006 Andrew Wakefield was called before the General Medical Council, charged with serious professional misconduct relating to research into the alleged link between autism and the triple MMR vaccine.

Medical research has acquired something of a bad reputation. Yet every time any one of us receives a prescription for antibiotics we benefit from research performed on others in the past. It is becoming a human guinea pig oneself, or letting one's child be so used, that may be an unattractive prospect. However, if medicine is to progress to combat cancer and continue the battle against diseases such as diabetes and multiple sclerosis, new drugs and procedures must be subject to trials.

In this chapter, we examine the role the law does and should play in the control of medical research involving human participants. Two European Directives, the Clinical Trials Directive 2001[8] and Good Clinical Practice (GCP) Directive 2005[9] instigated change across Europe. Some countries adapted their laws relating to all areas of clinical research, from epidemiology to complementary medicine. In England, the Medicines for Human Use (Clinical Trials) Regulations 2004, SI 2004/1031 (referred to as the Clinical Trials Regulations 2004) apply only to 'clinical trials of investigational medicinal products' (CTIMPs), defined essentially as trials of new pharmaceutical products. The regulation of research has undergone a period of unprecedented change, and there are more reforms yet to come. The overarching question is this: will the reformed system achieve an appropriate balance between the facilitation of good research and the protection of the rights and interests of research participants? In particular:

(1)   The authority to carry out research on the human adult derives from that person's consent. The first crucial question thus becomes, how satisfactory are the principles governing consent to participation in clinical research?

(2)   The law on medical treatment demands that the physician respects the confidences of his patient. How does this translate into medical research?

(3)   Finally, what provision does the law make for an individual suffering injury in the course of her participation in such clinical research?

---

5   See below at 16.8.
6   See J Savelescu, 'Two Deaths and Two Lessons' (2002) 28 *Journal of Medical Ethics* 1.
7   See below Chapter 19 at 19.2.
8   (EC) 2001/20.
9   (EC) 2005/28. The Medicines for Human Use (Clinical Trials) Regulations were duly amended: Medicines for Human Use (Clinical Trials) Amendment Regulations 2006, SI 2006/1928. The amended regulations came into force on 29 August 2006.

Clinical research[10] may be classified in a number of ways. Non-intrusive research involves no direct interference with the participant, for example research into medical records, epidemiological research. Intrusive research may be non-invasive (for example psychological inquiries) or invasive, involving actual contact with the patient's body (for example taking blood, administering drugs, testing new surgical techniques). Some research is combined with medical care, sometimes referred to as 'therapeutic research'. Some utilises volunteers who agree to participate in a research project not likely to confer any personal benefit to themselves. In previous versions of the Declaration of Helsinki[11] such research was categorised as 'non-therapeutic', and special restrictions recommended, but the distinction was abandoned in 2000.[12] It is not always logical to be more permissive of 'therapeutic' than 'non-therapeutic' research. Some research (such as pathogenesis and pathophysiology) does not fit neatly into either category.[13] Consequently, in the 2000 version, the category of 'non-therapeutic research' was removed and a new category of 'research combined with medical care' was introduced. The concepts remain broadly the same. The boundaries are still difficult to draw. Generally, the more invasive the research and the smaller the potential benefit to the participant, the greater are the ethical problems.

Research governance

16.2 Responsibility for the regulation of clinical research in the NHS is shared by local NHS research and development (R&D) management[14] and NHS research ethics committees (RECs). Special rules apply to clinical trials of investigational medicinal products (CTIMPs), which constitute around 15 per cent of research applications.[15] CTIMPs cannot commence without the authorisation of both an ethics committee and the UK licensing authority,[16] the MHRA. The MHRA, which subsumed the old Medicines Control Agency, provides the relevant assessment for clinical trials of medicines and devices. It must make its assessment within 60 days of receiving the application. If the MHRA gives approval and the clinical trial commences, then the MHRA takes on a monitoring role. As we saw in Chapter 10, the MHRA goes on to provide marketing authorisation, inspect the marketing processes and is also

---

10 This chapter will focus on clinical research. Wider aspects of health care research (including sociological research) are not covered here. See N Mays and C Pope (eds), *Qualitative Research in Health Care* (3rd edn, 2006) Blackwell; G Hek, P Moule, *Making Sense of Research: An Introduction for Health and Social Care Practitioners* (3rd edn, 2006) Sage Publications.

11 The Declaration is an international ethical guideline. The 1996 version is endorsed in the Medicines for Human Use (Clinical Trials) Regulations 2004, SI 2004/1031, Sch 1, Part 2, para 1.

12 World Medical Association, *The Declaration of Helsinki: Ethical Principles for Medical Research Involving Human Subjects* (2000) WMA General Assembly, Edinburgh Scotland. Clarifications were added in 2002 and 2004.

13 See, for example, RJ Levine, 'The Need to Revise the Declaration of Helsinki' (1999) 341 *New England Journal of Medicine* 531.

14 See R&D Directorate, Department of Health, *Best Research for Best Health* (2006) Ref 6050, which sets down the goals for NHS R&D over the next five years.

15 Department of Health, *Report of the Ad Hoc Advisory Group on the Operation of NHS RECs* (2005), para 3.2.

16 Medicines for Human Use (Clinical Trials) Regulations 2004, reg 11(3).

responsible for surveillance and enforcement. The MHRA's responsibilities in authorising CTIMPs are dual: it subjects proposals to a scientific assessment to ensure that participants are safe and it attempts to make the UK an attractive place to conduct research.[17] The two goals do not always sit comfortably together.[18]

More worrying than the possible shortcomings of the MHRA has been the limited governance of research which does not fall within the ambit of the Clinical Trials Regulations 2004. The Department of Health has taken steps to address this deficiency in its *Research Governance Framework for Health and Social Care*, first published in 2001 and significantly revised in 2005. Prior to this, monitoring of research was so ineffective that some research ethics committees took it upon themselves to monitor research.[19] This seemed the only way to ensure that researchers put into practice the guidance that the ethics committee provided. Now, all NHS organisations engaging in research are required to meet standards and manage risk through reporting, inspecting and reviewing internal systems. The framework clearly delineates the legal duties and responsibilities of sponsors, funders and researchers. The Healthcare Commission reviews compliance with the research governance framework as part of its general review of performance. If an organisation fails to comply then it is expected to develop proposals for improvement with its strategic health authority, or, in the event of significant failings, the Commission could advise the Secretary of State or Monitor (in the case of foundation trusts) to take special measures.[20]

Research ethics committees

16.3 The Clinical Trials Regulations 2004 require that CTIMPs have prior regulatory and ethical approval. Embarking on a trial without the prior sanction of a relevant ethics committee is a criminal offence.[21] We will say more about the constitution of ethics committees under the Clinical Trials Regulations 2004 shortly. First, it is important to note that outside the remit of the Clinical Trials Regulations 2004 a researcher contravenes no law in carrying out research without ethical approval. However, other sanctions and ethical guidance[22] deter any such practice. An NHS employee failing to seek approval from the relevant REC is likely to be disciplined by his employing trust. Outside the NHS, researchers may face disciplinary action by professional regulatory authorities. Conducting research without ethical review may constitute impaired 'fitness to practise'. In 2006, the General Medical Council

---

[17] See MHRA, *Business Plan for 2006–7* (2006), p 10.

[18] See *Expert Scientific Group on Phase One Clinical Trials* Final Report, and criticism of the MHRA in Chapter 10 at 10.10.

[19] See J Berry, 'Local Research Ethics Committees can Audit Ethical Standards in Research' (1997) 23 *Journal of Medical Ethics* 379 and E Pickworth, 'Should Local Research Ethics Committees Monitor Research They Have Approved?' (2000) 26 *Journal of Medical Ethics* 330.

[20] *Research Governance Framework for Health and Social Care* (2nd edn, 2005), para 5.7.

[21] Medicines for Human Use (Clinical Trials) Regulations 2004, reg 49.

[22] See Declaration of Helsinki, art 13; Council of Europe, *Additional Protocol to the Convention on Human Rights and Biomedicine, Concerning Biomedical Research* (2005), Art 9 (the UK is not a signatory).

instigated disciplinary action against Andrew Wakefield, the author of a 1998 *Lancet* paper linking autism and the MMR vaccine. Among ten counts of serious professional misconduct was the claim that no proper ethics committee approval was sought. Journal editors also play a monitoring role. One of the functions of the Committee on Publication Ethics[23] is to ensure that its members do not publish studies unless guidelines on ethical review are followed.

A number of ethics committees exist outside the NHS. These include ethical review committees set up by universities, private hospitals and pharmaceutical companies. Within the NHS, RECs comprise lay and medical individuals who advise as to the ethics of any NHS health care research and 'protect the dignity, rights, safety and well-being of all actual or potential research participants'.[24] They can also consider private sector research if requested to do so. RECs include up to 18 members from a balanced age and gender distribution. There should be a mixture of expert and lay members, the latter constituting at least one third of the membership. The quality of the people who volunteer to serve on NHS ethics committees, and their ability to exercise judgement, is fundamental to the process.

A troubled history

16.4 The Department of Health first recommended that district health authorities establish local research ethics committees (LRECs) in 1975. More detailed formal guidance was issued in 1991.[25] Each local health authority was required to set up at least one, and there were over 200 LRECs in all. Due to limited guidance and co-ordination, the review process was often inconsistent. Multi-centre researchers fared worst, facing a diversity of procedures and outcomes. In an effort to improve the system, multi-centre research ethics committees (MRECs) were introduced in 1997.[26] MRECs performed a single ethical review of research taking place in more than one research site and then passed the protocol on to LRECs to consider relevant local matters. The process remained unwieldy. The Central Office for NHS Research Ethics Committees (COREC) was established in 2000, to improve the system, issue guidance to RECs, manage the budget and appoint MRECs.[27] Strategic health authorities[28] took on the role of appointing authority for LRECs. In 2001, the Department of Health issued a *Research Governance Framework for Health and Social Care* and *Governance Arrangements for NHS RECs* (GAfREC), an updated version of which is expected in 2007. Researchers stepped up political

---

[23] See http://www.publicationethics.org.uk/.
[24] COREC, *Governance Arrangements for NHS Research Ethics Committees* (2001), para 2.2.
[25] Department of Health, *Local Research Ethics Committees*, HSG (91) 5. Replaced by COREC, *Governance Arrangements for NHS Research Ethics Committees*.
[26] Department of Health, *Multi-centre Research Ethics Committees*, HSG (97) 23. Replaced by COREC, *Governance Arrangements for NHS Research Ethics Committees*.
[27] The authority for COREC is now contained in regulation 5(4) of the Medicines for Human Use (Clinical Trials) Regulations 2004 by which the United Kingdom Ethics Committee Authority (UKECA) appointed COREC to provide advice and assistance to RECs.
[28] Reduced from 28 to 10 in July 2006.

pressure, aimed at reducing the level of bureaucracy and facilitating research, and, as a result, the National Patient Safety Agency (NPSA) took over responsibility for COREC in 2005.

Ethics committees and the Clinical Trials Regulations 2004

16.5 The implementation of the Clinical Trials Directive 2001[29] in the Medicines for Human Use (Clinical Trials) Regulations 2004 wrought further changes on the system. The 2004 Regulations delineate the responsibilities of funders, researchers, chief investigators and the organisation providing care. A Clinical Trials Tool Kit[30] was produced with practical help for the research community. New standard operating procedures for RECs were produced by COREC to take into account the Clinical Trials Regulations and other legislation (including the Health and Social Care (Community Health and Standards) Act 2003, Human Tissue Act 2004[31] and Mental Capacity Act 2005[32]).

The Clinical Trials Directive 2001 aims to facilitate research across Europe.[33] Strict time-limits are placed on ethics committee deliberations. In each Member State, the decision of one REC is valid for the whole of that country, thereby enabling research to cross borders within Europe. In addition to requiring standards of good clinical practice[34] the Directive demands the approval of a statutorily-recognised research ethics committee before research can commence or a protocol can be amended. In the UK, the approval of both a recognised REC and the licensing authority, the MHRA, is necessary.[35]

Under the Clinical Trials Regulations 2004, research ethics committees require independent statutory authority, provided by the newly formed United Kingdom Ethics Committee Authority.[36] Rather than giving all RECs statutory authority, the Ethics Committee Authority recognises certain RECs appointed by a range of authorities (including strategic health authorities, COREC, Universities and independent institutions). Other NHS RECs, established under COREC's *Governance Arrangements for NHS RECs*, together with other independent ethics committees may only review applications that do not relate to CTIMPs.

29   (EC) 2001/20.
30   See http://www.ct-toolkit.ac.uk/
31   See below, Chapter 19. See also Medical Research Council, *Human Tissue and Biological Samples for Use in Research* (2001, with addendum following passage of the Human Tissue Act 2004, added in 2005).
32   See NPSA, *Standard Operating Procedures for Research Ethics Committees* (2006, version 3.1).
33   E Cave and S Holm, 'New Governance Arrangements for Research Ethics Committees: is Facilitating Research Achieved at the Cost of Participants' Interests?' (2002) 28 *Journal of Medical Ethics* 318.
34   Medicines for Human Use (Clinical Trials) Regulations 2004, Part 4. See also Commission Directive (EC) 2005/28.
35   Medicines for Human Use (Clinical Trials) Regulations 2004, reg 12.
36   Medicines for Human Use (Clinical Trials) Regulations 2004, reg 5.

Though the Clinical Trials Regulations 2004 formally apply only to CTIMPs, COREC's standard operating procedures apply to *all* NHS RECs – whether or not they are recognised by the Ethics Committee Authority.[37] The *Governance Arrangements for NHS RECs* also apply, regardless of Ethics Committee Authority recognition. This, however, represents the limit of consistency engendered by the Clinical Trials Regulations. The failure to give statutory authority to all RECs has led to a complex system at a time when researchers feel stifled by bureaucracy. Medical professionals are hardened to the prolific use of acronyms, but the comprehension of new researchers must be sorely tested by a system in which UKECA-recognised NHSRECs review CTIMPs aided by MHU(CT)Regs whilst both UKECA-recognised and GAfREC-authorised NHSRECs review non-CTIMPS aided by GAfREC and SOPs, by COREC and NPSA.

Regulation 15(5) of the Clinical Trials Regulations 2004 limits the remit of research ethics committees, providing a list of relevant matters which the committee should consider. In summary these include a consideration of the relevance of the trial and its design; the balance of risks and benefits; the protocol; the suitability of the investigator and the facilities; the information sheet and procedure for obtaining informed consent; indemnity, insurance and compensation arrangements and payments to the participant and investigator.

Ethics committees are not required to concern themselves too much with the law:

> RECs should have due regard for the requirement of relevant regulatory agencies and of applicable laws. It is not for the REC to interpret regulations or laws, but they may indicate in their advice to the researcher and those institutions where they believe further consideration needs to be given to such matters.[38]

Nor is it any longer the business of the committee to review the scientific merit of the protocol. Peer reviewers and, where required, designated 'research ethics advisers' within COREC take on this role. The reduced autonomy of ethics committees is not easily borne by their members. It is often difficult to divorce law from ethics, or science from ethics. In the latter case, there are invariably members of the REC with considerable scientific experience and it is hard, and arguably unethical, for them to ignore issues that are central to the ethicality of the protocol.

A national research ethics service

16.6 COREC reduced the number of LRECs and made changes to the application process, including in 2004 a common application form. But even as teething troubles were addressed, disgruntled researchers prompted an ad hoc review commissioned by Lord Warner. The resulting report, which made

---

[37] Medicines for Human Use (Clinical Trials) Regulations 2004, reg 5.
[38] COREC, Governance Arrangements for NHS Research Ethics Committees (2001), para 2.6.

nine recommendations, was published in 2005.[39] The system will become a 'national research ethics *service*' (NRES). The NPSA have begun implementation.[40] The remit of ethics committees is subject to further controls: RECs will no longer review surveys and non-research activities that present no material ethical issues.[41] In England, at the time of writing, LRECs still handle site specific assessments, but reform is imminent. This role will be handed over to local NHS research and development management.[42] Further revision of the standard operating procedures is expected in June 2007 and a draft version 2 of *Governance Arrangements for NHS RECs* early in 2007. At the start of 2007, the number of RECs was reduced to 120 and the creation of 17 REC centres was underway in order to pool administrative resources.

A triage system will provide alternatives to full review where the protocol:

(1)   is outside the remit of the REC;
(2)   is insufficiently developed;
(3)   contains no material ethical issues; or
(4)   the committee requires expert advice.

Screening will identify such protocols, alongside existing validation processes. Paid 'national research ethics advisers' (recruited from REC chairs and members) will sign off cases falling into (3). In addition to providing 'streamlined review' the new advisers will also provide advice, training and feedback to the volunteer REC members; a tall order given that the NPSA proposes to fund only eight part-time advisers in England.[43]

Instead of designated 'multi-centre' and 'local' research ethics committees, committees with specialist interests are being developed. A researcher in mental health will not necessarily send his protocol to his nearest committee, instead he might forward it to a committee specialising in mental health research: he has choice.

Facilitating good research v patient protection

16.7 The ongoing reforms of the ethical review process focus on the facilitation of good research; efficiency, effectiveness and proportionality are key. Paragraph 5 of the Declaration of Helsinki states that: 'In medical research on human subjects, considerations related to the well-being of the human subject

---

[39]   Department of Health, *Report of the Ad Hoc Advisory Group on the Operation of NHS Research Ethics Committees* (2005). See AJ Dawson, 'The Ad Hoc Advisory Group's Proposals for Research Ethics Committees: A Mixture of the Timid, the Revolutionary and the Bizarre' (2005) 31 *Journal of Medical Ethics* 435.

[40]   NPSA, *Building on Improvement: Implementing the Recommendations of the Ad Hoc Advisory Group on the Operation of NHS RECs* (2006).

[41]   Accordingly, *Governance Arrangements for NHS Research Ethics Committees*, para 3.1 will be revised (expected in 2007).

[42]   See NPSA, *Updated COREC Business Plan 2006/7 and Pre-Planning Statement 2007/8* (2006), para 16.

[43]   NPSA, *Building on Improvement*, para 2.1.3.

should take precedence over the interests of science and society',[44] sentiments echoed in Article 2 of the European Convention on Human Rights and Biomedicine.[45] Both the Good Clinical Practice Directive and the Clinical Trials Directive refer to the Helsinki Declaration, as do the Clinical Trials Regulations 2004.[46]

Do the reforms achieve an appropriate balance? Some fear that the streamlined processes will benefit only the sponsors and researchers. Participants will be under-protected as a result.[47] We are less pessimistic. John Harris has persuasively argued that, provided the rights and welfare of research participants are adequately protected, there is a strong moral duty to perform and even to participate in good research.[48] Facilitating research is a laudable aim provided it is matched with suitable protections for participants.[49] Care will have to be taken to ensure that the new 'national research ethics advisers' are appropriately skilled; that checks are in place to ensure that only minimal risk studies bypass full committee review; and that committees and advisers receive detailed guidance on the meaning of 'no material ethical issues'. Because there is potential for drug companies to make handsome profits and researchers to benefit in terms of career advancement, it is particularly important that the rights and interests of research participants are safeguarded. This begs the question: how well do the Clinical Trials Regulations 2004 protect research participants? We attempt to answer that question in the following sections.

Consent to participation in trials

16.8 In 2000, allegations were made, albeit later largely not proven,[50] surrounding research carried out a decade before on premature babies at North Staffordshire Hospital. It was claimed the research was conducted without parents' consent.[51] Since 1964 the Declaration of Helsinki has sought

---

[44] *Ethical Principles for Medical Research Involving Human Participants* (1964, updated 2000; clarification added 2002 and 2004).

[45] Council of Europe (1997): '[T]he interests and welfare of the human being shall prevail over the sole interest of society or science.' Note that the Convention has not been signed by the UK.

[46] Note, though, that they make reference to the 1996 version rather than the controversial 2000 version. See E Cave, C Nichols, 'Reforming the Ethical Review System: Balancing the Rights and Interests of Research Participants with the Duty to Facilitate Good Research' (2007) 2 *Clinical Ethics*, forthcoming.

[47] See, for example, M Epstein, DL Wingate, 'Is the NHS Research Ethics Committees System to be Outsourced to a Low-cost Call Centre? Reflections on Human Research Ethics after the Warner Report' (2007) 33 *Journal of Medical Ethics* 45.

[48] J Harris, 'Scientific Research is a Moral Duty' (2005) 31 *Journal of Medical Ethics* 242.

[49] But see S Kerrison and AM Pollack, 'The Reform of UK Research Ethics Committees: Throwing out the Baby with the Bath Water' 31 (2005) *Journal of Medical Ethics* 487.

[50] See Editorial, 'Babies and Consent: Yet Another NHS Scandal' (2000) 320 *British Medical Journal* 1285.

[51] MP Samuals, DP Southall, 'Negative Extrathoracic Pressure in Treatment of Respiratory Failure in Infants and Young Children' (1989) 299 *British Medical Journal* 1253. There was a subsequent NHS review: NHS Executive, *West Midlands Regional Office Report of a Review of the Research Framework in North Staffordshire Hospital NHS Trust* (http://www.doh.gov.uk/wmro/northstaffs.htm).

to protect research participants' rights by demanding rigorous consent procedures. The fallout from disputes surrounding this controversial research contributed to the impetus for the 2001 Department of Health *Research Governance Framework for Health and Social Care*.[52] An updated version of the framework was produced in 2005, which states that informed consent is at the heart of ethical research and demands 'appropriate arrangements' for obtaining consent, and the review of those arrangements by an ethics committee.[53] Special rules apply to CTIMPs under the Clinical Trials Regulations 2004. Schedule 1, Part 2, paragraph 9 of the Regulations requires that 'subject to the other provisions of this Schedule relating to consent, freely given informed consent shall be obtained from every subject prior to clinical trial participation'. The Regulations go on to require that informed consent:

(a) is given freely after that person is informed of the nature, significance, implications and risks of the trial; and

(b) either:

(i) is evidenced in writing, dated and signed, or otherwise marked, by that person so as to indicate his consent, or

(ii) if the person is unable to sign or to mark a document so as to indicate his consent, is given orally in the presence of at least one witness and recorded in writing.[54]

Though informed consent of the participant is a prerequisite for ethical approval in most types of medical research, the Clinical Trials Regulations 2004 and, outside their remit, ethical codes of conduct accept limited circumstances where alternative safeguards are acceptable. Self–evidently, someone may be unable to consent by virtue of being a child or suffering from mental disability. In such circumstances, we shall see that other safeguards are put in place to protect the research participant.[55] Even in relation to competent adult participants, there may be trials where the risks to the participant might be minimal and the impracticalities of gaining consent tremendous. Thus, in some cases of epidemiological research (such as the collection of statistics on measles, for example) where the individual participant cannot be identified, an ethics committee might decide that obtaining consent is unnecessary.[56]

Even in trials such as epidemiological trials, however, consent must be obtained if data is not fully anonymised.[57] Article 20 of the Declaration of

---

[52] Department of Health, *Research Governance Framework for Health and Social Care* (2001; 2nd edn, 2005).

[53] Department of Health, *Research Governance Framework for Health and Social Care* (2nd edn, 2005), para 2.2.3.

[54] Schedule 1, Part 1, para 3(1), implementing Article 2(j) of Directive (EC) 2001/20. See also Schedule 1, Part 3, which sets out conditions of informed consent.

[55] See below, 16.10 and 16.11.

[56] General Medical Council, *Research: The Role and Responsibilities of Doctors* (2002), para 34.

[57] But see section 251 of the National Health Service Act 2006 (formerly section 60 of the Health and Social Care Act 2001), discussed below at 16.17.

Helsinki provides that 'the subjects must be volunteers and informed participants in the research project'. Article 22 outlines the importance of adequate information and Article 23[58] stresses the importance of volunteering. What does this mean in practice?

In any research on human beings, each potential participant must be adequately informed of the aims, methods, sources of funding, any possible conflicts of interest, institutional affiliations of the researcher, the anticipated benefits and potential risks of the study, and the discomfort it may entail. The participant should be informed of the right to abstain from the study or to withdraw consent to participate at any time without reprisal. After ensuring that the participant has understood the information, the researcher should then obtain the participant's freely-given informed consent, preferably in writing. If the consent cannot be obtained in writing, the non-written consent must be formally documented and witnessed.

The requirement of adequate information for consent to treatment has already been addressed in Chapter 5. We have seen that, gradually, the English courts are moving away from an exclusively professional standard of information disclosure. In the context of research, we would argue that the 'prudent patient' test governs what researchers must disclose to research participants.[59] COREC's *Governance Arrangements for NHS RECs* require that consent should usually involve a written consent form and information sheet, in addition to an oral explanation. A House of Commons Review led to new guidance being issued by COREC, directing researchers and ethics committees on the framing of information sheets.[60] The formal guidance offered to researchers is overtly patient-centred. The medical profession endorses that guidance. Only rarely, we would suggest, could it be logical or defensible[61] to depart from such unequivocal guidance.

Setting a stringent test for disclosure in the context of clinical research in Canada in *Halushka v University of Saskatchewan*,[62] Hall JA declared:

> There can be no exception to the ordinary requirements of disclosure in the case of research as there may well be in ordinary medical practice. The researcher does not have to balance the probable effect of lack of treatment against the risk involved in treatment itself. The example of risks being properly hidden

---

[58] Article 23 of the Declaration of Helsinki: 'When obtaining informed consent for the research project the physician should be particularly cautious if the subject is in a dependent relationship with the physician or may consent under duress. In that case, the informed consent should be obtained by a well-informed physician who is not engaged in the investigation and who is completely independent of this relationship.'

[59] COREC, *Governance Arrangements for NHS Research Ethics Committees* (2001), paras 9.17, 10.6. Under the NHS plan the 'good practice in consent initiative' seeks to review consent procedures to ensure a patient-centred standard.

[60] See House of Commons Health Committee, *The Influence of the Pharmaceutical Industry* Fourth Report of Session 2004–05, HC 42-I (2005). See COREC, *Guidance for Researchers: Information Sheets and Consent Forms* (2005, version 2).

[61] 'The use of these adjectives – responsible, reasonable and respectable – all show that the court has to be satisfied that the exponents of the body of opinion relied upon can demonstrate that such opinion has a logical basis.' Per Lord Browne-Wilkinson, *Bolitho v City and Hackney Health Authority* [1998] AC 232 at 778.

[62] (1965) 52 WWR 608.

from a patient when it is important that he should not worry can have no application in the field of research. The subject of medical experimentation is entitled to a full and frank disclosure of all the facts, probabilities and opinions which a reasonable man might be expected to consider before giving his consent.

Self-evidently, Hall JA's principle must be applied to volunteers. No one but the volunteer can be allowed to assess what risk he is prepared to accept for the community's welfare. This applies equally to patients who agree to become research participants. The doctor in such cases hopes that the patient may benefit from the experimental treatment. But that treatment remains experimental. The patient is exposed to additional, unquantifiable risk at least in part to benefit others not himself.

On the other hand, the volunteer is not free to accept any risk whatsoever. Research ethics committees will carefully assess the risk involved before sanctioning a research project. Special measures have been put in place to protect volunteers in first-in-man Phase 1 drug trial after the Northwick Park disaster in 2006.[63] New guidance for effective communication between ethics committees and the MHRA has been issued[64] and additional guidance will relate to safety issues in Phase 1 trials and, in the light of the manufacturers' limited liability insurance, the appropriate level of clinical trials insurance.[65]

Ethics committees will consider whether the volunteers are truly volunteers. Do medical students feel under compulsion to assist in trials mounted by their teachers? Do patients feel obliged to 'help' their doctor if he asks them to participate in research that is not related to their medical care?[66] Where resort is had to volunteers outside medical schools and hospital patients, payments are often made in this country. Amounts paid are usually relatively modest but may still constitute an inducement to impoverished students and the unemployed.[67] The principles of law are clear. Any degree of compulsion renders any written consent given invalid.[68] Proving compulsion might be the difficulty for a medical student. And for an unemployed 'volunteer', economic compulsion arising from his circumstances rather than any misconduct by the research team is as yet unrecognised in English law. Article 23 of the Declaration of Helsinki is clear that where any suspicion of duress might arise, an independent physician unconnected with the research project should seek the participant's consent.

---

[63] See above at 16.1.
[64] COREC, *Memorandum of Understanding Between MHRA, COREC and GTAC* (2006).
[65] See NPSA, *Updated COREC Business Plan 2006/7 and Pre-Planning Statement 2007/8* (2006), para 4.3.
[66] Department of Health and Royal College of Physicians of London guidelines both require patient consent forms to state expressly that whether or not the patient agrees to take part in the trial will not affect his medical care and that the patient is free to withdraw from the trial at any time.
[67] See P Bentley, PG Thacker, 'The Influence of Risk and Monetary Payment on the Research Participation Decision Making Process' (2004) 30 *Journal of Medical Ethics* 293. And see Wilkinson and Moore, 'Inducements in Research' (1997) 11 *Bioethics* 373, where it is argued that inducements are acceptable and promote individual autonomy.
[68] *Re T (Adult: Refusal of Medical Treatment)* [1992] 4 All ER 649.

The issue of free and full consent is central to the propriety and legality of clinical trials.[69] Should the public, and patients in particular, come to believe that there is a real likelihood of being involved in a trial unknowingly, or, having agreed to participate, discovering that they have been given inadequate or inaccurate information, the supply of volunteers for research will dry up and patients' confidence in general health care will be seriously undermined. The definition of what constitutes a proper consent is, as we have seen, far from easy.

Innovative therapy

16.9 There is another difficulty too. The line between experimenting on a patient and doing your utmost for him is blurred.[70] For example, if a doctor caring for patients with AIDS attempts a novel treatment as a last resort, knowing that there is no conventional treatment which will prolong the patient's life, has she crossed that line and made her patient a research participant?

In *Simms v Simms and JS v an NHS Trust*[71] it was held to be lawful to administer an experimental treatment that had never been tested on humans to two patients suffering from new variant Creutzfeldt-Jacob Disease. Both lacked the mental capacity to give consent themselves. Both faced a dismal prognosis given their degenerative and terminal condition. The risks of treatment were unknown but as some benefit was possible, Butler-Sloss P held that administration of the drug, Pentosan Polysulphate, by intracerebral infusion was in the best interests of the patients. *Simms* establishes that the use of innovative therapies in the best interests of the patient is not necessarily unlawful. Jonathan Simms' father fought for the treatment which might effect an improvement in his son's terrible condition. In *an NHS Trust v J*, the patient's family opposed the administration of innovative therapy.[72] J was in a persistent vegetative state (PVS) after suffering a brain haemorrhage three years earlier. Against the wishes of her family, withdrawal of artificial hydration and nutrition was postponed so that an innovative therapy could be administered. Two research papers had indicated that the insomnia drug Zolpidem sometimes enhanced neural responses in PVS patients. Experts held out little hope that it would work in J's case, but saw no harm in trying. The family disagreed. J had extensive neurological damage. Heightened awareness, if it could be brought about, would bring to her only distress. Sir Mark Potter P accepted the expert opinion that the therapy was in J's best interests and ordered it to proceed.

---

[69] See L Doyal, JS Tobias (eds), *Informed Consent in Medical Research* (2000) BMJ Publishing.

[70] JK Mason and GT Laurie, *Mason and McCall Smith's Law and Medical Ethics* (7th edn, 2006) OUP, pp 668–670.

[71] [2002] EWHC 2734 (Fam). See J Harrington, 'Deciding Best Interests' [2003] 3 *Web Journal of Current Legal Issues*.

[72] [2006] All ER (D) 73 (Dec). See further Chapter 20 at 20.15.

'Research' is poorly defined.[73] The divide between research and treatment and research and audit is blurred. A study that is labelled 'audit' will escape the onerous research governance process, whether or not it contains issues of ethical significance. What is needed is practical guidance for researchers and ethics committees based on the risk to the participant. In 2005, the Ad Hoc Advisory Group[74] recommended that the remit of RECs should not include non-research activities *if they present no material ethical issues*, which implied that non-research activities that contain ethical issues should be reviewed. COREC has rejected this implication. The reforms limit the remit of ethics committees without providing an adequate safety net for borderline studies which may fall outside the strict definitions of research but never the less warrant ethical review.

Children in medical research programmes

16.10 When can a child give her own consent to participation in a trial? When can she withhold that consent? If the child is incapable of giving an effective consent, may a parent give consent on her behalf? Once again, the answers depend on whether or not the study is governed by the Clinical Trials Regulations 2004.

For studies that fall outside the ambit of the Regulations, the House of Lords' ruling in *Gillick*[75] empowers a minor to consent to medical treatment when he or she has reached an age and individual maturity to judge what the treatment entails and assess its benefit and disadvantages. In the case of research combined with medical care, the test might be the same. If the child is over 16, the Family Law Reform Act 1969, which statutorily empowers minors over 16 to consent to medical treatment, will offer protection to the medical team. Legal requirements for consent of minors in research are supplemented with guidance from august bodies such as the Medical Research Council.[76] In 1991, Department of Health guidance to research ethics committees demanded that, despite a child satisfying the *Gillick* test, 'even for therapeutic research purposes it would ... be unacceptable not to have the consent of the parent or guardian where the child is under 16'.[77] It further required parental consent for 16- and 17-year-olds 'unless it is clearly in the child's best interests that the parents should not be informed'.[78] The current COREC guidance is

[73] See D Wade, 'Ethics, Audit and Research: All Shades of Grey' (2005) 330 *British Medical Journal* 468; T Lewens, 'Distinguishing Treatment from Research: A Functional Approach' (2006) 32 *Journal of Medical Ethics* 424.
[74] Department of Health, *Report of the Ad Hoc Advisory Group on the Operation of NHS RECs* (2005).
[75] *Gillick v West Norfolk and Wisbech Area Health Authority* [1984] QB 581.
[76] Medical Research Council, *Medical Research Involving Children* (2004).
[77] HSG (91) 5, para 4.
[78] This guidance has since been replaced by COREC, *Governance Arrangements for NHS Research Ethics Committees* (2001), which is silent on the issue.

surprisingly silent about the consent requirements for children.[79] More recently the Royal College of Paediatrics and Child Health[80] advised that where a child satisfies the *Gillick* test, he should also be able to consent to participation in research. And the Medical Research Council advises that, outside the ambit of the Clinical Trials Regulations 2004, *Gillick* will probably apply, though parental involvement should always be encouraged.[81]

What of research that confers no direct benefit on the child? There is no apparent reason why the *Gillick* ruling should not apply. The basis of the judgment is not limited to medical treatment alone but concerns the general capacity of older children to make decisions for themselves. Whenever researchers wish to include a research participant under 18, only the *Gillick* test can grant the minor herself authority to consent to participate in the trial. Section 8 of the Family Law Reform Act 1969, empowering young people between 16 and 18 to consent to medical treatment, is strictly limited to therapeutic and diagnostic interventions.[82] Lord Donaldson considered it to be 'highly improbable'[83] that a *Gillick* (or *'Fraser'*[84]) *competent* minor could consent to a procedure of no benefit to himself. The safest course of action where healthy adolescents are to be involved in a study falling outside the remit of the Clinical Trials Regulations 2004 remains to seek a dual consent from both the older child[85] and her parents.

What about younger children?[86] The law is unclear as to whether parental consent to research of no benefit to the child is of any effect.[87] Paediatricians emphasise the need for some degree of carefully controlled research on children.[88] Children respond differently to drugs, they suffer from illnesses not afflicting adults and, above all, their suffering when afflicted is particularly poignant. There is a plethora of ethical guidance on the subject from the British Medical Association, General Medical Council (1994), Royal College of Paediatricians and Child Health (2000) and Department of Health (2001).

---

79   COREC, *Governance Arrangements for NHS Research Ethics Committees* (2001), para 9.17c requires that the committee is satisfied as to 'clear justification for the intention to include in the research individuals who cannot consent, and a full account of the arrangements for obtaining consent or authorisation for the participation of such individuals'.

80   Royal College of Paediatrics and Child Health, 'Guidelines for the Ethical Conduct of Medical Research Involving Children' (2000) 82 *Ethics Advisory Committee in Archives of Disease in Childhood* 177.

81   Medical Research Council, *Medical Research Involving Children* (2004), para 5.3.1.a.

82   *Re W (A Minor) (Medical Treatment)* [1992] 4 All ER 627 at 635 and 647, CA.

83   *Re W (A Minor) (Medical Treatment)* [1992] 4 All ER 177 at 635, CA.

84   Lord Fraser promulgated the guidance in *Gillick*.

85   It is highly unlikely that a court would sanction including a *Gillick competent* minor in a trial against her will. Although no minor can veto treatment, refusal is always a very important consideration for doctors making judgments whether to proceed against the minor's wishes: *Re W (A Minor) (Medical Treatment)* [1992] 4 All ER 627 at 640, 645 and 648–649, CA.

86   Neonatal research poses particular problems: see SA Mason and C Megone, *Informed Consent in European Neonatal Research* (2001) Ashgate.

87   See, for example, the American case *Grimes v Kennedy Kreiger Institute*, Nos 128, 129, Sept Term, 2000, cert den 2001, in which the Appeal Court in Maryland ruled that parents cannot consent to their child's participation in non-therapeutic research.

88   See S Conroy, J McIntyre, I Choonara, TJ Stephenson, 'Drug Trials in Children: Problems and the Way Forward' (2000) 49 *British Journal of Clinical Pharmacology* 93.

More recently, the Medical Research Council, in *Medical Research Involving Children* (2004), states that 'it is ethical for a healthy child to participate in research as long as appropriate consent has been obtained, there is no more than minimal risk and the research is not against the child's interests'.[89]

Sometimes research provides treatment that confers little or no benefit on the individual patient-participant but can be used to help those who suffer from the same condition in the future. In these cases the Medical Research Council advises that even where the research poses greater than minimal risk, it might be acceptable after 'serious ethical consideration' for the research to go ahead. Factors such as the magnitude of the condition, probability of the research achieving its aims, resources and timing will contribute to this decision.[90]

In law, research can only be carried out on children if it is in their best interests. How can research of no benefit to the child ever be in his best interests? Do best interests include the interests of the community? The House of Lords in *S v S*[91] were asked to authorise a blood test on a child to determine his paternity. Lord Reid described the parental power to authorise such a test in this way:

> Surely a reasonable parent would have some regard for the general public interest and would not refuse a blood test unless he thought that would clearly be *against the interests of the child* (*emphasis added*).

Arguably where any risk to the child is minimal, parents may authorise any procedure which is not perceived as *against* the interests of the child. However the Clinical Trials Regulations 2004, which will cover most research on healthy children, take a different, altogether more restrictive, stance. In the event that the courts were asked to decide whether or not a parent could consent to his child taking part in research outside the ambit of the Clinical Trials Regulations that did not confer any direct benefit to the study group, it is likely that the courts would take a similar line.

The *Gillick* ruling does not apply to clinical trials of investigational medicinal products (CTIMPs). The Clinical Trials Regulations 2004[92] require that in CTIMPs, the written consent of the person with legal responsibility[93] for the child is obtained. In addition the child should be 'given information according to his capacity of understanding' whereupon his refusal to participate or request to withdraw from the trial must be 'considered'. Thus the Regulations do not require the child's informed consent even if he is capable of giving it. However the weight to be given to his refusal or request to withdraw should not depend on the effect it will have on the validity of the research results. Rather it will depend on the child's capacity and possibly on the effect withdrawal will have on his health. As we saw in Chapter 15, competent children are not always entitled to decline treatment that will save them from death or serious injury. Consider a 15-year-old girl with advanced malignant

---

[89] Medical Research Council, *Medical Research Involving Children* (2004), para 4.3.1.
[90] *Medical Research Involving Children*, para 4.3.
[91] [1972] AC 24.
[92] See Schedule 1, Part 4.
[93] The 'person with legal responsibility' will usually be a parent, guardian or the court.

melanoma which surgery and chemotherapy have failed to eradicate. Should she be free to refuse to join a randomised controlled trial testing a new vaccine designed to halt or slow disease progression? In one sense there is little difference between this scenario and the cases of *Re R* and *Re W*.[94] But even if the trial offers her her only chance of survival, can it be said to constitute a therapeutic necessity? The trial will almost certainly be placebo-controlled, in which case there is a chance that the forcible treatment will result in no benefit to the child whatsoever. Even if allocated to the active arm of the trial, the effects of the treatment are far from certain. Arguably, forcing a competent child to participate in this trial would constitute inhuman and degrading treatment, and offend Article 3 of the European Convention on Human Rights.

Research poses a more awkward problem where is it is not combined with medical care. The Clinical Trials Regulations 2004 state that children should only be enrolled in research where it 'can only be carried out on minors' and, more prohibitively, that 'some direct benefit for the group of patients involved in the clinical trial is to be obtained from that trial'.[95] Research of no direct benefit to the group of trial participants cannot be sanctioned, notwithstanding the consent of both child and legal representative, that the research poses minimal risk to the child and that it will benefit children in the future. However, whilst most Phase 1 studies involving adult volunteers test a drug on healthy volunteers who do not have the condition the drug is ultimately intended to treat, it is often the case that clinical trials involving children aim to test the efficacy of a drug currently licensed only for treatment of adults. Consequently, it is sometimes possible to establish direct benefit. However, in Phase 1 trials testing treatments for conditions specific to children, the Regulations take a restrictive approach.

Proper consent procedures do not necessarily ensure the protection of child research participants. In 2007, Andrew Wakefield faces General Medical Council proceedings relating to his part in research on autistic children, which allegedly involved unnecessary and invasive procedures (including lumbar punctures and colonoscopy). Further, it was revealed[96] that Dr Wakefield was in receipt of funding from the Legal Aid Scheme in respect of eleven of the research participants, the parents of whom were attempting to prove the link in order to get compensation. Sole responsibility for the consequent decline in the uptake of the triple vaccine does not rest with Wakefield; the Press, the *Lancet* and the medical profession must bear some of the blame. As for the conduct of the trial, it was presumably a single centre, non-CTIMP and would, were it repeated today, fail to come under the ambit of the Clinical Trials Regulations 2004. The additional safeguards contained therein would not be extended to this research.

---

[94] *Re R (A Minor) (Wardship: Consent to Treatment)* [1992] Fam 11; *Re W (A Minor) (Medical Treatment: Court's Jurisdiction)* [1993] Fam 64. Discussed in Chapter 15, at 15.21.

[95] Medicines for Human Use (Clinical Trials) Regulations 2004, Part 4, paras 9 and 10.

[96] B Deer, 'Revealed: MMR Research Scandal' (2004) Sunday Times, 22 February.

Adults who lack mental capacity[97]

16.11 As problematic as the question of research involving children is the question of research involving mentally ill, mentally-disabled, or unconscious patients. The Clinical Trials Regulations 2004 deal with clinical trials and the Mental Capacity Act 2005,[98] which comes into force in 2007,[99] deals with other research. Consistency between the two was inevitably too much to ask. According to the latter (discussed fully in Chapter 6), capacity is now assessed in a decision-specific test made at the relevant time. Where a person lacks capacity, her best interests, determined by reference to her previous wishes and the views of family and carers, will dictate the appropriate course of action. There is a notable exception to this rule: according to section 32(8) of the 2005 Act the duty to consult is waived if treatment is urgent or consultation is impracticable.

Special rules are put in place to govern research. Section 30 of the Mental Capacity Act 2005 states that intrusive research[100] is lawful if an 'appropriate body'[101] (normally a REC) agrees that the research is safe and relates to the person's impairing condition and that it cannot be done as effectively using people who have mental capacity. In addition, the research must produce a benefit to the person that outweighs any risk or burden, or it will derive new scientific knowledge[102] and it is of minimal risk to the person and can be carried out with minimal intrusion or interference with their privacy.[103]

Let us compare this with the arrangements for clinical trials under the Clinical Trials Regulations 2004. According to these Regulations, a clinical trial can only recruit adults lacking mental capacity if it relates 'directly to a life-threatening or debilitating clinical condition from which the subject suffers'[104] and '[t]here are grounds for expecting that administering the medicinal product to be tested in the trial will produce a benefit to the subject

---

[97] The Medical Research Council's guidance (*Adults who Lack the Capacity to Consent* (1991)) is, at the time of writing, being updated to take account of the Mental Capacity Act 2005.

[98] Mental Capacity Act 2005, s 30(3): 'A clinical trial which is subject to the provisions of clinical trials regulations is not to be treated as research for the purposes of this section.' For an analysis of the 2005 Act, see Chapter 6.

[99] Note that the Mental Capacity Act 2005 (Commencement No 1) (England and Wales) Order 2007 delays the commencement of sections 30–34 where a project started before 1 April 2007 but finishes before 1 April 2008. Also see the Mental Capacity Act 2005 (Loss of Capacity During Research Project) (England) Regulations 2007 (draft) which, if adopted, will give – subject to conditions – legal authority for the continuation of research which begins before 1 April 2007 during which the participant loses capacity to consent.

[100] In essence, intrusive research is research that would normally require consent. The Mental Capacity Act 2005, s 30(2) states: 'Research is intrusive if it is of a kind that would be unlawful if it was carried out – (a) on or in relation to a person who had capacity to consent to it, but (b) without his consent.'

[101] Section 30(4). Defined in the Mental Capacity Act 2005 (Appropriate Body) (England) Regulations 2006, SI 2006/2810, reg 2 as follows: '[T]he 'appropriate body' is a committee (a) established to advise on, or on matters which include, the ethics of intrusive research in relation to people who lack capacity to consent to it; and (b) which is recognised for those proposes by the Secretary of State.'

[102] Mental Capacity Act 2005, s 31(5).

[103] Mental Capacity Act 2005, s 31(6).

[104] Medicines for Human Use (Clinical Trials) Regulations 2004, Part 5, para 11.

outweighing the risks or produce no risk at all'.[105] Note that this test is stricter than the test applied under the Clinical Trials Regulations 2004 to children; there the benefit need only apply to the group as a whole, rather than to the individual participant. This is probably due to the necessity to prioritise research on children whose physiology is quite different to adults. It is also somewhat more restrictive than the equivalent section dealing with adults lacking capacity in the Mental Capacity Act 2005. Under the 2005 Act, the benefits do not necessarily have to outweigh the risks provided the study derives new scientific knowledge and is of 'minimal risk'. Under the Clinical Trial Regulations the research must either benefit the participant or produce 'no risk at all'.

Emergency research

16.12 Section 32(9) of the Mental Capacity Act 2005 provides an exception to the requirement to obtain consent where there is either 'prior agreement of a registered medical practitioner not involved in the trial or the researcher acts in accordance with a procedure approved by the appropriate body at the time the research project was approved'. An ethics committee will be unlikely to sanction research without the prior agreement of a medical practitioner, save in one situation: emergency research. Emergency research involves participants with life-threatening conditions who cannot give consent. It might, for example compare two methods of treatment of stroke on admission to hospital. Were it not for section 32(9), emergency research would be severely restricted.

No such exception was to be found in the original Clinical Trials Regulations 2004. Schedule 1, Part 4, para 4 (relating to minors) and Schedule 1, Part 5, para 4 (relating to adults lacking capacity) to the Regulations required that the prior consent of a legal representative must always be obtained where the proposed research participant lacks the capacity to give consent. Ideally, the legal representative will be a 'personal' one; a carer or family member. Otherwise a professional legal representative might be sought: 'A person not connected with the conduct of the trial who is (a) the doctor primarily responsible for the adult's medical treatment, or (b) a person nominated by the relevant health care provider (eg an acute NHS Trust or Health Board)'. Whilst this posed few problems in most cases, it presented insurmountable difficulties for some types of emergency research.

This was highlighted in the international TROICA trial[106] comparing two types of emergency treatment given when patients suffering cardiac arrest were brought into hospital by ambulance. In many cases a personal representative could not be immediately located and, given that treatment often had

---

[105] Medicines for Human Use (Clinical Trials) Regulations 2004, Part 5, para 9. Note that the requirements are not as stringent as those relating to a minor whereby some direct benefit for the group of patients is required (Part 4, para 10).

[106] Thrombolysis in Cardiac Arrest: a prospective, randomised, double-blind, placebo-controlled, multi-centre, parallel-group comparison trial led by Boehringer Ingelheim GmbH to evaluate the efficacy of tenecteplase during CPR as compared with standard treatment in patients suffering from out-of-hospital cardiac arrest.

to be administered within minutes by ambulance personnel, it was impracticable to utilise a professional representative. The ambulance personnel could not perform this role due to lack of independence. Yet the research was clearly valuable. Other countries across Europe had interpreted Article 5(a) of the Clinical Trials Directive more flexibly and the TROICA trial had been sanctioned. In England, the MHRA, concerned at the potential ill effects on emergency medicine, or perhaps at missing out on lucrative research, proposed an amendment in August 2005 sanctioning *deferred* consent. Accordingly, it was proposed that consent could be obtained within 24 hours of commencing the research treatment. The Medical Research Council thought this was not enough time and suggested 72 hours. But would this constitute a contravention of the Clinical Trials Directive? Beyleveld and Pattinson[107] argue that the provisions in the Directive 'unequivocally rule out both … no consent and deferred consent approaches to emergency research on medicinal products', that the position taken in the original Clinical Trials Regulations 2004 was correct. They argue that the duty to put the research participant before the interests of science prevents a purposive interpretation of the Directive.

Never the less, the Medicines for Human Use (Clinical Trials) Amendment (No 2) Regulations 2006,[108] which came into force in December 2006, promulgate a new interpretation of Article 5(a) of the Clinical Trials Directive. The 'deferred consent' model proposed by the MHRA was abandoned for a 'no consent' model. Accordingly an exception to the requirement that a legal representative gives consent on behalf of an adult who lacks capacity is created when:

(i)   treatment is required urgently;

(ii)   the nature of the trial also requires urgent action;

(iii)   it is not reasonably practicable to meet the conditions in paragraphs 1 to 5 of Part 5 (obtaining consent etc); and

(iv)   an ethics committee has given approval to the procedure under which the action is taken.

We now join a number of European countries awaiting a test case which will determine whether this flexible approach to interpretation of the Directive is legal. Would it not have been better to argue for the amendment of the Directive?[109]

Randomised controlled trials[110]

16.13   At the heart of much modern medical research lies the randomised controlled trial (RCT). Patients suffering from the same illness are divided into two groups and subjected to different treatments. Most commonly, either (a) one group will receive the conventional treatment, and another be given the

---

[107] See D Beyleveld, S Pattinson, 'Medical Research into Emergency Treatment: Regulatory Tensions in England and Wales' [2006] 5 *Web Journal of Current Legal Issues*.

[108] SI 2006/2984.

[109] See Beyleveld, Pattinson [2006] 5 *Web Journal of Current Legal Issues*.

[110] For trenchant criticism of randomised clinical trials, see J Penston, *Fiction and Fantasy in Medical Research: The Large Scale Randomised Trial* (2003) London Press.

experimental and hopefully more effective treatment, or (b) one group will be given a new drug, and the other a placebo.[111] For an outsider there are a number of worrying features to RCTs. First, there is again the question of consent. Second, there is concern that the control group is denied a chance of superior treatment. In particular, public anxiety was highlighted by a trial involving 3,000 women at risk of conceiving a spina bifida baby. Studies had shown that similar women appeared to suffer a reduced incidence of carrying a spina bifida baby if treated with special vitamin supplements. The trial involved randomising the women into four groups. One group received the full treatment under trial, another part only of the supplement, a third the other element of the supplement and the fourth a placebo. Why should any woman at risk be denied a treatment which *might* help her avoid a spina bifida conception? Further criticism of randomised trials includes this point, that while the control group in a test may be denied a benefit, people are also concerned at the risk to the experimental group. And finally, who controls and monitors RCTs?

There are doctors and researchers who believe that the RCT is most effective if conducted 'blind', that is the patient is told nothing at all.[112] The issue then is whether consent to treatment given generally is negated by unwitting participation in the RCT. The law will decide the issue on how closely related the RCT is to the condition under treatment and whether consent to treatment impliedly includes consent to what was done in the trial. At best, a patient asked to take part in an RCT will be told just that. The nature of the trial and the purpose of random allocation may be explained. Exactly what will be done to the patient cannot be explained, by virtue of the very nature of an RCT. Consent on the strength of a proper explanation of the trial and free acceptance by the patient of its random basis would appear both sufficient and necessary. Entering the patient in a random test with no explanation and no consent places the doctor at risk of an action for battery if the patient finds out. Fears that patients, if properly informed, will refuse to participate are natural. The erosion of personal freedom resulting from allowing 'blind' trials is not justified by those fears. A patient who will not agree to, or cannot understand the implications of, a trial should not be entered in that trial.[113]

---

[111] Note that paragraph 29 of the most recent version of the Declaration of Helsinki (2000) demands that new methods are tested 'against those of the best current prophylactic, diagnostic, and therapeutic methods'. Arguably this would compromise the scientific basis of research and even prevent research in developing countries where the cost of the best-proven treatment may be prohibitive. The new emphasis was so controversial (see HP Forster, E Emanuel, C Grady, 'The 2000 Revision of the Declaration of Helsinki: a Step Forward or More Confusion?' (2001) 358 *Lancet* 1449) that a note of clarification was added in 2002. Cases where placebo-controlled trials may be viewed as ethically acceptable despite the existence of proven therapy are listed. See also *Additional Protocol to the Convention on Human Rights and Biomedicine, Concerning Biomedical Research* (2005), Art 23(3).

[112] And see *Mason and McCall Smith's Law and Medical Ethics*, pp 667–668 on the ethical implications of a blind, randomised controlled trial on the treatment of Parkinsonism.

[113] See the useful discussion in SJ Edwards, RJ Lilford, DA Braunholtz, JC Jackson, J Hewison and J Thornton, 'Ethical Issues in the Design and Conduct of Randomised Controlled Trials' (1998) 2 *Health Technology Assessment* 1.

Apart from the questions of consent, the other means by which the courts may be invoked to consider the RCT arise when something goes wrong, and a participant suffers injury. Will the law enable him to obtain compensation?

Compensation for mishap

16.14 The Clinical Trials Directive requires that both sponsor and lead investigator are insured or indemnified before research can commence. Under the research governance framework, the sponsor of research is responsible for ensuring that appropriate insurance and indemnity arrangements are in place. In the NHS, R&D management permission, required at every research site before research can start, should not be granted unless NHS indemnity arrangements are in place. Unlike salaried employees of the NHS, many GPs and other independent practitioners must make their own indemnity or insurance arrangements with their professional bodies or the Medical Defence Union to protect themselves and their staff. In both cases, however, COREC advises[114] that research ethics committees leave the matter of indemnity and insurance in NHS research to the research governance process. They should, however, concern themselves with the adequacy of indemnity and insurance in research on private patients where the NHS governance research arrangements do not apply.

At present, compensation for personal injury suffered as a participant in a clinical trial is available only either to a participant who can prove negligence on the part of the operator of the trial, or on an *ex gratia* basis. Indemnity for non-negligent harm (caused through no discernible fault of an individual or institution involved) cannot be purchased by NHS bodies, and universities are finding the costs of such arrangements increasingly prohibitive. A claim in negligence may arise in two contexts in an RCT. First, a participant from the control group may complain that he was denied an improved prospect of cure. Second, participants from the experimental group may allege that unjustifiable risks were taken. Neither is likely to succeed. As long as conventional treatment of the control group remains proper medical practice, the control has no claim in negligence. As long as the novel procedure was a properly conducted piece of research, carried out in conformity with a well-founded and responsible body of medical opinion, the subject of that procedure is likely to fail.

Next, what about the case where something goes disastrously and unexpectedly wrong? The participant will not know why. It may be an inherent risk in the trial, it may be that the staff conducting the trial were negligent. The patients in the Northwick Park debacle[115] have already run into difficulties in their legal action. Not only did the MHRA conclude that the reaction was an 'unpredicted biological action', but TeGenro, the German manufacturer, offered an interim payment but then filed for bankruptcy with only limited

---

[114] COREC, *Guidance for RECs on GP Indemnity* (March 2006).
[115] See above at 16.1.

insurance. Parexel, who administered the drug may face claims, but, whilst the NHS will meet their immediate medical needs, the injured participants seem likely to go under-compensated.

In principle, carelessness by the research team, be it in selecting participants on the basis of their previous medical history, in the conduct of the trial or in monitoring of the effects of the trial, creates a remedy for the patient. Moreover, he also may have in theory a possible remedy against the ethics committee which approved the trial. It has been held that ethics committees can be subject to judicial review.[116] Arguably committees recognised by the UKECA have sufficient legal personality to be a defendant in a civil law suit. However, for those which lack statutory recognition, both the appointing strategic health authority and each individual ethics committee member of the committee have direct legal responsibilities to research participants.[117] Though there has yet to be an English case in which an ethics committee or committee member is held liable for acts or omissions in their ethics committee proceedings, now that committee members have detailed guidance on good practice, this possibility should not be discounted. The court would consider whether the committee acted negligently in approving a hazardous trial and failed in its duty to safeguard the interests of patients and volunteers. The claimant's problems lie in proof of negligence, just as any other patient-claimant's do.[118] And they are more acute: if proving negligence in the operation of standard procedures is difficult, how much more difficult is it to prove negligence in embarking on novel procedures?

No-fault compensation

16.15 Is the present law adequate as a means to provide compensation for injury suffered as a participant of medical research? Over 30 years ago the Pearson Commission[119] recommended that:

> Any volunteer for medical research or clinical trials who suffers severe damage as a result should have a cause of action, on the basis of strict liability, against the authority to whom he has consented to make himself available.[120]

Recent reforms in the NHS Redress Act 2006 create a tort-based scheme for low value claims within the NHS (see Chapter 9). The Act is unlikely to have any effect on compensation for research participants. To date, the Department of Health and the pharmaceutical industry have operated *ex gratia* compensation schemes. The injured participant's legal rights remain, in general, dependent on the vagaries of the law of negligence. When a research participant suffers injury in a drug trial he may, of course, gain some slight advantage from the regime of strict liability imposed on drug companies by the

---

[116] *R v Ethical Committee of St Mary's Hospital (Manchester), ex p H* [1988] 1 FLR 512.

[117] On the liability of ethics committees, see M Brazier, 'Liability of Ethics Committees' (1990) 6 *Professional Negligence* 186 and E Pickworth and M Brazier, 'Fees and Research Ethics Committees' (1999) 151 *Bulletin of Medical Ethics* 18.

[118] See Chapter 8 on the problems of litigation.

[119] See above, Chapter 9.

[120] Royal Commission on Civil Liability and Compensation for Personal Injury (1978) Cmnd 7054, paras 1340–1341.

Consumer Protection Act 1987. He still has to prove that his injury resulted from a defect in the drug, and that it was that defect which caused his injury. If the drug company chooses to dispute liability, once again the matter is clumsily resolved by adversarial proceedings.[121] An individual, volunteer or patient, who agrees to subject himself to risk in the cause of medical science and the better health of the community deserves better than this.

Extra-legally, drug companies in the UK recognise the research participant's moral right to compensation independent of proof of fault. The Association of British Pharmaceutical Companies (ABPI) operates an *ex gratia* scheme whereby any healthy volunteer in a drug trial mounted by an ABPI member will receive compensation for any injury arising from that trial. However, many drug trials relate to drugs manufactured by foreign companies. Such companies may not be ready to accept the ABPI guidelines. Department of Health guidance provides that ethics committees should be adequately reassured about 'whether there is provision in proportion to the risk for compensation/treatment in the case of injury/disability/death of a research participant attributable to participation in the research; the insurance and indemnity arrangements.'[122] Further, the Royal College of Physicians[123] advises research ethics committees that they should require from such companies a written agreement to provide for research participants 'at the least the same protection' as that offered by the ABPI. Such advice raises the interesting question whether a failure by a research ethics committee to obtain such assurances to safeguard research participants might constitute negligence on the part of the committee.

Patients agreeing to participate in research, and volunteers involved in non-drug trials, remain outside this informal no-fault provision. And the *ex gratia* nature of the ABPI scheme means that compensation remains dependent on the drug companies' generosity and is in no sense a right enjoyed by research participants.

The case for no-fault compensation of persons injured in the course of research has long received wide support among doctors.[124] The burden of compensating those injured in the course of research to benefit us all should have a wide base. A fund could be financed from all bodies promoting research, from the profession, the pharmaceutical industry and the Department of Health. The prospects for introduction of a scheme to compensate medical research victims along these lines may be brighter than prospects for a general no-fault scheme for all victims of medical accidents. Practical problems of definition, administration and finance will be faced, but with a will most difficulties could be overcome. A scheme limited to injury suffered as a research participant will confront one very real problem. Exactly who would be entitled to benefit under the scheme? Would eligibility be confined to healthy volunteers, such as those in the Northwick Park hospital disaster? The

---

[121] For the problems of establishing strict liability under the 1987 Act, see Chapter 10.
[122] COREC, *Governance Arrangements for NHS Research Ethics Committees*, para 9.15(l).
[123] Royal College of Physicians of London, *Research Involving Patients* (1991).
[124] See JM Barton, MS Macmillan and L Sawyer, 'The Compensation of Patients Injured in Clinical Trials' (1995) 21 *Journal of Medical Ethics* 166.

moral case for automatic compensation for that group is overwhelming. Volunteers put their health on the line with no hope of personal benefit. But what of patients used as participants in research into conditions unrelated to their illness? Should eligibility depend on the lack of any conferral of benefits from the research? Or should it extend to all research participants? If it did, the problem of deciding eligibility moves to determining when a patient suffers injury as a result of a research enterprise, as opposed to in the course of general health care which may include resorting to some novel procedure. These potential problems are not insuperable. They illustrate perhaps that a general scheme of compensation embracing all victims of medical mishap is to be preferred.

A second problem occurs where the threat of litigation is removed without the introduction of stringent measures to ensure accountability. In New Zealand in 1988, a public inquiry revealed a horrific tale.[125] An individual gynaecologist was convinced that orthodox opinion on cervical smear tests was wrong. A positive smear, he believed, was not a precursor of cervical cancer. No action should be taken until an actual malignancy was apparent. He recruited thousands of women into his trial using manifestly inadequate consent procedures. Many, many women suffered dreadfully when cancer did develop and by that stage of the disease they had to undergo painful invasive surgery. For years no other doctor dared speak out and challenge the investigator. New Zealand operates a no-fault system of compensation. The cervical smear trial started before that system was introduced. It will never be possible to know whether the knowledge that no patient could sue for their injuries either reinforced the investigator in his blind faith in his misguided theory or deterred his colleagues from taking action earlier, even if only out of self-protection. Recourse to court is a clumsy weapon, but it must not be taken from the research participant without affording him other safeguards. Litigation may provoke distrust, leading to public demand for all-embracing and stringent statutory controls on research. Abolishing legal liability in clinical research may provoke a scandal that will have the same effect unless existing controls are seen to operate effectively.

Research misconduct

16.16 Monitoring guards against research misconduct, which has been the subject of public outcry in recent years.[126] Career promotions are dependent on research publications and competition is fierce. In 1995, a high-ranking obstetrician and gynaecologist made headline news when it was discovered that he had forged a number of papers.[127] Two years later a former secretary of the Royal College of Physicians in Edinburgh was struck off the medical

---

[125] *Commission of Inquiry into the Treatment of Cervical Cancer and Other Related Matters at National Women's Hospital* (New Zealand, 1988), chaired by Judge Sylvia Cartwright.

[126] See M Farthing, R Horton, R Smith, 'Research Misconduct: Britain's Failure to Act' (2000) 321 *British Medical Journal* 1485.

[127] S Lock, 'Lessons from the Pearce affair: Handling Scientific Fraud' (1995) 310 *British Medical Journal* 1547.

register for research misconduct.[128] In 2002, a GP falsified research data.[129] Professional groups are subject to disciplinary action by the relevant regulatory bodies, such as the General Medical Council and the Nursing and Midwifery Council. In addition, an NHS Counter Fraud and Security Management Service operates to combat fraud in the NHS. Fraud, however, is only one species of research misconduct. The Committee on Publication Ethics[130] promulgates guidelines and a code of conduct for journals but not all misconduct comes to the attention of journal editors. A panel for Research Integrity in Health and Biomedical Sciences was set up in 2006, but its role is promotional and advisory. Investigations of research misconduct remain in the hands of employers or sponsors. Overall there remains a substantial imbalance between the monitoring of clinical trials and the monitoring of other research. Participants deserve the reassurance of a much more comprehensive monitoring system.

Confidentiality and medical research[131]

16.17 The Data Protection Act 1998 (implementing European Directive (EC) 95/46 on the Processing of Personal Data into UK law) came into effect in March 2000. An Information Commissioner registers the names of data controllers and a description of the processing of data by each. Medical researchers are among those who must in most cases register with the Commissioner. In addition to registration, researchers must also comply with the complex provisions of the 1998 Act, which demand special conditions be attached to the processing of 'sensitive data' (including all personal health data). The 1998 Act requires that explicit consent be obtained before personal health data is processed, but an exception is made in the case of medical research. However, the Act demands that 'personal data shall be processed fairly and lawfully'. This arguably places a duty on the researcher to apply the principles enshrined in the common law duty of confidentiality. Arguably, it goes further still.

The common law duty of confidentiality, which applies independently of the Data Protection Act 1998, is equally open to misinterpretation in relation to medical research. To advance the development of medicine and to enable research when completed to benefit other patients, the results of research must be published. Does publication of research findings amount to a breach of confidence to the patient? First, the patient, if he has given full and free consent to his participation in a trial, may at the same time agree to personal information being disclosed once the trial is completed and a report is prepared. This must be the preferable course of action. Whether in law disclosure in the course of a research project of confidential information about a patient without his consent amounts to an actionable breach of confidence

---

[128] C Dyer, 'Consultant Struck Off Over Research Fraud' (1997) 315 *British Medical Journal* 205.

[129] C Dyer, 'GP who Falsified Research Data Found Guilty of Professional Misconduct' (2001) 323 *British Medical Journal* 1388.

[130] See http://www.publicationethics.org.uk/.

[131] The common law duty of confidentiality and the Data Protection Act 1998 are explored in more detail in Chapter 4.

depends yet again on the nebulous test of whether that disclosure can be justified by the public interest in the advancement of the relevant research.

The General Medical Council[132] requires that, where practicable, researchers seek consent and anonymise data, and always keep disclosures to a minimum. It provides special requirements for researchers dealing with medical records and advises on the reporting of research data. Prior to 1999 it was generally assumed that it was not necessary to obtain the participant's consent to release data, provided that data was fully anonymised. In such a case neither the researcher nor any other individual can trace the data to a given research participant. The Data Protection Act 1998 does not apply when data is fully anonymised because the data is not considered 'personal'. The matter was put to the test in *R v Department of Health, ex p Source Informatics Ltd*,[133] which involved pharmacists who sold fully anonymised data to industry. Latham J held at first instance that such disclosure might breach confidentiality on the basis that consent could not be implied because the data was used for commercial purposes and was therefore not in the public interest. However, researchers breathed a sigh of relief when the decision was overturned in the Court of Appeal, where it was held that confidence would not be breached where the confider's identity was not disclosed.

What is clear is that disclosure should be limited to information strictly necessary to the project and that the anonymity of the patient must be protected. The NHS Ombudsman upheld a complaint from a young man who discovered in a medical textbook a full-frontal picture of his naked body. There are various means of achieving 'anonymity' – a much abused term. Full anonymisation offers greatest protection to research participants' confidentiality; however the research cannot then be linked to either the individual's past medical history or his future treatment. In most research projects a system of data coding is preferred. The codes can be broken in the event of adverse reaction and results can be linked to the individual's past medical history. Some researchers regard coded data as anonymised, but in fact the data is 'personal', the Data Protection Act 1998 applies and the common law duty of confidentiality will be breached if consent (be it express or implied) is not obtained before results are published.[134]

There is one limited exception to this rule. As we saw in Chapter 4, the controversial section 60 of the Health and Social Care Act 2001 (now section 251 of the National Health Service Act 2006) enables the Secretary of State to support the use of confidential patient information to improve the patient's medical care or in the public interest without the patient's consent provided there is no reasonably practicable alternative. Consequently, where it can be demonstrated that research is in the public interest, that anonymised patient data will not suffice and that it is impracticable to seek consent, an

---

132 General Medical Council, *Research: The Role and Responsibilities of Doctors* (2002). See also General Medical Council, *Good Medical Practice* (2006).
133 [1999] 4 All ER 185; [2000] 1 All ER 786, CA.
134 See J Strobl, E Cave, T Walley, 'Data Protection Legislation: Interpretation and Barriers to Research' (2000) 321 *British Medical Journal* 890.

application may be made under section 60 for approval of the research.[135] However, the research must still comply with data protection legislation.

Genetic privacy[136]

16.18 Genetic research generates significant public concern.[137] Some deem genetic research 'unnatural' or unethical. Others worry about the implications for their right to privacy under Article 8 of the European Convention on Human Rights.

As we saw in Chapter 4, Article 8 is transforming the law of confidentiality. Tighter controls on medical data were ushered in by the Data Protection Act 1998. It is getting harder for researchers to access the data they desire. They are required to protect the identity of participants and to prove that any non-consensual use of confidential data is in the public interest. In Iceland, much controversy was generated by the introduction of a national genetics database. Citizens' consent was implied unless they opted out.[138] The UK Biobank project[139] has also proved controversial. It is funded by the Department of Health, Scottish Executive, Medical Research Council and Wellcome Trust and aims to collect both data and samples on the health of 500,000 volunteers and analyse it over a period of 30 years. Consent of participants will be sought, but because it is not possible to predict all future research uses, the consent will be general rather than specific.[140]

In Chapter 19, we examine the law relating to the human body and its parts and the effects of the Human Tissue Act 2004. The doctrine of consent is central to this legislation. An exception exists for health-related research on living people where the tissue is unidentifiable and the project has received ethical approval[141] in accordance with the Human Tissue Act 2004 (Ethical Approval, Exceptions from Licensing and Supply of Information about Transplants) Regulations 2006. The REC must consider how tissue is to be disposed of and the means by which relatives are informed of results. Another exception exists by virtue of section 7(4) of the 2004 Act, which confers on the Secretary of State a power to deem consent to be in place, though it is envisaged that this will only be used where there is an overwhelming public interest in doing so.

The Genetic Interest Group[142] is concerned that insufficient weight is attached to the public interest in research. Concession to research in the

---

135 See Medical Research Council, *Personal Information in Medical Research* (2000, updated in 2003).

136 See G Laurie, *Genetic Privacy: A Challenge to Medico-Legal Norms* (2002) CUP.

137 Medical Research Council, *Public Perceptions of the Collection of Human Biological Samples* (2000).

138 Act on a Health Sector Database No 139/1998. See *Mason and McCall Smith's Law and Medical Ethics*, p 227.

139 See www.ukbiobank.ac.uk

140 See *UK Biobank Ethics Governance Framework* (2006, version 2), para B1.

141 By an authorised research ethics committee: see the Human Tissue Act 2004 (Ethical Approval, Exceptions from Licensing and Supply of Information about Transplants) Regulations 2006, SI 2006/1260, reg 2.

142 Genetics Interest Group, *Human Rights, Privacy and Medical Research* (2006), p 3.

Human Tissue Act 2004, it claims, is 'piecemeal, diffident and on occasion, virtually secret'. Could we be heading for a policy of 'ask or anonymise' that applies to both human tissue and data? Might the public interest threshold be set so high as to inhibit valuable research? It is unlikely. As we demonstrated in Chapter 4, the right to privacy under Article 8(1) of the European Convention on Human Rights is not absolute. It can be limited under Article 8(2),

> ... in the interests of national security, public safety or the economic well-being of the country, for the prevention of disorder or crime, for the protection of health or morals, or for the protection of the rights and freedoms of others.

Though there has been little case law on Article 8(2) in the context of medical confidentiality, the House of Lords in *R (S) v Chief Constable of South Yorkshire Police*[143] indicates how readily the judiciary will put the public interest before that of the individual. It was held that the retention and use of DNA and fingerprints by the police, after a suspect had been cleared of the offence, did not offend Article 8. Four of the Law Lords held that Article 8(1) was not invoked. Baroness Hale held that though there was an interference with privacy within the meaning of Article 8(1), it was justified as proportionate under Article 8(2). The information would not be made public and individuals were not identifiable to the 'untutored eye'. The retention of the samples to be used as comparators was appropriate.

The Government will not shackle researchers. Research is lucrative. Let us not forget that it also advances medicine and saves lives. In England and Wales, regulation and review of research is going through a period of unprecedented change. Efforts to facilitate good research have been matched by significant improvements in the level of participant safety. Provided this equilibrium is maintained (and midway through the reforms, this cannot yet be assumed), the changes are to be celebrated. On the other hand, implementation of the Clinical Trials Directive has resulted in a complex and frequently inconsistent system of ethical review. Whilst this is to be lamented, the quality and dedication of the much-maligned ethics committee members, and the vital importance of their role, must not be under-estimated.

[143] [2004] UKHL 39.

Chapter 17

DEFINING DEATH

17.1 The single certainty in human life is that we shall all die. Death cannot be evaded, though it may be delayed. Fifty years ago there would have been little debate about how to define death. None the less there is ample evidence that our ancestors feared that their physicians and their families might mistakenly anticipate their demise and one might find oneself buried alive.[1] Today, as we shall see, medical technology has created real questions about just how we identify the threshold between dying but alive, and death itself. The development of transplantation undoubtedly played a major role in prompting doctors to rethink definitions of death. It would be wrong to conclude that a desire to maximise the number of viable organs suitable for transplant is the only, or the most, important factor in the imperative need to define the moment of death. The question is far from straightforward and a legal definition of death is required for several purposes:

Defining death[2]

17.2 Defining death is difficult because, biologically, death is a process and not an event. Different organs and systems supporting the continuation of life cease to function successively, and at different times. The need to determine an exact or, at best, approximate time of death is important for many reasons. The law often requires such a finding.[3] Establishing the date of death may be important for property purposes. Until death is established, steps cannot be taken to obtain probate or letters of administration to that person's estate, and the interest of a beneficiary under a will is usually dependent upon the beneficiary surviving the testator. In some cases, when the testator and the beneficiary die at around the same time, it is important to know when each

---

[1] See J Bondeson, *Buried Alive: The Terrifying History of our Most Primal Fear* (2001) Norton.

[2] For an excellent analysis of all the medical and ethical conundrums surrounding a definition of death, see JK Mason and GT Laurie, *Mason and McCall Smith's Law and Medical Ethics* (7th edn, 2006) OUP, pp 464–476.

[3] The old common law 'year and a day' rule, which required that if a person was charged with murder his victim must have died within a year and a day of the unlawful act, was abolished by the Law Reform (Year and a Day Rule) Act 1996.

death took place. When two relatives die in a common accident, there may be a presumption that the elder died before the younger, unless evidence can be established as to the precise time of death of either; and the property consequences of this decision are significant.[4] There may also be tax factors. If a person gives away property before his death, that property may be free from inheritance tax, or be subject to less tax, only if he survives the gift for a specified period. There have been many stories written involving relatives of such donors going to great lengths to postpone or conceal the 'true moment' of death so that the donor 'survives' beyond the relevant statutory period for tax purposes. Another possibility may be that the spouse of a person who is either dead or dying may wish to remarry and, in the absence of clear evidence as to whether death has occurred, there may be a risk of bigamy. If the victim has a claim for damages for injuries sustained, the amount of damages will differ substantially between cases where the victim is comatose yet living, or dead.[5] And, self-evidently, doctors cannot remove organs for transplant under the rules governing cadaver donations unless the donor is in fact dead.

Determining whether a person was dead, once posed little difficulty. Historically, the key factors in the process used to determine whether death had occurred were the cessation of breathing and the cessation of heartbeat. Thus, the irreversible cessation of heartbeat and respiration implied death of a patient *as a whole*, although that did not necessarily imply the immediate death of every cell in the body. Doctors accepted and used traditional methods of establishing death. When someone's heart stopped beating and he stopped breathing, he was dead. Advances in medicine gradually demonstrated that this was not a valid test for all purposes: take, for example, elective cardiac arrest during open-heart surgery or cases of spontaneous cardiac arrest followed by successful resuscitation. The heart stops but the patient is not dead. Machines such as mechanical ventilators or respirators have effected major improvements in techniques of resuscitation and life-support for those who are desperately ill or injured. Where these efforts are successful and the patients recover, one may praise the advances in medical techniques. Sometimes such measures do not provide any satisfactory outcome, for example where the person's heart continues to beat on the machine long after breathing has stopped and his brain is irreversibly damaged. In such circumstances, keeping a body 'alive' on a machine can be as undesirable as it is pointless. It is distressing to relatives. It can have an adverse effect on nursing staff morale; the cost of maintaining the patient in such intensive care is high, and the use of machines in these cases can mean that they may be denied patients who are better able to benefit from them. Developments in life-support made rethinking death inevitable.

None the less, the principal trigger to rethinking our definition of death was the development of transplantation, which highlighted the need for speed in diagnosing death and removing organs from the body. Thus, pressures developed to consider a redefinition of death based upon a new concept of 'irreversible brain damage' or 'brain death'. This concept can be illustrated dramatically by considering a guillotine victim. Nobody would consider the

---

4   See the Law of Property Act 1925, s 184.
5   See *Lim Poh Choo v Camden and Islington Area Health Authority* [1980] AC 174.

body, after the head has been severed, to represent an individual living being; yet the decapitated body could be resuscitated and the organs kept 'alive' for a considerable period. In most cases, brain death follows the cessation of breathing and heartbeat in the dying process, but occasionally that order of events is reversed. This occurs as a result of severe damage to the brain itself, from perhaps a head injury or a spontaneous intracranial haemorrhage. In such cases, instead of failure of such vital functions as heartbeat and respiration eventually resulting in brain death, brain death results in the cessation of spontaneous respiration (normally followed within minutes by cardiac arrest). If, however, the patient is supported by artificial ventilation, the heartbeat can continue for some days and this will, for a time, enable the function in other organs, such as the liver and kidneys, to be maintained.

This condition of a 'state beyond coma' or 'irreversible coma' or 'brain death' was first advanced as a new criterion of death in 1968 in an influential report of an *ad hoc* Committee of the Harvard Medical School.[6] In such cases (it was said) a doctor could pronounce as dead a 'comatose' individual who had no discernible central nervous system activity, and then the ventilator could be switched off. The Harvard doctors stated that judgement of the existence of the various criteria of death was solely a medical issue. Using words such as 'coma' or 'comatose' was unhelpful and raised suspicion that concepts of death were being manipulated to make it easier to declare a patient 'dead'.[7]

Public opinion was unwilling to surrender control of such matters lightly to the medical profession. Unease was expressed about the relationship between attempts to redefine death and the needs of transplant surgeons to ensure that organs taken from a deceased person should be taken as soon as possible after death. In 1975, the British Transplantation Society expressed concern at the poor quality of cadaver kidneys being transplanted, mainly because of delay between the determination of death and the removal of the kidneys from the body. It was also important, for transplantation, that a ventilator should not be switched off permanently, but rather that the body be kept on the machine to preserve the quality of the organs until they were required. Two major fears were voiced. First, was the pressure to redefine death being made simply to enable transplant surgeons to obtain better results? Could it be said, for example, that potential transplant donors might be designated 'dead' at a point of time earlier than if they were not potential donors? Second, was it ethically or legally permissible to remove organs from a donor before the ventilator had been turned off? Because of doubts such as these, the British Transplantation Society recommended that the death of a potential organ donor should be certified by two doctors, neither of whom were a member of the transplant team and, most importantly, that the decision to stop a ventilator should be made quite independently of transplant considerations.

---

[6] 'A Definition of Irreversible Coma' (1968) 205 *Journal of the American Medical Association* 337.
[7] See *Mason and McCall Smith's Law and Medical Ethics*, p 468.

17.2 Defining Death

From the late 1970s the medical establishment in Britain[8] agreed that 'brain death'[9] or, preferably, 'brain stem death' (which is the 'irreversible loss of brain stem function') could be diagnosed with certainty; in these circumstances, the patient is dead whether or not the function of some organs, such as a heartbeat, is still maintained by artificial means.

Some commentators however, continued to reject the notion that 'death' could be equated with 'irreversible loss of brain stem function'.[10] They argued that only the cessation of the heartbeat truly indicated the end of life. Claims were made of 'mistakes'. Were patients who were not 'really' dead being diagnosed as brain-dead? Or were the few reported examples of such mistakes simply cases where the appropriate criteria for determining brain death had not been properly implemented? Was it possible that organs were being taken for transplant before a patient had died? The validity of procedures to establish 'brain death' had never, some argued, been rigorously tested. Short cuts in procedures were too often prompted by pressure from the transplant team anxious to 'get at' organs swiftly.

None the less, official endorsement of 'brain stem death' is to be found in both the Report of the Conference of the Royal Colleges of Medicine,[11] and now the Department of Health's Code of Practice,[12] which defines death as follows:

> Death entails the irreversible loss of those essential characteristics which are necessary to the existence of a living human person. ... [The] definition of death should be regarded as 'irreversible loss of the capacity for consciousness, combined with irreversible loss of the capacity to breathe'. The irreversible cessation of brain stem function (brain stem death) whether induced by intra-cranial events or the result of extra-cranial phenomena, such as hypoxia, will produce this clinical state and therefore brain stem death equates with the death of the individual.

The law

17.3 There is still no statutory definition of death in the UK. There is, however, little doubt that there is now sufficient judicial authority to support a definition of death based on 'brain stem death'. The question first arose where persons accused of murder claimed that it was not they who killed the victim, but the hospital team who disconnected the life-support machine. The courts

---

8   See Conference of Medical Royal Colleges and their Faculties in the UK, 'Diagnosis of Brain Death' [1976] 2 *British Medical Journal* 1187; 'Memorandum on the Diagnosis of Death' [1979] 1 *British Medical Journal* 332; C Pallis and DH Harley, *ABC of Brainstem Death* (2nd edn, 1996) BMJ Books.

9   For an analysis of the confusing terms in debates on 'brain death' see *Mason and McCall Smith's Law and Medical Ethics*, pp 468–469. See also D Price, *Legal and Ethical Aspects of Organ Transplantation* (2000) CUP, Chapter 1.

10 See M Evans, 'A Plea for the Heart' (1990) 3 *Bioethics* 227. Note that in Japan 'brain stem death' has only recently been accepted as a lawful definition of death: see J Wise, 'Japan to Allow Organ Transplants' (1997) 314 *British Medical Journal* 1298.

11 See Conference of Medical Royal Colleges and their Faculties in the UK [1976] 2 *British Medical Journal* 1187.

12 Department of Health, *Code of Practice for Diagnosis of Brain Stem Death* (HSC 1998/035).

did not react favourably, even though they side-stepped the issue as to what, in law, constitutes death. In *R v Malcherek*; *R v Steel*,[13] the Court of Appeal dealt with two such cases. The first defendant had stabbed his wife, who was taken to hospital and put on a life-support machine. When it was found she had irreversible brain damage, the ventilator was disconnected and shortly after that all her bodily functions ceased. The second defendant attacked a girl, causing her multiple skull fractures and severe brain damage. She too was taken to hospital and put on a life-support machine, which was disconnected when the doctors concluded that her brain had ceased to function. The Court of Appeal upheld the trial judges' decisions in each case not to leave the issue of causation to the jury, pointing out rather tartly that it was not the doctors, but the accused, who were on trial. The court took the crucial evidence to be that the original criminal acts by the defendants were continuing, operating and substantial causes of the death of their victims. In the ordinary case where treatment is given *bona fide* by competent and careful medical practitioners, evidence is not admissible to show that the treatment would not have been administered in the same way by other medical practitioners. Without exploring the definition of death, the court was not prepared to allow assailants to shelter behind technical arguments challenging standard medical procedures. Lord Lane CJ did go slightly further, saying:

> ... whatever the strict logic of the matter may be, it is perhaps somewhat bizarre to suggest ... that where a doctor tries his conscientious best to save the life of a patient brought to hospital *in extremis*, skilfully using sophisticated methods, drugs and machinery to do so, but fails in his attempt and therefore discontinues treatment he can be said to have caused the death of the patient.[14]

Re A[15] settles the matter. A two-year-old boy suffered a serious head injury. Doctors struggled to save his life and he was put on a ventilator. His condition deteriorated and tests established that he was, undoubtedly, brain stem dead. His parents vehemently opposed the decision to switch off the ventilator. The hospital sought a declaration that the doctors, in disconnecting the child from the ventilator, did not act unlawfully. Endorsing the definition of brain stem death now encapsulated in the Department of Health Code of Practice, the judge declared that the child was for all purposes legally dead. The House of Lords in *Airedale NHS Trust v Bland*[16] lent further authority to a legal definition of death dependent on proof of 'brain stem death'.

Should there be a statutory definition of death?

17.4 The case for a statutory definition of death is less compelling today than when such arguments were first advanced[17] as the courts have introduced a degree of certainty into the debate. Had there been a statutory definition of death in 1976, a definition based upon the long-standing medical criteria of

---

13   [1981] 2 All ER 422. And see *Finlayson v HM Advocate* 1978 SLT (Notes) 60.
14   [1981] 2 All ER 422 at 429.
15   [1992] 3 Med LR 303; and see *Mail Newspapers plc v Express Newspapers plc* [1987] FSR 90.
16   [1993] 1 All ER 821, HL. See below, Chapter 20.
17   For example, see the 14th Report of the Criminal Law Reform Committee, *Offences Against the Person* (1980) Cmnd 7844.

irreversible cessation of breathing and heartbeat, then the medical redefinition of death to take into account irreversible cessation of brain function would have no legal effect in those cases where there was a difference in time between the two definitions, until the existing definition had itself been changed by statute. As long as the matter is treated as a question of medical fact, changes in medical approach can be accommodated within the law without any requirement for further legislation.

Those in favour of legislation, however, regard the very ease with which, without legislation, definitions of death can, and have, alter as a source of disquiet. Doctors, supported by judges, change the goalposts. Visceral fears that doctors continue to be eager to declare A dead to give B her organs have not gone away.[18] A debate on a statutory definition of death would allow wide public involvement in that debate, and an opportunity for public education. Such a debate could also encompass other difficult issues surrounding defining death. There are those who argue that patients in a persistent vegetative state (PVS), such as Tony Bland,[19] are not dying but dead.[20] The destruction of the cortex and consequent loss of all cognitive function rendered Tony Bland, in that ghastly phrase, a 'human vegetable'. He had irreversibly lost personhood, and those capacities which made him distinctively human. Should we modify the definition of death so that patients in this state are also regarded as dead?[21] Some argue that this is the most sensible and most compassionate way of dealing with these persons. Criteria based on 'brain stem death' would be replaced by a concept of 'cognitive death'. But is this a decision that unelected judges should take by choosing to endorse flexible and developing definitions of death as valid if they accord with medical practice? Would a definition of death based on 'cortical or cognitive death' be comprehensible or acceptable to the public?

Formulating a statutory definition of death is not straightforward. Early attempts provided for alternative definitions: the long-established traditional definition and the new definition. This, it was said, would lead the public to believe that there are two separate phenomena of death, one being primarily for transplantation purposes. The American Uniform Brain Death Act (1978) served as a model for a number of states in the USA. It provides simply that 'for legal and medical purposes, an individual who has sustained irreversible cessation of all functioning of the brain, including the brain stem, is dead. A determination under this section must be made in accordance with reasonable medical standards.' It is difficult to see what this would add to English law, were it to be enacted. Such a statute would simply repeat and reinforce the Code of Practice currently operated voluntarily by the medical profession. Any doctor currently violating the Code by acting on a concept of 'cognitive death' in relation to his patients would have difficulty in justifying his actions in any subsequent legal or disciplinary proceedings. The more flexible means of

---

[18] See JM Appel, 'Defining Death: When Physicians and Family Disagree' (2005) 31 *Journal of Medical Ethics* 641.
[19] *Airedale NHS Trust v Bland* [1993] 2 All ER 821, HL. See below, Chapter 20.
[20] See Price, *Legal and Ethical Aspects of Organ Transplantation*, pp 61–72.
[21] See the arguments discussed in PDG Skegg, *Law, Ethics and Medicine* (1985) Clarendon Press.

regulation by a Code of Practice enable criteria for defining death to be examined and, where necessary, modified without the need to resort to amending legislation. Section 26(2)(d) of the Human Tissue Act 2004 empowers the Human Tissue Authority (HTA) to prepare a Code of Practice in relation to the definition of death, but for the purposes of that Act only. The HTA is well placed to consult widely in relation to its preparation of such a Code. It is regrettable that its Code of Practice would be narrowly focused within the 2004 Act as this could re-enforce fears that a different standard applies where the primary question is removal of organs and tissue from the body.[22]

Open debate about how we define death would allow two other questions to be explored, those relating to anencephalic infants and pregnant women. In anencephalic babies, criteria for 'brain stem death' are unworkable[23] as an anencephalic baby is born lacking a higher brain. He is bound to die, usually in a matter of days and, were his interests alone to be considered, such an infant would not be ventilated. Other babies are born with intact brains, but defective hearts or kidneys. Doctors may want to use organs from the anencephalic baby to save the life of a baby with other defective organs. If they allow the anencephalic baby to die 'normally', simply by ceasing to breathe, his organs will deteriorate so rapidly as to be useless. If the anencephalic baby is to be used as an organ donor, he must be ventilated. That poses a problem in defining *when* he dies. Tests for 'brain stem death' are not applicable to newborn babies, and there is some evidence that, if ventilated, an anencephalic infant's brain stem may remain active, 'alive', for some considerable period of time. If 'brain stem death' is inapplicable to anencephalic babies should we accept that the lack of any higher brain function renders the baby, so to speak, born dead?[24] Or is that confusing active euthanasia with defining death?

One objection, regardless of how we define death in such cases, is that in ventilating an anencephalic baby to retrieve her organs we use her solely as a means to an end. A similar problem surrounds ventilating brain-dead pregnant women.[25] If a pregnant woman suffers head injuries during pregnancy and brain stem death is diagnosed, should her corpse be ventilated to allow the foetus the opportunity to be delivered alive? Who should make such decisions? Where a woman has herself contemplated such a possibility and in an advance directive expressed her wish that her body be sustained so her child can live, the outcome might seem clearer. She has authorised the use of her body for that purpose. But such a use of a dead body is not contemplated in the Human Tissue Act 2004. The temptation for doctors wishing to comply with the 'dead' woman's instructions might be to fall back on earlier definitions of death based on cessation of heartbeat and declare that this

---

[22] See C Machado *et al*, 'A Definition of Human Death Should Not be Related to Organ Transplants' (2003) 29 *Journal of Medical Ethics* 201.

[23] See I Kennedy and A Grubb, *Medical Law: Text and Materials* (3rd edn, 2000) Butterworths, pp 2225–2237.

[24] See the Report of the Working Party of the Medical Royal Colleges, *Organ Transplantation in Neonates* (1988) sanctioning such a course of action.

[25] See *Mason and McCall Smith's Law and Medical Ethics*, pp 474–475. And see D Sperling, *Management of Post Mortem Pregnancy: Legal and Philosophical Aspects* (2000) Ashgate.

woman is thus not dead. What of instructions not to ventilate her 'corpse' from a woman in the later stages of pregnancy when a few further days in the womb might give the foetus a fighting chance of survival? Absent any instruction from the woman herself, does her husband, partner or parent have a right to determine whether or not the foetus survives? Or is this a case where an independent foetal interest can be asserted? Whatever conclusion is arrived at, the notion of 'brain-dead incubators'[26] challenges our understanding of death, and could undermine confidence in established definitions of brain stem death.[27]

The brutal reality may be that, however death is defined, and whether such a definition is enshrined in statute or not, diagnosing death will always be a matter of concern. Few people wish their final moments to be cut short by others. Accepting the death of someone close to you is more than an exercise in logic.

[26] See NS Peart, AV Campbell, AR Manara, 'Maintaining a Pregnancy Following Loss of Capacity' (2000) 8 *Medical Law Review* 275.
[27] *Mason and McCall Smith's Law and Medical Ethics*, p 475.

Chapter 18

ORGAN AND TISSUE TRANSPLANTATION

18.1 This chapter explores legal questions surrounding organ and tissue transplantation. It focuses solely on transplantation. Closely related questions relating to organ retention for the purposes of education and research are dealt with in Chapter 19.

In September 2006, new legislation came into effect in England, Wales and Northern Ireland. The Human Tissue Act 2004[1] is now the primary legislation regulating transplantation in those countries. Its origins owe more to the controversy surrounding revelations about the practice of organ retention than the needs of transplant medicine itself.[2] The Act is, unfortunately, both highly complex and difficult to understand.[3]

Certain sorts of tissue transplantation,[4] such as blood donation and skin grafts, have been routine for years. Tens of thousands of lives have been saved by bone marrow transplants. Despite the number of lives saved, organ donation has had a stormy history. Debates involving clinical, ethical, scientific, financial and resource considerations continue to rage. The 2004 Act has not stilled controversy. Public response to transplantation has often been erratic, influenced by publicity given to dramatic successes and failures. For example, in the early days of heart transplants stories which described transplant surgeons as 'human vultures', and claims of organs allegedly removed from bodies before 'real death' had occurred, contributed to excite concern and hostility. On the other hand, the media can be effective in publicising the benefit of transplantation and creating favourable public awareness about transplant medicine.

---

[1] The Act will not apply in Scotland (save for section 45 prohibiting the taking and analysis of DNA samples without consent). Separate legislation will apply in Scotland: see the Human Tissue (Scotland) Act 2006.

[2] See below at 19.2. As Mason and Laurie rightly say, '... the 2004 Act was born under the wrong star': JK Mason and GT Laurie, *Mason and McCall Smith's Law and Medical Ethics* (7th edn, 2006) OUP, p 493.

[3] For an overview of the Act, see D Price, 'The Human Tissue Act 2004' (2005) 68 *Modern Law Review* 798; M Brazier and S Fovargue, 'A Brief Guide to the Human Tissue Act 2004' (2006) 1 *Clinical Ethics* 26.

[4] On the general legal and ethical questions generated by transplantation, see D Price, *Legal and Ethical Aspects of Organ Transplantation* (2000) CUP.

Scientific developments in transplantation continue to be amazing. The principal problem remains the discrepancy between supply and demand.[5] The number of patients awaiting transplants is rising, and the number of transplants performed is falling. In 2005–06, 8,315 patients were registered as in need of a transplant.[6] The number of kidney transplants performed in 2005–06 was increased by 7 per cent from the previous year; liver transplants fell by 7 per cent; and cardiothoracic (heart/lung) transplants fell by 9 per cent. In 2005–06, 1,783 kidney or kidney and pancreas transplants were performed, but 6,906 patients were on the kidney transplant list.[7] 483 patients died while waiting for a solid organ transplant. Were it not for the increasing success of live donation and the ability to use one single cadaveric donor to perform multiple transplants, these figures would make more depressing reading. Much ink has been spilled exploring strategies to increase the supply of organs for transplant. Increasingly, the advantages of live donation, where that is feasible, are recognised and the number of live donations is rising fast. A market in organs from live 'donors' has powerful advocates, despite the continued ban on organ sales in the Human Tissue Act 2004. In the course of the passage of that Act through Parliament, attempts were made to introduce a system of 'presumed consent' for cadaveric donations. Proponents argued that doctors should be allowed to remove organs from the dead unless the deceased had registered an objection to organ donation. That attempt failed and the central principle of the 2004 Act is that all organ donations, from the living and the dead, must be authorised by an explicit consent. So now attempts to increase the numbers of organs available for transplant focus largely on improving ways of maintaining the quality of organs removed from deceased donors and increasing the use of living donors. The possibility of xenotransplantation, using genetically-modified organs harvested from non-human animals, remains on the agenda but looks less likely to materialise than five years ago.

Before examining the law in more detail, one or two points need to be understood about the mechanics of transplantation. First, the organ must be suitable for transplant – that means it must be healthy. The person from whom the organ is removed must be free of any systemic disease and the organ must retain a reasonable 'shelf life'. Most deaths occur in the elderly. Organs are now taken from an increasingly older range of cadaver donors, but those who die of progressive organ failure, common in the very old, are clearly unsuitable donors. Second, the organ must remain viable – in good condition. Either the transplant must take place a very short time after its removal from the donor, or means must be found to preserve it while it is transported to the potential recipient. Finally, there must be a tissue match between donor and recipient. A live transplant from a close relative is thus an optimal choice. A healthy sibling may be able to provide a matched organ that can be transplanted within minutes of its removal from the donor.

5   See the analysis in B New, M Solomon, R Dingwall, J McHale, *A Question of Give and Take? Improving the Supply of Donor Organs for Transplantation* (1994) Kings Fund Institute. Note, however, that far more people are considered eligible to receive a transplant than used to be the case.
6   See NHS Blood and Transplant, *Transplant Activity in the UK 2005–6*, pp 4–5 (6,698 on the active transplant list and 1,617 on the temporarily suspended transplants lists).
7   NHSBT, *Transplant Activity in the UK 2005–6*, pp 11–14.

The Human Tissue Act 2004: an overview

18.2 The Human Tissue Act 2004 now regulates most of the issues relating to the removal, retention and use of human body parts and tissue.[8] It repeals all previous legislation, including the Human Tissue Act 1961 and the Human Organ Transplants Act 1989.[9] The 2004 Act regulates all aspects of human transplantation, whether the organs (or tissue) are removed from the living or the dead. However, scanning the Act itself, the reader will find surprisingly few direct references to transplantation. The Act sets out rules for twelve scheduled purposes involving the use of human organs and tissue. Transplantation is just one of the twelve.[10] For the most part, the broad rules which the 2004 Act imposes apply generally to transplantation. Only a few sections of the Act apply exclusively to transplants. The Act itself offers no more than a framework to regulate transplantation. The details are supplied by Regulations to be made by the Department of Health, and Codes of Practice promulgated by the Human Tissue Authority (HTA).

The HTA is central to the 2004 Act.[11] The HTA is established to regulate all matters concerning the removal, storage, use and disposal of human tissue (except for gametes and embryos).[12] We shall see that the Authority has a number of special responsibilities in relation to transplants. The HTA must have a majority of lay members. Its remit is principally to regulate transplantation. Another authority, the NHS Blood and Transplant (NHSBT), is charged with operational matters relating to transplantation, and required to encourage donation and ensure the quality of the transplant service. The HTA will however also play a role in working to increase the number of organs made available for transplant. So, on 26 April 2006, the HTA promulgated a new policy designed to increase the numbers of living donors by allowing new kinds of altruistic donation.[13] However, the HTA will not have a long life. A Government White Paper proposes that the Human Tissue Authority and the Human Fertilisation and Embryology Authority should be merged to form a new Regulatory Authority for Tissue and Embryology (RATE).[14]

The Human Tissue Act 2004 'policed' by the HTA rests on a number of central tenets. Explicit consent to most forms of the use of organs and tissue is

---

[8] Section 53 of the 2004 Act adopts the term 'relevant material' and defines such material as '... material other than gametes, which consists of or includes human cells'. Embryos outside the human body, hair and nail clippings are expressly excluded from the Act. This very broad definition covers more than organs (such as kidneys) and tissue (such as bone marrow), but does not mean that every section of the Act applies to every speck of 'human material': see Price (2005) 68 *Modern Law Review* 798 at 800.

[9] The Human Tissue Act 2004 also repeals the Human Tissue Act (Northern Ireland) 1962, the Corneal Tissue Act 1986 and the Anatomy Act 1984.

[10] See Schedule 1, Part 1(7).

[11] See sections 13–15 and Schedule 2. Note that although different legislation applies in Scotland (the Human Tissue (Scotland) Act 2006), the HTA will perform various roles in Scotland.

[12] Already regulated by the Human Fertilisation and Embryology Authority: see above at Chapter 13.

[13] HTA, *Press Release* (26 April 2006).

[14] *Review of the Human Fertilisation and Embryology Act: Proposals for Revised Legislation (Including the Establishment of the Regulatory Authority for Tissue and Embryos* (2006) Cm 6989.

required. Criminal penalties attach to certain breaches of the Act. A number of activities relating to the removal and use of tissue, and the conduct of *post-mortem* examinations have to be licensed. Transplants do not require a licence, but certain kinds of transplant activities will require special approval from the HTA. Transplantation will be more closely regulated than used to be the case.

Live donor transplantation

18.3   For one person to subject himself to an unnecessary procedure for the benefit of another requires courage and altruism. A distinction must be made between donation of regenerative and non-regenerative organs. The blood donor undergoes temporary discomfort. His body replaces the blood he has lost. Blood and bone marrow are regenerative tissue. Some non-regenerative organs, such as the heart, are impossible for a living donor to donate in normal circumstances. However, what are possible are domino transplants, involving 'swaps' of heart and lungs. For example, a cystic fibrosis patient may need a heart and lung transplant. She receives a heart and lung from a cadaver organ. Her own healthy heart can, if she consents, be transplanted into another patient.[15]

The most common non-regenerative organ donated by a living person remains the kidney. 590 live kidney donations were performed in 2005–06 (over a quarter of all kidney transplants in that period), an increase of 24 per cent on the year before.[16] Techniques allowing transplants of lobes of the lung and sections of liver will increase the utility of live donations.[17] Nine living donor liver section transplants were performed in 2005–06.[18] The donor agrees to major surgery and accepts a significant risk to his own health. The law needs to be designed to ensure that such a donation is informed, truly voluntary, and not the result of coercion. And the British tradition has been that the donation of body products should be just that – a gift, not a sale. No part of a person's body should be treated as a commodity subject to the pressures of the market.[19] Section 32 of the Human Tissue Act 2004 continues the prohibition on sale of organs (or other bodily material) for transplantation, a ban initially imposed by the Human Organ Transplants Act 1989.[20] Markets remain illegal in the UK. Whether this should be so, we discuss later.

---

[15]   See Human Tissue Authority, *Code of Practice: Donation of Organs, Tissue and Cells for Transplantation* Code 2 (2006), paras 103–104.

[16]   See NHSBT, *Transplant Activity in the UK 2005–6*, p 17.

[17]   See Price, *Legal and Ethical Aspects of Organ Transplantation*, pp 217–225.

[18]   See NHSBT, *Transplant Activity in the UK 2005–6*, p 32.

[19]   See RM Titmuss, *The Gift Relationship: From Human Blood to Social Policy* (1971) Allen & Unwin.

[20]   This Act was rushed through Parliament as a hasty response to a scandal involving the sale of human kidneys by four impoverished Turkish citizens in circumstances where it seemed highly likely that the 'vendors' were cruelly exploited.

Adult donors

18.4 Difficult though it is to believe, in the early days of transplantation, doubts were cast about whether it was lawful for a person to agree to donate a solid organ, such as a kidney, to another during his lifetime. As we have seen, inflicting actual bodily harm on another person can constitute a crime regardless of consent.[21] By 1995, the Law Commission[22] could say with confidence that '... once a valid consent has been forthcoming, English law now treats as lawful donation of regenerative tissue and also non-regenerative tissue not essential to life'. The Human Tissue Act 2004 provides a statutory basis for live donation of organs and tissue for transplantation.

Sections 1 and 3 of the 2004 Act provide in effect that it is lawful to remove organs from a living adult for transplant with, but only with, his *appropriate* consent. The law empowers a person to choose to give a kidney, a lobe of her lung or section of liver to another in need of a transplant. But what is an appropriate consent? Living donors are often closely related to the potential recipient. The potential donor may be the only person whose compatibility is such that a relative's life can be saved.[23] In such circumstances, the psychological pressure can be enormous. It becomes crucially important to establish that the donor did give a genuinely free and informed consent. The Act itself does not define what appropriate means. That task is left to the HTA, which has set out guidance on consent in two key Codes of Practice.[24] Both Codes emphasise the need for good communication. The potential donor must be given information about what will be done and the risks to her. She must be given reliable information about the chances of success. She must be warned about some of the risks of tissue typing. Tests might reveal that apparent siblings are not full siblings. A donor could discover that her supposed father is not, after all, her biological parent. Donors should be offered counselling, given time to make a decision and re-assured that they are free to withdraw consent at any time up to the operation.

Nor is the donor's consent alone sufficient to make a live organ donation lawful. Under the Human Organ Transplants Act 1989, where the donor and recipient were not closely genetically related, it was a criminal offence to remove an organ for transplant without the authorisation of the Unrelated Live Transplant Authority (ULTRA). This rule was primarily designed to prevent covert sales of organs. The 1989 Act banned such sales, but the legislators suspected that organ vendors and purchasers might seek to bypass the ban. ULTRA had the task of ensuring that all apparently altruistic donations between strangers were truly altruistic. The law would be enforced, and potential donors could be protected from coercion or exploitation.

---

[21] See *R v Brown* [1993] 2 All ER 75, HL.
[22] Law Commission Consultation Paper No 139, *Consent in the Criminal Law* (1995) HMSO, para 8.32.
[23] In one American case a court, not surprisingly, refused to *order* the only possible donor to submit to a bone marrow transplant: *McFall v Shimp* (1978) 10 Pa D & C 3d.
[24] See Human Tissue Authority, *Code of Practice: Donation of Organs, Tissue and Cells for Transplantation* Code 2 (2006) and Human Tissue Authority, *Code of Practice: Consent* Code 1 (2006).

Section 33 of the Human Tissue Act 2004 extends the powers of the new HTA to oversee all live donations. The HTA must be satisfied that no money has changed hands and that other conditions prescribed by Regulations are met.[25] All potential donations, whether by a stranger, a friend or a family member, will be scrutinised. Is this right? The need to ensure a tissue match between donors and recipients means doctors will normally prefer a living donor closely related to the potential recipient. Close genetic relationships maximise the chances of a successful transplant. It might be argued that if we (as adults) choose to give a kidney or a section of liver to a dying sibling, this is nobody else's business. Within the family, emotional pressure may be as potent a threat to our freewill as poverty could be were sales of organs allowed. Questions must also be asked about donors' understanding of risk. The risk to a donor giving a kidney is small. The donor of a liver section faces a 1:200 risk of death.

The Regulations made under section 33 of the 2004 Act need to be read together with the HTA Code of Practice *Donation of Organs, Tissue and Cells for Transplantation*.[26] Doctors responsible for any potential live donor of a solid organ, part of an organ or bone marrow must refer the case to the HTA. The HTA must satisfy itself that the organ or bone marrow is not being sold. All live donations must be scrutinised to ensure a genuinely free consent has been given by the donor. The HTA will appoint independent assessors who will interview potential donors and recipients, satisfy themselves that the conditions set out by the HTA are fully met, and report to the HTA. The assessors will be specially trained and senior doctors. The Regulations and the Code of Practice distinguish between different kinds of live donation. When the donor and the recipient are genetically related or known to each other, what the HTA describes as 'genetically or emotionally related organ dona-tion', the assessor simply reports to the HTA and, on the basis of his approval, the donation may lawfully go ahead.

Three other sorts of live donation involving competent adults are identified, and more closely regulated. The first two involve an 'exchange' of donated organs.[27]

(1)   In a 'paired donation' a kidney will be removed from Donor A and given to someone who is a stranger to him. In return, a kidney removed from Donor B will be given to a relative or close friend of Donor A. Assume your husband needs a kidney transplant but you are not a suitable tissue match. If you agree to donate your kidney to B, a relative of B will provide a kidney for your spouse.

(2)   'Pooled donations' involve a linked series of 'paired donations'. For example, Donor A gives a kidney to the son of Donor B. Donor B gives a kidney to the husband of Donor C. Donor C's kidney is given to the wife of Donor A. These 'exchange' donations increase the likelihood of live donations. Should a brother be dying of renal failure and none of his relatives are a tissue match, his family could volunteer to give an

[25]   See the Human Tissue Act 2004 (Persons Who Lack Capacity to Consent and Transplants) Regulations 2006, SI 2006/1659.
[26]   See HTA, *Code of Practice* Code 2.
[27]   See SI 2006/1659, reg 1.12, and paras 94–96 of HTA, *Code of Practice* Code 2.

organ to someone else for whom one of them is a match. And then, in exchange, directly or indirectly, a relative of the recipient will donate an organ to the brother.

In both the above kinds of donation, two assessors must make a report which is then considered by a panel of at least three members of the HTA. The panel will decide whether or not to approve the donation.

(3) Finally there are wholly altruistic donations, where the donor gives an organ with no conditions, and no expectation of any exchange benefiting those close to her.[28] A rigorous procedure is set out to monitor such altruistic donations. The donor must undergo medical, surgical and psychiatric assessments. She must be interviewed by an independent assessor who will make recommendations to an HTA panel of at least three members.

Child donors

18.5 More difficult questions arise where organs or tissue are to be taken from children. Should children ever be used as organ donors?[29] In the USA, the courts sanctioned such a course of action nearly 50 years ago. The cases involved three sets of minor twins aged 19, 14 and 14 respectively. In each case, the healthy twin was willing to donate a kidney to his dying brother, but it was not clear whether the law permitted this. Applications were made to the court for guidance. The court focused on the psychiatric evidence given to show that each donor had been fully informed about the nature of the procedure and also that, if it were not possible to perform the operation and the sick twin were to die, there would be a resulting grave emotional impact of the surviving twin. This enabled the court to be satisfied in each case that the operation was for the benefit not only of the recipient but also of the donor, and that accordingly a parent was capable of giving consent to such a 'therapeutic' procedure, just as he could to any other medical treatment needed by his child.[30]

In England, until the Human Tissue Act 2004, this was a 'grey' area of law. It became routine practice for parents to authorise bone marrow donations (and skin grafts) from a healthy child to a sick sibling.[31] Solid organ donations from one living child to another appear to have been ruled out by the transplant community itself. Bone marrow donations[32] proceeded on the basis that the harvesting of bone marrow involves some discomfort, but minimal risk, for the donor child. The psychological benefit of a sibling's survival or well-being was said to outweigh any distress to the donors. The balance of

---

[28] See HTA, *Code of Practice* Code 2, paras 97–102.

[29] See D Price and A Garwood-Gowers, 'Transplantation from Minors: Are Children Other People's Medicine?' (1995) 1 *Contemporary Issues in Law* 1.

[30] Curran, 'A Problem of Consent: Kidney Transplantation in Minors' (1959) 34 *New York University Law Review* 891.

[31] See Price, *Legal and Ethical Aspects of Organ Transplantation*, pp 359–362.

[32] See now Human Tissue Authority, *Code of Practice: Donation of Allogeneic Bone Marrow and Peripheral Blood Stem Cells for Transplantation* Code 6 (2006).

burdens and benefits made the 'donation' a procedure in the best interests of the child and so an intervention parents could properly authorise. But how does a parent make an impartial evaluation of the interests of one child when the life of another child is at risk?

The Human Tissue Act 2004 clarifies the law. We deal first with children too young to consent on their own behalf. Where it is proposed to use such a child as a living donor, such a donation will require appropriate consent from a person with parental responsibility for the child.[33] That means in most cases consent from one of his parents.[34] It will not be strictly necessary for both parents to consent, even when they share parental responsibility for the child. Doctors may be wary of allowing a child to be used as a donor if his parents disagree. Parental authorisation alone will not suffice to make a donation by a minor lawful, even to a sibling. Just as with adult donors, the donation will need to be scrutinised by the HTA. Regulations made under the 2004 Act require that any proposal to use a child[35] as a solid organ donor must immediately be referred to the HTA for advice, and considered by a panel of three members of the Authority.[36] 'Children should be considered as living organ donors only in extremely rare circumstances'.[37]

What of older children? The younger set of American twins were 14. Even if legally not of an age to give independent consent, at 14 a child can be a party to the decision. Many 14-year-olds would be considered *Gillick competent*[38] in this country if what was in issue was therapeutic treatment.[39] Section 2(2) of the Human Tissue Act 2004 empowers the *Gillick competent* minor to donate organs and tissue. If a minor of 15 or 17 is considered sufficiently mature and intelligent to weigh up the benefits or risks of donating an organ, her consent will authorise the donation. Doctors and the HTA will be anxious to ensure that any such decision is fully understood by the young person and not subject to undue pressure from the family. So, as is the case with younger children, all proposed live donations of organs[40] involving *Gillick competent* minors will be further scrutinised by a panel of three from the HTA. The more mature teenager, not her parents, can decide to offer a kidney to her brother. The HTA will exert a more intense scrutiny of her decision than if she were 18. Should a minor be allowed to donate a kidney? If a beloved twin needed such a transplant, it is not difficult to suggest that the physical risk to a willing donor is outweighed by the emotional benefit.

---

[33] See section 2(3) of the Human Tissue Act 2004.
[34] Where parents are married or register the birth of the child together they automatically share parental responsibility. In other cases, the unmarried father will need either to seek an order granting him such parental responsibility or enter into a formal agreement with the mother: see above at 15.14.
[35] See SI 2006/1659, reg 12(2)(a).
[36] See HTA, *Code of Practice* Code 2, paras 27–36.
[37] HTA, *Code of Practice* Code 2, para 30.
[38] *Gillick v West Norfolk and Wisbech Area Health Authority* [1984] QB 581. See Chapter 15 at 15.18–15.19 for an explanation of *Gillick* competency.
[39] Prior to the Human Tissue Act 2004, it was doubtful whether any minor was legally competent to consent to organ donation: See *Re W (a minor) (medical treatment)* [1992] 4 All ER 627 at 635 and 647.
[40] For regulation of bone marrow donations, see HTA, *Code of Practice* Code 6, paras 45–52.

Mentally-incapacitated 'donors'

18.6 In the USA, in *Strunk v Strunk*[41] a 28-year-old married man who was dying of a fatal kidney disease sought the permission of the court for a kidney donation from his 27-year-old brother, who was said to have a mental age of six and who was detained in a mental institution. The Kentucky court emphasised the emotional and psychological dependence of the mentally-disabled sibling on his brother, and that his well-being would be jeopardised more severely by the loss of his brother than by the removal of a kidney. Accordingly, it applied a doctrine of 'substituted judgment', to allow the court to act as they believed the mentally-disabled brother would have acted had he possessed all his faculties, and gave consent on behalf of the donor. Subsequent cases in the USA[42] stressed that in authorising organ donation on behalf of a mentally-disabled adult the court must be fully satisfied that the interests of the donor will be served by the transplant. The benefits to him of his sibling's, or relative's, survival must be real, not speculative.[43]

Before the Human Tissue Act 2004 came into force, in *Re Y*,[44] Connell J granted a declaration that bone marrow donation from a severely learning-disabled woman of 25 to her 36-year-old sister, who was dying of leukaemia, was lawful. Of the elder sister's relations, only her learning-disabled sister proved to be a compatible donor. She was, it was agreed, incapable of giving consent to the procedure. The relationship between the sisters themselves was not especially close. The older sister's illness had meant that visits had become fewer. The relationship between the younger sister and her mother was close, as was the relationship between mother and her older, sick daughter. The judge found that if the older daughter died, her death would have an adverse impact on the mother. She would be less able to visit Y and much occupied in caring for her grandchild if the child's mother died. If the transplant went ahead the 'positive relationship' between Y and her mother would be enhanced, as would the relationship between the sisters. The risk and discomfort to Y would be minimal. Accordingly, it was in Y's best interests to allow the bone marrow transplant to go ahead. Connell J made it clear that he was not setting a precedent for kidney 'donation' by a learning-disabled person. He said:

> It is doubtful that this case would act as a useful precedent where the surgery involved is more intrusive than in this case ...

Should Connell J have sanctioned a transplant which amounted to enforced donation? The 'benefit' to Y seems somewhat remote on the facts of the case. Regulations[45] made under section 6 of the Human Tissue Act 2004 provide that organs or tissue can be removed from a person lacking mental capacity for transplant if, but only if, such a procedure is in that patient's best interests. Any such proposal would have to be referred to, and scrutinised by, the HTA.

---

[41]   (1969) 35 ALR (3d) 683.

[42]   See generally Price, *Legal and Ethical Aspects of Organ Transplantation*, pp 347–350.

[43]   See *Re Peslinski* 226 NW 2d 180 at 181 (Wisconsin); *Re Richardson* (1973) 284 So 2d 185.

[44]   *Re Y (Mental Incapacity: Bone Marrow Transplant)* [1997] Fam 110.

[45]   See SI 2006/1659, reg 12(3); HTA, *Code of Practice* Code 2, paras 21–26.

Moreover, the HTA has indicated that, prior to any consideration by the Authority, any proposal for such a donation must first receive the approval of a court.[46] It is difficult to see how the discomfort and surgery needed to remove a solid organ could be justified by a supposed emotional benefit. If the proposed donor cannot comprehend what is done to her, the balancing exercise becomes somewhat mythical.

Cadaver transplantation

18.7 Although the number of live donations is rising fast, the majority of organs for transplantation are still taken from people who have died rather than from living donors. As we shall see later[47] a person has no legal right at common law to determine what shall happen to his body after his death. A body, or part of it, cannot ordinarily be the subject matter of ownership, and normally it is the legal duty of the close relatives of a deceased or those who are in 'lawful possession' of the body to arrange for its disposal at the earliest opportunity. So it is not legally possible for a person to impose a duty upon others that she be cremated after death. All she can do is indicate that she desires to be cremated, and her executors or family are free to comply with or ignore such a wish as they see fit. At common law, a person has no legal power to donate organs from his body after his death; equally nobody has any right to interfere with a corpse, and any such interference would be a criminal act.[48] It was feared that cadaver transplantation might be illegal. Legislation was needed.

In 1952, the Corneal Grafting Act, later amended by the Corneal Tissue Act 1986, authorised the removal and use of eyes for therapeutic purposes in some circumstances. This statute attracted little publicity, nor was there much more public interest when, in 1961, the Human Tissue Act widened the law to cover any other parts of the body. Although the 1961 Act served as a model for similar legislation in many other countries, it proved to be unsatisfactory in almost every respect. It was repealed and replaced by the Human Tissue Act 2004.

Before examining the provisions of the 2004 Act in more detail, we need to address the problems with which the Act engages. What should be the basis on which organs can lawfully be removed from a dead body for transplant into another person? How can the law maximise the numbers of organs made available for transplant and ensure that organs can be removed and transplanted in a state likely to be 'fit for purpose'? The philosopher John Harris[49] proposed a radical and simple solution. Organ retrieval from the bodies of the dead should be lawful without any need for either the authorisation of the deceased or any consent from her family. A dead person has no interests

---

[46] HTA, *Code of Practice* Code 2, para 22.

[47] At 19.4.

[48] In *R v Lennox-Wright* [1973] Crim LR 529. An unqualified person removed eyes from a cadaver for further use in another hospital. He was successfully prosecuted for contravening section 1(4) of the Human Tissue Act 1961, which prohibits removal save 'by a fully registered medical practitioner'.

[49] J Harris, 'The Survival Lottery' (1975) 50 *Philosophy* 81.

sufficient to outweigh the needs of a patient whose life depends on a transplant. Organ conscription would replace organ donation. Harris[50] himself recognises that such a radical proposal would be highly unlikely to gain Parliamentary support and so has also endorsed a doctrine of 'presumed consent' as second best.

'Presumed consent', sometimes referred to as 'contracting out', means in effect that the law should allow organs to be removed for transplant unless the deceased had expressly put on record, for example, on a public register, that he had objected to such use. Relatives would lose any right of veto. A Private Member's Bill to introduce such a scheme was unsuccessfully presented to Parliament in March 2002. Such a law, which now exists in a number of European countries, should, in theory, enable surgeons to acquire all the organs they need – unless there happened to be a dramatic change in public attitude so that large numbers of people go to the trouble of registering their objections.

In France, however, the change in the law made little difference in practice.[51] Doctors remained unwilling to remove organs without the consent of the deceased's family. Other jurisdictions,[52] notably Belgium, have seen law reforms introducing 'presumed consent' rules for organ donation result in a significant increase in the number of cadaver organs transplanted. Belgium offers a particularly interesting test case for law reform. Laws implementing 'presumed consent' were implemented in one part of the country, but not universally. The available supply of organs rose sharply in the region where 'presumed consent' prevailed, but not elsewhere. The Belgian model prompted a number of distinguished lawyers, doctors and ethicists to renew the campaign for similar reform of the law in the UK.[53]

Another option would be a system of 'required request'. It is suggested that one of the main reasons for the shortfall in donor organs is the failure by doctors to ask relatives to agree cadaver organ donations. A number of American states[54] have enacted legislation requiring hospital staff to request permission from the deceased's family to remove suitable organs. The most comprehensive analysis of possible systems of organ retrieval was pessimistic about prospects of success. The King's Fund Report[55] suggested it was unlikely to work and might result in undue pressure being placed on families.

The enactment of the Human Tissue Act 2004 has, for now, ruled out reforms based on 'conscription', 'presumed consent' or 'required request'. The controversy generated by revelations that organs had been retained for research,

---

[50] J Harris, 'Law and Regulation of Retained Organs: The Ethical Issues' (2002) 22 *Legal Studies* 527.

[51] See R Redmond-Cooper, 'Transplants Opting-Out or In – the Implications' (1984) 134 *New Law Journal* 648.

[52] See generally Price, *Legal and Ethical Aspects of Organ Transplantation*, pp 83–126.

[53] See Kennedy *et al*, 'The Case for "Presumed Consent" in Organ Donation' (1998) 351 *Lancet* 1650.

[54] See I Kennedy and A Grubb, *Medical Law: Text and Materials* (3rd edn, 2000) Butterworths, pp 1048–1057.

[55] New, Solomon, Dingwall, McHale, *A Question of Give and Take? Improving the Supply of Donor Organs for Transplantation*, pp 60–63.

education and diagnosis without consent created a climate in which new laws even appearing to endorse an element of coercion would not command support. Explicit consent thus becomes the fundamental condition for all cadaver donations as much as donations by living donors. However, whatever the legal rules governing consent to donation, any principled basis for donation must also take account of the practical need for the shortest possible period between removal of an organ and its transplantation into the intended recipient. We noted earlier that a successful transplant requires that the organ to be transplanted remains viable – ie it has not, to put it brutally, begun to decay in the time between removal from the dead donor and implantation in the recipient. When a beating heart donor is used, the donor will usually have been on a ventilator and diagnosed as brain stem dead. Oxygen will have continued to perfuse his organs up to the time that the organs to be transplanted are removed. Suspicions of brain stem death may lead some families to question whether their relative – the donor – is really dead. However, the number of potential donors who are diagnosed as brain stem dead while on a ventilator remains small. One solution suggested some time ago, but not pursued, is elective ventilation.

At present, beating heart donors come from patients whose initial condition resulted in them being placed on a ventilator in the hope that treatment could be instituted to prolong their lives. Elective ventilation would involve patients dying from strokes or similar conditions being transferred to the intensive care unit and ventilated until brain stem death occurs. In this way, their organs are maintained in optimum condition for organ retrieval. Patients would be brain stem dead when organs are removed, but not legally dead when ventilated. Ventilation would be performed *solely* to enable the patient to become a potential organ donor and confer no benefit on him. Is elective ventilation lawful? There is nothing in the Human Tissue Act 2004 expressly authorising elective ventilation. And at the time a decision is made to transfer the patient to intensive care he is unlikely to be able to consent to such a procedure himself. The transfer to benefit the potential organ recipient is unlikely to be judged to be in the donor's interests[56] and might fall foul of section 4 of the Mental Capacity Act 2005.[57]

Should elective ventilation be lawful? The Law Commission's original report on the treatment of adults lacking mental capacity suggests that, with proper safeguards, such a procedure could be ethical and lawful. The Mental Capacity Act 2005 does not expressly implement this proposal. Perhaps two cases should be differentiated. If I choose not just to carry a donor card but to indicate that were I to suffer a stroke or other cerebral incident and recovery of consciousness was impossible, I should be ventilated to maximise my utility as an organ donor, that advance directive is as entitled to respect as any other. If I have expressed no such wish, should I, while still alive, be used as means to other ends even with my family's concurrence? The Mental Capacity Act 2005 gives statutory force to advance refusals of treatment but not alas, in

[56] See JV McHale, 'Elective Ventilation – Pragmatic Solution or Ethical Minefield? (1995) 11 *Professional Negligence* 23; and see *Mason and McCall Smith's Law and Medical Ethics*, pp 501–503.
[57] See above at 6.9–6.10.

this context, advance requests. Could one argue none the less that if we have expressly requested elective ventilation to bolster our wish to be organ donors, then that procedure does, paradoxically, become something done in our best interests?

Another strategy to increase the number of cadaver donations is to use non-beating heart donors.[58] The donors' hearts would have stopped and death would be diagnosed by the traditional cardio-respiratory criteria. Any organs to be used for donation need to be rushed to the recipients as lack of oxygenation will swiftly trigger the start of decay. Cold perfusion of the organ (or the whole body) will extend the time in which organs remain viable. Such a procedure needs to be done as soon as the heart stops beating, at a time when it cannot be ascertained if the deceased had consented to donation and relatives are not at the scene. Section 43 of the Human Tissue Act 2004 allows hospitals, or other relevant authorities, to take whatever steps immediately necessary to preserve parts of the body for transplantation. What is done must be the minimal and least invasive steps possible. It means this. A young man is brought into hospital after suffering inevitably fatal brain injuries in a road accident. His heart stops before his family can be contacted or even his identity ascertained. Doctors may lawfully use cold perfusion to preserve his organs until either it can be shown he had consented in advance to organ donation or his family can be contacted.[59]

The Human Tissue Act 2004

18.8 As we have reiterated, the Human Tissue Act 2004 adopts a principle of explicit consent for cadaver donation; Parliament expressly rejected calls to introduce a system of presumed consent. Removal of organs and tissue after death for the purposes of transplantation is governed by rules identical to those applying to removal for other purposes, such as medical research or education. When the proposed donor died over the age of 18, removal of organs for transplantation will be lawful if:[60]

(1)   the deceased himself gave appropriate consent before he died; *or* if he gave no consent, but nor did he veto organ donation;

(2)   consent is given by the deceased's nominated representative – that is a person expressly nominated by the deceased to make decisions about the use of his body parts before his death; *or* if the deceased neither made his own decision about donation nor nominated a representative;

(3)   consent is given by a close family member or friend – what is described as 'a person who stood in a qualifying relationship with the deceased before his death'.

Let us take each case in turn. When the deceased has made his own decision about donation of organs after his death, the 2004 Act provides that his consent alone is sufficient to authorise the transplant team to take his

---

[58]   In 2005–06, the number of non-beating heart donors rose to 125 – an increase of 44 per cent on the previous year (see NHSBT, *Transplant Activity in the UK*, p 4).

[59]   And see HTA, *Code of Practice* Code 2, paras 75–76.

[60]   Section 3(6).

organs.[61] In theory, the objections of his family carry no weight. But there are two difficulties. First, the 2004 Act prescribes no formalities to govern *post-mortem* donations for transplant.[62] There is no requirement that directions be given in writing. So, extra-legal measures to ensure easy access to information about donors are crucial. The first named author has carried a donor card for decades. It resides in her handbag. Should she be killed in a road accident, the handbag will not necessarily accompany her to the Casualty Unit where she is declared brain stem dead. A 1992 survey showed only 27 per cent of people had donor cards and only one in five carried their card with them at any time.[63] The NHS Organ Donation Register is thus of paramount importance. 13,122,056 potential donors were registered at the end of March 2006.[64] Where donation is a possibility, the first job for staff at the hospital where the potential donor dies is to check the register. When evidence of the deceased's wishes are available, his wishes should not be subject to any family veto. The objections of a grieving widower do not in law override his wife's authorisation. Implementing such a policy in practice will be harder. The HTA urges doctors to discuss this dilemma sensitively with the family. They should be encouraged to accept the deceased's wishes. The HTA's last sentence of advice on this matter is telling: 'There may never the less be cases in which donation is inappropriate and each case should be considered individually'.[65] We hope that this compassionate sentiment will not routinely be allowed to override the gift of life offered by the deceased.

The second means of authorising organ donation is by way of a nominated representative. The Human Tissue Act 2004 requires any such nomination to be in writing and witnessed. It may be asked why one should delegate such a task to someone else.[66] If a person has given the thought to donation required to make a nomination, you might expect her to express her own wishes directly. One reason for nominating a proxy may be a case where the potential donor is aware of divisions in her family about organ donation. The family might belong to a faith where more orthodox adherents rule out organ donation. The deceased may wish to ensure that authority to decide about uses of her body rests with a relative who shares her own views.

In the absence of express authorisation by the deceased or a proxy chosen by her, the power to donate organs falls to the family. The 2004 Act sets out a hierarchy of relatives.[67] Whilst the 1961 Act spoke vaguely of the need to ascertain that no 'surviving relative' objected to the removal of organs for transplant, the 2004 Act requires the consent of a relative (or, exceptionally, a friend) if no directions have been given by the deceased or her chosen proxy.

---

[61] And equally his veto will prohibit any removal of organs for transplant.
[62] Unlike donation for anatomical examination or public display.
[63] New, Solomon, Dingwall, McHale, *A Question of Give and Take? Improving the Supply of Donor Organs for Transplantation.*
[64] See NHSBT, *Transplant Activity in the UK*, p 58. Of 764 deceased donors in 2005–06, only 23 per cent were on the register.
[65] HTA, *Code of Practice* Code 2, para 40.
[66] Section 4.
[67] Section 27(4).

Staff seeking consent should first approach the deceased's spouse or partner.[68] If he or she declines to make a decision, or the deceased had no spouse or partner, those seeking consent then work their way through the following list:[69] (1) parent or child; (2) siblings; (3) grandparent or grandchild; (4) nephews or nieces; (5) step-parents; (6) half-siblings; (7) friend of longstanding. In what will often be the case, where more than one individual falls into any of these categories, the consent of one person alone will suffice to make removal of organs for transplant lawful.[70] Both authors are married, so our cases would be easy; our surviving husbands would decide whether our organs could be used for transplant. Should, alas, those same husbands not survive us, the decision would fall to Margot Brazier's adult daughter, and one of Emma Cave's surviving parents. Authorisation from one parent alone would suffice.

Unlike the Human Tissue Act 1961, section 2 of the 2004 Act expressly addresses cadaver donations from minors. It provides that where a person under 18 has given advance consent to organ donation at a point in her life when she was sufficiently mature and intelligent to make such a decision for herself, her consent authorises cadaver transplantation. The *Gillick competent* minor can determine what happens to her body after her death too. In theory, her parents have no say in the matter. Establishing *Gillick competence* retrospectively will be hard. Overriding grieving parents will be painful. Where a child has expressed no wishes of her own, the decision falls to a person with parental responsibility[71] immediately prior to her death. This will normally be her parents. Again, in theory, the consent of one parent alone will be enough.

Violating the Human Tissue Act 2004

18.9 One of the principal causes of the failure of the Human Tissue Act 1961 was that no provision was made for a criminal penalty or civil redress for breach of the Act.[72] The 2004 Act[73] imposes criminal sanctions for any failure to comply with the Act's rules requiring consent for removal of organs for transplant. Any removal of cadaver organs without appropriate consent is a criminal offence unless the surgeon removing the organs reasonably believes that he acts on the basis of such an appropriate consent. Any false representation that such a consent has been obtained is equally a criminal offence. Both offences carry the possibility of a jail sentence of up to three years.

---

[68] '[A] person is another's partner if the two of them (whether of different sexes or the same sex live as partners in an enduring family relationship': s 54 (8).
[69] See s 27(8).
[70] See s 27(6).
[71] If there is no such person (if, for example, parents and child died together in a road traffic collision), consent must be sought from the nearest qualifying relative – usually a grandparent.
[72] See PDG Skegg, 'Liability for the Unauthorised Removal of Cadavers Transplantation Material' (1974) 14 *Medicine, Science and the Law* 153.
[73] See s 5.

Some practical problems: the coroner

18.10 The kinds of death likely to yield organs for transplant are also the kinds of death likely to involve referral to the coroner. Where there is reason to believe that an inquest may have to be held on a body, or a *post-mortem* examination may be required by the coroner, it will also be necessary to obtain the consent of the coroner to the removal of any part of the body – which may delay the opportunity to remove organs. This may be the case particularly where a coroner regards his duty to act as coroner as being of greater importance than the secondary power which he has to authorise the use of organs before his coroner's duties are complete. In a controversial case in Leicester in 1980, the father of a girl who had died in a road accident had given surgeons permission to use any of her organs, including her heart, which had been removed by surgeons. At a subsequent inquest, the coroner complained that he had not given permission for the heart to be removed since permission had been sought from him only for the removal of a kidney. He therefore directed that in future written permission would have to be obtained from him and countersigned by a pathologist. This incident highlighted the problem that coroners, acting in pursuance of what they regarded as their legal duties, could adversely restrict the use of organs even where parents or other relatives had consented. It was for such reasons that the Home Secretary issued guidance to coroners, stressing that it was not part of a coroner's function to place obstacles in the way of the development of medical science or to take moral or ethical decisions in this matter, and that the coroners should assist rather than hinder the procedure for organ removal. A coroner should refuse his consent only where there might be later criminal proceedings in which the organ might be required as evidence, or if the organ itself might be the cause or partial cause of death, or where its removal might impede further inquiries.[74]

Some practical problems: establishing death

18.11 In Chapter 17, we noted that beating heart donors were not, under traditional definitions of death, strictly 'dead'. The needs of transplant medicine provided the impetus to reformulate that traditional view of death as the irreversible cessation of heartbeat and respiration. The difficulty in persuading the public that 'brain stem death' truly constitutes the death of a person has beset organ transplantation for decades. Fears have been voiced that doctors might have conflicting interests in that, on the one hand, their duty would be to act in the best interests of the ill or dying patient to keep him alive and yet, on the other, there might be pressures to certify a potential donor's death at the earliest possible moment to enable organs to be removed for the benefit of potential recipients.

In 1975, the British Transplantation Society sought to allay public fears by recommending a Code of Practice for Organ Transplantation Surgery (finally

[74]   HC (65) 1977. See also Home Office, *When Sudden Death Occurs: Coroners and Inquests* (2005), p 2, explaining how family can donate their relatives' tissues and organs for transplantation and stipulating that the coroner's consent is required.

agreed in 1979) to provide safeguards for those who needed reassurance about possible abuses of practice by over-zealous transplant teams.[75] Guidance to ensure that adequate steps to confirm a diagnosis of brain stem death are now to be found in the Department of Health Code of Practice[76] on the diagnosis of brain stem death. The Code requires (*inter alia*) that:

(1)   Before organs are removed from a body for transplant, death should be certified by two doctors, one of whom has been qualified for at least five years; neither of these doctors should be members of a transplantation team and at least one of them should be a consultant.

(2)   In cases of irreversible brain stem death, where respiration is dependent on mechanical ventilation, the decision to stop ventilation must have no connection with transplantation considerations. Two sets of tests should be carried out, the interval between the two to depend on clinical judgment.

(3)   Where it has been decided that brain stem death has occurred and mechanical ventilation is to be stopped, the question of organ removal should be discussed fully and sympathetically with available relatives so that their informed consent is obtained for the removal of organs either before or after mechanical ventilation is finally stopped.

A market in organs?

18.12 The thrust of current policy in relation to transplantation is to use public education to encourage voluntary altruistic donations. Whether that strategy will suffice to make up the shortfall in organs needed for transplant remains to be seen. Those who doubt its efficacy attack the tradition that has long held sway in the UK – the tradition that bodily products should be freely given and not traded.[77] Section 33 of the Human Tissue Act 2004 bans payments for live or cadaver organs, although it allows payment of expenses within conditions prescribed by the HTA.[78] The European Convention on Human Rights and Biomedicine[79] states forcefully,

The human body and its parts shall not, as such, give rise to financial gain.

In support of maintaining a prohibition of a market in organs are a cluster of arguments. They centre on four questions:

(1)   Would financial incentives to sell your own, or your deceased relative's organs, risk endangering the safety of organ transplants? In their anxiety to obtain payment might people conceal medical conditions which could endanger the recipient?[80]

---

[75]   For an argument that it should be permissible to remove organs before brain stem death is established, see J Savelescu, 'Death, Us and Our Bodies: Personal Reflections' (2003) 29 *Journal of Medical Ethics* 127.

[76]   HSC 1998/035, *A Code of Practice for the Diagnosis of Brain Stem Death* (1998) Department of Health.

[77]   J Radcliffe-Richards *et al*, 'The Case for Allowing Kidney Sales' (1998) 351 *Lancet* 1950.

[78]   See HTA, *Code of Practice* Code 2, paras 63–68.

[79]   Article 21.

[80]   At the heart of Titmuss's argument in *The Gift Relationship: From Human Blood to Social Policy*.

(2)   Is there a risk that financial pressure on potential vendors is such that they would give a less than voluntary and informed consent. There is evidence from the developing world that economic duress operates to pressure the poor into selling organs to the rich.

(3)   Is it intrinsically wrong that, even if properly informed, poorer people should 'have' to 'earn' part of their living by selling off body parts?

(4)   In sum, do markets degrade?[81]

Those proposing markets do so cautiously. They stress the vulnerability of the person needing the transplant. Her life is at risk. Harris and Erin argue that a regulated market,[82] where the NHS is the only permitted 'purchaser', would ensure (1) the quality of organs 'sold' and (2) rigorously monitor the consent process. Provision would be made to ensure that the vendor was adequately informed and acted freely. Fears of exploitation could be met in a regulated market. As to the distastefulness of the poor becoming organ banks, it is contended that, worldwide, the rich have benefits denied the poor. Mason and Laurie[83] question whether commercialism and altruism are irreconcilable values. They ask why one poor and needy person is allowed to risk his brain in the boxing ring, when another is barred from selling his kidney. They remind us that illegal markets across the world already exploit the poor. Janet Radcliffe-Richards,[84] leading the advocates for markets, sums up the debate:

> The weakness of the familiar arguments suggests that they are attempts to justify the deep feelings of repugnance which are the real driving force of the prohibition, and feelings of repugnance among the rich and healthy, no matter how strongly felt cannot justify removing the only hope of the destitute and dying. This is why we conclude that the issue should be considered again, with scrupulous impartiality.

For the most part, advocates for markets focus on living vendors. But why not allow payments for cadaver organs? The risk of harming the donor's health is nil. 'Donors' might see the promise of an organ for payment as an alternative, or a supplement, to life insurance. Relatives auctioning off Grandma's kidneys might be distasteful, unless your child was dying for want of a kidney. Mason and Laurie[85] find '... payment for organs of the dead far less easy to justify than payment to a living donor'. But they somewhat reluctantly suggest that this may come to pass. The justification for banning payments needs more careful thought. The 'safety' arguments advanced by Titmuss[86] have proved fallible in the context of blood donation.[87] In permitting 'paired' and 'pooled' donations, inducements are sanctioned. The potential 'reward' of a kidney for your relative may be a much more powerful inducement than money.

---

[81] See M Radin, 'Market – Inalienability' (1987) 100 *Harvard Law Review* 1849; N Duxbury, 'Do Markets Degrade?' [1996] 59 *Modern Law Review* 331.

[82] See C Erin and J Harris, 'An Ethical Market in Human Organs' (2003) 29 *Journal of Medical Ethics* 137.

[83] *Mason and McCall Smith's Law and Medical Ethics*, pp 490–491.

[84] Radcliffe-Richards *et al* (1998) 351 *Lancet* 1950.

[85] *Mason and McCall Smith's Law and Medical Ethics*, pp 504.

[86] Titmuss, *The Gift Relationship: From Human Blood to Social Policy*.

[87] See AM Farrell, 'Is the Gift Still Good? Examining the Politics and Regulation of Blood Safety in the European Union' (2006) 14 *Medical Law Review* 155.

Xenotransplantation

18.13 A once much-vaunted development in the field of organ transplantation involves the use of non-human animals. Non-human animal to human transplant attempts are not new. Early efforts resulted in disastrous rejection episodes. Scientists responded by seeking to develop procedures to modify the genetic make-up of pigs to provide tailor-made organs suitable to transplant into humans. The technical progress with xenotransplantation has been slow. The range of problems associated with it is vast.[88] Is it right to use non-human animals in this way?[89] What about infection risks? How will the first human volunteers be recruited? The Government initially responded cautiously, setting up an interim regulatory body, the United Kingdom Xenotransplantation Interim Regulation Authority (UKXIRA).[90] For those that are satisfied that breeding animals for transplant is ethical, the major problem becomes the risk to humans. Zoonoses are diseases that cross the species barrier, as it is feared the latest lethal form of avian flu may do. Might genetically engineered pigs carry viruses harmless to pigs, but lethal to humans? In the light of this risk, it is argued that xenograft recipients would have to consent to lifelong monitoring, sterilisation and abstention from unprotected sexual intercourse. How would such draconian rules be policed? Should recipients be allowed to create risks for us all?[91] In 2006 the Government announced its decision to abolish UKXIRA, and UKXIRA ceased to exist from 12 December 2006. New guidance suggests that the Medical and Healthcare Products Regulatory Authority (MHRA) and research ethics committees (RECs) are now suitably equipped to make any necessary decisions about clinical trials of xenografts in humans.[92]

Liability for mishaps[93]

18.14 A number of questions about potential liability arise if organ transplantation goes awry. A failed transplant will not of itself give rise to any legal claim by the recipient. The renal surgeon does not guarantee success any more than any other medical practitioner. But what if, for example, donated blood or kidneys prove to be infected, perhaps with HIV? Might the donor, or the transplant team, be liable in tort? It would seem unchallengeable that donors owe a duty of care to recipients which is breached by a donor knowingly

---

[88] See M Fox and J McHale, 'Xenotransplantation: The Ethical and Legal Ramifications' (1998) 6 *Medical Law Review* 42; Nuffield Council on Bioethics, *Animal to Human Transplants* (1996).

[89] See W Cartwright, 'The Pig, The Transplant Surgeon and the Nuffield Council' (1996) 4 *Medical Law Review* 250.

[90] See HSC 1998/126; and Report of the Advisory Group on the Ethics of Xenotransplantation, *Animal Tissue into Humans* (1996); Department of Health, *The Government Response to 'Animal Tissue into Humans'* (1997).

[91] See S Fovargue, 'Consenting to Bio-Risk: Xenotransplantation and the Law' (2005) 25 *Legal Studies* 405.

[92] See Department of Health, *Xenotransplantation Guidance* (2006). As to the efficacy of the MHRA and RECs, see above, Chapter 16.

[93] In *Urbanski v Patel* (1978) 84 DLR (3d) 650, the donor claimed that the defendant's negligence in removing his daughter's only kidney caused injury (the loss of his kidney) to him.

donating organs or tissue when he is aware that he is infected by, say, hepatitis or HIV.[94] The recipient's problem may be tracing the donor. Public policy grounds for protecting the anonymity of donors may be found to outweigh the recipient's individual right of action.[95]

Realistically any claim in respect of contaminated body products will be brought against the hospital supplying those products. Actions in negligence against the Department of Health by haemophiliacs who contracted HIV from contaminated Factor 8 were settled out of court.[96] The Pearson Commission recommended that strict liability should be imposed on authorities responsible for the supply of human blood and organs. It is now clear that the Consumer Protection Act 1987, imposing strict liability for defective products, includes human tissue in its definition of a product.[97]

Foetal tissue and neonatal transplants

18.15   The potential for the use of foetal tissue for transplantation has aroused much ethical debate. Foetal brain cells can be taken from aborted foetuses and transplanted into the brains of patients with Parkinson's disease, in the hope of improving the recipient's condition. In 1989, a committee chaired by the Rev Dr Polkinghorne reported and recommended a Code of Practice for the use of foetuses and foetal material in research and treatment.[98] Many of the fears about the use of foetal tissue focus on concerns that women with relatives suffering from Parkinson's disease might deliberately become pregnant, intending to abort the foetus to provide the needed brain cells. The law is relatively simple. Any abortion must conform to the provisions of the Abortion Act 1967. The Code of Practice mandates that any question of the use of foetal tissue must be independent of decisions relating to the management of the pregnancy. The only remaining question is whether the woman's consent is needed before doctors may make use of the aborted foetus. The Code of Practice requires such consent, but whether consent is mandatory in law is less clear. Does the woman own the foetus, so that 'misuse' of it is an interference with her property? Even if the foetus is 'property' – which we doubt – has she, in making the decision to abort, abandoned her property? The development of stem cell therapy is likely, in any case, to overtake the debate in use of foetal tissue.

A rather different question arises in relation to anencephalic neonates. Could a baby born without a brain be used as a donor of organs for a baby born with a defective heart? As we have seen, criteria of brain stem death are not

---

[94]   And might be criminally liable for causing grievous bodily harm? See *R v Dica* [2004] 3 All ER 593, CA.
[95]   A Scottish court so found in relation to a claim against a blood donor: see *AB v Scottish Blood Transfusion Service* [1990] SLR 263.
[96]   See above at 10.1.
[97]   See *A v The National Blood Authority* [2001] Lloyd's Rep Med 187 discussed fully above at 10.6.
[98]   *Review of the Guidance on the Research Use of Fetuses and Fetal Material* (1989) Cm 762.

applicable to newborn infants.[99] The Department of Health Code of Practice[100] on diagnosis of brain stem death none the less endorses the removal of organs for donation (with parental consent) when 'two doctors, who are not members of the transplant team, agree that spontaneous respiration has ceased'.

Transplantation: the future

18.16 The most important single issue in the context of organ and tissue transplantation is to find means of ensuring an adequate supply of organs within the framework established by the Human Tissue Act 2004. New possibilities of extending live donor transplantation will have to be explored. Means of ensuring more adequate supply of cadaver kidneys will continue to be sought. Are the ethical doubts about, for example, sale of organs, elective ventilation and foetal tissue transplants sufficiently grave to rule out their use? Should the ban on conditional donation, whereby families seek to place some restrictions on who may benefit from a cadaver donation, be revisited? An attempt to restrict donation to persons of one's own racial group, or religious persuasion, appears fairly odious at first sight.[101] But might some forms of conditional donation seem more acceptable? What of this example? A young man dies in a road accident. His twin sister has end-stage renal failure. His parents are prepared to donate all his organs if one of his kidneys is made available to his sister.

One further matter should be noted. Doctors are acquiring the skills to transplant more and more organs. French doctors have performed a partial face transplant. British doctors have been given permission to move towards the first full face transplant. Fears that the recipient will be identical to the donor are misplaced. Practical and medical questions abound. But it is doubtful that face transplants pose any new ethical or legal questions.[102] Controversy about such transplants may however re-kindle more general concerns about transplant medicine.

---

[99] See above at 17.4.
[100] See 1998/035, *A Code of Practice for the Diagnosis of Brain Stem Death* (1998) Department of Health, para 3.3. See also Report of the Working Party of the Medical Royal Colleges, *Organ Transplantation in Neonates* (1998) (discussed in *Mason and McCall Smith's Law and Medical Ethics*, pp 505–510).
[101] See Department of Health, *An Investigation into Conditional Organ Donation* (2000).
[102] See RS Hartman, 'Face Values: Challenges of Transplant Technology' (2005) 31 *American Journal of Law and Medicine* 7.

Chapter 19

THE HUMAN BODY AND ITS PARTS

19.1 We take our bodies for granted most of the time. The purpose of our organs and tissue is to sustain us, the people who live in those bodies. We refer without reflection to 'our' hands, 'our' hearts. Whether that language of ownership is reflected in the law may be doubted. What is beyond doubt is that our human body parts have value to others.[1] 'My' kidney may save 'your' life. That kidney could become 'yours' while I remain alive. 'My' heart could also save your 'life', but only when my 'life' has ended. Once again, in modern times, it was the development of transplantation that highlighted the usefulness of human body parts, taken from both the living and the dead. However, doctors and scientists have been learning from the bodies, and body parts, of the dead for centuries. Medicine has developed from the knowledge gathered from the dissection of corpses. Dissection, however good its ends, has a murky history.[2] Bodies were stolen in the seventeenth and eighteenth centuries. The Anatomy Act 1832 conscripted the bodies of the poor to help train medical students in anatomy and provide material for early medical research. In the twentieth century, the public knew little about practices whereby doctors retained organs and tissue for both research and education. Post-mortem examinations were rarely discussed. Only when the controversy surrounding organ retention erupted at the end of the last century was the public gaze fixed on the uses of bodies and their parts.

In this chapter, we examine how (outwith the context of transplantation) English law regulates the removal, retention and uses of human body parts and we consider how far (if at all) we own our own bodies. We revisit those parts of the Human Tissue Act 2004 not examined in Chapter 18.

Removal of body parts from the dead

19.2 It was organ retention from the bodies of the dead that resulted in the enactment of the Human Tissue Act 2004. For this reason we reverse the natural order, and consider first the questions relating to the use of corpses

---

[1] See M Brazier, 'Human(s) (as) Medicine(s)' in SAM McLean (ed), *Do No Harm* (2006) Ashgate, p 187.

[2] See R Richardson, *Death, Dissection and the Destitute* (2nd edn, 2000) Chicago Press.

before addressing retention of organs and tissue from the living. In the course of the Inquiry[3] established in 1998 to investigate the paediatric cardiac service at Bristol Royal Infirmary, evidence emerged of a widespread practice of organ and tissue retention. Over a long period of time, organs and tissue had been taken at, or after, post-mortem examinations from children's bodies and used '... for a variety of purposes, including audit, medical education and research, or had simply been stored'. The Bristol Inquiry Team, led by Professor Ian Kennedy, issued an Interim Report *Removal and Retention of Human Material*[4] in May 2000. The Report noted that these practices had become an '... issue of great and grave concern' generating an outcry not confined to the Bristol parents. Worse was to follow. Almost in passing one of the witnesses to the Bristol Inquiry, Professor RH Anderson, in explaining the benefits of retaining hearts for educational purposes, noted the existence of many collections of children's hearts elsewhere. The largest collection, he commented, was at the Royal Liverpool Children's Hospital (Alder Hey). His evidence prompted the Department of Health to set up an Independent Confidential Inquiry under section 2 of the National Health Service Act 1977, chaired by Michael Redfern QC. The Inquiry was instructed to investigate the removal and disposal of human organs and tissue following post-mortem examinations at Alder Hey.

The Redfern Report,[5] published in January 2001, proved to be political dynamite. It revealed longstanding practices of removing and retaining children's organs without the consent or even knowledge of their grieving parents. In some cases, infants were literally stripped of all their organs and what was returned to their families was an 'empty shell'. In a horrifying number of cases, organs and tissue retained were simply stored. They were put to no good use. In some instances, the whole of a foetus or still born infant was kept and stored in pots. The Report is 535 pages long. It addresses not just the original wrong of retaining organs, but subsequent mishandling of organ return and a range of other appalling practices and mismanagement. In this chapter, we focus on the legal issues arising out of organ retention.

Simultaneously with the publication of the Redfern Report, the Chief Medical Officer published a census carried out to ascertain the extent of organ retention since 1970 across the NHS in England and Wales.[6] What became apparent was that practices whereby pathologists simply took and retained human material after *post-mortem* examination were routine. The extent to which the deceased's family was involved at all in such decisions varied radically. What was clear was that adequate and free consent was rarely

3   *Learning from Bristol: The Report of the Public Inquiry into Children's Heart Surgery at the Bristol Royal Infirmary 1984–1995* (2001) Cm 5207(1).

4   The Inquiry into the Management of Care of Children Receiving Complex Heart Surgery at the Bristol Royal Infirmary Interim Report, *Removal and Retention of Human Material* (available at www.bristol-inquiry.org.uk) (hereafter Bristol Interim Report).

5   *The Royal Liverpool Children's Inquiry Report* (2001) HC 12–11 (hereafter the Redfern Report).

6   Department of Health, *Report of a Census of Organs and Tissue Retained by Pathology Services in England* (2001).

obtained, or even thought necessary. Nor was this a practice limited to children. Many families were to learn about organs stripped from adult relatives.[7]

The value of taking and retaining organs after *post-mortem* examination in certain cases should not be doubted. Ascertaining the cause of death is self-evidently important. And often, especially with infants, tests on organs and tissue may have crucial value to the child's family. Investigations which reveal genetic disease may be the key to helping that family have further healthy children. In the wider public interest, medical research is dependent on access to human organs and tissue. Medical education requires such material. One simple example illustrates the educational use of human organs. If a child dies tragically and is found to have a grossly abnormal heart, retaining that heart so that paediatric surgeons can examine it before attempting to operate on and save the life of a child with a similar abnormality makes sense. It can only be ethical to do so with the family's consent. For the devout Jew or Muslim, it is a religious imperative to bury the body intact. For other families, the pain of not laying their relative to rest complete is overwhelming. However, for many families involved in the organ retention controversy, what motivated their anger was the loss of control over their relative's burial or cremation. Many relatives said publicly that had they been consulted they would have agreed to doctors retaining the organs of the dead child or other relative. They would have been content to 'gift' some parts of the body to achieve good ends, ends fully explained to them. What they abominated was the lack of respect shown to them and their relative. They felt that someone whom they loved dearly had been treated as a mere convenience, treated with contempt.[8]

Post-mortem examinations

19.3 Before looking at the law relating to retention of dead bodies, organs and tissue, we need to say a little about *post-mortem* examinations – sometimes referred to as autopsies. A *post-mortem* examination is conducted by a pathologist to investigate (*inter alia*) the cause of a death, and to understand more fully the nature of the patient's disease, including an evaluation of any medical or surgical treatment given to him. Such examinations are a key tool of modern scientific medicine. One distinguished doctor and philosopher has said, 'Of all the clinical disciplines, pathology is the one

---

[7] See, in particular, Department of Health, *The Investigation of Events that Followed the Death of Cyril Mark Isaacs* (2003). The Bristol Interim Report, the Redfern Report and the Chief Medical Officer all made extensive recommendations about how the NHS should seek to manage and resolve the process of informing families about organ retention and organ return, about support for families and how to resolve past controversies as well as how the law should be reformed. The Secretary of State established a special health authority, the NHS Retained Organs Commission, to manage the process by which NHS trusts provide information to families about organ retention, oversee the process of organ return, act as an advocate for families, and develop a new regulatory framework for organ and tissue retention.

[8] For diametrically opposed views about the ethics of organ retention, see J Harris, 'Law and Regulation of Retained Organs: the Ethical Issues' (2002) 22 *Legal Studies* 527; M Brazier, 'Retained Organs: Ethics and Humanity' (2002) 22 *Legal Studies* 550.

that most directly reflects the demystification of the human body that has made scientific medicine so effective and so humane'.[9] To the lay person, what is done to the body in a full *post-mortem* examination may seem grisly. The body is opened and organs removed, weighed and sometimes dissected. In some cases, organs must be retained for a period of time to be treated before they can be fully examined, or organs and tissue may be sent away for tests elsewhere. Some religious faiths, including Orthodox Judaism and Islam, mandate the swift burial of the intact body. *Post-mortem* examinations (save in exceptional circumstances)[10] thus offend those faiths.[11]

Post-mortem examinations in this country can either be compulsory on the orders of the coroner, or voluntary, conducted with the consent of the deceased or his family. We shall refer to this latter form of *post-mortem* examination as a hospital autopsy.

Post-mortem examinations must be distinguished from anatomical examinations. Anatomical examinations involve what is more commonly known as dissection. People donate their whole bodies to medical schools to assist in medical education, primarily to educate students in human anatomy and train them in dissection.

The law before 2004: complex and obscure[12]

19.4 Doctors, especially pathologists, endured odium in the wake of revelations in the Bristol Interim and Redfern Reports. Some of the blame lay with the unsatisfactory state of the law prior to the Human Tissue Act 2004. The Bristol Interim Report said simply but tellingly:

> ... we have no doubt that the complexity and obscurity of the current law will be manifest to all. Equally we have no doubt that there will be general agreement that this state of affairs is regrettable and in need of attention.[13]

Prior to the 2004 Act, a complicated mixture of ancient common law principles and statutes governed the retention and use of body parts taken from the dead. The common law asserted that there was 'no property in a corpse'.[14] This principle remains untouched by the 2004 Act. When a family member dies his family have no claim by which they can assert 'this is now our body and we have unfettered rights to dispose of it or its parts'. However, the executors or administrators of the deceased's estate are subject, ultimately, to a common law duty to dispose of the body decently. This duty confers on

---

9   See R Tallis, *Hippocratic Oaths: Medicine and Its Discontents* (2004) Atlantic Books, p 195.

10   See, for example, M Lamm, *The Jewish Way in Death and Mourning* (1998) Jonathan David, p 100; A Sheikh and AR Gartrad, *Caring for Muslim Patients* (2000) Radcliffe Medical Press, p 107.

11   One option may be to carry out a limited *post-mortem*, so restricting the intrusion on the body: see generally, *Guidelines on Autopsy Practice* (2005) Royal College of Pathologists.

12   See D Price, 'From Cosmos and Damian to Van Velzen: The Human Tissue Saga Continues' (2003) 11 *Medical Law Review* 1.

13   At p 20.

14   *Doodeward v Spence* (1908) 6 CLR 406. And see below at 19.9.

them a right to possession of the body to fulfil that duty of decent disposal of the body.[15] Several Acts of Parliament touched on the lawful use of dead bodies. The three key statutes were the Anatomy Act 1984, the Human Tissue Act 1961 and the Coroners Act 1988.

The Anatomy Act 1984 enabled people to donate their bodies or their parts for use for anatomical examination. The details of the 1984 Act were in some ways as fuzzy as was the case with the Human Tissue Act 1961. The framework for the use of donated bodies was, however, closely regulated, and subject to the supervision of HM Inspector of Anatomy. Violation of the Anatomy Act 1984 resulted in criminal liability. The Anatomy Act worked well, within a culture of respect for the donors of the bodies given to medical schools. However, it was that vast majority of cases not regulated by the Anatomy Act which provoked the controversy around organ retention. First, a distinction must be made between removal of organs and tissue after a hospital autopsy, and removal of body parts subsequent to a coroner's *post-mortem* examination. The Human Tissue Act 1961 governed removal and retention of organs after a hospital autopsy. It provided that where no coroner's inquiry was likely, the person lawfully in possession of the body (the hospital) could authorise an autopsy where, after:

> ... such reasonable enquiry as may be practicable, there is no reason to believe:
> (a) that the deceased had expressed an objection to his body being so used after his death ... or (b) that the surviving spouse or any surviving relative objects to his body being so dealt with.[16]

Under the 1961 Act, a person was not empowered to authorise an autopsy on himself in advance of his death. If body parts were to be retained after completion of the autopsy, a further enquiry was supposed to establish that there was no objection to retention and use of those parts. 'Consent' to an autopsy should not have been judged to presume consent (or no objection) to organ retention.

In relation to transplants, doctors were reluctant to exercise the powers granted by the Human Tissue Act 1961. They sought positive and explicit consent from families before removing organs for transplant. In the context of organ retention, the opposite ethos seems to have prevailed. The 1961 Act was obscure. It did not require explicit consent. Rather it set up a 'no objection' rule. Put crudely, hospitals thought that they could take organs and tissue for purposes of education and research if no family member voiced dissent. The Bristol Interim Report suggests that even where families were asked their views and expressed no objection, 'agreement' both to hospital autopsies and subsequent removal of body parts was often given with little understanding of what was entailed. It might be an 'agreement' given at a time of great personal trauma, for example shortly after the death of a child. In some cases, families, knowing nothing of the distinction between hospital autopsies and coroners' *post-mortem* examinations, did not realise that they had a right to object. The use of the word 'tissue' confused people. Understandably, lay people assumed

---

[15]   *Williams v Williams* (1882) 20 Ch D 659.
[16]   See ss 1(2) and 2(2). See also PDG Skegg, 'The Use of Corpses for Medical Education and Research: The Legal Requirements' (1991) 31 *Medicine, Science and the Law* 345.

that in agreeing to the removal of tissue, they agreed to doctors taking small specimens from organs, not whole organs. The Redfern Report revealed a bleaker picture. Organs had been taken and stored without even a pretence of seeking the family's views. The flaws in the Human Tissue Act 1961 became patent. Even if it could be shown to have been flouted, the lack of sanctions punishing violation of the Act rendered it toothless.

The position in relation to coroners' *post-mortem* examinations was no better. The overwhelming majority of *post-mortems* are performed on the orders of the coroner. Put briefly,[17] a coroner may order a *post-mortem* if he is informed that the body of the deceased is lying within his district and there is reasonable cause to suspect that the deceased:

(a) died a violent or unnatural death; (b) has died a sudden death of which the cause is unknown; or (c) has died in prison or such a place or in such circumstances as to require an inquest under any other Act.[18]

The Registration of Births and Deaths Regulations 1987 elaborate on the rules governing which deaths must be reported to the coroner, placing an emphasis on reporting surgical deaths or deaths where some medical negligence may have occurred.[19] A pathologist carrying out a coroner's *post-mortem* examination acts under the coroner's authority. The original Rule 9 of the Coroner's Rules placed a duty on the pathologist to remove and preserve 'materials' which in his opinion bore on the cause of death. If a baby died in the course of cardiac surgery, the pathologist might lawfully remove and retain his heart until it was possible to ascertain why the infant died. However, there was no power to retain organs for research or teaching purposes. Once the cause of death was established, neither the coroner nor the pathologist had any further legal power to retain body parts. Such 'material' should have been disposed of, unless the relatives of the deceased authorised retention for research or teaching purposes. In practice, coroners simply allowed pathologists to do what they wished with human material no longer required for the purposes of verifying cause of death. Pathologists, in ignorance of the law in many cases, retained organs and tissue over long periods of time and for a multiplicity of purposes. By 2001, NHS hospitals were in possession of literally tens of thousands of organs and vast collections of blocks and tissue slides. Leading teaching hospitals and medical museums such as the Royal College of Surgeons had extensive archival material of body parts, some including collections long predating the NHS.

The Human Tissue Act 2004: the dead[20]

19.5 The Human Tissue Act 2004 came into force in September 2006 and governs the removal, retention and use of body parts taken from the dead,

---

[17] For a much fuller account, see the Bristol Interim Report, Annex B 'Law and Guidelines'.
[18] Coroners Act 1988, s 8(1).
[19] SI 1987/2088, reg 41(e).
[20] See D Price, 'The Human Tissue Act 2004' (2005) 68 *Modern Law Review* 798; K Liddell and A Hall, 'Beyond Bristol and Alder Hey: The Future Regulation of Human Tissue' (2005) 13 *Medical Law Review* 170.

except where body parts are removed and retained solely for the purpose of investigating a death under the authority of the coroner. The 2004 Act also governs the performance of hospital autopsies. The Anatomy Act 1984 and the Human Tissue Act 1961 are wholly repealed. The 2004 Act, as we have seen, makes 'appropriate' consent the fundamental principle governing retention and use of whole bodies and body parts. It also introduces extensive regulation of hospital autopsies and retention and use of both bodies and what is 'relevant material'.[21] It is tortuous to read. It does not apply in Scotland.[22]

Let us start with the circumstances in which it is lawful to conduct a *post-mortem* examination. All *post-mortem* examinations must now be performed in premises licensed by the Human Tissue Authority (HTA). The 2004 Act does not govern when a *post-mortem* examination can be ordered by the coroner. So if a person dies suddenly in hospital and there is suspicion that her death may be as a result of some crime or medical malpractice, the coroner will be informed. If the coroner orders a *post-mortem* examination, the family (at present) have no formal right to object. But there are many other circumstances when doctors might want to conduct a *post-mortem* examination. There may be uncertainty about the exact cause of death. There may be a wish to learn more about why treatment failed, as well as the underlying disease or injury. Doctors (and families) may want to explore whether any genetic factors are implicated in the deceased patient's disease. Any such hospital autopsy will be lawful only if[23] the deceased himself gave appropriate consent to the autopsy in advance of his death, such consent is given by his nominated representative[24] or, failing any advance consent by the deceased or authorisation by his nominated representative, appropriate consent is obtained from a person who stood in a qualifying relationship to the deceased.[25] Whatever the purpose of the hospital autopsy, be it to determine the cause of death, investigate the effect of treatment on him or examine genetic factors, what is done can only be done with consent.[26]

Should doctors wish to retain body parts after the hospital autopsy, explicit consent to both the retention, and the projected use of those parts, must be obtained additionally, and separately, from any consent to the autopsy.[27] Imagine that, knowing she is dying from ovarian cancer, a woman consents in advance to an autopsy – especially in order to assess any genetic risk to her daughters. In the course of the autopsy, pathologists identify further tumours

---

21 Defining organs and tissue and attaining a common understanding of those terms proved to be a major problem in the controversy surrounding organ retention. The Human Tissue Act 2004 regulates all 'relevant material' (defined in s 53 as 'material, other than gametes, which consists of or includes human cells' but excluding embryos outside the human body (regulated by the Human Fertilisation and Embryology Authority) and hair and nail from the body of a living person).

22 See the Human Tissue (Scotland) Act 2006.

23 Human Tissue Act 2004, ss 1, 3 and Sch 1, paras 2 and 3.

24 Human Tissue Act 2004, s 4.

25 For discussion of who constitutes such a person, see above at 18.8.

26 The bare rules of the Human Tissue Act 2004 are elaborated in this context by two Codes of Practice: Human Tissue Authority, *Code of Practice: Consent* Code 1 (2006) and Human Tissue Authority, *Code of Practice: Post Mortem Examination* Code 3 (2006).

27 See the Human Tissue Act 2004, s 1 and Sch 1.

in her kidneys and liver. They want to retain those organs for further investigation and research. For such retention and use to be lawful, appropriate consent will have to be obtained from the woman's husband or partner, if she had one, or from one of her daughters. Retention of body parts from the dead must be authorised by appropriate consent, be the purpose of retention, research, audit, education, performance assessment, public health monitoring or surveillance.[28]

Although no consent is required when the coroner orders a *post-mortem* examination, once that examination is complete should a pathologist wish to retain body parts removed in the course of that investigation, appropriate consent must be sought to make such retention and any projected use of those parts lawful. If our hypothetical patient who died of ovarian cancer died unexpectedly on the operating table, the coroner may well order a *post-mortem*. Should the examination establish that her death was in no sense caused by any error or lack of care, but pathologists still wish to retain her organs, consent must be sought for the retention and use of those organs even though it was not required for the *post-mortem* examination itself. Amendments to the Coroner's Rules[29] now require that a coroner ordering a *post-mortem* examination and notified about retention of organs and tissue must inform the deceased's family (*inter alia*) that organs and tissue will be retained, about the options once examination of retained material is complete and (if the relatives wish the material to be returned to them) about what arrangements may need to be made.[30]

Somewhat surprisingly, the Human Tissue Act 2004 prescribes no formalities for consent to a hospital autopsy, or to retention and use of organs after *post-mortem* examination. There is no rule requiring that consent must be given in writing. Greater formality is required for two particular uses of dead bodies and their parts. A person who wishes to donate his body for anatomical examination or for public display must (normally) do so in writing and in the presence of at least one witness.[31] Moreover, *only* the individual himself can donate his body to anatomical examination[32] or public display. Should the authors of this book die in advance of our respective husbands having expressed no instruction about the use of our corpses, those husbands could authorise a hospital autopsy and donate our organs and tissue for medical research or education. Only we can donate our whole bodies to the local medical school or gain a strange sort of immortality in exhibitions such as *Bodyworlds*, where plastinated human bodies are on display as public 'entertainment'.

Section 2 of the Human Tissue Act 2004 makes express provision in relation to children and young people who die before reaching the age of maturity at 18. If a young person was sufficiently mature and intelligent to make an

---

[28] See also HTA, *Code of Practice: The Removal, Storage and Disposal of Human Organs and Tissues* Code 5 (2006).

[29] Coroners (Amendment) Rules 2005, SI 2005/420.

[30] And see HTA, *Code of Practice* Code 3, paras 27–34.

[31] See s 3(4) and (5).

[32] For further information about anatomical examination, see HTA, *Code of Practice: Anatomical Examination* Code 4 (2006).

advance direction about the conduct of an autopsy or retention of body parts, her advance direction authorises implementation of her wishes. A *Gillick competent*[33] minor can in theory determine what happens to her body after death.[34] Establishing *Gillick competence* retrospectively after death will not be easy. In relation to younger children, normally parents will be the designated decision-makers. Autopsy and organ retention are lawful only on the basis of appropriate consent from a person with parental responsibility[35] for the dead child. Consent from one parent alone will suffice to make the relevant activity lawful. Overriding an objecting bereaved parent will pose ethical and practical difficulties. Consider this dilemma. A child dies of cancer at the age of four. His Orthodox Jewish father objects to any retention of his organs. His mother desperately wants to know if his disease has any genetic implications for her other children, and so want his organs retained and samples tested.

The Human Tissue Act 2004: the living

19.6 The Human Tissue Act 2004 was enacted in the wake of controversy about the (mis)use of the bodies of the dead. The 2004 Act, however, also regulates the retention and use of 'material' from living patients. So if a patient undergoes surgery to remove a diseased organ, the Act regulates the conditions in which doctors may retain that organ for teaching or research purposes. And the wide definition given to 'material'[36] within the 2004 Act means that not only is retention of whole organs regulated, but also that of any specimen, including cells (however small that may be). The original Human Tissue Bill imposed almost the same regime of requirements for explicit consent in relation to such surgical or surplus tissue from living patients, as for body parts removed and retained from the dead. The Bill caused an outcry, with senior scientists claiming that such burdensome rules would paralyse medicine.[37] Hence, as we shall see, a modified set of rules now govern retention of surgical or surplus tissue.[38]

The 2004 Act does not regulate the initial removal of body parts from the living. That continues to be governed by the common law. Any surgery is normally unlawful and a criminal assault unless properly authorised by the patient's consent. A hysterectomy on a mentally-competent woman self-evidently requires her consent. But what if doctors want to retain her diseased uterus, either to help train medical students or to pursue research into the kind of cancer that necessitated the surgery? Must doctors seek the woman's explicit consent to retain her uterus, or even any specimens of diseased tissue?

---

[33]   *Gillick v West Norfolk and Wisbech Area Health Authority* [1984] QB 581. See Chapter 15 at 15.18–15.19 for an explanation of *Gillick* competency.

[34]   See s 2(3). Only such a *Gillick competent* minor can authorise donation of her body for anatomical examination or public display. Parents cannot donate their children's bodies for such purposes.

[35]   See ss 1, 2 and Sch 1. Where there is not such a person, the nearest person in a qualifying relationship to the dead child is the designated decision-maker.

[36]   See s 53 and above at 19.5.

[37]   See P Furness and R Sullivan, 'The Human Tissue Bill' (2004) 328 *British Medical Journal* 533.

[38]   See Liddell and Hall (2005) 13 *Medical Law Review* 170.

It depends on their purpose.[39] If retention is intended for the purposes of audit, education or training, performance assessment, public health monitoring or quality assurance, her consent may be presumed.[40]

Retention to acquire genetic or other information relevant to others will normally require an explicit consent.[41] Retention for research will require such a consent if the identity of the patient will be ascertainable. The 2004 Act empowers the Secretary of State to make regulations allowing retention of material from the living for research, without an explicit consent, where the research has been ethically approved by an accredited research ethics committee and the 'source' of the material has been anonymised.[42] Research on surgical or surplus tissue taken from one of the authors would have to be explicitly authorised by us if researchers will be able to discover that the source is Brazier or Cave. Very often, researchers will require this information to be able to, for example, access our medical records. Only research, approved by a research ethics committee, where that link is *not* necessary, and has not been broken, will not require our explicit consent.[43]

The final version of the 2004 Act operates on the assumption that more people have little concern about what happens to 'bits of their body' removed at surgery. They would be indifferent to whether such 'bits' were incinerated or put to some good use. Two *caveats* should be stated:

(1) Some religious faiths attach an almost equal value to parts separated from the living body as from the dead. When an Orthodox Jew has to have a limb amputated, he will make arrangements for that limb to be stored and ultimately interred with him.

(2) Surplus tissue is not necessarily mere 'waste'. It can be the source of crucial and sensitive genetic information. It can be the source of medical advances of commercial value. We will return to this question a little later.

'Appropriate consent'

19.7 We have so far indicated when an explicit consent is required by the Human Tissue Act 2004. The Act refers to 'appropriate consent'. Just what those two words may mean is crucial to how the Act will operate in practice. The HTA is expressly required by the 2004 Act to address what constitutes consent and does so in a number of Codes of Practice, including a general

---

[39] See generally HTA, *Code of Practice* Code 5, paras 46–53.
[40] See s 1(d) and (f) and Sch 1.
[41] However, see s 7, which provides that the HTA can in exceptional circumstances, where the original donor of the material cannot be traced, dispense with the need for consent.
[42] See s 1(7), (8) and (9); see also the Human Tissue Act 2004 (Ethical Approval, Exceptions from Licensing and Supply of Information About Transplants Regulations) 2006, SI 2006/1260.
[43] Section 6 empowers the Secretary of State to make regulations relating to 'deemed consent' by persons who lack the requisite mental capacity to consent on their own behalf. See also the Human Tissue Act 2004 (Persons Who Lack Capacity to Consent and Transplants) Regulations 2006, SI 2006/1659, regs 3, 8.

Code on Consent[44] and more specific Codes relating to consent to *post-mortem* examinations[45] and consent to removal, retention and storage of tissue.[46] The HTA stresses that seeking consent '... is a process which involves listening, discussing and questioning so as to arrive at a shared understanding' – a signed form is not necessarily an indication that such an understanding has been reached.[47] A valid consent must be given voluntarily and on the basis of sufficient information. What degree of information is sufficient is difficult. Some families asked to consent to a hospital autopsy and organ retention may not want comprehensive and graphic descriptions of what will be done to their newly-dead relative.[48] Some living patients will be happy simply to 'give away' excess tissue or diseased organs uninterested in their fate. Doctors should not, however, assume either that acute distress in the first case or indifference in the second justifies failing to *offer* information. A number of families brought claims against hospitals retaining organs without consent. In *AB v Leeds Teaching Hospital NHS Trust*,[49] the judge stressed that (even under the old Human Tissue Act 1961) families were '... entitled to have their wishes in respect of their deceased (relative's) body respected and complied with ... those wishes cannot be complied with unless it is explained to the (relative) what is involved'. He rejected any blanket view that information would have been distressing to all relatives, saying: 'In so far as it involved the exercise of a therapeutic privilege it was one which does not appear to have been exercised on a case by case basis'.

We would suggest that the Act requires that doctors offer to disclose to the person giving consent all the information that any reasonable lay person would need to make a sensible choice about whether or not to give the requested consent.[50] Especially in the context of sudden bereavement, time and support for the decision-maker will be crucial. Information must neither be withheld nor forced on the unwilling recipient. Evidence of compliance with HTA Codes of Practice will weigh strongly with the courts.

In the context of retention for research, one particularly thorny question surfaces. Must consent be specific to every research use of the relevant material? Or will a general consent suffice? If a woman agrees to consent to retention of her diseased uterus for research into one form of cancer therapy and in the course of that research other, more promising lines of research emerge, must she be contacted to give specific consent to this further research? The HTA seems to endorse the applicability of a *general* consent.[51] Donors may be asked to make an unconditional gift of their tissue (or that of their deceased relative). The key factor will be to establish what kind of consent was sought and given. Did the patient or relative consent only to the use of the

---

44 HTA, *Code of Practice* Code 1.
45 HTA, *Code of Practice* Code 3.
46 HTA, *Code of Practice* Code 5.
47 HTA, *Code of Practice* Code 1, para 92.
48 See D Knowles, 'Parental Consent to the Post Mortem Removal and Retention of Organs' (2001) 18 *Journal of Applied Philosophy* 215.
49 [2004] EWHC 644 (QB).
50 Modelled on Lord Woolf's definition of informed consent in *Pearce v United Bristol Healthcare NHS Trust* (1999) 48 BMLR 118 (discussed above at 5.7).
51 See HTA, *Code of Practice* Code 1, paras 104–106.

relevant material for Project X, or did they consent to surrender all control of that material and 'gift' the body parts in question to the hospital or university?

Regulation

19.8 We have focused in this chapter on the legal requirements for consent to removal, retention and use of body parts. The Human Tissue Act 2004 also imposes substantial regulatory requirements on such activities. We touch on these only briefly. As we saw in relation to transplantation, the HTA plays a major role in regulation. Its mandate to prepare Codes of Practice means that the HTA will profoundly influence how the 2004 Act works in practice.[52] More directly, a number of activities now require a licence from the HTA.[53] These include carrying out anatomical examinations and storing anatomical specimens. Medical schools will now have to be licensed by the HTA to carry out and train students in dissection.[54] *Post-mortem* examinations must be carried out in licensed premises. Storage of any body or part of a body for any of the purposes covered by the 2004 Act must be licensed, as must the use of bodies and their parts for public display. Pathology museums and archives of tissue will also need to be licensed in respect of acquisitions after the Act came into force. It remains lawful to retain existing holdings (even where there is no evidence of consent).[55] The HTA none the less advises that if the views of the deceased person or their relatives are known, those views '… must be respected',[56] and it gives extensive advice on the respectful disposal of existing holdings.[57]

The 2004 Act, unlike its predecessor, the Human Tissue Act 1961, has teeth. Proceeding without appropriate consent where consent is required is a criminal offence unless the person reasonably believed that he acted on the basis of an appropriate consent.[58] In the context of consent to the removal and retention of body parts from the dead, a practical question besets obtaining consent. If, for example, a child dies of leukaemia, it is usually the treating clinicians who will approach the family to seek consent to an autopsy and subsequent retention of material. But it is the pathologist who will carry out the autopsy and retain any material. Pathologists will need to ensure that they have a reasonable basis for a belief in consent and that, in most cases, will mean evidence in writing of consent. To ensure doctors charged with seeking consent do their part, it is also a criminal offence to represent falsely to

---

[52] See ss 26 and 27.
[53] See s 16. Note that it is proposed that the HTA be merged with the Human Fertilisation and Embryology Authority to form a new Regulatory Authority for Tissue and Embryos (RATE): see above at 13.1.
[54] Continuing the regulatory regime previously imposed by the Anatomy Act 1984; and see the Human Tissue Act 2004, ss 16(2)(a), 17 and 18.
[55] See s 9. The licensing requirement does not apply to bodies of people who died before the 2004 Act came into force and are at least 100 years' old (ie archaeologists are exempt).
[56] HTA, *Code of Practice* Code 5, para 45.
[57] HTA, *Code of Practice* Code 5, Appendix A.
[58] See s 5(1).

another that appropriate consent has been obtained.[59] Carrying out unlicensed activities where such a licence is required equally engages criminal liability.[60]

Ownership of body parts[61]

19.9 The vexed question of whether we own our bodies is only fleetingly addressed in the Human Tissue Act 2004. We noted earlier the ancient common law assumption that there is no property in a corpse. That statement must be qualified. Consider the Egyptian mummies held in the British Museum. Do they belong to the British Museum? Or might we lawfully help ourselves to one or two? *R v Kelly*[62] confirmed that once a body or body parts had been changed in nature by work done on them, such parts become capable of being property. A technician was accused of stealing body parts from the Royal College of Surgeons and selling them to an artist who wished to use the parts as moulds for his sculptures. Both were charged with theft. Their defence was the College did not own the parts and so they could not steal them. Upholding the convictions, the Court of Appeal found that body parts became capable of being property for the purposes of the Theft Act 1968 because they had '… acquired different attributes by virtue of the application of skills, such as dissection or preservation technology, for exhibition or teaching purposes'. The notion of 'property' however is complex in this context. The Court of Appeal in *Kelly* did not find that the Royal College of Surgeons *owned* the stolen body parts. A right to lawful possession of property is all that is required for that property to be stolen from you. The English Court of Appeal concurred with their Australian brethren in *Doodeward v Spence*;[63] in that case Griffith CJ spoke of a body and its parts becoming the subject of property. He said:

> … when a person has by the lawful exercise of work or skills so dealt with a human body or part of a human body that it has acquired some attributes differentiating it from a mere corpse awaiting burial he requires a right to retain possession of it, at least as against any person not entitled to have delivered to him for the purpose of burial.

Does it follow from *Kelly* that whenever organs or tissue have been retained and, for example, preserved in formalin or put in blocks, the hospital in possession of the specimen can assert a property right to it? *Dobson v North Tyneside Health Authority*[64] undermines such an argument. The family of a woman who had died of a brain tumour brought a claim in clinical negligence against the health authority, alleging failure to diagnose her condition sufficiently swiftly to offer her effective treatment. To succeed in their claim, they needed to ensure that their expert witnesses could examine samples of the brain. The brain had been removed at a coroner's *post-mortem*, preserved in

[59] See s 5(2).
[60] See s 25.
[61] See JW Harris, 'Who Owns My Body?' (1996) 16 *Oxford Journal of Legal Studies* 55.
[62] [1998] 3 All ER 741.
[63] (1908) 6 CLR 406 at 413–444.
[64] [1996] 4 All ER 474.

paraffin and later disposed of. The family sued the hospital for conversion, alleging unlawful disposal of the brain. They argued that on completion of the coroner's investigation the family were entitled to the return of the brain. They enjoyed either ownership or, at least, a right of possession of the deceased's brain. The Court of Appeal dismissed their claim. Fixing the brain in paraffin was not a sufficient exercise of skill or labour to give that brain any different attributes to the organ initially removed from the body in the course of the *post-mortem*. There was:

> ... nothing ... to suggest that the actual preservation of the brain after the post mortem was on a par with stuffing or embalming a corpse or preserving an anatomical or pathological specimen for collection or with preserving a human freak such as a double-headed foetus that had some value for exhibition purposes.[65]

Identifying exactly what must be done to transform an organ taken from a body into property is difficult. It must, though, be noted that at one point in *Kelly*[66] Rose LJ suggested that the common law could develop to recognise a body part as property even without the acquisition of different attributes if it had acquired '... a use or significance beyond ... mere existence'. Rose LJ even suggested that in such a case outright ownership may be recognised. In *AB v Leeds Hospital NHS Trust*[67] parents whose deceased children had been subject to *post-mortem* examinations and organ retention without their consent brought claims for psychiatric injury to themselves and wrongful interference with the bodies of the children. Gage J, rejecting the latter claim, reasserted the rule of 'no property in a corpse'. He also confirmed that, none the less, separated parts of the body subjected to the application of work and skill might become property – the property of he who expended that work and skill. So, pathologists who dissected and fixed organs from the body and transformed them into blocks and slides could acquire ownership of that 'property'. The skill and labour rule creates an odd paradox whereby our bodies and their parts are not our property (or at least do not form part of our estate) but put '... to the uses of medicine, their body parts become, as if by magic, property, but property owned by persons unknown for purposes unforeseen by the deceased'.[68]

Questions of property in separated parts of the living body pose further questions.[69] Intellectual property raises its head.[70] The Human Tissue Act 2004 offers little help. In section 32 prohibiting commercial dealings in body parts for transplant purposes, the Act exempts from this prohibition 'material which is the subject of property because of an application of human skill'.[71] The Human Tissue Bill had originally sought to ban commercial

---

[65] [1996] 4 All ER 479, per Peter Gibson LJ.
[66] [1998] 3 All ER 741 at 750.
[67] [2004] EWHC 644 (QB).
[68] See Brazier (2002) 22 *Legal Studies* 550 at 563.
[69] See JK Mason and GT Laurie, *Mason and McCall Smith's Law and Medical Ethics* (7th edn, 2006) OUP, pp. 511–525.
[70] *Mason and McCall Smith's Law and Medical Ethics*, pp 529–538.
[71] See s 32(9)(c).

dealings in body parts for any purposes. Does its amendment indicate that trade in body parts for research and other purposes is common and acceptable to Government, at least?

The fundamental question of whether we should own our bodies would constitute a book of its own. We might ask, does it matter? The Human Tissue Act 2004 grants us and our families fairly extensive control of what may be done with our bodies and their component parts. A number of reasons suggest that it might matter. Common law dicta that there was no property in a corpse did not derive from any belief that such bodies were without value. Quite the contrary – the dead should not be seen '… as other inanimate objects, but were to be treated quite differently, even reverently'.[72] Our bodies were too valuable to be 'things', to be mere property. Would classifying bodies as property devalue them?

However there is no avoiding the evidence that in the modern world bodies have certain sorts of tangible value. Sometimes this value is crudely commercial. Consider the famous case of Mr Moore.[73] Cell lines developed from his excised and diseased spleen made his doctor $15m and much greater profits for the drug company who bought the potential cell line. Yet Mr Moore was held to have no ownership rights in the body part removed. Another value secreted in our body parts is our genetic information. What may seem to be redundant surplus tissue carries within it information about the whole of our health and much about ourselves. We may prefer to retain control of that information.

Until recently proponents of property models and bodies tended to be motivated by a belief in markets in human tissue. We should own our bodies so we can sell them. The debate is much more sophisticated now. Mason and Laurie[74] have made a powerful case for a modified property model.[75]

Reforming the role of the coroner

19.10 The organ retention controversy prompted as many questions about the role of the coroner as it did about retention of organs per se. The Shipman Inquiry also casts doubt about how far in 2007 the ancient office of the coroner meets modern needs.[76] A review of the coroners' service made a number of recommendations for reform, including granting more rights to relatives.[77] In 2006, the Department of Constitutional Affairs introduced a

---

[72] See P Matthews, 'The Man of Property' (1995) 3 *Medical Law Review* 237 at 254.

[73] *Moore v Regents of the University of California* 793 P 2d 479 (Cal 1950).

[74] JK Mason and GT Laurie, 'Consent or property. Dealing with the Body and its Parts in the Shadow of Bristol and Alder Hey' (2001) 64 *Modern Law Review* 710.

[75] And see L Skene, 'Property Rights in Human Bodies, Body Parts and Tissue: Regulatory Contexts and Proposals for New Laws' (2002) 22 *Legal Studies* 102.

[76] See in this context, the Third Report of the Shipman Inquiry, *Death Certification and the Investigation of Death by Coroners* (2003) Cm 5854.

[77] *Report of a Fundamental Review of Death Certification and Coroner Services* (2003) Cm 5831 (The Luce Report).

draft Coroners Bill.[78] The Bill seeks to modernise the role of the coroner in several ways. What is most relevant to this chapter, is the objective of the Bill to ensure that the coronial system provides a better service to bereaved people, so families will be granted rights of appeal against decisions to require a *post-mortem*. A new Coroners Act is intended to draw a line beneath the controversy surrounding organ retention. Just as the Human Tissue Act 2004 struggles to balance public interests in health and medical science against individual and family interests, so the Coroners Bill struggles to balance such interests against the needs of the criminal justice system.

---

[78] Department of Constitutional Affairs, *Coroner Reform: The Government's Draft Bill – Improving death investigation in England and Wales* (2006) Cm 6849.

Chapter 20

THE END OF LIFE

20.1 Society has never been comfortable with issues surrounding the process of dying; and as health care staff are involved with the dying, they inevitably become involved in ethical as well as medical dilemmas. These dilemmas are, first, whether efforts should always be made to keep a dying person alive in spite of the additional suffering incurred by that person and the cost in terms of human dignity; and, second, when, if ever, attempts may be made to hasten death when there is excessive suffering and when the cause is hopeless.

The practice of what some regard as 'striving officiously to keep alive' has been facilitated by the increase in high technology equipment, much of it capable of being used to postpone inevitable death for a time. The benefits of such equipment may often be great; yet there is a cost, both in human and economic terms. Further treatment may sometimes be said to be futile. A vast literature has developed around the concept of medical futility.[1] The very word generates controversy. Mason and Laurie[2] prefer to talk of non-productive treatment, treatment which cannot offer even a minimal likelihood of benefit to the patient. Part of the difficulty in this debate is the problem of separating human and economic considerations. Refusing to order doctors to continue to ventilate a severely injured infant, Balcombe LJ said openly:

> ... [A]n order which may have the effect at compelling a doctor or heath authority to make available scarce resources and to a particular child ... might require the health authority to put J on a ventilator in an intensive care unit, and thereby possibly deny the benefit of those limited resources to a child who was much more likely than J to benefit from them.[3]

Language invoking medical futility could be seen as disguising rationing decisions, or even covert euthanasia. Whatever the economic considerations, few would deny the personal cost to the patient and to those close to the patient in terms of human dignity. Do the 'rights' of patients include the right to die with dignity? If so, does that 'right' extend to being 'helped to die'? In preserving and sustaining the life of a patient with a hopeless prognosis, is it in

---

[1] JK Mason and GT Laurie, *Mason and McCall Smith's Law and Medical Ethics* (7th edn, 2006) OUP, Chapter 16.

[2] *Mason and McCall Smith's Law and Medical Ethics*, p 542.

[3] *Re J (a Minor) (wardship: medical treatment)* [1992] 4 All ER 614 at 625, CA.

the interests of the patient, the family or the doctor to prolong his suffering? Unlimited access to technology may sometimes be as cruel as the illness itself. Doctors concerned with terminally ill patients must make professional and human decisions to give up treatment which may be merely sustaining the function of the organs, and turn to appropriate care at the terminal stage.

In 1993, the tragic case of Tony Bland thrust this question into the public domain.[4] Did the law demand that a young man grievously injured in the horrific disaster at Hillsborough Football Stadium should continue to be kept alive by artificial means? The Law Lords concluded that it did not. The *Bland* judgment rekindled debates on euthanasia, albeit their Lordships and many commentators[5] vehemently rejected suggestions that the decision to allow Tony Bland to die was in any sense sanctioning euthanasia.[6]

The Mental Capacity Act 2005 comes into force in October 2007. The Act sets down principles by which the social and medical care of persons lacking the mental capacity to make their own decisions should be conducted. A Code of Practice (in draft form at the time of writing) provides guidance on the interpretation of the Act. We examine the wider effects of the Act in Chapter 6. In this chapter, we will consider the implications of the Act for end of life decisions relating to adults lacking capacity. During the passage of the Mental Capacity Bill through Parliament, some feared that the Act would introduce euthanasia 'by the back door' for patients lacking mental capacity.[7] As we shall see, these fears were largely unfounded.

Tony Bland lacked the capacity to make his own decisions. But what of patients who retain capacity? Since *Bland*, the courts have been deluged with cases seeking clearer definition of an individual's right to determine the manner of her death, or life. The Human Rights Act 1998 focused attention on what exactly is entailed in the right to life embodied in Article 2 of the European Convention on Human Rights. Does the prohibition on inhuman and degrading treatment in Article 3 assist those dying in distress? Does a right to privacy in Article 8 encompass autonomy in decisions on the end of life? Case law remains confused and confusing.

In 2002, the President of the Family Division endorsed a tetraplegic patient's right to demand that doctors switch off the ventilator keeping her alive,[8] but when Dianne Pretty argued that she had a right to assisted suicide, the House of Lords found against her.[9] Doctors cannot be forced to administer treatment which they believe to be clinically unnecessary, futile or inappropriate. Does this include artificial nutrition and hydration (ANH)? The Court of Appeal held that it does.[10] An appeal to the European Court of Human Rights was

---

[4]   *Airedale NHS Trust v Bland* [1993] 1 All ER 821, HL.
[5]   *Mason and McCall Smith's Law and Medical Ethics*, p 582.
[6]   See in particular *Airedale NHS Trust v Bland* [1993] 1 All ER 821 at 856, HL, per Hoffman LJ.
[7]   D Mason, 'Euthanasia by the Back Door?' (2004) 154 *New Law Journal* 321.
[8]   *B v An NHS Trust* [2002] EWHC 429.
[9]   *R (Pretty) v DPP* [2002] 1 All ER 1, HL. Mrs Pretty's appeal to the European Court of Human Rights also failed: *Pretty v United Kingdom* (2002) 35 EHHR 1.
[10] *R (on the application of Burke) v General Medical Council* [2005] EWCA Civ 1003.

ruled inadmissible.[11] Nor are the courts the only forum for debates on the end of life. In 2006, Lord Joffe's third attempt to enshrine a right to assisted suicide in law was defeated in the House of Lords by a vote of 148 to 100. Opponents argue for the sanctity of life and for better palliative care.[12]

The *Concise Oxford Dictionary* defines euthanasia as 'Gentle and easy death; bringing about of this, especially in case of incurable and painful disease'. It is a term much used, and misused. It may be popularly invoked to include conduct characterised as 'mercy killing' when somebody, usually a relative, deliberately and specifically performs some act, such as administering a drug, to accelerate death and terminate suffering. Prosecutions for mercy killing, while rare, are sometimes reported, and the courts deal with such cases with compassion. Such cases of mercy killing, where doctors are not usually directly involved, may be termed 'active euthanasia', in contrast to 'passive euthanasia' (which might describe, for example, withholding of life-support treatment). The terminology of the debate is complex and confusing.[13] Active euthanasia involves an act done deliberately designed to shorten life, by however short a span. *Active* euthanasia may involve *voluntary* euthanasia where the act done, the killing of the patient, is done at her specific request. *Non-voluntary* euthanasia may be the term used to refer to ending the life of someone who cannot express a view on the prolongation of her life at the relevant time. A proxy speaks on her behalf and what is done is done, at least purportedly, for the patient's own good. *Involuntary* euthanasia involves killing a person without her, or any proxy, authority. The patient's life may be ended for what others perceive as her good, or could be terminated because of the burden her continued life places on society. *Passive* euthanasia can itself be voluntary, non-voluntary or involuntary. As we shall see, any boundary between passive and active euthanasia is less clear than it might at first be thought to be.

Attitudes to euthanasia in all its forms are changing.[14] Physicians themselves are more disposed to accept, in theory, some limited form of active euthanasia – or at least physician-assisted suicide. Surprisingly large numbers of doctors are prepared to confess in private that they have participated in active voluntary euthanasia.[15] The uncertainties and doubts which affect public attitudes towards the euthanasia debate are compounded by misunderstanding about, and lack of clarity in, the relevant law. We must now examine the present state of the law in England, to see how it applies to the various situations in which the medical profession becomes involved.

11   *Burke v United Kingdom* [2006] App 19807/06.
12   The Government recently promised to double funds for palliative care in the White Paper, *Our Health, Our Care, Our Say* (2006), para 4.102
13   See *Mason and McCall Smith's Law and Medical Ethics*, pp 599–600; but see also E Jackson, *Medical Law: Text, Cases and Materials* (2006) OUP, pp 911–912.
14   See S Ost, *An Analytical Study of the Legal, Moral and Ethical Aspects of the Living Phenomenon of Euthanasia* (2003) Edwin Mellen Press; H Biggs, *Euthanasia, Death with Dignity and the Law* (2001) Hart Publishing.
15   See, for example, C Norton, 'Family Doctors Admit helping Thousands of Patients to Die' (1998) Sunday Times, 15 November.

Murder, suicide and assisting suicide

20.2 Deliberately taking the life of another person, whether that person is dying or not, constitutes the crime of murder. Accordingly, any doctor who, no matter how compassionately, practises voluntary euthanasia or mercy killing can be charged with murder, if the facts can be clearly established. As Lord Mustill puts it:

> ... 'mercy killing' by active means is murder ... that the doctor's motives are kindly will for some, although not for all, transform the moral quality of his act, but this makes no difference in law.[16]

A doctor convicted of murder faces a mandatory life sentence in jail. Dr Cox was in a sense lucky.[17] He injected his patient, Mrs Lilian Boyes, with potassium chloride. Mrs Boyes suffered unbearable pain from rheumatoid arthritis and begged Dr Cox to end her suffering. Potassium chloride stops the heart. It kills and has no therapeutic or painkilling properties. Before Dr Cox's action came to the attention of the police, Mrs Boyes was cremated. It could not therefore be proved beyond reasonable doubt that the injection administered by Dr Cox killed her. Dr Cox was convicted only of attempted murder. The judge imposed a suspended sentence and the General Medical Council (GMC) allowed him to continue to practise subject to certain conditions. Had the link between his action and Mrs Boyes's death been clearly established, no such merciful course would have been open to the judge. Active euthanasia, whatever the circumstances, equals murder in English law – though we wonder if a sympathetic jury might not strive to avoid conviction in such a case.[18]

Double effect

20.3 The only exception to that rule was spelt out by Devlin J in the case of *R v Adams*[19] in 1957. Dr Adams was charged with the murder of an 81-year-old patient who had suffered a stroke; it was alleged that he had prescribed and administered such large quantities of drugs, especially heroin and morphine, that he must have known that the drugs would kill her. In his summing-up to the jury, Devlin J first stated:

> ... it does not matter whether her death was inevitable and her days were numbered. If her life was cut short by weeks or months it was just as much murder as if it was cut short by years. There has been much discussion as to when doctors might be justified in administering drugs which would shorten life. Cases of severe pain were suggested and also cases of helpless misery. The law knows no special defence in this category ...

However he went on to say:

16   *Airedale NHS Trust v Bland* [1993] 1 All ER 821 at 850, HL.
17   *R v Cox* (1992) 12 BMLR 38. See E Jackson, 'Whose Death Is It Anyway? Euthanasia and the Medical Profession' (2004) 57 *Current Legal Problems* 415.
18   See Jackson, *Medical Law: Text, Cases and Materials*, pp 912–914.
19   *R v Adams* [1957] Crim LR 773.

... but that does not mean that a doctor who was aiding the sick and dying had to calculate in minutes, or even hours, perhaps, not in days or weeks, the effect on a patient's life of the medicines which he would administer. If the first purpose of medicine – the restoration of health – could no longer be achieved, there was still much for the doctor to do and he was entitled to do all that was proper and necessary to relieve pain and suffering even if the measures he took might incidentally shorten life by hours or perhaps even longer. The doctor who decided whether or not to administer the drug could not do his job, if he were thinking in terms of hours or months of life. Dr Adams's defence was that the treatment was designed to promote comfort, and if it was the right and proper treatment, the fact that it shortened life did not convict him of murder.

Devlin J introduced into English law a version of the 'double effect' principle, whereby if one act has two inevitable consequences, one good and one evil, the act may be morally acceptable in certain circumstances. His ruling is endorsed in *Bland*.[20] It is not crystal clear in its meaning. In one passage, Devlin J referred to the incidental shortening of life by hours and, in another passage, he referred to the shortening of life by hours or months. It must be a matter of judgment in each case.[21] Clearly he was dealing with terminally ill patients where, in order to alleviate pain, it is permissible to disregard the fact that the treatment involved may accelerate the patient's death.

At the time of writing, the matter is about to be put to the test in the High Court.[22] Kelly Taylor, who suffers from both Eisenmenger's syndrome and Klippel-Feil syndrome, which affect her heart, lungs and spine, has as little as a year to live. She is in constant pain and asserts that her life is intolerable. She is allergic to some of the drugs used to treat her condition. Doctors have been unable to alleviate her pain. Mrs Taylor wants neither to starve to death, nor to travel abroad for assisted suicide. She argues that the refusal of doctors to administer enough morphine to induce a coma-like state (but which poses a risk of killing her) is 'inhuman or degrading treatment' under Article 3 of the European Convention on Human Rights, and breaches her right to privacy under Article 8. Her argument is not that doctors should be forced to administer the treatment, but that doctors should not deny it to her without trying to find a doctor willing to carry it out.[23] Mrs Taylor has prepared an advance directive refusing treatment. If the requested dose of morphine is administered, and her advance directive is valid and applicable, she will die.

[20] *Airedale NHS Trust v Bland* [1993] 1 All ER 821 at 868. But consider the impact of *R v Woollin* [1999] 1 AC 82 (jury may infer intent to kill even if causing death is not the accused's primary purpose); see Jackson, *Medical Law: Text, Cases and Materials*, p 923.

[21] See, for example, the investigation surrounding 43 cases of patient deaths under GP Howard Martin. Martin was cleared of murdering three patients by injecting them with morphine, at Teeside Crown Court in 2005: see 'Morphine Doctor Cleared of Murder' (2005) Times, 14 December. Further investigation followed and, at the time of writing, Dr Martin remains suspended by the GMC (GMC Interim Order No 0525365).

[22] See G Slapper, 'The Law Exposed: Assisted Suicide' (2007) Times, 15 February.

[23] But see Select Committee on the Assisted Dying for the Terminally Ill Bill, HL Paper 86 (2005), para 269(c)(8), which recommended that 'any new bill should not place on a physician with conscientious objection the duty to refer an applicant for assisted suicide or voluntary euthanasia to another physician without such objection; it should provide adequate protection for all health care professionals who may be involved in any way in such an application; and it should ensure that the position of persons working in multi-disciplinary teams is adequately protected'.

Will the doctrine of double effect stretch this far? It seems unlikely, but the distinction is a fine one. Mrs Taylor undoubtedly intends her death to result from the administration of morphine, but, arguably, the doctor's aim will be quite different – the alleviation of pain. Perhaps Mrs Taylor's case would stand a better chance if she could find a doctor willing to administer the drug and to stand up for his right to do so in court.

The application of laws relating to murder and suicide are central to an understanding of the law controlling treatment of the dying. It will be appropriate to consider first the case of the 'competent' patient, that is a person with full legal and mental capacity, who is aware of what is happening and who may wish to make decisions himself about his quality of life – the way he will be treated and how he will continue to live or die. Second, the case of the adult 'incompetent' patient will be considered – unconscious patients or persons who do not have the mental or physical capacity to make their own wishes known at the relevant times.[24]

Competent patients: is there a 'right' to die?

20.4 Does a patient have a 'right' to die? The answer will depend on the circumstances in which she seeks to exercise such a 'right'. The Court of Appeal in *Re T*[25] made it clear that an adult, mentally-competent patient enjoys an absolute right to refuse further treatment even where refusing treatment means certain death. A patient who is terminally ill, or who, even if not terminally ill, suffers from intractable pain or unbearable disability can refuse further treatment. The only *caveat* is that the evidence that her refusal of treatment was free and informed must be unequivocal. Her reasons to refuse treatment are not material. A patient dying of cancer has the right to say 'no more', however strongly her doctor may argue that more chemo-therapy would offer her some additional months of life. A person paralysed by multiple sclerosis can refuse to be ventilated. A patient whose condition is no longer bearable to her can take her own life if she has access to the means to do so, and is still independently capable of such action. There is a right to prevent others forcing you to live.

The first major difficulty is this. A patient who wishes to die may already be receiving life-sustaining treatment. She is hooked up to a ventilator or receiving artificial nutrition via a naso-gastric tube or intravenous drip. She wants her life support withdrawn and to be permitted to die. Intrinsically, her position seems indistinguishable from the patient who refuses further chemo-therapy or instructs her doctors not to ventilate her. However, someone will have to intervene in this scenario, to switch off the ventilator or remove the feeding tube. Will a doctor who does the relevant act risk prosecution for murder or assisting suicide?

---

[24]   It should be noted, of course, that it may not always be an easy issue to determine whether a person is clinically or legally competent: see above, Chapter 6. Children and infants are considered in Chapter 15.

[25]   *Re T (Adult: Refusal of Treatment)* [1992] 4 All ER 469, CA (discussed in Chapter 5 at 5.2).

The decision in *Airedale NHS Trust v Bland*[26] made it clear that if a doctor disconnects a patient from life-support at her specific request, that act does not constitute either murder or assisting suicide. *Bland* exposes the fragility of distinctions made between active and passive euthanasia.[27] Three principles emerge from *Bland*:

(1)   Treatment involving any invasive procedure constitutes a battery, unless authorised by the patient or, if he is unable to authorise his own treatment, it is justified by other lawful authority.

(2)   Continuing invasive treatment once justification for that treatment is withdrawn becomes a battery and therefore unlawful.

(3)   Artificial nutrition and hydration constitutes treatment as much as drug therapy or ventilation. If a patient instructs doctors to switch off a ventilator or withdraw a naso-gastric tube, failure to act on those instructions renders continuing treatment unlawful.

In *B v An NHS Trust*,[28] Ms B suffered a haemorrhage in the spinal column in her neck. Her condition deteriorated rapidly. Within two years she was paralysed from the neck down and could breathe only supported by a ventilator. Doctors told her that she was unlikely to recover. Rehabilitation programmes to allow her to live outside hospital on the ventilator were proposed to her. Ms B was adamant that she did not want to survive in such a condition. She instructed doctors to switch off the ventilator. The doctors treating her refused, citing conscientious objections to such a course of action and challenging Ms B's mental capacity to refuse further treatment. Butler-Sloss P held that Ms B retained mental capacity.[29] That being the case, continuing to ventilate her against her will was unlawful. She was entitled to demand that the ventilator be switched off, though not to require an individual clinician to act contrary to his conscience. Yet there can be no doubt that switching off a ventilator or removing a naso-gastric tube is an act hastening death. In *Bland*, the Law Lords skirt around the logical implications of their findings. Lord Browne-Wilkinson is honest in his appreciation of the dilemma. He says:

> Mr Munby QC ... submits that the removal of the naso-gastric tube necessary to provide artificial feeding and the discontinuation of the existing regime of artificial feeding constitute positive acts of commission. I do not accept this. Apart from the act of removing the naso-gastric tube, the mere failure to continue to do what you have previously done is not, in any ordinary sense to do anything positive; on the contrary it is by definition an omission to do what you have previously done.

> The positive act of removing the naso-gastric tube presents more difficulty. It is undoubtedly a positive act, similar to switching off a ventilator in the case of a patient whose life is being sustained by artificial ventilation. But in my

---

[26]   [1993] 1 All ER 821, HL; and see *Nancy B v Hôtel Dieu de Quebec* (1992) 86 DLR (4th) 385 (Canada); *Auckland Area Health Board v A-S* [1993] 1 NZLR 235 (New Zealand); *Bouvia v Superior Court* (1986) 225 Cal Reptr 297.

[27]   But see A McGee, 'Finding a Way Through the Ethical and Legal Maze: Withdrawal of Medical Treatment and Euthanasia' (2005) 13 *Medical Law Review* 357 and J Keown, 'A Futile Defence of Bland: A Reply to Andrew McGee' (2005) 13 *Medical Law Review* 393.

[28]   [2002] EWHC 429 (Fam).

[29]   Discussed more fully above at 6.3.

judgment in neither case should the act be classified as positive, since to do so would be to introduce intolerable fine distinctions. If instead of removing the naso-gastric tube, it was left in place but no further nutrients were provided for the tube to convey to the patients' stomach, that would not be a positive act ... if the switching off of a ventilator were to be classified as a positive act, exactly the same result can be achieved by installing a time-clock which requires to be reset every 12 hours; the failure to reset the machine could not be classified as a positive act. In my judgment, essentially what is being done is to omit to feed or ventilate; the removal of the naso-gastric tube or the switching off a ventilator are merely incidents of that omission.[30]

Eliding acts and omissions enable the Law Lords to achieve the desired result. Consider its implications.[31] James is sustained by a ventilator. He asks his wife, Claire, to switch it off because his doctor refuses to do so. James rejects advice to seek a declaration from the courts to overturn his doctors' advice. Reluctantly, Claire pulls the switch and James dies. Is Claire exempt from a charge of murder, or is a *Bland* defence exclusive to doctors? In the light of *B v An NHS Trust*, could Claire argue thus? Continuing to ventilate James against his will constitutes the tort of battery and the crime of assault. When Claire switched off the ventilator all she did was use reasonable measures to prevent a crime. Then there is the most awkward question of all. What of the patient whose illness renders their life intolerable, but who are not reliant on treatment or life support to survive? Their condition is such that they cannot take their own life.

Assisted suicide

20.5 Since the Suicide Act 1961, it is no longer a criminal offence to commit, or attempt to commit, suicide. However, the Act does provide that 'a person who aids, abets, counsels or procures the suicide of another, or an attempt by another to commit suicide, shall be liable on conviction ... to a term not exceeding fourteen years'.[32] It is a crime that may be committed for diverse reasons, ranging from the avaricious to the compassionate. In *R v McShane*,[33] a daughter was found guilty of trying to persuade her 89-year-old mother in a nursing home to kill herself so that she could inherit her estate. A secret camera installed by the police showed the daughter handing her mother drugs concealed in a packet of sweets, and pinning a note on her dress saying 'Don't bungle it'!

Clear evidence of aiding and abetting a particular act of suicide is necessary before a prosecution can be successful. In *Attorney-General v Able*,[34] the court was asked to declare that it was an offence for the Voluntary Euthanasia Society to sell a booklet to its members aged 25 and over, setting out in some detail various ways in which individuals could commit suicide. The Society,

---

[30] [1993] 1 All ER 821.
[31] See Jackson, *Medical Law: Text, Cases and Materials*, p 425.
[32] Section 2(1) of the Suicide Act 1961. Prosecution requires the consent of the Director of Public Prosecutions: see s 2(4).
[33] (1977) 66 Cr App Rep 97.
[34] [1984] QB 795.

which campaigned for the introduction of voluntary euthanasia legislation, claimed that, pending such legislation, they saw no alternative to supplying on request the necessary information to enable its members to bring about 'their own deliverance'. The Society neither advocated nor deplored suicide; it had a neutral stance and regarded such decisions as matters of personal belief and judgement. Evidence in the case suggested that over a period of 18 months after the first distribution of the booklet, there were 15 cases of suicide linked to the booklet and 19 suicides where documents were found which showed that the deceased was a member of, or had corresponded with, the Society. The court concluded that in most cases the supply of the booklet would not constitute an offence. Normally, a member requesting the booklet would not make clear his intentions, and the booklet would be supplied without any knowledge by the supplier of whether it was required for general information, research or because suicide was contemplated. To establish an offence, it would have to be proved that the Society distributed the booklet to a person who, at the time of the distribution, was known to be contemplating suicide, with the intention of assisting and encouraging that person to commit suicide by means of the booklet's contents, and – further – that that person was in fact assisted and encouraged by the booklet to commit or attempt to commit suicide.

In the same way, a doctor who knowingly provides someone with sufficient tablets with which to end a life, and advises how best to take them, risks prosecution. In 2005, much publicity was given to the case of Dr Michael Irwin, who visited his friend, Patrick Kneen, with 60 Temazepam pills which he had prescribed for himself. When he arrived, Kneen, who suffered from terminal prostate cancer, was too ill to swallow. Dr Irwin's intention to commit a criminal act led to his being struck off the register by the General Medical Council.[35] However, in many cases it might be difficult to prove that a doctor who had supplied drugs to a patient was responsible for the patient taking an overdose.

The well-informed and able may kill themselves. The patient dying of degenerative disease, or in the terminal throes of cancer, may need help to do so. If Jane can breathe only with the aid of a ventilator, she can require her doctor to switch off the ventilator. If Jane is slowly choking to death with motor neurone disease, but can still swallow enough lethal sleeping tablets, Jane can end her misery. If Jane is so weakened by the disease that she cannot reach for the tablets or swallow, she must endure her suffering.

An increasing number of commentators now advance the case for legalising physician-assisted suicide.[36] But what does this mean? The Oregon Death with Dignity Act 1994[37] allows doctors to comply with a patient's request for medication to end their life. But this does not meet the truly hard cases where

[33]   C Dyer, 'GP is Disciplined for Willingness to Help Friend Commit Suicide' (2005) 331 *British Medical Journal* 717.

[36]   Notably and eloquently, DW Meyers and JK Mason, 'Physician Assisted Suicide: A Second View from Mid-Atlantic' (1999) 29 *Anglo-American Law Review* 39.

[37]   Discussed below at 20.18. See also I Kennedy and A Grubb, *Medical Law: Text and Materials* (2000) Butterworths, p 1950.

the patient, even if supplied with medication, cannot take the dose independently. As we shall see, recent attempts to introduce legislation legalising physician-assisted suicide in England and Wales have proved unsuccessful.

The patient who cannot commit suicide

20.6   Does the patient who cannot, or does not, wish to administer the means of suicide himself have a right to assistance? Articles 2, 3, 8, 9 and 14 of the European Convention on Human Rights have been employed, to date unsuccessfully, in defence of such a right.

This matter first came before the UK courts in the sad case of Dianne Pretty. Mrs Pretty was dying of motor neurone disease. Gradually she had lost all ability to use her muscles. She could barely speak and could not swallow. She was fed by a tube. Mrs Pretty sought an assurance from the Director of Public Prosecutions (DPP) that no charge would be brought against her husband should he help her to die at a time of her choice. The DPP refused to give any such assurance. Mrs Pretty brought an application for judicial review. She argued that the DPP acted unlawfully. He failed to pay due regard to Mrs Pretty's fundamental human rights. Her application failed before the Divisional Court,[38] as did her subsequent appeal to the House of Lords.[39] She took her case to the European Court of Human Rights at Strasbourg, but lost again.[40] The Law Lords held that the decision not to promise immunity to Mr Pretty should he help his wife to die was not, in the circumstances, amenable to judicial review.[41]

What human rights arguments did Mrs Pretty raise? It was put to the judges that Article 2, endorsing the right to life, carried with it the corollary of a right to die at a time and in a manner of one's own choosing. The Law Lords were unimpressed. They could read nothing into Article 2 to confer a right to be helped to die. Lord Bingham regarded Article 2 as embodying the traditional doctrine of sanctity of life. He put it thus:

> Whatever the benefits which, in the view of many, attach to voluntary euthanasia, physician-assisted suicide and suicide without the intervention of a physician, these are not benefits which derive protection from an article framed to protect the sanctity of life.[42]

Nor did an argument based on Article 3, prohibiting inhuman or degrading treatment, find any greater favour. Dignity in sickness and dying should be protected. Nothing in Article 3 conferred a positive obligation to help an individual end her life.[43] The Divisional Court declared:

---

[38]   [2001] EWHC Admin 788.
[39]   [2002] 1 All ER 1, HL.
[40]   *Pretty v United Kingdom* (2002) 35 EHHR 1.
[41]   Although at least some of their Lordships left open the question of whether on different facts such an application might succeed.
[42]   [2002] 1 All ER 1 at 7, HL. The ECtHR concurred that Article 2 'could not be interpreted as involving a negative aspect'.
[43]   But see the persuasive arguments of J Coggon, 'Could the Right to Die with Dignity Represent a New Right to Die in English Law ?' (2006) 12 *Medical Law Review* 219.

... far from having the effect contended for by Mr Havers, articles 2 and 3 between them are aimed at the protection and preservation of life and the dignity of life, because of its fundamental value, not only to the individual but also to the community as a whole. It is to stand the whole purpose of these articles on its head to say that they are aimed at protecting a person's right to procure their own death.[44]

In the Lords, Lord Bingham[45] doubted whether any positive obligation to prevent citizens being subjected to degrading treatment could translate into a duty to ensure a person could seek help to die. Lord Steyn was clear that '... article 3 was not engaged'. It was:

... singularly inapt to convey the idea that the state must guarantee to individuals a right to die with the deliberate assistance of third parties. So radical a step, infringing the sanctity of life principle, would have required far more explicit wording.[46]

Lord Hope[47] was not convinced that Mrs Pretty's condition met the minimum level of severity required in Article 3. Since she could not be compelled to accept treatment and, in his view, palliative treatment was available, Lord Hope doubted that her state was degrading.[48]

Arguments centred on Article 8, the right to respect for private and family life, fared a little better. The Divisional Court conceded that Article 8 could extend to embrace a right to bodily integrity, including a right to refuse life-saving treatment. They were even prepared to assume Article 8(1) could extend to a right to be allowed to take one's own life. In some of their speeches, the Law Lords suggest Article 8 does not go that far. Lord Steyn puts it bluntly:

... article 8 prohibits interference with the way in which an individual leads his life and it does not relate to the manner in which he wishes to die.[49]

All their Lordships concurred with the Divisional Court that even if some sort of right to choose one's manner of dying can be inferred from Articles 8(1), Article 8(2), placing restrictions on privacy rights, justifies the state in criminalising assisted suicide. The need to afford protection for vulnerable people, especially the elderly, justifies the provisions of the Suicide Act 1961 as they stand. Lord Bingham says:

It is not hard to imagine that an elderly person, in the absence of any pressure, might opt for a premature end to life if that were available, not from a desire to die or a willingness to stop living, but from a desire to stop being a burden to others.[50]

Arguments grounded on Articles 9 and 14 of the Convention also failed. Two policy questions perhaps influenced the judges in the Divisional Court and the

44 [2001] EWHC Admin 788 at para 51.
45 [2002] 1 All ER 1 at 11–12, HL.
46 At 29.
47 At 37.
48 At 37.
49 At 29.
50 At 18. A view endorsed by the ECtHR.

Lords. First, note that Mrs Pretty did not seek physician-assisted suicide, but her husband's help to die. The Divisional Court noted:

> We are not being asked to approve physician assisted suicide in carefully defined circumstances with carefully defined safeguards. We are being asked to allow a family member to help a loved one die, in circumstances of which we know nothing, in a way of which we know nothing, and with no continuing scrutiny by any outside person.[51]

Second, the Law Lords were much exercised by the European scope of the Convention. Lord Steyn made this point:

> The fact is that among the 41 member states ... there are deep cultural and religious differences in regard to euthanasia and assisted suicide. The legalisation of euthanasia and assisted suicide as adopted in the Netherlands would be unacceptable in predominantly Roman Catholic countries in Europe. The idea that the European Convention requires states to render lawful euthanasia and assisted suicide (as opposed to allowing democratically elected legislatures to adopt measures to that effect) must therefore be approached with caution.[52]

The last (judicial) word on physician-assisted suicide may still be to come. Hopes that Parliament will take this burden from judges have so far proved unfounded.

Death tourism

20.7 With the development of the freedom of movement in Europe, some patients have travelled abroad to take advantage of laws permissive of assisted suicide in a practice labelled 'death tourism'. In Switzerland, assisted suicide is not illegal provided it is not motivated by self-serving ends. The practice of assisting suicide is not limited to doctors, and suicide organisations in Switzerland are some of the few in the world willing to accept foreign patients.[53] The English courts are powerless to intervene unless someone 'aids, abets, counsels or procures the suicide of another'. Many applicants are too ill to make all the arrangements themselves and are helped by a doctor or loved one. For the DPP, there seems to be a great difference between promising immunity and giving the consent necessary to secure a conviction. Though technically it remains a crime to aid and abet suicide, the DPP has proved loath to exercise its discretion. Neither has the Crown Prosecution Service (CPS) set guidelines to clarify the legal position.

In *Re Z (An Adult: Capacity)*,[54] Mr Z informed his local authority that he and his wife, Mrs Z, would travel to Switzerland where arrangements had been made for her to end her life at the Zurich-based assisted-suicide clinic, Dignitas. Could the court prevent him from assisting his wife? The judge

---

[51] [2001] EWHC Admin 788 at para 60. See also [2002] 1 All ER 1 at 21, per Lord Bingham.

[52] At 27.

[53] Since the Swiss clinic Dignitas was set up in 1998, there have reportedly been 450 assisted suicides, of which 42 were Britons: see D Foggo, 'Chain of Suicide Clinics Planned' (2006) *Sunday Times*, 16 April.

[54] [2004] EWHC 2817 (Fam). See P DeCruz, 'The Terminally Ill Adult Seeking Assisted Suicide Abroad' (2005) 13 *Medical Law Review* 257.

satisfied himself that Mrs Z remained competent and was not subject to any undue influence. The decision to travel to Switzerland was hers. Any question of her husband's criminal liability was a matter for the DPP, who had not authorised any prosecution:

> [A]lthough an act may be criminal, it is not always in the public interest to prosecute in respect of it.[55]

If in the future, Ludwig Minelli, the founder of Dignitas, is successful in his plans to offer his services to a wider range of individuals, including those suffering from chronic depression,[56] might the DPP take a more proactive role?

Would the courts be as permissive of *doctors* helping patients to travel to assisted suicide clinics? Since Dr Michael Irwin was struck off the medical register by the GMC, he has admitted to helping six terminally ill people travel to Dignitas in Switzerland through his organisation TLC ('The Last Choice'). He is awaiting a decision by the CPS as to whether or not to prosecute. It is a long time coming.

The unconscious patient

20.8 What of the fate of the patient whose illness or injury has rendered him unconscious and unlikely ever to regain consciousness? What test should be employed to determine the appropriate course of action? Two tests were examined in Chapter 6, the substituted judgment test and the best interests test.

The substituted judgment test was employed in the seminal American case of Karen Quinlan,[57] a young woman who, suddenly stricken with illness, lay in a coma attached to a life-support machine. Although she was not brain stem dead, her doctors were satisfied that there was no hope that she would ever recover a cognitive state: she was characterised as being in a 'chronic, persistent, vegetative condition' kept alive only with the assistance of a ventilator. Karen's parents decided that it would be best for her to be removed from the life-support machine. Accordingly, her father applied to the court to be appointed her guardian and claimed that, as guardian, he would be entitled to authorise the discontinuance of all 'extraordinary' medical procedures sustaining Karen Quinlan's life. The Supreme Court of New Jersey upheld the father's claim. First, had Karen Quinlan been conscious and lucid, she would have had a right, just like Ms B, to decide to discontinue life-support treatment in circumstances where it was simply prolonging for a short period a terminal condition. She was not conscious or lucid. Second, because of her condition, her father was appointed guardian and the question then arose whether he could make a decision of that kind on her behalf. He was entitled to go to the court to seek assistance, and the court was prepared to 'don the

---

55 *Re Z (An Adult: Capacity)* [2004] EWHC 2817 (Fam), per Hedley J at para 14.
56 J Shakespeare, 'A Date with Death' (2006) Sunday Times, 16 April.
57 *Re Quinlan* 355 A 2d 647 (1976). See also *Cruzan v Director Missouri Department of Health* (1990) 110 S Ct 2841 (USA Supreme Court).

mental mantle of Karen Quinlan' to make a decision for her which she would have made had she been able to do so. Thus, by applying a 'substituted judgment' test, the court decided that if, upon the concurrence of the guardian and the family of the patient, the attending physicians should conclude that there was no reasonable possibility of her ever emerging from her comatose condition to a cognitive state and that the life-support apparatus should be discontinued, they should consult with the Hospital Ethics Committee and, if that body agreed, the life-support system might be withdrawn, without any civil or criminal liability on the part of any participant. Following that judgment, a Hospital Ethics Committee was convened and the decision was taken to remove the life-support system machine. It is an interesting reflection on the fallibility of human judgement that withdrawal of the life-support system did not lead to a swift death, and Karen Quinlan survived for ten long years after falling into the coma.

Where relatives disagree as to the appropriate course of action, the substituted judgment test can result in acrimonious legal action. Another American example involves the tragic case of Terri Schiavo, who collapsed at home in 1990 and was resuscitated by emergency services. She went into a coma and was diagnosed as being in a persistent vegetative state three years later. The cause of the collapse was not determined, but her husband and guardian, Michael Schiavo, successfully settled a malpractice suit out of court. Various therapies failed to improve Mrs Schiavo's condition and, in 1998, Mr Schiavo filed a petition for the removal of ANH tubes. He argued that Mrs Schiavo would not have wanted to continue living in these circumstances. Her Roman Catholic parents vehemently disagreed. The judge ordered the removal of ANH in 2000. The tubes were removed but reinserted pending the outcome of a series of challenges to Mr Schiavo's guardianship. He had a new partner, yet he remained married to Mrs Schiavo and his guardianship was affirmed. Challenges were also mounted on the basis that Mrs Schiavo was not actually in PVS. These too were unsuccessful. The tubes were removed again in 2003. A week later, legislation was passed allowing Governor Jeb Bush to inter- vene.[58] Her tubes were reinserted and the legal battle resumed. In 2004, Governor Bush's legislation was deemed unconstitutional:[59] it was a clear abuse of the doctrine of separation of powers. In early 2005, the order was made for the tubes to be removed for the third time. Publicity reached fever pitch. In a final bid to overrule the judges, Governor Bush passed a private Bill enabling the case to be transferred to the federal courts. Mrs Schiavo's parents' case was turned down and the US Supreme Court denied *certiorari* on each of the five occasions it was sought.[60] Mrs Schiavo's ANH tubes were removed for

---

[58]   State of Florida, House Bill No 35-E, which later was passed into Law as Florida Public Law, Chapter 2003–418.

[59]   *Jeb Bush, Governor of Florida v Michael Schiavo, Guardian of Theresa Schiavo*, Case Number SC04–925, Florida Supreme Court, 23 September 2004.

[60]   *Schindler v Schiavo*, No 04A801, 2005 WL 615863 (17 March 2005); *Schindler v Schiavo*, No 00A926 (2000); *Bush v Schiavo*, 125 S Ct 1086 (2005); *Committee on Government Reform v Schiavo*, No 04A811, 2005 WL 636582 (US, 18 March 2005); *Respondent Michael Schiavo's Opposition to Application for Injunction*, Case No 04A-825 (24 March 2005).

the third and final time in March 2005, and she died 13 days later. Difficult decisions remain difficult whether the legal test is best interests or substituted judgment.

English law has rejected a test whereby the next of kin should automatically enjoy proxy powers of consent. Instead, both case law and the Mental Capacity Act 2005 embrace a modified best interests test. The Mental Capacity Act introduces important changes in practice. There is a new Court of Protection which can appoint a 'deputy' to act for the patient. Alternatively, the patient himself can, whilst competent, appoint a donee of a lasting power of attorney (LPA) to make certain decisions on his behalf if, or when, he loses capacity to make them himself. He may also make an advance directive refusing treatment. Decisions of the LPA and the relevance and applicability of advance directives are subject to stringent controls.[61] The best interest test survives the reform, and earlier case law remains relevant to illustrate how the 2005 Act will work. As we shall see, the best interests test involves a careful balancing of the sanctity of life, the quality of life and the individual's rights and interests in dignity and autonomy.

Bland: crossing the Rubicon?[62]

20.9 At 17, Tony Bland suffered crush injuries at Hillsborough football stadium. He suffered catastrophic and irreversible damage to his brain. The condition from which he suffered is known as a persistent vegetative state (PVS).[63] He had lost all cortical (higher brain) function, but his brain stem continued to operate. PVS patients continue to breathe independently and their digestion continues to function. Tony Bland was incapable of voluntary movement and could feel no pain. He could not see or hear, taste or smell.[64] He remained alive, fed through a tube. All his excretory functions were managed mechanically. Doctors were agreed that there was no hope of recovery of any sort. In this condition, the young man existed for two years until, with the concurrence of his family, the hospital applied for a declaration that they might lawfully discontinue artificial nutrition and hydration. The House of Lords unanimously granted that declaration.

We have seen[65] how their Lordships managed to find that withdrawing the naso-gastric tube was not an act hastening death such as to expose doctors to

---

61 See below at 20.13.
62 *Airedale NHS Trust v Bland* [1993] 1 All ER 821, HL.
63 On which see B Jennett, *The Vegetative State: Medical Facts, Ethical and Legal Dilemmas* (2002) CUP. According to the NHS Direct Health Encyclopaedia (available at www.nhsdirect.nhs.uk), a person in a vegetative state for one month is said to be in a 'persistent vegetative state'. A person in a persistent vegetative state for more than a year is said to be in a 'permanent vegetative state'. We refer to the '*persistent* vegetative state', indicating that the condition is continuing. The British Medical Association and the Royal College of Physicians prefer the term 'persistent vegetative state'. Permanency is a prediction that is ultimately uncertain. See BMA, *Treatment Decisions for Patients in Persistent Vegetative State* (2006); RCP, *The Vegetative State: Guidance on Diagnosis and Management* (2003).

64 This incontrovertible physical evidence and irreparable damage to the brain distinguishes *Bland* from some subsequent cases.
65 Above at 20.1.

liability for murder. Tony Bland, however, could not instruct his doctors to cease treatment. Unlike in the Karen Quinlan case in the USA, his family could not seek to be appointed as guardians of their adult son. The Law Lords fell back on *F v West Berkshire Health Authority*.[66] When a patient was incapable of deciding whether to continue treatment for himself, what could lawfully be done to him depended on what constituted treatment in his best interests and in conformity to responsible medical practice. For Lords Goff, Keith and Lowry, the evidence of medical opinion and professional guidelines on diagnosis and confirmation of PVS allowed them to conclude that, as Tony Bland received no benefit from treatment, it was not in his best interests to continue naso-gastric feeding. They reasoned that the regime of artificial feeding constitutes treatment and an overwhelming body of medical opinion supported withdrawing artificial nutrition and hydration from patients confirmed in PVS. Therefore withdrawing 'treatment' was lawful.

Lord Mustill acknowledged[67] the complexity of best interests in this context. Tony Bland was not suffering; he felt no pain:

> By ending his life the doctors will not relieve him of a burden become intolerable, for others carry the burden and he has none. What other considerations could make it better for him to die now rather than later? None that we can measure, for of death we know nothing. The distressing truth which must not be shirked, is that the proposed conduct is not in the best interests of Anthony Bland, for he has no best interests of any kind.

Lord Mustill turned traditional analyses of best interests on their heads. He looked at the justification for what was being done to Tony Bland's body – the tubes feeding him, the tubes excreting his waste. Absent evidence that such invasive treatments were necessary to promote his best interests, they were themselves unlawful, a trespass on the youth's unconscious body. Thus treatment not in his interests could and must be withdrawn. *Bland* is an exceptional, difficult case. No-one could fail to sympathise with his family whose child was breathing, but effectively a 'living corpse'. Yet where does *Bland* lead?[68] Can something as basic as feeding be withheld to bring about death? Would this mean staff caring for a patient in advanced stages of dementia who could swallow, but did not demand food, could stop spoon-feeding?

The Law Lords saw the dangers of their decision. They advised that before treatment was discontinued, a declaration should be sought from the courts. They warned that their ruling covered only patients in PVS. They sought to restrain any slide down slippery slopes. Withdrawal of artificial nutrition and hydration required evidence that:

(1)   every effort should have been made to provide rehabilitation for at least six months;

---

[66] [1989] 2 All ER 545, discussed fully above at 6.5.
[67] [1993] 1 All ER 821 at 894, HL.
[68] For critical appraisal of *Bland*, see JM Finnis, 'Bland: Crossing the Rubicon?' (1993) 109 *Law Quarterly Review* 329; J Keown, 'Restoring Moral and Intellectual Shape to the Law after *Bland*' (1997) 113 *Law Quarterly Review* 481.

(2)   diagnosis of irreversible PVS should not be considered confirmed until at least twelve months after the injury;

(3)   diagnosis should be agreed by two independent doctors; and

(4)   generally the views of the patient's immediate family will be given great weight.[69]

Bland is a limited and cautious decision. Even on its own facts it provokes numerous questions. The experts who gave evidence in Bland expressed total confidence in medical ability to judge that a patient was irreversibly in PVS. Others are more dubious, concerned that diagnosis may be mistaken and arguing that, in some cases, intensive treatment can result in limited recovery.[70] The legerdemain by which their Lordships classified removal of a feeding tube as an omission not an act provokes charges of covert legalisation of euthanasia.[71] Lord Mustill[72] recognised that it is difficult to find any moral difference between inaction resulting in a slow death and action resulting in a swift one. Can the legal distinction be maintained?[73] If it is a matter of policy rather than legal principle, then should the mantra of sanctity of life be swapped for that of quality of life and euthanasia legalised?[74] If Tony Bland's life was sacred for itself, not its quality, how can withholding basic food and water be acceptable?

After Bland: PVS to 'near PVS'

20.10 Decisions which followed *Bland* indicate that *Bland* has led to radical change in the law governing the ending of life. The carefully constituted limitations built into *Bland* to keep that decision within bounds were eroded step by step. In *Frenchay Healthcare NHS Trust v S*,[75] the patient was said to have been in PVS for two-and-a-half years following a drug overdose. His feeding tube was accidentally disconnected. The hospital immediately sought a declaration that it could lawfully refrain from re-inserting the tube. The Court of Appeal granted the declaration in haste and without any independent medical opinion confirming that S was irreversibly in PVS. The court recognised that the evidence as to S's condition was neither as unanimous nor as emphatic as in *Bland*. The judges found that in the emergency which had arisen because of the disconnection of the tube, there was no benefit conferred on S by re-inserting the tube. Indeed, following Lord Browne-Wilkinson's reasoning in *Bland*, it might be construed as an assault on S to do so. In these

---

[69]   And see British Medical Association, *Withholding and Withdrawing Life-Prolonging Medical Treatment: Guidance for Decision-Making* (2nd edn, 2001) (updated 2005); *Guidelines on Treatment of Patients in Persistent Vegetative State* (2006).

[70]   See K Andrews, 'Recovery of Patients after Four Months or More in the Persistent Vegetative State' (1993) 306 *British Medical Journal* 1597; K Andrews, 'Patients in the Persistent Vegetative State: Problems in their Long Term Management' (1993) 306 *British Medical Journal* 1600.

[71]   See the incisive arguments in Finnis (1993) 109 *Law Quarterly Review* 329 and Keown (1997) 113 *Law Quarterly Review* 481.

[72]   [1993] AC 789 at 885.

[73]   See L Doyal, 'Dignity in Dying Should Include the Legalization of Non-Voluntary Euthanasia' (2006) 1(2) *Clinical Ethics* 65.

[74]   See P Singer, *Rethinking Life and Death* (1994) OUP, p 75.

[75]   [1994] 2 All ER 403.

circumstances, the further inquiry necessary to take an independent medical opinion could be dispensed with. A fortuitous event affected the criteria set out in *Bland* to protect patients. On the facts, some doubt exists whether S was truly in PVS. There was evidence of restlessness and distress for which S was receiving medication.[76] Condition 3 set by Lord Goff in *Bland*, independent evidence confirming PVS, survived barely a year.

Subsequent decisions eroded the *Bland* limitations yet further. In *Re D*,[77] the patient had suffered serious brain damage after a road accident. As in *Frenchay*, her feeding tube became disconnected. Stephen Brown P accepted evidence that D's condition did not fully conform to guidelines for diagnosis of PVS laid down by the Royal College of Physicians (RCP). He was satisfied that there was 'no evidence of any meaningful life whatsoever' and held that it was lawful to refrain from re-inserting the tube. In *Re H*[78] a 43-year-old woman had suffered brain injuries in a car crash. She retained some rudimentary awareness and, like D, did not fit squarely within the RCP definition of PVS. The President of the Family Division approved cessation of artificial feeding. He was '... satisfied that it is in the best interests of this patient that the life sustaining treatment currently being artificially administered should be brought to a conclusion.'[79]

After Bland: beyond PVS?

20.11 Another lesson which may be drawn from post-*Bland* cases on PVS, or near PVS, is that PVS cases are no longer 'special'. Nor is withdrawal of feeding seen as much more of a dilemma than withdrawal of any other form of treatment, such as dialysis.[80] The *Practice Note*[81] setting out procedures to obtain court sanction to withdraw treatment from an adult lacking mental capacity embraces PVS within a wider range of medical and welfare disputes leading to litigation. Each case turns on the best interests of the patient. Best interests is a phrase easy to utter and difficult to interpret. It inevitably involves judgments of quality of life. In *Re D*,[82] a patient who had been hospitalised for much of his life with serious psychiatric illness developed renal failure and required dialysis. D lacked mental capacity to consent to treatment and often would not be co-operative in dialysis treatment. To continue dialysis he might have to be anaesthetised on each occasion. The judge ruled that it was not in the patient's interest to impose dialysis on him where, in the doctors' opinion, 'it is not reasonably practicable to do so'.

In *W Healthcare NHS Trust v H*,[83] the feeding tube of a 59-year-old multiple sclerosis sufferer, KH, fell out. KH was conscious, but lacked the capacity to

---

[76] See J Stone, 'Withholding of Life-Sustaining Treatment' (1995) 145 *New Law Journal* 354.
[77] *Re D (Medical Treatment)* [1998] 1 FLR 411.
[78] *Re H (A Patient)* [1998] 2 FLR 36.
[79] [1998] 2 FLR 36 at 41.
[80] For example, *Re D (Medical Treatment: Mentally Disabled Patient)* [1998] 2 FLR 22.
[81] *Practice Note (Official Solicitor: Declaratory Proceedings: Medical and Welfare Decisions for Adults who Lack Capacity)* [2001] 2 FLR 158.
[82] *Re D (Medical Treatment)* [1998] FLR 411.
[83] [2004] EWCA Civ 1324.

make her own decisions. She recognised nobody, had difficulty swallowing and had required a feeding tube for the past five years. The family opposed the carers' wish to replace the tube. In the absence of a valid advance directive, the court held that it was in KH's best interests for the tube to be reinserted: death by starvation would be even less dignified than the death she would face if the feeding tube was reinserted.[84] Whether judges like it or not, the effect of the long series of judicial decisions relating to withdrawal of treatment is that judges are making life or death decisions.[85]

A right to artificial nutrition and hydration?

20.12 The entry into force of the Human Rights Act 1998 raised questions about the legality of the reasoning in *Bland* and the cases which followed *Bland*. Were decisions to cease feeding, especially to withdraw ANH, lawful? Or did they contravene Article 2 of the European Convention on Human Rights (protecting the right to life)? In *NHS Trust A v M*,[86] the President of the Family Division ruled that in the circumstances of cases such as *Bland*, where a recovery allowing the patient to enjoy any sort of cognitive abilities was nigh on impossible, nothing in Article 2 required measures to ensure prolongation of survival.

The General Medical Council produced guidance in 2002 indicating that, where a patient's disease is severe and the prognosis poor, ANH will not always be appropriate – even if death is not imminent.[87] This prompted Leslie Burke, who suffers from a degenerative neurological condition, cerebellar ataxia, to fight for the right to artificial nutrition and hydration in the event that he is unable to voice his wishes. His condition gradually reduces his co-ordination while his mental faculties are unimpaired. He will lose the abilities to walk, hear, see and swallow. He could make an advance directive, but was worried that, after a significant deterioration, the GMC guidance would sanction the discontinuation of ANH in spite of it, and that he would be aware of great pain and suffering caused by malnutrition and dehydration. His argument was that, in his personal view, knowing as he does the likely progression of his disease, ANH will never be futile.

Mr Burke argued that the GMC guidance offended his human rights in four ways. First, the right to life in Article 2(1) contains both a negative obligation not to unlawfully take life and a positive obligation to protect it. The guidance failed to adequately protect his life. Second, by failing to protect him from

---

[84] [2004] EWCA Civ 1324, per Brooke LJ at paras 22 and 27.

[85] A series of cases involving the withdrawal of treatment from children is examined above in Chapter 15 at 15.6. See *Re K (a child)* [2006] EWHC 1007 (Fam); *An NHS Trust v MB (A Child by CAFCASS as Guardian ad litem)* [2006] EWHC 507 (Fam); *Wyatt v Portsmouth NHS Trust* [2005] EWCA Civ 1181; *ReL (A Child)* [2004] EWHC 2713 (Fam).

[86] [2001] 1 All ER 801; and see E Wicks, 'The Right to Refuse Medical Treatment Under the European Convention on Human Rights' (2001) 9 *Medical Law Review* 17.

[87] General Medical Council, *Withholding and Withdrawing Life-Prolonging Treatments: Good Practice in Decision-Making* (2002). Paragraph 16 provides: '... Doctors must take account of patients' preferences when providing treatment. However, where a patient wishes to have a treatment that – in the doctor's considered view – is not clinically indicated, there is no ethical or legal obligation on the doctor to provide it.'

death by malnutrition and dehydration, it offended Article 3 (which protects him from inhuman and degrading treatment). Third, by failing to give his advance directive legal force, the guidance offended Article 8 (which protects his right to a private and family life). Finally, it discriminated against those incapable of making a competent decision and therefore offended Article 14. At first instance, it was held that the GMC guidance was incompatible with sections 3 and 8 of the Human Rights Act 1998.[88] Munby J's decision was controversial because it suggested a positive right to demand treatment that was not, in the doctors' views, in the patient's medical best interests.[89] Could the principle be extended beyond the provision of ANH, to other forms of treatment? The GMC feared that it might and took the case to the Court of Appeal, where Munby J's decision was overturned.[90] Mr Burke's concerns, the court held, were already addressed by the law: where a competent patient indicates his wish to be kept alive through ANH, a doctor who deliberately brings that life to an end by removing ANH may be guilty of murder. Mr Burke was more concerned about what should happen in the event that he loses capacity. The court is clear. Doctors cannot be forced to administer treatment which they believe to be clinically unnecessary, futile or inappropriate. There is no discrimination, as the law applies equally to both a competent patient demanding treatment and an incompetent patient whose demands are expressed through an advance directive. Doctors are guided by the indistinct and complex concepts of futility and best interests. The Court of Appeal decision (on the facts of this case) is a blow to patient autonomy and a victory for medical paternalism.

In 2006, Leslie Burke lodged an appeal with the European Court of Human Rights. His application was ruled inadmissible.[91] There was no imminent risk that ANH would be withdrawn in circumstances that would lead to death by malnutrition and dehydration. In many ways, Mr Burke made his case too early: the emphasis on 'imminent' risk and the court's view that no issue arose under Articles 2, 3 and 8 on the basis that 'the applicant cannot pre-determine the administration of specific treatment in future unknown circumstances'[92] must come as a blow given that, by the time the issues are 'imminent', Mr Burke is unlikely to be competent to bring the proceedings himself. Never the less, the court affirms the position taken in the Court of Appeal that the GMC guidelines do not have legal status and make no recommendations contrary to the law. Nor is there any discrimination within the meaning of Article 14: neither competent nor incompetent patients can require a doctor to provide treatment that he does not believe is clinically justified.

---

[88] *R (on the application of Burke) v General Medical Council* [2004] EWHC 1879 (Admin).
[89] See R Gillon, 'Why the GMC is Right to Appeal Over Life-prolonging Treatment' (2004) 329 *British Medical Journal* 810. In support of the High Court judgment see H Biggs, 'In Whose Best Interests: Who Knows?' (2006) 1(2) *Clinical Ethics* 90; D Gurnham, 'Losing the Wood for the Trees: Burke and the Court of Appeal' (2006) 14 *Medical Law Review* 253. See also Coggon (2006) 12 *Medical Law Review* 219, who argues that a right to die with dignity cannot exist if a right to die does not.
[90] *R (on the application of Burke) v General Medical Council* [2005] EWCA Civ 1003.
[91] *Burke v United Kingdom* [2006] App 19807/06.
[92] [2006] App 19807/06, per Casadevall J.

As we shall see, section 4(5) of the Mental Capacity Act 2005 offers further guidance. It provides that decisions relating to life-sustaining treatment must not be motivated by a desire to bring about the patient's death. Does this mean that there is a positive obligation on doctors to provide life-sustaining treatment? This is unlikely. The draft Code of Practice provides that:

> Doctors must give special consideration to written statements that ask for life-sustaining treatment, such as artificial nutrition and hydration (ANH). Wherever possible, all steps should be taken to prolong life. However, in exceptional cases, or where the patient is close to death, the provision of ANH may cause great suffering and loss of dignity. Doctors must take account of the patient's wishes as set out in the written statement but weigh these carefully against all other relevant factors in deciding whether it is in the best interests of the patient to provide or continue ANH. Doctors sometimes must apply to the Court of Protection where there is doubt about the patient's best interests.[93]

Mr Burke's remaining options are to make an advance directive refusing treatment or, when the Mental Capacity Act 2005 comes into force, to appoint a lasting power of attorney.

The Mental Capacity Act 2005[94]

20.13 The Mental Capacity Act 2005 will come fully into force by October 2007. The Act governs decision-making on behalf of adults who temporarily or permanently lack mental capacity. It endorses the modified best interests test employed by case law, but introduces a number of important practical changes. A new Court of Protection, established by section 45 of the Act, is pivotal to the new regime. The court will be supported by a new officer, the public guardian. The powers of the Court of Protection extend only to granting declarations relating to a patient's capacity to determine her own treatment and the lawfulness of decisions taken on her behalf. The court may also appoint a 'deputy' to make welfare and treatment decisions on behalf of the patient lacking capacity.[95]

How will the 2005 Act affect end of life decisions? As we have seen, the test of lawfulness remains the best interests of the patient. But an element of substituted judgment is incorporated into the statutory checklist for best interests. Decision-makers must give due consideration to the patient's previous wishes, beliefs and values.[96] So Mr Burke's wish to prolong his life would have to be taken into account even after the Act comes into force. Particular attention must be paid to any written statement made by the patient when he had capacity.[97] But though an advance directive purporting to *demand*

---

[93] Department for Constitutional Affairs, *Mental Capacity Act 2005 Draft Code of Practice* (CP 05/06), para 4.28. See also para 4.29.
[94] See also above, Chapter 6.
[95] Section 16. The deputies' powers are limited by s 20. Section 20(5) provides: 'A deputy may not refuse consent to the carrying out or continuation of life-sustaining treatment in relation to P.'
[96] Section 4(6)(b).
[97] Section 4(6)(a); and see ss 24–26 on advance decisions to refuse treatment.

treatment may be persuasive, it is not binding.[98] Many patients in Mr Burke's condition might prefer to ensure that life-sustaining treatment is not prolonged. We saw in Chapter 6 that advance decisions to *refuse* treatment are not valid if:

- the treatment in question 'is not the treatment specified in the advance decision';
- 'any circumstances specified in the advance decision are absent' or
- 'there are reasonable grounds for believing that circumstances exist which [the patient] did not anticipate at the time of his advance decision and which would have affected his decision had he anticipated them'.[99]

In addition, where the advance decision to refuse treatment relates to life-sustaining treatment, special conditions apply. It must incorporate a statement that the decision stands, even if life is at risk. It must be in writing, signed, witnessed and verified by the author.[100] If so it is as binding as a statement refusing life-sustaining treatment made by a competent patient such as Ms B. Yet there is no requirement that the patient discusses the content or implications of the statement with a health professional or that he be fully informed.

Alternatively, a competent patient may appoint a proxy to act for her via a lasting power of attorney (LPA) and make decisions on her behalf in the event that she loses capacity.[101] The powers of the LPA are wider than those of the enduring power of attorney which it replaces, potentially encompassing both welfare and financial matters. Again, special conditions apply if the proxy is to make decisions regarding life-sustaining treatment. The proxy may only make such decisions if the donor of the LPA expressly enabled him to do so.[102] Even then, the decision of a proxy is subject to the conditions of the 2005 Act. If the proxy and the doctors or carers disagree about what is in the best interests of the patient, the court will usually be called upon to make a decision or declaration. As we shall see, the court as 'decision-maker' will be guided, but not bound, by the views of the proxy.

Whoever is making the crucial decision – doctors, any attorney or the court – section 4(5) of the Mental Capacity Act 2005 contains special considerations relating to life-sustaining treatment, which is defined as 'treatment which in the view of a person providing health care for the person concerned is necessary to sustain life':

> Where the determination relates to life-sustaining treatment [the person making the decision] must not, in considering whether the treatment is in the best interests of the person concerned, be motivated by a desire to bring about his death.[103]

---

[98] This was also the case in common law: *R (on the application of Burke) v GMC* [2005] EWCA Civ 1003 at para 35.
[99] Section 25(1).
[100] See s 25(5)–(6).
[101] Lasting powers of attorneys are governed by ss 9–14.
[102] See s 11(8)(a).
[103] Section 4(10).

This peculiar statement was framed to appease those who feared that the Mental Capacity Act 2005 would sanction covert euthanasia. It 'forbids the decision-maker from being motivated by any such desire to bring about the death of the person lacking capacity in his/her assessment of what is in that person's best interests'.[104] We are at a loss to define 'desire' in this context. The draft Code of Practice states:

> ... there will be some limited number of cases, for example in the final stages of terminal illness, where treatment is futile or where there is no prospect of recovery. In such cases it may be in the best interests of the patient to withdraw or withhold treatment ...[105]

The draft Code recognises that those making the treatment decision might wish the patient dead (either to ease his suffering or for other reasons) but insists that this is not the motivation for the discontinuation of treatment.

The role of the courts

20.14 It is good practice to seek prior judicial sanction in cases of dispute or uncertainty as to a patient's capacity or his best interests, but is there a legal requirement to do so? We saw in Chapter 6 that there is not. In *Burke*, Lord Phillips MR stated:

> Good practice may require medical practitioners to seek such a declaration where the legality of proposed treatment is in doubt. This is not, however, something that they are required to do as a matter of law.[106]

Nor does the Mental Capacity Act 2005 mandate resort to court. Its Code of Practice will advise that a declaration should be sought in certain circumstances, including any proposal to withdraw ANII.[107] The Act maintains that transgression of the Code by certain individuals (including health care professionals) will be 'taken into account in proceedings in any court or tribunal'.[108] Most controversial cases are, therefore, likely to appear before the Court of Protection. However, as we noted in Chapter 6,[109] where there is consensus regarding a course of action, there may be no-one to enforce recourse to the court. The patient will lack an advocate, and have no-one to speak on his behalf.

---

[104] Department for Constitutional Affairs, *Mental Capacity Act 2005 Draft Code of Practice* (CP 05/06), para 4.28.

[105] Department for Constitutional Affairs, *Mental Capacity Act 2005 Draft Code of Practice* (CP 05/06), para 4.27. See also J Coggon, 'Ignoring the Moral and Intellectual Shape of the Law after *Bland*: The Unintended Side-Effect of a Sorry Compromise' (2007) 27 *Legal Studies* 110.

[106] [2005] EWCA Civ 1003 at para 80.

[107] For fuller advice, see Department for Constitutional Affairs, *Mental Capacity Act 2005 Draft Code of Practice* (CP 05/06), paras 7.9 and 7.17–7.23.

[108] Sections 42(4) and 42(5).

[109] At 6.16.

Where there is disagreement as to the proposed course of action and an application to the Court of Protection is made, how will the courts determine what is in the patients' best interests? What weight is given to the views of carers and family members?

Where carers disagree

20.15 In *Bland, Frenchay, D* and *H*, the patient's family supported the doctors' judgment to cease treatment. The Mental Capacity Act 2005 gives statutory force to a process of consultation with all those concerned with the patient's care – formalising the less clear requirements of consultation under the common law. Under the Act, any decision-maker must take into consideration the past and present wishes and feelings of the patient[110] and, where appropriate and practicable, the views of carers, family, LPAs and court-appointed deputies when determining best interests.[111] But what happens when these views conflict? Pre-Mental Capacity Act 2005 case law gives some guidance.

In *Re G*,[112] G suffered serious injuries while riding his motorcycle. In the course of attempts to resuscitate him, he suffered a heart attack which resulted in the interruption of blood flow to his brain. He was diagnosed as being in PVS, a state in which he had lain for nearly two years at the time of the application to court to withdraw feeding. G's wife and mother remained devoted to him and visited regularly. G's wife somewhat reluctantly supported the application to withdraw feeding from G. His mother opposed the application. Stephen Brown P said that he was satisfied that doctors had taken into account all the views of G's family. The mother's views could not prevail against what was considered to be the best interests of the patient. It might be argued that the wife's judgment should be preferred. This is not the basis of the finding in G. The judge seems to give relatively little weight to any relative's views. He says:

> It would indeed be an appalling burden to place upon any relative to transfer as it were the responsibility for making a decision in a case of this nature to that relative. In this case, the responsibility must ultimately remain with the doctors in charge of the case, albeit taking fully into account views of relatives.[113]

In *NHS Trust v A*,[114] there was disagreement between the NHS Trust and the family, and also between medical experts. An 86-year-old man suffered a heart attack and was brought into intensive care. His heart, lungs and kidneys were artificially supported and he was given artificial nutrition. A was sentient and made attempts to remove the tubes. Given the remote likelihood of any meaningful recovery, it was proposed that he should be given palliative care only. The family disagreed and their expert medical witness stated that A might have a 20 per cent chance of recovery. At first instance, it was held that

---

[110] Section 4(6)(a) and (b).
[111] Section 4(7).
[112] *Re G (Persistent Vegetative State)* [1995] 2 FCR 46.
[113] [1995] 2 FCR 46 at 51.
[114] [2005] EWCA Civ 1145.

A lacked capacity to decide and that it was not in his best interests to continue treatment that would not improve his condition. A's son appealed, arguing that the judge had not taken into consideration the family's views and, in particular, their religious beliefs. Further, it was argued that, applying *Bolam v City & Hackney Health Authority*,[115] if a responsible body of medical opinion did not support the view that withdrawal of treatment was in A's best interests, then the court had no authority to hold to the contrary. The appeal was dismissed. The court, and not the doctors, were responsible for deciding what was in A's best interests, which go wider than medical interests alone. The judge at first instance had taken into account the religious and other views of the family. The views were 'material' but not 'governing factors' in determining the patient's best interests.[116]

In *NHS Trust v J*,[117] the court once again had to declare whether withdrawal of ANH was in the best interests of a patient in circumstances where the doctors and family disagreed, but here the family proposed the immediate withdrawal of treatment. The Official Solicitor, an officer appointed by the court when no other person is either suitable or willing to act, proposed a delay. J suffered a subarachnoid and interventricular brain haemorrhage whilst on holiday in 2003. She was without oxygen for around twelve minutes, which experts agreed was likely to cause profound and permanent brain damage. J was in PVS for three years whereupon the trust sought a declaration from the court that J lacked capacity, and that it was not in her best interests to continue ANH. J's husband, mother and two daughters supported the application. Sir Mark Potter P would have granted the application,[118] but the Official Solicitor opposed the immediate grant of the declarations on the basis of two research articles indicating the potential of the insomnia drug Zolpidem to enhance the neural responses of patients in PVS. The expert witness doubted the drug would work on account of J's age and the nature of her brain injury, but saw no harm in trying. Zolpidem is not harmful and any effect on neural activity is immediate: no response within 45 minutes would indicate that the drug had not worked. The family, however, opposed it. They were concerned that J would not have wanted her life prolonged in this way, and that the experimental use of the drug might induce a sense of awareness that would be distressing for both J and her family. Even if the drug worked, J would have no meaningful quality of life. Sir Mark Potter was much impressed by the expert medical evidence. He declared that J lacked capacity to make a decision and that a three-day course of Zolpidem was in her best interests. He did so with a view to a return to court if the drug failed to have an effect, in which case there is no reason why the removal of ANH would not be declared lawful.

The views of family, it seems, have little weight. Will this change? Under the Mental Capacity Act 2005, the relevance and weight of the various considerations going to best interests depends upon who is the decision-maker. What if the patient has appointed a proxy, someone with a lasting power of attorney?

[115] [1957] 2 All ER 118, discussed fully in Chapter 7.
[116] [2005] EWCA Civ 1145 at para 59, per Waller LJ.
[117] [2006] All ER (D) 290 (Nov).
[118] [2006] All ER (D) 290 (Nov) at para 31.

We have seen that the powers of proxies do extend in some circumstances to decisions about life-sustaining treatment. Does this herald a new era of substituted judgment, with the proxy more likely to make the decision that she believes the donor would have wanted? Three factors limit the powers of the new attorney. First, such a proxy can only make decisions concerning the continuation of life-sustaining treatment if expressly authorised to do so by the patient. Second, she must act in the best interests of the patient, which include the duty to consult other interested parties and the requirement that she must not be motivated by a desire to bring about the patient's death. Where her views conflict with those of the doctors, the draft Code of Practice recommends that life-sustaining treatment is continued until clarification is obtained from the court.[119] Which leads us to the final restriction: where the outcome of a decision is very serious, as in the proposed withdrawal of ANH[120] for example, it is still good practice to bring each case before the court. Where the court is the decision-maker, it must merely 'take into account, if it is practicable and appropriate to consult them'[121] the views of (*inter alia*) the attorney. Despite the extended powers of proxies and the statutory recognition of advance directives, best interests rather than substituted judgments remains the dominant test.

DNAR orders[122]

20.16 DNAR (do not attempt resuscitation) orders are not expressly referred to in the Mental Capacity Act 2005. What is in issue is not withdrawing treatment, but whether or not the patient should be resuscitated if he suffers a cardiac arrest. Whose decision should determine whether or not a DNAR order is made? In some cases, the patient can be consulted. Where she lacks capacity, an advance refusal of treatment may be effective. Where the donor expressly authorises it, the LPA may 'authorise the giving or refusing of consent to the carrying out or continuation of life-sustaining treatment'.[123] In other cases, guidelines on DNAR make it clear that decision-making is not an exclusively medical role. The patient's wishes, if known, must be respected.

Guidelines developed jointly between the British Medical Association and the Royal College of Nursing[124] suggest that it is appropriate to consider a DNAR order if the following conditions are met:

(1)   The patient's condition is such that effective cardio-pulmonary resuscitation (CPR) will not be successful.

(2)   Where there is no benefit in restarting the patient's heart (if, for example, imminent death cannot be avoided).

---

[119] Department for Constitutional Affairs, *Mental Capacity Act 2005 Draft Code of Practice* (CP 05/06), para 6.18.
[120] Department for Constitutional Affairs, *Mental Capacity Act 2005 Draft Code of Practice* (CP 05/06), para 5.18.
[121] Section 4(7).
[122] See also the discussion of *Re Wyatt* [2004] EWHC 2247 (Fam); [2005] EWHC 693 (Fam); [2005] EWCA Civ 1181; [2005] EWHC 2902; [2006] EWHC 319 (Fam) in Chapter 15.
[123] Section 11(8)(a).
[124] See BMA/RCN, *Decisions Relating to Cardio-Pulmonary Resuscitation* (2002), para 10.

(3)   Where the expected benefit is outweighed by the burdens (where there is a high risk of substantial brain damage, for example).

Where a DNAR order has not been made and the wishes of the patient are unknown, CPR should be attempted if cardiac or pulmonary arrest occurs. Responsibility for a DNAR decision rests with the consultant or GP in charge. Decisions should be made on the basis of appropriate consultation with other staff and the patient's family.

Fears about DNAR decisions focus on *who* makes the decision about life or death, whether such decisions may be made arbitrarily or in a discriminatory fashion, and whether the patient will be treated well once a DNAR order is in place.[125] DNAR orders are made more often in relation to elderly patients. That of itself may not be surprising. It is the quality of decision-making which counts and how prospects of successful resuscitation and future quality of life are assessed. A greater number of very elderly patients who are also gravely ill may be more unlikely to recover than their grandchildren in their twenties and thirties. Disturbingly, Mason and Laurie note that the relevance of the age factor often depends on the age of the physician making the decision.[126] Junior doctors in particular require training to understand the needs of their elderly patients. The criteria governing the assessment of the patient and the weight given to his or her family's wishes should not vary with age.

The validity of DNAR orders came before the English courts in *Re R (adult: medical treatment)*.[127] R was 23. He was born with a severe malformation of the brain. He developed epilepsy in infancy, suffered from multiple disabilities and had no real means of communicating with others. He had severe and debilitating intestinal troubles, including ulcers 'all the way through his guts'. His only real response to others seems to have been to being cuddled. He appeared to experience quite acute pain. He was not in PVS or anything akin to 'near PVS'. Since he was 19, he had lived in a nursing home, attending a day centre and going home to his devoted family most weekends. In the year before the court proceedings, R had been hospitalised five times. His doctors, with the full agreement of R's parents, issued a DNAR order. Should R suffer from a life-threatening condition involving a cardiac arrest he should not be resuscitated. Staff at R's day centre were concerned about the use of DNAR orders in R's case, and made an application for judicial review of the order. The NHS trust responsible for R's care sought a declaration both to declare the DNAR order lawful and to support a wider non-treatment policy, including withdrawing nutrition and hydration. This part of the trust's application was later withdrawn. Sir Stephen Brown P upheld the DNAR order. He was persuaded that the evidence established that, in cases such as R, CPR was unlikely to succeed. Indeed the very process might do R further injury. R had never been able to articulate his wishes. None the less, the judge concluded that it was permissible to consider the patient's quality of life in assessing his best interests. DNAR orders do not involve measures to

---

[125] See R Dobson, 'Stroke Patients with "Do Not Resuscitate" Orders are Treated Worse Than Those Without' (2005) 331 *British Medical Journal* 926.
[126] *Mason and McCall Smith's Law and Medical Ethics*, p 637.
[127] (1996) 31 BMLR 127.

terminate life or accelerate death. Where continued existence involved a life 'so afflicted as to be intolerable',[128] policies designed to limit life-saving intervention could be approved. In the absence of consent from the patient, the decision to institute a DNAR order should usually be made by the physicians, family and carers. Recourse to the courts is rare indeed and should be reserved for cases of serious disagreement.

The euthanasia debate[129]

20.17   English law is imprecise and uncertain. Doctors cannot always be given clear advice about the legality of various procedures. Is this fair to the medical profession? Is it right that some doctors, even acting with the best of motives, may under a screen of silence do things which they believe may be unlawful? There is some evidence that doctors practise covert euthanasia.[130] If what is taking place in medical practice is acceptable to society, it is argued that the law should be changed to set out clearly the parameters within which doctors should be acting. If society disapproves of certain procedures, how can they be controlled? Is it right, again, for the law to be left obscure, yet when clear evidence of euthanasia occurs prosecutors may elect not to enforce the law? On the other hand, there are those who oppose legislation on the grounds that the current fudge allows for maximum flexibility for a caring medical profession. McCall Smith[131] has argued that:

> The current state of the law can be defended as the embodiment of a moral compromise which satisfies the needs of a delicately nuanced problem.

Once any proposal to clarify the current fudge surfaces, opinions polarise sharply. Pro-life campaigners sought to unsuccessfully reverse the decision in *Bland*[132] and to encourage police and prosecutors to pursue vigorously any evidence of covert euthanasia. Supporters of voluntary euthanasia argue their contrary case with equal passion. As Kennedy and Grubb note, '... whenever the topic of voluntary euthanasia is broached, rational argument becomes an early casualty'.[133]

The case for voluntary euthanasia is deceptively simple. It rests on the principle of autonomy. The individual is the '... final determinant of his or her destiny'.[134] We enjoy the right to control our death just as we enjoy the right

---

[128] See *Re J (a minor) (Wardship: Medical Treatment)* [1990] 3 All ER 930, CA.

[129] See generally, J Keown (ed), *Euthanasia Examined: Ethical, Legal and Clinical Perspectives* (1995) CUP; M Otlowski, *Voluntary Euthanasia and the Common Law* (1997) Clarendon Press.

[130] See RS Magnusson, 'Above Ground, Below Ground' (2004) 30 *Journal of Medical Ethics* 441; Ost, *An Analytical Study of the Legal, Moral and Ethical Aspects of the Living Phenomenon of Euthanasia*; Biggs, *Euthanasia, Death with Dignity and the Law*; J Keown, *Euthanasia, Ethics and Public Policy* (2002) CUP.

[131] See A McCall Smith, 'Euthanasia: The Strengths of the Middle Ground' (1994) 7 *Medical Law Review* 198.

[132] In the Medical Treatment (Prevention of Euthanasia) Bill discussed in J Keown, 'Dehydrating Bodies: the *Bland* Case, the Winterton Bill' in A Bainham, SD Slater, M Richards (eds), *Body Lore and Laws* (2002) Hart Publishing, p 245.

[133] Kennedy and Grubb, *Medical Law: Text and Materials*, p 1997.

[134] See Otlowski, *Voluntary Euthanasia and the Common Law*, p 189.

to control our lives. Moreover, dignity and welfare, it is contended, impel us to allow the individual the right to end an intolerable life. A compassionate society should not force people dying, or living with pain and disability, to continue to live. The patient in the terminal stages of motor neurone disease should not be compelled to suffer all the consequences of a drawn-out death. Human rights are invoked in support of the pro-euthanasia case. Article 3 of the European Convention on Human Rights prohibits inhuman and degrading treatment. Does the absence of a euthanasia option in effect impose such degrading treatment? Article 8 protects our private and family lives. Do laws preventing my doctor, or indeed my husband, from helping me to end an intolerable life violate my privacy? We have seen that the Law Lords, and the European Court of Human Rights, in *Pretty*[135] were unmoved by such legal arguments. The ethical debate continues.

Those opposed to legislation permitting voluntary euthanasia advance several objections. For many, though not all, opponents of euthanasia, central to their opposition is their commitment to the doctrine of sanctity of life.[136] However, other concerns are voiced. Just how voluntary would such euthanasia be? Would the introduction of such laws result in a change of attitude by society towards the sanctity of life generally, towards the elderly, infirm and the mortally sick? Would the existence of such laws impose pressures upon elderly and terminally ill patients to seek euthanasia, rather than remain a burden on relatives or on society? Would the existence of such legislation provide opportunities for fraud and abuse, and undermine the relationship of trust between doctor and patient? How easy would it be to apply such a law?

Let us examine what form legislation might take. Two rather different sorts of laws might be envisaged – both of which have models in other jurisdictions. Legislation could sanction physician-assisted suicide (as is now the case in the State of Oregon, USA) or could allow voluntary active euthanasia (as is the case in the Netherlands and Belgium).

Physician-assisted suicide[137]

20.18 The Oregon Death with Dignity Act 1994 came into force in 1997. It applies only to adults who have been diagnosed as terminally ill. A prescription for oral medication is the only assistance sanctioned. Direct assistance with suicide is prohibited.

Lord Joffe's Patient (Assisted Dying) Bill 2003 was modelled on the Oregon Act, but incorporated voluntary euthanasia for those physically incapable of taking the final steps to end their life. It did not progress beyond a Second Reading. His ill-fated Assisted Dying for the Terminally Ill Bill 2004 ran out of time. It was more restrictive than the 2003 Bill, applying only to terminally ill patients and including a requirement for a discussion of the option of

---

[135] See above at 20.6.
[136] See L Gormally (ed), *Euthanasia, Clinical Practice and the Law* (1994) The Linacre Centre.
[137] For another model of assisted dying, see P Lewis, 'The Evolution of Assisted Dying in France: A Third Way?' (2006) 14 *Medical Law Review* 44.

palliative care. The Select Committee on the Assisted Dying for the Terminally Ill Bill reported in April 2005.[138] Nine recommendations were made for any future bills, including (*inter alia*):

- a clearer delineation between euthanasia and physician-assisted suicide;
- a statement of the actions which a doctor may or may not take in providing assisted suicide or administering voluntary euthanasia;
- a clinical definition of terminal illness (if terminal illness is a qualifying condition); and
- a definition of mental competence so as to differentiate between applicants lacking mental capacity and those suffering a mental disorder.[139]

Lord Joffe accepted four of the nine recommendations when introducing his third Bill in 2005. It was outvoted in the House of Lords by 148 to 100. Lord Joffe promised to reintroduce the Bill and the Government indicated that it would not block a further hearing.

Active euthanasia

20.19 Meyers and Mason[140] envisaged the doctor 'providing or *administering* a lethal dose of medication'. But, surely, a lethal injection performed by the doctor must be killing, not simply assisting suicide? Do we have to resort to complex mechanical devices whereby the doctor sets up a machine to inject the patient with her lethal dose and somehow (maybe via a computer) she triggers the mechanism delivering the injection? The line between assisted suicide and killing becomes as fragile as the artificiality of the current law. In *Pretty*, Lord Bingham[141] exposed the dilemma:

> If article 2 does confer a right of self-determination in relation to life and death, and if a person were so gravely disabled as to be unable to perform any act whatsoever to cause his or her own death, it would necessarily follow in logic that such a person would have a right to be killed at the hands of a third party ...

In the Netherlands, an informal agreement between the prosecution authorities and the medical profession allowed active euthanasia for several years. The *Postma*[142] case was the first in a series of rulings easing restrictions on euthanasia. Dr Postma gave his disabled mother, who had previously attempted suicide and no longer wanted to live, a fatal dose of morphine. The court imposed a suspended sentence of one week's imprisonment and indicated that euthanasia might be acceptable provided that the patient was incurably ill, was suffering unbearably, had requested assisted suicide, and that the act was performed by the patient's own doctor or in consultation with her. Nine years later, the prosecution authorities agreed not to prosecute any

---

138 HL Paper 86.
139 HL Paper 86, para 269(c).
140 (1999) 29 *Anglo-American Law Review* 39.
141 *R (on the application of Pretty) v DPP* [2002] 1 All ER 1 at 6–7, HL.
142 *Nederlandse Jurisprudentie* 1973 No 183 District Court of Leeuwarden, 21 February 1973.

doctor who ended his patient's life within the parameters set by agreed guidelines.[143] The patient must have freely requested 'help in dying' and the physician must assure himself that that request is truly voluntary and well considered. The patient and his doctor must be satisfied that there are no other means of relieving the patient's suffering or other incurable condition. A second doctor must be consulted. It is estimated that thousands of patients each year have opted for active euthanasia in the Netherlands, perhaps 2.7 per cent of all reported deaths.[144] None the less, until 2000, euthanasia remained formally unlawful in the Netherlands. Legislation to give legal effect to the earlier informal arrangements came into force in 2002.[145] Controversially, individuals can make advance requests for euthanasia and children over twelve may request it – though, until they are 16, parental assent is required.[146]

The impact of Dutch practice and their new laws is much debated. Opponents argue[147] (*inter alia*) that (1) the incidence of active euthanasia is under-reported, (2) there is evidence of termination of life without an explicit request from the patient (in perhaps as many as one in five cases), (3) withdrawal of treatment with minimal safeguards is common, and (4) depressed and mentally-disturbed patients are helped to die. The nub of the case is that what is supposed to be a limited provision to allow free and informed choices by competent patients to end their lives has become a convenient means of disposing of the elderly and grievously sick. Supporters[148] equally passionately refute these allegations. Dispassionate analysis of how voluntary euthanasia 'works' in the Netherlands is hard to find.

The first Euthanasia Bill in this country was introduced into Parliament in 1936. The Bill was quickly rejected.

Another Voluntary Euthanasia Bill, introduced in 1969, was designed to allow a patient or prospective patient to sign in advance a declaration requesting the administration of euthanasia if he was believed to be suffering from a fatal illness or was incapable of rational existence. Again, the Bill failed.

Subsequent Bills in the mid-1970s were more modest and attempted to avoid being seen as attempts to legalise euthanasia or 'mercy killing'. In the wake of the decision in *Bland*, the House of Lords set up a Select Committee on Medical Ethics[149] to investigate legal, ethical and social issues surrounding treatment decisions at the end of life. The Committee endorsed the judges' ruling in *Bland*, commended (but refused to endorse) legislation to give effect

---

[143] *Wertheim, Nederlandse Jurisprudentie* 1982 No 63 Rotterdam Criminal Court.

[144] See *Mason and McCall Smith's Law and Medical Ethics*, p 606.

[145] Termination of Life on Request and Assisted Suicide (Review Procedures) Act 2000. Discussed in J de Haan, 'The New Dutch Law on Euthanasia' (2002) 10 *Medical Law Review* 57.

[146] Discussed in Jackson, *Medical Law: Text, Cases and Materials*, p 963.

[147] See J Keown, 'The Law and Practice of Euthanasia in the Netherlands' (1992) 108 *Law Quarterly Review* 51; H Jochenson and J Keown, 'Voluntary Euthanasia under Control? Further Empirical Evidence from the Netherlands' (1999) 25 *Journal of Medical Ethics* 16.

[148] JM Van Delden, 'Slippery Slopes in Flat Countries – a Response' (1999) 25 *Journal of Medical Ethics* 22.

[149] *Report of the Select Committee on Medical Ethics* HL-21 (1993–94).

to advance directives, and in total delivered a Report of almost amazing banality. Their recommendations, in effect, were no change and leave such difficult questions to the doctors. The Report came out firmly against legalising voluntary euthanasia. Their Lordships considered that argument based on autonomy, the right to choose to die constituted '... insufficient reason to weaken society's prohibition on intentional killing'. It was not, in their view, possible to set secure limits on voluntary euthanasia, and vulnerable people might be pressured into requesting early death. Moreover, there was good evidence that palliative care could relieve pain and distress in the majority of cases.

Though, in 2005, the British Medical Association changed its policy on assisted dying from one of opposition to one of neutrality,[150] the Royal College of General Practitioners and the Royal College of Physicians maintain their opposition to both physician-assisted suicide and voluntary euthanasia. Moreover, in a spectacular U-turn, the BMA reverted to opposition in 2006.[151] Physician-assisted suicide and voluntary active euthanasia have public backing,[152] but without the support of doctors, legislation faces an uncertain future. The debate intensifies and it does not seem to move on.

---

[150] Available at: http://www.bma.org.uk/ap.nsf/Content/AssistedDyingDebate.

[151] N Hawkes, 'Doctors Reject Making Euthanasia Legal' (2006) Times, 29 June; British Medical Association, *End-of-Life Decisions* (2006), p 4.

[152] See British Social Attitudes Survey published 24 January 2007, which revealed that 80 per cent would support a law allowing doctors to end the life of a patient with an incurable or painful illness from which they will die. See also L Ward and J Carvel, 'Four out of Five Want to Give Doctors the Rights to End Life of Terminally Ill Patients in Pain' (2007) Guardian, 24 January.

Index

Index

Index

Index

Index

Index

Index

Index